T0189637

IFIP Advances in Information and Communication Technology 663

Editor-in-Chief

Kai Rannenberg, Goethe University Frankfurt, Germany

Editorial Board Members

IFIP – The International Federation for Information Processing

IFIP was founded in 1960 under the auspices of UNESCO, following the first World Computer Congress held in Paris the previous year. A federation for societies working in information processing, IFIP's aim is two-fold: to support information processing in the countries of its members and to encourage technology transfer to developing nations. As its mission statement clearly states:

IFIP is the global non-profit federation of societies of ICT professionals that aims at achieving a worldwide professional and socially responsible development and application of information and communication technologies.

IFIP is a non-profit-making organization, run almost solely by 2500 volunteers. It operates through a number of technical committees and working groups, which organize events and publications. IFIP's events range from large international open conferences to working conferences and local seminars.

The flagship event is the IFIP World Computer Congress, at which both invited and contributed papers are presented. Contributed papers are rigorously refereed and the rejection rate is high.

As with the Congress, participation in the open conferences is open to all and papers may be invited or submitted. Again, submitted papers are stringently refereed.

The working conferences are structured differently. They are usually run by a working group and attendance is generally smaller and occasionally by invitation only. Their purpose is to create an atmosphere conducive to innovation and development. Refereeing is also rigorous and papers are subjected to extensive group discussion.

Publications arising from IFIP events vary. The papers presented at the IFIP World Computer Congress and at open conferences are published as conference proceedings, while the results of the working conferences are often published as collections of selected and edited papers.

IFIP distinguishes three types of institutional membership: Country Representative Members, Members at Large, and Associate Members. The type of organization that can apply for membership is a wide variety and includes national or international societies of individual computer scientists/ICT professionals, associations or federations of such societies, government institutions/government related organizations, national or international research institutes or consortia, universities, academies of sciences, companies, national or international associations or federations of companies.

More information about this series at https://link.springer.com/bookseries/6102

Duck Young Kim · Gregor von Cieminski ·
David Romero (Eds.)

Advances in Production Management Systems

Smart Manufacturing and Logistics Systems: Turning Ideas into Action

IFIP WG 5.7 International Conference, APMS 2022
Gyeongju, South Korea, September 25–29, 2022
Proceedings, Part I

 Springer

Editors
Duck Young Kim (i)
Pohang University of Science and
Technology
Pohang, Korea (Republic of)

Gregor von Cieminski (i)
ZF Friedrichshafen AG
Friedrichshafen, Germany

David Romero (i)
Tecnológico de Monterrey
Mexico City, Mexico

ISSN 1868-4238   ISSN 1868-422X   (electronic)
IFIP Advances in Information and Communication Technology
ISBN 978-3-031-16409-5   ISBN 978-3-031-16407-1   (eBook)
https://doi.org/10.1007/978-3-031-16407-1

This Springer imprint is published by the registered company Springer Nature Switzerland AG
The registered company address is: Gewerbestrasse 11, 6330 Cham, Switzerland

Preface

Over the past few years, we have been going through tough times with the COVID-19 pandemic. This coincides with other fundamental risks to the global economy. If we look at the manufacturing and logistics industries, we have experienced an ever more challenging environment in the global supply chains and networks. Sustainable energy management and global environmental issues are no longer just regulations but top priorities for competitiveness and even survival. Most manufacturers and logistics providers have nowadays to operate in very volatile, uncertain, complex, and ambiguous market conditions. For example, product lifecycles are becoming shorter and shorter; customers' demands are turning out to be highly unpredictable and unbounded; raw material and energy prices are being subject to sharp increases; and transport, logistics, and distribution systems are being demanded with almost impossible delivery times, all threatening the break-even point of manufacturing and logistics enterprises.

To meet these urgent business and operational challenges, many studies on manufacturing and logistics management systems have been conducted in academia. Some research topics such as Industry 4.0, digital transformation, and cyber-physical production systems are buzzwords in many consulting firms without concrete action plans. Therefore, the International Conference on Advances in Production Management Systems (APMS 2022) in Gyeongju, South Korea, aimed to bridge the gap between academia and industry in the development of next-generation smart and sustainable manufacturing and logistics systems. The conference spotlighted internationally renowned keynote speakers from academia and industry, and the active participation of manufacturers, their suppliers, and logistics service providers.

A large international panel of experts reviewed 153 submissions (with a minimum of two single-blind reviews per paper) and selected the best 139 papers to be included in the proceedings of APMS 2022, which are organized into two parts. The topics of special interest in the first part include AI and Data-driven Production Management; Smart Manufacturing and Industry 4.0; Simulation and Model-driven Production Management; Service Systems Design, Engineering and Management; Industrial Digital Transformation; Sustainable Production Management; Digital Supply Networks; and Urban Mobility and City Logistics.

The conference featured special sessions to empathize with the real challenges of today's industry, and accordingly, to exchange valuable knowledge and promote discussions about new answers while emphasizing how to turn technological advances into business solutions. The following important topics were actively discussed in the special sessions and these topics are included in the second part of the APMS 2022 proceedings: Development of Circular Business Solutions and Product-Service Systems through Digital Twins; "Farm-to-Fork" Production Management in Food Supply Chains; Digital Transformation Approaches in Production Management; Smart Supply Chain and Production in Society 5.0 Era; Service and Operations Management in the

Context of Digitally-enabled Product-Service Systems; Sustainable and Digital Servitization; Manufacturing Models and Practices for Eco-efficient, Circular and Regenerative Industrial Systems; Cognitive and Autonomous AI in Manufacturing and Supply Chains; Operators 4.0 and Human-Technology Integration in Smart Manufacturing and Logistics Environments; Cyber-Physical Systems for Smart Assembly and Logistics in Automotive Industry; and Trends, Challenges and Applications of Digital Lean Paradigm.

APMS 2022 was supported by the International Federation of Information Processing (IFIP), and it was organized by the IFIP Working Group 5.7 on Advances in Production Management Systems (APMS) established in 1978, the Department of Industrial and Management Engineering of Pohang University of Science and Technology (POSTECH), the Korean Institute of Industrial Engineers (KIIE), and the Institute for Industrial Systems Innovation of Seoul National University. The conference was also supported by four leading journals: Production Planning & Control (PPC), the International Journal of Production Research (IJPR), the International Journal of Logistics Research and Applications (IJLRA), and the International Journal of Industrial Engineering and Management (IJIEM).

We would like to give very special thanks to the members of the IFIP Working Group 5.7, the Program Committee, the Organizing Committee, and the Advisory Board, along with the reviewers of each submission. Finally, we deeply appreciate the generous financial support from our sponsors, namely, Pohang Iron and Steel Company (POSCO), POSTECH, and the Institute for Industrial Systems Innovation of Seoul National University.

September 2022

Duck Young Kim
Gregor von Cieminski
David Romero

Organization

Honorary Co-chairs

Dimitris Kiritsis   École Polytechnique Fédérale de Lausanne,
                             Switzerland
Chi-Hyuck Jun   Pohang University of Science and Technology,
                             South Korea

Conference Chair

Duck Young Kim   Pohang University of Science and Technology,
                             South Korea

Conference Co-chair

Gregor Von Cieminski   ZF Friedrichshafen, Germany

Program Chair

David Romero   Tecnológico de Monterrey, Mexico

Organizing Committee Chair

Minseok Song   Pohang University of Science and Technology,
                             South Korea

Program Committee

Dong Ho Lee   Hanyang University, South Korea
Sang Do Noh   Sungkyunkwan University, South Korea
Kyungsik Lee   Seoul National University, South Korea
Hong-Bae Jun   Hongik University, South Korea
Xuehao Feng   Zhejiang University, China
Thorsten Wuest   West Virginia University, USA
Paolo Gaiardelli   University of Bergamo, Italy
Mélanie Despeisse   Chalmers University of Technology, Sweden

Advisory Board

Alexandre Dolgui   IMT Atlantique, France
Bojan Lalić   University of Novi Sad, Serbia
Farhad Ameri   Texas State University, USA

Ilkyeong Moon	Seoul National University, South Korea
Hermann Lödding	Technische Universität Hamburg, Germany
Marco Taisch	Politecnico di Milano, Italy
Andrew Kusiak	University of Iowa, USA
Volker Stich	RWTH Aachen, Germany
Vittal Prabhu	Pennsylvania State University, USA
Jai-Hyun Byun	Gyeongsang National University, South Korea

Organizing Committee

Dong Gu Choi	Pohang University of Science and Technology, South Korea
Kwangmin Jung	Pohang University of Science and Technology, South Korea
Kwangyeol Ryu	Pusan National University, South Korea
Jongho Shin	Chosun University, South Korea
Sujeong Baek	Hanbat National University, South Korea

Marco Garetti Doctoral Workshop Co-chairs

| David Romero | Tecnológico de Monterrey, Mexico |
| Jannicke Baalsrud Hauge | KTH Royal Institute of Technology, Sweden, and BIBA, Germany |

Contents – Part I

Smart Manufacturing and Industry 4.0

Simulation and Model-Driven Production Management

Service Systems Design, Engineering and Management

Industrial Digital Transformation

Sustainable Production Management

Digital Supply Networks

Contents – Part II

Digital Transformation Approaches in Production Management

Smart Supply Chain and Production in Society 5.0 Era

**Service and Operations Management in the Context
of Digitally-Enabled Product-Service Systems**

Sustainable and Digital Servitization

Manufacturing Models and Practices for Eco-Efficient, Circular and Regenerative Industrial Systems

Cognitive and Autonomous AI in Manufacturing and Supply Chains

Trends, Challenges and Applications of Digital Lean Paradigm

AI and Data-Driven Production Management

Improving Accuracy of Time Series Forecasting by Applying an ARIMA-ANN Hybrid Model

Hadid Wahedi[1], Kacper Wrona[1], Mads Heltoft[1], Sarkaft Saleh[1(✉)],
Thomas Roum Knudsen[1], Ulrik Bendixen[1], Izabela Nielsen[1], Subrata Saha[1],
and Gregers Sandager Borup[2]

[1] Department of Materials and Production, Aalborg University, 9220 Aalborg East,
Denmark
{hwahed17,kwrona21,mhelto18,ssaleh18,trkn17,
ubendi18}@student.aau.dk, {izabela,saha}@mp.aau.dk
[2] SKIOLD A/S, 9300 Sæby, Denmark
gsb@skiold.com

Abstract. Accurate demand forecasting is critical for any small and medium-sized manufacturer. Limited structured data sources commonly prevent small and medium-sized manufacturers from improving forecasting accuracy, affecting overall performance. We classified products, then implemented a hybrid forecasting method and compared the outcome with Exponential smoothing, ARIMA, LSTM, and ANN forecasting techniques. Numerical results demonstrate that a selection of forecasting methods is not independent of product categorization. For slow-moving products, careful consideration is required. The hybrid ARIMA-ANN method can outperform some existing techniques and lead to higher prediction accuracy, by capturing both linear and nonlinear variations.

Keywords: Machine learning · Forecasting · ARIMA-ANN

1 Introduction

Demand forecasting is the focal point of making informed strategic and operational business decisions such as procurement, capacity planning, and inventory control. Accurate forecasting facilitates small and medium-sized manufacturers to make informed business decisions [21]. Commonly, the manufacturers experience uncertainty and irregular demand patterns throughout the year, where demand patterns consists of both linear and nonlinear components. Therefore, improving forecasting accuracy can substantially enhance delivery performance and profitability by reducing the probability of shortages.

© IFIP International Federation for Information Processing 2022
Published by Springer Nature Switzerland AG 2022
D. Y. Kim et al. (Eds.): APMS 2022, IFIP AICT 663, pp. 3–10, 2022.
https://doi.org/10.1007/978-3-031-16407-1_1

Product classification and demand forecasting should not be considered separately [6]. Determining the proper forecasting approach is always crucial. The forecast of finished products seeks to model customer demand over time, concerning quantity and a time horizon to plan for customers' requests for quotes. On the other hand, forecasting on raw materials aim to optimize inventory, minimise capital tied up in raw material, smooth the production run, etc. [20]. Since the distribution of demand during lead times is used to secure replenishment and order points of inventory, the degree of accuracy is a crucial aspect of successful inventory management to secure delivery promise. However, almost every product shows random irregular patterns [12,22], that standard statistical methods might fail to capture. We present a brief overview of the methods used in this study in Table 1.

Table 1. Literature review

Study	Method	Strength	Weakness
[22]	Exponential smoothing	Simplicity and inexpensive, the model can easily be adjusted to changes.	Take limited observations into account.
[8,9]	ARIMA	Ability to generate accuracy in forecasting when time series data is stationary. Flexible in representing several types of time series.	Inefficient in modelling complex nonlinear patterns.
[25]	ANN	Showcases ANNs ability to comprehend, approximate and model problems that are complex in nature and underlines the strength of ANN in predictive outcomes.	ANN generates approximations which serve as solutions to different learning problems.
[1,2,16,28]	LSTM forecasting model	LSTM solves vanishing gradient problems, enabling the model to cope with long-term dependency between the observations.	Can only capture nonlinear patterns. The distribution of errors on the test set some- times equal to the validation set.
[11,24]	Gated Recurrent Unit	Collects relationship from massive data sequences without losing information from previous inputs.	A vast amount of data needed for optimal performance.
[4,17,29]	Hybrid forecasting ARIMA and ANN	The ability to comprehend linear and nonlinear patterns; hybrid models copes better with unstable and changing patterns in data	The optimal ANN architecture can vary with products and be challenging to implement

The core analysis of this paper is the outtake of well-known forecasting frameworks such as Exponential smoothing, ARIMA, LSTM, and ANN. A hybridization of ARIMA and ANN methods consisting of linear and nonlinear components is implemented. In cases where limited historical data is available, the most common time-series forecasting techniques, Exponential smoothing, ARIMA, and bootstrapping, have proven to yield undesirable accuracy scores [12]. To investigate if other and more complex methods could produce more accurate results on the limited data, a hybrid ARIMA-ANN model has been implemented.

Researchers proposed various raw material categorization methods, based on the usage rate (e.g., slow, medium, and fast-moving), cost per unit (e.g., A-B-C analysis) and part criticality [5,26]. Categorizations can be helpful when conducting forecasts and making decisions, while the variation of consumption patterns can differ significantly in each category [6]. For example, fast-moving materials are often used and might not need to keep inventory long, whereas slow-moving materials remain in stock for extended periods. Slow-moving raw materials has the highest impact, implying that having these raw materials in inventory ties up capital significantly more than fast-moving raw materials.

This study is based on collaboration with the Danish manufacturer, SKIOLD A/S. The company provides the most innovative and reliable manufactured solutions for the agricultural industry, from fieldwork to livestock. A pilot study was initiated to answer the following key research questions: Does product classification affect the forecasting method selection? Can hybridization improve forecasting accuracy, and which computational intelligence methods will yield the highest accuracy? The main objective of forecasting is to improve the overall performance of manufacturers. However, in this study, the objective was analyzing the interaction of forecasting method selection and product categorization.

2   A Case Study

This case study was conducted in collaboration with SKIOLD A/S, located in Denmark, which previously experienced considerable challenges with demand forecasting and production planning that have had the negative consequence of poor delivery performance. The stochastic nature of the demand has made it difficult for the collaboration partner to determine a forecasting approach, as the data contains both linear and nonlinear components.

This case study was conducted with a bottom-up approach to experiment and analyze outcomes of forecasting techniques on a disaggregated product level, based on monthly consumption in the period 2017–2021. The first three years (36 data points) were used as the training set for the different forecasting models. The following 12 month's data are used as a test set. Finally, six months' data is used as a validation set. The following criteria are considered when categorizing the raw materials based on the consumption during the study period from 2017 to 2021: (i) slow-moving materials if the amount consumed is less than 10,000 units/year, (ii) medium-moving if the consumption is 10,001 to 50,000 units/year and (iii) fast-moving if the consumption is above or equal to 50,001 units/year. A detailed overview of the analysis is presented in Fig. 1a.

3   Methods

A brief overview of each method used in this study is presented below:

Auto-Regressive Integrated Moving Average (ARIMA)(p,d,q) modeling is essentially an exploratory data-oriented technique with the flexibility of fitting an appropriate model. The stochastic nature of the time series can be approximated using the auto-correlation function (ACF) and partial auto-correlation function (PACF). It will help to extract information such as trend, periodicity component, serial correlation, etc. [15]. Using the ARIMA model for forecasting, it is presumed that the demand series is stationary and homoscedastic. While implementing ARIMA, the following five steps was integrated: (I) data preparation, (II) model selection based on p (order of auto-regressive part), d (order of the moving-average process), and q (order of the difference) (III) estimation, (IV) diagnostic checking based on Augmented Dickey-Fuller test, and (V) accuracy measure based on MAPE, MSE, and MAE [14].

Artificial Neural Network (ANN) is a computational intelligence model that simulates how the human brain learns and processes information. It is expected to have fewer miss-specifications in the data-driven approach (e.g., ANN) than in parametric methods (e.g., ARIMA). Standard ANN models are based on neurons that compose the input layer, which is then processed in the hidden layer and sent to the output. The number of hidden layers, the number of neurons in each layer, and the weights between neurons in various layers affect the model's performance [19]. The ANN method is extensively used for forecasting [3] due to its advantages in replicating complex system behavior [13].

Long Short-Term Memory (LSTM) is a sub-class of Recurrent Neural Network (RNN) for sequential dependent data. The primary distinction between RNN and LSTM is that the latter can hold long-range time dependency information and appropriately map input and output data. The LSTM network differs from traditional perceptron architecture (e.g., ANN) because it has a cell and gates that govern information flow. An input gate, a forget gate, an internal state (cell memory), and an output gate are all part of the LSTM. Each cell guarantees the reliability of information transmission and avoids the problem of loss of gradient[10,18].

The **hybrid ARIMA-ANN** approach implemented in this study has two key steps. The linear component of the data is analyzed by applying the ARIMA model in the first step. Later, a suitable ANN architecture was identified to cope with the nonlinear pattern of the data. Therefore, the hybrid model consists of both linear and nonlinear components as [29]:

$$y_t = L_t + N_t \tag{1}$$

where L_t represents the linear component of the model at a time, t and N_t represent the nonlinear component at time t, and y_t represents the implemented hybrid method consisting of linear and nonlinear components. First, the ARIMA model is implemented to predict the linear components. The corresponding residuals obtained from the ARIMA model ($e_t = y_t + \hat{L}_t$, where e_t denotes the residual at time t, and $\hat{L}$ represents the forecast value from the estimated relationship) are then used as input for the ANN model, which can be presented as:

$$e_t = f(e_{t-1}, e_{t-2}, ..., e_{t-n}) + \varepsilon_t \qquad (2)$$

where n represents the number of input nodes, f is a nonlinear function determined by the neural networks, and ε_t is the white noise. If Eq. 2 is denoted as $\hat{N}_t$, then the hybrid forecast at time t is defined as:

$$\hat{y}_t = \hat{L}_t + \hat{N}_t \qquad (3)$$

Figure 1b represents the detail of the hybrid ARIMA-ANN framework.

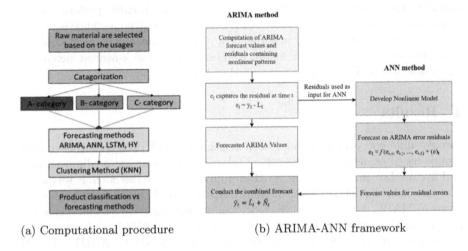

(a) Computational procedure   (b) ARIMA-ANN framework

Fig. 1. The detail computational scheme and hybrid-ANN methods

The hybrid model takes advantage of the unique features and strengths of both the ARIMA and the ANN models in capturing linear and nonlinear patterns and is commonly expected to yield more accurate results. Note that the hybrid ARIMA and LSTM is not relevant for this analysis, while the LSTM model does not perform optimally when the sample size is too small [7,27,30].

To ensure good performance, an optimization of the following hyperparameters was conducted, while implementing each method [1]. (i) **Epoch size**: An epoch stands for training the neural network with all the training data for one cycle (10–200); (ii) **Batch size**: The batch size defines the number of samples that is propagated through the network (1–4); (iii) **Number of hidden layers**: The hidden layer performs a nonlinear transformation to the input and produces an output (1–2); (iv) **Number of neurons**: A neuron is a mathematical function that is the weighted average of its input, this sum is passed through a nonlinear function, often called the activation function, (e.g., ReLU) (8–200); (v) **Dropout**

rate: The dropout rate influence the performance of neural networks by enhancing model regularization to reduce overfitting of predictions (0–20%). For example, suppose the number of neurons is too small. In that case, the system will be unable to memorize all the information required to achieve optimal prediction, or if it is too high, the system will overfit the training instances. Similarly, if a high epoch value is set, the system will overfit the predictions. Conversely, if a low epoch value is set, the system will underfit the optimal prediction. The following performance measures have been used, namely(i) Mean absolute error (MAE)= $\frac{1}{n}\sum_{t=1}^{n}|a_t - \hat{y}_t|$, (ii) Mean absolute percentage error (MAPE)= $\frac{1}{n}\sum_{t=1}^{n}\left|\frac{a_t - \hat{y}_t}{a_t}\right|$, and (iii) Mean squared error (MSE)=$\frac{1}{n}\sum_{t=1}^{n}(a_t - \hat{y}_t)^2$ are considered, where a_t is the actual observation and $\hat{y}_t$ is the predicted value.

The **k-nearest neighbors (KNN)** algorithm is one of the simplest similarity-based artificial learning algorithms, offering reliable performance in many contexts. The primary notion behind classifying a given instance is to have the closest neighbor instances in terms of a preset distance. The most common class then determines the new instance's class among the k-nearest neighbors. The value of k (=3) must be chosen a priori [23].

4   Results

Twenty different products have been considered and categorized into three groups based on usage rate. Eleven are slow-moving, four are medium-moving, and five are fast-moving products. After applying all five methods, it was found that the hybrid ARIMA-ANN method outperforms all other four methods in terms of MAPE, MAE, and MSE. One medium moving product had conflicting performance measures, where both LSTM and hybrid ARIMA-ANN can lead to higher forecast accuracy. However, for slow mowing products, ARIMA, LSTM, ANN, or hybrid ARIMA-ANN can lead to higher accuracy under different performance measures. Therefore, a careful secretion is warranted when considering slow moving products. KNN was applied to conduct a F-test. The results suggests that whether to select LSTM or hybrid ARIMA-ANN significantly impacts defining clusters. Clusters centers are also different.

Literature highlights the need for product categorization and forecast accuracy estimation. Several authors argue that forecasting is essential for the A-category of items. However, when looking at the BOM, the absence of one of the components can degrade the delivery performance of the manufacturers, while they are not keeping excess inventory for each item. Therefore, forecasting for all item categories is always crucial, and thereby careful data-driven methodology can support those medium-sized manufacturers for appropriate future planning.

5   Conclusion

The empirical results from this case study show that a hybrid model which captures both linear and nonlinear components improves the accuracy of forecasted demand. Additionally, the hybrid model is a relevant approach that overcomes traditional forecast methods' problematic or undesirable accuracy scores based on similar data sets with a short historical record lacking trends, cycles, and seasonality. The proposed hybrid model can further aid the operational decision-making of inventory management-related raw materials.

The study's main contribution is that although only twenty products from three different categories have been considered, the study can be further extended to numerous categories. The managers need to classify products and slow-moving products; they should not rely on any blind selection. It is also found that instead of applying ARIMA or LSTM, the hybrid ARIMA-ANN method can ensure higher forecast accuracy. As a future study, we will integrate the forecast results with inventory replenishment decisions to study the impact of forecast accuracy on cost or space-saving. [19] Additionally, larger data-sets than utilized in this study will further compliment the use of deep learning models for time series forecasts in similar cases.

References

1. Abbasimehr, H., Shabani, M., Yousefi, M.: An optimized model using LSTM network for demand forecasting. Comput. Ind. Eng. **143**, 106435 (2020)
2. Abbasimehr, H., Paki, R.: Improving time series forecasting using LSTM and attention models. J. Ambient Intell. Human. Comput. **13**(1), 673–691 (2022)
3. Ahmad, A.S., et al.: A review on applications of ANN and SVM for building electrical energy consumption forecasting. Renew. Sustain. Energy Rev. **33**, 102–109 (2014)
4. Babu, C.N., Reddy, B.E.: A moving-average filter based hybrid ARIMA-ANN model for forecasting time series data. Appl. Soft Comput. **23**, 27–38 (2014)
5. Boylan, J.E., Syntetos, A.A.: The accuracy of intermittent demand estimates. Int. J. Forecast. **21**(2), 303–314 (2005)
6. Boylan, J.E., Syntetos, A.A.: Spare parts management: a review of forecasting research and extensions. IMA J. Manag. Math. **21**(3), 227–237 (2010)
7. Bocewicz, G., Nielsen, P., Banaszak, Z.A., Dang, V.Q.: Cyclic steady state refinement: multimodal processes perspective. In: Frick, J., Laugen, B.T. (eds.) APMS 2011. IAICT, vol. 384, pp. 18–26. Springer, Heidelberg (2012). https://doi.org/10.1007/978-3-642-33980-6_3
8. Box, G.E., Jenkins, G.M., Reinsel, G.C., Ljung, G.M.: Time Series Analysis: Forecasting and Control. John Wiley & Sons, Hoboken (2015)
9. Büyükşahin, Ü.Ç., Ertekin, Ş: Improving forecasting accuracy of time series data using a new ARIMA-ANN hybrid method and empirical mode decomposition. Neurocomputing **361**, 151–163 (2019)
10. Chandriah, K.K., Naraganahalli, R.V.: RNN/LSTM with modified Adam optimizer in deep learning approach for automobile spare parts demand forecasting. Multimedia Tools Appl. **80**(17), 26145–26159 (2021)
11. Chaudhuri, K.D., Alkan, B.: A hybrid extreme learning machine model with harris hawks optimisation algorithm: an optimised model for product demand forecasting applications. Appl. Intell., 1–17 (2022)
12. Dolgui, A., Pashkevich, M.: On the performance of binomial and beta-binomial models of demand forecasting for multiple slow-moving inventory items. Comput. Oper. Res. **35**(3), 893–905 (2008)

13. Efendigil, T., Önüt, S., Kahraman, C.: A decision support system for demand forecasting with artificial neural networks and neuro-fuzzy models: a comparative analysis. Expert Syst. Appl. **36**(3), 6697–6707 (2009)
14. Gilbert, K.: An ARIMA supply chain model. Manag. Sci. **51**(2), 305–310 (2005)
15. Ho, S.L., Xie, M.: The use of ARIMA models for reliability forecasting and analysis. Comput. Ind. Eng. **35**(1–2), 213–216 (1998)
16. Kantasa-Ard, A., Nouiri, M., Bekrar, A., Ait el Cadi, A., Sallez, Y.: Machine learning for demand forecasting in the physical internet: a case study of agricultural products in Thailand. Int. J. Prod. Res. **59**(24), 7491–7515 (2021)
17. Khashei, M., Bijari, M.: A novel hybridization of artificial neural networks and ARIMA models for time series forecasting. Appl. Soft Comput. **11**(2), 2664–2675 (2011)
18. Kim, M., Lee, J., Lee, C., Jeong, J.: Framework of 2D KDE and LSTM-Based Forecasting for Cost-Effective Inventory Management in Smart Manufacturing. Appl. Sci. **12**(5), 2380 (2022)
19. Kourentzes, N., Trapero, J.R., Barrow, D.K.: Optimising forecasting models for inventory planning. Int. J. Prod. Econ. **225**, 107597 (2020)
20. Lesmana, E., Subartini, B., Jabar, D.A.: Analysis of forecasting and inventory control of raw material supplies in PT INDAC INT'L. In: IOP Conference Series: Materials Science and Engineering, vol. 332, no. 1, p. 012015. IOP Publishing (2018)
21. Nielsen, P., Michna, Z., Do, N.A.D.: An empirical investigation of lead time distributions. In: Grabot, B., Vallespir, B., Gomes, S., Bouras, A., Kiritsis, D. (eds.) APMS 2014. IAICT, vol. 438, pp. 435–442. Springer, Heidelberg (2014). https://doi.org/10.1007/978-3-662-44739-0_53
22. Olesen, J., et al.: Joint effect of forecasting and lot-sizing method on cost minimization objective of a manufacturer: a case study. Appl. Comput. Sci. **16**(4), 21–36 (2020)
23. Rawnaque, F.S.: Technological advancements and opportunities in Neuromarketing: a systematic review. Brain Inf. **7**(1), 1–19 (2020)
24. Sajjad, M., et al.: A novel CNN-GRU-based hybrid approach for short-term residential load forecasting. IEEE Access **8**, 143759–143768 (2020)
25. Shanmuganathan, S.: Artificial neural network modelling: an introduction. In: Shanmuganathan, S., Samarasinghe, S. (eds.) Artificial Neural Network Modelling. SCI, vol. 628, pp. 1–14. Springer, Cham (2016). https://doi.org/10.1007/978-3-319-28495-8_1
26. Syntetos, A.A., Boylan, J.E., Croston, J.D.: On the categorization of demand patterns. J. Oper. Res. Soc. **56**(5), 495–503 (2005)
27. Thibbotuwawa, A., Nielsen, P., Bocewicz, G., Banaszak, Z.: UAVs fleet mission planning subject to weather fore-cast and energy consumption constraints. In: Conference on Automation, pp. 104–114. Springer, Cham (2019). https://doi.org/10.1007/978-3-030-13273-6_11
28. Van Houdt, G., Mosquera, C., Nápoles, G.: A review on the long short-term memory model. Artif. Intell. Rev. **53**(8), 5929–5955 (2020)
29. Zhang, G.P.: Time series forecasting using a hybrid ARIMA and neural network model. Neurocomputing **50**, 159–175 (2003)
30. Zhang, R., Song, H., Chen, Q., Wang, Y., Wang, S., Li, Y.: Comparison of ARIMA and LSTM for prediction of hemorrhagic fever at different time scales in China. Plos one **17**(1), e0262009 (2022)

Fault Detection in Automatic Manufacturing Processes via 2D Image Analysis Using a Combined CNN–LSTM Model

Na Hyeon Yu and Sujeong Baek[✉]

Hanbat National University, Daejeon 34158, Republic of Korea
sbaek@hanbat.ac.kr

Abstract. Artificial intelligence, automated sensors, and robots have improved the production efficiency in smart factories. Real-time monitoring and quick responses are important to prevent time losses and increased costs caused by abnormal situations in an automated manufacturing process with several actuators. In this study, we explicitly analyzed only sequential 2D image data from a webcam to detect faults in an automatic manufacturing process without any additional sensors. A model combining a convolutional neural network and long-short term memory was used to reflect the characteristics of sequential processes. When a current process image was applied to the model, it predicted the corresponding future image captured by the camera 1 s later. For training, only image datasets collected during normal manufacturing process operations were used. The prediction error of the training datasets was used for threshold calculation to detect faults. For validation and verification, we collected image datasets for two fault types; the proposed model demonstrated the highest detection accuracy with a dynamic threshold.

Keywords: 2D image data · Fault detection · Convolutional neural network · Long short-term memory

1 Introduction

Since the 4th industrial revolution, several efforts have been dedicated towards the adoption of automated and intelligent systems in factories in an attempt to develop smart factories. In smart factories, productivity can be improved by combining artificial intelligence and the Internet of Things [1]. In an automated manufacturing process consisting of multiple actuators and sensors, a late response to abnormal conditions may lead to time losses and increased costs and reduce process efficiency. Thus, process monitoring and fault detection are important for efficient operation in an automated manufacturing system [2]. Generally, fault detection in mechanical systems is performed through analysis of analog sensor data, including vibration and temperature signals. Yang *et al.* collected sensor data using a Raspberry Pi microcontroller and created a fault detection algorithm using a convolutional neural network (CNN) model to identify the occurrence

© IFIP International Federation for Information Processing 2022
Published by Springer Nature Switzerland AG 2022
D. Y. Kim et al. (Eds.): APMS 2022, IFIP AICT 663, pp. 11–18, 2022.
https://doi.org/10.1007/978-3-031-16407-1_2

of a fault in an installed sensor in real time [3]. Lim *et al.* developed a fault prediction model by analyzing waveforms of voltage and current signals collected from the power distribution system [4]. The proposed model was found to demonstrate better performance than simple algorithms adopted in the commercial power distribution intelligence system. However, the model required additional sensors, which resulted in corresponding additional costs. In addition, it was also necessary to consider the type, number, and location of the sensors before fault detection model development. For example, Song and Baek conducted real-time fault detection for a sequential manufacturing process using programmable logic controller's digital control signals [5]. They observed a detection delay, but the current situation could not be improved. A possible solution was to install a new sensor at the beginning of the conveyor or analyze the process monitoring images rather than sensor signals.

As mentioned above, in recent years, several studies using 2D images for fault detection and diagnosis have been conducted. Chen *et al.* extracted relevant features by converting the collected sensor signals into the frequency domain for improving the performance of bearing fault diagnosis. After training a CNN, a long-short term memory (LSTM) was used to identify the type of faults, and the approach demonstrated good performance even in the presence of abundant noise [6]. Jalayer *et al.* proposed a contextual LSTM technique that reflected spatio-temporal features for the detection and diagnosis of faults in rotational machinery [7]. The features were extracted by applying fast Fourier transform to the collected data, following which a CNN and an LSTM were used. The approach demonstrated better performance than other basic deep learning models. However, so far, previous studies conducted on fault detection have usually adopted sensor signal transformed images as representative inputs; therefore, dedicated signal preprocessing is still required to generate representative input images.

To skip the elaborate preprocessing step required for input data, in this study, we aimed to detect the current state using only process images captured via a webcam. We used sequential 2D monitoring images captured by a webcam to monitor the process operation status, and we detected faulty situations in an automation process by explicitly analyzing the captured images. We conducted resizing operations as an image preprocessing task. For fault detection, a model combining a CNN and an LSTM was used to consider temporal characteristics of the recorded images and to reflect the characteristics of a sequential process.

2   2D Image Data Collection from an Automated Laser-Marking Process

In this study, we collected datasets from a laser-marking process that is installed at Hanbat National University. Typically, the laser-marking process imprints specific letters and a QR code on a product in the production process, inhere a universal serial bus (USB). A pneumatic gripper moves the USB along the target workbench; when a pallet with a USB arrives at a pre-determined position, laser-marking is performed on the USB. To collect 2D monitoring image data, a camera (Logitech C922 PRO HD STREAM WEBCAM) was installed on top of the testbed to capture all movements from the start to the end of the process. During this period, images were captured at a rate of 1 image/s using Python programming.

During normal process operation, the time elapsed between the entrance of a pallet until the next process is approximately 64 s. If a fault occurs because the pallet enters without a USB or the laser-marking machine is turned off, the process is suddenly terminated at a certain instant, and the operations are halted; note that in our study, for data analysis, 64 sequential images were captured after the process began (the average process time in normal operation). A total of 3,840 images were collected during 30 normal process cycles and 30 abnormal process cycles; 64 images were continuously captured per process cycle, as shown in Table 1. For fault detection, two arbitrary faulty states were generated during the process: (i) a pallet entering without a USB (Fault type I), and (ii) no laser marking due to machine error (Fault type II). These detailed situations are illustrated in Fig. 1. Hereafter, we use "normal data" and "faulty data" to indicate the 2D image datasets collected during normal process operations and abnormal process operations, respectively.

Table 1. Number of image datasets collected during normal and abnormal process operations.

	Number of process cycles	Number of images in one cycle	Total number of images
Normal data	30	64	1920
Faulty data	30	64	1920

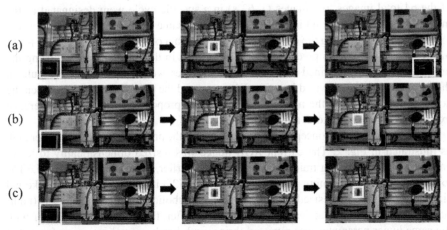

(a)

(b)

(c)

Fig. 1. 2D images collected from laser-marking process in normal and faulty states: (a) Normal data; (b) Faulty data from Fault type I (pallet without USB); (c) Faulty data from Fault type II (no laser-marking operation). Red boxes indicate the difference between normal and abnormal process status at the same time step.

3 Fault Detection via a CNN with an LSTM

As the collected datasets could not be easily analyzed via conventional statistical infer-ence, we used an artificial neural network (ANN). In an ANN, high-dimensional input data are planarized in one dimension (as a concatenated vector) and connected to a fully connected layer for classification (normal or fault state). However, as the dimen-sion increases, data loss occurs more easily during planarizing (concatenating multiple rows). In particular, image data are generally composed of three or more dimensions, as two-dimensional RGB images are collected in the form of a time series. Thus, if the existing fully connected layer is identically used with a concatenated vector, spatial information may be lost, rendering fault detection difficult [8]. To effectively detect faults using 2D sequential images, we used a neural network with convolutional layers (CNN) to consider spatial information [9]. CNNs extract significant features while maintaining the input data form for a 2D image; thus, there is no loss in the spatial information, and the output has the same dimensionality as the input data [10]. The data collected in this study were in the form of a time series, which could describe a sequential process over time. To reflect time-variant characteristics, a CNN algorithm combined with an LSTM, instead of a simple CNN, was used [11–13]. In this regard, several studies are currently under way to analyze spatio-temporal characteristics by using a combination model of CNN and LSTM. Huang *et al.* proposed a CNN–LSTM model that is capable of provid-ing time information on fault occurrences during chemical processes [14]. Jalayer *et al.* proposed a contextual LSTM technique that identified spatial features through a CNN and temporal features through an LSTM for fault detection in a rotating machine [7].

The model requires only normal data. However, as a supervised learning model, the next $(i + 1)^{th}$ image is always generated as the model output. In our analysis, out of the 64 total images, 63 images (1–63 s) in a specific cycle were designated as the model input, and another 63 images (2–64 s) in the same cycle were designated as the model output. By training the corresponding output data of the ith image as the $(i + 1)^{th}$ image, it was possible to predict the next movement in the process. Finally, using the predicted and actual obtained $(i + 1)^{th}$ images together, we attempted to detect faults in the process with unsupervised learning. We compared the pixel differences between the actual future image and the image predicted by the proposed model. If the difference exceeded a certain threshold, a fault was identified.

Using this detection concept, the final structure of the proposed model was generated, as illustrated in Fig. 2. The current RGB image was resized dimensionality to lower computation costs during training. As mentioned earlier, in the first CNN and LSTM to 18 × 32 to reduce combination layer (ConvLSTM2D layer), 64 filters with a kernel size of applied to the resized image, and the hyperbolic tangent 3 × 3 were (tanh) function was used as an activation function. Thereafter, the ConvLSTM2D layer with the same hyper-parameter was repeated thrice, with batch normalization performed at each layer. After all the ConvLSTM2D layers and batch normalizations were completed, a convolution layer with three dimensions (Conv3D) was applied using three filters with a kernel size of 3 × 3 × 3, and the sigmoid function was used as an activation function. Detailed hyper-parameter information is presented in Table 2. A general CNN has a binary classification; the output label is either 0 or 1. Thus, binary cross-entropy is usually used as a loss function [15]. However, the proposed method predicts the next consecutive image. In other words, the model output consists of continuous values rather than discrete labels. Thus, the mean squared error (MSE), the average squared difference between the predicted values and the actual values [16], was used as a loss function. If the MSE value between the predicted image and the actual future image (collected after 1 s) was greater than the threshold value, it was determined that a fault occurred in the process.

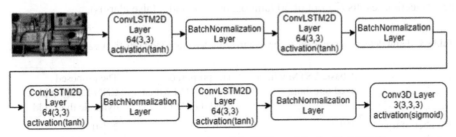

Fig. 2. Structure of proposed model (CNN combined with LSTM).

Table 2. Optimized hyper-parameter of the proposed CNN model with an LSTM for predicting the next future image.

Hyper-parameter	Value
Optimizer function	Adam
Loss equation	Mean squared error
Batch size	8
Number of epochs	400

4   Fault Detection Results for the CNN Algorithm with an LSTM

A threshold value for fault detection must be determined during the training phase. In this study, we employed two thresholding methods: (i) a fixed threshold and (ii) a dynamic threshold. The fixed threshold is a method in which all the trained datasets are correctly classified as normal datasets based on the maximum value of the MSE in the datasets obtained through normal processes (hereafter referred to as normal datasets). On the contrary, the dynamic threshold method proceeds by considering the characteristics of each time zone [17]. A dynamic threshold consists of *n-1* values (63 values in this paper), which are the summation of the average value and six times the standard deviation of the MSE values for each time zone. Each calculation result is considered as the threshold at each time point.

Based on this concept, 30 normal datasets were used to develop the trained model; additionally, 30 datasets (hereafter called as faulty datasets) were further collected to analyze the fault detection performance. Figure 1 depicts faulty situations encountered in obtaining the faulty datasets. To test the performance of the proposed model, the model was compared to a basic LSTM model. On applying the fixed threshold method to the basic LSTM model, it resulted in 14 fault occurrence alarms for 30 faulty datasets. However, all the fault alarms were identified as false alarms, as shown in Table 3. The proposed CNN-LSTM model with a fixed threshold demonstrated better detection results: 8 faults were correctly detected among 30 detection alarms (for every fault situation). Finally, the proposed fault detection model with a dynamic threshold demonstrated the best detection results (27 out of 30 fault occurrence and 3 false alarms).

Table 3. Fault detection accuracy according to fault detection methods (analyzing test datasets).

	A basic LSTM with a fixed threshold	The proposed CNN-LSTM with a fixed threshold	The proposed CNN-LSTM with a dynamic threshold
Number of true positives	0/30	8/30	27/30

For a more detailed analysis of the detection results, we monitored the detection time. The fault detection time for the best fault detection model (CNN-LSTM with the dynamic threshold) is also summarized in Table 4, according to the fault types. In the case of Fault Type I, a pallet entered without a USB, an actual fault occurred within 3.6 s on average, and the model detected the corresponding fault occurrences within approximately 3.5 s, which is almost identical to the actual fault occurrence time. In the case of Fault Type II, a process error occurred due to a fault in the laser-marking operation, an actual fault occurred within 38.5 s on average, and the proposed model detected the fault occurrences within 40 s, which indicated a slight delay. The obtained detection results appear satisfactory; however, the model demonstrates a limitation in predicting fault occurrences: it can judge only the current situation. If a fault is detected by the proposed model before it actually occurs (for example, more than 2 s early), it would be highly probable of an erroneous detection (false alarm). In addition, as the faults considered in this study do not result from deterioration or machine aging, they cannot be predicted in advance (fairly early). To address this limitation, information recorded for the purpose of manufacturing management (such as operation time of a cylinder or conveyor) should be collected using given images and analyzed using target values.

Table 4. Time information for actual fault occurrence and detection by the proposed model (CNN-LSTM with a dynamic threshold) for two fault types.

	Average time of actual fault occurrence	Average time of fault detection
Fault type I	3.6	3.5
Fault type II	38.5	40.0

5 Conclusion

In this study, a fault detection model was developed for an automated manufacturing process; 2D images were analyzed instead of the addition of another analog sensor. To consider the characteristics of sequential 2D image data captured by a webcam, fault detection was performed using a CNN algorithm combined with an LSTM. The algorithm predicted the next image (in this paper, 1 s later) by analyzing the current image. Using the predicted image, faults were detected by comparing pixel differences between the predicted and actual images. To improve the detection performance, two different thresholding methods were employed: a fixed threshold and a dynamic threshold. To compare the performance, three different detection models were analyzed: a basic LSTM with a fixed threshold, the proposed CNN-LSTM with a fixed threshold, and the proposed CNN-LSTM with a dynamic threshold. In terms of the detection rate and detection time, CNN-LSTM with a dynamic threshold demonstrated the best performance. In summary, because the proposed method employs only 2D sequential images recorded using a camera, it can be easily applied to any discrete manufacturing process, provided that monitoring images can be captured using a camera. In addition, we attempted to exclude detailed preprocessing steps for better utilization.

However, there is still further scope for improvement in the detection performance. For example, in the proposed model, equally weighted training for each pixel was conducted, but each pixel might have different attention, for example more attention to an actuator's significant movement and less attention to background. In future, the fault detection performance can also be improved by analyzing significant areas in the captured images. To effectively diagnose and repair a detected fault, various bits of information, such as the type of faults and corresponding repair methods, can be automatically derived better depending on the fault detection results.

Acknowledgement. This work was supported by project for Industry-Academic Cooperation Based Platform R&D funded Korea Ministry of SMEs and Startups in 2020 (Project No. S3025721), and supported by project for Industry-Academic Cooperation Based Platform R&D funded Korea Ministry of SMEs and Startups in 2020 (Project No. S3025825).

This paper was also supported by Korea Institute for Advancement of Technology (KIAT) grant funded by the Korea Government (MOTIE). (P0012744, HRD program for industrial innovation).

References

1. Seo, I.B., Cho, Y.B.: Comparison and analysis of chest X-ray-based deep learning loss function performance. J. Korea Inst. Info. Comm. Eng. **25**(8), 1046–1052 (2021)
2. Song, G.W., Kim, B.S., Choi, W.S.: RCM based failure-prediction system for equipment. In: Proceedings of 2010 Fall Korean Society of Mechanical Engineers, pp. 1281–1286. The Korean Society Mechanical Engineering, Republic of Korea (2010)
3. Yang, J.W., Lee, Y.D., Koo, I.S.: Timely sensor fault detection scheme based on deep learning. J. Inst. Internet, Broadcast. Comm. **20**(1), 163–169 (2020)
4. Lim, H.G., Han, K.H., Kim, Y.S., Kim, J.H.: Algorithm for detection of fault through analysis of waveform from voltage and current in distribution system. In: Proceedings of 2016 Fall Korean Institute of Electrical Engineers Conference, pp. 101–104. Korean Institute of Electrical Engineers, Republic of Korea (2016)

5. Song, Y.U., Baek, S.J.: Real-time fault detection in discrete manufacturing systems via LSTM model based on PLC digital control signals. J. Korean Soc. Ind. Syst. Eng. **44**(2), 115–123 (2021)
6. Chen, X., Zhang, B., Gao, D.: Bearing fault diagnosis base on multi-scale CNN and LSTM model. J. Intell. Manuf. **32**(4), 971–987 (2020). https://doi.org/10.1007/s10845-020-01600-2
7. Jalayer, M., Orsenigo, C., Vercellis, C.: Fault detection and diagnosis for rotating machinery: a model based on convolutional LSTM, fast Fourier and continuous wavelet transforms. Comput. Ind. **125**, 103378 (2021)
8. Kim, Y.S., Kim, N.H., Kim, J.H.: Hardware architecture of artificial neural network for large-scale network applications, In: Proceedings of 2015 Summer Annual Conference of Institute of Electronics and Information Engineers, pp. 72–75. The Institute of Electronics and Information Engineers, Republic of Korea (2015)
9. Kang, H.J.: SoftMax computation in CNN using input maximum value. J. Korea Inst. Inf. Comm. Eng. **26**(2), 325–328 (2022)
10. Lim, J.Y., Kim, D.H., Noh, T.W., Lee, B.K.: Remaining useful life prediction for lithium-ion batteries using EMD-CNN-LSTM hybrid method. Trans. Korean Inst. Power Electr. **27**(1), 48–55 (2021)
11. Lee, H.H., Hong, N.Y., Lee, T.W.: Comparison of prediction for multivariate time series between LSTM and VARX. J. Korean Data Inf. Sci. Soc. **33**(1), 35–47 (2022)
12. Kim, K.T., Lee, B.M., Kim, J.W.: Feasibility of deep learning algorithms for binary classification problems. J. Korean Intell. Inf. Syst. Soc. **23**(1), 95–108 (2017)
13. Cho, T.S., Lee, M.H., Kim, M.S., Song, B.H., Park, P.K.: Heating furnace temperature control system of anomaly detection method using LSTM autoencoder, In: Proceedings of 2021 Korean Institute of Electrical Engineers Conference, pp. 269–270. Korean Institute of Electrical Engineers, Republic of Korea (2021)
14. Huang, T., Zhang, Q., Tang, X., Zhao, S., Lu, X.: A novel fault diagnosis method based on CNN and LSTM and its application in fault diagnosis for complex systems. Artif. Intell. Rev. **55**, 1289–1315 (2022)
15. Kim, Y.H., Woo, G.M. Kim, H.B., Park, H.H.: Life pattern-based depression prediction machine learning method using NHANES dataset, In: Proceedings of the Korean Institute of Communication Sciences Conference, pp. 81–82. Korean Institute of Communication Sciences, Republic of Korea (2021)
16. Son, S.J., Chen, T.J., Park, A.R., Baek, S.J.: Spectrum data compression using ResNet-convolutional autoencoder based neural network. J. Korea Academia-Ind. Coop. Soc. **22**(12), 135–143 (2021)
17. Yu, N.H., Baek, S.: Improving next image prediction performance using dynamic threshold for deep learning based fault detection in automated systems. In: Proceedings of the Korean Society of Mechanical Engineers Conference, p. 32. The Korean Society of Mechanical Engineers, Republic of Korea (2022)

An Automated Machine Learning Framework for Predictive Analytics in Quality Control

Mattheos Fikardos[1]([⊠]) [iD], Katerina Lepenioti[1] [iD], Alexandros Bousdekis[1] [iD], Enrica Bosani[2], Dimitris Apostolou[1] [iD], and Gregoris Mentzas[1] [iD]

[1] Information Management Unit (IMU), Institute of Communication and Computer Systems (ICCS), National Technical University of Athens (NTUA), Athens, Greece
{mfikardos,klepenioti,albous,dapost,gmentzas}@mail.ntua.gr
[2] Whirlpool EMEA, Benton Harbor, USA
enrica_bosani@whirlpool.com

Abstract. Developments in Machine Learning (ML) in the last years resulted in taking as granted their usage and their necessity clear in areas such as manufacturing and quality control. Such areas include case specific requirements and restrictions that require the human expert's knowledge and effort to apply the ML algorithms efficiently. This paper proposes a framework architecture that utilizes Automated Machine Learning (AutoML) to minimize human intervention while constructing and maintaining ML models for quality control. The data analyst gives the setting for multiple configurations while designing predictive quality models which are automatically optimized and maintained. Moreover, experiments are conducted to test the framework in both the performance of the prediction models and the time needed to construct the models.

Keywords: Machine learning · Automated machine learning · Quality control · Predictive quality

1 Introduction

Quality of products and processes have increasingly concerned the manufacturing firms because negative consequences do not show up until the product is actually produced or worse, until the customer returns it [1, 2]. Predictive quality moves beyond traditional quality evaluation methods towards extracting useful insights from various data sources with the use of Machine Learning (ML) in an Industry 4.0 context [1]. Even though well-known methodologies like the Cross-Industry Standard Process for Data Mining (CRISP-DM) [3] can be applied, their generic approach does not consider domain-specific requirements in manufacturing quality procedures [4]. This limitation requires the data analyst and the production expert to work alongside the AutoML pipeline.

In this paper, we propose the use of AutoML in methodologies similar to CRISP-DM that can facilitate their implementation in a predictive quality context. Despite the fact that extensive research for ML in manufacturing has already been conducted [5,

© IFIP International Federation for Information Processing 2022
Published by Springer Nature Switzerland AG 2022
D. Y. Kim et al. (Eds.): APMS 2022, IFIP AICT 663, pp. 19–26, 2022.
https://doi.org/10.1007/978-3-031-16407-1_3

6], highlighting advantages, challenges and applications, research on AutoML in the manufacturing quality function is still in preliminary stages [4, 7–9]. However, AutoML has the potential to reduce time-consuming tasks of constructing ML models for quality procedures, allowing the data analyst to devote more time on data integration and deployment. In this way, the human intervention in ML model configuration is minimized since the algorithms are automatically updated and optimized based on new data.

The rest of the paper is organized as follows. Section 2 outlines the theoretical background on AutoML. Section 3 presents our proposed approach for AutoML in predictive quality. Section 4 describes the implementation of the proposed approach in a real-life scenario of white goods production. Section 5 concludes the paper and presents our plans for future work.

2   Theoretical Background on Automated Machine Learning

AutoML aims to simplify and automate the whole ML pipeline, giving the opportunity to domain experts to utilize ML without deep knowledge about the technologies and the need of a data analyst [10]. The most fundamental concept of AutoML is the Hyper Parameter Optimization (HPO) problem where hyperparameters are automatically tunned for ML systems to optimize their performance [10] for problems such as classification, regression and time series forecasting. As of today, further developments to the field of AutoML added additional capabilities to the AutoML pipeline: *Data Preparation, Feature Engineering, Model Generation* and *Model Evaluation* [11].

The *Data Preparation* and *Feature Engineering* steps are associated with the available data used for the ML algorithms. The former includes actions for collecting, cleaning and augmenting the data, with the latter includes actions for extracting, selecting and constructing features. In the *Model Generation* step, a search is executed with the goal of finding the best performing model for the predictions, such as k-nearest neighbors (KNN) [12], Support Vector Machines (SVM) [13], Neural Networks (NN), etc. The *Model Evaluation* step is responsible for evaluating the generated models based on predefined metrics and runs in parallel to the Model Generation step. The evaluation of the generated models is used for optimization of existing models and the construction of new models. The search procedure of AutoML terminates based on predefined restrictions, such as the performance of the models or the time passed.

From a technical perspective, AutoML attracted a lot of research interest resulting in several AutoML frameworks, such as: Autokeras [14], FEDOT [15] and TPOT [16]. Additionally, research focusing on benchmarking several AutoML frameworks [17, 18] concludes that they do not outperform humans yet but give promising results.

3   The Proposed Approach for Automated Machine Learning in Predictive Quality

The proposed approach focuses on the development of dynamic ML algorithms using AutoML to minimize human intervention in model configuration. The proposed approach is divided into two phases: the ***Design phase*** and the ***Runtime phase***, as depicted in Fig. 1. In a nutshell the *Data analyst* based on technical and case specific knowledge designs the ML models used for the predictions which are then used by the *Quality Expert* for predictions and are automatically updated when new data are available for training. Compared with the traditional process of creating and maintaining ML models for quality control, the *Data Analyst* would spend valuable time constructing models. Even though the data preprocessing algorithms may exist, the HPO and fine tuning of the models would have been performed via trial and error from the *Data Analyst*.

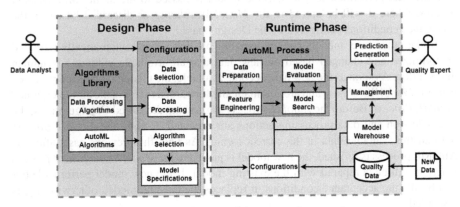

Fig. 1. The architecture of the proposed approach.

3.1 Design Phase

The Design phase is executed by the data analyst, who is responsible for defining the necessary configurations that bootstrap the analysis solving the predictive quality problem under examination by employing the available *AutoML algorithms*. The Design phase consists of two components, *Configuration* and *Algorithms Library*. During the *Configuration*, the data analyst must first select which of the available quality data are required for the predictions to be carried out. After the *Data Selection*, if necessary, the data analyst can apply *Data Processing Algorithms* from the *Algorithms Library*, which may include data cleaning, data augmentation, feature extraction and feature selection.

Regarding the ML algorithms, the data analyst specifies the AutoML algorithm that will search for the best predictive model, also found in the *Algorithms Library*. For the *Algorithm Selection*, the data analyst can define the configuration of the selected AutoML algorithm, e.g., construction parameters for the model, metrics for evaluation, and termination conditions. With the *Model Specifications*, additional case specific configurations can be made, such as model acceptance conditions and output formats, that will be used by the *Model Management* process during the Runtime phase.

3.2 Runtime Phase

The Runtime phase is responsible for executing the *AutoML process* and the *Model Management* of the constructed models. It can start either when the data analyst creates new configurations or when new data become available for existing models.

In the first case, after the data analyst completes the configuration for the predictive quality problem, the *Configurations* are stored for later use and the *AutoML process starts* searching for a model. During that process, additional data processing actions may be executed from the AutoML algorithm at the Data Preparation and Feature Engineering steps. After the input data transformations have been completed, the algorithm starts the search by constructing several models followed by the evaluation and optimization of the candidate ones. When the search step finishes, a single model is selected as the model with the best performance. The selected model is passed to the *Model Management* process, where it will be stored in the *Model Warehouse* or discarded based on the acceptance conditions configured in the Design phase.

In the other case, models already used for predictions are automatically retrained or optimized and changed based on new data that are available without any human intervention. As soon as the new data become available, the related models are retrieved from the *Model Warehouse* and are automatically forwarded to repeat the aforementioned *AutoML Process*. Before the *AutoML process* starts using the stored Configurations, the data selection and data processing actions are executed, feeding the *AutoML process* with all the available data in the correct format. As with the previous case, after the AutoML process is finished, the new model is passed to the *Model Management* process where it will be compared with the existing model. If the new model performs better and fulfills the acceptance conditions, it replaces the existing model, otherwise it gets discarded.

In both cases the *Model Management* process can retrieve the corresponding model for a prediction and pass the model to the *Prediction Generation* process to execute predictions. The generated predictions are then communicated to the quality expert, in order to support the predictive quality-related decisions.

4   Application to a White Goods Production Use Case

4.1   Use Case Description

In the Whirlpool production model, the whole white goods production is tested from quality and safety point of view in order to ensure a high standard level of product quality to final customers. The use case under examination deals with the microwave production line. At the end of the production line, random inspections are made from employees to detect defective products, which are subsequently repaired or replaced. During the quality control, several features of the products and the tests are recorded, including their Defect Groups which are used as categories for similar Defects. In this scenario, we opted to predict the Defect Group of the defective products and the number of orders found with defects for the following days. The former is a classification problem while the latter is a Regression/Timeseries forecasting problem.

4.2   Dataset

Based on the available data sources, we constructed a Quality Control Data Model as shown in Fig. 2. The main entity in the Quality Control Data Model is the Defect Instance which maps all the entries from the data. Common attributes are used as reference fields for other entities such as the Product, the Part and the Defect Type, which provide further information about the Defect Instance. This Data Model gave us the ability to better manage the available data and retrieve additional information if needed. The experiments were performed based on a limited amount of data. The dataset consisted of 25655 entries during a span of 270 Days and included a total of 38 features from which we extracted each entity as a Defect Instance.

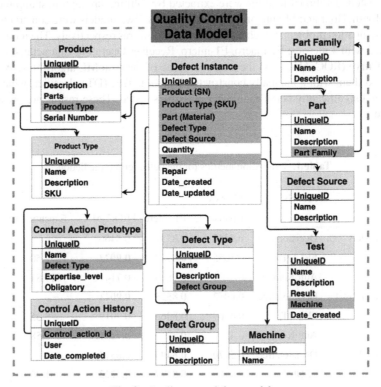

Fig. 2. Quality control data model

4.3   Results

The proposed approach was implemented with the Python libraries AutoKeras and Fedot. Specifically, the Structured Data Regressor and the Structured Data Classifier are used from the AutoKeras library, in order to find the best performing Neural Network (NN) for the predictions, and the Fedot library in order to compose a chain of data-preprocessing and ML models. In our experiments, 3 models were implemented for each algorithm as follows: 1) an *initial model* trained only with the 80% of the available data, 2) a *retrained model* which was the initial model retrained with all the available data and 3) a *new model* that started the AutoML process from scratch with all the available data. The *retrained* and the *new* model were automatically trained following the proposed approach with the configurations made by the *initial model*. Additionally, regarding the execution time of the experiments that follow the values are based on configured stopping conditions, which can be changed resulting in different values.

Predict Defect Group. Starting with the configuration, data processing algorithms were used to select 6 features of the Defect Instances: The Date Created, the Product Type (SKU), the Defect Source, the Station ID and the Part Family. From the first one, the Date Created, additional features were extracted by splitting up the timestamp into the Year, Month, Hour and Minute of the recorded defect. Two models were constructed for this classification problem, which use Fedot and AutoKeras respectively. The models are evaluated with 4 metrics: F1-macro, F1-micro, Receiver Operating Characteristic Area Under Curve (ROC-AUC) and the execution time of the AutoML algorithms. We also compared them with a manually constructed Decision Tree (DT) classifier, which had performed significantly better than other classifiers tested. These results are presented in Table 1.

Table 1. Evaluation metrics for the defect group prediction

	Models	Metrics			
		F1-macro	F1-micro	ROC-AUC	Execution time (s)
Initial models	Decision tree	**0.5347**	0.8331	0.8466	–
	FEDOT	0.5055	**0.8363**	**0.9023**	1212.50
	AutoKeras	0.4509	0.7813	0.7141	1019.81
Retrained models	Decision tree	**0.6052**	**0.8525**	**0.9041**	–
	FEDOT	0.4969	0.8368	0.9019	9.35
	AutoKeras	0.4510	0.7813	0.7141	0.58
New models	Decision tree	**0.5170**	**0.8403**	0.8514	–
	FEDOT	0.4909	0.8277	**0.8722**	91.96
	AutoKeras	0.4631	0.7681	0.7177	953.36

Even though the DT classifier outperformed the other models in almost all cases, the AutoML proposed models with an acceptable performance, while the FEDOT model has a similar performance with the DT. The models trained with all the available data performed slightly better than the initial ones and the execution time for AutoML algorithms is also acceptable, especially in the case of the *retrained models*. Finally, it is important to note the significance of choosing the evaluation metric for the model acceptance conditions, since this may affect the selection of the model.

Predict Defective orders. With data preprocessing, the Defect Instances were summed based on the attribute Date Created to produce the needed timeseries. Two models were constructed by selecting two AutoML algorithms: the Fedot by configuring the problem as timeseries, and the TimeSeriesForecaster of the AutoKeras. The performance of these models is evaluated with the Mean Square Error (MSE), the Mean Absolute Error (MAE) and the execution time of the AutoML algorithms, as shown in Table 2.

From the evaluation metrics we observe that both AutoML algorithms have performed well. In the case of the *initial models*, the metrics values are worse due to the inadequate data for training. As in the previous results the execution time follows the same pattern and all the models were proposed in a reasonable amount of time.

Table 2. Table captions should be placed above the tables.

	Models	Metrics		
		MSE	MAE	Execution time (s)
Initial models	FEDOT	0.2338	0.2017	101.88
	AutoKeras	**0.0402**	**0.1624**	187.39
Retrained models	FEDOT	0.1361	**0.1002**	0.32
	AutoKeras	**0.0201**	0.1082	2.57
New models	FEDOT	0.1391	**0.0988**	127.48
	AutoKeras	**0.0191**	0.1036	11.17

5 Conclusions and Future Work

In this paper we proposed a framework for predictive quality using AutoML algorithms, where the human supervision is decreased as existing prediction models are automatically optimized based on new data. By reducing the effort needed to construct and maintain prediction models, the data analyst can devote more time to inspect and understand case-specific requirements. From the experimental results we concluded that by leveraging AutoML algorithms, good performing models can be acquired and automatically optimized in a reasonable amount of time.

The growing interest in the AutoML field in the last few years provides a promising future for its development and applications. As the automated steps of AutoML are improved, their ability to adapt or incorporate case specific requirements or restrictions paves the way for its extensive application to predictive quality. In our future work, we plan to examine in depth various configurations in the proposed framework, and test more AutoML algorithms in the predictive quality context.

Acknowledgements. This work is partly funded by the European Union's Horizon 2020 project COALA "COgnitive Assisted agile manufacturing for a LAbor force supported by trustworthy Artificial Intelligence" (Grant agreement No 957296). The work presented here reflects only the authors' view and the European Commission is not responsible for any use that may be made of the information it contains.

References

1. Zonnenshain, A., Kenett, R.S.: Quality 4.0—the challenging future of quality engineering. Qual. Eng. **32**(4), 614–626 (2020)
2. Bousdekis, A., Wellsandt, S., Bosani, E., Lepenioti, K., Apostolou, D., Hribernik, K., Mentzas, G.: Human-AI collaboration in quality control with augmented manufacturing analytics. In: Dolgui, A., Bernard, A., Lemoine, D., von Cieminski, G., Romero, D. (eds.) Advances in Production Management Systems. Artificial Intelligence for Sustainable and Resilient Production Systems: IFIP WG 5.7 International Conference, APMS 2021, Nantes, France, September 5–9, 2021, Proceedings, Part IV, pp. 303–310. Springer International Publishing, Cham (2021). https://doi.org/10.1007/978-3-030-85910-7_32
3. Chapman, P., Clinton, J., Kerber, R., Khabaza, T., Reinartz, T.P., Shearer, C., Wirth, R.: CRISP-DM 1.0: Step-by-step data mining guide (2000)
4. Krauß, J., Pacheco, B.M., Zang, H.M., Schmitt, R.H.: Automated machine learning for predictive quality in production. Procedia CIRP **93**, 443–448 (2020)
5. Wuest, T., Weimer, D., Irgens, C., Thoben, K.D.: Machine learning in manufacturing: advantages, challenges, and applications. Prod. Manuf. Res. **4**(1), 23–45 (2016)
6. Dogan, A., Birant, D.: Machine learning and data mining in manufacturing. Expert Syst. Appl. **166**, 114060 (2021)
7. Ferreira, L., Pilastri, A., Sousa, Vítor., Romano, F., Cortez, P.: Prediction of maintenance equipment failures using automated machine learning. In: Yin, H., et al. (eds.) Intelligent Data Engineering and Automated Learning – IDEAL 2021: 22nd International Conference, IDEAL 2021, Manchester, UK, November 25–27, 2021, Proceedings, pp. 259–267. Springer International Publishing, Cham (2021). https://doi.org/10.1007/978-3-030-91608-4_26
8. Gerling, A., Ziekow, H., Hess, A., Schreier, U., Seiffer, C., Abdeslam, D.O.: Comparison of algorithms for error prediction in manufacturing with automl and a cost-based metric. J. Intell. Manuf. **33**(2), 555–573 (2022). https://doi.org/10.1007/s10845-021-01890-0
9. Ribeiro, R., Pilastri, A., Moura, C., Rodrigues, F., Rocha, R., Cortez, P.: Predicting the tear strength of woven fabrics via automated machine learning: an application of the CRISP-DM methodology (2020)
10. Hutter, F., Kotthoff, L., Vanschoren, J. (eds.): Automated Machine Learning: Methods, Systems, Challenges. Springer International Publishing, Cham (2019). https://doi.org/10.1007/978-3-030-05318-5
11. He, X., Zhao, K., Chu, X.: AutoML: a survey of the state-of-the-art. Knowl.-Based Syst. **212**, 106622 (2021)
12. Altman, N.S.: An introduction to kernel and nearest-neighbor nonparametric regression. Am. Stat. **46**(3), 175–185 (1992)
13. Cortes, C., Vapnik, V.: Support-vector networks. Mach. Learn. **20**(3), 273–297 (1995)
14. Jin, H., Song, Q., Hu, X.: Auto-keras: an efficient neural architecture search system. In: Proceedings of the 25th ACM SIGKDD International Conference on Knowledge Discovery & Data Mining, pp. 1946–1956 (2019)
15. Nikitin, N.O., et al.: Automated evolutionary approach for the design of composite machine learning pipelines. Future Gener. Comput. Syst. **127**, 109–125 (2022)
16. Olson, R.S., Moore, J.H.: TPOT: a tree-based pipeline optimization tool for automating machine learning. In: Workshop on Automatic Machine Learning, pp. 66–74. PMLR (2016)
17. Gijsbers, P., LeDell, E., Thomas, J., Poirier, S., Bischl, B., Vanschoren, J.: An open source AutoML benchmark. arXiv preprint arXiv:1907.00909 (2019)
18. Zöller, M.A., Huber, M.F.: Benchmark and survey of automated machine learning frameworks. J. Artif. Intell. Res. **70**, 409–472 (2021)

Comparison of Machine Learning's- and Humans'- Ability to Consistently Classify Anomalies in Cylinder Locks

Tim Andersson[✉], Markus Bohlin, Tomas Olsson, and Mats Ahlskog

Mälardalen University, Eskilstuna, Sweden
{Tim.Andersson,Markus.Bohlin,Tomas.Olsson,Mats.Ahlskog}@mdu.se

Abstract. Historically, cylinder locks' quality has been tested manually by human operators after full assembly. The frequency and the characteristics of the testing procedure for these locks wear the operators' wrists and lead to varying results of the quality control. The consistency in the quality control is an important factor for the expected lifetime of the locks which is why the industry seeks an automated solution. This study evaluates how consistently the operators can classify a collection of locks, using their tactile sense, compared to a more objective approach, using torque measurements and Machine Learning (ML). These locks were deliberately chosen because they are prone to get inconsistent classifications, which means that there is no ground truth of how to classify them. The ML algorithms were therefore evaluated with two different labeling approaches, one based on the results from the operators, using their tactile sense to classify into 'working' or 'faulty' locks, and a second approach by letting an unsupervised learner create two clusters of the data which were then labeled by an expert using visual inspection of the torque diagrams. The results show that an ML-solution, trained with the second approach, can classify mechanical anomalies, based on torque data, more consistently compared to operators, using their tactile sense. These findings are a crucial milestone for the further development of a fully automated test procedure that has the potential to increase the reliability of the quality control and remove an injury-prone task from the operators.

Keywords: Machine learning · Binary classification · Torque data · Multiple experts · Cylinder lock

1 Introduction

The result from the production process for mechanical parts is dependent on the quality of the material, machinery, personnel, environment, and measurements. These factors will eventually cause dimensional deviations that exceed the given tolerances [1]. A product that is an assembly of several parts will inherently be sensitive to these deviations. In this article, a type of pin-tumbler cylinder lock mechanism is considered [2]. A lock consists of tens of moving parts, see Fig. 1, where a deviation from the given tolerances

© IFIP International Federation for Information Processing 2022
Published by Springer Nature Switzerland AG 2022
D. Y. Kim et al. (Eds.): APMS 2022, IFIP AICT 663, pp. 27–34, 2022.
https://doi.org/10.1007/978-3-031-16407-1_4

in the production process can result in increased friction or an unsmooth jerky motion when the lock is operated. The locks get tested at the very end of the assembly process, before packaging for delivery, to ensure the quality of the product. It is not possible to detect faults by a visual inspection, instead, testing is done by experienced operators that subjectively decide upon the quality of a lock by using their tactile sense when turning the lock mechanism with the corresponding key, an operation which unfortunately can lead to substantial wear of the operators' wrists. The faults that can occur during the production of the lock mechanism can easily be detected when the lock needs relatively high torque to operate, but in other cases, it is not easy to detect faults, such as when the lock has not been oiled properly. Therefore, different operators might classify these locks as both working and faulty. The result of inconsistent classifications can lead to greater variation in the expected lifetime of a lock. The purpose of this research is to investigate the possibility of an automated solution to objectively test locks by analyzing the required torque to turn the key 360 degrees. An automated method can potentially increase the reliability in the testing phase and remove a monotonous and injury-prone task from the operators. When analyzing sensor data, it is common to use Machine Learning (ML) because of its ability to effectively detect patterns in high dimensional datasets [3]. The main research questions this study seeks to answer are, how consistent can the operators classify locks, using their tactile sense, compared to an automated solution, using torque data and ML, and is the operator's tactile sense suitable to use as a source of labels for the training of the ML algorithms? This study evaluates three different ML algorithms' ability to consistently classify mechanical anomalies in the locks with two different approaches to create labels for the training dataset, the results are then compared to the operators' ability. The company where this study was done, is one of the largest manufacturers in the world of different types of locks. Furthermore, to the best of our knowledge, this paper is the first published study on an automated solution for quality control of locks. It is therefore expected that the results from this study are of great interest for this industry but also, for other applications where fault detection is done by rotating a mechanical system.

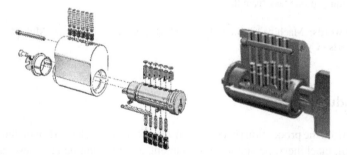

Fig. 1. Illustration of the cylinder lock that was used in this study [4].

2   Literature Review

Today's harsh global competition forces the industry to constantly improve its cost-efficiency. To achieve this, it is important to minimize downtime of the systems and machinery which has led to constant monitoring of products' health status to predict when corrective actions are needed based on sensor data, this is called Predictive Maintenance (PdM) [3]. This is similar to what this study seeks to achieve in the context of locks. Although the PdM method can lead to an improved lifetime and downtime its success is highly dependent on the sensor data and the gained insights the model is based upon [5]. The PdM method often needs to handle high-dimensional datasets and ML has proven to be successful for such tasks which are why ML algorithms are often used [3]. Two common methods in ML are called supervised- and unsupervised- learning [6]. In this study, both a supervised and an unsupervised learning approach were used. Supervised learning is an agent that learns a function based on a set of input-output pairs, i.e. labeled observations, that can map the input to output. These input-output pairs are assumed to be correct and can therefore act as a ground truth. However, if the data are labeled by multiple experts, as in this study, the labels can be contradictory and affect the classification results negatively. To counteract this problem there exist different methods to develop consensus models, such as majority voting, which was used in this study, but also more complex approaches [7]. In contrast, an unsupervised learner finds patterns in the input without any explicit feedback. Unsupervised learners often have the task of clustering observations based on similar properties. In [3] the authors reviewed 36 different papers that have used ML algorithms in PdM implementations where it can be seen that Support Vector Machine (SVM), Decision Tree (DT), K-Nearest Neighbor (KNN) and K-Means have been frequently implemented. When developing ML algorithms for classification tasks every class should be represented equally often in the dataset to avoid the algorithm getting biased towards a specific class, and hence poor performance [8]. In essence, it is in practice often easier to get data regarding a normal condition of a system compared to an abnormal condition, but in many cases, it is the anomalies that are of interest. To solve skewed datasets a synthetic dataset can be generated based on the original dataset with methods for balancing minority classes, for example, SMOTE [9], which is the approach used in this paper.

3   Method and Implementation

To evaluate the operators' ability to consistently classify mechanical anomalies, using their tactile sense, a test was designed where 9 different operators were instructed to classify the same collection of 46 unused locks as either 'faulty' or 'working' according to their opinion of the quality. The set of locks was deliberately chosen because they had not been lubricated properly for three years after they were stored, which should result in a higher frequency of minor mechanical anomalies that can typically be difficult to detect with the human tactile sense. The test resulted in 413 votes in total (one of the operators forgot to classify a single lock). The distribution of all votes between the two classes were 84% 'working and 16% 'faulty'. For assessing the inconsistency of the operators, we compute the majority vote fraction, that is, the percentage of votes consistent with the majority vote for each lock. A low majority vote fraction indicates a low consistency between operators and vice versa. For instance, if 5 voted 'working' and 4 voted 'faulty', then the majority vote is 'working' and the majority vote fraction is about 56%, which is a low consistency. Given that we have only 9 operators, this is the lowest possible value of consistency. In contrast, if all operators voted the same, we would have a fraction of 100% which is the highest possible value of consistency.

3.1 Collecting, Processing and Labeling of Torque Data

The operators use their tactile sense to detect anomalies related to the change in the needed torque to turn the key when the lock is faulty, which is the reason why the automated solution used a torque measuring machine to collect data. To get a similar evaluation of the automated solution's consistency, we collected 9 different torque measurements per lock that then could be classified by the ML algorithm in order to get 9 different "votes" corresponding to the votes from the 9 operators (however, due to the missing data, one of the locks was tested 8 times). The machine collects the data with a torque transducer by holding the cylinder in a fixed position while turning the cylinder core with the corresponding key during a constant angular velocity of 30 degrees per second for 360 degree-turn in an angular position system with a resolution of 0.1 degrees resulting in 3600 measuring points for each lock. All measuring instruments are subjected to a specific degree of variations in their measuring results depending on the instrument's precision and surrounding noise. This means that 9 repeated torque measurements from the same lock will all be unique. The torque transducer used in this study has a range of 0.1–200 Nm and a sensitivity of 0.02 Nm [10]. Approximately 0.5% of the torque measurements for different angles lost data when they experienced a sudden change in friction resulting from the lack of lubrication. This is due to the cycle time of 1 ms that the computer reads the torque transducer with. The spring-effect that occurs from the sudden change of friction will force the lock to rotate too fast and therefore resulting in missed readings. This was solved by using linear interpolation [11] with the neighboring values. It is a common understanding that an ML algorithm will not perform any better than the labeled data it has been trained on. Since it is already known that the subjective evaluations of the locks' quality done by the operators' tactile sense can give inconsistent results, the ML algorithms are trained using two different labeling methods. This approach makes it possible to evaluate how the two different labeling methods will affect the classification results from the ML algorithms.

Tactile Sense Labeling. The operators have only knowledge of classifying the locks based on their tactile sense, so an alternative method was used to label the torque measurements. The first set of reference labels is created based on the classification results from the operators. The torque measurements from a specific lock are labeled such that it has the same fraction between the two different labels as the operators' labels for the same lock. To minimize the effect on the training result from variations in the measurements that originates from a specific lock, the torque measurements were randomly chosen to belong to a specific class fraction. For example, lock x was labeled 'faulty' 5 times and 4 times as 'working' by the operators when they used their tactile sense, this means that 5 torque measurements were randomly labeled as 'faulty and 4 were randomly labeled as 'working' for the same lock. This approach was repeated 10 times to be able to calculate an average result from 10 different evaluations for each of the sets of labels for the torque dataset.

Cluster Labeling. The second set of reference labels was created by letting an unsupervised learner, named k-means, divide the dataset into two different clusters such that the sum of the squared Euclidian distances from each measurement-point to the cluster centroid is minimized. By visual inspection of the torque diagrams from the two clusters, an expert identified one cluster that contained torque measurements with more torque anomalies, see Fig. 2. This cluster's torque measurements were labeled as 'faulty' and the other cluster as 'working'. This resulted in a dataset with 37% of the torque measurements labeled as 'working' and 63% labeled as 'faulty'. The method of analyzing torque diagrams from locks has not been evaluated before which means there is no established ground truth so the size and labels for the clusters are not important, the main focus is consistency.

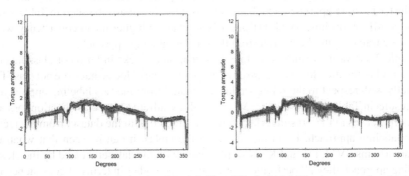

Fig. 2. Torque diagrams labeled as 'working' (left) and 'faulty' (right) by an expert after clustering using the k-means method.

3.2 Training and Evaluation

The ML algorithms SVM, DT and KNN were chosen in this study because they are commonly used in similar applications. The ML algorithms were initially trained on a synthetic dataset based on the original torque dataset using a systematic parameter variation with a Bayesian Optimization algorithm [12] to get suitable parameters for the ML algorithms. The purpose of this was to give the different ML algorithms optimal circumstances for the training on the real dataset to be able to compare the methods' results knowing that they probably have the optimal settings. All the ML algorithms were tested by excluding all the data gathered from one lock from the dataset and the rest of the data from all the other locks were used as a training dataset i.e. leave-one-out cross-validation [13]. The training dataset was balanced with the method SMOTE. This process was done iteratively for every lock in the dataset until all the torque measurements from each lock have been classified. The final labels from an ML algorithm for all 46 locks were chosen based on how the majority of the torque measurements that originate from the same lock were classified. Similar to the operators, the uncertainty and inconsistency of the ML algorithms were assessed using the majority label fraction for each lock i.e. consistency, and then the average consistency for the two classes was calculated. The processing of the collected data and the implementation of the algorithms were all done in MATLAB [14].

4   Results

In the tables below are the experimental results from the classification of locks. The tables are structured such that the results related to a dataset created with a specific labeling approach are located in the corresponding column named after the used labeling approach. Table 1 shows how consistent the torque measurements that originate from the same lock were labeled at mean consistency. The results show that the tactile sense labeling approach resulted in a dataset with a low mean consistency of 86 and 61% for the 'working' and 'faulty' classes respectively compared to the corresponding values for the cluster labeling approach which are 97 and 98%. It can also be seen in Table 1 that the three ML algorithms SVM, DT and KNN achieved higher mean consistency when they were trained with the dataset from the cluster labeling approach.

Table 2 shows the results from the classification of locks in terms of classification loss. The classification loss is expressed as the percentage of locks that were not classified correctly with respect to the reference labels created from the two labeling approaches. The results in Table 2 show that the ML algorithms suffered high classification loss and great differences in their results when they were trained with the dataset from the tactile sense labeling approach. From the results in the tables, it can be seen that when the ML algorithms SVM, DT and KNN were trained with the dataset created by the cluster labeling approach they all performed similarly to each other in terms of consistency but SVM outperformed DT and KNN in terms of classification loss.

Table 1. Mean (μ) and standard deviation of consistency for each ML algorithm

	Tactile sense labeling [%]				Cluster labeling [%]			
	Working		Faulty		Working		Faulty	
	μ	σ	μ	σ	μ	σ	μ	σ
Dataset	86	11	61	8	97	7	98	8
SVM	100	3	–	–	95	11	98	8
KNN	80	16	81	18	94	14	95	13
DT	86	15	75	18	94	12	95	13

Table 2. Classification loss i.e. percentage of locks that were not classified correctly for each class.

	Tactile sense labeling [%]		Cluster labeling [%]	
	Working	*Faulty*	*Working*	*Faulty*
SVM	0	100	0	0
KNN	45	50	17	3
DT	20	100	12	10

5 Conclusion and Discussion

In this study, a comparison has been made regarding how consistent the operators can classify mechanical anomalies in locks into two groups, named 'faulty' and 'working', using their tactile sense compared to an automated solution using torque measurements and machine learning. The results from this study show that operators are likely to achieve about 74% consistency on average when asked to repeatedly classify mechanical anomalies in locks resulting from the lack of lubrication. The corresponding values for the automated solution are 96% when trained using the cluster labeling approach and 88% when trained with the tactile sense labeling approach. However, when ML algorithms were trained with the tactile sense labeling approach, they suffered 53% classification loss, on average, as compared to only 7% with the cluster labeling approach. An observation during the experiments that could partially explain this was that the operators rotated the locks faster and with greater variation in their techniques compared to the automated test machine. When the machine rotated the locks, some of them started to oscillate, this did not happen for the operators. It was possible to recreate this phenomenon when an operator rotated the key inside the lock with the same angular velocity as the test machine. This shows that the angular velocity is vital for certain behaviors to arise and can be an explanation for why the operators are not as consistent as the test machine to classify the locks since they all have different testing techniques. From the results in this paper, it can be concluded that the automated solution can measure torque variations in the locks such that the ML algorithms (SVM, DT and KNN) can achieve higher consistency in their classifications, compared to the operators. Furthermore, it seems promising to use a more objective labeling approach such as the cluster labeling approach augmented with expert judgment. An established ground truth regarding how to evaluate torque diagrams could be used in a similar approach to categorize different types of mechanical anomalies automatically, and, possibly, with even higher consistency and precision than either of the variants hitherto investigated. The approach of using torque measurements and ML to detect anomalies of a rotating mechanical system has been done before [15] but, mapping each measurement to an angular position seems to be less common. The advantage of this mapping, compared to using regular time series data, is that there are no phase shifts between the observations which minimize the need for preprocessing of the data.

5.1 Threat to the Validity and Future Work

This study is done on a small sample of 46 locks and with just 9 operators to compare with. These factors are an obvious threat to the external validity of this study. The test was performed by letting the operators follow a set of instructions without supervision. This means that there is no way of knowing if they followed the instructions correctly or if they performed the test with their best intentions and during the training, synthetic data were used to get balanced datasets, these factors are a threat to the internal validity of the study. The next step in this research is to gather more data from locks directly from the assembly line where the faults are likely to be more distinct and therefore consistently classified by the operators, but also further research needs to be made on how to recognize a working/faulty lock based on torque data. This would make it possible for the operators to use the machine to evaluate the quality by visual inspection of the torque diagram instead of using their tactile sense. This removes the monotonous task of manual testing of these locks during the development of the ML algorithms but also provides the possibility for a more reliable dataset for minor mechanical anomalies which were not consistently classified with the current tactile sense testing method.

References

1. Krynke, M., Knop, K., Mielczarek, K.: Identifying variables that influence manufacturing product quality. Prod. Eng. Arch. **4**, 22–25 (2014)
2. Pulford, G.W.: High-Security Mechanical Locks: An Encyclopedic Reference. Elsevier Inc., San Diego (2007)
3. Carvalho, T.P., et al.: A systematic literature review of machine learning methods applied to predictive maintenance. Comput. Ind. Eng. **137** (2019). https://doi.org/10.1016/j.cie.2019.106024
4. Case company: Service manual. Case company (2016)
5. Wickern, V.M.Z.: Challenges and reliability of predictive maintenance. Rhine-Waal (2019)
6. Russell, S., Norvig, P.: Forms of learning. In: Artificial Intelligence a Modern Approach, 3rd edn, pp. 693–695. Prentice Hall, New Jersey (2010)
7. Valizadegan, H., Nguyen, Q., Hauskrecht, M.: Learning classification models from multiple experts. J. Biomed. Inf. **46**, 1125–1135 (2013). https://doi.org/10.1016/j.jbi.2013.08.007
8. Japkowicz, N., Stephen, S.: The class imbalance problem: a systematic study. Intell. Data Anal. **6**, 429–449 (2002)
9. Chawla, N.V., Bowyer, K.W., Hall, L.O., Kegelmeyer, W.P.: SMOTE: synthetic minority over-sampling technique. J. Artif. Intell. Res. **16** (2002). https://doi.org/10.1613/jair.953
10. Messtechnik, H.B.: T21WN Torque Transducer. https://www.hbm.com/en/7343/t21wn-torque-meter-with-cylindrical-shaft-stubs, Accessed 29 Apr 2022
11. Caruso, C., Quarta, F.: Interpolation methods comparison. Comput. Math. Appl. **35**, 109–126 (1998). https://doi.org/10.1016/S0898-1221(98)00101-1
12. MathWorks: Bayesian Optimization Algorithm. https://se.mathworks.com/help/stats/bayesian-optimization-algorithm.html#bvaz8tr-1, Accessed 29 Apr 2022
13. Russel, S., Norvig, P.: Leave-one-out cross-validation. In: Artificial Intelligence a Modern Approach, 3rd edn, p. 708. Prentice Hall, New Jersey (2010). Accessed 29 Apr 2022
14. MathWorks: MATLAB. https://se.mathworks.com/products/matlab.html, Accessed 29 Apr 2022
15. Reddy, M.C.S., Sekhar, A.S.: Detection and monitoring of coupling misalignment in rotors using torque measurements. Measurement **61**, 111–122 (2015). https://doi.org/10.1016/J.MEASUREMENT.2014.10.031

Geometric Design Process Automation with Artificial Intelligence

Jörg Brünnhäußer[1]([⊠]), Pascal Lünnemann[1], Ursina Bisang[1], Ruslan Novikov[1], Florian Flachmeier[2], and Mario Wolff[2]

[1] Fraunhofer Institute for Production Systems and Design Technology, Pascalstraße 8-9, 10587 Berlin, Germany
joerg.bruennhaeusser@ipk.fraunhofer.de
[2] BASF Polyurethanes GmbH, Elastogranstr. 60, 49448 Lemförde, Germany

Abstract. Design tasks are largely performed manually by engineers, while machine learning is increasingly able to support and partially automate this process to save time or costs. The prerequisite for this is that the necessary data for training is available. This paper investigates whether it is possible to use data-driven methods to support the design of jounce bumpers at BASF. Based on the analysis of the use case, the geometry of the jounce bumper is approximated with a spline to generate suitable data for training. Based on this, data for training the machine learning model is generated and simulated. In the training process, the appropriate feedforward neural network and the best combination of hyperparameters are determined. In the subsequent evaluation process, it is shown that it is possible to predict the geometries of jounce bumpers with our proof of concept. Finally, the results are discussed, the limitations are shown and the next steps to further improve ssthe results are reflected.

Keywords: Design automation · Machine learning · Data-driven design · Synthetic data

1 Introduction

Automation in engineering combined with continuous data management has led to a comprehensive stock of design-describing data in many companies over the years. Depending on the management, documentation and quality, these could be used as a basis for establishing data-driven algorithms for further automation and support in engineering. This paper discusses research on a case study concerning the potential of automated geometry generation using machine learning on this very data, and presents a possibility of using synthetic data for design automation of components of high geometric similarity and high variation in behavior.

The case study carried out and considered here addresses jounce bumpers (see Fig. 1). As an essential element in the suspension system, jounce bumpers, together with the coil spring and shock absorber, provide the non-linear behavior while protecting the shock

D. Y. Kim et al. (Eds.): APMS 2022, IFIP AICT 663, pp. 35–42, 2022.
https://doi.org/10.1007/978-3-031-16407-1_5

absorber from damage under high loads. The design of jounce bumpers Lemförde, is very complex and time-consuming. The development process of the jounce bumper is integrated into the product development processes of the automotive OEM. Starting from the vehicle design, the BASF engineering department receives a description of the jounce bumper to be developed, including the boundary conditions and costs to be considered. Essential data are the bump behavior to be mapped (e.g. on the basis of a load-deflection curve), as well as the limiting installation space. The designs can be continuously and automatically loaded, parameterized in the CAD environment and then subsequently simulated.

Within the framework of this procedure, numerous product-describing data in relation to the bump behavior have been created over the years. This information could therefore contain comprehensive knowledge from which machine learning (ML) models for assisting or improving the design process can be derived. One possibility to do this would be to train a machine learning model to imitate the simulation to speed up validation or train another model to generate suitable designs, based on these validations. The approach we chose is to teach a model to generate suitable designs from simulated requirements. This decision

Fig. 1. Profile of a jounce bumper.

was made as the current simulation works well even though not fast enough to be used as objective function in model training, it fulfils its current task and anecdotal evidence implies that is very hard to imitate the simulation. In the following, reflecting on the case study, the method of a multivariate regression in the form of a feedforward neural network is presented based on the literature review. Following the implementation of this method, findings are explained and discussed.

2 Literature Review

The potential for using artificial intelligence for design automation is widely known. In particular, due to the increasing variability of products as a result of higher individualization [1, 2]. At the most basic level, a distinction can be made between approaches that integrate simulations into the automation of the design [3] (for example, generative design approaches) and those that use the results of representative simulations to generate substitute models [2]. Using generative design, unlike when using machine learning more constraints and rules have to be defined. Krish [4] showed that a generative design approach is suitable for complex multi-criteria design problems. The paper proposed a method that starts with a CAD genotype and varies it randomly within specific limits. After that the designs are filtered and the resulting designs can be adapted by an engineer.

In contrast, artificial intelligence methods do not need the manual setup of many specific rules because they try to learn those rules implicitly from data. Data-driven services are becoming more and more important due to their ability to make correct predictions in very complex situations where deterministic systems would be either very difficult to develop or very time consuming in generating results. Shah et. al. For instance are using a multi-target regression model to extract the parameters of a single-diode model of photovoltaic modules [5]. The model accelerates the performance evaluation of photovoltaic modules. This work uses basic machine learning algorithms like SVM or random forest instead of neural networks.

Another approach combines generative exploration and machine learning: in Oh et. al. [6] generative adversarial networks are used to create different optimized design options. Then, anomaly detection can be used to identify new designs. This helps the designer to spot relevant results. Jang et. al. [7] propose reinforcement learning to get a high amount of diverse topology designs. On the downside, the computational effort of this approach seems to be high. Multioutput regression is a supervised learning technique that is used to learn a function to predict multiple connected output values from a single input [8]. Multioutput regression can be used for different things, Shah et. al. [5] uses it to extract the parameters of photovoltaic cells and we use it to generate jounce bumper designs. The use of simulations for digital mock-ups is common when designing products as [9] show in their literature review, this is the original purpose of the BASF tool used during the data creation step, but we employ it differently from the original purpose to generate our training data.

3   Method

Our approach was based on the CRISP-DM [10]. The underlying user story is about specifying the requirements of a bumper and getting an improved design as a result. Next, we analyzed the data with the subject matter experts. An available database contains all the designs simulated so far. It contains about 14.000 designs with basic information such as density, dimensions and block height, load-deflection curves calculated from the simulation stored and about 400 optional parameters to describe the bumper. Figure 2 shows the basic concept for solving the user story. The requirements, which include the desired force-displacement curve, are the input for a machine learning model. The model is to predict a suitable new shock absorber geometry, which is the output. Analysis of the data revealed that the complex form of the geometric description by 400 - often optional and therefore empty - parameters are not ideal for training a machine learning model.

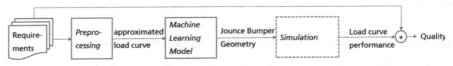

Fig. 2. Concept to predict and evaluate jounce bumper geometries.

One possible solution is to use a simplified model to describe the geometry of the shock absorber, which has significantly fewer parameters. However, it is very difficult to map the relation between the simplified geometry and the original geometry. To solve this problem and to make an estimation of the usability in ML models beforehand, a geometry model of a specific jounce bumper was created based on two splines (inner and outer geometry of the rotationally symmetric part) and these were varied in a regular way to create many different designs for the training process. The generated designs were then simulated to determine their load behavior. This procedure resulted in a synthetic data set, which, however, does not take the existing data into account. In addition to the geometry-describing data and behavioral data from the simulation, the consideration of the requirements is particularly relevant for an application in the design process. The requirements describe the necessary load-deflection curves as well as geometric limitations of the available installation space. These data result from the simulation and can be derived from the geometry-describing data. Thus, there is a complete description system of the geometric parameters with associated load-deflection curves. Based on this data, a feedforward neural network was trained, which attempts to learn the relationship between requirements and suitable geometries. In the final step, the evaluation of the model's predictions was carried out. Besides the basic evaluation in terms of mathematical metrics, such as the squared error, different load-deflection curves of generated bumpers were compared with those from the requirements.

3.1 Generation and Variation of Spline-Based Jounce Bumper Geometry

The geometry variations were generated by repeatedly varying specified measurement variables. The resulting permutations of the template geometry formed the basis of the simulation data used in our machine learning process. The template geometry used, was a custom-build spline-based jounce bumper in STP format with the splines being second order 'B-spline-curves with knots'.

The spline curve as well as other measurement variables were read and processed by a custom Python script. The processed data points were set in relation to define thresholds and ranges within which the variation could be performed. We minimized the amount of potentially unstable geometries as far as possible, by limiting the range in which the measurement variables of the template geometry could be modified. However, stricter thresholds may lead to variations with features too similar, which in turn could negatively impact the performance of the machine learning process. Each change in the spline curve and geometry was performed using a modifiable step range and increment range using simple script functions. For the initial test, about 18000 geometries were generated. The outputs are STP geometry files that are used in simulation stages to calculate the load-deflection curves for the requirements used in the machine learning process.

3.2 Data Preparation and Training of Machine Learning Model

After the splines were varied as described above and simulated, the corresponding requirements were generated with a Python script: For the measurements of the piston rod, cup and striker, the measurements of the attachment parts used for the simulation were taken as requirements. To describe the load-deflection curve, 6 points were taken from the load distribution in regular intervals, from these a polynomial of the 5th grade was calculated. Although it does not describe the load-deflection curve perfectly, the level of detail is sufficient for a proof of concept.

As inputs of the machine learning model, we used the height of the jounce bumper, the size of the cup, the striker and the piston rod, as well as the coefficients of the polynomial of the load-deflection curve and the block height (minimum height to which a jounce bumper can be compressed to. Labels are the x- and y-coordinates for 10 points of each of the two splines which describe the inner and outer geometry, as well as the density the generated jounce bumper should have. Both the input and the labels for the training data were standardised to have mean zero and a standard deviation of one.

To predict the multiple spline points as well as the density of the jounce bumper that is described by the splines, multi-output regression was determined to be the most suitable approach. A feedforward neural network was chosen. The model was trained on 70% of the generated data using Adam [11] as an optimisation algorithm and the mean squared error (MSE) as loss. The remaining data was used to track the training process and to test the model on data not seen during training.

To find a good size for the hidden layers as well as learning rate, the dropout rate and the batch size, hyperparameter tuning was done. We specifically used an evolutionary approach to find the most suitable hyperparameters[1]. The best performing neural network had four fully connected hidden layers and a Dropout-layer after every fully connected layer. The activation function of the hidden layers was ReLU [12] and for the final layer we didn't use any activation function. The data preparation and the training of the neural network was implemented in several Jupyter notebooks. The PyTorch framework [13] was used for the training process and the model is compact enough to train it on a personal computer.

4 Results and Discussion

To evaluate the machine learning, the MSE (prediction-label-relation) and R^2 (fitting-quality) were evaluated. In addition, 10 jounce bumpers that were generated from the test data (not used during training) were randomly chosen and their behavior was simulated. Furthermore, one actual requirement was fed to the model and the resulting jounce bumper was simulated, too.

The generated jounce bumpers were evaluated for two qualities: Behavior in the simulation and fit to the requirements. Although the general deformation behavior was acceptable to good in most cases, the prediction of the initial stiffness by splines showed a design weakness. These splines predicted a much higher initial stiffness than the requirements as well as the later simulation. Also, the adherence to the design space must be ensured, as deviation will result in a lack of confidence in the method.

Figure 3 shows the difference between requirements and the jounce bumpers generated according to them. Large differences in height were caused by the polynomial curve describing the load-deflection curve having a wrong height at the y-intercept when compared to the original load-deflection curve[2]. The differences for inner and outer radius will have to be investigated further to remedy all differences in geometry between requirement and output in future iterations.

---

[1] The chosen hyperparameters are 18 neurons in the first hidden layer, 33 neurons in the second one, 40 in the third one and 78 in the fourth and final hidden layer. The learning rate is 0.0073, dropout rate 0.057 and the batch size 512, we trained the model for 900 epochs and chose to use a version saved at epoch 860, as we found it has the best validation performance of the epochs we trained to.

[2] The model does not optimize in this case for the actual height, but for the height of the polynomial at the y-intercept, which should be identical to the height of the jounce bumper as this point describes the height of the jounce bumper when no load is applied.

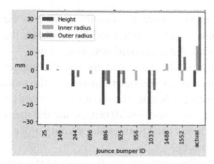 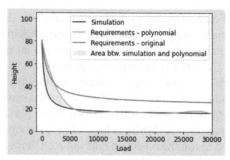

Fig. 3. Deviation from the requirements to the predicted jounce bumper geometry.

Fig. 4. A load-deflection curve where the requirements are not met (ID: 1488)

Figure 4 contain examples for the load-deflection curves simulated for two jounce bumpers[3].

The curves show that the model is able to generate jounce bumpers that will have a similar load-deflection curve to the polynomial requirement curve, especially at higher loads. For lower loads the jounce bumper's height tends to decrease more rapidly than that of the polynomial. In this the simulation of the jounce bumper and the simulation that supplied the green requirements curve are more similar and the early flattening of compression in the simulated curves seems to be one behavior of the load-deflection curves that the polynomial curves cannot replicate well. Still, it is encouraging that the model is able to learn the supplied curve in some cases, as shown in Fig. 3. Figure 3 also illustrates the case stated above that the model conforms to the height implied by the polynomial, not the required height, when it generates a jounce bumper. Furthermore, the jounce bumper in Fig. 4 would not be chosen by an engineer, because the area between the actual requirement curve and the simulated one is too large and therefore the generated jounce bumper does not fulfill the actual design goal on the most important criterion.

Based on the results it seems possible to predict jounce bumper geometries from requirements with ML and specifically with a feedforward neural network and the approach of using splines to approximate the geometry of jounce bumpers.

The measured MSE is low on the test data, indicating that the requirement load-deflection curves are fairly closely followed, as are the geometry requirements. Further investigation indicates that the model is only able to make good predictions because it meets the training label, which was the approximated load-deflection curves. But those curves are not very close to the original ones. Therefore, the approximation of the requirements with a polynomial curve seems to be a critical problem of this approach. Another challenge will certainly be the provision of training data for realistic applications, since in this case, for example, the add-on parts were varied only minimally and the installation

---

[3] The green curve describes the original requirement, based on the simulation of the jounce bumpers generated as described in Sect. 3.1, the orange curve shows the polynomial approximating the original requirement and the blue curve describes the load-deflection curve that was simulated for the jounce bumper generated by the machine learning model.

space was also varied only in rough steps. However, as long as the simulation cannot be significantly accelerated, the provision of large training data is difficult.

5 Conclusion

The aim of the case study presented here was to investigate whether machine learning methods can be applied to the BASF process of designing jounce bumpers based on historical design data. To do this, we identified a user story and created a concept for training an ML model. The available data and the related model were not transferable in their complexity to a representative, general geometry model. The development of an alternative spline-based geometry model and the generation of synthetic data of the spring behavior led to first insights, though. The sample showed a reliable correlation of the load-deflection curve, which, however, cannot be sufficiently approximated by a polynomial function to the nominal parametric.

The reason for this seems to be the approach of the representation of the expected behavior where alternative substitute functions are used in further research. Further potential obviously results from the consideration of further test data. In addition, it will be examined whether the synthetic data can be created more comprehensively if a substitute model is used instead of a simulation.

The approach followed here addresses products and components that are always very similar in their basic structure, but very different in their individual functional requirements. On the one hand, this enables the design of a controllable geometry model and, on the other hand, the prediction of the functional behavior in alternative geometries. The gathered evidence suggest that intelligent models can be created based on synthetic data. This approach is not applicable to components that vary greatly in their geometric structure. Here, approaches that directly integrate FEM simulations seem more promising.

Overall, the study shows that it is not always possible to use existing development data for the qualification of AI algorithms, but that artificial data can be used instead. In general, however, this shows the potential for supporting engineering.

References

1. Papakostas, N., Ramasubramanian, A.K.: Digital technologies as a solution to complexity caused by mass personalization. In: Design and Operation of Production Networks for Mass Personalization in the Era of Cloud Technology, pp. 153–180. Elsevier (2022)
2. Papakostas, N., Ramasubramanian, A.K.: Chapter 6 - Digital technologies as a solution to complexity caused by mass personalization. In: Mourtzis D. (ed.) Design and Operation of Production Networks for Mass Personalization in the Era of Cloud Technology, pp. 153–180. Elsevier (2022)
3. Mourtzis, D., Angelopoulos, J., Panopoulos, N.: Design of an intelligent robotic end effector based on topology optimization in the concept of industry 4.0. In: Andersen, A.-L., et al. (eds.) CARV/MCPC -2021. LNME, pp. 182–189. Springer, Cham (2022). https://doi.org/10.1007/978-3-030-90700-6_20
4. Krish, S.: A practical generative design method. Comput. Aided Des. **43**, 88–100 (2011). https://doi.org/10.1016/j.cad.2010.09.009

5. Shah, R.: Solar cell parameters extraction using multi-target regression methods. In: Leonowicz, Z. (ed.) Conference proceedings 2020 IEEE International Conference on Environment and Electrical Engineering and 2020 IEEE Industrial and Commercial Power Systems Europe (EEEIC/I & CPS Europe), 9–12 June, 2020, Madrid, Spain: The 2020 Edition Will be Held on Scheduled Days From 09th to 12th June 2020 in Web Streaming, pp. 1–6. IEEE, Piscataway (2020)
6. Oh, S., Jung, Y., Kim, S., et al.: Deep generative design: integration of topology optimization and generative models. J. Mech. Des. **141** (2019). https://doi.org/10.1115/1.4044229
7. Jang, S., Yoo, S., Kang, N.: Generative design by reinforcement learning: enhancing the diversity of topology optimization designs (2020)
8. Borchani, H., Varando, G., Bielza, C., et al.: A survey on multi-output regression. WIREs Data Min. Knowl. Disc. **5**, 216–233 (2015). https://doi.org/10.1002/widm.1157
9. Mourtzis, D.: Simulation in the design and operation of manufacturing systems: state of the art and new trends. Int. J. Prod. Res. **58**, 1927–1949 (2020). https://doi.org/10.1080/00207543.2019.1636321
10. Wirth, R., Hipp, J.: Crisp-dm: towards a standard process modell for data mining (2000)
11. Kingma, D.P., Ba, J.: Adam: a method for stochastic optimization (2014)
12. Nair, V., Hinton, G.E.: Rectified linear units improve restricted boltzmann machines. In: Fürnkranz, J., Joachims T. (eds.) Proceedings of the 27th International Conference on Machine Learning (ICML-10), 21–24 June 2010, pp. 807–814. Omnipress, Haifa (2010)
13. Paszke, A., Gross, S., Massa, F., et al.: PyTorch: an imperative style, high-performance deep learning library. In: Wallach, H., Larochelle, H., Beygelzimer, A., et al. (eds.) Advances in Neural Information Processing Systems, vol 32. Curran Associates, Inc. (2019)

Case-Study-Based Requirements Analysis of Manufacturing Companies for Auto-ML Solutions

Günther Schuh, Max-Ferdinand Stroh, and Justus Benning[✉]

FIR, Institute for Industrial Management at RWTH Aachen University, Campus-Boulevard 55, 52074 Aachen, Germany
justus.benning@fir.rwth-aachen.de

Abstract. Methods of machine learning (ML) are difficult for manufacturing companies to employ productively. Data science is not their core skill, and acquiring talent is expensive. Automated machine learning (Auto-ML) aims to alleviate this, democratizing machine learning by introducing elements such as low-code or no-code functionalities into its model creation process. Due to the dynamic vendor market of Auto-ML, it is difficult for manufacturing companies to successfully implement this technology. Different solutions as well as constantly changing requirements and functional scopes make a correct software selection difficult. This paper aims to alleviate said challenge by providing a longlist of requirements that companies should pay attention to when selecting a solution for their use case. The paper is part of a larger research effort, in which a structured selection process for Auto-ML solutions in manufacturing companies is designed. The longlist itself is the result of six case studies of different manufacturing companies, following the method of case study research by Eisenhardt. A total of 75 distinct requirements were identified, spanning the entire machine learning and modeling pipeline.

Keywords: Machine learning · Auto-ML · Requirements · Manufacturing

1 Introduction

Manufacturing remains one of the most promising areas for the application of machine learning. However, since data science is not a core competency of manufacturing companies, they are severely affected by the lack of experts in this field [1]. Automated machine learning (Auto-ML) is defined as both the concept as well as the underlying technology to accelerate the development lifecycle of machine learning models through automation [2]. It therefore addresses this problem by democratizing and simplifying the machine learning value chain process, from data acquisition to model validation.

1.1 Background and Overall Research Goal

Software solutions that integrate Auto-ML functionalities have seen a surge in popularity over the last year, resulting in a dynamic vendor market, as software providers try to offer

D. Y. Kim et al. (Eds.): APMS 2022, IFIP AICT 663, pp. 43–50, 2022.
https://doi.org/10.1007/978-3-031-16407-1_6

unique solutions to creating machine learning models without data science expertise [3]. This market proves to be a challenge for manufacturing companies, as they still struggle to build knowledge about the basics of artificial intelligence [4], making the choice of an apt Auto-ML solution for their use cases a complex challenge. This paper aims to alleviate said challenge by providing a longlist of requirements that companies should pay attention to when selecting a solution for their use case. The paper is part of a larger research effort, in which a structured selection process for Auto-ML solutions in manufacturing companies is designed (see Fig. 1).

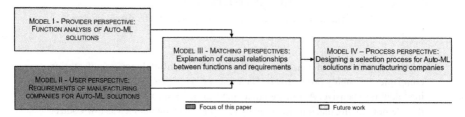

Fig. 1. Overall research goal and context of this paper

Simultaneously in another research effort, a descriptive model is being developed which comprises the functions of current Auto-ML solutions in the form of a function tree. In successive endeavors, these two models will be combined to match the user and the product perspective. This will yield in an explanatory model that links requirements of manufacturing companies to functions of Auto-ML solutions. In a final step, this model will be integrated into a structured selection process that companies can use.

1.2   State of the Art and Current Research

Most of the current literature regarding Auto-ML focuses on benchmarking the performance of the underlying algorithms or applying the technology to existing optimization and prediction problems. Publications that focus on the requirements of users are limited. While no sources have been found that provide a longlist of requirements for manufacturing companies, there is research that evaluates the user perspective on the technology, which will be briefly introduced here.

Krauß et al. analyse the applicability of Auto-ML for a predictive use case in a production context. However, the requirements which they test against are purely focused on model performance [5]. Crisan and Fiore-Gartland conduct an experiment focusing on human-machine-interaction of user and Auto-ML systems. In their setup, they implicitly regard requirements such as degree of automation and interpretability of the models. However, their research is not focused on the manufacturing sector and leaves out requirements that are posed by non-human entities, such as the legal framework or the organizational structure of the company [6]. Elshawi et al. conduct a survey of current Auto-ML solutions and look at functions as well as functional requirements. Still, their focus lies on the technical description of the solutions themselves [7] The same thing holds true for the benchmarking survey of Zöller and Huber [8]. In their paper, Xin et al. conducted interviews with experienced Auto-ML users to provide general guidelines for applying these solutions in companies. A part of their results contains a subjective rating of solutions regarding criteria like explainability and ease of use. Thus, it provided a good reference point for the completeness of the longlist created in this paper, even though it lacks the focus on the manufacturing sector [9].

1.3 Delineation of the Term Requirements Used in the Context of this Paper

The term requirements used in the context of this paper follows the definition by the IEEE Standard Glossary of Software Engineering Terminology. Requirements are defined as "a condition or capability needed by a user to solve a problem or achieve an objective" [10]. This includes technical requirements as well as the economic objectives that the stakeholders of Auto-ML strive to achieve by employing the technology.

2 Methodology

In order to investigate which requirements are relevant when selecting an Auto-ML solution from the perspective of manufacturing companies, theory building according to Eisenhardt was applied [11]. The case study research method was selected due to its capability of describing and explaining novel phenomena with relatively sparse information [12]. Furthermore, as this paper deals with the descriptive part of the overall research goal (see Fig. 1), methods that focus on prescriptive knowledge, such as design science research, were excluded. The method used comprises of a complete process for building theory from case studies, which is especially suitable for investigating new areas of research like the one at hand. At the beginning of the case study research process, questions were formulated for the interviews. Table 1 shows the final questionnaire. It contains 16 open-ended questions and served as the basis for the case studies, which were conducted as semi-open interviews.

Table 1. Final questionnaire

No	Question
1	What is the current state of implementation of ML in your company?
2	What challenges do you see in the introduction and usage of ML?
3	What goals do you want to achieve by using an Auto-ML solution?
4	Which usage scenarios should be realized in your company with the help of an Auto-ML solution?
5	Which working steps are to be optimized using Auto-ML?
6	Who should be responsible for creating models? Who should use them?
7	Is Auto-ML intended to compensate for a specific expertise?

(continued)

Table 1. (*continued*)

No	Question
8	Which communication interfaces are essential for you?
9	Are there other requirements for software, such as guidelines?
10	What are your requirements for the performance of an Auto-ML model?
11	What are your requirements for the transparency and explainability of an Auto-ML model?
12	How do you envision optimal user interaction with an Auto-ML solution?
13	How should data visualization be implemented in your opinion?
14	In which cases would you like to be notified?
15	How should the system behave in the event of an error?
16	Do you have any other requirements for an Auto-ML solution that have not been mentioned yet?

Table 2. Case subject data

Case number	Manufactured product/industry sector	AI use case
1	Agricultural machinery	Demand forecasting
2	Cutting machinery	Predictive quality
3	Trailers and cargo equipment	Production control
4	Medical equipment	Predictive maintenance
5	Plant supplier for the metallurgical industry	Customer relations
6	Coating and surface solutions	Predictive maintenance

In total, 6 case studies with machine learning users and digitalization officers from manufacturing companies were conducted. Data about the enterprises and case studies is given in Table 2.

To reach closure, i.e., to determine that enough case studies have been conducted theoretical saturation must be reached. That means, that the incremental improvement to the results become minimal [11]. The sixth case study only yielded in three new requirements (compared to 72 total recorded requirements at that point, cf. Fig. 2). Due to the high redundancy at this point, the case number was capped at six.

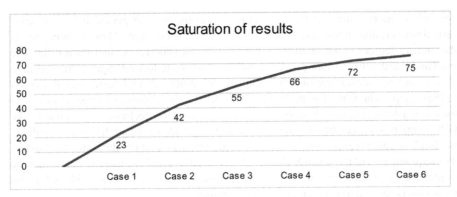

Fig. 2. Saturation of results according to Eisenhardt

3 Results

In total, 75 unique requirements were synthesized in the case study research process. To aid readability of this paper while fully disclosing the research results, the longlist of requirements can be downloaded via hyperlink under [13]. In this section, general observations derived from the requirements will be shared.

First, the requirements were clustered according to the model creation process steps for automated machine learning which is roughly based on the analyses of Zöller and Huber [8] (cf. Fig. 3).

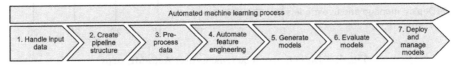

Fig. 3. Auto-ML process steps used for categorizing the requirements

Although slight variations exist to this process, for the context of this analysis there are assumed to be seven distinct steps to creating and using models with Auto-ML-solutions. They start with handling the input data and end with the deployment and management of the finished models. A superordinate step (zero) was introduced, as a significant portion of the requirements did not match a distinct step but rather referred to Auto-ML solutions in general. In the following paragraph, the clusters and patterns of the requirements within them will be described.

The requirements of step zero (superordinate step) either described economic considerations that were expected of the application of Auto-ML or constraints, that the company had regarding the use of IT solutions, such as a cloud strategy or data protection guidelines. The requirements of cluster one ("handle input data") consisted mainly of the various data sources (e.g., SQL databases) that companies need the solutions to integrate seamlessly. The second cluster ("create pipeline structure") showed an interesting dichotomy. Although this step is a field of high concern for researchers, as there are various mathematical challenges yet to be solved, the user perspective is not concerned with the algorithms and techniques that the software offers. They are interested in the varying degrees of automation vs. control that the underlying algorithms offer. The third and fourth cluster ("pre-process data" and "automate feature engineering") paint a similar picture, as users are mainly occupied with efficiency and degree of automation of these steps. The fifth cluster, "generate models" showed themes of user control and interaction during the model creation process as well as more technical requirements like GPU-support to reduce training times. The defining topic of the sixth cluster, "evaluate models", is transparency, both about model performance and the decisions they make. The requirements of the seventh cluster "deploy, manage and use models" show that the digital units want to distribute their finished models as efficiently as possible, while the model users require transparent, easy to use models.

To give an overview over the 75 distinct requirements and their clusters, the distribution of requirements is shown in Fig. 4.

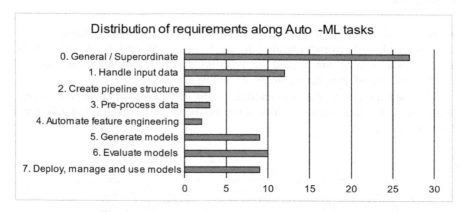

Fig. 4. Distribution of requirements over Auto-ML steps

This graphic should not be interpreted as a scoreboard that indicates which steps are the most important in Auto-ML, because the requirements are not weighted in any way. However, it gives an impression which steps manufacturing companies are concerned with when they think about solving their AI use cases with Auto-ML-solutions.

In an additional analysis, the requirements were categorized according to the three goals of Auto-ML according to Crisan and Fiore-Gartland. In their work, which is concerned with the interaction of humans with Auto-ML-systems, they synthesize three objectives that companies can achieve with employing Auto-ML. The first is automating routine work, the second is rapid prototyping of models to solve business problems, and the third and final is democratizing machine learning and data science [6]. The distribution is shown in Fig. 5. Some of the requirements did not match the three goals (e.g., compliance or legal requirements) and are subsumed in the "other" category.

The graphic shows a rather balanced distribution of goals, with automation being the main goal of manufacturing companies, closely followed by rapid prototyping and democratization of machine learning.

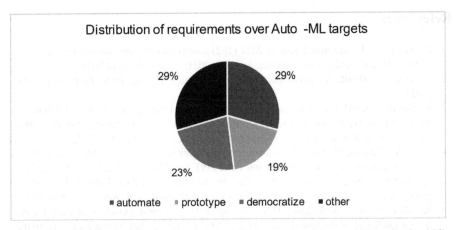

Fig. 5. Distribution of requirements over Auto-ML targets after Crisan and Fiore-Gartland [6]

4   Discussion

The results of the paper are subject to the characteristic weaknesses of case study research, which tend to be overly complex or narrow models that do not generalize well [11]. To mitigate this risk, the a-priori variables have been selected from a wide range of sources, yielding in a diverse questionnaire. However, before the applicability of the results needs to be further validated once all partial models have been created and the Auto-ML selection process is used in the industry. Furthermore, the longlist focuses on specific requirements regarding Auto-ML-solutions. General procurement criteria, which virtually every enterprise has, are not included. Thus, an application of this longlist should always be supplemented by the usual economic considerations. General criteria for selecting and employing innovative technologies in enterprises are well researched and can be found in works such as [14] and [15].

5   Summary and Outlook

In this paper, the authors derived 75 distinct requirements of manufacturing companies for Auto-ML-solutions from six case studies using the research method of Eisenhardt. The requirements were clustered according to the model creation process and their distribution along these steps is shown. Furthermore, the requirements were assigned to the three goals of Auto-ML according to Crisan and Fiore-Gartland, showing a rather even distribution along the objectives. In successive research efforts, these user-centric results need to be matched to the solution provider perspective, i.e., the functions that current Auto-ML solutions offer. Furthermore, the synthesized stakeholder groups will be analysed. This will yield in a structured selection process for Auto-ML solutions in manufacturing companies.

References

1. Reder, B.: Studie Machine Learning 2021 (2021). https://www.lufthansa-industry-solutions.com/de-de/studien/idg-studie-machine-learning-2021. Accessed 2 Sept 2021
2. Masood, A., Sherif, A.: Automated Machine Learning, 1st edn. Packt Publishing, Safari (2021)
3. Statista Research Department: Number of AI/ML service offerings at hyperscale CSPs worldwide 2020–2021, by provider (2022). https://www.statista.com/statistics/1268286/worldwide-ai-machine-learning-service-offerings-hyperscalers/. Accessed 7 Mar 2022
4. Kaul, A., Schieler, M., Hans, C.: Künstliche Intelligenz im europäischen Mittelstand. Status quo, Perspektiven und was jetzt zu tun ist (2019). https://www.uni-saarland.de/fileadmin/upload/lehrstuhl/kaul/Universita%CC%88t_des_Saarlandes_Ku%CC%88nstliche_Intelligenz_im_europa%CC%88ischen_Mittelstand_2019-10_digital.pdf. Accessed 7 Mar 2022
5. Krauß, J., Pacheco, B.M., Zang, H.M., Schmitt, R.H.: Automated machine learning for predictive quality in production. Procedia CIRP **93**, 443–448 (2020). https://doi.org/10.1016/j.procir.2020.04.039
6. Crisan, A., Fiore-Gartland, B.: Fits and starts: enterprise use of AutoML and the role of humans in the loop. In: Kitamura, Y. (ed.) Proceedings of the 2021 CHI Conference on Human Factors in Computing Systems. CHI 2021: CHI Conference on Human Factors in Computing Systems, Yokohama Japan, 08–13 May 2021, pp. 1–15. Association for Computing Machinery, New York (2021). https://doi.org/10.1145/3411764.3445775
7. Elshawi, R., Maher, M., Sakr, S.: Automated machine learning: state-of-the-art and open challenges (2019). http://arxiv.org/pdf/1906.02287v2
8. Zöller, M.-A., Huber, M.F.: Benchmark and survey of automated machine learning frameworks. J. Artif. Intell. Res. **70**, 409–474 (2021)
9. Xin, D., Wu, E.Y., Lee, D.J.-L., Salehi, N., Parameswaran, A.: Whither AutoML? understanding the role of automation in machine learning workflows (2021). http://arxiv.org/pdf/2101.04834v1
10. IEEE Standards Board: IEEE Standard Glossary of Software Engineering Terminology, New York (IEEE Std 610.12–1990) (1990). http://www.informatik.htw-dresden.de/~hauptman/SEI/IEEE_Standard_Glossary_of_Software_Engineering_Terminology%20.pdf. Accessed 25 June 2022
11. Eisenhardt, K.M.: Building theories form case studies. Acad. Manag. Rev. **14**, 532–550 (1989)
12. Sprinz, D., Wolinsky, Y. (eds.): Models, Numbers, and Cases. Methods for studying international relations, 2nd edn. University of Michigan Press, Ann Arbor (2007)
13. Justus Benning: Case-Study-Based Requirements Analysis of Manufacturing Companies for Auto-ML solutions. Long List of Requirements (2022). https://github.com/BenningJustus/APMS-Longlist/raw/main/APMS_Requirements_Long-List_public_Bn.xlsx
14. Schuh, G.: Innovationsmanagement. Springer, Heidelberg (2012) https://doi.org/10.1007/978-3-642-25050-7
15. Schuh, G., Klappert, S.: Technologiemanagement. Springer, Heidelberg (2011). https://doi.org/10.1007/978-3-642-12530-0.

Optimization of Production Processes in SMEs: Practical Methodology for the Acquisition of Process Information

Heiner Winkler[1（✉）], Felix Franke[2], Susanne Franke[2], and Ralph Riedel[3]

[1] Chemnitz University of Technology, 09125 Chemnitz, Germany
heiner.winkler@mb.tu-chemnitz.de
[2] d-Opt GmbH, Oberneumarker Street 59, 08496 Neumark, Germany
[3] University of Applied Sciences Zwickau, 08056 Zwickau, Germany

Abstract. Production companies are increasingly required to flexibly adapt to competitive situations and, hence, aim to ensure that their production processes have optimal outcome. This combines requirements e.g. on product quality, production time and costs as well as process variability. The cornerstone for optimizing current processes lies in a thorough understanding of these requirements in order to derive optimization potential that can efficiently be realized. Business process modelling provides such a comprehensive view on the processes and accurately reflects the existing workflows – given that all necessary information is considered and acquired accordingly. This includes not only the company's goals and the production processes themselves, but also the implicit knowledge on these processes of the employees. For many companies, a proper systematization and combined realization of these steps is a challenge. We present a practical methodology for acquiring the relevant production process information as basis for a proper process modelling. We develop a generic procedure which is tailored to the characteristics of small and medium-sized companies and describe the goal, the requirements, the methodology as well as a practical application including benefits and limitations. The methodology provides a structured approach for the systematic mapping of heterogeneous production processes and builds the foundation to detect optimization potential.

Keywords: Process modelling · Optimization of production processes · Information acquisition

1 Introduction

Meeting the needs of today's globalized market has become a distinct competitive edge for production companies. This requires a high transparency on the production process to react appropriately and flexibly to varying customers' wishes and to adapt to different batch sizes. In addition to the requirement of achieving the punctual delivery of high-quality products at a reasonable cost, small and medium-sized enterprises (SME) in Europe and Asia face typical challenges like the lack of financial, technological and

D. Y. Kim et al. (Eds.): APMS 2022, IFIP AICT 663, pp. 51–59, 2022.
https://doi.org/10.1007/978-3-031-16407-1_7

networking resources [6, 15]. Consequently, companies are searching for cost-efficient solutions, specifically addressing their needs and unique situation, to optimize their production processes. This ranges from the retrofitting of existing assets (like machines) over the automated integration of expert knowledge to the implementation of lean approaches [11].

To identify suitable optimization potential, a thorough process analysis is inevitable. The appropriate level of detail and the cost-benefit-ratio of this analysis have to be considered carefully. Depending on the company's goals (e.g. throughput time reduction, AI-based quality control), the potential use of the information builds the basis for the relevant data and knowledge that needs to be acquired. The paper focuses on the formulation of a procedure to efficiently perform this information acquisition and simultaneously create a profound knowledge gain of the employees on the production process chain and the interconnections of the sub-processes.

We present an application-oriented method for the acquisition of information regarding the production process which allows a straightforward realization of digital transformation and optimization processes in SME. This information includes machines, products, relevant data (e.g. order-related) and expert knowledge (e.g. adaptations of the production plan, specific characteristics regarding machine utilization). The approach is tailored to production companies of SME-type as it addresses their special requirements like handling the available process documentation, including the rather high amount of employees' expert knowledge and producing as little additional costs for e.g. software tools as possible. According to the typical steps for process analysis [13], we concentrate on the information acquisition and thereby providing transparency on the production process.

The paper is structured as follows. Section 2 comprises the theoretical background and the state of the art. In Sect. 3, the methodology for the process analysis is described. A practical application in a production company is presented in Sect. 4, whereas Sect. 5 addresses further research questions.

2 Theoretical Background and Related Work

Results on the model-based approach as basis for production process analysis and optimization can already be found in the literature. The model of a production process with respect to realizing a proper quality management is given in [1]. Here, a general process model is developed that allows a statistical analysis of the process, containing e.g. the statistical distribution and the method for determining the capability and performance (in the sense of long-term capability) of the process. However, aspects beyond statistical process evaluation are not considered here.

A conceptual reference model for identifying and organizing production data is given in [2], which aims at analysing and finding relations between the five dimensions production, plant hierarchy, process, context and resources. The approach however concentrates on the organization of digital factory data and does not take the connection with human expert knowledge into account.

In [3], both the product and its production process including their mutual connections are mapped. This allows the modelling of a configurable product as a directed multigraph, a set of (process) model and coupling constraints. Such an instance of the model provides a configured product and the executable process for its production. Similarly, an approach to design a manufacturing system is presented in [12]. Both do however not aim at mapping the existing process chain.

Special focus on production control is set in [7], where a Petri net approach is presented in order to map production process-relevant data, which includes data on the products and on the production facility. Even though we concentrate on the optimization of production processes rather than production control, environmental factors are a relevant aspect for us as well. A systematic literature overview on data acquisition is presented in [4], which reveals that this field is highly granular and realizations differ across machines, processes and on the plant level.

In conclusion, the acquisition of the relevant information for process modelling is crucial for creating proper and meaningful images of the real processes. While process modelling itself is a highly investigated topic, the practical realization of the information acquisition has rarely been addressed in the literature, and to our best knowledge there exist no standardized procedures or methods.

3 Methodology

The methodology presented below aims at acquiring information on production process chains. It was developed by applying action design research [14], combining the scientific study of a problem with the application in a real-life situation. Its goal is to generate prescriptive design knowledge by learning from the realization and evaluation in an organizational setting [10]. This was achieved by developing the methodology together with a production company of SME-type which has the typical characteristics we want to address: the motivation to improve the production process, a partly digitized production process with both high-technological machinery and machinery in need of retrofit, a significant amount of implicit knowledge of the employees. One advantage of the methodology is its generalizability since the company-specific requirements (e.g. level of digitalization) and the varying goals (ranging from simple retrofit to complex real-rime data analysis) are considered in the process. Additionally, as it is described in the upcoming paragraph, it is the goal to take into account and acquire all relevant information and knowledge of the company's employees. Therefore, the respective employees are assigned various roles. The methodology can be applied to SMEs of different size and complexity as it is process- instead of enterprise-oriented. Depending on the availability of different participants, certain roles can be condensed. As company-internals, at least a decision-maker and an implementer must be involved.

We start by defining the relevant roles and designate the respective participants. First, a process analyst (who can be internal, but usually is external) being familiar with the methodology has to be included for implementation as well as guidance of the company's participants. On the company's part, a decision-maker (e.g. CEO or manager) is needed for formulating the target of the production process optimization. Furthermore, a superordinate technology employee (the implementer) has to be involved, who functions as knowledge carrier and interface between the process analyst and the company's employees. Regarding every production sub-process that is considered, both a worker performing this process and having profound knowledge on it (mainly for the information acquisition; especially in small enterprises, this might be the technology employee) as well as the respective team leader (for further inquiries and the final release; this role can be taken by the decision-maker) are included. With the inclusion of the different participants, a holistic view on the processes, the acquisition of all available knowledge as well as a proper release process is guaranteed.

The procedure is illustrated in Fig. 1. After laying the foundations by defining the target and choosing the respective relevant process chain, the acquisition of every sub-process information is iteratively achieved by the conducting three steps visualized in the middle part. These three steps have to be performed for each sub-process individually (and chronologically according to their appearance within the process chain) such that in the end, the outcome builds the basis for process optimization.

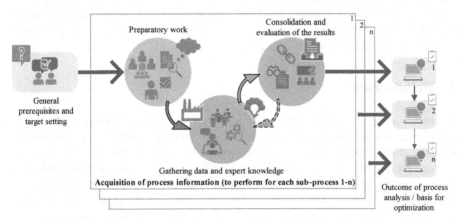

Fig. 1. Visualization of the proposed methodology.

General Prerequisites and Target Setting: Using the top-down-principle, a product family as reference object for the process optimization is defined. Therefore, first an overview over the available product families is created. A prioritized choice is found by evaluating certain criteria, which are split into primary (core) and secondary (supporting) ones: Primary criteria, representing economic and technological factors, depict the strategic view of the management (by key performance indicators, business environment, orientation and competitive differentiation of the company) and the operational view w.r.t. the manufacturing process (by production quantities, importance and impact of production know-how). The availability of relevant product/process information (e.g. test plans, work instructions) is included as secondary criterion since it facilitates the successful implementation of the procedure and, hence, influences the quality of the subsequent process optimization. To gather the relevant information to evaluate these criteria, the process analyst interviews a decision-maker of the company to get an overview of the company's typology (e.g. size, vertical integration). Then, the shop floor is visited to get a deeper understanding of the workflow. Expert interviews with a technology employee who has profound knowledge on the production process complete the first insight. Now the reference product is chosen, and a flow chart of the relevant sub-process of the product family as well as first rough drafts of event-driven process chains (EPC) are created by the process analyst and the technology employee. EPCs were chosen because of their easy understanding for the company and their expedient use ([9]; for a further discussion, see Sect. 5).

Preparatory Work: The next three steps regard the acquisition of detailed information on the relevant sub-processes. First, the planned procedure is announced to the worker who is responsible for the execution of the considered sub-process, with focus on their respective involvement. Furthermore, a preliminary short briefing between the process analyst and the technology employee in which the rough draft of the respective EPC is discussed helps to establish a uniform level of knowledge. New information gathered from this discussion is included in the EPC.

Gathering Data and Expert Knowledge: The worker responsible for the execution of the sub-process is consulted. He or she gives a detailed description of his or her tasks and simultaneously executes them on the respective machine/workstation etc., while the process analyst documents this knowledge. Note that this does not only include the typical work steps, used machines or software but might also address implicit knowledge like machine parametrization or typically arising problems. The focus is explicitly set on the standard procedure and not on rarely occurring exceptions. The technology employee, combining knowledge both on the acquisition procedure and on the company's practical processes, connects the internal staff and external analysts. To raise the worker's motivation to participate and to include a maximum amount of (implicit) knowledge (e.g. regarding information flow, parametrization tasks, interaction with other work steps), he or she is asked about his or her view on necessary or possible need for optimization. Finally, the process analyst describes the further procedure to make the upcoming involvement of the worker transparent.

Consolidation and Evaluation of the Results: The process analyst adds the new information to the roughly designed EPC and transforms it into a detailed one, which is then reviewed and improved by both the technology employee and, afterwards, the worker responsible for executing the sub-process. The final release of the EPC is done by the team leader. If he or she does not approve of the latest version, corrections are performed by the team leader and the technology employee, which corresponds to the arrow in Fig. 1 leading back to the gathering of expert knowledge. The worker responsible for the sub-process is informed about the changes (as a benefit, internal differences in the understanding of the processes are clarified). A subsequent check regarding semantic accuracy and comprehensibility is made by the process analyst.

These three steps are repeated iteratively until every sub-process has been considered and the respective information is acquired.

Outcome: As a result of the methodology, every sub-process of the process chain is mapped as a process model, e.g. EPC (as in our case), Business Process Model and Notation (BPMN), Unified Modelling Language. This includes information on the technical infrastructure, the used machines, hard- and software, relevant data and parametrizations, involved employees, material and information flow, informal information regarding the overarching interaction of the sub-process (e.g. communication in case of high reject rate) as well as sub-process-specific and overall suggestions for improvement. Hence, the information of the process chain is systematized and the connections between the different sub-processes are made transparent.

4   Practical Application

The procedure was developed using action design research methodology in cooperation with a company producing tools (needles for knitting machines) in a high vertical integration (ranging from stamping of the raw material over forming to heat treatments). Since needles are very delicate easily damageable, a comprehensive know-how is inevitable for high production stability. Within a research and development project funded by the German Federal Ministry of Education and Research, the initially rarely digitized production process is optimized using AI-based data analysis to automatically identify variations in the product quality for critical sub-processes.

The process analysis was realized using the procedure introduced above. For the chosen product, a process chain containing 20 sub-processes was identified and investigated. Due to the pandemic situation, on-site visits were only possible in the early stages. The majority of information acquisition and interviews with the company were performed online. The most important perceptions are summarized in Table 1.

Table 1. Perceptions regarding the practical implementation of the methodology.

General prerequisites and target setting
– difficult to conduct digitally as on-site visit of running production (layout, size, routes and temporal relations) is required for overall understanding (especially in the context of complex production processes)
Preparatory work
– during the repetitive cycles of the acquisition process, the gradual qualification of the technology employee led to more efficient realization
Gathering data and expert knowledge
– usage of EPC for modelling, which are easy to understand and map all relevant information, facilitates communication with employees
Consolidation and evaluation of the results
– it is useful to plan additional time for the final release of the EPCs to account for possible (un-)availability of the team leaders

(continued)

Table 1. (*continued*)

General prerequisites and target setting
Acquisition of process information

– a digital conduction, which was necessary due to the pandemic situation, had no negative influence on the results (however, photo documentation in this case is highly recommended); this allows more flexibility in scheduling appointments with employees

– the rather high amount of repetitive check cycles involving different employees has various positive effects:

o implicit employee knowledge is transferred into explicit one

o the awareness of employees for their own sub-processes, the neighboring ones and the whole process chain has risen significantly, which led to an increased sense of responsibility for the product and a reduction of uncertainties

o cross validation of employee and team leader raises quality of EPCs

o increased knowledge of employees in process modelling and information acquisition

o optimization potential becomes more transparent and is iteratively refined due to the gained knowledge, transparency and understanding of the processes and their interrelations

5 Further Discussion and Outlook

The initial application of the methodology in the above-mentioned company proved to be a successful starting point for the digitization of the production line and the realization of an automatic process monitoring to reduce the reject rate. The information acquisition, specifically the documentation, led to the involved employees' raised transparency on the processes' complexity as well as interconnections and intrinsically motivated them to actively suggest improvements on the sub-processes. Especially in the project's production process optimization context, this proved to be a profound basis for conducting the actual realization steps.

Even though the process requires a significant commitment of (personal) resources, the step-by-step realization leads to higher transparency and an expedient competence development of the involved employees. The knowledge gain regarding the processes builds the basis for continuous improvement processes and, hence, a wide range of optimization potential. The direct availability of the structured information builds the basis for certification programs (e.g. for a quality management system), leading to a better competitiveness. Applying the methodology is the starting point for the creation of digital twins of assets like machines, products etc. Furthermore, the formulated assets and their underlying architecture allow a risk analysis w.r.t. data security.

For process modelling, EPCs were prioritized because of their easy use and expandability. Additionally, they were understood well by employees who initially were unfamiliar with process modelling. For our further research and application, we intend to use BPMNs from start (note that EPCs can be used to create BPMNs). Hence, the results are also usable in connection with BPMN workflow engines for the visualization of the operational processes and the identification of optimization potential. This is especially of high interest considering platforms (like BaSys [8]) that provide standardized solutions for the optimization of production processes.

The derived information can also serve for maturity models as the thorough analysis of the production processes' actual state allows a straightforward evaluation of the current maturity level and the derivation of the necessary steps to achieve the envisioned target (this is a typical procedure in the context of retrofitting, see e.g. [5]).

The experience and know-how of the involved employees significantly influence the pace and quality of the information acquisition. A high benefit arises for a high vertical integration and a large amount of (differing) sub-processes due to the binding of (expensive) technology employees. It is part of our future research to develop an assessment logic for the economic evaluation w.r.t. the company's initial goals (e.g. basis for digitalization, AI-based production process optimization or certification).

Acknowledgements

 SPONSORED BY THE

Federal Ministry of Education and Research

The project *ProDaTEX: Data-driven production optimization through digitalized process chains in the textile industry* (01IS21077) is funded by the German Federal Ministry of Education and Research.

References

1. Alot, Z.: The model of the production process for the quality management. Found. Manag **9**(1), 43–60 (2017)
2. Boniotti, G., Cocca, P., Marciano, F., Marini, A., Stefana, E., Vernuccio, F.: A conceptual reference model for smart factory production data. In: Dolgui, A., Bernard, A., Lemoine, D., von Cieminski, G., Romero, D. (eds.) APMS 2021. IAICT, vol. 633, pp. 110–118. Springer, Cham (2021). https://doi.org/10.1007/978-3-030-85910-7_12
3. Campagna, D., Formisano, A.: Product and production process modeling and configuration. Fund. Inf. **124**(4), 403–425 (2013)
4. Ekwaro-Osire, H., Wiesner, S., Thoben, K.-D.: Data acquisition for energy efficient manufacturing: a systematic literature review. In: Dolgui, A., Bernard, A., Lemoine, D., von Cieminski, G., Romero, D. (eds.) APMS 2021. IAICT, vol. 633, pp. 129–137. Springer, Cham (2021). https://doi.org/10.1007/978-3-030-85910-7_14
5. Franke, F., Franke, S., Riedel, R.: Retrofit concept for textile production. In: Lalic, B., Majstorovic, V., Marjanovic, U., von Cieminski, G., Romero, D. (eds.) APMS 2020. IAICT, vol. 592, pp. 74–82. Springer, Cham (2020). https://doi.org/10.1007/978-3-030-57997-5_9
6. Gherghina, S.C., Botezatu, M.A., Hosszu, A., Simionescu, L.N.: Small and medium-sized enterprises (SMEs): the engine of economic growth through investments and innovation. Sustainability **12**(1), 347 (2020)
7. Gradisar, D., Music, G.: Production-process modelling based on production-management data: a Petri net approach. Int. J. Comput. Integr. Manuf. **20**(8), 794–810 (2008)
8. Kuhn, T.: BaSys 4.0. The Middleware for Industrie 4.0. Fraunhofer Institute for Experimental Software Engineering IESE (2019)
9. Nizioł, P., Wiśniewski, K.K., Ligęza, A.: Characteristic and comparison of UML, BPMN and EPC based on process models of a training company. Ann. Comput. Sci. Inf. Syst. **26**, 193–200 (2021)

10. Petersson, A.M., Lundberg, J.: Applying action design research (ADR) to develop concept generation and selection methods. Procedia CIRP **50**, 222–227 (2016)
11. Powell, D., Romero, D., Gaiardelli, P., Cimini, C., Cavalieri, S.: Towards digital lean cyber-physical production systems: industry 4.0 technologies as enablers of leaner production. In: Moon, I., Lee, G.M., Park, J., Kiritsis, D., von Cieminski, G. (eds.) APMS 2018. IAICT, vol. 536, pp. 353–362. Springer, Cham (2018). https://doi.org/10.1007/978-3-319-99707-0_44
12. Ramírez, J., Molina, A.: Improving manufacturing system design by instantiation of the integrated product, process and manufacturing system development reference framework. In: Dolgui, A., Bernard, A., Lemoine, D., von Cieminski, G., Romero, D. (eds.) APMS 2021. IAICT, vol. 634, pp. 99–107. Springer, Cham (2021). https://doi.org/10.1007/978-3-030-85914-5_11
13. Riskadayanti, O., Yuniaristanto, Sutopo, W., Hisjam, M.: Discrete-event simulation of a production process for increasing the efficiency of a newspaper production. In: IOP Conference Series: Materials Science and Engineering, vol. 495 (2019)
14. Sein, M., Henfridsson, O., Purao, S., Rossi, M., Lindgren, R.: Action design research. MIS Q. **35**(1), 37–56 (2011)
15. Yoshino, N., Taghizadeh-Hesary, F.: Major challenges facing small and medium-sized enterprises in Asia and solutions for mitigating them. Asian Dev. Bank Institute (2016)

Average Flow Time Estimation and Its Application for Storage Relocation in an Order Picking System

Jeongwon Park[1], Permata Vallentino Eko Joatiko[2], Chiwoo Park[3], and Soondo Hong[2(✉)]

[1] Major in Industrial Data Science and Engineering, Department of Industrial Engineering, Pusan National University, Busan 46241, South Korea
[2] Department of Industrial Engineering, Pusan National University, Busan 46241, South Korea
soondo.hong@pusan.ac.kr
[3] Department of Industrial and Manufacturing Engineering, Florida State University, Tallahassee, FL 32306, USA

Abstract. This study proposes an average flow time estimation model based on Gaussian process regression that can be applied to adjust the storage locations of partial products and manages demand fluctuations and other dynamic order picking issues. We use the historical order picking data of a progressive zone picking system to extract features for the model. Subsequently, we train the estimation model and acquire the new storage location assignment by relocating part of the total products based on the estimated average flow time from the learning model. We test the proposed model using a simulation model based on a real cosmetic company's distribution center in South Korea. The simulation results indicate that the proposed model improves the performance by 9.61% with four relocation operations compared with the original storage location assignment before reassignment. The proposed model shows significant effectiveness when workloads are unbalanced, even in environments with high product diversity. We conclude that the proposed model could improve the productivity of real distribution centers with fewer reassignment operations.

Keywords: Facility logistics · Order picking · Flow time estimation · Storage location assignment · Warehouse

1 Introduction

The correct relocation of products assists in maintaining performance when warehouses and distribution centers (DCs hereafter) experience demand fluctuations and other problems that affect order picking operations. Balancing workloads minimizes the possibility of congestion in progressive zone picking systems [1]. Pan et al. [2] used a genetic algorithm for storage location assignments, and Chen et al. [3] formulated a mathematical model and used the tabu search algorithm to relocate items in a warehouse considering

© IFIP International Federation for Information Processing 2022
Published by Springer Nature Switzerland AG 2022
D. Y. Kim et al. (Eds.): APMS 2022, IFIP AICT 663, pp. 60–66, 2022.
https://doi.org/10.1007/978-3-031-16407-1_8

the relocation effort. To avoid relocating an entire warehouse inventory, Accorsi et al. [4] proposed a bi-objective integer linear programming model for an adaptive storage allocation policy. Kim and Hong [5] developed a dynamic storage location assignment method in progressive zone picking with a bypass conveyor system and S/R crane. They regarded the dynamic storage assignment problem deterministically and formulated the problem using mixed-integer programming. In this study, we extend [5] by including Gaussian process regression in solving the dynamic storage location assignment problem. We develop an average flow time estimation model to evaluate the expected increase in performance from the relocation operation as a response to demand fluctuation. Then we optimize the storage location assignment by searching for the new storage locations that will yield the minimum estimated average flow time.

2 Problem Definition

2.1 Progressive Zone Picking System

We consider a progressive zone picking system with an S/R crane consisting of z zones with r racks and a picker per zone, as shown in Fig. 1. The pickers assigned to picking zones fill totes with an order's products and place the totes on a conveyor that transports them throughout the zones to an unloading station. If a zone's buffer is full, totes bypass the zone to avoid blocking and return after recirculation.

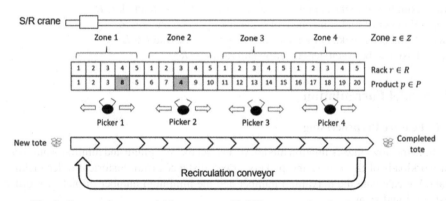

Fig. 1. Progressive zone picking system with S/R crane and recirculation conveyor

In this study, we assume that a product occupies one pick face. A picker loads product p into the tote from the assigned pick face k. When pickers start or finish order picking, they are at their depot stations located in the middle of each zone. The flow time of order o is the interval between the moment a tote enters the picking system and when the order is complete. The S/R crane transfers products to storage locations.

We obtain the average flow time $\overline{FT}$ from the sum of the flow times of the orders divided by the number of orders. An order list l is a group of orders processed within the same shift or time slot. We let w_l^k be the number of picks at pick face k in order list l, and K_z and K_r be the set of pick faces allocated in zone z, and the set of pick faces allocated in rack position r, respectively. We formulate the total number of picks in zone z of order list l as:

$$zw_{lz} = \sum_{k \in K_z} w_{lk}.$$

and the total number of picks in rack r of order list l as:

$$rw_{lr} = \sum_{k \in K_r} w_{lk}.$$

We use the following notations and parameters.

Set and its indices

O, o Set of orders and its indices $o \in O$
L, l Set of order lists and its indices $l \in L$
Z, z Set of zones and its indices $z \in Z$
R, r Set of racks and its indices $r \in R$
P, p Set of products and its indices $p \in P$
K, k Set of pick faces and its indices $k \in K$

Parameters

w_{lk} Number of picks at pick face k of order list l, $\forall l \in L$ and $k \in K$
zw_{lz} Number of picks in zone z of order list l, $\forall l \in L$ and $z \in Z$
rw_{lr} Number of picks in rack r of order list l, $\forall l \in L$ and $l \in L$
d_r Distance between depot station and rack $r \in R$

3   Model Formulation

3.1   Feature Preprocessing

To train the flow time estimation model, we extract the maximum and minimum numbers of workloads of the zones, and pickers' travel distances from historical order picking data. We calculate the maximum number and the minimum number of picks for order lists l, x_l^1 and x_l^2 as:

$$x_l^1 = \max_{\forall z \in Z} zw_{lz},$$

$$x_l^2 = \min_{\forall z \in Z} zw_{lz}.$$

and pickers' total travel distance of order list l as x_l^3 as:

$$x_l^3 = \sum_{r \in R} d_r \cdot rw_{lr}$$

Last, we merge x_l^1, x_l^2, and x_l^3 to form matrix X which is the input or feature.

3.2 Average Flow Time Estimation

Historical data from order picking system are noisy observations due to measurement errors and the influence of workload balance, rack storage policies, sequencing, etc., on order picking performance. Based on the definition of the Gaussian process adapted from Schulz et al. [6], Rasmussen and Williams [7], we formulate the joint probability of noisy observed data (X, X_*, y) and posterior function f_* as:

$$\begin{bmatrix} y \\ f_* \end{bmatrix} \sim \mathcal{N}\left(0, \begin{bmatrix} K(X, X) + \sigma_n^2 I & K(X, X_*) \\ K(X_*, X) & K(X, X_*) \end{bmatrix}\right),$$

where σ_n controls the noise level. In this study, X and X_* denote the training input and testing input, respectively, y denotes the training target (see Joatiko [8] for the details of the estimation model with the Gaussian process).

Prediction using the Gaussian process depends entirely on the kernel function Mackay [9]. The kernel function expresses the dependence of the two observations, x_i and x_j. We use a Gaussian kernel combined with a linear kernel as the kernel function. We formulate test target y_* the mean function of the posterior distribution as:

$$p(f_*|X_*, X, y) = \mathcal{N}\left(\overline{f_*}, \mathrm{cov}(f_*)\right).$$

To identify an optimal storage location, we use average flow time estimation. We measure the accuracy of the average flow time estimation model using the Pearson correlation coefficient, also called Pearson's r. Figure 2 shows the correlation along with Pearson's r value between the real value and the predicted value of 200 order lists using several experimental configurations as described in Sect. 4. We obtain real values using simulation and predicted values using the proposed flow time estimation model.

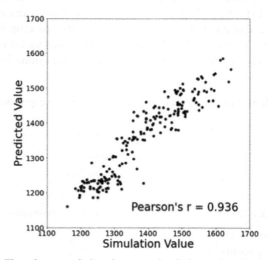

Fig. 2. Flow time correlations between simulation and prediction values

3.3 Storage Relocation Procedure

As mentioned, proper assignments of storage locations determine the best storage locations for the products in the order lists with minimal labor and cost. We assume a constant picking time per picker and that each picker picks each product independently. We assume identical zone size and rack size and that the termination time of the relocation operation is unknown because relocation times vary in practice.

We generate a candidate for the new storage assignment by switching the locations of two products. We consider only two products to switch at a time because we assume an unknown termination time. Thus, the total number of possible candidates is a combination of two of the total number of products $\binom{|P|}{2}$. We evaluate the $\overline{FT}$ of each candidate using the proposed average flow time estimation and select the pair of products estimated to have the minimum $\overline{FT}$ if we switch them.

If more time is available to relocate the products again after the relocation operation, we use the same relocation procedure for the new storage assignment. Stage n denotes the number of switched pairs as determined by the experience of management, considering the number of storage locations that can be reassigned.

4 Experiment and Results

4.1 Experiment

Table 1 shows the order picking system's configuration based on the real DC. We base the size of each order on uniform distribution and base the picker's travel time to pick each product on its storage location. Classes A, B, and C differentiate the storage locations in each zone. We set each zone's buffer size at 3 and the constant work-in-process level (CONWIP) at 60. We train the estimation model on 300 order lists and test them with 200 different order lists. According to the workload distribution among zones, 40% of the order lists are classified as the balanced scenario and the remaining 60% as the unbalanced scenario. We use Python 3.7 and the scikit-learn toolbox to construct the model and Tecnomatix© Plant Simulation 12 to generate the synthetic historical data.

Table 1. Configuration of the order picking system experiment

Parameter	Values
Number of zones	8
Number of products	96, 144
Order size	*Uniform* (3,10)
Size of the rack in each zone	3 rows × 6 columns
Number of orders in each order list	100
Number of switched pairs (n)	1, 2, 3, 4

4.2 Experiment Results

We defined performance improvement as the $\overline{FT}$ reduction percentage relative to the initial storage assignment (n = 0). Table 2 shows the performance improvement of the proposed model from n = 1 to n = 4 depending on the number of products. To measure performance, we first consider the number of products to be 96. The proposed model yields an average improvement of 3.29% in one relocation operation and an average improvement of 8.44% in four relocation operations.

Table 2. Performance improvement of the proposed model

Scenario	Improvement percentage (%)							
	$|P| = 96$				$|P| = 144$			
	$n = 1$	$n = 2$	$n = 3$	$n = 4$	$n = 1$	$n = 2$	$n = 3$	$n = 4$
Balance	1.30	1.85	2.38	2.63	1.76	2.98	3.65	4.16
Unbalanced	4.62	7.86	10.44	12.31	4.95	8.59	11.23	13.24
Average	3.29	5.46	7.22	8.44	3.67	6.34	8.20	9.61

Next, to analyze performance with high product diversity, we consider the number of products to be 144. The proposed model yields an average improvement of 3.67% in one relocation operation and an average improvement of 9.61% in four relocation operations. For both the unbalanced and the balanced scenarios, the improvement increases as the number of switched pairs increases, but the improvement in the unbalanced scenario is higher.

5   Conclusion

An average flow time estimation model was proposed to optimize storage location assignments in a progressive zone picking system considering the number of relocated products. Experiments based on a real DC showed that the proposed model successfully shortens the average flow time of order lists with a limited number of relocated products and that the proposed model significantly shortens the average flow time in an environment with high product diversity.

Having extracted features from historical data that were roughly related to the real workload balance of the real DC's picking system, future research will study the preprocessing step to confirm whether it could improve the accuracy of the proposed model. Further experiments will consider environments when stochastic picking times and pickers' capacities are not the same.

Despite the proposed model's performance, there is a risk that it will not achieve sufficient improvement considering relocation costs if there is not much room for improvement, or if the estimation model is not sufficiently trained. Future research will investigate all possible search procedures and approaches to guarantee estimates suitable for Gaussian process-based optimization.

Acknowledgements. This work was supported by 2022 BK21 FOUR Program of Pusan National University and was supported by the National Research Foundation of Korea (NRF) grant funded by the Korean government (MSIT) (No. NRF-2020R1A2C2004320). This work was also supported by the Brain Pool Fellowship of the National Research Foundation of Korea (No. NRF-2019H1D3A2A01100649).

References

1. Jane, C.C.: Storage location assignment in a distribution center. Int. J. Phys. Distrib. Logist. Manag. **30**(1), 55–71 (2000)
2. Pan, J.C.-H., Shih, P.-H., Wu, M.-H., Lin, J.-H.: A storage assignment heuristic method based on genetic algorithm for a pick-and-pass warehousing system. Comput. Ind. Eng. **81**, 1–13 (2015)
3. Chen, L., Langevin, A., Riopel, D.: A tabu search algorithm for the relocation problem in a warehousing system. Int. J. Prod. Econ. **129**(1), 147–156 (2011)
4. Accorsi, R., Baruffaldi, G., Manzini, R.: Picking efficiency and stock safety: a bi-objective storage assignment policy for temperature-sensitive products. Comput. Ind. Eng. **115**, 240–252 (2018)
5. Kim, J., Hong, S.: A dynamic storage location assignment model for a progressive bypass zone picking system with an S/R crane. J. Oper. Res. Soc. **73**, 1–12 (2021)
6. Schulz, E., Speekenbrink, M., Krause, A.: A tutorial on Gaussian process regression: Modelling, exploring, and exploiting functions. J. Math. Psychol. **85**, 1–16 (2018)
7. Rasmussen, C.E., Williams, C.K.I.: Gaussian Processes for Machine Learning. MIT Press, Cambridge (2006)
8. Joatiko, P.V.E.: A Data-driven yard template planning in a transshipment hub (2020)
9. Mackay, D.J.C.: Introduction to Gaussian processes. NATO ASI Ser. F: Comput. Syst. Sci. **168**, 133–165 (1998)

Smart Manufacturing and Industry 4.0

Analyzing Operations on a Manufacturing Line Using Geospatial Intelligence Technologies

Takeshi Kurata[1]($\boxtimes$) (iD), Munenori Harada[2], Katsuko Nakahira[2], Takashi Maehata[3],
Yoshinori Ito[4], and Hideki Aso[4]

[1] Human Augmentation Research Center, AIST, Chiba, Japan
t.kurata@aist.go.jp
[2] Faculty of Engineering, Nagaoka University of Technology, Nagano, Japan
[3] IoT R&D Center, Sumitomo Electric Industries, Ltd., Osaka, Japan
[4] IoT Acceleration Lab, J-Power Systems Co. Ltd., Ibaraki, Japan

Abstract. This paper reports on a case study of work analysis using geospatial intelligence technologies conducted on a manufacturing line at a J-Power Systems (JPS) plant in FY2020. First, an overview of the workplace, the purpose of the analysis, and the types of data used in the analysis is presented. Next, we describe the data processing methods developed in the preparatory phase of the analysis, and finally, we report the results and discussion of the work analysis.

Keywords: Geospatial intelligence (GSI) · Indoor positioning · Machine learning · Manufacturing line · Work analysis

1 Introduction

Health and productivity management (HPM) [1–3] is realized by simultaneously improving labor productivity and Quality of Working (QoW) in a well-balanced manner. Since it is necessary to deal with a wide range of issues for that, engineering and Digital Transformation (DX) approaches are essential. On the other hand, it has been reported that 60–80% of information is related to location information [4] and that humans spend approximately 90% of their time indoors [5]. Therefore, geospatial intelligence (GSI), especially indoor GSI, which supports problem solving by linking geospatial data with other data, is expected to be an effective means to promote DX and HPM [6, 7]. This paper reports on a case study of work analysis using indoor GSI technologies conducted on manufacturing lines (MLs) at a JPS plant.

The area was about 1,800 m^2 rectangle in size. An indoor positioning system [8] and a PLC were installed to collect data to determine the position of each worker and the state of each equipment (Fig. 1). There are three MLs with three workers in charge of one line each. The leader of the MLs manages the entire work area, and sometimes works in cooperation with other workers as needed.

The main objective of this work analysis was to investigate the feasibility of (1) improving the operation rate, and it also included feasibility studies on (2) automating

D. Y. Kim et al. (Eds.): APMS 2022, IFIP AICT 663, pp. 69–76, 2022.
https://doi.org/10.1007/978-3-031-16407-1_9

work records and (3) visualizing work transitions, respectively, and (4) confirming the value of work skills. From the perspective of HPM, (1) to (4) are all related to productivity, and (2) to (4) are related to QoW (physical/mental load reduction, transparency of work status, and skill improvement).

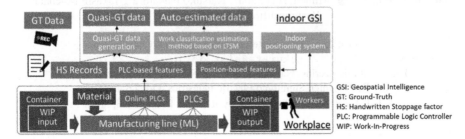

Fig. 1. Workplace overview and the indoor GSI.

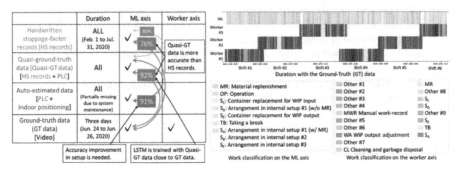

Fig. 2. Types of time-series work classification data (left), breakdown of work classifications, as well as the GT values and work-shift overlaps (right).

2 Basics of This Work Analysis Case Study

In the actual case study presented in this paper, work analysis was conducted in the area containing the work-in-progress (WIP) manufacturing process at a JPS plant [7].

We use four types of time-series work classification data for different purposes as shown in Fig. 2-left, which are along the "ML axis" or the "worker axis" where The ML axis indicates the time axis of each ML, and the worker axis indicates the time axis of each worker.

The "ground-truth (GT) data" were prepared manually by visual inspection using recorded video for three days of work. Only the GT data have both the ML axis and the worker axis. The handwritten stoppage-factor records (hereinafter referred to as "HS records") are daily handwritten records kept by workers in the workplace. The "quasi-GT data" are generated by integrating the HS records and PLC data using the method described in Sect. 3.1. Since both HS records and PLC data are constantly obtained onsite, they can be easily scaled up. The "auto-estimated data" are the estimation results of a method based on machine learning (LSTM: Long short-term memory) [9] using PLC data and positioning data as described in Sect. 3.2. All three types of data are along the ML axis. Figure 2-right shows the breakdown of work classifications, as well as the GT values and work shift overlaps for workers #1, #2, and #3.

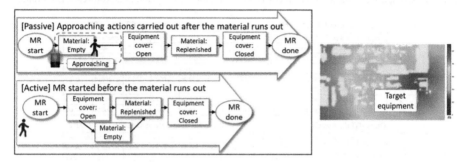

Fig. 3. MR detection process (left), Travel distance map for position-based features (right).

3 Methodology of Work Analysis on ML Axes

3.1 Quasi-Ground-Truth Data Generation

The HS records contain no missing data along the ML axis. However, there are two significant issues for investigating the feasibility of improving the operation rate. One is that the start and end times of each record are rounded off, and the other is that "material replenishment (MR)" works are not included in the records even if they are supposed to be one of major stoppage factors for the MLs.

Meanwhile, because IoT transition is still underway in the workplace, PLC data that can be sent to the server and used for analysis are limited.

In this case study, we developed a method to generate "quasi-GT data" that are more accurate in time and include MR works by integrating HS records and PLC data. The method mainly consists of a process to make time recording more accurate using PLC data and an MR detection process. This section outlines the latter, which is also used to extract one of PLC-based features for LSTM.

With PLC data, it is possible to grasp each status of "out of material" and "open/closed status of the equipment cover". We developed a method for detecting MR works by identifying the state transitions caused by their combinations, as shown in Fig. 3-left. Note that "arrangement in internal setup #1 (with MR)", "container replacement for WIP input", and "arrangement in internal setup #1 (without MR)," which are S_A, S_C, and S_D respectively, are related setups that are difficult to separate in the machine learning described below, so we deal with them collectively in this case study.

The accuracy of the quasi-GT data generation method, including the MR detection process, was evaluated by comparing the HS records, GT data, and quasi-GT data, respectively. Comparison of the GT and quasi-GT data (Table 1-bottom-left) confirmed that the quasi-GT data can be generated with an accuracy of approximately 92%, that it is possible to obtain data closer to the GT data than HS records (Table 1-top-left), and that it is possible to automatically record operation (OP) and MR with the high accuracy of 96% and 93% respectively by using PLC data.

Table 1. Comparisons between HS records, GT data, Quasi-GT data, and Auto-estimated data.

HS Records vs GT data: 76%

	recall	precision	f1	time ratio	time (sec.)
OTHER	41.3%	66.8%	51.0%	61.9%	11,096
OP	97.6%	66.5%	79.1%	146.7%	63,148
MR	0.0%			0.0%	23,575
$S_A S_C S_D$	88.2%	95.6%	91.8%	92.2%	25,696
S_B	100.0%	65.2%	78.9%	153.5%	2,346
S_E	81.1%	90.5%	85.6%	89.6%	11,045
TB	96.8%	95.9%	96.3%	100.9%	21,400

HS Records vs Quasi-GT data: 80%

	recall	precision	f1	time ratio	time (sec.)
OTHER	40.5%	100.0%	57.7%	40.5%	16,948
OP	100.0%	65.3%	79.0%	153.2%	60,486
MR	0.0%			0.0%	22,072
$S_A S_C S_D$	100.0%	100.0%	100.0%	100.0%	23,700
S_B	100.0%	100.0%	100.0%	100.0%	3,600
S_E	100.0%	100.0%	100.0%	100.0%	9,900
TB	100.0%	100.0%	100.0%	100.0%	21,600

Quasi-GT data vs GT data: 92%

	recall	precision	f1	time ratio	time (sec.)
OTHER	88.8%	58.2%	70.3%	152.7%	11,096
OP	93.6%	97.7%	95.6%	95.8%	63,148
MR	90.4%	96.6%	93.4%	93.6%	23,575
$S_A S_C S_D$	88.2%	95.6%	91.8%	92.2%	25,696
S_B	100.0%	65.2%	78.9%	153.5%	2,346
S_E	81.1%	90.5%	85.6%	89.6%	11,045
TB	96.8%	95.9%	96.3%	100.9%	21,400

Auto-estimated data vs Quasi-GT data: 91%

	recall	precision	f1	time ratio	time (sec.)
OTHER TB	88.2%	80.2%	84.0%	110.0%	24,130
OP	95.4%	96.7%	96.0%	98.6%	54,808
MR	94.6%	95.9%	95.2%	98.6%	20,982
$S_A S_C S_D$	73.6%	77.5%	75.5%	94.9%	11,671
S_B					0
S_E	76.6%	86.4%	81.2%	88.7%	6,900

3.2 Automatic Recording Based on LSTM

To achieve automatic recording of work classifications in addition to OP and MR without HS records, we developed a work classification estimation method based on LTSM using 47 features derived from PLC data and 9 features derived from positioning data. Besides the features obtained using the MR detection process described above, internal-setup features were also designed based on PLC data. Although they are more coarse-grained than work classifications such as OP, MR, and S series denoted as S_*, it can represent each state such as the first and second half of setup, and several types of machine operations during setup.

As for features based on positioning data, we designed 9 distance features each of which represents the travel distance for a worker to reach each target equipment. For efficiency, maps of travel distances from each equipment, as shown in Fig. 3-right, are pre-computed and stored. In addition, the time spent in each work area is also used as one of features by defining work areas that are assumed to correlate strongly with some of specific works in the work classification.

Either the GT or quasi-GT data can be used for LSTM training. Although the GT data are more accurate, they are only available for three days in this case study and are very expensive to prepare in actual operation. In contract, we can obtain the quasi-GT data continuously, and they are close enough to the GT data as shown in the previous section. For these reasons, LSTM training was conducted using the quasi-GT data.

We evaluated the accuracy of the LSTM-based method. Since the purpose of work classification estimation was to automatically generate data comparable to the quasi-GT data, which contributes to elimination of manual recording works, the comparison target here was the quasi-GT data. As a result of evaluation by k-fold cross-validation (K = 3), the estimation accuracy was about 91% (Table 1-bottom-right). Note that K = 3 was used for this evaluation since there are state sequences the occurrence frequency of which is small with respect to the length of whole data.

While OP and MR are highly accurate thanks to each detection process that constitutes the quasi-GT data generation method, there was room for improvement for estimating S_* each of which is internal-setup-related work classification. As shown in Table 1-bottom-left, comparing the GT data, the accuracy of S_* in the quasi-GT data is not so high for the training data, and it may have affected the accuracy of the estimation. One of the practical issues for improving the quality of training data is not to increase the burden in the workplace for collecting high-quality training data. In addition, to estimate S_* involving no equipment controls, it is crucial to obtain the workers' status because PLC data is not available. Therefore, positional data is expected to play an important role in identifying the status of workers.

3.3 Indoor Positioning

The integrated positioning method used in this case study consists of BLE (Bluetooth Low Energy) positioning, PDR (Pedestrian Dead Reckoning), and map matching [8]. Since the data for international indoor positioning competitions [10, 11] were collected at the same workplace as this case study, here we use the competition data for performance evaluation. As a result, CE50, a representative accuracy indicator, was 4.39 m (Reference: CE50 in AIST's method [12, 13] was 2.73 m).

At the target workplace, solar BLE beacons (Fujitsu PulsarGum) were installed for the maintenance-free advantage. The shortest advertisement transmission interval is 1.28 s, however, depending on the amount of electricity generated by solar power, the transmission interval may be longer. It may cause passing it unnoticed. Compared to warehouses where visual work is often required everywhere, in manufacturing sites, there are many areas where the luminance level is not sufficient such as aisles and other areas where visual work is not required. In such environments, the advertisement transmission interval is getting longer. Therefore, it would be possible to improve the positioning accuracy and the quality of features related to setup works by installing battery-powered beacons, which have shorter and more constant transmission intervals than solar beacons, in critical areas where PLC data is not available for work classification.

4   Work Analysis on Manufacturing Line Axis

We conducted work analysis using the quasi-GT data and GT data instead of using the results of the work classification estimation by machine learning since it was still in the feasibility study phase during this case study. This section reports on the quasi-GT data-based analysis on the ML axis.

Figure 4-left shows a state transition diagram of the work classification, that is, the work process model. The transitions from OP clearly identify that the major stoppage factor is MR and that the main setup workflow after OP is "S_C to {S_A or S_D} to S_E." Since it is possible to perform simulations based on such models as in Ref. [14], preliminary evaluations with the model are expected for efficient 'Kaizen' of these MLs and the similar MLs in the future.

There are 3,230 OPs in the quasi-GT data with 406 operation cycle. Note that we define one operation cycle as a cycle consisting of (1) setting a full WIP container on the input side to the ML, (2) running the ML, (3) consuming the WIP, and (4) removing the empty WIP container. As shown in Fig. 4-right, there was a weak positive correlation between the operation rate and the continuous operation time (operation time per run) within each cycle. These results implies that the longer the continuous operation time is, the higher the operation rate is.

As each ML requires a brief stop for MR, we also analyzed MR and the approaching actions to the equipment for MR. Comparing the HS records with the quasi-GT data confirmed that 34% of time for OP in the HS records were MR (Fig. 6-middle-right). It was also found that the approaching time obtained by the MR work detection process (Fig. 3-left) accounted for 36% of the MR time. Based on these results, if all approaching times that take longer than the median were replaced by the median, the operation rate could be improved by 3%.

We also compared differences in operation rates depending on whether MR was passive or active. A passive cycle is one in which all approaching actions are carried out after the material runs out, and an active cycle is one that includes at least one MR started before the material runs out. The analysis confirmed that the median operation rates for passive and active cycles are 47% and 49%, respectively, and that the variation in operation rates is greater for passive cycles (Fig. 6-top-right).

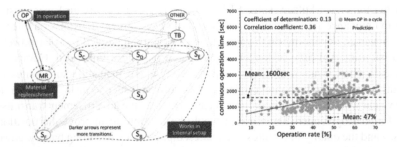

Fig. 4. Quasi-GT data-based transition diagram on the ML axis (left), Operation rate and continuous operation time within each cycle (right).

5   Work Analysis on Manufacturing-Line and Worker Axes

Obtaining the correspondence matrix between each work classification on the ML and worker axes from the GT data, we confirmed that "WIP output adjustment (WA)" (adjustment of the position of WIP output in the container) occupies about half of the time in OP, the ratio of "manual work record (MWR)" in OP to MWR except in OP is 2:1, and about half of "cleaning and garbage disposal (CL)" is done during internal setup.

The percentage of time for WA in OP averaged 47%, the lowest 35%, and the highest 60% (Fig. 5). For example, if the ratio is kept not to exceed 40%, the reduction in WA is equivalent to 9% of time for OP. By allocating the reduction in OP to other works (such as HR, CL, advance execution of internal setup, etc.), downtime is expected to be reduced. Improving work skills contributes to the reduction of time for WA, and it is expected to lead to higher operation rates and more rewarding work. In addition, although automation of WA is not currently underway, the effect is not small.

If MWR and CL were performed in OP in Shifts #1, #2, #3, and #5 as the same rate as the high-skilled worker in Shift #4, the average time for the increase of MWR and CL would be equivalent to 8% of time for OP. Although the 9% estimated above for WA reduction in OP is only an average, the increase of MWR and CL is expected to be within the range of the WA reduction.

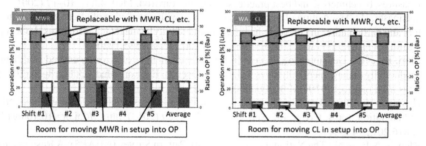

Fig. 5. WA (WIP output adjustment) and MWR (manual work record) in OP (left), WA and CL (cleaning and garbage disposal) in OP (right).

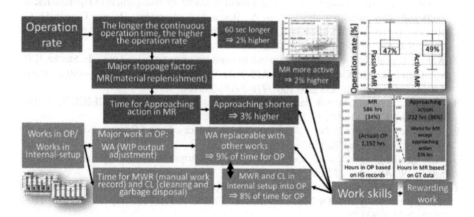

Fig. 6. Candidate metrics related to the operation rate and work skills.

6   Conclusion

This paper reported on the case study of work analysis using GSI technologies on MLs at the JPS plant. First, regarding the improvement of the operation rate, we were able to extract candidates of metrics related to the operation rate and work skills as shown in Fig. 6. Next, regarding the automation of MWR, it was shown that although sufficient accuracy was obtained in estimating OP and MR, there is room for improvement in the accuracy of estimating S∗. In particular, it was found that improving the accuracy of indoor positioning is required to obtain the workers' status in the actual workplace.

The feasibility of visualizing work transitions was demonstrated by generating the work process model (Fig. 4-left) using the quasi-GT data. In addition, it was confirmed that the "active MR metrics" and replacement of WA in Figs. 5 and 6 are deeply related to work skills which contribute to QoW.

References

1. Goetzel, R.Z., et al.: Health and productivity management: establishing key performance measures, benchmarks, and best practices. J. Occup. Environ. Med. **43**(1), 10–17 (2001)
2. Takahashi, H.: Association of organizational factors with knowledge of effectiveness indicators and participation in corporate health and productivity management programs. J. Occup. Health 63(1), e12205 (2021). https://doi.org/10.1002/1348-9585.12205
3. Mori, K., et al.: Development, success factors, and challenges of government-led health and productivity management initiatives in Japan. J. Occupa. Environ. Med. **63**(1), 18–26 (2021). https://doi.org/10.1097/JOM.0000000000002002
4. Hahmann, S., Burghardt, D.: How much information is geospatially referenced? networks and cognition. Int. J. Geogr. Inf. Sci. **27**(6), 1171–1189 (2013). https://doi.org/10.1080/136 58816.2012.743664
5. Klepeis, N.E., et al.: The National Human Activity Pattern Survey (NHAPS): A Resource for Assessing Exposure to Environmental Pollutants, Lawrence Berkeley National Laboratory (2001)
6. Kurata, T.: Geospatial intelligence for health and productivity management in Japanese restaurants and other industries. In: Dolgui, A., Bernard, A., Lemoine, D., von Cieminski, G., Romero, D. (eds.) APMS 2021. IAICT, vol. 632, pp. 206–214. Springer, Cham (2021). https://doi.org/10.1007/978-3-030-85906-0_23
7. Kurata, T., et al.: IoH technologies into indoor manufacturing sites. In: Ameri, F., Stecke, K.E., von Cieminski, G., Kiritsis, D. (eds.) APMS 2019. IAICT, vol. 567, pp. 372–380. Springer, Cham (2019). https://doi.org/10.1007/978-3-030-29996-5_43
8. Maehata, T., et al.: Sensor data fusion for indoor positioning system. IEICE Tech. Rep 120(204), RCS2020–106, pp.75–79 (2020)
9. Hochreiter, S., Schmidhuber, J.: Long short-term memory. Neural Comput. **9**(8), 1735–1780 (1997). https://doi.org/10.1162/neco.1997.9.8.1735
10. xDR Challenge in industrial Scenarios 2019 (2019). https://unit.aist.go.jp/harc/xDR-Challenge-2019/, Accessed 24 Mar 2022
11. Potorti, F., et al.: Off-line evaluation of indoor positioning systems in different scenarios: The experiences from IPIN 2020 competition. IEEE Sens. J. (2021). https://doi.org/10.1109/JSEN.2021.3083149
12. Kourogi, M., Kurata, T.: Personal positioning based on walking locomotion analysis with self-contained sensors and a wearable camera. In: Proceedings of ISMAR, pp. 103–112 (2003). https://doi.org/10.1109/ISMAR.2003.1240693
13. Ichikari, R., et al., Complementary integration of PDR with absolute positioning methods based on time-series consistency. In: Proceedings of IPIN, Work-in-Progress, pp. 4–7 (2016)
14. Myokan, T., et al.: Pre-evaluation of Kaizen plan considering efficiency and employee satisfaction by simulation using data assimilation -toward constructing Kaizen support framework-. In: Proceedings of ICServ, p. 7 (2016)

Strategic Alignment and Industry 4.0: An Exploratory Study with Eleven Companies

Gilberto Francisco de Oliveira[1]([⊠]) ⓘ, Rodrigo Franco Gonçalves[1] ⓘ,
and Fernando José Barbin Laurindo[2] ⓘ

[1] Universidade Paulista – UNIP, São Paulo, SP, Brasil
gilberto.oliveira18@aluno.unip.br
[2] Escola Politécnica da Universidade de São Paulo – EPUSP, São Paulo, SP, Brasil

Abstract. The technologies that make up the Industry 4.0 umbrella provide organizations with efficiency and flexibility, but without alignment with organizational strategies, below-average results can be achieved in comparison with the market. In order to avoid this failure, investments in I4.0 must support current or explore new business strategies. The present work aims to analyze how eleven companies located in Brazil can be typified in technological transformation alignment perspective by model of Henderson and Venkatraman. The eleven companies are large companies with consolidated initiatives to implement Industry 4.0. In the findings, it was possible to identify that the dominant adequacy to the strategic alignment model remains valid, despite the enabling technologies of Industry 4.0 to be recent. It is also highlighted the degree of concern about the type of strategic alignment chosen by these companies, which results in a temporary competitive advantage, as it allows imitation by other competing companies by not creating value in the customers' view.

Keywords: Industry 4.0 · Industrie 4.0 · Strategic alignment · Henderson and Venkatraman Model · Technology transformation · Competitive advantage

1 Introduction

There is a widespread paradigm that Industry 4.0 (I4.0) increases firm performance to the highest levels of competitiveness [1]. The technological tools that make the I4.0 possible bring advantages, such as better quality with lower production costs; customized production; process flexibility and efficient use of resources [2]. In contrast to the positive aspects, there are several risks involved in implementing I4.0 to consider when deciding to implement it. Of these, the lack of adherence to corporate strategic alignment stands out [3].

The business strategy is the result of the confrontation between the essential competencies of the organization in the face of opportunities and threats identified in the external environment. Core competencies increase the organization's competitive advantages (valuable, rare, expensive and non-replaceable) [4]. Information Technology and Digital

© IFIP International Federation for Information Processing 2022
Published by Springer Nature Switzerland AG 2022
D. Y. Kim et al. (Eds.): APMS 2022, IFIP AICT 663, pp. 77–84, 2022.
https://doi.org/10.1007/978-3-031-16407-1_10

Communication (ITDC) plays a leading role in strategic alignment, and in the model proposed by Henderson & Venkatraman [5], it occurs in a bidirectional way [6]. However, despite the fact that I4.0 is essentially based on ITDC [1], there is no consolidated version of strategic alignment and one of the justifications lies in the fact that it is a relatively new area of study [3].

From the premise that the new technologies of I4.0 can contribute to the organizational strategy. The objective of this paper is to verify the application of Technological Transformation of the strategic alignment model between ITDC and Business developed by Henderson and Venkatrama [5] for companies that adopt I4.0 embedded technologies, for this, eleven companies located in the state of São Paulo, Brazil, were analyzed in a sample selected by convenience.

2   Theoretical Background

2.1   Industry 4.0

The I4.0 is related to the strong integration with industrial processes, aiming to improve quality, add value to activities and eliminate waste, mainly qualifying the data flow providing speed in transmission [7]. Organizations benefit from technologies covered in I4.0 in flexibility, real-time capacity monitoring, decentralization, modularity, operational and energy efficiency, interoperability, service orientation, virtualization, and sustainability [8].

The gains achieved with I4.0 have managed to break an important paradigm in production management, by making production in volume and variety more flexible without increasing cost [9]. The technologies that comprise I4.0 are broad, according to the literature, but the most used are Big Data Analytics, CPS, IoT, and Artificial Intelligence [2, 10–12].

2.2   Strategic Alignment Model

The literature defines "strategic alignment" as the process of transforming business strategy into actions that ensure that business objectives are supported [6]. Strategic alignment between business and ITDC means the synchronization between consolidated strategic business initiatives and the choices made in ITDC solutions and their governance, to achieve the maximum potential for results [13]. Authors have dedicated themselves to studying strategic alignment, since, in a dynamic market, efficiency in achieving business results is dependent on how ITDC is exploited by the organization [14]. The seminal model of Henderson and Venkatraman [5] is used to typify preponderant alignment [15].

The model develops four perspectives of dominant alignment by which an organization can be characterized [5]. The first two have a business strategy as a driving force: strategy execution and technology transformation, and the other two perspectives: competitive potential and service level, explore how information technology can enable new or improved business strategies with organizational implications [15].

In perspective two: technology transformation, the assessment of the implementation of the business strategy is based on the ITDC strategy and the articulation between infrastructure needs and the information system process. There is a more prominent adherence to this perspective by companies when observing the application of I4.0 technologies [16]. This represents a tendency to apply ITDC solutions that can bring more flexibility to manufacturing operations until product delivery, without necessarily changing the business strategy [17]. Companies that adopt technology solutions embedded in I4.0 tend to give technology the ability to act preventively in their production processes, thus supporting decision making [2]. Technologies are essentially dedicated to improving to get data in operational processes and from this data, extracting information in an agile and efficient way [19]. Greater agility in data collection and processing enables decentralization and independence in decision-making in production cells [20]. The autonomy gained from digitalization enables vertical and horizontal integrations [21, 22], in addition to the ability to share operational information in real-time with different hierarchical levels of the company [9]. The technological transformation advocated with perspective two of the strategic alignment model is not just the result of the acquisition of new technologies with the adaptation of the factory layout [23], it also depends on the training of people all over the organization to obtain superior results in the attribution of their functions [24].

3   Research Method

The present work can be considered exploratory research [25]. Therefore, it is intended to analyze the adherence of organizations with initiatives to implement I4.0 technologies to the model of Henderson & Verkatraman [5] in its perspective Technological Transformation. The research question that motivated the study was "How are companies that apply emerging technologies from I4.0 positioned in perspective technological transformation of the strategic alignment proposed by Henderson and Venkatrama?".

Methodological steps were followed to give consistency to the research process. Initially, it was performed a literature review to identify the theoretical basis, in which knowledge was obtained to identify the research question that guided the proposed study. With the literature review and the research question formulated, the next step was to determine the research protocol to carry out the data collection.

The data collection stage took place between May and June 2021, with eleven responding companies located in the state of São Paulo. A structured questionnaire based on a theoretical study was applied to the response of employees who occupy decision-making positions in these companies. The choice of the responding companies was based on the indication of market professionals and academics and for having already participated in research on the maturity in the implementation of emerging technologies of I4.0 [26].

The questionnaire has fourteen assertions, in which the respondent chooses between a Likert Scale ranging from 1 to 5. Where 1 means "totally disagree" and 5, he "totally agree" with the statement. The questionnaire was developed on a Web platform. The assertions were formulated from the findings in theory about characteristics of the technological transformation perspective and, thus, verify the existence and degree of strategic alignment in a company.

Table 1 addresses the assertions presented in the questionnaire, with the reference authors.

Table 1. Questionnaire

At the company, I work for:	Support
has confidence in its technologies to support decision-making and acts, based on the implemented technologies, in a preventive	[20]
manages to capture data in all its operational processes and organize it to derive value from it	[19]
has autonomous cells, that is, they operate independently in the entire manufacturing operation	[20]
has activity digitization that helps management	[21]
has vertical integration (the information sharing from the shop floor to company executives) and horizontal integration (the connection between all sectors of the production chain)	[21]
all those responsible for dealing with implemented Industry 4.0 technologies have the knowledge and skills to perform this role	[24]
can proactively plan for future occurrences because of the implemented Industry 4.0 technologies	[2]
has adapted the structure and layout throughout the entire manufacturing area to receive Industry 4.0 technologies	[23]
has high levels of standardization in processes and products, following norms and specifications	[2]
uses integrated systems throughout the manufacturing unit that allow the sharing of data information from the factory floor with the operational and executive levels	[9]
uses technologies such as Big Data Analytics, CPS, IoT, and Artificial Intelligence in all its manufacturing processes	[2, 10–12, 27]
has a management system for all logistical links, from supplier data, and inventory, to sales	[21]
has systems capable of accumulating knowledge and autonomously making decisions, performing analyzes of the results accumulated in the manufacturing operations	[22]
has systems capable of accumulating knowledge and making decisions in a semi-autonomous way (with human intervention), performing analyzes of the results accumulated in the manufacturing operations	[22]

Source: Prepared by the authors

4   Results and Discussion

Preliminary to the questionnaire, on adherence to perspective two of the model by Henderson and Venkatraman [5], questions were asked that helped to typify the respondent company, and the compilation of the eleven companies is presented in Table 2.

Table 2. Typification of respondent companies

	Type of industry	Range of number of employees	Annual billing range
Company 1	Metallurgical	10 to 49	Between BRL 360 thousand and BRL 4.8 million
Company 2	Electronics	50 to 249	Greater than BRL 300 million
Company 3	Cosmetics	250 or more	Greater than BRL 300 million
Company 4	Chemistry	0 to 9	Between BRL 360 thousand and BRL 4.8 million
Company 5	Metallurgical	50 to 249	Between BRL 360 thousand and BRL 4.8 million
Company 6	Metallurgical	250 or more	Greater than BRL 300 million
Company 7	Steel Mill	250 or more	Greater than BRL 300 million
Company 8	Mining	250 or more	Greater than BRL 300 million
Company 9	Metallurgical	250 or more	Greater than BRL 300 million
Company 10	Cosmetic	250 or more	Greater than BRL 300 million
Company 11	Automobile	250 or more	Greater than BRL 300 million

Source: Prepared by the authors

As shown in Table 2, the number of employees combined with the billing classify the companies surveyed can be considered as large. There is a variety of areas of activity, and in the metallurgical segment, there are four companies, followed by the cosmetics area with two companies interviewed.

The level of training and experience of the respondents were also mapped. The minimum training is higher education, with more than 4 years in the company, all of them occupying a management position in the companies they operate.

Table 3 shows the data collected from the fourteen assertions, the sum was tabulated and calculated for each respondent company, considering that the higher the total value, with seventy being the maximum, the greater the company's adherence to perspective two of the strategic alignment model of Henderson and Venkatraman [5].

Company 7 was the only one that the respondent scored with the highest value on the scale for all assertions, something expected of the high level of investment in recent years in innovative technologies of the company in the steel segment, mainly aimed at improving the ability to collect and transfer data in your processes. Company 8 had the lowest average, although, with high dispersion, the result is linked to the

Table 3. Sum of points by company where 70 is the maximum value

Company	1	2	3	4	5	6	7	8	9	10	11
Sum	44	51	42	42	42	66	70	33	42	59	58

Source: Prepared by the authors

company's operating segment (mining) in which investments in I4.0 technologies do not confirm perspective two of strategic alignment as dominant, because there are occasional and dispersed applications of new technologies in their manufacturing processes. The other companies, to a lesser and greater degree, corroborate the understanding that the strategic alignment has been guided by the use of ITDC enablers of I4.0 to improve production processes, as recommended by the strategic alignment model of Henderson and Venkatrama [5].

5   Conclusion

The emerging technologies of I4.0 have contributed companies to be more agile in their production processes. Agility is achieved by collecting, transforming and transmitting data more quickly to decision makers. However, the mere availability of new technologies does not mean a return of superior results if there is not an adequate strategic alignment.

In the eleven companies studied, it was possible to identify the predominant adherence to perspective technological transformation, in which the technologies structured in I4.0 aim to support the organizational strategy. On the one hand, it means obtaining results in a pragmatic with improved levels of information, but the competitive advantage that comes from this perspective is temporary, as it is easily imitated by other competitors. Organizations interested in achieving perennial competitive results should align efforts in the application of I4.0 technologies to offer differentiated, customized products and services focused on servitization, as recommended by perspectives three and four of the strategic alignment model.

Although new digital transformation technologies can be applied to many manufacturing processes, their access is still restricted to large companies due to the high investment required. This characteristic was identified in the eleven companies studied when analyzing their size and revenue.

Analyzing how obtaining new technologies incorporated into I4.0 is converting into benefits in the strategic field plays an important role, as argued by Karpovsky [14]. Supporting a proposition to be tested in future works, named here as P1.

P1. Organizations that apply the new I4.0 technologies adhering to their business strategies can obtain a higher return on investment.

Although there is no consolidated model to typify the companies that align the new technologies of the I4.0 to their strategies. The model by Henderson and Venkatraman [5], published in 1993, proved to be adequate to characterize the companies studied from the perspective of technological transformation, but there is another gap for study, declared in the proposition to be tested in future works regarding the applicability of the other perspectives.

P2. The application and use of new technologies incorporated in I4.0 can characterize organizations in any of the four perspectives of strategic alignment, depending on the way they were implemented.

The presented propositions have the limitation of the few respondents, opening opportunities for future research, in which the methodological procedures could be either case studies or surveys.

As in any research, there are limitations inherent to the methodology, such as considering a restricted group of companies, and not being possible to generalize the findings, which opens the opportunity for further research with a larger sample base.

This study was partially financed by the Coordination for the Improvement of Higher Education Personnel - Brazil (CAPES) – Financial Code 001.

References

1. Tyas, W.P., Hutama, J.K.P.: Strategy and innovation of home based enterprises for local development in the 4.0 era: a bibliographic study. In: IOP Conference Series Earth Environment Science, vol. 673, no. 1, pp. 0–14 (2021)
2. Kamble, S.S., et al.: Smart manufacturing process and system automation–a critical review of the standards and envisioned scenarios. J. Manuf. Syst. **56**(4), 312–325 (2020)
3. Cordeiro, G.A., Ordóñez, R.E.C., Ferro, R.: Theoretical proposal of steps for the implementation of the Industry 4.0 concept. Brazilian J. Oper. Prod. Manag. **16**(2), 166–179 (2019)
4. Hitt, M.A., Ireland, R.D., Hoskisson, R.E.: Administração Estratégica. Cengage Learning Edições (2008)
5. Henderson, J.C., Venkatraman, H.: Strategic alignment: leveraging information technology for transforming organizations. IBM Syst. J. **38**(2.3), 472–484 (1993)
6. Fernandes, A.A., Abreu, V.F.: implantando a governança de TI: da estratégia à Gestão dos Processos e Serviços. BRASPORT, Rio de Janeito (2014)
7. Gadekar, R., Sarkar, B., Gadekar, A.: Assessment of key success factors for Industry 4.0 implementation in manufacturing industry using EDAS. Int. J. Innov. Eng. Sci. **6**(1), 1–11 (2021)
8. Nosalska, K., Piątek, Z.M., Mazurek, G., Rzadca, R.: Industry 4.0: coherent definition framework with technological and organizational interdependencies. J. Manuf. Technol. Manag. **31**(5), 837–862 (2019)
9. Lee, C.K.M., Lin, B.B., Ng, K.K.H., Lv, Y.Q., Tai, W.C.: Smart robotic mobile fulfillment system with dynamic conflict-free strategies considering cyber-physical integration. Adv. Eng. Inf. **42**, 100998 (2019)
10. Culot, G., Orzes, G., Sartor, M., Nassimbeni, G.: The future of manufacturing: a delphi-based scenario analysis on Industry 4.0. Technol. Forecast. Soc. Change **157**, 120092 (2020)
11. El Zant, C., Benfriha, K., Loubère, S., Aoussat, A., Adjoul, O.: A design methodology for modular processes orchestration. CIRP J. Manuf. Sci. Technol. **35**, 106–117 (2021)
12. Zheng, T., Ardolino, M., Bacchetti, A., Perona, M.: The applications of Industry 4.0 technologies in manufacturing context: a systematic literature review. Int. J. Prod. Res. **59**(6), 1922–1954 (2021)
13. Mitropoulos, S.: An integrated model for formulation, alignment, execution and evaluation of business and IT strategies. Int. J. Bus. Syst. Res. **15**(1), 90–111 (2021)
14. Karpovsky, A., Galliers, R.D.: Aligning in practice: from current cases to a new agenda. J. Inf. Technol. **30**(2), 136–160 (2015)

15. Ullah, A., Lai, R.: A systematic review of business and information technology alignment. ACM Trans. Manag. Inf. Syst. **4**(1), 1–30 (2013)
16. Ghobakhloo, M., Fathi, M.: Corporate survival in Industry 4.0 era: the enabling role of lean-digitized manufacturing. J. Manuf. Technol. Manag. **31**(1), 1–30 (2020). https://doi.org/10.1108/JMTM-11-2018-0417
17. Gajsek, B., Marolt, J., Rupnik, B., Lerher, T., Sternad, M.: Using maturity model and discrete-event simulation for Industry 4.0 implementation. Int. J. Simul. Model. **18**(3), 488–499 (2019)
18. Lang, S., Reggelin, T., Jobran, M., Hofmann, W.: Towards a modular, decentralized and digital Industry 4.0 learning factory, pp. 123–128 (2018)
19. Ribeiro, P.P., de M. Lopes, C., Correia, A.M.: Avaliação da gestão de estoque em uma microempresa de autopeças utilizando a curva abc como ferramenta de apoio. Rev. CEREUS **12**(2), 130–145 (2020)
20. Hoffmann Souza, M.L., da Costa, C.A., de Oliveira Ramos, G., da Rosa Righi, R.: A survey on decision-making based on system reliability in the context of Industry 4.0. J. Manuf. Syst. **56**, 133–156 (2020)
21. Belinski, R., Peixe, A.M.M., Frederico, G.F., Garza-Reyes, J.A.: Organizational learning and Industry 4.0: findings from a systematic literature review and research agenda. Benchmarking **27**(8), 2435–2457 (2020)
22. Kamble, S.S., Gunasekaran, A., Sharma, R.: Analysis of the driving and dependence power of barriers to adopt industry 4.0 in Indian manufacturing industry. Comput. Ind. **101**, 107–119 (2018)
23. Espinola, A.J.C., da Si. Diniz, R., de Oliveira, G.F.: Níveis De Ocupação No Brasil Com a Indústria 4.0: Desafio Ou Caos? Rev. FATEC SEBRAE EM DEBATE Gestão, Tecnol. e Negócios **07**(11), 41 (2020)
24. Pacchini, A.P.T., Lucato, W.C., Facchini, F., Mummolo, G.: The degree of readiness for the implementation of Industry 4.0. Comput. Ind. **113**, 103125 (2019)
25. Stebbins, R.A.: Exploratory Research in the Social Sciences: Qualitative Reserach Methods Series, vol. 48. Sage University Paper, Thousand Oaks (2001)
26. Pereira, G.B., Nogueira, G.C., Oliveira, G.F.: Maturity in Industry 4.0: study in eleven companies located in greater São (2021)
27. Buchi, G., Cugno, M., Castagnoli, R.: Smart factory performance and Industry 4.0. Technol. Forecast. Soc. Change **150**, 119790 (2020)

Industry 4.0: A Case Study on Strategy and Innovation in a Brazilian Auto Parts Company

Sergio Miele Ruggero[1]([✉]) [ID], Nilza Aparecida dos Santos[1,2] [ID],
and Marcia Terra da Silva[1] [ID]

[1] Programa de Engenharia da Produção – Universidade Paulista, São Paulo,
SP 04026-002, Brazil
miele326@gmail.com, marcia.terra@uol.com.br
[2] FATEC, Cotia, SP 06702-155, Brazil

Abstract. Innovation in small and medium-sized companies can be favored by the use of technologies covered by Industry 4.0 and differentiated strategies can be decisive for competitiveness. Although smaller companies are slower in terms of implementing technologies when compared to large organizations, they denote innovation capacity and strategies. The method used to carry out this paper was a single case study in a medium-sized auto parts company located in São Paulo/Brazil. The results showed that the company studied broke the pattern and found a strategic way out to face the challenges of using new technologies. The digitization project implemented by the company, supported by some of the pillars of Industry 4.0, provided positive results for its internal processes and paved the way for the creation of a digital competence school and a startup to offer digital solutions in a practical and competitive way. The strategy adopted by the company corroborates the perspective that to take advantage of Industry 4.0 opportunities, new business models need to be considered.

Keywords: Industry 4.0 · Competitiveness · Digital transformation · Business models

1 Introduction

The use of technologies covered by Industry 4.0 can favor innovation in small and medium-sized companies and offer benefits for improving the efficiency of their internal processes. Opportunities related to the use of these technologies can expand the range of benefits to be obtained from business model innovation [1].

The innovation strategies added to Industry 4.0 are presented differently in relation to the size of the companies. While for large companies these strategies are guided by business models centered on novelty, smaller companies rely on business models centered on the efficiency of their processes [2].

D. Y. Kim et al. (Eds.): APMS 2022, IFIP AICT 663, pp. 85–92, 2022.
https://doi.org/10.1007/978-3-031-16407-1_11

Small and medium-sized companies play an important role in the debate on digital transformation and new business development. Although they have a competitive disadvantage compared to large companies, given their limitations in technical and financial resources, they have innovation capabilities and strategies [3] and as a result can generate new flexible organizational processes and structures [4].

In this way, Industry 4.0 technologies can promote changes in production processes and allow the development of new business models and new forms of management and organizational strategies [5]. The necessary requirements and benefits that small and medium-sized companies can obtain with the implementation of Industry 4.0 are still little explored in the literature and generate research gaps [6].

This paper aims to fill part of these gaps through the following question: How are small and medium-sized auto parts companies in Brazil adapting their strategies for the transition to Industry 4.0? Aiming to identify and analyze the innovation strategy in a medium-sized auto parts company, in Brazil, for the implementation of technologies covered by Industry 4.0.

In the search for an answer to the proposed question, the case of an auto parts company was chosen as the object of analysis, whose innovation strategy differs from the standard established by others of the same size and segment, as will be discussed in the results section.

2 Literature Review

Industry 4.0 has an important and long-term strategic impact on global industrial development, as it signals a growing demand for research on the issues, challenges, and solutions related to the design, implementation, and management of smart manufacturing systems [7]. In this way, it represents a technology based opportunity to change the way companies generate value for their customers [8].

In this context, companies seek to understand how Industry 4.0 can impact professional skills and competencies and the company's organizational structure [9], also discussing the role of these new technologies in the creation or destruction of jobs [10]. However, despite the impact of the use of new technologies, especially digitalization and advanced automation, on the workforce, the human role within the smart manufacturing system is expected to remain dominant [11].

On the other hand, the difficulty of obtaining qualified labor for small and medium-sized companies can make it difficult for them to develop the expertise necessary for the successful implementation and use of digital manufacturing technologies [12]. In addition, in many cases, companies underestimate the cost and difficulties of introducing new technical solutions into an organized system, a problem that is more critical for small and medium-sized companies, despite having greater adaptability [13].

Therefore, companies must develop skills to provide employees with a sense of ownership, trust and a culture of interconnectivity and information transparency [14], in order to take advantage of technologies to adapt new processes to the detriment of the organization's redesign.

Another aspect to be highlighted deals with innovation management, which refers to the company's ability to adjust to market changes and promote the organization's adaptability through learning and the balance between knowledge and technological exploitation [15].

In turn, a business model can be considered an architecture of product and information flows, which includes the description of the various business actors and their functions, composed of a system of interdependent activities that goes beyond the limits of the focal company [16].

It is also considered that in relation to the use of new technologies, companies can present different levels of maturity and the integration of these various technologies can generate solutions according to the needs of each company [17].

Thus, despite the difficulties mentioned, companies must start a digital transformation journey, which considers changes throughout the company, including its organization, physical infrastructure, human resources, process and operations management and manufacturing technologies [18].

In this context, the transition to Industry 4.0 is presented as a possible path for companies in the search for competitiveness. Therefore, it will be necessary to define manufacturing models and plan transformation programs [19]. Therefore, this transition should not be seen as the solution to the challenges to be faced, but as a strategy to rethink the business model as a whole [9].

3   Method

The method used to carry out this paper was the single case study, which is characterized by a way of investigating an empirical topic in depth, through a set of pre-specified procedures, which reveals "how" and "why" questions and contributes to the construction of theory [20]. For the selection of the case under analysis, aspects related to the use of technologies covered by industry 4.0, innovation strategies and business model were considered.

The case chosen as the object of analysis is a medium-sized auto parts company, located in São Paulo/Brazil, which has been operating in the automotive market for over 50 years. The choice of the case is justified by the strategic differential that the company presents in relation to others in the same segment and size. Data were collected in the second half of 2021 through semi-structured open interviews with a focus on strategies aimed at Industry 4.0 and through direct observations.

The interview was conducted with the CEO of the company, as he is the person involved with all processes relevant to digital transformation. In addition to the questions proposed in the interview, some information was spontaneously provided by the respondent and is portrayed in the results and discussions.

Direct observations were carried out during a technical visit to the factory premises and it was monitored by the managers of each area. During the visit, it was possible to know the details of the production processes and technologies used, which allowed a better foundation and favored the conduction of the interview with the chief executive officer.

All stages of the research ensured confidentiality to the participating company regarding the identification of the company and the research respondent. Thus, throughout this paper, the company will be named as "Innovative company".

4 Results and Discussions

The results found in the search are shown in tables and figures. Table 1 shows the questions and a summary of the answers obtained on strategies and competences of the company studied.

Table 1. Strategy and competence for industry 4.0

	Questions	Answers
1	How do you rate your ability and skills to adapt to technological changes?	Open and receptive to technological changes, without preexisting paradigms
2	How do you consider the alignment of your company's strategies and organizational culture to Industry 4.0?	The company's culture was already open to changes, which facilitated alignment with innovation strategies
3	How can the transition affect your company's competitiveness?	Opening the way for new business, making the company more competitive
4	What strategies does your company use to make the transition to Industry 4.0?	Systemic vision, training of personnel and exchange of knowledge and experiences
5	Are the strategies adopted by the company bringing results? Which are?	It motivated teams, productivity gains, creation of an independent business unit (startup) and a digital competence school
6	How does the market influence the decision to invest in new technologies?	For the competitiveness and survival of the company in a sustainable way
7	Has the digital transformation caused changes in the organizational structure and strategic planning of the company?	An artificial intelligence department was created and strategic planning began to prioritize new business models

Source: Prepared by the authors

In the analysis of the questions (Table 1), it was observed that the company has a broad and differentiated vision to carry out the transition since its proposals and directions include innovative strategies that go beyond the internal environment and the standard business model. This differentiated aspect contrasts with the idea that smaller companies are guided by business models centered on the efficiency of their processes, while large companies prioritize business models centered on novelty [2].

The company's main manager considers himself an open-minded professional, just as the company's culture is open to change. Regarding the use of new technologies, the respondent used the expression "it is necessary to think big", in order to outline strategies with a broad and systemic view, corroborating the perspective that new business models require companies to obtain new ways of thinking. Inside and outside the corporate environment [21].

In the search for competitiveness, companies need to plan transformation programs [19], which is in line with the interviewee's perspective, for whom the use of technologies can open paths for new business and make the company more competitive.

Regarding the choice of strategies to carry out the transition, although the researched company could acquire new machines (option A), it opted for a digitalization process focused on maximizing human capacity, using existing machines and equipment (option B). The interviewee justifies that the choice for the digitization project was due to the high investment required for the acquisition of new machines.

However, it emphasizes that the decision to invest can be affected by the competitiveness of the market and the need for the company to survive in a sustainable way, corroborating the idea that the adaptation of companies to market changes can occur through learning and the balance between knowledge versus technological exploitation [15].

For a better understanding of some answers about the strategies adopted, Fig. 1 illustrates the "anxieties" raised by the manager, the strategic solutions found, the means used and the results obtained.

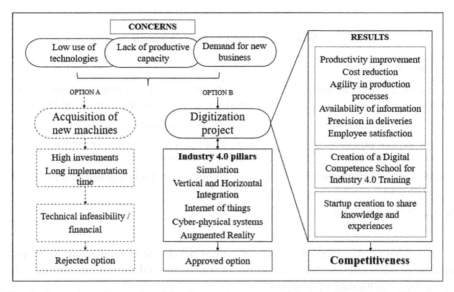

Fig. 1. Concerns and strategies of the "Innovative company" (Source: Prepared by the authors)

According to spontaneous statements by the interviewee, the awakening of the anxieties raised (Fig. 1) occurred due to the company's inability to participate in the competition of a new business, given the lack of productive capacity. Added to this issue was the low use of technologies and the search for new market demands, which could significantly transform your company.

The digitization project started in 2018 was supported by some of the pillars of Industry 4.0, which provided opportunities for results such as improved productivity, cost reduction, agility in production processes, availability of information, precision in deliveries and employee satisfaction.

Regarding the adaptation of employees to the use of these new technologies, in the opinion of the interviewee, at first there was resistance to changes, which was undone by the perception that technology can be an ally and not a threat to the worker. An issue also addressed in the literature which discusses the role of technology in the creation or destruction of jobs [10].

In addition to the internal results obtained, the digitalization project, thinking about the sustainability of the ecosystem, paved the way for the creation of a school of digital competence to prepare for Industry 4.0, with a view to training young people from the local community and employees' children.

An important aspect to highlight is the difficulty of obtaining labor for small and medium-sized companies can make it difficult to implement and use digital manufacturing technologies [12], in this way the creation of the school of digital competence can be seen as a tool for the sustainability of the company's ecosystem.

Before finishing the explanations in Fig. 1, regarding the creation of the startup, it is worth detailing the actions and results obtained with the implementation of the digitization project, as shown in Table 2.

Table 2. Digitization project strategy

Actions	Results
Formation of a corporate intelligence group	Stimulation of creativity; Broader participation of employees; Maximization of human capacity
Installation of sensors in a business unit	Autonomous data capture of variables
Creation of best pattern recognition algorithms in real time	Optimization of processes and consumption of materials, and guidance of operators
Creation of a command system and activity record	Establishes human-machine communication in real time

Source: Prepared by the authors

As stated by the interviewee, all the actions developed to implement the project brought good results as evidenced (Fig. 1) which justified the investment made in technology and training of employees.

Still, in relation to the return on investment, the company creatively adopted an innovative strategy with the creation of a digital competence school and a startup to offer digital solutions to other companies in a practical and competitive way.

It should be noted that this new business unit is independent and is not subordinated to the formal structure of company. In this way, the team formed for the development and implementation of the digitization project began to divide its activities between the referenced company and the startup.

The strategies adopted by "Innovative company" validate the perspective that to take advantage of the potential provided by Industry 4.0, new business models need to be considered to improve the efficiency of the process as a whole [22].

5 Conclusions

The objective of this study was to identify and analyze the innovation strategy in an auto parts company, in Brazil, for the implementation of technologies covered by Industry 4.0. The analysis of the case studied made it possible to understand how a medium-sized auto parts company adapted its strategies to transition to Industry 4.0.

The results indicated that differentiated strategies, with the involvement of top management, and the participation of employees with creativity and innovation, can facilitate the path to the use of new technologies, even in smaller companies.

The digitization project implemented met its main objective of maximizing human capacity and opened the door to other innovative strategies and creative responses, both with the foundation of the school of digital competence and the creation of a startup.

The startup was configured as a bold business model to offer services with digital solutions in a practical and competitive way. In this way, it provided innovation by incorporating, independently, the provision of technological services, with the use of skilled labor and the know-how acquired in the development of the digitization project.

The school of digital competence collaborated with the company's strategy to increase the density of knowledge and promote the qualification of the workforce in a continuous way since the school's initial proposal was to qualify the local community and employees' children in relation to the technologies covered by the Industry 4.0.

The main contribution of this paper was to identify how the strategy for using technologies can make room for creating new businesses and managing companies in the automotive sector. Based on the findings, this paper advanced some steps to fill research gaps on necessary requirements and the benefits generated by the implementation of Industry 4.0 in small and medium-sized companies.

As with all research, especially as it is a single case study, the results obtained cannot be generalized to all companies. As a proposal for future studies, it is recommended to analyze the organizational impact of the implementation of new technologies in smaller companies.

Acknowledgment. This study was financed in part by the Coordenação de Aperfeiçoamento de Pessoal de Nível Superior - Brasil (CAPES) - Finance Code.

References

1. Frank, A.G., Mendes, G.H., Ayala, N.F., Ghezzi, A.: Servitization and industry 4.0 convergence in the digital transformation of product firms: a business model innovation perspective. Technol. Forecast. Soc. Change **210**, 15–26 (2019)
2. Julian, M.M., Oana, B., Kai-Ingo, V.: The role of absorptive capacity and innovation strategy in the design of industry 4.0 business models - a comparison between SMEs and large enterprises. Eur. Manag. J. **39**(3):333–343 (2011). ISSN 0263–2373
3. Del, G., Scuotto, M., Papa, V., Tarba, A., Bresciani, S.Y., Warkentin, M.: A self- tuning model for smart manufacturing SMEs: effects on digital innovation. J. Prod. Innov Manag. **38**, 68–89 (2021)
4. Felin, T., Powell, T.C.: Designing organizations for dynamic capabilities. Calif. Manag. Rev. **58**(4), 78–96 (2016)

5. Zheng, T., Ardolino, M., Bacchetti, A., Perona, M., Zanardini, M.: The impacts of Industry 4.0: a descriptive survey in the Italian manufacturing sector. J. Manuf. Technol. Manag. **13**(2), 137–150 (2019). 1741–038X

6. Moeuf, A., Pellerin, R., Lamouri, S., Tamayo-Giraldo, S., Barbaray, R.: The industrial management of SMEs in the era of Industry 4.0. Int. J. Prod. Res. **56**(3), 1–19 (2017)

7. Xu, L.D., Xu, E.L., Li, L.: Industry 4.0: state of the art and future trends. Int. J. Prod. Res. **56**(8), 2841–2962 (2018)

8. Oesterreich, T.D., Teuteberg, F.: Understanding the implications of digitisation and automation in the context of Industry 4.0: a triangulation approach and elements of a research agenda for the construction industry. Comput. Ind. **83**, 121–139 (2016)

9. Erol, S., Schumacher, A., Sihn, W.: Strategic guidance towards Industry 4.0–a three-stage process model. In: International Conference on Competitive Manufacturing, vol. 9, no. 1, pp. 495–501 (2016)

10. Weber, E.: Industry 4.0 job-producer or employment-destroyer? AB Forschungsbericht, vol. 2 (2016)

11. Jäger, A., Ranz, F.: Industry 4.0: challenges for the human factor in future production scenarios. In: 4th Conference on Learning Factories (2014)

12. Krishnan, T., Scullion, H.: Talent management and dynamic view of talent in small and medium enterprises. Hum. Resour. Manag. Rev. **27**(3), 431–441 (2017)

13. Cimini, C., Boffelli, A., Lagorio, A., Kalchschmidt, M., Pinto, R.: How do industry 4.0 technologies influence organisational change? an empirical analysis of Italian SMEs. J. Manuf. Technol. Manag. **32**(3), 695–721 (2021)

14. Stentoft, J., Adsbøll Wickstrøm, K., Philipsen, K., Haug, A.: Drivers and barriers for Industry 4.0 readiness and practice: empirical evidence from small and medium-sized manufacturers. Prod. Plan. Control **32**(10), 811–828 (2021)

15. Reeves, M., Zeng, M., Venjara, A.: The self-tuning enterprise. Harv. Bus. Rev. **93**(6), 77–83 (2015)

16. Wieland, H., Hartmann, N.N., Vargo, S.L.: Business models as service strategy. J. Acad. Mark. Sci. **45**(6), 925–943 (2017). https://doi.org/10.1007/s11747-017-0531-z

17. Vermulm, R.: Políticas para o desenvolvimento da indústria 4.0 no Brasil. São Paulo: [s.n.] (2018). http://web.bndes.gov.br/bib/jspui/handle/1408/15486

18. Gilchrist, A.: Industry 4.0: The Industrial Internet of Things. Apress, Berkeley (2016)

19. Almada-Lobo, F.: The Industry 4.0 revolution and the future of manufacturing execution systems (MES). J. Innov. Manag. **3**(4), 16–21 (2016)

20. Yin, R.K.: Estudo de caso: planejamento e métodos, 5th edn. Bookman, Porto Alegre (2015)

21. Ehret, M., Wirtz, J.: Unlocking value from machines: business models and the industrial internet of things. J. Mark. Manag. **30**(1/2), 111–130 (2017)

22. Müller, J.M., Buliga, O., Voigt, K.I.: Fortune favors the prepared: how SMEs approach business model innovations in Industry 4.0. Technol. Forecast. Soc. Change **132**, 2e17 (2018)

Industry 4.0 and Supply Chain Integration: A Case Study in an Auto Parts Company in Brazil

Nilza Aparecida dos Santos[1,2]([mail]) (iD), Sergio Miele Ruggero[1] (iD),
and Marcia Terra da Silva[1] (iD)

[1] Programa de Engenharia da Produção – Universidade Paulista, São Paulo SP 04026-002,
Brazil
nilzaasantos7@gmail.com
[2] FATEC, Cotia SP 06702-155, Brazil

Abstract. The use of technologies embraced by Industry 4.0 drives integration and collaboration between companies in order to expand borders for other organizations, thus allowing the intelligent use of data and favoring integration throughout the supply chain. To carry out this article, the method used was a single case study in a medium-sized auto parts company, located in Greater São Paulo/Brazil. The results showed that data connectivity is important to enable the use of technologies in the automotive chain and strengthen the relationship between suppliers and customers and that greater efficiency can be obtained by the dissemination of technologies throughout the chain. It is noteworthy that the expectations of results to be obtained by the integrated use of technologies in the client-supplier relationship, can favor innovation and improve the efficiency of internal and external processes.

Keywords: Industry 4.0 · Integration · Collaboration · Automotive chain

1 Introduction

The concept of Industry 4.0 appears at the beginning of the 21st century, based on a productive structure with information, communication, automation, production, and business processes [1], which can transform traditional supply chains into chains of digital supplies [2].

Digital transformation can connect companies and customers, and provide transparency, reliability, and effectiveness through the intelligent use of data throughout the chain [3]. In this way, the technologies encompassed by Industry 4.0 can favor integration in order to make organizations smarter [4].

Considered one of the main mechanisms for industrial organization, integration [5] driven by advanced and connected technologies, can expand the boundaries of companies to other organizations and stakeholders [6].

D. Y. Kim et al. (Eds.): APMS 2022, IFIP AICT 663, pp. 93–100, 2022.
https://doi.org/10.1007/978-3-031-16407-1_12

In the context of Industry 4.0, integration, from an internal perspective, can enable information to be shared across different sectors and hierarchical levels within the company, while horizontal integration is established through collaboration between two or more companies in pursuit of common goals.

However, even if the relationship between customer and supplier can be favored by the use of new technologies so that everyone can benefit from a possible integration, it is necessary that smaller companies also have access to technological innovations.

Thus, even though larger companies have access to technologies, exclusive use within the company hampers the competitive advantage that could be unlocked and accelerated by sharing data along the supply chain [7].

In Brazil, it is considered that there are many challenges for companies to be able to use technologies related to Industry 4.0, such as investments in equipment with digital technologies, an adaptation of layouts, processes, relationships between companies, and management of the production chain [8].

Although the challenges are present in the different sectors of the Brazilian economy, the automotive chain, composed of automakers and auto parts, stands out for its participation in the GDP (Gross Domestic Product), for the generation of jobs, investments in innovation, and for significant linkages in its production processes [9], and therefore it is the sector chosen for study in this article.

The use of new technologies, of course, promotes relevant changes in how supply chains are managed and opens research gaps on this issue [10], since few studies explore the subject.

Seeking to fill part of these gaps, the study of this article consists of understanding how the use of Industry 4.0 technologies can facilitate the integration of the supply chain in auto parts companies in Brazil, aiming to analyze the conditions and challenges for the integration of the supply chain considering Industry 4.0 technologies, from the perspective of an auto parts company.

2 Literature Review

The use of Industry 4.0 technologies can provide the supply chain with the opportunity to trace materials and products, collect and analyze processes, collect data in real-time and improve production, storage and transport communication [11].

A supply chain is considered to be the aggregation of interdependent organizations that coordinate activities and share common adaptive challenges [12]. In this way, the integration of internal operations and the ability to coordinate between customers and suppliers can enable the efficiency of production processes [13].

The attributes of a digitized supply chain are real-time communication and collaboration between customers, suppliers, and partners based on shared and standardized data across platforms in a network of companies [14]. The concept of integration is considered one of the pillars of Industry 4.0 [15] added new technologies can make companies more intelligent and integrated [16].

In this way, communication within the same company at different hierarchical levels can occur through vertical integration, which can provide more flexible production systems, while horizontal integration facilitates cooperation between different companies [17].

The collaboration between companies is an element of integration capable of providing joint work between organizations to create a competitive advantage [18]. Thus, for collaboration to occur throughout the chain, vertical integration is first necessary, followed by horizontal integration [19].

The use of new technologies can give companies a competitive advantage [20], including in the automotive industry. However, some companies will only walk the path of transition when this reality is also relevant to smaller companies [21].

It is also noteworthy that a closer relationship between customer-supplier can bring a positive result for the success of manufacturing companies since suppliers can provide new knowledge, skills, and working methods [22]. In addition, new business models require industries to think about the internal and external environment [23].

In this way, the shared understanding of concepts related to Industry 4.0 among different companies can boost innovation strategies [24], since knowledge about technology beyond their companies can improve process efficiency [25].

3   Method

To carry out this article, the methodology used was exploratory, through a single, longitudinal case study. Because it is characterized by the "how" and "why" questions about a set of contemporary events, it allows for in-depth investigation and preservation of the holistic and meaningful properties of real-life events [26].

The case chosen was a medium-sized auto parts company, supplier to the main vehicle manufacturers operating in Brazil. In order to maintain confidentiality regarding the identity of the company and to maintain the research protocol, throughout this article it will be referred to as "Company X".

Data collection was carried out through an open semi-structured interview with the supply chain director of "Company X". The interview was divided into two blocks: 1) Use of Industry 4.0 technologies in the automotive chain; 2) Integration and collaboration in the automotive chain.

Data were also collected during a technical visit with on-site observations and physical artifacts about a project developed by "Company X", which was pointed out by the respondent during the interview.

The main aspect addressed in this article refers to two links in the studied chain: the customer and the supplier. It is worth explaining that auto parts within the automotive chain are suppliers of automakers, but they also assume the role of the customer with regard to their raw material suppliers.

4   Results and Discussions

The results obtained are presented in the following tables and figures. Tables 1 and 2 present the syntheses of the interview, in which the respondent puts his perceptions as a supplier of the automakers and as a customer of sub-suppliers.

Table 1. Use of Industry 4.0 technologies in the automotive chain

Questions		Finds
1	Why is it important for your customer to have access to Industry 4.0 technologies?	To enable data connectivity and streamline information
2	How important is your supplier to these technologies?	Strengthen customer-supplier relationships and establish partnerships
3	Is it possible to automate the data collection at different stages of the chain?	Possible with the use of specific technologies and real-time control
4	Is it possible to exchange information in real-time, speed up sharing, and track the product along the chain? And what would be the expected results?	It will only be possible if the different links have access to technology and connectivity. Agility, data accuracy, delivery reliability, and traceability
5	Regarding the supply chain, do you consider it to be customer-centric?	Yes, because the customer will guide the demand and service deadlines

Source: Prepared by the authors

In the analysis of this group of questions, it was found that the customer is the central object of the supply chain, and data connectivity is important to enable the use of technologies in the automotive chain and to strengthen the relationship between suppliers and customers.

He also highlighted that the interest in the use of new technologies is linked to the possibilities of results of the investment made, which corroborates with research [8] that indicate that the level of investment in Brazil continues to be oriented toward obtaining productivity gains and cost reduction.

Another important aspect pointed out in the interview refers to the access and dissemination of technology along the chain, in line with the very conception of the supply chain, which is configured as the aggregation of interdependent organizations that coordinate activities and share common challenges of adaptation [12].

The other group of issues analyzed concerns the integration and collaboration in the automotive chain, as shown in Table 2.

Table 2. Integration and collaboration in the automotive chain

Questions		Finds
1	How your company institutionalizes collaboration on Industry 4.0 topics with external partners, suppliers, and customers	Some clients consider carrying out joint projects, as long as there is a possibility of earnings
2	How do you assess the degree of integration of your horizontal value chain, in which aspects is this integration important?	The horizontal integration allows the proximity between the customer's needs and what is being produced by the supplier

(continued)

Table 2. (*continued*)

Questions		Finds
3	How do you assess the degree of integration of your vertical value chain?	Partial in production processes
4	Is it important for customers, suppliers, and partners to communicate and collaborate in real-time based on shared and standardized data across platforms in a network?	Yes, the company is also developing a project with the supplier to share data with a view to reducing the storage area and the material stock started in 2021
5	Can the use of new technologies along the chain generate new forms of integration and collaboration among chain members?	Technology makes integration and collaboration more agile, efficient, and reliable

Source: Prepared by the authors

The answers to this group of questions denote the importance of the client-supplier relationship, but the development of common projects is suggested through the possibility of gains for both parties.

The interviewee states that technology can make integration and collaboration more agile, efficient, and reliable, but on the other hand it is important to note the challenges regarding the choice of appropriate technology for each company [27].

The closer relationship between customer-supplier makes it possible to obtain positive results for companies since suppliers can provide new knowledge, skills, and working methods [22], corroborating the interviewee's position in which horizontal integration it promotes the approximation between the customer's needs and what is being produced by the supplier, in addition to facilitating the logistics service.

Another important finding of this analysis was to identify that "Company X" has been developing a project with one of its suppliers to share data to reduce the storage area and material stock, as illustrated in Fig. 1.

Based on the data collected, it was possible to identify the steps taken by the company studied to implement a project to optimize inventories. The motivations that generated the need to develop this project refer to problems related to the level of stock, physical space, movement of materials, and various risks.

The project originates from real problems that involved actors from different companies. In this case, "Company X" becomes the client and the other company participating in the project becomes the sub-supplier. The common problems faced by the two companies, as depicted in Fig. 1, led to the need to use new technologies and opened up opportunities for collaboration between them.

The choice of sub-supplier to carry out this partnership was guided by the identification of common problems, the number of items supplied to "Company X", the high added value of the products, and the location of the sub-supplier.

The project aimed to optimize and make stock levels more flexible and was structured using Industry 4.0 technologies. Based on the analysis of the problems faced by the two companies, a strategy was drawn up to create an integrated system for programming and controlling materials, which would meet mutual needs.

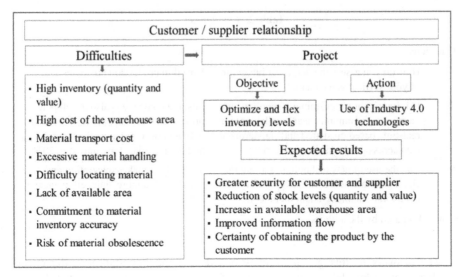

Fig. 1. Project topics "Company X" and sub-supplier (Source: Prepared by the authors)

To operationalize the project, the two companies started to make use of an inter-mediary database, together with dedicated software to organize, control, and monitor in real-time the processes related to material management. The system used through digitalization allows greater integration of processes throughout the supply chain.

This integrated system allowed the customer to have direct access to the supplier's inventory data in relation to scheduled material, while the supplier has access to the customer's scheduling needs in real-time.

The preliminary results signaled the direction of meeting the expectations of the companies, which can be confirmed by the continuous monitoring and control since the project started in 2021. The preliminary signaling of the results can be reinforced by the fact that the use of new technologies can give companies a competitive advantage [20].

The analysis of the case in question, combined with the interviewee's statements, evidence the importance of Industry 4.0 technologies to promote integration between customer and supplier, corroborating the view that sharing the use of these technolo-gies between different companies can boost innovation strategies [24], and improve the efficiency of internal and external processes [25].

5   Conclusion

In the search to answer how the use of Industry 4.0 technologies can facilitate the integration of the supply chain in auto parts companies in Brazil, this article aimed to analyze the conditions and challenges for the integration of the supply chain considering the technologies of Industry 4.0.

From the perspective of the auto parts company, the importance of connectivity was verified to enable the use of technologies in the chain and to strengthen the relationship between suppliers and customers. In the case studied, integration appears as a collaborative process that began with the identification of difficulties common to participating companies about inventory management, which culminated in the development of a project for optimization.

What triggered the process to develop the project was the problems common to the companies, whose solution was based on collaboration between customer and supplier for the use of new technologies that provided better management and optimization of inventories in the participating companies.

It was found that this type of initiative opens the way for the process of horizontal integration to occur more broadly, in the sense of propagating itself in the supply chain. However, for this to happen, access to technology must be disseminated along this chain.

The main contribution of this article was to verify how the use of technologies can facilitate the integration of the supply chain in auto parts companies in Brazil, as well as the integration and collaboration in the chain can enable the participating companies to face the challenges for the use of technologies related to the Industry 4.0.

The present research does not conclude conclusions on the proposed question, especially as it is a single case study. Thus, the results obtained cannot be generalized to all companies. As a proposal for future studies, it is recommended to verify the conditions and challenges for the supply chain integration of other links in the automotive chain.

Acknowledgment. This study was financed in part by the Coordenação de Aperfeiçoamento de Pessoal de Nível Superior - Brasil (CAPES) - Finance Code".

References

1. Bahrin, M.A.K., Othman, M.F., Nor, N.H., Azli, M.F.T.: Industry 4.0: a review on industrial automation and robotic. Jurnal Teknologi (Sci. Eng.) **78**(6–13) (2016)
2. Queiroz, M.M., Pereira, S.C.F., Telles, R., Machado, M.C.: Industry 4.0 and digital supply chain capabilities: a framework for understanding digitalisation challenges and opportunities. Benchmarking Int. J. **28**(5), 1761–1782 (2021)
3. Zekhnini, K., Cherrafi, A., Bouhaddou, I., Benghabrit, Y., Garza-Reyes, E.: Supply chain management 4.0: a literature review and research framework. Benchmarking Int. J. **28**(2), 465–501 (2021)
4. Khan, M., Xiaotong, W., Xiaolong, X., Dou, W.: Big data challenges and opportunities in the hype of Industry 4.0. In: 2017 IEEE International Conference on Communications (ICC), pp. 1–6 (2017)
5. Schuh, G., Potente, T., Wesch-Potente C., Weber, A.R., Prote, J.P.: Collaboration mechanisms to increase productivity in the context of Industrie 4.0. In: Robust Manufacturing Conference, Procedia CIRP, vol. 19, pp. 51–56 (2014)
6. Ibarra, D., Ganzarain, J., Igartua, J.I.: Business model innovation through Industry 4.0: a review. Procedia Manufact. **22**, 4–10 (2018)
7. World Economic Forum Homepage. Fourth Industrial Revolution: Beacons of Technology and Innovation in Manufacturing. http://www3.weforum.org. Accessed 21 Aug 2021
8. CNI - Confederação Nacional Da Indústria - Industry 2027 Risks and Opportunities for Brazil in the face of disruptive innovations. Brasília (2018)

9. Daudt, G.M.; Willcox, L.D.: Indústria automotiva. Automotive industry. In: Puga, F.P., Castro, L.B (Org.). Visão 2035: Brasil, país desenvolvido: agendas setoriais para alcance da meta. 1st edn. Rio de Janeiro: Banco Nacional de Desenvolvimento Econômico e Social, pp. 183–208 (2018)
10. Hofmann, E., Rüsch, M.: Industry 4.0 and the current status as well as future prospects on logistics. Comput. Ind. **89**, 23–34 (2017)
11. Xu, L., Viriyasitavat, W.: Application of blockchain in collaborative Internet-of-Things services. IEEE Trans. Comput. Soc. Syst. **6**(6), 1295–1305 (2019)
12. Pidun, U., Reeves, M., Schüssler, M.: Do you need a business ecosystem? (2019). www.bcg.com/en-us/publications/2019/do-you-need-business-ecosystem.aspx. Accessed 10 Oct 2021
13. Tomas, R.N., Alcantara, R.L.C.: Modelos para gestão de riscos em cadeias de suprimentos: revisão, análise e diretrizes para futuras pesquisas. Gest. Prod., São Carlos, **20** (3) (2013)
14. Wu, L., Yue, X., Jin, A., Yen, D.C.: Smart supply chain management: a review and implications for future research. Int. J. Logistics Manage. **27**(2), 395–417 (2016)
15. Lu, Y.: Industry 4.0: a survey on technologies, applications and open research issues. J. Ind. Inf. Integr. **6**, 1–10 (2017)
16. Suri, K., Cuccuru, A., Cadavid, J., Gérard, S., Gaaloul, W., Tata, S.: Model-based development of modular complex systems for accomplishing system integration for Industry 4.0. In: 5th International Conference on Model-Driven Engineering and Software Development, pp. 487–495 (2017)
17. Wang, S., Wan, J., Li, D., Zang, C.: Implementing smart factory of Industrie 4.0: an outlook. Int. J. Distrib. Sens. Networks **12**(1), 3159805 (2016)
18. Wiengarten, F., Humphreys, P., Cao, G., Fynes, B., Mckittrick, A.: Collaborative supply chain practices and performance: exploring the key role of information quality. Supply Chain Manage. Int. J. **15**(6), 463–473 (2010)
19. Sanchez, M., Exposito, E., Aguilar, J.: Industry 4.0: survey from a system integration perspective. Int. J. Comput. Integrated Manufact. **33**(10–11), 1017–1041 (2020)
20. Trstenjak, M., Cosi, P.: Process planning in Industry 4.0 environment. Procedia Manufacturing. In: 27th International Conference on Flexible Automation and Intelligent Manufacturing, FAIM2017, vol. 1, 27–30 June, Modena, Italy. Elsevier (2017)
21. Oesterreich, T.D., Teuteberg, F.: Understanding the implications of digitisation and automation in the context of Industry 4.0: a triangulation approach and elements of a research agenda for the construction industry. Comput. Ind. **83**, 121–139 (2016)
22. Porter, M.E., Heppelmann, J.E.: How smart, connected products are transforming companies. Harv. Bus. Rev. **93**(10), 96e114 (2015)
23. Frank, A.G., Mendes, G.H., Ayala, N.F., Ghezzi, A.: Servitization and Industry 4.0 convergence in the digital transformation of product firms: a business model innovation perspective. Technological Forecasting and Social Change (2019, in press)
24. Müller, J.M., Buliga, O., Voigt, K.-I.: The role of absorptive capacity and innovation strategy in the design of industry 4.0 business models - A comparison between SMEs and large enterprises. Eur. Manage. J. **39**(3), 333–343. ISSN 0263–2373 (2021)
25. Kiel, D., Müller, J.M., Arnold, C., Voigt, K.I.: Sustainable industrial value creation: benefits and challenges of Industry 4.0. Int. J. Innov. Manage. **21**(8), 1740015 (2017)
26. Yin, R.K.: Estudo de caso: planejamento e métodos. 5th edn. Porto Alegre, Bookman (2015)
27. Sousa Jabbour, A.B.L., Jabbour, C.J.C., Foropon, C., Filho, M.G.: When titans meet – can Industry 4.0 revolutionise the environmentally-sustainable manufacturing wave? The role of critical success factors. Technol. Forecast. Soc. Change **132**(7), 18–25 (2018)

User-Centric Digital Assistance with Smart Tools for Manual Assembly Processes

Simon Piontek$^{(\boxtimes)}$ and Hermann Lödding$^{(\boxtimes)}$

Hamburg University of Technology, Hamburg, Germany
{simon.piontek,loedding}@tuhh.de

Abstract. To efficiently leverage digitalization potentials for large proportions of manual processes, workers must be integrated in the digital world in a seamless manner. This paper contributes to the ongoing research on Digital Assistance Systems. In particular, manual assembly processes in aircraft production are scrutinized to identify specific requirements for such a system. Following the resulting analysis, we propose a concept for user-centric digital assistance that uses smart, localized hand tools and provides workers with information based on a digital twin of the product and the production process. The proposed digital assistance system accurately tracks the tool position and enables event-based and bidirectional data flow between workers and a digital twin. The tools are automatically configured with the correct process parameters based on their current position. Quality and progress are documented and ultimately operations and everyday efforts are simplified. The concept is examined for its potentials on productivity and quality in manual assembly processes. The results show that further development of the concept promises significant improvements in manual work.

Keywords: Digital assistance · Smart tools · Digital twin · User-Centric design

1 Introduction

1.1 Motivation

Looking at the aircraft industry, increasing overall demand as well as rising product variants and complexities [1, 2] amplify the necessity of assisting workers. Product complexity leads to error-prone manual labor and paper-based information accumulations on the shop floor. This has immediate effects on labor productivity and quality. Such deficits in terms of value-added work can be targeted to optimize manual operations. Worker states can be structured in a generic work cycle of work preparation, work execution and follow-up processes [3]. Necessary technology for assisting these parts is already on the market. Nevertheless, technologically enhanced hand tools are not used and most digital assistance systems focus on the work preparation elements of information and material procurement, and component as well as site preparation in one-off production (e.g., [4, 5]). Deficits prevail especially in the documentation of work (follow-up) and in error prevention and optimization of work execution.

© IFIP International Federation for Information Processing 2022
Published by Springer Nature Switzerland AG 2022
D. Y. Kim et al. (Eds.): APMS 2022, IFIP AICT 663, pp. 101–109, 2022.
https://doi.org/10.1007/978-3-031-16407-1_13

However, the amount of time spent on work preparation in series production is significantly lower than in one-off production. Worker acceptance of assistance systems may suffer if increased handling of the digital document is necessary. This underlines the necessity of improving further elements of work cycles in series production. Hence, this paper proposes a user-centric, scalable, and dynamic solution that integrates digital information assistance with smart hand tools which are both connected to a digital twin to optimize the entire workflow of manual assembly in aircraft manufacturing.

1.2 Current State of Research

Digital assistance systems are developing rapidly in the industrial context, leading to an abundance of approaches to support assembly operations [2]. User-centered system development places the worker at the center to raise efficiency and usability and will regularly re-evaluate expectations and worker feedback. The goal is to assure that the system will fulfill its intended purpose and thereby leads to higher effectiveness [6] and is crucial in the development of digital assistance systems [7].

Figure 1 shows the user model in the context of assembly processes and hence the elements which can be digitally enhanced and optimized. It consists of the worker at the center, the information that is provided, the tools and means of production necessary for the work tasks, the product (or parts to assemble), and the environment in which the human works. Digital assistance systems should address and improve these elements to achieve a comprehensive digital integration over most of the generic work cycle.

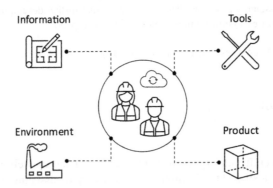

Fig. 1. User model in the context of assembly processes

By digitally enhancing these elements the performance requirements of work tasks and workers capabilities are aligned to reduce training times, search times and operating errors [9]. Looking at the current state in research, most approaches focus on the optimization of information provision. Functionalities and features aim to provide process information and instructions in relation to real world objects. Information is filtered and visualized in accordance with work progress and in reference to specific components and means of production to improve work preparation and to ensure correctness [8, 9]. While this influences work preparation, it does not influence work execution itself in the sense that the assistance system can intervene and support in the work process. An exception is the use of smart tools for optimizing manual drilling processes in aircraft manufacturing developed by Hintze et al. [1]. Semi-automatic drilling units were developed, which can be monitored regarding position- and process-data and can be configured depending on their position in the process. Process and quality control of work tasks are feasible. However, this solution relies on a static database and server and therefore lacks integration with informational assistance.

To comprehensively support the worker over the entire work cycle, a concept that revolves around a digital twin and comprises smart tools, digital information assistance and other processing services in a unified namespace is needed. The idea is to use the digital twin to control hand-held tools such as drilling machines by leveraging bidirectional data transmission between physical and digital entities. Assembly guidance can be dynamically updated in real-time and process performance can be predicted and controlled [10]. Including workers and variable manual processes requires adaptive assistance systems that include context sensitive information from the environment, e.g., sensors and localization systems [7, 8]. A digital twin of a manual process which can integrate sensors dynamically through modular interfaces and that includes scalable services to react to new data streams is needed.

2 Manual Assembly Processes

The aircraft industry manufactures highly complex products. Due to bad accessibility and changing product variants, many of the work processes are still manual. This suits the frame of the proposed digital assistance concept and offers possibilities of transferring knowledge from one-off production to series production. To find relevant tasks and current deficits in the industry, a thorough analysis of fuselage assembly processes was conducted. Workers in a fuselage completion workstation were investigated and consulted regarding their everyday workflows and required assistance.

2.1 Aircraft Structure Assembly Processes

In the context of assembling aircraft structures and subsystems, operations can often be grouped into: Preparation of work, drilling of boreholes, and joining the components through riveting connections. Preparing the assembly consists of finding correct tools, production means and information of positioning parts to be assembled in the fuselage structure. Components must be fixated with production means and clamps as well as shims to compensate voids. Workers rely on complex working documents to find information in textual elements, which often describe work steps and assembly positions using the frames and stringers of the fuselage.

Drilling and riveting are characterized as work execution and have similar properties. Information about different areas and process parameters (e.g., drilling and tightening torque, feed rates, collar types, connecting joints) must be repeatedly procured and memorized, examining technical drawings and various execution instructions. Accordingly, machines have to be configured regarding their offsets, status of tool wear, clearance and process parameters. Quality and progress are often assessed and documented manually at the end of a shift.

2.2 Core Tasks and Deficits

Core tasks can be identified along the process. Figure 2 shows the relation of relevant tasks to the generic work cycle and correlating elements of the user model to assist the worker.

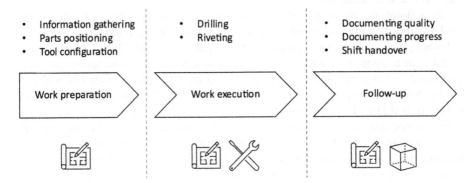

Fig. 2. Core tasks and influencing elements of user model

The way these tasks are usually carried out is inadequate in several aspects: Information must be gathered by skimming through several different documents and locations. The complexity of information leads to a trade-off between spending time on searching and memorizing information or working based on experience and being more prone to errors. Configuration of tools and equipment is thus prone to setting wrong process parameters or not adjusting them in time. Resulting drilling and riveting errors can lead to severe quality issues and high costs. Subsequent documentation of quality and progress usually is recorded on paper after visual assessment. This is especially problematic if offset heads are used to work on points with difficult accessibility and can lead to a lack of transparency in actual torque used for the processes. Additionally, current work

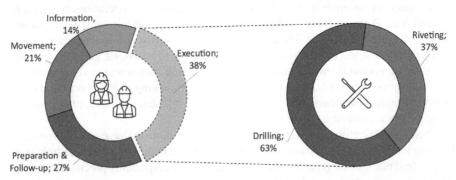

Fig. 3. State proportions in fuselage assembly processes (*information proportion was increased by 10% after consulting with experts; Preparation & Follow-up was decreased accordingly*)

progress must be explained at shift change, at which point it is documented for controlling purposes. Figure 3 shows portions of methods-time measurement elements for the process, underlining the necessity of assisting all elements of the work cycle.

3   Digital Assistance Concept

The proposed digital assistance concept contains three main elements:

- **Digital twin.** A digital twin is the core component and is accessible as a platform, being the key to both scalability and functionality.
- **Smart tools.** Smart tools with highly accurate position sensors receive the correct process parameters and send the actual values to the digital twin.
- **Digital information assistance.** Information- and tool-based processes are assisted by creating means to efficiently provide information as well as interact with workers and write information back to the system.

Figure 4 provides a schematic overview of the concept elements and their connections.

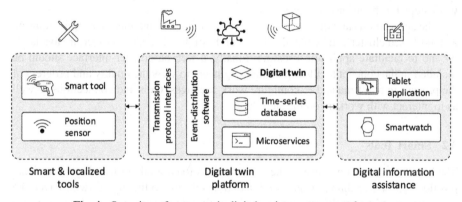

Fig. 4. Overview of user-centric digital assistance concept elements

The concept is built upon the specifics of the analyzed manual processes but also enables the seamless integration of further elements and sensors as well as logic modules in the form of microservices. At this point in time, the concept is in the process of being implemented. This means that a basic platform of the digital twin has been implemented that can provide modular client interfaces and microservices. Furthermore, there are prototypes of the smart hand tools that are being further developed in terms of their industrial applicability and data interfaces for integration into the concept. Similarly, existing software development kits for digital information assistance are being further developed in terms of their synchronization with the digital twin and extensions for information filtering on smartwatches. The following descriptions of the concept elements can thus be regarded as a target state.

3.1 Digital Twin Platform

The digital twin is planned to act as core of the digitalization concept, as it will map the physical process and product to a digital entity using real-time data transmission from several sources. It is embedded in a platform that enables clients (software and hardware elements of the concept) to establish connections using different interfaces and transmission protocols and then bridges information to different modules using event-distribution software. The basic structural components and interfaces are already set up for testing purposes. Once the client connections are established, the event-distribution software allows microservices to subscribe to data messages and react according to workflow information. The platform enables and hosts the microservices that can access information from the centralized repository of data for various purposes, e.g., to optimize work execution in real-time or to feed machine-learning algorithms to learn from data correlation over time.

The envisioned purpose of the proposed modular structure is to allow new logic and software modules to be created and integrated seamlessly. Regarding the analyzed assembly processes, the intended use is to integrate and connect smart hand tools, position sensors and digital information assistance. On the other hand, the platform should integrate product data, workplans and process data from enterprise resource planning systems. 3D product models can be used to derive process parameters for the tools and work steps for the information assistance.

The applications and microservices will be running as containerized applications on a cloud-based cluster and be handled by an orchestrator. The idea is to ensure availability and to facilitate application scaling. Finally, a web-based user-interface should be included in the concept to allow planning engineers to view the quality and progress of the process in real time and to configure work packages, tools and connections as well as to interact with workers on the shopfloor.

3.2 Smart Tools

The key to the envisioned use of the smart tools is to equip them with highly accurate position sensors, enabling event-based data transmission to the digital twin. Given the requirements of assembly environments, the positioning accuracy needs to be approximately 10 mm to ensure accurate allocation to the correct drilling and riveting points. In addition, the tools will be equipped with an integrated chip and sensor technology that allows the effective recording of torque-force curves to enable conclusions to be drawn about the quality of boreholes and rivets. Determining and configuring which process parameters and tool attachments are being used, completes the system.

A bidirectional and low-latency connection to the digital twin facilitates the collected sensor data to be simultaneously evaluated in process by the platform's various logic modules, for example to take countermeasures in the event of mishandling. Via the communication of the position data, correct process parameters can be automatically adjusted. Moreover, the clearance can be denied if an incorrect attachment or a worn tool is about to be used. This avoids errors caused by using wrong machine configurations and simultaneously optimizes the assembly workflow by reducing necessary information gathering and configuration tasks to a minimum.

The comparison of data recording close to the active point and the torque fed in allows the calculation of wear in tool and attachment. Hence, there is no need to release tools only for a limited number of operations and for certain material pairings, which reduces maintenance measures. Besides the mentioned optimizations, the progress and quality of each machine operation is automatically documented in the digital twin.

3.3 Digital Information Assistance

To assist workers in information procurement combining a tablet as main information device and a smartwatch for crucial in-process information is recommended. The idea is to use a smartwatch to display information during work execution that reassures the worker of correctly operating. For example, the currently used torque can be displayed or visual aids can show directions to the next drilling or riveting point. Tactile feedback can be given when errors are about to be made and for more complex problems workers can be referred to the tablet. The tablet is used to display information in form of small work packages, e.g., preparatory steps of positioning components or overviews of drilling steps. Connecting it to the 3D product model allows to visualize complex information in reference to the product element of the user model. Role-based information layouts assure optimal filtering for each organizational entity.

A bidirectional connection to the digital twin will assure consistent up-to-date information about progress and quality so workers can visually confirm the current status if desired. This is likely to simplify both shift handover and collaboration as well as information procurement in general. By confirming work steps, the progress is automatically documented for tool-independent process steps. Errors and comments can be recorded in relation to these steps and collaboration with employees of indirect areas is possible. Combining these elements leads to an effective assistance of workers in preparation, execution and follow-up.

4   Potentials for Productivity and Quality

The idea of the digital assistance concept is to provide workers with an optimized and technologically augmented workflow as follows: After establishing the connection to the digital twin and the initial job synchronization, process guidance via the digital information assistant displays the current progress and next work step. With regard to drilling and riveting, the workers receive an optimized suggestion for the machining sequence and can then seamlessly carry out the steps with the smart hand tools while these are automatically configured or blocked in the event of mishandling. Progress and quality are automatically documented by the system and workers can concentrate on the execution without being exposed to the trade-off between information procurement and being prone to errors. Workflows can be optimized through data accumulation and machine-learning algorithms over time. Figure 5 shows a detail of the proposed workflow with the example of a seat rail assembly. The tablet will be used for processes like positioning the rail and preparing for the task. The smart tool used to drill holes and rivet the rail to the fuselage structure, will be automatically configured and the smart watch will display information such as current process parameters and potential errors.

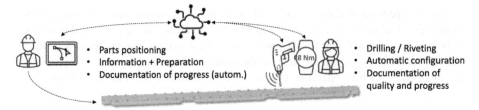

Fig. 5. Information provision and augmented execution in seat rail assembly

The described workflow holds various benefits compared to the current situation in assembly. Productivity and quality potentials are created, for example, in that core tasks are partly eliminated and partly simplified. The need for tool configuration and the respective documentation of progress or quality is eliminated. In addition, information provision is significantly improved and preparatory steps are simplified by visualizing the task. The execution of drilling and riveting becomes more efficient because constant checking of parameters is not needed and the machining sequence is suggested by the system in an optimized way. Collaboration between employees is enabled more intuitively and lengthy shift handovers can be better managed. All in all, the non-value-adding state proportions in fuselage assembly processes can be significantly reduced.

Finally, further potentials arise through the modular and seamless structure of the digital assistance concept, as it will enable future integration and utilization of benefits in the unified namespace. Dynamic flexibility is created through decoupling the client-interfaces from the event-distribution inside of the platform, allowing further sensors and data sources to be included. The long-term acceptance and implementation of the digital assistance concept in existing corporate structures thus becomes more likely.

5   Outlook

As of now, the digital assistance system is in the early stages of development. Nevertheless, the concept presented has been coordinated with the development partners and will be elaborated via feedback cycles with the industry in order to facilitate a transfer of the results. To verify the potential improvements of productivity and quality, a testable demonstrator will be developed and then tested and evaluated in the investigated assembly process. If the potentials can be realized, the concept will be transferred to industry to achieve long-term integration. The ultimate goal of our research is to improve quality and productivity in aircraft industry. The modular and platform-independent concept combining localized production means with bidirectional data flows also promises the potential to improve application scenarios in various industries.

By developing a systematic approach of configuring interfaces and new modules for the digital twin platform, the implementation of new data streams could then be designed in such a way that desired functionality is ensured for diverse applications. The approach should focus on matching the requirements of the digital twin use case with the characteristics of data transmission protocols and transmission technologies and propose a configuration accordingly.

Acknowledgement. The authors would like to thank Bundes-Ministerium für Wirtschaft und Klimaschutz (BMWK) for funding the project "Software architecture for a digital twin and connection of a digital assistance system to worker guidance, smart hand tools and location system". (Project No. 20W1922E).

References

1. Hintze, W., et al.: Digital assistance systems for smart drillings units in aircraft structural assembly. In: 7th International Workshop of Aircraft System Technologies (AST 2019), pp. 255–266, Hamburg (2019)
2. Hinrichsen, S., Riediger, D., Unrau, A.: Assistance systems in manual assembly. In: Proceedings of 6th International Conference on Production Engineering and Management, pp. 3–14, Lemgo (2016)
3. Tietze, F.: Analyse und Verbesserung der Arbeitsproduktivität in der Unikatproduktion. Wissen schafft Innovation (32), Hamburg (2017)
4. Halata, P.: Augmented-Reality-gestützte Informationsbereitstellung für die Unikatproduktion. Wissen schafft Innovation (35), Hamburg (2018)
5. Mueller, R., Vette, M., Scholer, M. Ball, J.: Assembly assistance and position data feedback by means of projection lasers. In: SAE 2016 Aerospace Manufacturing and Automated Fastening Conference and Exhibition, Detroit (2016)
6. Abras, C., Maloney-Krichmar, D., Preece, J.: Encyclopedia of Human-Computer Interaction, 1st edn. Sage Publications, Bainbridge, Thousand Oaks (2004)
7. Apt, W., Schubert, M., Wischmann, S.: Digitale Assistenzsysteme – Perspektiven und Herausforderungen für den Einsatz in Industrie und Dienstleistungen. Autonomik Industrie 4.0, Berlin (2018)
8. Hold, P., Erol, S., Reisinger, G., Sihn, W.: Planning and evaluation of digital assistance systems. Procedia Manufact. **9**, 143–150 (2017)
9. Rost, R.: Digitale Assistenzsysteme in der Industrie: Visualisierungskonzept. TUHH Universitätsbibliothek, Hamburg (2021)
10. Qiu, C., Zhou, S., Liu, Z., Gao, Q., Tan, J.: Digital assembly technology based on augmented reality and digital twins: a review. Virtual Reality Intell. Hardware **1**(6), 597–610 (2019)

Building Digital Shadows for Production Control

Günther Schuh[ID], Andreas Gützlaff[ID], Judith Fulterer[ID],
and Annkristin Hermann[✉][ID]

Laboratory for Machine Tools and Production Engineering (WZL) of RWTH Aachen
University, Campus-Boulevard 30, Aachen 52074, Germany
{g.schuh,a.guetzlaff,j.fulterer,a.hermann}@wzl.rwth-aachen.de

Abstract. Digital Shadows can support stakeholders in production control by providing context-aware and aggregated information serving a specific task and thus supporting in the decision-making. In this paper, we propose a methodology for building Digital Shadows with focus on production control. We identify the building blocks for defining Digital Shadows consisting of purpose, models and data. Furthermore, we suggest an implementation for the methodology as a decision support tool for the stakeholders in production control. Finally, we illustrate the use of our methodology on the basis of a exemplary use-case of production control.

Keywords: Digital shadows · Production control

1 Introduction

Digital Shadows are a research area within the Internet of Production, a German Cluster of Excellence at RWTH Aachen University. Digital Shadows support the decision process by providing the relevant information. [1] For this purpose, data from different sources is collected, aggregated and analyzed [2]. Models are used to aggregate, link and analyze the data to generate the relevant information [3]. Digital Shadows are a promising approach to improve production systems by providing access to relevant information increasing the decision-quality [4].

Production control is well suited for the use of digital shadows due to the complexity of decisions [5]. The aim of production control is to realise the production plan, taking into account short-term disruptions [6]. However, responding to short-term disruptions is a challenge [7]. The task of the production controller is to decide on appropriate changes in the production processes [7]. These decisions have an impact on the overall system and are difficult to map using existing IT-systems due to the high complexity caused by multiple interactions and dependencies in production [8]. This leads to a local optimization of production control [9].

This paper introduces a methodology for describing and implementing Digital Shadows in production control. First, an overview of the theoretical background of Digital Shadows and Digital Twins is given. In Sect. 3 the methodology to

ⓒ IFIP International Federation for Information Processing 2022
Published by Springer Nature Switzerland AG 2022
D. Y. Kim et al. (Eds.): APMS 2022, IFIP AICT 663, pp. 110–117, 2022.
https://doi.org/10.1007/978-3-031-16407-1_14

build Digital Shadows is illustrated. An use case explains the application of the methodology. Finally, a conclusion on the current state is drawn with an outlook on future work.

2   Scientific Basics

In the following, the theoretical foundations of Digital Shadow and its application for production planning and control are considered. First, a distinction is made between the terms model, Digital Twin and Digital Shadow. The main differentiating aspect is the flow of information between the digital and the physical object. A digital model is a digital illustration of an existing or planned physical object. It does not include any form of automated data exchange between the physical object and the digital object. The digital representation may contain a more or less detailed description of the physical object. The Digital shadow follows the physical object on the basis of an automatic one-way data flow. The Digital Twin is an extension of the Digital Shadow in that the data flows between an existing physical object and a digital object are fully integrated in both directions. [5] Since the Digital Shadow is to be used for a purpose-oriented application [10], it will be considered in the remainder of the paper.

A Digital Shadow is defined as a set of contextual records and their aggregation and abstraction, collected in relation to a system for a specific purpose in relation to the original system [11]. A Digital Shadow is composed of aggregated data traces as well as models [12]. The goal of using the Digital Shadow is to provide data-based support in the complex decision-making process and only present the relevant information to the user to reduce complexity [4,13].

The Digital Shadow provides all information needed to successfully perform a task and make a decision. In context on manufacturing the objective of a Digital Shadow is to improve decision-quality and the performance. [4] In addition to this, the Digital Shadow can reduce the increasing complexity and information quantity of information systems for the user, by providing only with the relevant information [4]. To ensure this, it is essential to provide the information at the right time and in the right place [14,15]. The information is generated with the help of a Digital Shadow by linking, aggregating and analysing the data traces from corresponding models [16,17]. Data traces can originate from different sources and consist of time-dependent data, variable data and metadata. They describe a past as well as the current state [17–19]. Sensors used to collect the required data enable real-time bidirectional data communication between the physical system and the virtual system using integration technology that includes communication interface and security. Then the Digital Twin uses the analysis techniques to analyse the data for specific purposes and provides response based on the simulation results and directs further action to the physical system. [20] The application of the Digital Shadow for production planning and control offers enormous as the user receives the necessary information in complex decision situations such as on-time delivery, lead time, capacity utilization and inventory [21]. To this end, initial approaches have already been tested to support a capacity control decision. As a result, the Digital Shadow provides the relevant information for decision-supporting production control. Therefore data of various systems and domains are aggregated to the required detail level. This relevant information includes configuration, costs and logistical target variables such as on-time delivery, lead time, capacity utilization and inventory [17].

3   Methodology to Build Digital Shadows

As stated in Sect. 2 Digital Shadows aim to support the decision process by providing the necessary information. Current research focuses on the description of Digital Shadows but does not provide an approach to implement Digital Shadows in practice. Aim of this research is to develop a methodology enabling production planner and controller to describe Digital Shadows so software engineers can implement them. Using the methodology decisions, models and data trace of Digital Shadows are specified.

3.1   Decisions

Each Digital Shadow supports a specific decision, like the termination of the order release or capacity control. In this methodology the elements decision problem, purpose, information needs and assessment dimensions describe a decision.

First, a decision problem of PPC is selected. It is described via the scope of consideration, the potential scope for solutions as well as the goal of the decision. For the example termination of order release all open orders with a specific due date are part of the scope of consideration and solution. The goal of the is to identify which of the orders should be released next to fulfill the logistical target values best.

The purpose of the decision is determined based on the decision problem. The purpose specifies the target of the Digital Shadow and is, either an optimization of a target value or an information on critical disturbances. For the termination of the order release a purpose can be the determination of the optimal release date.

The information requirements can be derived from the purpose. If the purpose is an optimization, the user requires information on the target values as well as the necessary parameter adjustments. So for the order release optimization not only the order release date but also information on material and resource availability are required. If the purpose is to identify critical disturbances users need information regarding the disturbance and the effects of the disturbance.

The assessment dimensions are used to evaluate the provided solutions. In PPC, these are typically the logistical target values and costs. The best evaluated alternative solutions are provided to the users. Based on the quantitative evaluation they can make a decision.

3.2 Models

Models represent the link between the information requirements and the data. Models can be either structure models or behavior models.

Structure models describe the relationships of the system and correlation between different models, these are e.g. ontologies or UML models. In the context of the Digital Shadow, structure models serve to identify and link the necessary behavior models. A structure models is described based on structure model type (e.g. ontology), aggregation level (e.g. meta model, application model) and the described system (e.g. actors, interrelationships).

Behavior models display the interdependencies within the system, these are e.g. simulations or AI-algorithms. They model the effect of system state change, e.g. the effect an order rescheduling on the overall delivery dates. To charcerize a behavior model production controller need to describe the model properties as well as the required input data and the output information. The model's input data is characterised via the required data sets (attributes), the data structure and the data quality. Even though behavior models in the digital shadow can exchanged the general goal of the model must be described by the properties. Based on these specification the best fitting model can be selected. The properties include the calculation aim (e.g. minimisation of throughput time), behaviour of the model (online/offline), global quality of the model (precision), and local quality of the model (interpretability, explainability). Additionally, adaptability and robustness of the model can be described. The information output is characterised and described in terms of accuracy.

3.3 Data Trace

In order to generate the information needed to make a decision, the relevant data traces of the system must be queried. A data trace consists of data points and metadata. Data points are the parameter values stored in the IT-systems. For the production control, relevant data points are, for example, order number, material availability or the delivery date required by the customer. For each decision specific data points in different aggregation levels are required. However, there are similar requirements for different decisions, for example, almost all decisions require data on the production orders such as the order number, the work plan and the planned end date. Once a Digital Shadow has been described, further digital shadows can be modelled with less effort.

The metadata is used to characterize the data points. Examples for meta data are data attribute characteristics (e.g. order number, customer), data storage location (e.g. ERP System), time of storage, data type, data origin (e.g. recording person, sensor), update frequency (e.g. every second, daily) and data format (e.g. image data).

Figure 1 gives an overview over the elements of the Digital Shadow. After the elements of Digital Shadows are described by production planner and controller a Digital Shadow can be implemented.

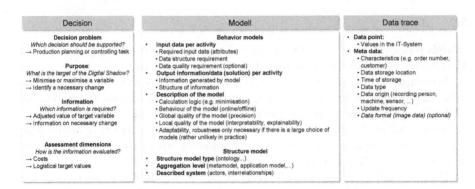

Fig. 1. Building elements of a digital shadow

3.4 Implementation

For the implementation of a Digital Shadow, an infrastructure on the basis of a web application can be used to illustrate the building and setting of a Digital Shadow into action. A web application can be represented through two main components: the frontend and the backend. On the frontend, the user has the ability to interact with a graphical interface to build a Digital Shadow and call its output. The backend handles all interactions with the frontend in the background and forward processed results for graphical representation on the user interface. In context of implementing a Digital Shadow, the user has the ability on the frontend to either select from a set of predefined Digital Shadows or define a new one.

Building a new Digital Shadow requires from the user to select the involved models from a model catalogue. The model catalogue contains all possible models, such as behavioral models (e.g. simulation, optimization) along with meta-information on the nature of inputs and outputs that are expected with each model. Considering each model as a black-box, most models rely on data for the input and delivers results as processed data in the output. For example, given a combinatorial optimization problem (e.g. TSP, VRP), an optimization model needs as an input to have access to data from production (e.g. cost matrix) along with the underlying objective, cost function and constraints. The access to the required data is described in the model meta-information by data queries that target corresponding data sources (e.g. the cost matrix is defined in the ERP system, which can be acquired through an SQL query target its underlying database management system). Note that for executing the data queries, it is important that the backend has established data connections to the corresponding data sources.

The user has the ability through a model editor on the frontend to combine different models by linking the inputs to the outputs accordingly and thus chaining between the models. The chaining allows for structuring the execution of the models leading to the results that serve the ultimate goal from defining the Digital Shadow. The model catalogue is hosted on a database with references to models (including where they are stored and what dependencies they have). Moreover, the model catalogue takes care of providing the required models as well as their execution to delivers the results back to the frontend depending on the user interactions. In case inconsistencies (e.g. missing data values, corrupted queries) are detected in terms of the definition of a model or their meta-information in the model catalogue, the backend warns the user on the frontend about the irregularities.

4   Digital Shadows for Production Control

In this section the building of a Digital Shadow is demonstrated for the example capacity controlling. First the decision is described. A production controller needs to decide if a change in the utilisation of the capacities is necessary. The capacity plan of the next week is the considered scope. The scope of solution are adaptions of the production and capacity plan of the next week. The purpose is to inform the production controller if there is a critical disturbance and which possible actions can be performed to reduce the impact of the disturbance. The required information is the necessary capacity and production plan changes. The evaluation criteria are the adherence to due dates, the machines' utilization, and the expected manufacturing costs. To generate the required information different three behavior models are necessary. One model is required to identify capacity disturbances leading to critical disturbances of the production plan. The model provides information indicating the critical resources and orders. The input data are the capacity plan, production plan and current state of the production. A data mining a approach is used to identify the capacity disturbances. The second model, a optimization model, has the goal to identify possible changes of capacities and the production orders in order. These generate different capacity scenarios. This model contains for each resource possible capacity changes like additional shifts or increase of speed. The required input data are necessary resource changes. The third model is necessary to calculate the production plan based on the adapted capacities and evaluate the new production plan. In this use case a simulation model is used. The three models are linked to each other. The first model generates input data for the second and the third uses the results from the second model. The required data are determined by the first model and are all data regarding the planned and current capacity and production orders. For the orders the current working plan, planned start and end date (current production plan) as well as is data are relevant. For the resources (machines and personnel) the shift plan, availability, technical attributes for machines and qualification for personnel are the relevant input data. In addition the costs are needed to evaluate the alternative solutions. Necessary costs in the use case are machine costs, personnel costs, costs for late delivery and costs for additional capacity (e.g. external production, overtime). Now the production controller can decide which capacity changes to make based on quantitative information. The advantage compared to existing ERP solutions is that in the Digital Shadow different models can be easily linked. Additionally, the if there is a better model the model can be changed. Also the user gets the right information and does not need to search for the information in different IT-Systems.

5   Summary

This paper introduced a methodology to build Digital Shadows in Production Control. The main elements of Digital Shadows are decisions, models and data traces. The methodology gives a procedure to describe the elements for production controllers. Based on the description, Digital Shadows can be implemented in software. An use case in the field of production control details the application of the methodology to describe Digital Shadows.

In contrast to existing IT-software Digital Shadows provide the relevant information for a decision to the user. Additionally, different models can be easily combined. In further research more Digital Shadows should be described and implemented to improve the methodology and to ensure comprehensive decision support in production control.

Acknowledgements. Funded by the Deutsche Forschungsgemeinschaft (DFG, German Research Foundation) under Germany's Excellence Strategy - EXC-2023 Internet of Production - 390621612.

References

1. Riesener, M., Schuh, G., Dölle, C., Tönnes, C.: The digital shadow as enabler for data analytics in product life cycle managemen. Procedia CIRP **26**, 729–734 (2019)
2. Tao, F., Cheng, J., Qi, Q., Zhang, M., Zhang, H., Sui, F.: Digital twin-driven product design, manufacturing and service with big data. Int. J. Adv. Manuf. Technol. **94**(9–12), 3563–3576 (2018)
3. Schuh, G., et al.: Effizientere produktion mit digitalen schatten. Zeitschrift für wirtschaftlichen Fabrikbetrieb **115**(s1), 105–107 (2020)
4. Schuh, G., Gützlaff, A., Sauermann, F., Maibaum, J.: Digital shadows as an enabler for the internet of production. In: Lalic, B., Majstorovic, V., Marjanovic, U., von Cieminski, G., Romero, D. (eds.) APMS 2020. IAICT, vol. 591, pp. 179–186. Springer, Cham (2020). https://doi.org/10.1007/978-3-030-57993-7_21
5. Kritzinger, W., Karner, M., Traar, G., Henjes, J., Sihn, W.: Digital twin in manufacturing: a categorical literature review and classification. IFAC-PapersOnLine **51**(11), 1016–1022 (2018)
6. Schuh, G., Stich, V.: Produktionsplanung und-steuerung 1: Grundlagen der PPS. Springer, Berlin, Heidelberg (2012). 4, überarbeitete auflage ed
7. Steinlein, F., Liu, Y., Stich, V.: Development of a decision support app for short term production control to improve the adherence to delivery dates. In: Nyhuis, P., Herberger, D., Hübner, M. (eds.), Proceedings of the 1st Conference on Production Systems and Logistics (CPSL 2020) (Hannover), pp. 438–447, Institutionelles Repositorium der Leibniz Universität Hannover, Hannover (2020)

8. Scherwitz, P., et al.: Digitale transformation in der produktioinsplanung und - steuerung: Ergebnisse einer gemeinsamen studie der produktionstechnischen institute fraunhofer igcv, ifa, ipmt und wzl. Zeitschrift für wirtschaftlichen Fabrikbetrieb ZWF **115**(4), 252–256 (2020)
9. Kunath, M., Winkler, H.: Integrating the digital twin of the manufacturing system into a decision support system for improving the order management process. Procedia CIRP **72**, 225–231 (2018)
10. Becker, F., et al.: A conceptual model for digital shadows in industry and its application. In: Ghose, A., Horkoff, J., Silva Souza, V.E., Parsons, J., Evermann, J. (eds.) ER 2021. LNCS, vol. 13011, pp. 271–281. Springer, Cham (2021). https://doi.org/10.1007/978-3-030-89022-3_22
11. Bibow, P., et al.: Model-driven development of a digital twin for injection molding. In: Dustdar, S., Yu, E., Salinesi, C., Rieu, D., Pant, V. (eds.) CAiSE 2020. LNCS, vol. 12127, pp. 85–100. Springer, Cham (2020). https://doi.org/10.1007/978-3-030-49435-3_6
12. Brecher, C., Buchsbaum, M., Storms, S.: Control from the cloud: edge computing, services and digital shadow for automation technologies. In: 2019 International Conference on Robotics and Automation (ICRA), pp. 9327–9333. IEEE (2019)
13. Qi, Q., Tao, F.: Digital twin and big data towards smart manufacturing and industry 4.0: 360 degree comparison. IEEE Access **6**, 3585–3593 (2018)
14. Bauernhansl, T., Hartleif, S., Felix, T.: The digital shadow of production-a concept for the effective and efficient information supply in dynamic industrial environments. Procedia CIRP **72**, 69–74 (2018)
15. Pause, D., et al.: Task-specific decision support systems in multi-level production systems based on the digital shadow. In: 2019 IEEE International Conference on Industrial Cyber Physical Systems (ICPS), pp. 603–608. IEEE (2019)
16. Riesener, M., Dölle, C., Schuh, G., Tönnes, C.: Framework for defining information quality based on data attributes within the digital shadow using LDA. Procedia CIRP **83**, 304–310 (2019)
17. Schuh, G., Gützlaff, A., Schmidhuber, M., Maibaum, J.: Development of digital shadows for production control (2021). ESSN: 2701-6277
18. Schuh, G., Dölle, C., Tönnes, C.: Methodology for the derivation of a digital shadow for engineering management. In: 2018 IEEE Technology and Engineering Management Conference (TEMSCON), pp. 1–6. IEEE (2018)
19. Stecken, J., Ebel, M., Bartelt, M., Poeppelbuss, J., Kuhlenkötter, B.: Digital shadow platform as an innovative business model. Procedia CIRP **83**, 204–209 (2019)
20. Parott, A., Warshaw, L.: Industry 4.0 and the digital twin: manufacturing meets its match, Retrieved January, vol. 23, p. 2019 (2017)
21. Kubenke, J., Roh, P., Kunz, A.: Assessing the efficiency of information retrieval from the digital shadow at the shop floor using it assistive systems. Mechatronics, pp. 202–209 (2018)

Does Industry 4.0 Matter to Automotive SME Suppliers? The Role of Advanced Digital Technologies in the Strategic Work of Firms in the Swedish Automotive Valley

Kristian Ericsson[✉], Seyoum Eshetu Birkie, and Monica Bellgran

Department of Sustainable Production Development, Production Management, KTH Royal
Institute of Technology, Södertälje, Sweden
kerics@kth.se

Abstract. Automotive small and medium-sized enterprise (SME) suppliers are
important players in many national economies. They are currently facing increased
pressure to manage the undergoing, demanding changes in the automotive industry. One proposed way for the firms to manage is to introduce Industry 4.0 (I4.0)
technologies in their production, but for this to happen the firms need to consider
such technologies in their strategic work. In this study, insights were gathered
through interviews with representatives from 24 SME durable goods suppliers
within automotive in Sweden, to find out what role I4.0 technologies play in their
business-level strategic work. The findings show that these firms do not seem to
consider the introduction of I4.0 technologies in production in their strategic work.
The firms also do not include any other kind of long-term improvement programs
in production in their strategizing. This goes against recommendations from several prior studies, which have emphasized the importance of I4.0 technologies
in production for the future competitiveness of automotive SME suppliers. This
study contributes to the discussion on how automotive SME suppliers can use
I4.0 technologies strategically in their production, by being the first to empirically
investigate the role of production in these firms' strategic work.

Keywords: Industry 4.0 · Industrial digital transformation · Business strategy ·
SME · Automotive

1 Introduction

The automotive industry is a core sector in most industrialized nations [1]. For some
countries it is the largest source of exports overall [2]. However, the automotive industry
is currently undergoing demanding changes. The firms are under increased pressure to
conduct their business aligned with a sustainable development (particularly the environmental dimension) [3], increase their pace and complexity of innovation [4], and
consider radical technological shifts in their business activities [5]. These demanding

© IFIP International Federation for Information Processing 2022
Published by Springer Nature Switzerland AG 2022
D. Y. Kim et al. (Eds.): APMS 2022, IFIP AICT 663, pp. 118–125, 2022.
https://doi.org/10.1007/978-3-031-16407-1_15

changes add to an already difficult competitive situation for firms in the automotive industry [6].

One substantial group of companies within the industry are automotive Small and medium-sized enterprises (SMEs). SMEs are important players in the business landscape overall; in the EU they make up over 99% of all companies, employ more than 50% of the workforce, and have a more than 50% share of the value added ([7, 8]). Automotive SMEs are a big part of the economies in some European countries [9] and their importance have increased [10]. Hence, the ability of these companies to manage the changes in the industry is of importance to several national economies.

To stay competitive in this environment, automotive SMEs will have to improve and adapt several functions in their organisations, and a particularly important function for automotive SME suppliers is production [3]. Prior literature has suggested numerous approaches with which automotive SME suppliers can increase their performance in production, like (a) to introduce lean manufacturing [11], (b) to introduce "Industry 4.0" (I4.0)/smart manufacturing ([5, 12]), and (c) to build networks around manufacturing [13], among others.

Since alternative (b) has been branded as "the next enabler of performance improvement" and is assumed to bring with it "a potential revolution" in manufacturing [14], it is justified to investigate this alternative further. Several studies have evaluated how I4.0 technologies can be used to enhance performance in production in automotive SME suppliers ([15–17]). According to these studies, I4.0 technologies have the potential to enhance the performance in production, and subsequently allow automotive SME suppliers to remain competitive, and should therefore be purposefully included in the business-level strategic work of these firms.

However, no studies have so far investigated the inclusion of I4.0 technologies in the strategic work of automotive SME suppliers ("strategic work" in this case referring to both the strategy formulation and -implementation). The existence of strategic benefits from I4.0 technologies in production has been pointed out, but the process of converting this knowledge within the firms into long-term actions has so far not been investigated, although this process is essential to achieve the strategic benefits.

The research presented in this paper addresses this gap by exploring what role I4.0 technologies play in the strategic work of automotive SME suppliers in Sweden. The research objective is to evaluate how the members of these SMEs choose to position I4.0 technologies as strategic alternatives to manage the demanding changes in the automotive industry. The research question guiding the study is:

– RQ: What role does the introduction of I4.0 technologies in production play in the business-level strategic work of automotive SME suppliers?

By investigating the SMEs' strategic work, this study can give insights about under what conditions I4.0 technologies are regarded suitable, feasible and acceptable strategic alternatives for these firms.

2 State of the Art

Industry 4.0 has been defined as "a new industrial transformation that aims to connect people and things anytime, anyplace, with anything and anyone, ideally using any path/network and any service" [18, p. 1]. It includes advanced digital technologies, like smart worker technologies, smart equipment technologies, data analytics technologies, network technologies, etc. [18], referred to as "I4.0 technologies".

Prior literature, that has investigated how automotive SME suppliers can achieve increased performance in production through the adoption of I4.0 technologies, typically relate their studies to the strategic situation in the automotive industry. However, these studies usually present strategic recommendations, rather than investigate the strategic work done in practice in their target companies.

Some studies evaluate what different, strategic potentials I4.0 technologies carry for automotive SME suppliers. For example, strategic benefits of individual technologies, like Cloud-Based Advanced Planning and Scheduling Systems [16] and Discrete Event Simulators [17]. Other examples include more general inquiries on how I4.0 technologies will influence key strategy factors, like business models [12].

Other studies assume that I4.0 technologies carry strategic potential and proceed to investigate how I4.0 technologies are best implemented. These are for example studies suggesting procedures for the gradual implementation of I4.0 technologies in automotive SME suppliers [19]. Other studies describe how these companies implement I4.0 [20], or more generally describe facilitators and obstacles when implementing I4.0 technologies (e.g. [15, 21]).

However, no studies have been found that describe strategic work regarding production among automotive SME suppliers, although there are several theoretical frameworks for general SMEs [22]. Questions on how the firms decide if and how to integrate I4.0 technologies in production, to either respond to changes in their surroundings or try to influence their surroundings, have largely remained unanswered.

Prior scholars have pointed out that the competitiveness and resilience of general SMEs can, in part, be attributed to their strategic work, and their use of technology [23]. It should therefore be possible to evaluate the potential, future competitiveness of the automotive SME suppliers based on their strategic work, particularly concerning technology. This study aims to carry out this evaluation concerning I4.0 technologies, and thereby provide insights about the probable future competitiveness of a group of firms with great importance for several national economies.

3 Method

An exploratory case study was conducted to fulfil the research objective. The study was carried out in parallel to a study about the future of automotive in the Mälaren Valley in Sweden ("Fordonsdalen Stockholm") with authors working on both studies.

Representatives from twenty-four automotive SMEs were interviewed, being limited to firms with less than 250 employees and suppliers of physical, durable goods to automotive firms. All SMEs came from the Mälaren Valley-cluster of automotive companies, which is the second largest automotive cluster in Sweden [1].

The respondents were selected by the firms when asked for employees with insights into (a) the situation in the automotive industry at large, and (b how the firm carries out strategy work. Ten of the respondents were CEOs or regional CEOs, eight were sales managers/CSOs, two were heads of regions, and four had other similarly central roles in the strategic work of SMEs. The firms produced auto parts, auto materials, auto subsystems and production tools for OEMs.

The interviews conducted were semi-structured and held via videoconferencing during late 2020 and the first half of 2021. Since the interviews took place during the COVID-19 pandemic, it's possible that the respondents were occupied with managing the short-term situation rather than strategic work. However, the respondents mentioned stress from demanding changes in automotive rather than from the pandemic.

To avoid false positives, where respondents would claim I4.0 technologies were more prevalent in their strategic work than in reality, the researchers refrained from mentioning digital technologies. The interviews were introduced as being about the SMEs' business-level strategic work, and would begin with open, general questions and proceed into a level of detail where I4.0 technologies in production would inevitably be mentioned if included in the strategic work.

To better understand negatives, where respondents would not talk of I4.0 technologies, two forms of negatives where specifically probed for. The first form where firms that did not carry out any qualitative strategic work at all, or only did rough estimates. To filter out such firms, the respondents were asked to supply their prognoses of the future of the Swedish automotive industry until 2030. Their answers were then compared to a compilation of relatively fresh expert prognoses about industry trends until 2030 (the compilation has been published in a report: [1] pp. 21–54). In cases where the respondents' prognoses of the Swedish automotive industry deviated substantially from the compilation, the firms' strategic work were regarded as of low quality.

The second form of negatives were firms with less advanced production capabilities, for which I4.0 technologies were not (yet) a realistic strategic alternative. To filter out such firms, the answers were probed for other, already established long-term improvement programs in production, like Lean Manufacturing, Six Sigma, various forms of automation, ERP systems, etc. SMEs that mentioned any of these, but not I4.0, would be considered too early in their production development to host I4.0.

All interviews were recorded, and the recordings were later reviewed for quotes and summarising key statements. These were, in turn, eventually gathered to form the high-level results of this study.

4 Results

The respondent's prognoses about the demanding changes in the automotive industry were well aligned with the compilation of expert prognoses. The respondents usually mentioned a large share of the compilation, and the most central topics from the compilation were also considered central tropics by the respondents.

Using this knowledge, the respondents had made efforts to predict how the demanding changes in the automotive industry at large would influence their immediate business situation. The respondents could also give reasonable justifications for their prognoses, which further indicates that business-level strategic work was well established among these firms.

Based on their predictions of the changes to their immediate business situation, the firms had generated alternative, high-level strategic measures to adapt to these changes. Some commonly mentioned high-level measures were:

- To increase the level of Sustainable Development in the firm, to make it one of their unique selling points.
- To engage in collaborative innovation endeavours with other automotive firms.
- To improve the firm's product portfolios with more product and service bundles, product and software bundles, and products for electric vehicles.
- To enhance the firm's skills and budget used for research and development in the areas of electrical vehicles and digital tools.

Going deeper into these high-level measures, firms mentioned the use of I4.0 technologies in their product offerings. This could be, for example, including AI in the software parts of the product and software bundles, or creating functions for gathering and big data analysis of user data. However, no respondents mentioned the integration of I4.0 technologies in production as alternative, high-level strategic measures.

Additionally, none of the already established long-term improvement programs in production (referred to above: Lean Manufacturing, Six Sigma…) were mentioned. Very few of the alternative measures mentioned by the respondents were situated in their production function. That is: few respondents made a connection between their strategic work and any long-term improvement programs in production. When the respondents did mention methods to adapt and improve production, they referred to it as something enabling other long-term responses, than long-term responses in their own right. In sum, the lack of evidence that the respondents connected strategic manoeuvring to increased performance in production, was not exclusive to I4.0-enabled performance increases, but to performance increases in production in general.

5   Analysis and Discussion

The results of the study indicate that automotive SME suppliers in Sweden do not include the introduction of I4.0 technologies in production in their strategic work. They also do not seem to consider any other kinds of long-term improvement program in production. The indicated answer to the research question is therefore that I4.0 technologies play no role, which goes against recommendations from prior studies, which pointed out long-term improvement programs in production as suitable strategic measures for automotive SME suppliers (e.g. [16, 17, 24]).

The respondents had insights about industry trends, and few firms were labelled as doing low quality strategic work. The respondents were informed of I4.0 technologies and their potential. Several respondents did discuss the use of I4.0 technologies outside of production to reach strategic goals – for example to capture use data from their customers – but not within production. Some respondents were critical towards the use of digital tools in general, but more as inconvenience than antagonism.

It is possible that the respondents were not working close enough to production to see the potential of I4.0 technologies in that environment. However, most firms interviewed had only around 10–20 employees, and an investment in I4.0 technologies in production would be a major investment, so it is improbable that there were discussions of introducing I4.0 in production without the respondents being informed.

It is also possible that I4.0 technologies have not yet reached a level of maturity and sufficiently low costs to come in question as a strategic measure for automotive SME suppliers. However, the respondents were evidently informed of the rapid advances of digital technologies, including their lowered costs, and since the strategic timeframe investigated was between 2021 and 2030, it is unlikely that many of them would dismiss I4.0 technologies as too futuristic or expensive all the way until then.

After ruling out these possible causes as to why the respondents did not mention I4.0 technologies, no conclusive causes could be identified despite the rich data.

The most probable causes with support from the empirical data are the personal opinions of the respondents. The respondents gave indication of viewing their production as strategically insignificant. For example, the respondents frequently mentioned bundles between physical products and services, and physical products and software, as appropriate, innovative next steps for their firms. Comparing to these, production alone had come to be viewed as unfashionable and strategically uninteresting.

Regardless of the causes, and instead looking at what consequences these apparent, contradicting views will have, it depends on the point of view chosen. Assuming the view of prior authors, that claim that the technologies play an important part in the future competitiveness of these firms (e.g. [15, 21]), the consequences of not considering them would be drastically reduced future competitiveness. Assuming instead the respondents' view, the importance of I4.0 technologies has been exaggerated, and the greatest risk probably lies in firms being stressed into implementing complex technology that has little actual potential.

Clearly, further empirical research is needed to understand what actual opportunities and risks arise for automotive SME suppliers that choose to integrate I4.0 technologies in their manufacturing.

6 Conclusions

Our results indicate that the introduction of I4.0 technologies in production is not considered in the business-level strategic work of Swedish automotive SME suppliers. This goes against recommendations from prior studies, which have emphasized the importance of I4.0 technologies in the production for the competitiveness of these firms. This study is the first to empirically investigate the role of production in automotive SME suppliers' strategic work, and thereby contributes to the larger discussion on how these firms can make strategic use of I4.0 technologies in production.

It is apparent that the strategic considerations of automotive supplier SMEs and those of prior studies diverge. A recommendation for future research would therefore be to narrow this gap by further investigating how strategic work is carried out in automotive SME suppliers. Enhanced insights about the strategic work might reveal how they select which long-term initiatives (like I4.0 technologies in production) to consider, and not, and why production seems to be so absent in the strategic work.

Another area that might need attention is the relationship between the introduction of I4.0 technologies in production, and the introduction of the same technologies in the products being produced. It is possible that the latter type of introduction will eventually stimulate the former, and since respondents showed apparent interest in the latter, this might lead to enhanced interest for I4.0 technologies in production.

Acknowledgements. The authors would like to thank the Swedish Agency for Economic and Regional Growth via the European Regional Development Fund for the funding of the project, and Laith Butty, Sarkis Khatchadourian, Emelie Rhenman and Josefine Sohlman for their valuable contribution to the data gathering for this study.

References

1. Butty, L., Khatchadourian, S., Rhenman, E., Sohlman, J.: Fordonsindustrins framtida behov: En kartläggning av små- och medelstora företag i Stockholmsregionen (2021). http://www.rufs.se/publikationer/20212/fordonsindustrins-framtida-behov/
2. Hill, T.: Manufacturing Strategy: The Strategic Management of the Manufacturing Function. Macmillan Press Ltd., Basingstoke, Hants (1993)
3. O'Brien, C.: Sustainable production - a new paradigm for a new millennium. Int. J. Prod. Econ. **60**, 1–7 (1999). https://doi.org/10.1016/S0925-5273(98)00126-1
4. Fallah, M.H., Lechler, T.G.: Global innovation performance: Strategic challenges for multinational corporations. J. Eng. Technol. Manag. JET-M **25**(1–2), 58–74 (2008). https://doi.org/10.1016/J.JENGTECMAN.2008.01.008
5. Dodourova, M., Bevis, K.: Networking innovation in the European car industry: does the open innovation model fit? Transp. Res. Part A Policy Pract. **69**, 252–271 (2014). https://doi.org/10.1016/J.TRA.2014.08.021
6. Ili, S., Albers, A., Miller, S.: Open innovation in the automotive industry. R D Manag. **40**(3), 246–255 (2010). https://doi.org/10.1111/J.1467-9310.2010.00595.X
7. Airaksinen, A., Luomaranta, H., Alajääskö, P., Roodhuijzen, A.: Statistics on Small and Medium-sized Enterprises: Dependent and Independent SMEs and Large Enterprises (2015). http://ec.europa.eu/eurostat/statistics-explained/index.php/Statistics_on_small_and_medium-sized_enterprises
8. German Federal Ministry of Economic Affairs and Energy, "German Mittelstand: Motor der deutschen Wirtschaft," Berlin (2014)
9. Thun, J.H., Drüke, M., Hoenig, D.: Managing uncertainty-an empirical analysis of supply chain risk management in small and medium-sized enterprises. Int. J. Prod. Res. **49**(18), 5511–5525 (2011). https://doi.org/10.1080/00207543.2011.563901
10. Rutherford, T., Holmes, J.: 'The flea on the tail of the dog': power in global production networks and the restructuring of Canadian automotive clusters. J. Econ. Geogr. **8**(4), 519–544 (2008). https://doi.org/10.1093/JEG/LBN014
11. Miller, G., Pawloski, J., Standridge, C.: A case study of lean, sustainable manufacturing. J. Ind. Eng. Manag. **3**(1), 11–32 (2010). https://doi.org/10.3926/JIEM.2010.V3N1.P11-32
12. Müller, J.M., Buliga, O., Voigt, K.I.: Fortune favors the prepared: how SMEs approach business model innovations in Industry 4.0. Technol. Forecast. Soc. Change **132**, 2–17 (2018)
13. Karlsson, C., Sköld, M.: Forms of innovation openness in global automotive groups. Int. J. Automot. Technol. Manag. **13**(1), 1–17 (2013). https://doi.org/10.1504/IJATM.2013.052776

14. Buer, S.-V. V., Semini, M., Ola Strandhagen, J., Sgarbossa, F., Strandhagen, J.O., Sgarbossa, F.: The complementary effect of lean manufacturing and digitalisation on operational performance. Int. J. Prod. Res. **59**(7), 1976–1992 (2021). https://doi.org/10.1080/00207543.2020. 1790684
15. Arcidiacono, F., Ancarani, A., Di Mauro, C., Schupp, F.: Where the rubber meets the road. Industry 4.0 among SMEs in the automotive sector. IEEE Eng. Manag. Rev. **47**(4), 86–93 (2019). https://doi.org/10.1109/EMR.2019.2932965
16. Liu, J.L., Wang, L.C., Chu, P.C.: Development of a cloud-based advanced planning and scheduling system for automotive parts manufacturing industry. Procedia Manuf. **38**, 1532–1539 (2019). https://doi.org/10.1016/j.promfg.2020.01.133
17. Martínez, E., Cortés, D., Ramírez, J., Obregón, M.G., Molina, A.: Analysis of productivity and profitability of a SME through collaborative networks using discrete event simulation tool: an automotive case study. In: Camarinha-Matos, L.M., Afsarmanesh, H., Ortiz, A. (eds.) PRO-VE 2020. IAICT, vol. 598, pp. 406–417. Springer, Cham (2020). https://doi.org/10. 1007/978-3-030-62412-5_33
18. Calabrese, A., Dora, M., Levialdi Ghiron, N., Tiburzi, L.: Industry's 4.0 transformation process: how to start, where to aim, what to be aware of. Prod. Plan. Control (2020). https://doi. org/10.1080/09537287.2020.1830315
19. Pinto, B., Silva, F.J.G., Costa, T., Campilho, R.D.S.G., Pereira, M.T.: A strategic model to take the first step towards Industry 4.0 in SMEs. Procedia Manuf. **38**, 637–645 (2019). https:// doi.org/10.1016/j.promfg.2020.01.082
20. Nagy, J., Oláh, J., Erdei, E., Máté, D., Popp, J.: The role and impact of Industry 4.0 and the Internet of Things on the business strategy of the value chain-the case of Hungary. Sustain **10**, 3491 (2018). https://doi.org/10.3390/su10103491
21. Mattsson, S., Centerholt, V., Bryntesson, P., Banehag, G.: Insufficient knowledge in industrial digitalization - Promising perspective from female suppliers. Procedia Manuf. **38**, 832–839 (2019). https://doi.org/10.1016/j.promfg.2020.01.164
22. Löfving, M., Säfsten, K., Winroth, M.: Manufacturing strategy frameworks suitable for SMEs. J. Manuf. Technol. Manag. **25**(1), 7–26 (2014). https://doi.org/10.1108/JMTM-08-2012-0081
23. Gunasekaran, A., Rai, B.K., Griffin, M.: Resilience and competitiveness of small and medium size enterprises: an empirical research. Int. J. Prod. Res. **49**(18), 5489–5509 (2011). https:// doi.org/10.1080/00207543.2011.563831
24. Müller, C., Grunewald, M., Spengler, T.S.: Redundant configuration of robotic assembly lines with stochastic failures. Int. J. Prod. Res. **56**(10), 3662–3682 (2018). https://doi.org/10.1080/ 00207543.2017.1406672

Automating Quality Control Based on Machine Vision Towards Automotive 4.0

Dimitris Mourtzis$^{(\boxtimes)}$ ⓘ, John Angelopoulos ⓘ, Angelos Nektarios Arvanitis, and Nikos Panopoulos ⓘ

Laboratory for Manufacturing Systems and Automation, Department of Mechanical Engineering and Aeronautics, University of Patras, 26504 Rio Patras, Greece
mourtzis@lms.mech.upatras.gr

Abstract. By virtue of the increased automation, digitization, and digitalization of manufacturing and production systems a constantly growing amount of data, also known as Big Data Sets, are produced. Thus, techniques, in particular Machine Learning (ML) and Artificial Intelligence (AI), to utilize and organize Big Data Sets for the benefit of contemporary industries are in need. High-quality products are in great demand, especially under the framework of Mass Customization. Machine Vision (MV) algorithms in combination with precision manipulation offered by robotics can be valuable towards this direction. Therefore, the contribution of this research work is focused on the design and development of a framework for automating the quality inspection of parts towards the creation of an Intelligent Manufacturing Cell (IMC). The applicability of the proposed framework is validated in a car differential case study derived from the automotive industry, achieving mesh quality of 98.7%, with minimal voids based on 64 image samples.

Keywords: Manufacturing systems · Artificial Intelligence (AI) · Machine Learning (ML) · Machine Vision (MV) · Automotive 4.0

1 Introduction and State of the Art

Lately, the digitization and the digitalization of manufacturing has obtained a fair amount of scientific consideration [1, 2]. The key drivers/challenges for modern manufacturing and production systems can be summarized to are the volatility in demand, the requirements for increased quality, customized products, as well as the emerge of flexible supply chains [3]. Hence, companies are focusing on the development of new strategies based on the integration of automation and flexibility, such as AI, ML, MV and Computer-Aided Technologies (CAx). The main challenges for AI integration are, i) reasoning, ii) representation, iii) knowledge, learning, iv) natural language processing, v) planning, perception and vi) precision object manipulation. The gap between AI and natural intelligence has led to the creation of two models, in particular the structuralist and the functionalist. Concretely, structuralist models loosely mimic human mind, in areas of basic intelligence operations, such as logic and reasoning. On the other hand,

D. Y. Kim et al. (Eds.): APMS 2022, IFIP AICT 663, pp. 126–134, 2022.
https://doi.org/10.1007/978-3-031-16407-1_16

functionalist models correlate data to its computer counterpart [4]. Overall, AI constitutes a set of technologies and techniques enabling computers and machines to develop intelligence [5, 6]. Consequently, machine tools must become more intelligent, capable of constructing a solid correspondence framework among them and supporting Human-Machine Interface (HMI) [7, 8]. Furthermore, communication networks and structures like Wireless Sensor Networks and Industrial Networks (ModBus, ProfiBus), are important for establishing communication channels between various systems. Cyber-Physical Systems (CPS) consist of smart machines and other production facilities aiming at a more organized production [9]. MV is the mix of strategies and innovation providing an imaging-based programmed review and examination for applications, e.g. investigation, process control, quality control, robot guidance etc. [10] The rising of automation has transformed complex activities manufacturing into direct step by step methodologies that can be repeated by machines [11]. Ma et al. [12], performed an optical inspection for blister defect detection for lithium-ion batteries based on the development of a "DenseNet" architecture. Staar et al. in [13] proposed a modern triplet architecture for Convolutional Neural Networks (CNN), applied two data augmentation methods and trained the algorithm on three diverse datasets, for improving the algorithm's accuracy. Similarly, Pachner et al. [14] and Lokrantz et al. [15], focused on the entirety of a production process instead of the final visual inspection. Lokrantz model was a Bayesian network capable of recognizing quality deviations in two dissimilar manufacturing processes. On the other hand, Pachner, create a model of a decision tree to gain insights about the effects of several process parameters on the floss of the final product for the optimized manufacturing process of powder coating [14]. Sumesh et al. [16] in their research work have proposed a method for the quality classification of welding processes by utilizing a random forest and (J48) decision tree. Based on the literature investigation, quality control in manufacturing is still an open challenge. Furthermore, robotics have not yet been fully integrated to support such activities in modern manufacturing environments. Thus, the contribution of this research work is focused on the design and development of a framework for automating the quality inspection in modern manufacturing and production systems in the automotive industry, utilizing MV and ML techniques, that will be embedded in an IMC [7, 17].

2   Manufacturing Cell Model

The IMC is a combination of three machines, as illustrated in Fig. 1. The MV module consists of a depth camera and a robot. A 3D printer is also integrated for the production of additively manufactured components. Third, a CNC milling machine is utilized for light machining operations, as resulted by the CAD comparison module.

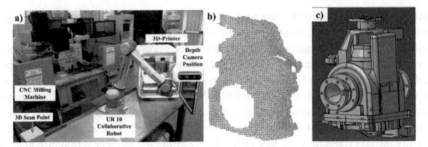

Fig. 1. a) Cell layout, b) STL of the differential, c) CAD of the differential

Taking into consideration the increased volume and variation of produced parts in the automotive industry the proposed framework is based on the utilization of a differential, due to its complicated geometries. The differential consists of 6 gears, 1 input shaft, 2 output shafts and a housing for the gears and bearings.

3   Problem Formulation and System Architecture

The proposed framework relies on the development of methods for the creation of a point cloud with the use of a robot, and the conversion to CAD file, in order to compare it versus the CAD file of the manufactured part. The general system architecture is presented in Fig. 2.

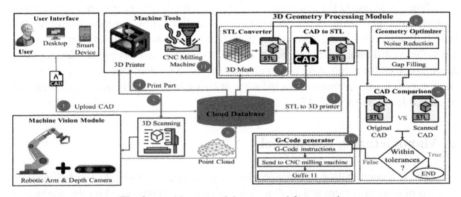

Fig. 2. Architecture of the proposed framework

As illustrated in Fig. 2, the overall procedure of the framework is divided into two sections: pre-processing and processing. In the pre-processing stage, the user imports the CAD file to the Cloud Database, then the file is converted to an STL and automatically imported to the 3D-Printer. After the component is printed, the robot automatically transfers it to the scanning position. The robot then scans the component, with the use of the depth camera, and 64-point cloud images are captured and uploaded to the Cloud. Afterwards, the noise elimination and the alignment of the images into groups are performed. The point cloud groups are automatically converted to 3D meshes. This conversion starts by applying the Poisson disk sampling in which each point of the cloud is subjected to an independent Bernoulli trial in order to determine if an element should be part of the sample, using Eq. 1.

$$\pi_{ij} = \pi_i \times \pi_j \tag{1}$$

where πi is the point population, πj is the point population that is sampled and π_{ij} is the single sample of points of the Poisson disk sampling. The next steps are the computation of Normals for the aforementioned sets of points (n) and the procedure of rendering. Finally, the Ball Pivoting Algorithm (BPA) is applied [18], in order to reconstruct the surface, and ultimately create the mesh. Starting by determine a seed triangle ($\tau = \sigma i, \sigma j$, σk, where $\sigma i, \sigma j, \sigma k$ the vertices of the triangle), which contains three datasets relative to the radius R, the BPA pivots a (virtual) ball of a given radius R (in this paper case R = 0.03 mm) around the already formed edges (e(i, j), e(j, k) and e(k, i)) until it touches another point, forming another triangle. The interaction continues until all reachable edges have been attempted. In this manner the BPA is producing a large number of equal triangles, that finally form the mesh.

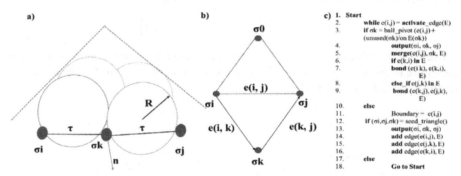

Fig. 3. a) Ball Pivoting Formation, b) Join operation of the Ball Pivoting Algorithm, c) Pseudocode for Ball Pivoting Algorithm

The BPA uses the existing points without creating new ones. A pseudocode is illustrated in Fig. 3c, in order to depict the reasoning of the BPA. Then the file is extracted as an STL. Hence, 16 meshes in an STL formation are generated. Following, is the bonding of the 16 meshes to form one single, three-dimensional mesh, that will be geometrical optimized, by the smoothing of the edges and the filling of holes that may occur, from the bonding procedure. The BPA uses the existing points without creating new ones. In Fig. 4, it is visible that, both the point cloud and mesh files are immediately acquiring a three-dimensional shape, due to the bonding procedure.

The last phase of the pre-processing is the conversion of the STL file to a 3D CAD file, which will then pass in the processing phase. During the processing phase, the original CAD and the one the user acquired from the pre-processing phase are compared, using the deviation algorithm. If any deviations are detected, the UR10 will automatically transfer

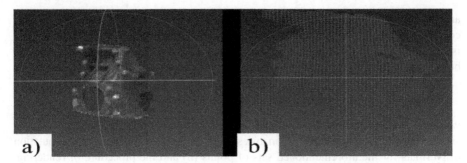

Fig. 4. a) Point cloud of differential, b) mesh of differential

the differential to the CNC-working center, to apply the deviations. If there are not any deviations, then the part is transferred to the buffer. The proposed method is based on the implementation of a k-nearest neighbor (k-NN) classification algorithm. The algorithm automatically detects the center of the CAD file in the Cartesian coordinate system. Afterwards, based on the user-selected accuracy (n), the edges of the original CAD are divided with n dots and the distance between each point and the origin is calculated. Then the algorithm detects if there are any deviations (Fig. 5).

$$C_n = \left[k_n(x_n, y_n, z_n) - d_n(x_n, y_n, z_n) \right] \tag{2}$$

where Cn is the value of the n-th (x, y, z) point of the deviation matrix, and k_n and d_n are the cartesian distances of the original and the scanned item respectively. The deviation results are saved to matrix C (Eq. 2).

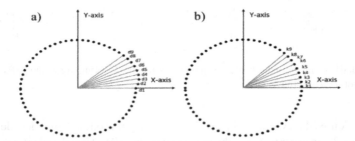

Fig. 5. Deviation algorithm principle: a) scanned item converted to CAD, b) original CAD

This matrix has n rows and 3 columns (for axes X, Y, Z).

$$C = \begin{bmatrix} -1.2 & -2.43 & -1.44 & \cdots & 0 & \cdots & 0 \\ -1.75 & -1.86 & -2.22 & \cdots & 0 & \cdots & 0 \\ 0 & 0 & 0 & \cdots & 0 & \cdots & -1.11 \end{bmatrix} \tag{3}$$

Afterwards, the algorithm shorts the negative coordinates, and convert them into g-code to be uploaded to the milling machine controller via the Cloud Database. This algorithm operates similarly with the BPA. The deviation algorithm rolls a virtual ball, starting from the center of the CAD towards every edge of the three-dimensional CAD file. After each algorithm recursion, the deviation algorithm measures the distance from center-to-edge. Every time a distance is measured for both the original and printed CAD, the Cartesian coordinates of this edge, are imported to their respective distance matrix. Upon completion of measurements the two distance matrixes of both the original and printed CAD are created ($[D_O] - [D_P]$), the final deviations matrix is formed by their subtraction.

$$[C] = \left[D_{O,i,j,k}\right] - \left[D_{P,i,j,k}\right] \tag{4}$$

where, [C], is the deviation matrix, $\left[D_{O,i,j,k}\right]$ is the distance matrix of the original CAD, and $\left[D_{P,i,j,k}\right]$ is the distance matrix of the printed CAD.

4   Method Implementation

Regarding the IMC, the machines used are a 3D Systems Cube Trio 3D-Printer, an UR 10 robot integrated with an Intel RealSense D435 depth camera for the 3D scanning, and an XYZ RMX 2500 milling machine. From a software point of view, the GUI have been developed in Unity 3D game engine, both as a mobile application and a desktop stand-alone application. The code scripts for the GUIs have been developed in MS™ Visual Studio IDE (Integrated Development Environment) in C#, and in Python for the CAD comparison algorithm. MeshLab has also been utilized as a middleware for parsing

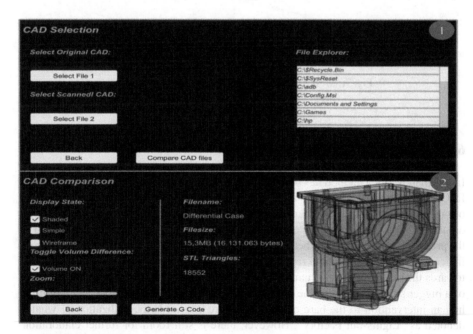

Fig. 6. 1) CAD selection GUI; 2) CAD comparison GUI, with deviation highlighted

the 3D point cloud and the conversion to CAD format. The robot's path was designed in the RoboDK software and exported as a universal report (urp) file for uploading to the controller. The GUIs are displayed in Fig. 6.

5 Results and Discussion

The quality of the mesh grid is essential for the successful operation of the framework, which is also depended to the point cloud quality. Concretely, a more detailed point cloud data can result to a more solid final mesh. The experimentation began by capturing only four images of the differential (one image per side). The resulting mesh is of poor quality (see Fig. 7a) with multiple voids. Thus, several experiments were conducted, increasing the sampling rate each time. The best results have been obtained for 64 sample images. Beyond this sampling rate, the quality improved, but cavities were formed. As illustrated in Fig. 7, for 64 samples the quality of the mesh is 98.7%, with minimal voids.

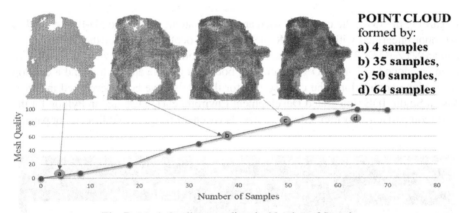

POINT CLOUD
formed by:
a) 4 samples
b) 35 samples,
c) 50 samples,
d) 64 samples

Fig. 7. Mesh Quality regarding the Number of Samples

6 Concluding Remarks and Outlook

In this manuscript a method has been proposed for improving the automation level of an IMC via the utilization of a MV algorithm and a robotic arm for the quality inspection of manufactured products. The key contribution of this research work lies in the development of an algorithm for the comparison of CAD files prior and postproduction of the products/components. Furthermore, the results presented in the previous paragraphs indicate that the precision and repeatability of robotic arms has to be further exploited towards the direction of 3D scanning and quality control. The presented method is part of a bigger solution, towards the complete automation of the shop-floor level, limiting human intervention to the bare minimum required, towards the realization of what is denoted as "Lights-out Factory". However, there is still room for further elaboration. More specifically, since robotic manipulators can multipurposed, future research work, will be focused on the development of an intelligent robotic end effector, which will enable the robotic arm to handle different geometries, and use a separate end effector for the depth camera. Concretely, the cell presented, will be integrated with an automatic tool changer for the end effector, enabling the robot to select through a wider variety of tools. By extension the cell can be further optimized in order to utilize the robot in light machining operations instead of using the CNC milling machine, and thus achieve greater energy economy. Future work will also be head towards the further elaboration of the CAD conversion and comparison algorithm, in order to reduce geometry voids and eliminate surface imperfections (e.g. casting marks) that do not affect the operation of the component but appear as deviation from the original CAD (which has a totally smooth surface).

References

1. Liu, C., Zheng, P., Xu, X.: Digitalisation and servitisation of machine tools in the era of Industry 4.0: a review. Int. J. Prod. Res. 1–33 (2021). https://doi.org/10.1080/00207543.2021.1969462
2. Mourtzis, D.: Simulation in the design and operation of manufacturing systems: state of the art and new trends. Int. J. Prod. Res. 58(7), 1927–1949 (2020). https://doi.org/10.1080/00207543.2019.1636321
3. Wang, X., Wang, Y., Tao, F., Liu, A.: New paradigm of data-driven smart customisation through digital twin. J. Manuf. Syst. 58, 270–280. https://doi.org/10.1016/j.jmsy.2020.07.023
4. Lieto, A., Lebiere, C., Oltramari, A.: The knowledge level in cognitive architectures: current limitations and possible developments. Cogn. Syst. Res. 48, 39–55 (2018). https://doi.org/10.1016/j.cogsys.2017.05.001
5. Aydin, N., Ray, Y., Zhong, X.L., Bogdan, I.-E.: Review of machine learning technologies and artificial intelligence in modern manufacturing systems. In: Mourtzis, D. (ed.) Design and Operation of Production Networks for Mass Personalization in the Era of Cloud Technology. Elsevier, Amsterdam, pp. 317–348 (2022). https://doi.org/10.1016/B978-0-12-823657-4.00002-6
6. Yang, T., Yi, X., Lu, S., Johansson, K.H., Chai, T.: Intelligent manufacturing for the process industry driven by industrial artificial intelligence. Engineering 7(9), 1224–1230 (2021). https://doi.org/10.1016/j.eng.2021.04.023
7. Dogan, A., Birant, D.: Machine learning and data mining in manufacturing. Expert Syst. Appl. 166, 114060 (2021). https://doi.org/10.1016/j.eswa.2020.114060
8. Mourtzis, D.: Machine Tool 4.0 in the Era of Digital Manufacturing (2020). https://doi.org/10.46354/i3m.2020.emss.060
9. Weichert, D., Link, P., Stoll, A., Rüping, S., Ihlenfeldt, S., Wrobel, S.: A review of machine learning for the optimization of production processes. Int. J. Adv. Manuf. Technol. 104(5–8), 1889–1902 (2019). https://doi.org/10.1007/s00170-019-03988-5
10. Yin, S., Ji, W., Wang, L.: A machine learning based energy efficient trajectory planning approach for industrial robots. Procedia CIRP 81, 429–434 (2019). https://doi.org/10.1016/j.procir.2019.03.074
11. Mourtzis, D., Angelopoulos, J., Dimitrakopoulos, G.: Design and development of a flexible manufacturing cell in the concept of learning factory paradigm for the education of generation 4.0 engineers. Procedia Manuf. 45, 361–366 (2020). https://doi.org/10.1016/j.promfg.2020.04.035

12. Ma, L., Xie, W., Zhang, Y.: Blister defect detection based on convolutional neural network for polymer lithium-ion battery. Appl. Sci. **9**(6), 1085 (2019). https://doi.org/10.3390/app906 1085
13. Staar, B., Lütjen, M., Freitag, M.: Anomaly detection with convolutional neural networks for industrial surface inspection. Procedia CIRP **79**, 484–489 (2019). https://doi.org/10.1016/j.procir.2019.02.123
14. Pachner, S., Miethlinger, J.: Smart data analysis for optimized manufacturing of powder coatings on co-rotating twin screw extruders. AIP Conf. Proc. **2055**(1), 070010 (2019). https://doi.org/10.1063/1.5084854
15. Lokrantz, A., Gustavsson, E., Jirstrand, M.: Root cause analysis of failures and quality deviations in manufacturing using machine learning. Procedia CIRP **72**, 1057–1066 (2018). https://doi.org/10.1016/j.procir.2018.03.229
16. Sumesh, A., Rameshkumar, K., Mohandas, K., Babu, R.-S.: Use of machine learning algorithms for weld quality monitoring using acoustic signature. Procedia Comput. Sci. **50**, 316–322 (2015). https://doi.org/10.1016/j.procs.2015.04.042
17. Tsurumine, Y., Cui, Y., Uchibe, E., Matsubara, T.: Deep reinforcement learning with smooth policy update: application to robotic cloth manipulation. Robot. Autonom. Syst. **112**, 72–83 (2019). https://doi.org/10.1016/j.robot.2018.11.004
18. Bernardini, F., Mittleman, J., Rushmeier, H., Silva, C., Taubin, G.: The ball-pivoting algorithm for surface reconstruction. IEEE Trans. Visualization Comput. Graph. **5**(4), 349–359 (1999). https://doi.org/10.1109/2945.817351

Evaluation of Potential Benefits of Augmented Reality for Industrial Services

Stephan Bollinger[1], Volker Stich[2], Lennard Holst[2], Florian Defèr[2], and Florian Schuldt[2(✉)]

[1] YNCORIS GmbH & Co., KG, Industriestr. 300, 50354 Hürth, Germany
[2] Research Institute for Industrial Management (FIR) at RWTH Aachen, Campus-Boulevard 55, 52074 Aachen, Germany
`Florian.Schuldt@fir.rwth-aachen.de`

Abstract. Augmented reality seems to offer great potential benefits in the field of industrial services. However, the question of the exact benefits, both monetary and qualitative, is difficult to evaluate, as is the case with IT investments in general. Within the framework of the DM4AR research project, an evaluation model was therefore developed. Based on group discussions and interviews on potential AR use cases, a list of monetary and qualitative benefits was compiled to form the basis for selecting suitable evaluation modules in the existing literature. These include an impact chain analysis in the form of a strategy map, a monetary evaluation as a calculation of the return on investment, based on the assumptions of the use case as well as existing studies, and a qualitative evaluation in the form of a utility analysis. The outcome is an evaluation model in the form of a multi-perspective approach that considers the impact of AR in the four perspectives of the balanced scorecard (financial, customer, internal business processes, learning and growth). The results of the qualitative and monetary evaluation can be summarized in a 2D matrix to support decision-making.

Keywords: Augmented reality · Potential benefits · Evaluation · Return on investment

1 Introduction

The topic of Augmented Reality (AR) is becoming increasingly relevant in industrial practice [1]. This is primarily due to technological advances in the areas of graphics processors, displays and RAM [2]. AR glasses and handheld devices such as tablets or smartphones can superimpose computer-generated objects on the user's natural perspective and thus provide context-related information [3].

In contrast to virtual reality (VR), the focus is on the real environment in which work can be performed on real objects [4]. AR technology therefore can offer great potential in the area of industrial services, in which activities are carried out for the inspection, maintenance, repair and optimization of machines and systems [5].

© IFIP International Federation for Information Processing 2022
Published by Springer Nature Switzerland AG 2022
D. Y. Kim et al. (Eds.): APMS 2022, IFIP AICT 663, pp. 135–144, 2022.
https://doi.org/10.1007/978-3-031-16407-1_17

However, as with IT investments in general, the question of ex ante evaluation of the benefits is difficult, since qualitative effects are often expected as well and a one-dimensional evaluation (only financial indicators) is therefore not necessarily expedient, although monetary values are ultimately the deciding factor in an investment decision [6]. In the literature, there are various criteria for evaluating AR, but often no reproducible methodology [7].

In the research project "Data Management for Augmented Reality" (DM4AR), group discussions and interviews with relevant stakeholders were used to analyze various AR use cases, their potential benefits, and impacts on the company. Based on this, a multi-perspective approach [8] was chosen for a balanced evaluation and suitable evaluation modules for monetary and qualitative benefits were selected from existing literature. The evaluation should already be possible at an early stage in the implementation process, when only an elaborated use case concept is available [9]. To validate the model, a first application was conducted by the project team at YNCORIS. The superior goal of this work is therefore to evaluate the benefit of the usage of AR in industrial service not only monetarily but holistically. This represents a gain in knowledge to the extent that only the monetary evaluation has been in the foreground up to now.

2   State of the Art

There are already some approaches that allow different forms of evaluation and consider the content focus of AR and industrial service in different ways. The utility analysis or scoring model, as a classical evaluation approach of the multi-criteria decision analysis, enables a qualitative evaluation, where the uni-dimensional methods of the economic investment calculation are not sufficient [10]. The four perspectives of the Balanced Scorecard (BSC) by Kaplan and Norton can be used to assess the impact on the entire company and also consider the potential of information systems as part of the learning and growth perspective [11].

Schuh et al. developed a procedure to evaluate Industry 4.0 use cases at an early stage by using a two-part approach, monetary in the form of the payoff method and non-monetary in the form of the aforementioned utility analysis. The results are compiled in a portfolio matrix [9]. In their multi-criteria evaluation of industrial assistance systems, Zigart and Schlund provide an overview of possible evaluation methods. For a balanced evaluation, five perspectives are considered, based on the BSC. However, a precise methodology for the application and consolidation of the results is not provided [12]. Müller et al. developed a multi-perspective approach [8] primarily for evaluating controlling application systems, but it is also applicable to information systems in general [13]. Different evaluation methods are assigned here to the various potential benefits to enable an adequate evaluation of these benefits.

Concrete return on investment calculations for the use of AR are made by Forrester Research, Inc. in their Total Economic Impact approach [14, 15], as well as by the AR for Enterprise Alliance (AREA) [16]. Both use data from fictitious enterprise use cases for this purpose.

3 Model for Evaluating Potential Benefits of Augmented Reality in Industrial Service

3.1 Identification and Classification of Potential Benefits of AR

In the considerations of possible use cases in the DM4AR research project and an additional literature review, various potential benefits of AR technology were identified. Potential benefits, as all possible positive effects of an investment on the company's objectives [13], can be differentiated according to their quantifiability and their monetary evaluability [17]. Table 1 categorizes the potential of AR technology in terms of its monetary value. The potentials that can be monetarily valued are primarily those that can lead directly to cost savings but also to increases in revenue.

Table 1. Categorization of potential benefits of AR

Monetizable benefits	Non-monetizable benefits
• Increase service productivity	• Improve data currency & quality
• Increase expert productivity	• Improve knowledge transfer
• Reduce process lead time	• Increase flexibility
–Operational processes more efficient	• Improve employee satisfaction
–Support processes more efficient	• Increase transparency
–Avoid waiting/driving times	• Ensure compliance
Improve service quality	• Improve safety/working conditions
–Avoid rework & follow-up visits	• Promote sustainability
–Improve error identification	• Improve service quality
• Reduce training time	• Reduce customer complaints
• Avoid travel/trip costs	• Shorten response time
• Reduce material costs	• Reduce customer downtime
• Increase turnover	• Differentiate service offerings
	• Improve corporate brand awareness
	• Improve customer satisfaction

3.2 Methodology – Multi-perspective Approach

The basic structure of the methodology for evaluating the potential benefits is based on the multi-perspective approach [8]. The advantage here is that suitable evaluation methods can be selected depending on the type of potential benefit. The identified potential benefits can be grouped into several overarching categories. For a balanced view of the impact on the overall company or business unit, these categories should cover all four perspectives of the BSC (see Fig. 1). Different evaluation methods can then be assigned to the various categories. For the evaluation of AR usage in industrial service, three different evaluation methods were selected: The strategy map of the BSC as an impact chain analysis, a calculation of the return on investment for monetary evaluation, and the qualitative evaluation in the form of a utility analysis. The monetary evaluation includes the financial perspective and those improvements in processes and quality that can be monetized, such as reduced process times and increased first-time fixed rates (FTFR). All other factors are only evaluated qualitatively. To combine the monetary and qualitative assessment into a decision-making framework, a two-dimensional matrix can be used to plot the utility score against the ROI. Different areas can recommend implementation, refrain, or further discussion. This specific multi-perspective evaluation model is explicitly designed for the AR application use case (see Fig. 1).

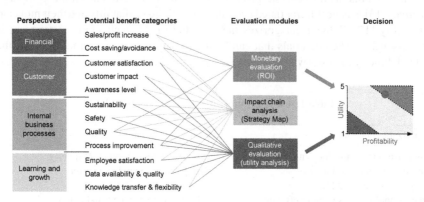

Fig. 1. Overview of the evaluation model based on a multi-perspective approach

3.3 Cause-Effect Relations of Potential Benefits – Strategy Map

The strategy map as an impact chain analysis is less of an evaluation procedure, but it does reveal the dependencies of the various potential benefits and thus ensures transparency and a better understanding. Another advantage is that all potential benefits can be considered in this analysis. In this way, it also provides the basis for considerations in the later evaluation procedures. As mentioned in the introduction, this specific strategy map is based on group discussions and interviews with relevant stakeholders of different AR use cases.

Starting from the potentials offered by a new information system, it is possible to infer the consequential effects for the other perspectives all the way to the financial result for the company through logical linkage (see Fig. 2). The benefits of an AR information system initially have a positive impact on the employees by empowering them for new tasks and increasing their flexibility, which leads to increased employee satisfaction. From a process perspective, this results in increased service productivity by shortening the training time for new employees, reducing process cycle times, eliminating trips and travel, and saving materials. This also promotes sustainability. Security and compliance can be ensured through workflows and checklists that provide contextual security guidance, whereas automated documentation leads to greater transparency. In combination with better empowerment of employees, this also increases the quality of work. There are also direct positive effects for the customer. Faster response times and more efficient processes reduce plant downtime. At the same time, the increased quality leads to fewer complaints. Through AR, differentiated service offers can be made to differentiate from the competition. All in all, this leads to increased customer satisfaction, can also raise the company's brand awareness and result in sales increases. Together with cost savings on the process side, this leads to a positive ROI.

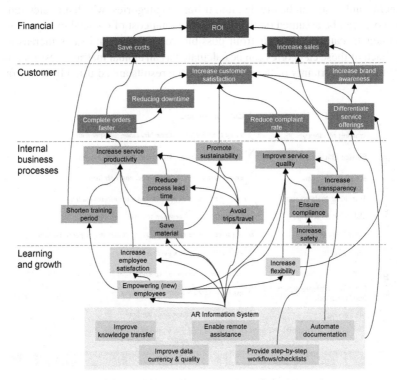

Fig. 2. Strategy Map for AR in maintenance

3.4 Monetary Evaluation – ROI

The monetary evaluation should lead to transparency in the question of whether the use of augmented reality in industrial service also leads to a measurable return on investment (ROI). In a 2018 survey, 62% of respondents answered that this is the case [18]. Direct added value for the company can result from efficiency gains, more flexible employee deployment, time or cost savings in both training and processes, and improved quality [1]. ROI can generally be calculated using the following formula [14]:

$$ROI = \text{net benefits} / \text{costs} = (\text{benefits} - \text{costs}) / \text{costs} \tag{1}$$

The ROI thus compares the benefits with the costs. For the calculation, the cash flows associated with the use of AR must be estimated and their present value (PV) determined by discounting them to the valuation date using a discount rate i and a period t. A typical assessment period for IT investments of 3 years [16] was selected.

$$PV = \text{cash flow} \times (1+i)^{-t} \tag{2}$$

Benefits and costs can be divided into different categories, which are later summed up. The costs can be assumed on the basis of the total cost of ownership approach [19] and the benefit categories result from possible cost savings and sales increases (see Fig. 3). Each of these categories can be calculated as an annual metric by estimation. To account for the uncertainty of the assumptions, the results are adjusted by a risk factor.

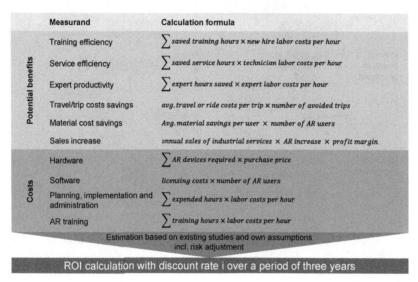

	Measurand	Calculation formula
Potential benefits	Training efficiency	$\sum$ *saved training hours × new hire labor costs per hour*
	Service efficiency	$\sum$ *saved service hours × technician labor costs per hour*
	Expert productivity	$\sum$ *expert hours saved × expert labor costs per hour*
	Travel/trip costs savings	*avg. travel or ride costs per trip × number of avoided trips*
	Material cost savings	*Avg. material savings per user × number of AR users*
	Sales increase	*annual sales of industrial services × AR increase × profit margin*
Costs	Hardware	$\sum$ *AR devices required × purchase price*
	Software	*licensing costs × number of AR users*
	Planning, implementation and administration	$\sum$ *expended hours × labor costs per hour*
	AR training	$\sum$ *training hours × labor costs per hour*

Estimation based on existing studies and own assumptions incl. risk adjustment

ROI calculation with discount rate i over a period of three years

Fig. 3. Benefit and cost categories with related calculation formula

Benefits

Newly hired technicians in industrial service initially accompany experienced employees for the first few months before working independently. AR can shorten this training time and thus increase new hire productivity. Less qualified employees can be deployed earlier in the field if they are guided by AR assistance and can call in an experienced employee via remote support in the event of a problem. Service efficiencies result from service technician efficiencies with AR support, shortened process cycle times, and reduced rework due to increased first-time fix rates. The productivity of experts or operations managers can be increased, as they spend less time on documentation, staff training and knowledge transfer, and on-site visits.

The use of AR can make trips to the site obsolete through remote support and increased FTFR. The greater the distance, the greater will be the savings. For regional companies, only the transportation costs are saved, but for globally active service providers, high travel costs including flight, hotel and expenses can be avoided.

Material costs can also be saved, e.g. for paper, printer ink or even personal protective equipment (PPE). Attributing an increase in sales to a particular technology is difficult, as it is not possible to establish exactly which factors are responsible for the customer's decision to buy [16]. For the sake of completeness, however, this potential benefit was also included in the evaluation.

Costs

When selecting AR hardware, companies have several options. The AR visualization can be displayed through AR glasses, but also on a tablet or smartphone. However, the hardware should be determined by the use case, e.g. the need for hands-free work favors glasses. One advantage of handhelds, however, is that they are already in widespread use in many companies and thus incur only minor additional hardware costs [20].

The use of an AR software solution requires licensing costs per user, which must be taken into account too. The time and cost, as well as expertise and employee acceptance, required to successfully implement an AR solution should not be underestimated. While the remote function is implemented quickly, a significantly greater effort must be made for work instructions and 3D visualizations, which have to be iteratively improved until the application delivers the added value for the user. [15] Lastly, personnel costs during employee training for AR technology must also be considered.

Exemplary ROI Calculation

To validate the model, an exemplary calculation of the ROI for a possible application scenario at YNCORIS was carried out (see Fig. 4). Existing studies on improvements from AR [14–16, 18, 21, 22] can be used as a reference to better estimate the potential benefits. In the further course of the project, the evaluation can be carried out again with more precise information, e.g., through own tests on process efficiencies.

	Year 0	Year 1	Year 2	Year 3	Total	Present value
Total costs	477.452 €	247.458 €	386.208 €	345.063 €	1.456.181 €	1.280.845 €
Total benefits	0 €	524.980 €	1.258.038 €	1.563.928 €	3.346.947 €	2.691.958 €
Net benefits	-477.452 €	277.523 €	871.830 €	1.218.865 €	1.890.766 €	1.411.114 €

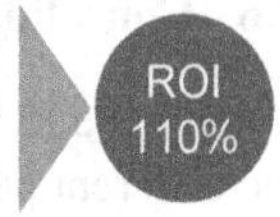

ROI 110%

Fig. 4. Exemplary ROI calculation of a possible AR implementation at YNCORIS

3.5 Qualitative Evaluation – Utility Analysis

The purely monetary evaluation does not consider many of the identified potential benefits. The utility analysis is a suitable instrument for evaluating the benefits of AR technology in qualitative terms as well. It was originally developed to compare different alternatives [10]. In this case, this purpose is slightly modified by evaluating the changes to the status quo. However, another use case can be the comparison between different application options in terms of teams or business segments.

This module evaluates the benefit categories of all perspectives except financial. Quality and process improvements were also partially evaluated in monetary terms, but this is not possible for other potential benefits in these categories, such as improved transparency, which is why these are also evaluated qualitatively.

The rating is based on a cardinal scale of 1–5, with the mean value of 3 corresponding to no change compared to the status quo (see Table 2).

Table 2. Cardinal scale for qualitative evaluation

1	2	3	4	5
Strong deterioration/neg. Impact	Slight deterioration/neg. Impact	No change/impact	Slight improvement/pos. Impact	Strong improvement/pos. Impact

In the customer perspective, it can be evaluated whether there are direct effects (pos./neg.) on the customer and how customer satisfaction and brand awareness change. In the internal process perspective, safety and sustainability are assessed in addition to process and quality changes. And in the learning and growth perspective, changes in data timeliness and quality, knowledge transfer and flexibility, and the impact on employee satisfaction are evaluated. Preferences of the decision makers, which should be selected in an interdisciplinary and use case dependent manner, can be taken into account by weighting the different criteria, e.g. by pairwise comparison [9]. The qualitative score is calculated by multiplying the criteria values by the respective weighting and then summing them up [17]. When evaluating the criteria, the challenges and risks of AR use should also be considered. These include network connectivity, IT security, privacy rights of employees, user-friendliness and user acceptance, 'motion sickness' and a possible increased distance between service technician and customer [15, 23].

3.6 Consolidation of Results and Decision Support – 2D-Matrix

Finally, the ROI and the score of the utility analysis (total score, or the partial scores of the different perspectives) can be compared in a two-dimensional coordinate system of profitability and qualitative utility (see Fig. 1). The further up on the right the application scenario can be plotted, the more beneficial the implementation of the project. The area at the bottom left, on the other hand, represents an unfavorable implementation. If the point lies in between, further discussions and investigations may be necessary. Each company must determine the exact ranges according to its own preferences in order to perform an appropriate assessment in each case. An example of such an assessment is included in Fig. 1.

4 Conclusion

The model presented enables an initial evaluation of AR use in industrial service, both economically and qualitatively. In doing so, it can be used to evaluate AR technology in general based on a possible use case, or to compare different application scenarios.

The model is being tested with different use cases as part of the DM4AR project. The evaluation is based on own assumptions and data from previous studies, which can be replaced at a later stage with improved information from own user tests and time and motion studies, for example before the approval of piloting or the approval of roll-out. In addition, the evaluation of concrete hardware and software solutions and their impact on users should also be investigated in a next step. Additionally, subject evaluations need to be conducted regarding the usability and task load of the use of AR applications.

References

1. Adelmann, R.: Augmented Reality in der industriellen Praxis. In: Orsolits, H., Lackner, M. (eds.) Virtual Reality und Augmented Reality in der Digitalen Produktion, pp. 7–32. Springer Fachmedien Wiesbaden, Wiesbaden (2020)
2. Kind, S., Ferdinand, J.-P., Jetzke, T., Richter, S., Weide, S.: Virtual and augmented reality. Status quo, Herausforderungen und zukünftige Entwicklungen (2019). https://www.tab-beim-bundestag.de/de/pdf/publikationen/berichte/TAB-Arbeitsbericht-ab180.pdf. Accessed 4 Nov 2021
3. Syberfeldt, A., Danielsson, O., Gustavsson, P.: Augmented reality smart glass-es in the smart factory: product evaluation guidelines and review of available products. IEEE Access **5**, 9118–9130 (2017). https://doi.org/10.1109/ACCESS.2017.2703952
4. Shinde, G.R.: Internet of things integrated augmented reality. In: SpringerBriefs in Applied Sciences and Technology Ser. Springer Singapore Pte. Limited, Singapore (2021)
5. DIN EN 13306: DIN EN 13306:2018–02, Instandhaltung_- Begriffe der Instandhaltung; Dreisprachige Fassung EN_13306:2017. Beuth Verlag GmbH, Berlin ICS 01.040.03, 03.080.10(13306:2018–02) (2018)
6. Kesten, R., Müller, A., Schröder, H.: IT-Controlling. Messung und Steuerung des Wertbeitrags der IT, 1st edn. Vahlen, München (2007)
7. Zigart, T., Schlund, S.: Evaluation of augmented reality technologies in manufacturing – a literature review. In: Nunes, I.L. (ed.) Advances in Human Fac-tors and Systems Interaction. Proceedings of the AHFE 2020 Virtual Confer-ence on Human Factors and Systems Inter-action, USA, 16–20 July 2020, vol. 1207. Springer eBook Collection, vol. 1207, 1st edn., pp. 75–82. Springer, Cham (2020)
8. Müller, A., Lang, J., Hess, T.: Wirtschaftlichkeit von Controlling-Anwendungssystemen: Konzeption und Erprobung eines Multiperspektiven-Ansatzes. In: Hess, T. (ed.) Anwen-dungssysteme im Controlling: Was treibt die Entwicklung? ZfCM-Sonderheft, vol. 2, pp. 58–66. Gabler Verlag, Wiesbaden, s.l. (2003)
9. Schuh, G., et al.: Industrie 4.0: Implement it! Ein Leitfaden zur erfolgreichen Implementierung von Industrie 4.0-Lösungen, 1st edn. Werkzeugmaschinenlabor der Rheinisch-Westfälischen Technischen Hochschule Aachen, Aachen (2018)
10. Zangemeister, C.: Nutzwertanalyse in der Systemtechnik. Eine Methodik zur multidimen-sionalen Bewertung und Auswahl von Projektalternativen. Teilw. zugl.: Berlin, Univ., Diss., 1970, 5th edn. Books on Demand, Norderstedt (2014)
11. Kaplan, R.S., Norton, D.P.: The Balanced Scorecard. Translating Strategy into Action. HBS Press, Harvard (1996
12. Zigart, T., Schlund, S.: Multikriterielle Evaluation von industriellen Assistenzsystemen am Beispiel von Augmented Reality-Anwendungen in der Produktion. In: Gesellschaft für Arbeitswissenschaft e.V. (ed.) GfA-Frühjahrskongress 2020 // Digitale Arbeit, digitaler Wandel, digitaler Mensch? Digitaler Wandel, digitale Arbeit, digitaler Mensch? // 66. Kongress der

Gesellschaft für Arbeitswissenschaft, TU Berlin, Fachgebiet Mensch-Maschine-Systeme/HU Berlin, Professur Ingenieurpsychologie, Berlin, 16–18 März 2020, pp. 1–5. GfA-Press, Dortmund (2020)

13. Becker, A.: Nutzenpotenziale und Herausforderungen Service-orientierter Architekturen. SpringerLink Bücher. Gabler, Wiesbaden (2011)

14. Forrester Research, Inc.: The Total Economic Impact™ Of PTC Vuforia. Cost Savings And Business Benefits Enabled By Industrial Augmented Reality (2019). https://www.ptc.com/-/media/Files/PDFs/Augmented-Reality/The-Total-Economic-Impact-of-PTC-Vuforia_2019.pdf. Accessed 24 Nov 2021

15. Forrester Research, Inc.: The Total Economic Impact Of Mixed Reality Using Microsoft HoloLens 2 (2021). https://download.microsoft.com/download/e/1/3/e1364937-5f62-4a0c-bb9e-664c270ad4fe/Forrester-Total-Economic-Impact-Mixed-Reality-Microsoft-HoloLens-2_Cover.pdf. Accessed 14 Feb 2022

16. AR for Enterprise Alliance (AREA): Case Study – ROI Analysis for AR Use in Maintenance & Repair Operations (2017). http://thearea.org/wp-content/uploads/2018/05/AREA-Enterprise-AR-ROI-Case-Study.pdf. Accessed 24 Jan 2022

17. Pietsch, T.: Bewertung von Informations- und Kommunikationssystemen. Ein Vergleich betriebswirtschaftlicher Verfahren, 2nd edn. E. Schmidt, Berlin (2003)

18. Mainelli, T.: How augmented reality drives real-world gains in services, training, sales and marketing, and manufacturing (2018). https://www.ptc.com/-/media/Files/PDFs/IoT/IDC-AR-Use-Cases-Report.pdf. Accessed 18 Oct 2021

19. Mieritz, L., Kirwin, B.: Defining gartner total cost of ownership (2005). https://barsand.files.wordpress.com/2015/03/gartner_tco.pdf. Accessed 11 Apr2022

20. Llamas, R.T., Dialani, M.: Augmented reality is ready and open for business (2020). https://www.ptc.com/-/media/Files/PDFs/Augmented-Reality/IDC-AR-Is-Ready-and-Open-for-Business.pdf. Accessed 24 Jan 2022

21. Lyden, S.: Fix it right the first time: first-time fix rate calculation (2015). https://fsd.servicemax.com/2015/04/13/first-time-fix-rate-field-service-metrics-that-matter/. Accessed 15 Jan 2022

22. Porter, M.E., Heppelmann, J.E.: Why every organization needs an augmented reality strategy. Harv. Bus. Rev. **95**(2017), 46–57 (2017)

23. Gutsche, K., Eigenstetter, M.: Dienstleistungsproduktivität in der smarten Produktion. Mensch und Automation in der industriellen Instandhaltung. wt (2019). https://doi.org/10.37544/1436-4980-2019-07-08-4

Lean Digital Twins in Production Machines: Case Study in Pharmaceutical Industry

Leandro Nunes da Silva$^{(\boxtimes)}$ ⓘ and Rodrigo Franco Gonçalves ⓘ

Universidade Paulista – UNIP, São Paulo SP, Brasil
leandro.silva405@aluno.unip.br

Abstract. The present work has the objective to present a lean digital twin applied in a production line of medications in a pharmaceutical industry. Digital twins are standardization of design of software or digital representations of an active. The proposal of a lean digital twin starts from the concept of lean manufacture. The adoption of a practical solution, agile, flexible, innovative and efficient meets a framework that cuts costs and risks from long and time-consuming projects, but with applicability and investment return in a shorter time. Adjusts of the product or process are more dynamic and its efficiency is validated in a short period. The focus of its development is to identify the main problems and present a solution in a general manner and easy understanding. A lean digital twin requires a reduced effort in its development from the hypothesis and evaluations of the problem to be solved and it is dimensioned according to each life cycle previously evaluated.

Keywords: Digital twin · Lean digital twin · Pharmaceutical industry

1 Introduction

Throughout many years the pharmaceutical industry has been attracting the attention of society, academics and big governments and private corporations. Pandemics outbreaks, degenerative diseases, and the aging of the populations have made this sector very important and fundamental in the social wellbeing of each citizen.

This sector is in the avant-garde of the development of high technological products that help to cure and treat ill patients. Biotechnology, digital twins, internet of things, Big Data, Blockchain, among others technologies from the so called 4.0 industry, take these two areas to a higher position inside the manufactory.

These technologies meet the needs and expectations of the population, providing a better quality in the products, management of patients and providing tools to improve the quality of life and the products. Among them the digital twin has arisen as a promising tool for the pharmaceutical industry concerning digitalization of the production line and processes inside the manufacture and patient care.

Even though, and in spite of great advantages of the digital twin, the researchers and authors ensure that it is far from being consolidated in its application in the industry of medications and similar.

© IFIP International Federation for Information Processing 2022
Published by Springer Nature Switzerland AG 2022
D. Y. Kim et al. (Eds.): APMS 2022, IFIP AICT 663, pp. 145–151, 2022.
https://doi.org/10.1007/978-3-031-16407-1_18

The biggest part of the applications is focused on the simulations of substances or parts of the processes. Others are the applications of big technological companies which do it in a wide fashion demanding huge financial investments.

Thanks to this a lot of projects and applications end up getting undermined and some do not meet the particular demands in each case inside the production line.

The objective of this work is to present a solution that fills this gap: leaning digital twin focusing on a dynamic application in the pharmaceutical industry.

To do so it has been developed a leaning digital twin with devices of the internet of things, sensors, camera and interface man-machine in one powder compressor machine to produce pills with two layers.

The machine in which the twinning was made had its main functions transferred to the virtual world and received new functions in the real world. For this interaction was made a connection via communication protocol joining the two worlds.

To understand how the work was done the following sections describe the theory referential, including applications and studies of digital twin in the pharmaceutical industry and health area e medical care in the Sect. 2. In Sect. 3 is described the real world equipment, the lean digital twin, its concepts and implementation. In Sect. 4 discussions and results are presented. Finally, in Sect. 5 there is the conclusion and proposals for future works.

2 Theoretical References

2.1 The Concept of Digital Twin

The digital twin, in its fundamental concept, is described as the representation of a device, machine, equipment or real-world system to the digital world. Its application in the modeling of goods tangibles or not tangibles joins these two universes.

It is this union that differs from simulators. The modeling used by digital twins gets mixed up with simulators in the majority of the works. What makes them distinctive is the interaction which the digital twin has (or might have) with his real twin.

Basically, its model is described by physical product, virtual product and its connections. This proposal was presented by Michael Grieves [1], in 2003, in his work about the "life cycle of product management". In spite of this concept not being profoundly specific, it has been conceived as a preliminary form of conceptualization.

Some authors make reference to the concept introduced by teacher Greeves but they also report the review made by National Aeronautics and Space Administration (NASA), in 2012, bringing a new reevaluation of the concepts, with a new perspective about the digital twin, defining it as a simulation Multiphysics, multiscale, probabilistic, high-fidelity which translates the state of the twin, based on its historic, capture of data by sensors in real time and modeling and physical model [2].

2.2 Pharmaceutical Industry Application

The application of digital twins in the pharmaceutical industry has grown a lot recently. In spite of this evolution, researchers assure that this process is just in the initial phase and far from being consolidated [3].

In [4] one better application of the digital twins in the industry lacks a pattern that improves the production of modeling tools.

In [5], it presents one application with focus on the dynamism of the production line, synchronizing data in real time, and coming from the equipment for future analyzes.

The work of [6] describes the theoretical modeling of a powder compressing through a digital twin, and also its continuum process of working in the real world.

In a similar study, [7] explains the modeling mathematics of one coated pill machine and how it could be generated as a digital twin of it.

In [8] shows the development of one digital twin for a continuum process with low demand for a mixture of pharmaceutical powder.

In [9] explores the benefits of the simulation to a later adoption of the digital twin in the production line of the multinational pharmaceutical Roche GmbH for supporting the decision in real time of the manufacturing process.

The work of [10] presents one proposal of digital twin in supply chain in the pharmaceutical industry, focusing gaps observed in systems ERP, without considering a product or physical service and the use of a digital twin in co-property with the product or service.

In [11] has proposed a digital twin for projects of processes based on Quality by Design (QbD) in the pharmaceutical industry. In this work he used a device Arduino together with automation devices for a better valorization of the biomass, adapting the extraction process to the comportment of the extracted components.

3 Development and Application in the Machine

The machine modeling in the digital world was a powder compress (Fig. 1a), in use in the primary production line of solids. Its origin is from a German manufacturer, from 2007. Its weight, according to the manufacturer, is 1855 kg. It works in shifts of 24 h a day, seven days a week.

The machine works with a capacity to produce between 15000 and 30000 pills per hour (4 to 8 pills per second respectively) because of its current physical conditions.

Information, such as pressure made by punctures hydraulic and pneumatic parts, powders feeders, physical dimensions and signals of the logical controller programmable of the machine were considered irrelevant. So, this information does not add value and was kept out of the digital twin.

Among the relevant information can be cited the distance between the matrixes (shape of the pills) of 34 mm and the diameter of each matrix, of 10 mm. The direction of turn of the table, the perimeter and the position of the discard of the pill also formed were taken in consideration to the digital twin.

We called Lean Digital Twin the idea of only representing the aspects that really add value: information that can improve quality, reduce lead time, loss and costs [12, 13]. The Lean Digital Twin utilizes minimum modeling characteristics; only functions that add value to the process, reducing the modeling and implementation costs.

The lean digital twin electronics was constructed in an Arduino Mega board, placed onboard for prototyping, with a simple plant representation (not 3D representation) in the digital user interface. In it were added additional boards to treat the signals received

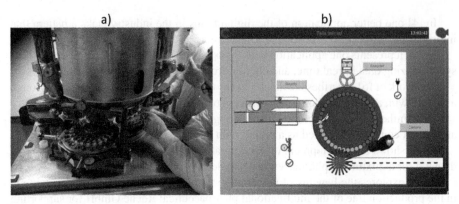

Fig. 1. a) Real world powder compressor; b) powder compressor Lean digital twin. Finished prototype. (Source: the authors)

by sensors and sending command signals for acting installed in the real twin, as well as, the board for communication and an interface screen between the two (Fig. 1b).

The flow chart presented in the Fig. 2 shows the functioning of the software of the lean digital twin integrated to the real twin.

A camera to register the pills in the matrixes was installed. The communication of the camera controller with the lean digital twin is realized by a net Ethernet and Modbus protocol. The data are transmitted almost instantaneously. The lean digital twin updated the information by a transmission rate between 100 and 200 ms to the screen that makes it possible to visualize the event of the movement of the matrixes almost without delays (considering the speed of the nominal work of 15000 and 30000 pills per hour (between each pill there are125 ms in the highest and 250 ms in the lowest).

The camera is installed after the first filling of powder from the matrix and just after the insertion in the nucleon where there is no interference in the acquisition of the image of the pill's nucleon inserted inside the matrix.

Previously established and evaluated the presence of the nucleon inside the pill, the turn of the table and the movement verified, the next step is to realize the transfer of this signal until the segregation of the product considered approved and the product to be rejected.

An encoder programmable was installed by contact to the turntable. It was parameterized so each pulse corresponded to a certain distance measure. When starting moving the pulses begin to be transmitted. For each lap, a certain quantity of pulses is generated, according to what was initially programmed through the software supplied by the encoder manufacturer. For each application, one millimeter of distance corresponds to three pulses in the encoder.

One resolution of three pulses per millimeter was considered to provide precision of reading realized by the encoder. This information assures the exact moment of the inspection of the pill inserted, located inside the matrix and also the moment of the expulsion of the defected pill to be rejected in the exit of the machine.

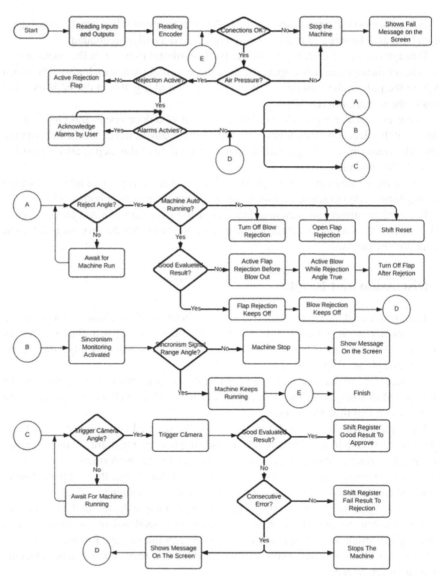

Fig. 2. Flow chart of the functioning of software of the lean digital twin (Source: from the author)

To determine the speed and the functioning of the machine in turning, two inductive sensors were added to identify each passage of puncture and know the rotation direction of the table.

The lean digital twin determines the expulsion of the pill to be rejected. It is realized when the lean digital twin determines the end of the cycle.

In the end of the movement cycle of the pill there is a transfer gutter for two recipients to accommodate the pills according to their previous evaluation.

Two actuators electropneumatic (solenoids valves) were installed, one to blow (eject) the bad pill and the other to make the opening of the door (flap) redundant.

Through one valve electro pneumatic, the lean digital twin sends the command to blow the air through the holes opened in one piece of real twin, which also serves as a guide to the pills in the turn table exit in the direction of a gutter in the table exit that leads to the segregation recipients.

To ensure that these pills do not mix in the gutter a door opens and closes at the moment of this decision. This door is prompted by the lean digital twin together with the blow valve, ensuring one bigger redundancy on the safety of this step against a possible mix with the good pills.

For the interaction between the parts, real and virtual, was put one interface screen man machine (IHM) touch screen so the operator can interact with both worlds.

The configurations and parameterizations of the twins are realized by the user in IHM, which serves as the interface of the lean digital twin. All the process is followed in real time by the user.

4   Discussion and Results

The lean twinning of the compressor was the best alternative found to solve the problem. The automatization is not capable to solving with efficiency and with the same results without a significant rise in the implementation costs and pieces availability, considering the available physical space.

It is necessary to put sensors in excess to know the exact position of each pill in the matrixes and as a new controller to meet the cyclic speed, as well as, interactivity with an interface in real time by the user.

A complete twinning, with 3D modeling and high-speed communication, is more expensive, involving more company sectors, big suppliers or integrators of digital twins, software developers, cutting edge advanced equipment and performance, larger team and more time consumed in the system integration. In this sense, the company project sector had considered that the better solution was the lean twinning.

The lean digital twin was also useful to give a new sense in the use of the equipment. It made possible the digitalization of an equipment considered old without modern technological resources widespread nowadays through the so-called industry 4.0, in a kind of digital retrofit. It was possible to integrate digital systems and virtual in a machine almost all mechanized.

Some obstacles were found along the twinning compressor project. The first one was the impossibility to connect to the internet but soon it was realized that it was not necessary. All the contact and interactivity were made in real time, by the sensors, with the virtual side.

5   Conclusion and Future Works

This work had the objective to use a lean digital twin applied in the pharmaceutical industry. In one powder compressor to make double coated pills in manufactory demonstrated its viability as a process improvement tool and allowed a longer life to the machine.

The digital twin also can be an efficient tool able to provide a longer life to machines and equipment. It is very important in the pharmaceutical industry which follows rigid processes and manufacturing protocols. These protocols do not permit change machines frequently, let alone the high costs to acquire one.

From this project, the new step is to integrate the lean digital twin in an internal communication net between machines (machine to machine – M2M), with the application of block chain to validate parameters modifications done by the digital twin and/or by the users via interface.

References

1. Grieves, M., Vickers, J.: Digital twin: mitigating unpredictable, undesirable emergent behavior in complex systems. In: Kahlen, F.-J., Flumerfelt, S., Alves, A. (eds.) Transdisciplinary perspectives on complex systems, pp. 85–113. Springer, Cham (2017). https://doi.org/10.1007/978-3-319-38756-7_4
2. Glaessgen, E., Stargel, D.: The digital twin paradigm for future NASA and US Air Force vehicles. In: 53rd AIAA/ASME/ASCE/AHS/ASC Structures, 14th AIAA Structural Dynamics and Materials Conference 20th AIAA/ASME/AHS Adaptive Structures Conference, p. 1818 (2012)
3. Augustine, P.: The industry use cases for the digital twin idea. In: Advances in Computers. Elsevier, pp. 79–105 (2020)
4. Tao, F., et al.: Digital twin in industry: state-of-the-art. IEEE Trans. Ind. Inf. **15**(4), 2405–2415 (2018)
5. Negri, E., Pandhare, V., Cattaneo, L., Singh, J., Macchi, M., Lee, J.: Field-synchronized digital twin framework for production scheduling with uncertainty. J. Intell. Manuf. **32**(4), 1207–1228 (2020). https://doi.org/10.1007/s10845-020-01685-9
6. Martin, N.L., et al.: Process modeling and simulation of tableting—an agent-based simulation methodology for direct compression. Pharmaceutics **13**(7), 996 (2021)
7. Ochsenbein, D.R., et al.: Industrial application of heat-and mass balance model for fluid-bed granulation for technology transfer and design space exploration. Int. J. Pharm. X **1**, 100028 (2019)
8. Beke, Á.K., et al.: Digital twin of low dosage continuous powder blending–Artificial neural networks and residence time distribution models. Eur. J. Pharm. Biopharm. **169**, 64–77 (2021)
9. Spindler, J., Kec, T., Ley, T.: Lead-time and risk reduction assessment of a sterile drug product manufacturing line using simulation. Comput. Chem. Eng. **152**, 107401 (2021)
10. Marmolejo-Saucedo, J.A.: Design and development of digital twins: a case study in supply chains. Mob. Networks Appl. **25**(6), 2141–2160 (2020)
11. Uhlenbrock, L., et al.: Digital twin for extraction process design and operation. Processes **8**(7), 866 (2020)
12. Ohno, T., Bodek, N.: Toyota Production System: Beyond Large-Scale Production. Productivity Press, New York (2019)
13. Womack, J.P., Jones, D.T., Roos, D.: The Machine that Changed the World: The Story of Lean Production–Toyota's Secret Weapon in the Global Car Wars that is now Revolutionizing World Industry. Simon and Schuster, New York (2007)

Reconfigurable Manufacturing Systems from a Sustainability Perspective: A Systematic Literature Review

Martha Orellano⬛, Rachel Campos Sabioni(✉)⬛, and Adriana Pacheco⬛

Capgemini Engineering. Direction Recherche and Innovation France, 4 avenue Didier Daurat, 31700 Blagnac, France
rachel.campos-sabioni@capgemini.com

Abstract. Reconfigurable Manufacturing Systems (RMS) are a promising manufacturing paradigm able to quickly respond to changing market needs while being economically viable. The RMS core characteristics can potentially contribute to coping with the sustainability global needs, regarding the three sustainability pillars (i.e., economic, environmental, and social). The aim of this paper is to survey the existing literature on sustainability in RMS context. Throughout a systematic literature review using the PRISMA method, 31 papers were selected for qualitative analysis. Those works were classified according to the three sustainability pillars and the RMS design and operational issues, their main contributions were analyzed, and some research gaps were identified.

Keywords: Sustainability · Reconfigurable manufacturing systems · Changeable manufacturing systems · Sustainable manufacturing

1 Introduction

Historically, manufacturing systems have been a critical driver for the growth of the global economy [1, 2]. However, given the current panorama with a growing population, an increasing demand for product differentiation, the increase of pollution, the accelerated resource depletion and the climate change, productive systems should be environmentally and socially responsible as well as economically efficient [1–3].

From the need to respond to an unpredictable and changeable market facing sustainability issues, emerged the Reconfigurable Manufacturing System (RMS), which combines the high throughput of Dedicated Manufacturing Systems (DMS) and the flexibility of Flexible Manufacturing Systems (FMS) (Table 1). RMS is considered as one of the most suitable production systems to meet the sustainability requirements thanks to its six key characteristics (i.e., modularity, integrability, convertibility, scalability, diagnosability, customization) [1, 4]. These characteristics are directly related to the system's ability to reconfigure, at function and/or capacity level, to meet new market requirements all over its lifecycle. Thanks to the RMS's ability to reconfigure, these systems potentially have longer lifecycles by remaining economically viable. From a social point of view,

D. Y. Kim et al. (Eds.): APMS 2022, IFIP AICT 663, pp. 152–159, 2022.
https://doi.org/10.1007/978-3-031-16407-1_19

RMS promotes the employees' skills improvement against hyper-specialization, typical in the mass production paradigm [5]. Throughout a systematic literature review using the PRISMA method, this article investigates 31 papers addressing RMS design and operational issues from a sustainability perspective.

Table 1. RMS features versus DMS and FMS ones. Adapted from Koren [6].

	DMS	FMS	RMS
System structure	Fixed	Changeable	Changeable
Machine structure	Fixed	Fixed	Changeable
System focus	Single part	Machine	Part/product family (PF)
Flexibility	No	Yes	Customized around PF
Scalability	No	Yes	Yes
Productivity	Very high	Low	High
Lifetime cost*	High	High	Medium

* *To produce multiple parts simultaneously at variable demand.*

The remainder of this paper is structured as follows: Sect. 2 presents the methodology implemented to address the research questions. Section 3 summarizes the reviewed literature and classifies the articles according to the sustainability pillars and the addressed RMS issues. Section 4 analyses the articles' contributions according to the three sustainability pillars. Conclusions and research perspectives are presented in Sect. 5.

2   Research Methodology

The literature review has been performed following the main phases of the PRISMA method (i.e., identification, screening, eligibility, and inclusion) as shown in Fig. 1 [7]. The research question guiding this review: *What is the state of the art regarding the three sustainability pillars in reconfigurable manufacturing systems (RMS)?*

Firstly, for the identification phase, a set of keywords was defined concerning the research question and the two main research fields addressed in this paper (i.e., RMS and sustainability). Advanced research was carried out with the aid of Boolean operators. The keywords included the combination of ("reconfigurable manufacturing" OR "changeable manufacturing") AND ("Sustainability" AND ("environment*" OR "social" OR "economic")). The keywords were searched by "Title" and "Field" using EBSCO and SCOPUS search engines. The timeframe considered was delimited between 1999 and 2022. This research only included English written works. A total of 85 documents were identified at this step. After a duplicate removal, 79 works were gathered, and an abstract analysis was performed resulting in 41 works selected for full-text analysis. Finally, a total of 31 papers were selected for further analysis.

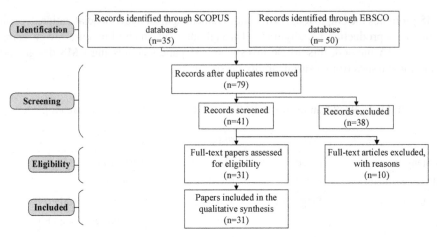

Fig. 1. PRISMA framework.

3   Sustainability in RMS Literature

Table 2 summarizes the original research papers selected from literature review. They were analyzed according to their associated sustainability pillar and the addressed RMS design and operational issues.

Table 2. Classification of works addressing sustainability in RMS.

Sustainability Pillars	Process planning	Production planning/Scheduling	Layout design	System configuration design	Workforce reconfiguration	Other
Environmental	[8–15]	[3, 12, 13, 16–19]	[13, 19–22]	[23, 24]		[25–27]
Social	[12, 28]	[12, 18]	[29, 30]	[24]	[31, 32]	
Economic	[8, 11–15]	[12, 13, 16–19]	[13, 16, 17, 19, 20]	[24]		

The environmental pillar arouses a lot of interest in RMS [3, 8, 16, 20, 21]. Besides, the social aspects are weakly studied, and the contributions are mostly theoretical [5, 29–31]. Finally, while social and environmental aspects are mostly related to sustainability issues, the economic aspect has been broadly studied in RMS literature mainly as a performance criterion, without sustainability perspective. In this research only papers addressing the economic aspect with a focus on sustainability were considered.

The main RMS issues identified in the related literature and described in Table 2 are: i) Process planning, ii) production planning or scheduling, iii) layout design, iv) system configuration design (i.e., configuration at system/layout and machine levels) and v) workforce reconfiguration. While the four first topics are often addressed as main issues in RMS, in this review the workforce configuration arises as relatively new RMS topic, evidencing the relevance of investigating the human within the RMS.

The articles related exclusively to the social pillar were classified into a new category, «workforce re-configuration» which considers the human as an RMS resource that needs to be optimised [32].

Recent literature reviews were also analyzed to position the contribution of this work [4, 33]. Battaïa et al. [4] introduce the three sustainability pillars but focus on the energy efficient RMS, while Dahmani et al. [33] address the economic and environmental pillars, without considering the social one.

4 The Pillars of Sustainability in RMS

4.1 Environmental Pillar

Environmental issues in RMS appear as the main sustainability pillar since they were addressed by more than 80% of the papers in Table 2. Most of them present approaches to minimise environmental impacts on the RMS while optimising the process planning [8–15], production planning/scheduling [3, 12, 13, 16–19], layout design [13, 19–22], or system configuration design [23, 24].

According to the international standards ISO 14001:2015 [34] and ISO 26000:2010 [35] the environmental pillar includes four main impact categories: i) Resource utilisation, ii) Pollution, iii) Climate change, and iv) Environment preservation.

In the reviewed literature, only the resource utilisation is broadly discussed, since most of the papers minimize energy consumption [4, 16, 18, 23]. This leads to the emergency of REMS (Reconfigurable energy-efficient manufacturing systems) [23]. REMS are a category of RMS whose components can switch to an energy-efficient mode when they are inactive in each configuration, and turn back into a working mode when needed [4, 23]. It is noted that the high academic interest on the optimisation of energy consumption in RMS is directly linked to the reduction of production costs and not to a real environmental consciousness [16, 19]. Few papers consider the pollution and climate change, focusing respectively on the hazardous waste generated from the production process, and the greenhouse gas emissions (GHG) linked to the energy consumption [8, 9, 21]. Most of these studies are still numerical and inputs are estimated. Therefore, further research is needed to investigate how environmental-related data could be collected from real applications to calculate sustainability KPIs.

Although some authors highlight the importance of the lifecycle perspective in RMS environmental pillar there is a lack of studies in this subject [4]. For instance, Brunoe et al. [25] analyse the RMS convertibility potential to enable circularity strategies, comparing three scenarios to manage the end of life (EOL) of products. However, their proposal is limited to the product, and does not address RMS EOL issues. Besides, Bi et al. appear as the only addressing RMS EOL through 4R strategies (reusing, recycling, redesigning and recovery) to reconfigure obsolete machines for new functionalities. According to Battaïa et al. [4], RMS systems potentially have longer lifecycles than traditional ones, thanks to their ability to be reconfigured. The above highlights the interest of developing further research concerning the lifecycle analysis of RMS.

4.2 Social Pillar

The social pillar appeared as the least investigated in this RMS literature review, and most of the works remain theoretical. Except by Yazdani et al. [12], which maximized the number of employees per machine in order to increase the employability in the industry location. The few studies dedicated exclusively to the social pillar focus on ergonomics [5, 29, 30], and more recent research addresses organisational aspects of the workforce [31, 32].

The ergonomics studies are based on the work of Cheikh et al. [30], which proposes a set of indicators such as movement repeatability, musculoskeletal trouble, and bad working conditions (e.g., noise). The authors highlight the pertinence of measuring ergonomics because RMS can lead to a higher level of repetitive tasks than traditional manufacturing systems (e.g., frequent assembly and disassembly movements to reconfigure the system).

Hashemi-Petroodi et al. [32] carried out a literature review on the workforce configuration, demonstrating the lack of studies on this subject. The authors claim that a joint reconfiguration of workers and machines can increase the RMS adaptability and robustness. Nevertheless, there is still no work simultaneously investigating machines and human reconfiguration abilities in RMS. Besides, the skills and cognitive development of employees are weakly discussed in the RMS literature. Only Korder et al. [31] propose a theoretical framework that describes different skill levels of employees in an RMS context. Nevertheless, this contribution remains theoretical and practical approaches are still lacking.

Three main conclusions can be drawn out from the social issues in RMS literature. Firstly, the ergonomics is the most developed social aspect, supported by existing ergonomics metrics broader applied in manufacturing, which means that those metrics are not specific to RMS context but used in a generic way. Secondly, there is a research opportunity regarding the impact of the Industry 4.0 technologies on the workforce organisation (e.g., human-machine collaboration or cobotics, sensors, actuators, etc.). Finally, more research can be done regarding employees' skills in RMS context. Concerning this latter, we propose considering an employee as a set of competences and skills able to evolve in the RMS environment.

4.3 Economic Pillar

Beyond the typical costs considered in any manufacturing system (e.g., cost of raw material, labour, and processing, etc.), most of research include RMS specific metrics as the cost of changing the system configuration, including machines and/or tools changes. Two types of costs related to sustainability issues have been identified in this literature review. The first one is the energy consumption cost and more recently, works have been addressing the GHG emissions and hazardous waste disposal cost.

Singh et al. [16] propose an optimisation method using cost metrics related to the system investment, maintenance, and energy consumption. Concerning the energy consumption cost, the authors consider an average energy price, without modelling the energy fluctuation prices or time-of-use (TOU). Nevertheless, energy prices can vary along the day (e.g., on-peak, mid-peak, and off-peak hours), and depending on the day (i.e., labour day, weekend) or year season [4, 19]. In this line, Ghanei and Algeddawy [17, 19] propose a mathematical model to maximize RMS sustainability considering the energy TOU, namely the calculation of the energy consumption cost for each task, at the exact time of the day in which the task is performed.

Khettabi et al. [36] and Khezri et al. [9] propose multi-objective optimisation methods for process plan generation, in which one of the objective functions corresponds to the total production cost. They focus on two environmental metrics for the cost calculation: disposal cost for hazardous liquid waste, and disposal cost for GHG emissions, without considering the energy consumption.

Most of the reviewed papers address the economic pillar of sustainability from a cost-driven perspective. An important economic criterion that was not considered by any of the works is the return on investment (ROI). As stated by Andersen et al. [37], justifying investments in RMS and its reconfiguration potential in the first steps of its implementation is essential; therefore, future works optimizing the RMS design could consider the ROI.

5 Conclusion and Research Perspectives

In this article, we perform a systematic literature review of 31 works to explore the research advances and opportunities regarding sustainability in the RMS context. The reviewed literature is classified and analysed throughout the lens of the three pillars of sustainability and the main topics of RMS.

The literature reveals an increasing interest in incorporating sustainability issues in the RMS design, since most of the reviewed papers were published in the last four years. However, most of them remain theoretical and practical applications are still missing. Further, there is still a lack of research simultaneously addressing the three sustainability pillars. The environmental pillar is the most addressed with a focus on energy consumption minimization. The economic pillar often includes environmental related costs, besides typical operational ones. The social pillar appears as the least addressed in literature and most of the related papers focus on ergonomic aspects.

For future research, we suggest the development of more application-oriented approaches to holistically evaluate the sustainability of RMS, in order to help indus-trials to go towards more sustainable reconfigurable manufacturing systems. Regarding environmental issues, we suggest future research to investigate how circular strategies can be applied during the RMS design and reconfiguration. Considering social pillar, further research can be done on the employee skills and their cognitive development required to adapt in new RMS configuration contexts. Seeing the operator as an evolutive resource can highly impact the resource assignment decisions as well as the reconfiguration and operational management, since qualified operators become capable of manage and anticipate the difficulties encountered in the production systems.

References

1. Bi, Z.: Revisiting system paradigms from the viewpoint of manufacturing sustainability. Sustainability 3(9), 1323–1340 (2011)

2. Koren, Y., Gu, X., Badurdeen, F., Jawahir, I.S.: Sustainable living factories for next generation manufacturing. Procedia Manuf. **21**, 26–36 (2018). https://doi.org/10.1016/j.promfg.2018.02.091
3. Choi, Y.-C., Xirouchakis, P.: A holistic production planning approach in a reconfigurable manufacturing system with energy consumption and environmental effects. Int. J. Comput. Integr. Manuf. **28**(4), 379–394 (2015)
4. Battaïa, O., Benyoucef, L., Delorme, X., Dolgui, A., Thevenin, S.: Sustainable and Energy Efficient Reconfigurable Manufacturing Systems, pp. 189–203 (2019)
5. Bortolini, M., Botti, L., Galizia, F.G., Mora, C.: Safety, ergonomics and human factors in reconfigurable manufacturing systems. In: Benyoucef, L. (ed.) Reconfigurable Manufacturing Systems: From Design to Implementation. SSAM, pp. 123–138. Springer, Cham (2020). https://doi.org/10.1007/978-3-030-28782-5_6
6. Koren, Y.: The Global Manufacturing Revolution: Product-Process-Business Integration and Reconfigurable Systems. Wiley, Hoboken (2010)
7. Moher, D., et al.: Preferred reporting items for systematic review and meta-analysis protocols (PRISMA-P) 2015 statement. Syst. Rev. **4**(1), 1 (2015)
8. Khettabi, I., Benyoucef, L., Boutiche, M.A.: Sustainable reconfigurable manufacturing system design using adapted multi-objective evolutionary-based approaches. Int. J. Adv. Manuf. Technol. **115**(11–12), 3741–3759 (2021). https://doi.org/10.1007/s00170-021-07337-3
9. Khezri, A., Benderbal, H.H., Benyoucef, L.: Towards a sustainable reconfigurable manufacturing system (SRMS): multi-objective based approaches for process plan generation problem. Int. J. Prod. Res. **59**(15), 4533–4558 (2021)
10. Massimi, E., Khezri, A., Benderbal, H.H., Benyoucef, L.: A heuristic-based non-linear mixed integer approach for optimizing modularity and integrability in a sustainable reconfigurable manufacturing environment. Int. J. Adv. Manuf. Technol. **108**(7), 1997–2020 (2020)
11. Touzout, F., Benyoucef, L.: Multi-objective sustainable process plan generation in a reconfigurable manufacturing environment: exact and adapted evolutionary approaches. Int. J. Prod. Res. **57**(8), 2531–2547 (2019)
12. Yazdani, M.A., Khezri, A., Benyoucef, L.: Process and production planning for sustainable reconfigurable manufacturing systems (SRMSs): multi-objective exact and heuristic-based approaches. Int. J. Adv. Manuf. Technol. **119**(7–8), 4519–4540 (2022)
13. Gao, S., Daaboul, J., Le Duigou, J.: Process planning scheduling, and layout optimization for multi-unit mass-customized products in sustainable reconfigurable manufacturing system. Sustainability **13**(23), 13323 (2021)
14. Khettabi, I., Boutiche, M.A., Benyoucef, L.: NSGA-II vs NSGA-III for the sustainable multi-objective process plan generation in a reconfigurable manufacturing environment. IFAC Pap. **54**(1), 683–688 (2021)
15. Khettabi, I., Benyoucef, L., Amine Boutiche, M.: Sustainable multi-objective process planning in reconfigurable manufacturing environment: adapted new dynamic NSGA-II vs New NSGA-III (2022). https://doi.org/10.1080/00207543.2022.2044537
16. Singh, P., Madan, J., Singh, H.: Economically sustainable configuration selection in reconfigurable manufacturing system, pp. 457–466 (2021)
17. Ghanei, S., AlGeddawy, T.: An integrated multi-period layout planning and scheduling model for sustainable reconfigurable manufacturing systems. J. Adv. Manuf. Syst. **19**(01), 31–64 (2020)
18. Akbar, M., Irohara, T.: Scheduling for sustainable manufacturing: a review. J. Clean. Prod. **205**, 866–883 (2018)
19. Ghanei, S., Algeddawy, T.: A new model for sustainable changeability and production planning. Procedia CIRP **57**, 522–526 (2016). https://doi.org/10.1016/j.procir.2016.11.090
20. Huang, A., Badurdeen, F., Jawahir, I.S.: Towards developing sustainable reconfigurable manufacturing systems. Procedia Manuf. **17**, 1136–1143 (2018)

21. Kurniadi, K.A., Ryu, K.: Development of multi-disciplinary green-BOM to maintain sustainability in reconfigurable manufacturing systems. Sustainability **13**(17), 9533 (2021)
22. Kurniadi, K.A., Ryu, K.: Maintaining sustainability in reconfigurable manufacturing systems featuring green-BOM. Int. J. Precis. Eng. Manuf. Green Technol. **7**(3), 755–767 (2020). https://doi.org/10.1007/s40684-020-00215-5
23. Zhang, J., et al.: Modeling and verification of reconfigurable and energy-efficient manufacturing systems. Discrete Dyn. Nat. Soc. **2015**, 1–14 (2015)
24. Azab, A., ElMaraghy, H., Nyhuis, P., Pachow-Frauenhofer, J., Schmidt, M.: Mechanics of change: a framework to reconfigure manufacturing systems. CIRP J. Manuf. Sci. Technol. **6**(2), 110–119 (2013). https://doi.org/10.1016/j.cirpj.2012.12.002
25. Brunoe, T.D., Andersen, A.-L., Nielsen, K.: Changeable manufacturing systems supporting circular supply chains. Procedia CIRP **81**, 1423–1428 (2019)
26. Dubey, R., Gunasekaran, A., Helo, P., Papadopoulos, T., Childe, S.J., Sahay, B.: Explaining the impact of reconfigurable manufacturing systems on environmental performance: the role of top management and organizational culture. J. Clean. Prod. **141**, 56–66 (2017)
27. Bi, Z., Pomalaza-raez, C., Singh, Z., Nicolette-Baker, A., Pettit, B., Heckley, C.: Reconfiguring machines to achieve system adaptability and sustainability: a practical case study. Proc. Inst. Mech. Eng. Part B J. Eng. Manuf. **228**(12), 1676–1688 (2014)
28. Bortolini, M., Botti, L., Galizia, F.G., Regattieri, A.: Bi-objective design and management of reconfigurable manufacturing systems to optimize technical and ergonomic performances. Appl. Sci. **11**(1), 263 (2020). https://doi.org/10.3390/app11010263
29. Bougrine, A., Darmoul, S., Hajri-Gabouj, S.: TOPSIS based multi-criteria reconfiguration of manufacturing systems considering operational and ergonomic indicators. In: 2017 International Conference on Advanced Systems and Electric Technologies (IC_ASET), pp. 329–334, January 2017
30. Cheikh, S., Hajri-Gabouj, S., Darmoul, S.: Manufacturing configuration selection under arduous working conditions: A multi-criteria decision approach, Piscataway, vol. 25, pp. 32–33, March 2016
31. Korder, S., Tropschuh, B., Reinhart, G.: A competence-based description of employees in reconfigurable manufacturing systems. In: Advances in Production Management Systems. Production Management for the Factory of the Future, Cham, pp. 257–264 (2019)
32. Hashemi-Petroodi, S.E., Dolgui, A., Kovalev, S., Kovalyov, M.Y., Thevenin, S.: Workforce reconfiguration strategies in manufacturing systems: a state of the art. Int. J. Prod. Res. **59**(22), 6721–6744 (2020)
33. Dahmani, A., Benyoucef, L., Mercantini, J.-M.: Toward sustainable reconfigurable manufacturing systems (SRMS): past, present, and future. Procedia Comput. Sci. **200**, 1605–1614 (2022)
34. ISO 14001: Environmental management systems, 3rd edn. (2015)
35. ISO 26000: Guidance on social responsibility, 1st edn. vol. 22 (2010)
36. Khettabi, I., Benyoucef, L., Boutiche, M.: Sustainable Reconfigurable Manufacturing System Design Using Adapted Multi-Objective Evolutionary Based Approaches (2021). https://doi.org/10.1080/00207543.2022.2044537
37. Andersen, A.-L., Brunoe, T., Nielsen, K., Rösiö, C.: Towards a generic design method for reconfigurable manufacturing systems - Analysis and synthesis of current design methods and evaluation of supportive tools. J. Manuf. Syst. **42**, 179–195 (2017)

Manufacturing Repurposing: A Literature Review

Wan Ri Ho$^{(\boxtimes)}$ ⏺, Omid Maghazei ⏺, and Torbjørn Netland ⏺

ETH Zürich, Zürich, Switzerland
who@ethz.ch

Abstract. Manufacturing repurposing was a rapid response strategy to overcome shortages of critical healthcare products during the Covid-19 pandemic. Many companies repurposed facilities to manufacture products such as ventilators and hand sanitizers in response to the skyrocketing demand. Manufacturing repurposing was a widespread practice during the early months of the Covid-19 pandemic. This systematic literature review consolidates the fragmented literature on manufacturing repurposing and identifies potential research opportunities in production and operations management. Using a systematic approach, we identified and reviewed 29 articles on manufacturing repurposing and report the findings from both descriptive and thematic analyses. We identified four main themes in the manufacturing repurposing literature: (1) barriers and success factors (2) role of the supply chain, (3) role of innovation, and (4) role of digital technologies. We conclude with a research agenda that suggests three promising lenses for future research on manufacturing repurposing: (1) dynamic capabilities, (2) supply chain resilience, and (3) network perspectives.

Keywords: Manufacturing repurposing · Literature review · Covid-19

1 Introduction

In response to the worldwide shortage of critical healthcare items caused by the Covid-19 pandemic, many firms engaged in manufacturing repurposing [1, 2]. Manufacturing repurposing involves repurposing production capacities, capabilities, know-how, and facilities to manufacture new-to-the-firm products. Although manufacturing repurposing is not a new phenomenon—for example, repurposing is common during wartime [e.g., 3] and emergencies [e.g., 4]—it has been experienced at a completely different scale during the Covid-19 pandemic. Before the pandemic, repurposing had not received much research interest, resulting in a very limited and fragmented literature base. This is changing; several academic papers and numerous media reports have been published over the past two years discussing manufacturing repurposing in different ways and forms. In this paper, our research objective is to conduct a systematic literature review of the state of the literature on manufacturing repurposing and propose a research agenda.

Literature reviews map a field of study and form a baseline for theory development [5]. Conducting a literature review on manufacturing repurposing allows us to

© IFIP International Federation for Information Processing 2022
Published by Springer Nature Switzerland AG 2022
D. Y. Kim et al. (Eds.): APMS 2022, IFIP AICT 663, pp. 160–172, 2022.
https://doi.org/10.1007/978-3-031-16407-1_20

reflect on multiple aspects of this emerging and multifaceted phenomenon, such as origins, strengths, flaws, contradictions, interdependencies, and boundary conditions [5]. It also allows the identification of best practices and summarizes empirical studies of performance outcomes. In addition, by studying and summarizing the state-of-the-art, a literature review allows for identifying research gaps and—through that—developing a research agenda.

This paper is structured as follows. Section 2 explains our systematic approach to conducting the literature review. In Sect. 3, we report our main findings from thematic analysis. In Sect. 4, we develop an agenda for future research based on the gaps and under-developed discussions in the extant literature. Section 5 concludes.

2 Methodology

This literature review is based on the structured method suggested by Tranfield *et al.* [6]. The summary of our review process is shown in Fig. 1.

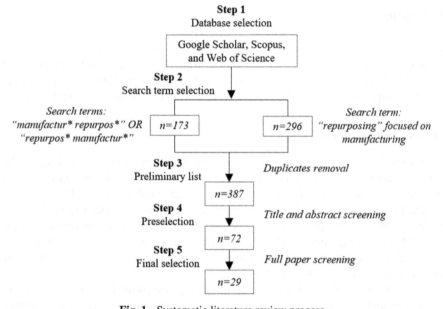

Fig. 1. Systematic literature review process

In the first step, we selected three databases: Google Scholar, Scopus, and Web of Science. In the second step, we conducted a manual search using "manufacturing repurposing" or "repurpose manufacturing" as the main search terms adapted to each database's search function. We further expanded our search term into "repurposing" and filtering it down to articles only containing the word "manufacturing." Taken together, we collected 469 articles. In the third step, we cross-checked our database for duplicates resulting in 378 articles. In the fourth step, we then preselected papers by screening titles and abstracts, resulting in 72 preselected articles. In this step, we excluded articles that, for example, discussed purely technical and engineering aspects of repurposing [e.g., 7]. In the fifth step, we read the full articles to identify the final sample, through which we selected 29 papers to be included in the review (see Appendix). The main exclusion criterion at this step was concerning the papers discussing, for example, drug repurposing [e.g., 8] or medical devices repurposing [e.g., 9].

To analyze the final selected articles, we followed a six-step thematic analysis method suggested by Braun and Clarke [10]. In the first step, the articles were independently reviewed and *coded* by the research team. In particular, we searched for constituents of manufacturing repurposing and applied theoretical lenses. In the second phase, the codes were cross-checked through iterative discussions leading to the generation of *initial codes*. This was followed by the third step of clustering the codes into *themes*. In the fourth phase, these themes were reviewed by the research team to generate a *thematic map* of analysis. In the fifth phase, the thematic maps were collated to construct the constituents of the manufacturing repurposing phenomenon as well as potential theoretical lenses for future research. In the sixth phase, the findings were documented and summarized.

3   Findings

In this section, we first provide a descriptive analysis of the extant literature followed by a summary of the clustered themes of manufacturing repurposing which emerged from our thematic analysis: (1) barriers and success factors of manufacturing repurposing, (2) role of the supply chain, (3) role of innovation, and (4) role of digital technologies.

3.1 Descriptive Analysis

Our results show that manufacturing repurposing has rarely been discussed before the Covid-19 pandemic. There are, however, some notable exceptions. For instance, in 2018, Ciortea et al. [11] explore multi-agent systems to design scalable and flexible agent-based manufacturing systems, which allows engineers to program and repurpose manufacturing lines without interruption. In the same year, Fisher et. al. [12] also mentioned how Cloud Manufacturing could likely impact manufacturing repurposing operations with its flexibility and scalability. Despite these rare mentions, manufacturing repurposing has emerged as a distinct field of study since 2020.

Our analysis revealed four main themes in the manufacturing repurposing literature: (1) barriers and success factors of manufacturing repurposing, (2) role of the supply chain, (3) role of innovation, and (4) role of digital technologies.

3.2 Barriers and Success Factors of Manufacturing Repurposing

The first main theme involves the ways companies set out to manufacture entirely new products. For instance, Okorie et al. [13] identify and assess enablers such as organizational flexibility, expertise and know-how, technological capacities and capabilities, and barriers such as insufficient resources, funding limitations, and time pressure, impacting manufacturing repurposing initiatives. Poduval et al. [14] focus more on barriers that can hinder repurposing existing manufacturing settings and classify them into 11 categories, including strategic, cultural, technological, financial, regulatory, sourcing, and innovation. Poduval et al. [14] then employ structured approaches to delineate interdependencies among the identified barrier to improve decision-making processes and increase the success of viable manufacturing repurposing projects. In a literature review on how Covid-19 impacts manufacturing, Kapoor et al. [15] identify the regulatory aspects during the execution of manufacturing repurposing projects, including medical safety and protocols, design qualifications, and testing procedures. Moreover, Kapoor et al. [15] explain reconfigurability capabilities and manufacturing flexibility—through which firms adapt their production lines and capacities—as enablers for repurposing.

3.3 Role of Supply Chain in Manufacturing Repurposing

The second main theme is concerned with the supply chain aspects of manufacturing repurposing. Ivanov [16] highlights the insufficient discussions around the integration of pandemic-like disruptions within the supply chain resilience literature and proposes manufacturing repurposing as one of the adaptation strategies to increase resilience in supply chains. Falcone et al. [17] analyze the impact of structural networks—in particular, firms' supply chain network and CEO network—and identify that firms' entrepreneurial positions in supply chain and CEO networks increase the success of operational repurposing. Falcone et al. [17] also explain the connections between supply chain plasticity—defined as a firm's "capability of rapidly making major changes to a supply chain to accommodate significant shifts in the business environment" [18]—and manufacturing repurposing. Shokrani [19] outlines the role of "alternative" supply chains that remain underused during emergencies to mobilize repurposing of domestic mass-production capacities to produce items at excessively high demand.

3.4 Role of Innovation in Manufacturing Repurposing

The third main theme involves innovation aspects of manufacturing repurposing. Companies using open innovation in their repurposing projects demonstrated better results due to (1) collaborations in product design and reducing design iterations, (2) complementing manufacturing capacities and increasing productivity, and (3) repurposing existing technologies than developing new ones [14, 20]. Liu et al. [20] examine how shared purpose accelerates the innovation process through the concept of exaptation—"an ability to 'pivot'… from one function to another, without the need for a long and costly development process" [20, p. 2] Schwabe et al. [21] developed a maturity model based on repurposing projects during the Covid-19 pandemic to conceptualize the speed of innovation diffusion from ideation to market saturation.

3.5 Role of Digital Technologies in Manufacturing Repurposing

The fourth main theme is the role of digital technologies in manufacturing repurposing. Digital technologies were seen as key enablers for manufacturing, repurposing, and navigating disruptions [22–24]. Examples include using digital fabrication tools in maker spaces [25]; additive manufacturing to produce face shields [13], and digital supply chain twin to track network states in real-time [16]. Soldatos et al. [26] show how different Industry 4.0 technologies such as digital platforms can accelerate manufacturing repurposing projects.

4 Research Agenda

The literature on manufacturing repurposing is still at its infancy, which offers many opportunities for future research. Our literature review revealed currently underdeveloped yet high-potential areas of research. We identify three particularly promising lenses for future studies of manufacturing repurposing: (1) dynamic capabilities, (2) supply chain resilience, and (3) networks.

4.1 A Dynamic Capabilities Lens on Manufacturing Repurposing

The extant literature on manufacturing repurposing, to some extent, highlights the importance of quick adaptations in product- and process-related routines [21, 27–29], which is akin to the concept of *dynamic capabilities*. Dynamic capabilities are "the capacity to renew competences to achieve congruence with the changing business environment" by "appropriately adapting, integrating, and reconfiguring internal and external organizational skills, resources, and functional competencies to match the requirements of a changing environment" (i.e., capabilities) [30, p. 515]. OM scholars could further conceptualize the role of dynamic capabilities and investigate planning, implementation, and integration and the impact of such changeovers on firms' operations and supply chains during repurposing projects. Moreover, a promising research area involves the exploration of specific dynamic capabilities that firms should develop prior to likely future disruptions. For instance, it is a worthwhile research area to examine how manufacturing flexibility could enhance dynamic capabilities and thus increase firms' preparedness for repurposing initiatives.

4.2 A Supply Chain Resilience Lens on Manufacturing Repurposing

During the early stages of the Covid-19 pandemic, many scholars focused on increasing the supply chain's resilience to improve responsiveness against likely disruptions [31, 32]. Focusing on manufacturing repurposing, this literature review reveals a research gap about differences, opportunities and challenges, and synergies of various strategies. For example, increasing supply chain resilience versus building manufacturing repurposing capabilities—to overcome sudden increases of demand and immediate shortages of critical items such as healthcare products during pandemic-like disruptions. Although this distinction is echoed in the studies conducted by Schumacher et al. [29], there is little research on each strategy's characteristics and consequences.

4.3 A Network Lens on Manufacturing Repurposing

The reviewed articles outline the importance of building a network to enhance manufacturing repurposing projects [15–17]. However, network analysis in manufacturing repurposing projects provides a promising path for future research [cf. 33]. Particularly relevant for products with high complexity, such as ventilators (i.e., multiple components with strict regulations and standards), companies built networks of actors with diverse expertise to complement each other's resources, capabilities, know-how, capacities, technologies, and infrastructure, among others, during manufacturing repurposing projects. Analyzing manufacturing repurposing from a network perspective and using network visualizations can be an interesting future research direction for OM scholars.

5 Conclusion

This paper provided the first systematic literature review on the phenomenon of manufacturing repurposing. A total of 29 papers were systematically selected and reviewed through thematic analysis. We identified four main themes in the manufacturing repurposing literature, including barriers and success factors involved, supply chain issues, innovation-related issues, and the role of digital technologies. We call for more research on manufacturing repurposing, and encourage scholars to consider studying it with one or more of the following lenses: dynamic capabilities, supply chain resilience, or network perspectives.

Appendix

(See Table 1).

Table 1 Summary of the final selected papers included in this literature review

Authors	Title	Source	Year	Summary
Akoum and Achi (2021)	Reimagining innovation amid the COVID-19 Pandemic: Insights from the WISH innovation programme	Report	2021	Discuss the effect of the pandemic on innovation and the need for speed, and cross-sectorial approach
Betti et al. (2020)	From perfume to hand sanitiser, TVs to face masks: How companies are changing track to fight COVID-19	News report	2020	Discuss the motivation, complexity, approach, and potential of manufacturing repurposing
Castañeda-Navarrete et al. (2020)	COVID-19's impacts on global value chains, as seen in the apparel industry	Centre for Technology Management Working Paper Series	2020	Provide an analysis on the impact of Covid-19 on the apparel industry and identify key policies to address the challenges
Chien et al. (2020)	A Positive-Pressure Environment Disposable Shield (PEDS) for COVID-19 Health Care Worker Protection	Prehospital and Disaster Medicine	2020	Discuss the repurposing of a positive pressure head isolation unit from materials available
Ciortea et al. (2018)	Repurposing manufacturing lines on the fly with multi-agent systems for the Web of Things	Proceedings of the 17th International Conference on Autonomous Agents and Multiagent Systems	2018	Present an approach to design scalable and flexible agent-based manufacturing systems

(continued)

Table 1 (*continued*)

Authors	Title	Source	Year	Summary
Correa et al. (2020)	Protecting productive assets during the COVID-19 pandemic	Report	2020	Discuss manufacturing repurposing as a flexible and fast response for manufacturing
Corsini and Leal-Ayala (2020)	The role of industrial digitalisation in post-Covid-19 manufacturing recovery, diversification, and resilience	Cambridge Industrial Innovation Policy	2020	The role of digitalization post-Covid-19 globally
Corsini et al. (2020)	Critical factors for implementing open-source hardware in a crisis: lessons learned from the COVID-19 pandemic	Journal of Open Hardware	2020	Discuss the role of open-source hardware and its potential post Covid-19
El-Aziz et al. (2021)	The role of emerging technologies for combating COVID-19 pandemic	Studies in Systems, Decision and Control	2021	Provide an overview of digital technologies as a response to Covid-19
Falcone et al. (2022)	Supply chain plasticity during a global disruption: Effects of CEO and supply chain networks on operational repurposing	Journal of Business Logistics	2022	Propose a stepwise weight assessment ratio analysis on firms' supply chain plasticity vs repurposing capabilities

(*continued*)

Table 1 (*continued*)

Authors	Title	Source	Year	Summary
Fisher et al. (2018)	Cloud manufacturing as a sustainable process manufacturing route	Journal of Manufacturing Systems	2018	Discuss the potential of cloud manufacturing to provide scalability and flexibility in repurposing manufacturing
Hanapi and Hanapi (2021)	Repurposing typical institutional hall as temporary Covid-19 quarantine stations In Johor: A review study in KKTM	International Journal of Integrated Engineering	2021	Explore the physical repurposing of facilities based on a case study methodology
Ivanov (2021)	Supply chain viability and the COVID-19 pandemic: A conceptual and formal generalisation of four major adaptation strategies	International Journal of Production Research	2021	Propose repurposing as one of four adaptation strategies for supply chain viabilities
Kapoor et al. (2021)	How is COVID-19 altering the manufacturing landscape? A literature review of imminent challenges and management interventions	Annals of Operations Research	2021	Provide a literature review on manufacturing during Covid-19 and a research agenda
Liu et al. (2021)	Accelerated innovation through repurposing: Exaptation of design and manufacturing in response to COVID-19	R&D Management	2021	Study the effect of shared purpose in driving change in the innovation processes

(*continued*)

Table 1 (*continued*)

Authors	Titles	Journal	Year	Summary
López-Gómez et al. (2020)	COVID-19 critical supplies: The manufacturing repurposing challenge	United Nations Industrial Development Organization	2020	Define manufacturing repurposing as a response solution to address global shortages
Magelssen (2020)	Jindal school researchers examine COVID-19 impact on manufacturing	News report	2020	Examine manufacturers response to Covid-19 discuss the lack of capability among manufacturers
Malik et al. (2020)	Repurposing factories with robotics in the face of COVID-19	Materials and Design	2020	Discuss the potential of cobots in expediting repurposing manufacturing
Mamo (2020)	Insights from Africa's Covid-19 response: Repurposing manufacturing	Tony Blair Institute for Global Change	2020	Discuss the potential of pivoting to local manufacturing with the collaboration of public and private sectors
Moerchel et al. (2020)	Identifying crisis-critical intellectual property challenges during the Covid-19 pandemic: A scenario analysis and conceptual extrapolation of innovation ecosystem dynamics using a visual mapping approach	Centre for Technology Management	2020	Identify crisis associated challenges and IP specific dynamic developments
Okorie et al. (2020)	Manufacturing in the time of COVID-19: An assessment of barriers and enablers	IEEE Engineering Management Review	2020	Propose a best practice framework for a successful pivot to major disruptions
Poduval et al. (2021)	Barriers in repurposing an existing manufacturing plant: A total interpretive structural modeling (TISM) approach	Operations Management Research	2021	Explore a total interpretative structural modelling (TISM) approach to analyze barriers of manufacturing repurposing

(*continued*)

Table 1 (*continued*)

Authors	Titles	Journal	Year	Summary
Puślecki et al. (2021)	Development of innovation cooperation in the time of COVID-19 pandemic	European Research Studies Journal	2021	Discuss the development of partnerships and R&D alliances during and post pandemic
Robinson (2020)	The companies repurposing manufacturing to make key medical kit during Covid-19 pandemic	News report	2020	Describe the various manufacturing repurposing initiatives from different manufacturers
Schumacher et al. (2021)	Strategies to manage product recalls in the COVID-19 pandemic: an exploratory case study of PPE supply chains	World Economic Forum	2021	Discuss the response of firms to product recalls and the effect of institutional actors
Schwabe et al. (2021)	A maturity model for rapid diffusion of innovation in high value manufacturing	Procedia CIRP	2021	Develop a maturity model for forecasting innovation in projects including manufacturing repurposing
Shokrani et al. (2020)	Exploration of alternative supply chains and distributed manufacturing in response to COVID-19; a case study of medical face shields	Materials and Design	2020	Propose a simplified face shield design through an assortment of alternative supply chains
Soldatos et al. (2021)	Digital platform and operator 4.0 services for manufacturing repurposing during COVID19	IFIP Advances in Information and Communication Technology	2021	Provide an introduction of digital solutions for manufacturing repurposing transformations
Tondel and Ahair-we (2020)	Policy coherence issues emerging from COVID-19 with a focus on healthcare supply chains	Development Policy Review	2020	Discuss the implications of policy on healthcare supply chains to better manage the effects of globalization

References

1. Netland, T.: A better answer to the ventilator shortage as the pandemic rages on (2020)
2. López-Gómez, B.C., Corsini, L., Leal-Ayala, D., Fokeer, S.: COVID-19 critical supplies : The manufacturing repurposing challenge. (2020)
3. Overy, R.: War and Economy in the Third Reich. Oxford University Press, Oxford (1994)
4. Nishiguchi, T., Beaudet, A.: The Toyota group and the Aisin fire. Sloan Manag. Rev. **40**(1), 49–59 (1998)
5. Post, C., Sarala, R., Gatrell, C., Prescott, J.E.: Advancing theory with review articles. J. Manag. Stud. **57**(2), 351–376 (2020)
6. Tranfield, D., Denyer, D., Smart, P.: Towards a methodology for developing evidence-informed management knowledge by means of systematic review. Br. J. Manag. **14**, 207–222 (2003)
7. Throup, J., et al.: Rapid repurposing of pulp and paper mills, biorefineries, and breweries for lignocellulosic sugar production in global food catastrophes. Food Bioprod. Process. **131**, 22–39 (2022)
8. Von Krogh, G., Kucukkeles, B., Ben-Menahem, S.M.: Lessons in rapid innovation from the covid-19 pandemic. MIT Sloan Manag. Rev. **61**(4), 8–10 (2020)
9. Loomba, A.: Repurposing medical devices for LRCs. IEEE Sustainability Considerations (2014)
10. Braun, V., Clarke, V.: Using thematic analysis in psychology. Qualitative Res. Psychol. **3**(2), 77–101 (2006)
11. Ciortea, A., Mayer, S., Michahelles, F.: Repurposing manufacturing lines on the fly with multi-agent systems for the web of things. In: Proceedings of the 17th International Conference on Autonomous Agents and Multiagent Systems (AAMAS 2018), pp. 813–822 (2018)
12. Fisher, O., Watson, N., Porcu, L., Bacon, D., Rigley, M., Gomes, R.L.: Cloud manufacturing as a sustainable process manufacturing route. J. Manuf. Syst. **47**, 53–68 (2018)
13. Okorie, O., Subramoniam, R., Charnley, F., Patsavellas, J., Widdifield, D., Salonitis, K.: Manufacturing in the time of COVID-19: an assessment of barriers and enablers. IEEE Eng. Manage. Rev. **48**, 167–175 (2020)
14. Poduval, A., et al.: Barriers in repurposing an existing manufacturing plant : a total interpretive structural modeling (TISM) approach. Operations Manag. Res. (2021)
15. Kapoor, K., Bigdeli, A.Z., Dwivedi, Y.K., Raman, R.: How is COVID-19 altering the manufacturing landscape? a literature review of imminent challenges and management interventions. Ann. Oper. Res. (2021)
16. Ivanov, D.: Supply chain viability and the COVID-19 pandemic: a conceptual and formal generalisation of four major adaptation strategies. Int. J. Prod. Res. **59**, 3535–3552 (2021)
17. Falcone, E.C., Fugate, B.S., Dobrzykowski, D.D.: Supply chain plasticity during a global disruption: Effects of CEO and supply chain networks on operational repurposing. J. Bus. Logist. **43**(1), 116–139 (2022)
18. Zinn, W., Goldsby, T.J.: Supply chain plasticity: redesigning supply chains to meet major environmental change. J. Bus. Logist. **40**(3), 184–186 (2019)
19. Shokrani, A., Loukaides, E.G., Elias, E., Lunt, A.J.G.: Exploration of alternative supply chains and distributed manufacturing in response to COVID-19: a case study of medical face shields. Mater. Des. **192**, 1–3 (2020)
20. Liu, W., Beltagui, A., Ye, S.: Accelerated innovation through repurposing: exaptation of design and manufacturing in response to COVID-19. R&D Manag., 1–17 (2021)
21. Schwabe, O., et al.: A maturity model for rapid diffusion of innovation in high value manufacturing. Procedia CIRP **96**, 195–200 (2021)

22. El-Aziz, A.A.A., Khalifa, N.E.M., Darwsih, A., Hassanien, A.E.: The role of emerging technologies for combating COVID-19 pandemic. Stud. Syst. Decis. Control **322**, 3–19 (2021)
23. Majeed, A., Oun Hwang, S.: Data-driven analytics leveraging artificial intelligence in the era of COVID-19: an insightful review of recent developments. Symmetry **14**(1) (2021)
24. Malik, A.A., Masood, T., Kousar, R.: Repurposing factories with robotics in the face of COVID-19. Sci. Robot. **5**(43), 17–22 (2020)
25. Corsini, L., Dammicco, V., Moultrie, J.: Critical factors for implementing open source hardware in a crisis: lessons learned from the COVID-19 pandemic. J. Open Hardw. **4**, 1–11 (2020)
26. Soldatos, J., et al.: Digital platform and operator 4.0 services for manufacturing repurposing during COVID19. In: IFIP International Federation for Information Processing, pp. 311–320. Springer, Switzerland (2021)
27. Robinson, D.: The companies repurposing manufacturing to make key medical kit during Covid-19 pandemic. NS Med. Dev. (2020)
28. Binder, S., et al.: African national public health institutes responses to COVID-19: innovations, systems changes, and challenges. Health Secur. **19**, 498–507 (2021)
29. Schumacher, R., Glew, R., Tsolakis, N., Kumar, M.: Strategies to manage product recalls in the COVID-19 pandemic: an exploratory case study of PPE supply chains. Contin. Resil. Rev. **3**, 64–78 (2021)
30. Teece, D.J., Pisano, G., Shuen, A.: Dynamic capabilities and strategic management. Strat. Manag. J. **18**(7), 509–533 (1997)
31. Phillips, W., Roehrich, J.K., Kapletia, D., Alexander, E.: Global value chain reconfiguration and COVID-19: investigating the case for more resilient redistributed models of production. Calif. Manag. Rev. **64**, 71–96 (2022)
32. Gereffi, G., Pananond, P., Pedersen, T.: Resilience decoded: the role of firms, global value chains, and the state in COVID-19 medical supplies. Calif. Manag. Rev. **64**(2), 46–70 (2022)
33. Choudhary, N., Ramkumar, M., Schoenherr, T., Rana, N.P.: Assessing supply chain resilience during the pandemic using network analysis. IEEE Trans. Eng. Manag., 1–14 (2021)

Autonomization and Digitalization: Index of Last Mile 4.0 Inclusive Transition

Adriana Saraceni[(✉)], Rozali Oleko, Lisi Guan, Adarsh Bagaria, and Lieven Quintens

Maastricht University, Maastricht, The Netherlands
a.saraceni@maastrichtuniversity.nl

Abstract. While autonomization and digitalization solutions appear beneficial within last mile delivery process, the literature on these solutions remain fragmented and distributed across different themes among various research papers. This paper aims to assemble some of the prominent solutions and outline their key characteristics to guide our researchers in future studies. To do so, this paper first extensively investigates the available literature and presents the most prominent solutions in a prioritization and categorization method (PCM) approach. Where these solutions currently stand in the perspective of inclusive last mile 4.0 transition is then discussed in our findings.

Keywords: Autonomization · Digitalization · Last mile delivery · Last mile 4.0 · Big data · Logistics 4.0

1 Introduction

Innovative solutions based on autonomization and digitalization (A&D) appear promising in logistics, given that their employment can contribute to cost-reduction, operational competitiveness, and environmental sustainability (Winkelhaus and Groose 2020, Hahn 2019, Seghezzi et al. 2020, Xu et al. 2020). While several stages of supply chain are becoming more automated each day, the last piece of this chain, the last mile delivery, faces complex struggles to completely automate its processes. *Increase in demand*—online purchases have been increasing with a rapid pace (Kiba-Janiak et al. 2021, Mucowska 2021, Tsai and Tiwasing 2021, Simoni et al. 2019, Zhou et al. 2020, Aurambout et al. 2019), triggered largely by the current Covid19 pandemic (Wang et al. 2021). While higher demands lead to higher congestions, Winkelhaus and Groose (2020) build the logistics 4.0 framework that integrates the modern technological solutions that help in building future strategies and accomplish the tasks. *Customer expectations*—companies are called to address increasing consumers' expectations related to a delivery's timeliness, costs, or environment impact (Comi and Savchenko 2021, Kiba-Janiak et al. 2021, Rossolov et al. 2021, Tsai and Tiwasing 2021, Saetta and Caldarelli 2020, Viu-Roig and Alvarez-Palau 2020). *Driver Shortages*—Last mile delivery is explained to be 'physically demanding' with 'strict time constraints'. Over the last years, there is an increasing gap in the shortage of drivers and warehouse handlers available, which

© IFIP International Federation for Information Processing 2022
Published by Springer Nature Switzerland AG 2022
D. Y. Kim et al. (Eds.): APMS 2022, IFIP AICT 663, pp. 173–182, 2022.
https://doi.org/10.1007/978-3-031-16407-1_21

motivates to look for alternative solutions. A&D has proven to provide high efficiency, while keeping up with the accelerating growth, in other verticals of supply chain, fostering the inclusive transition of last mile delivery within logistic 4.0. However, manifold implications are associated to the implementation of A&D in last mile, from regulatory specificities (Hoffmann and Prause 2018, Elsayed and Mohamed 2020), to customers' acceptance (Mangiaracina et al. 2019, Tsai and Tiwasing 2021), to job losses paradigm, social impact (Feng et al. 2017) and beyond. Due the aforementioned, not many studies have taken the lenses of the new solutions to the inclusive transition of the last mile into Logistic 4.0. This paper takes the challenge to index A&D references based on different areas of importance. Our findings argue the currently stands of A&D in the perspective of inclusive last mile 4.0 transition. In the results, we indicate the viability and the time frame of optimization possibilities.

2 Literature Review

By performing an interdisciplinary assessment of existing literature, this research was able to assemble several viable last-mile innovative solutions recently identified by researchers, namely unmanned aerial vehicles, autonomously driving robots, underground delivery, parcel lockers, reception boxes, customer's car trunks. It was also identified that big data, dynamic pricing and crowdsourcing logistics (Kiba-Janiak et al. 2021, Ranieri et al. 2018). Main solutions are discussed in the sequence.

Unmanned Aerial Vehicles (UAVs): commonly referred as 'drones', can be employed to deliver a parcel to a final destination (Bosona 2020, Di Puglia Pugliese et al. 2020, Elsayed and Mohamed 2020, Seghezzi et al. 2020, Aurambout et al. 2019, Maghazei and Netland 2019, Zhu 2019, Ranieri et al. 2018). Drones can navigate to such a destination and deposit a parcel by means of an embedded GPS (Mangiaracina et al. 2019), and subsequently return to their point of departure following the delivery. Researchers have assessed both stable optimal locations of such departures and returns (Aurambout et al. 2019), as well as the feasibility of moving locations via the use of trucks (Di Puglia Pugliese et al. 2020, Mangiaracina et al. 2019). There is contribution towards environmental sustainability and their potential to reduce the GHG emissions (Elsayed and Mohamed 2020, Mangiaracina et al. 2019).

Autonomously Driving Robots: can be defined as "[…] self-driving road vehicles that, moving on determined and controlled paths […]" (Mangiaracina et al. 2019, p. 14). Researchers have distinguished between semi-autonomous and fully autonomous vehicles (Ranieri et al. 2018) and have assessed possibilities for the optimization of existing ground robot prototypes such as FURBOT (Silvestri et al. 2019). Benefits relates of minimizing last-mile delivery costs while existing regulatory could be associated challenges to their application (Seghezzi et al. 2020; Hoffmann and Prause 2018).

Big Data: appears as a well-established information technology solution in last mile delivery within the literature explored with "ability to transform entire business processes." (Feng et al. 2017, p. 2) and to increase performance efficiency (Kiba-Janiak et al. 2021, Bosona 2020, Fosso Wamba 2020, Sarma et al. 2020, Dubey et al. 2019,

Hahn 2019, Feng et al. 2017). Their application forms a significant aspect of Logistics 4.0, as it is directly associated to digital technologies that enable the formation of (semi) autonomous networks.

Parcel Lockers or Cabinets: refer to "[…] a form of self-service technology used for customer pick-up and return of e-purchased goods." (Vakulenko et al. 2019, p. 3). Specifically, "[…] a locker can be opened with a unique pickup code sent by e-mail or short message service on one's own phone." (Ranieri et al. 2018, p. 8). Researchers have established the existence of facilitating conditions related to the usage of parcel lockers as a factor increasing this solution's acceptance (Tsai and Tiwasing 2021, Zhou et al. 2020). The benefit of this solution in minimizing last-mile delivery costs is straightforward (Kiba-Janiak et al. 2021, Bosona 2020, Mangiaracina et al. 2019, Zhu 2019, Florio et al. 2018), as it eradicates face-to-face human interaction of customers and couriers and thus can be distinguished from the similar solution of pick-up points (Mucowska 2021, Mangiaracina et al. 2019).

There are several other solutions identified during our literature search. One such solution pertains to the use of destination locations owned by customers. Such locations can be either fixed, namely 'reception boxes' situated in a customer's residence (Hoffmann and Prause 2018), or shifting, by means of delivery in a 'customer's car trunk'. While the value of those solutions in minimizing last-mile delivery costs is similar to parcel lockers and straightforward (Mangiaracina et al. 2019, Florio et al. 2018).

Another solution is that of 'Dynamic pricing', namely "[…] associating different delivery prices to different time windows." (Mangiaracina et al. 2019, p.14). This aims to optimize the last-mile delivery process by considering customers' preferences. The benefits of this solution in minimizing last-mile delivery costs of e-grocery delivery have been established (Mangiaracina et al. 2019). Whereas 'Crowdsourcing logistics' is a term referring to the possibility of engaging people directly in the last mile delivery process per se, by "outsourcing the delivery of the goods to 'common' people that give their availability for bringing the parcel from a point of collection, generally a warehouse or a store, to a point of delivery" (Lazarević and Dobrodolac 2020, p. 2). While the benefits of this solution in minimizing last-mile delivery costs have been established (Ghaderi et al. 2022, Kiba-Janiak et al. 2021, Bosona 2020, Lazarević and Dobrodolac 2020, Mangiaracina et al. 2019, Zhu 2019), further research is needed in order to better assess the value of different crowdsourcing logistics business models (Mangiaracina et al. 2019, p. 16), given that the application of this solution may incur negative externalities (Simoni et al. 2019, Zhu 2019).

3 Methodology

To index all automation and digitalization solutions technologies which are viable solutions to address last-mile delivery inefficiencies, we have compiled available literature in Sect. 2 according to various A&D solutions. We have identified four verticals upon which the characteristics of each autonomous solution are highlighted. While 'benefits' and 'challenges' remain the most studied characteristics among the papers reviewed, 'efficiency' and 'implementation time frame' make up the four verticals.

Taking the premise of the inclusive transition of the last mile into Logistic 4.0, the prioritization and categorization method (PCM) is then applied as following: High, Moderate, and Low. E.g. 'High' cost benefit is where the potential to realize cost benefits through using a particular solution shows great prospect. Furthermore, where enough information is not available to make an educated inference, 'N/I' is highlighted. The results provide where these innovations currently stand.

4 Results and Discussion

Where do These Innovations Currently Stand? The use of both UAVs and Autonomous robots as optimization solutions has been frequently examined. Researchers have created analytical models based on the employment of drones or robots, with the aim of minimizing last mile delivery costs (Di Puglia Pugliese et al. 2020, Aurambout et al. 2019, Silvestri et al. 2019) or introducing a sustainable delivery solution (Elsayed and Mohamed 2020). Table 1 gives an overview of the characteristics of A&D solutions being studied.

Table 1. Characteristics of inclusive Last Mile 4.0 transition

	Benefits		Challenges		Time frame	Efficiency
	Cost	Environmental	Legal	Technological	Optimization possibility	
UAV's	Moderate-Low	High	High	High	Long term	Moderate
Autonomous robots	Moderate	High	High	High	Mid term	High
Parcel lockers	High	High	Low	Moderate	In use	Moderate
Big data	High	High	Low	Moderate	In use	High
Reception boxes	Moderate	Low	Low	Low	Short term	Moderate
Dynamic pricing	High	Moderate	Low	Low	In Use	Low
Crowdsourcing	High	Moderate	N/I	Moderate	Short term	Moderate

Research involving collaboration with companies that have opted for the use of drones or robots (Hoffmann and Prause 2018) is fundamental to identify the practical challenges of their application. Customer acceptance as well as on their societal impact could identify unforeseen complexities of their use. Parcel lockers and the customers' behaviour are valuable insights regarding factors that impact on their initial intention to adopt new solutions (Tsai and Tiwasing 2021, Zhou et al. 2020), as factors that impact the continuation of its use (Vakulenko et al. 2019). Big data applications have been thoroughly studied by the academia. Within the literature examined, the Internet of Things has been identified as the principal application of Logistics 4.0 (Winkelhaus and Grosse 2020), and attention has been given to the increasing dependence of SCM on big data use, the importance of data manipulation capacity as well as on questions regarding data quality (Feng et al. 2017). Regarding the last-mile, researchers have established that their use has a positive impact towards cost minimization (Kiba-Janiak et al. 2021, Bosona 2020, Fosso Wamba 2020, Sarma et al. 2020, Dubey et al. 2019, Hahn 2019, Feng et al. 2017) based on the creation of analytical and simulation models (Sarma et al. 2020, Shan et al. 2019, Zhang et al. 2019). The use of Information and Communication Technologies (ICT) has been associated with collaborative urban logistics, the optimization of transport management and routing city logistics as well as innovative mobility infrastructure (Ranieri et al. 2018).

5 Conclusion

While A&D is poised to provide numerous benefits within the last mile delivery process, inclusive potential for last mile 4.0—literature on this subject remains to be fragmented and distributed across numerous research papers in different themes. This paper introduces several reasons why A&D is sought after to provide solutions to the challenges last mile process currently faces. Supply Chain Management is poised to be one of the biggest benefactors of A&D, however their implementation in last mile is still limited to theory. Even then so, there is a keen interest in the research community to understand the applications of these solutions in transition to a last mile 4.0. With the proposed index of current solutions and time frame of optimization possibilities, we thus argue the inclusive transition of the last mile within Logistic 4.0. Future research can delve deep into other inclusive last mile 4.0 characteristics.

Acknowledgements. The authors would like to thank the OP Zuid program awarded funding. The project is made possible, in part, by financial support from the European Union (European Fund for Regional Development), OP-Zuid, the Province of North Brabant, the Province of Limburg and the Ministry of Economic Affairs and Climate.

Appendices

Appendix 1. Measurement and Data Structure—'Benefits'

Benefit level	Benefit dimension	Item examples and references
High	Cost	**Parcel lockers** (Viu-Roig and Alvarez-Palau 2020, Mangiaracina et al. 2019, Vakulenko et al. 2019, Zhu 2019) **Big data** (Saetta and Caldarelli 2020, Sarma et al. 2020, Xu et al. 2020, Dubey et al. 2019, Hahn 2019, Winkelhaus and Grosse 2020, Zhang et al. 2019, Ranieri et al. 2018) **Dynamic pricing** Mangiaracina et al. (2019) **Crowdsourcing** Comi and Savchenko (2021), Kiba-Janiak et al. (2021), Seghezzi et al. (2020), Viu-Roig and Alvarez-Palau (2020), Mangiaracina et al. (2019), Florio et al. (2018)
	Environment	**UAV's** (Elsayed and Mohamed 2020, Lazarević and Dobrodolac 2020, Mangiaracina et al. 2019, Zhu 2019) **Autonomous robots** (Lazarević and Dobrodolac 2020, Mangiaracina et al. 2019, Ranieri et al. 2018) **Parcel lockers** (Mucowska 2021, Viu-Roig and Alvarez-Palau 2020) **Big data** (Mucowska 2021, Bosona 2020, Fosso Wamba 2020, Saetta and Caldarelli 2020, Shan et al. 2019, Winkelhaus and Grosse 2020, Ranieri et al. 2018)
Moderate	Cost	**UAV's** (Bosona 2020, Di Puglia Pugliese et al. 2020, Lazarević and Dobrodolac 2020, Aurambout et al. 2019, Maghazei and Netland 2019, Mangiaracina et al. 2019, Zhu 2019) **Autonomous robots** (Lazarević and Dobrodolac 2020, Mangiaracina et al. 2019, Hoffmann and Prause 2018, Ranieri et al. 2018) **Reception boxes** (Viu-Roig and Alvarez-Palau 2020, Mangiaracina et al. 2019)
	Environment	**Dynamic pricing** Mangiaracina et al. (2019) **Crowdsourcing** Ghaderi et al. (2022), Comi and Savchenko (2021), Kiba-Janiak et al. (2021), Mucowska (2021), Simoni et al. (2019), Viu-Roig and Alvarez-Palau (2020)
Low	Environment	**Reception boxes** Viu-Roig and Alvarez-Palau (2020), Mangiaracina et al. (2019)

Appendix 2. Measurement and Data Structure—'Challenges'

Challenges level	Challenges dimension	Item examples and references
High	Legal	**UAV's** (Bosona 2020, Elsayed and Mohamed 2020, Lazarević and Dobrodolac 2020, Viu-Roig and Alvarez-Palau 2020) **Autonomous robots** (Viu-Roig and Alvarez-Palau 2020, Hoffmann and Prause 2018, Ranieri et al. 2018)

(continued)

(continued)

Challenges level	Challenges dimension	Item examples and references
	Technology	**UAV's** (Bosona 2020) **Autonomous robots** (Lazarević and Dobrodolac 2020, Ranieri et al. 2018)
Moderate	Technology	**Parcel lockers** (Tsai and Tiwasing 2021, Vakulenko et al. 2019) **Big data** (Bosona 2020, Shan et al. 2019, Winkelhaus and Grosse 2020) **Crowdsourcing** (Ghaderi et al. 2022, Seghezzi et al. 2020)
Low	Legal	**Parcel lockers** (Tsai and Tiwasing 2021) **Big data** (Shan et al. 2019) **Reception boxes** (Mangiaracina et al. 2019) **Dynamic pricing** (Mangiaracina et al. 2019)
	Technology	**Reception boxes** (Mangiaracina et al. 2019) **Dynamic pricing** (Mangiaracina et al. 2019)

Appendix 3. Measurement and Data Structure—'Implementation Time Frame'

Implementation time frame	Item examples and references
Long-term	**UAV's** (Lazarević and Dobrodolac 2020, Bosona 2020, Viu-Roig and Alvarez-Palau 2020)
Mid-term	**Autonomous robots** (Kiba-Janiak et al. 2021)
Short-term	**Reception boxes** (Mangiaracina et al. 2019, Florio et al. 2018) **Crowdsourcing** (Kiba-Janiak et al. 2021, Mangiaracina et al. 2019, Florio et al. 2018)
In use	**Parcel lockers** (Tsai and Tiwasing 2021, Zhou et al. 2020, Vakulenko et al. 2019, Ranieri et al. 2018) **Big Data** (Fosso Wamba 2020, Sarma et al. 2020, Dubey et al. 2019, Hahn 2019, Shan et al. 2019, Zhang et al. 2019) **Dynamic pricing** (Mangiaracina et al. 2019)

Appendix 4. Measurement and Data Structure—'Efficiency'

Efficiency: optimization possibility	Item examples and references
High	**Autonomous robots** (Lazarević and Dobrodolac 2020, Silvestri et al. 2019, Ranieri et al. 2018) **Big data** (Fosso Wamba 2020, Saetta and Caldarelli, 2020, Sarma et al. 2020, Dubey et al. 2019, Hahn 2019, Shan et al. 2019, Zhang et al. 2019)

(continued)

(*continued*)

Efficiency: optimization possibility	Item examples and references
Moderate	**UAV's** (Di Puglia Pugliese et al. 2020, Aurambout et al. 2019, Maghazei and Netland 2019) **Parcel lockers** (Zhou et al. 2020, Mangiaracina et al. 2019) **Reception boxes** (Florio et al. 2018) **Crowdsourcing** (Ghaderi et al. 2022, Seghezzi et al. 2020, Simoni et al. 2019, Mangiaracina et al. 2019, Florio et al. 2018)
Low	**Dynamic pricing** (Mangiaracina et al. 2019)

References

Aurambout, J.-P., Gkoumas, K., Ciuffo, B.: Last mile delivery by drones: an estimation of viable market potential and access to citizens across European cities. Eur. Transp. Res. Rev. **11**(1), 1–21 (2019). https://doi.org/10.1186/s12544-019-0368-2

Bosona, T.: Urban freight last mile logistics—challenges and opportunities to improve sustainability: a literature review. Sustainability **12**(21), 8769 (2020). https://doi.org/10.3390/su12218769

Comi, A.: A modelling framework to forecast urban goods flows. Res. Transp. Econ. **80**, 100827 (2020). https://doi.org/10.1016/j.retrec.2020.100827

Comi, A., Savchenko, L.: Last-mile delivering: analysis of environment-friendly transport. Sustain. Cities Soc. **74**, 103213 (2021). https://doi.org/10.1016/j.scs.2021.103213

Di Puglia Pugliese, L., Macrina, G., Guerriero, F.: Trucks and drones cooperation in the last-mile delivery process. Networks (2020). https://doi.org/10.1002/net.22015

Dubey, R., et al.: Big data analytics and organizational culture as complements to swift trust and collaborative performance in the humanitarian supply chain. Int. J. Prod. Econ. **210**, 120–136 (2019). https://doi.org/10.1016/j.ijpe.2019.01.023

Elsayed, M., Mohamed, M.: The impact of airspace regulations on unmanned aerial vehicles in last-mile operation. Transp. Res. Part D Transp. Environ. **87**, 102480 (2020). https://doi.org/10.1016/j.trd.2020.102480

Feng, Y., Zhu, Q., Lai, K.: Corporate social responsibility for supply chain management: a literature review and bibliometric analysis. J. Clean. Prod. **158**, 296–307 (2017). https://doi.org/10.1016/j.jclepro.2017.05.018

Florio, A., Feillet, D., Hartl, R.: The delivery problem: optimizing hit rates in e-commerce deliveries. Transp. Res. Part B Methodol. **117**, 455–472 (2018). https://doi.org/10.1016/j.trb.2018.09.011

Fosso Wamba, S.: Humanitarian supply chain: a bibliometric analysis and future research directions. Ann. Oper. Res. (2020). https://doi.org/10.1007/s10479-020-03594-9

Ghaderi, H., Tsai, P.-W., Zhang, L.: An integrated crowdshipping framework for green last mile delivery. Sustain. Cities Soc. **78**, 103552 (2022). https://doi.org/10.1016/j.scs.2021.103552

Hahn, G.: Industry 4.0: a supply chain innovation perspective. Int. J. Prod. Res. **58**(5), 1425–1441 (2019)

Hoffmann, T., Prause, G.: On the regulatory framework for last-mile delivery robots. Machines **6**(3), 33 (2018). https://doi.org/10.3390/machines6030033

Kiba-Janiak, M., Marcinkowski, J., Jagoda, A., Skowrońska, A.: Sustainable last mile delivery on e-commerce market in cities from the perspective of various stakeholders. Literature review. Sustain. Cities Soc. **71**, 102984 (2021). https://doi.org/10.1016/j.scs.2021.102984

Lazarević, D., Dobrodolac, M.: Sustainability trends in the postal systems of last-mile delivery. Perner's Contacts **15**(1) (2020). https://doi.org/10.46585/pc.2020.1.1547

Maghazei, O., Netland, T.: Drones in manufacturing: exploring opportunities for research and practice. J. Manuf. Technol. Manag. **31**(6), 1237–1259 (2019). https://doi.org/10.1108/jmtm-03-2019-0099

Mangiaracina, R., Perego, A., Seghezzi, A., Tumino, A.: Innovative solutions to increase last-mile delivery efficiency in B2C e-commerce: a literature review. Int. J. Phys. Distrib. Logist. Manag. **49**(9), 901–920 (2019). https://doi.org/10.1108/ijpdlm-02-2019-0048

Mucowska, M.: Trends of environmentally sustainable solutions of urban last-mile deliveries on the E-commerce market—a literature review. Sustainability **13**, 5894 (2021)

Ranieri, L., Digiesi, S., Silvestri, B., Roccotelli, M.: A review of last mile logistics innovations in an externalities cost reduction vision. Sustainability **10**(3), 782 (2018). https://doi.org/10.3390/su10030782

Rossolov, A., Rossolova, H., Holguín-Veras, J.: Online and in-store purchase behavior: shopping channel choice in a developing economy. Transportation **48**(6), 3143–3179 (2021). https://doi.org/10.1007/s11116-020-10163-3

Saetta, S., Caldarelli, V.: How to increase the sustainability of the agri-food supply chain through innovations in 4.0 perspective: a first case study analysis. Procedia Manuf. **42**, 333–336 (2020). https://doi.org/10.1016/j.promfg.2020.02.083

Sarma, D., Das, A., Bera, U.: Uncertain demand estimation with optimization of time and cost using Facebook disaster map in emergency relief operation. Appl. Soft Comput. **87**, 105992 (2020). https://doi.org/10.1016/j.asoc.2019.105992

Seghezzi, A., Mangiaracina, R., Tumino, A., Perego, A.: 'Pony express' crowdsourcing logistics for last-mile delivery in B2C e-commerce: an economic analysis. Int. J. Logist. Res. Appl., 1–17 (2020). https://doi.org/10.1080/13675567.2020.1766428

Shan, S., Zhao, F., Wei, Y., Liu, M.: Disaster management 2.0: a real-time disaster damage assessment model based on mobile social media data—a case study of Weibo (Chinese Twitter). Saf. Sci. **115**, 393–413 (2019). https://doi.org/10.1016/j.ssci.2019.02.029

Silvestri, P., Zoppi, M., Molfino, R.: Dynamic investigation on a new robotized vehicle for urban freight transport. Simul. Model. Pract. Theory **96**, 101938 (2019). https://doi.org/10.1016/j.simpat.2019.101938

Simoni, M.D., Marcucci, E., Gatta, V., Claudel, C.G.: Potential last-mile impacts of crowdshipping services: a simulation-based evaluation. Transportation **47**(4), 1933–1954 (2019). https://doi.org/10.1007/s11116-019-10028-4

Supply Chain Security Working Group: U.S. Chamber of Commerce (2021). https://www.uschamber.com/

Tsai, Y., Tiwasing, P.: Customers' intention to adopt smart lockers in last-mile delivery service: a multi-theory perspective. J. Retail. Consum. Serv. **61**, 102514 (2021). https://doi.org/10.1016/j.jretconser.2021.102514

Vakulenko, Y., Shams, P., Hellström, D., Hjort, K.: Service innovation in e-commerce last mile delivery: mapping the e-customer journey. J. Bus. Res. **101**, 461–468 (2019). https://doi.org/10.1016/j.jbusres.2019.01.016

Viu-Roig, M., Alvarez-Palau, E.: The Impact of E-commerce-related last-mile logistics on cities: a systematic literature review. Sustainability **12**(16), 6492 (2020). https://doi.org/10.3390/su12166492

Wang, X. (Cara), Kim, W., Holguín-Veras, J., Schmid, J.: Adoption of delivery services in light of the COVID pandemic: Who and how long? Transp. Res. Part A Policy Pract. **154**, 270–286 (2021). https://doi.org/10.1016/j.tra.2021.10.012

Winkelhaus, S., Grosse, E.H.: Logistics 4.0: a systematic review towards a new logistics system. Int. J. Prod. Res. **58**, 1, 18–43 (2020). https://doi.org/10.1080/00207543.2019.1612964

Xu, S., Zhang, X., Feng, L., Yang, W.: Disruption risks in supply chain management: a literature review based on bibliometric analysis. Int. J. Prod. Res. **58**(11), 3508–3526 (2020). https://doi.org/10.1080/00207543.2020.1717011

Zhang, Y., Sun, L., Hu, X., Zhao, C.: Order consolidation for the last-mile split delivery in online retailing. Transp. Res. Part E Logist. Transp. Rev. **122**, 309–327 (2019). https://doi.org/10.1016/j.tre.2018.12.011

Zhou, M., Zhao, L., Kong, N., Campy, K., Xu, G., Zhu, G., et al.: Understanding consumers' behavior to adopt self-service parcel services for last-mile delivery. J. Retail. Consum. Serv. **52**, 101911 (2020). https://doi.org/10.1016/j.jretconser.2019.101911. https://doi.org/10.1080/00207543.2019.1641642

Zhu, Y.: The status & future trend of the last mile distribution mode in Chinese cities. In: Proceedings of the 2019 2nd International Conference on Education, Economics and Social Science (ICEESS 2019). Atlantis Press. https://www.atlantis-press.com/proceedings/iceess-19/125920647. Accessed 11 July 2021

An Approach to Digitalising the Manufacturing Steps of Large-Scale Components by Using an Industrial Pilot Case

Kay Burow[1]([✉]) [iD], Patrick Klein[1] [iD], and Klaus-Dieter Thoben[2] [iD]

[1] BIBA – Bremer Institut für Produktion und Logistik GmbH, Hochschulring 20,
28359 Bremen, Germany
{bow,klp}@biba.uni-bremen.de

[2] Institute for Integrated Product Development, University of Bremen, Badgasteiner Straße 1,
28359 Bremen, Germany
tho@biba.uni-bremen.de

Abstract. Although Industry 4.0 is a widespread word and is expected to be found everywhere, a deeper look shows that, depending on the application, its entire implementation throughout manufacturing is finite and has enormous potential for higher levels of integration.

Many complex parts and components are still fabricated and checked manually by workers, especially in large-scale components and vessels; these processes are far beyond digitalised input. With a specific pilot case in mind, the authors work on an approach to include data and implement this knowledge to digitalise the manufacturing process. Therefore, input data (e.g., requirements from the manufacturer, technical constraints, CAD files) are collected and allocated, and the fabrication status is checked.

This paper focuses on a digital mapping for the manufacturing of large-scale components to receive a digital thread, particularly an oil and gas piping vessel (industrial pilot case). The goal is to visualise a target-performance comparison for quality checking to locate missing auxiliary components and fabrication deviations. The individual steps shall be listed, connected and cross-linked to have a digital thread of the until now still manual process.

Keywords: Digitalisation · Digital thread · Large-scale components

1 Introduction

During the past last years, the terms Industry 4.0 and digitalisation have become more and more common. In sectors like automation, digital mapping, digital threads, and digital twins are typical tools [1]. Applications in logistics like the delivery service of Amazon are in a highly digital and flexible state. Individual orders and access to the supply chain up to intervening running orders are possible [2]. Large Enterprises (LE), especially in logistics, have a well-developed implementation towards digitalisation using interconnected services, data and information transfer and monitoring.

D. Y. Kim et al. (Eds.): APMS 2022, IFIP AICT 663, pp. 183–189, 2022.
https://doi.org/10.1007/978-3-031-16407-1_22

For Industry 4.0, it is clear that for a high level of digitalisation, the processes must be transparent and connected (e.g. network, cloud-based); data and information exchange also must be done digitally.

Where digital twins picture a digital counterpart of physical objects or processes with all its connections and dependencies, a digital thread focuses on the traceability of a single set of related data between digital and physical worlds. Figure 1 shows the concept of a digital thread through an Engineering model throughout the entire lifecycle [3] and links the different steps together. Depending on the required information and its limited complexity, a digital thread can help better understand a product's related processes and data flows.

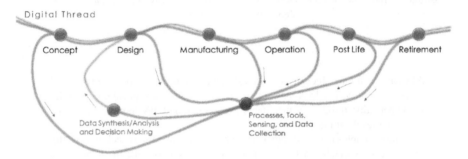

Fig. 1. Engineering design with a Digital Thread [3]

Nevertheless, for small and midsize enterprises (SME) and manufacturing chains with unique or single-part fabrication, the production processes are often only at the beginning of digitalisation. In addition, SMEs lack knowledge in converting their existing manual processes into a digital way. Converting is also a matter of efficiency and price.

Other sectors like Aerospace have their difficulties with the fabrication in only small numbers and extremely hard requirements in manufacturing, quality and documentation [4]. Also, for the manufacture of large-scale components, similar difficulties exist. Here, we must differentiate between the concept and transformation of a smart factory for mass production (e.g., large numbers of items) and the individual implementation of concrete customised components.

Handling and manufacturing large-scale components are still very challenging and lack digitalised processes, especially in combination with SMEs and their difficulties towards digitalisation [5].

In this paper, we consider the manufacturing processes of vessels for oil and gas piping as an example and later pilot case. These vessels (see Fig. 2) are massive in size and are partly manufactured by hand. In addition, the later quality check is also to be done manually, which means workers check every detail and attachment if they are in the proper position, angle and connected by measuring the fabricated model and checking/comparing it with the design model.

One difficulty is the small number of fabricated components, which are mostly unique and designed for one purpose on customer's demand. Also, different stakeholders work together, from the concept over the design phase to the manufactured model, and have to

Fig. 2. Large-scale component (vessel) for oil and gas piping [6]

exchange data and information. To optimise this manual process, a digital thread that will map the different fabrication steps could help to receive a digital approach. Moreover, the data flows can be integrated (e.g., input, output), which can be transformed into a closed-loop for manufacturing.

2 Approach and Methodology

As stated in the previous section, depending on the field of application, manufacturing processes are partly still on the level of Industry 3.0, meaning a lot of work is done by paper and manually with digitalised processes just at the start [7].

Having a particular product in hand with the general focus on manufacturing of large-scale components, the idea is to develop a solution with a general approach. This is adopted for a particular pilot case on the one hand, and on the other hand, the general approach shall serve for transmission to other applications in large-scale manufacturing.

The first step is to analyse the existing manufacturing process and map it, including the flows of information (e.g. input/output data) and technical requirements from the manufacturer.

The general mapping is done by AutomationML, a neutral and XML-based data format that supports data storage and exchange. It further offers the possibility of integrating all kinds of information (e.g., values, files) [8]. Depending on the used software, APIs (application programming interface) allow to import and export data between AutomationML. For example, values in CAD files can be exported and changed in AutomationML.

Furthermore, for the pilot case, the focus lies in evaluating the fabricated component. This means that we need different information from different stakeholders (e.g., CAD model, 3D scan/point cloud, technical requirements). The explicit mapping concerns the pilot case; here, the quality check of a fabricated vessel. The main idea is to compare two models and analyse their deviations. Figure 3 shows the general idea, which can be divided into three parts:

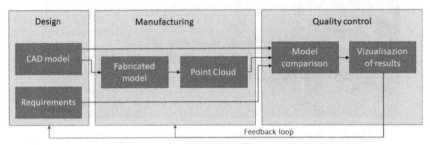

Fig. 3. Simplified concept of the digital thread for the process chain as the specification for AutomationML

- Design includes CAD files, technical drawings, models and technical requirements as well as manufacturing constraints
- Manufacturing includes the fabrication of components and a digital image of the model as a point cloud. Therefore, a 3D scan was made of the fabricated model and provided to us in a point cloud format; manufacturing can consist of multiple fabrication steps, depending on the complexity of the model and is done in iteration loops
- Quality control - the input data from the design phase are compared with the fabricated model, e.g., a point cloud model made by a scan with the help of the requirements

Therefore, two models are necessary. The first is the design model, the CAD model, and the second is the fabricated model. A manufacturer visualisation shall be achieved, which lists and highlights all deviations between the CAD model and point cloud (target-performance comparison). The list can be used for selected targets (deviations) and will show necessary examination as digital content.

3 Pilot Case: Visualisation for Quality Checking

In this section, a deeper look at details is done to understand our idea better. Connecting processes do not make them "smart". It also depends on the correct information in the right place.

For the quality check, the first step is checking for eccentricity and whether the vessel is within tolerances. The next step during manufacturing is to attach all auxiliary components such as flanges, valves, mounts, etc. Every vessel is divided into sections; before two sections are connected/welded, a quality check is necessary. Workers do these checks. They check each detail for position, angle, determent and proper placement by measuring from a reference edge to every single component, also double-checking with the bill of materials. An approach that is very time-consuming and expensive gives freedom for failure due to tired workers of monotonous work and lack of concentration.

Our approach offers a solution to reduce the manual work to specific items. For comparison and visualisation, we use open-source software. Here, we work with Cloud-Compare [9], which includes all necessary tools for quality checks. Nevertheless, the input data require preprocessing. CloudCompare demands specific import formats and both models have to be in the same scale and units. Partly it is done via AutomationML and the CAD software Inventor, which can convert and provide the required format and possess an API for AutomationML.

The procedure is based on the concept shown in Fig. 3 and considers only quality control. Input data is the CAD model, the 3D scan as a point cloud of the fabricated model and the technical requirements. Also, the bill of materials is required for all the components (e.g. pipes, flanges, mounts) attached to the main vessel from the manufacturing phase.

The quality check is done in multiple steps but customised for this solution.

1. Preprocessing input data
2. Check and visualise for completeness
3. Check and visualise for deviations
4. Collect, list and allocate each position of 1 and 2.
5. Recirculation of all positions towards the manufacturer for further arrangements

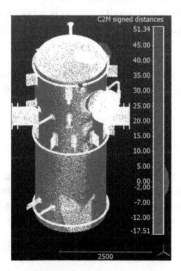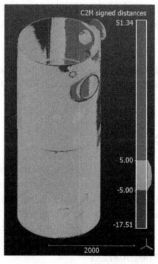

Fig. 4. Comparison of CAD model and point cloud; Left: checking for missing parts (white: CAD model, red: point cloud); Right: Visualisation of deviations - green is within the tolerance, red above and blue below (Color figure online)

As a basis for the pilot case, the AutomationML approach is used, and the single steps are implemented. After receiving all required information for the design and manufacturing, the quality check can be done and results in a list for the designer and manufacturer for further checking. Figure 4 shows exemplarily the results of the first two steps. Used was a partly fabricated vessel for the first examination. Instead of checking every single attachment, only the deviations have to be checked.

4   Conclusion

We found and described a way to depict and transform manual processes in a digital thread and work on a specific implementation through a pilot case. This digital thread will help improve the quality checking by reducing the effort of manual work. Further, digitalising the entire manufacturing process allows data and information to be easily integrated and exchanged between the stakeholders. So far, we can import, adapt and provide the input data for CloudCompare to start with the comparison algorithms. The connection between AutomationML and CloudCompare is the next big step.

5   Discussion and Outlook

Nevertheless, the project is still running, and a lot of work has to be done. Continuing work is the flow of information towards the AutomationML implementation to achieve a complete digital thread.

Parallel, the pilot line with its particular goal has to be completed with steps 4 and 5 to complete the circle of information and gives us the feedback loop.

Defining an API that links AutmationML with CloudCompare is a task that could not yet be achieved. The data is imported manually and exported as a list in an Excel file.

Acknowledgements. This work was supported by the European Union's Horizon 2020 research and innovation programme under the PENELOPE project under grant agreement No. 958303.

References

1. Industry 4.0 is Enabling a New Era of Manufacturing Intelligence and Analytics. https://www.forbes.com/sites/louiscolumbus/2016/08/07/industry-4-0-is-enabling-a-new-era-of-manufacturing-intelligence-and-analytics/?sh=65984bcc7ad9. Accessed 14 May 2022
2. The Amazon's supply chain competitive advantage. http://www.strategy4.org/my-blog/the-amazons-supply-chain-competitive-advantage. Accessed 14 May 2022
3. Singh, V., Willcox, K.E.: Engineering Design with Digital Thread. AIAAJ (2018). https://doi.org/10.2514/1.J057255
4. Industry 4.0 within the Aerospace Sector: Prepare for Takeoff. https://manufacturing.cioreview.com/cxoinsight/industry-40-within-the-aerospace-sector-prepare-for-takeoff-nid-32049-cid-34.html. Accessed 14 May 2022

5. Cotrino, A., Sebastián, M.A., González-Gaya, C.: Industry 4.0 roadmap: implementation for small and medium-sized enterprises, Appl. Sci. **10**(23), 8566 (2020). https://doi.org/10.3390/app10238566
6. Large scale manufactured vessel for oil and gas piping. https://www.idesa.net/references/cat-manufacturing-en.html. Accessed 14 May 2022
7. Bakkari, M., Khatory A., Industry 4.0: Strategy for More Sustainable Industrial Development in SMEs, April 2017
8. What is AutomationML. https://www.automationml.org/about-automationml/automationml/. Accessed 14 May 2022
9. CloudCompare Homepage. https://www.cloudcompare.org. Accessed 14 May 20225

A Rubric for Implementing Explainable AI in Production Logistics

Amita Singh[✉][iD], Erik Flores Garcia[iD], Yongkuk Jeong[iD],
and Magnus Wiktorsson[iD]

KTH Royal Institute of Technology, Södertälje 151 36, Stockholm, Sweden
{amitas,efs01,yongkuk,magwik}@kth.se

Abstract. With the advent of Industry 4.0, the world is witnessing increasing use of data and data-driven services. This phenomenon has penetrated through different sectors of production including logistics. The purpose of this study is to explore the use of Artificial Intelligence (AI) and Machine Learning (ML) in production logistics. This paper is the first step in the direction of understanding the complexity of AI and ML algorithms and thus explaining the black-box-like characteristics of these algorithms. This is coupled with the definition of eXplainable AI (XAI) in the domain. The paper furthers describes the needs for XAI and consequently presents a rubric for implementing XAI in the domain of production logistics and discusses it in detail.

Keywords: Production logistics · Explainable artificial intelligence · Explainability · Interpretability

1 Introduction

For many years artificial intelligence (AI) has mostly focussed on theory without looking a the applications of the real world [27]. However, this is changing with the help of improved learning algorithms, more computational power at hand, and easier access to data enabled advances in the field leading to wider industrial adoption of AI [20]. AI and ML are seeping into our everyday lives in different domains, ranging from medicine and healthcare [2,13,14,36] to banking sectors [21,26] and the domain of production logistics is no different [23,38,42]. The AI and ML techniques have demonstrated remarkable potential in these varied fields [5]. These techniques can benefit from the fact that they can learn automatically based on the historical data and that they can learn from experience while predicting results for new data.

However, with the increasing capacity of these models to be able to predict accurately, the complexity of these AI/ML models are increasing. Many AI algorithms are considered black box when they deal will a large number of data points for training. This black-box-like characteristic is a major roadblock

Supported by Vinnova funded project EXPLAIN.

when it comes to implementing these results [39]. Additionally, since users lack the ability to explain the results obtained through the implementation of these AI algorithms it becomes difficult to trust the results. Wang et al. [41] describe this as preventing "responsible exploitation" of their decisions by users. This phenomenon thus gives rise to the need to motivate these decisions through explanations resulting in more interest in eXplainable AI (XAI) [4].

Researchers and practitioners have started using XAI extensively in the field of medicine and healthcare [2,31,33] as it involves decisions of utmost importance. However, this phenomenon has evolved in different aspects of business domains. Production logistics is one such business domain where this change is taking place. Through this work the authors want to define XAI in terms of what it means in the domain of production logistics and why it is needed. The paper then describes a rubric for implementing XAI in production logistics.

The remainder of the paper is structured as follows: Sect. 2 describes the related work in the field production logistics and AI/ML followed by the reasons why XAI is an emerging and urgent need for production logistics. In Sect. 4, we discuss a set of rules for implementing XAI in the domain and the paper ends with a conclusion.

2   XAI in Production Logistics

In literature, production logistics is described as a system that deals with planning, coordinating and service functions to carry out manufacturing activities [40]. Production logistics refers to all activities involving the transportation of materials and information in a factory. This definition has been reinforced in literature by several other works [30,40]. In time dimension, the scope of produciton logistics is spread over the endpoints from where demand of a product is determined to the point where it is fulfilled which includes flow of product, service or information crossing entrepreneurial and state boundaries [43]. Coordination of these complex systems poses a challenge to both academicians and practitioners.

Nowadays, AI and ML are creeping into the solution space of almost all domains as we discussed earlier and so is the case of production logistic [22]. Next, we describe, in short, artificial intelligence and machine learning followed by the definition of explaninable AI (XAI) in the domain of production logistics.

With the advent of Industry 4.0 machine learning and artificial intelligence has come to the forefront of problem-solving in production domains. With the growing complexity of AI and ML models, it is becoming increasingly important to understand and decode the complexity in order to take informed and understandable decisions.

However, so far there is no concrete definition of XAI in the domain for production and the research team of this work believes that as a first step it is important to understand and define XAI in this domain.

It is important to note that we in this paper adopt the definitions of explainability and interpretability and hence the difference between the two as per the literature [1,29].

We understand XAI in production logistics as the capability to assist users in understanding the AI models with clear reasoning behind them that enables users to use, trust, verify and validate the outputs produced that eventually helps in building rigorous business models and facilitates business needs.

3 Reasons for XAI in Production Logistics

In this section, we discuss what are the core needs for explanation of AI and where do they stem from. The research team based on existing literature and based on the discussions found these needs or reasons for XAI in the domain of production logistics.

The first purpose of XAI in production logistics comprehends justifying the results of a model. AI propelled research and the results are reported to have yielded controversial results [1,10,19] which demands more and more justification for the results presented through AI. XAI should thus be able to provide explaination for a decision-making specifically for unexpected results [1]. This would give provable and auditable results which further defend that algorithms are fair and logical thus building trust in AI. According to the authors, these characteristics of being provable and auditable would play an important role in the implementing XAI and encouraging AI in production logistics. Furthermore, these explanations provide compliance with legislation in the domain of production logistics.

The second reason to employ XAI in produciton logistics is to be able to control. According to Adadi and Berrada [1], explainability can help prevent untoward events by giving more insights into a model which, in turn, provides visibility over vulnerabilities and flaws. This can prove to be an important aspect in supply chain and production systems where flaws in AI models can lead to disruption on an assembly line leading to, for example, shortage of material or bottleneck in the assembly.

Explainability to evaluate AI models in production logistics for us mean that both domain experts, logistics planners and software developers, how to evaluate and compare different models. This would require understanding the models in depth to check how the results are yielded and how models perform with changing input criteria.

If the model is explained well, it can then be improved as well. This forms a part of continuous improvement which forms the basis for lean management in production logistics. If planners responsible for logistics in companies understand why a certain output is produced, it will make it possible for the planners to improve it. From the developers' perspective, the increased visibility over vulnerabilities in the model help understand and debug the problem thus giving enhanced performance of the AI model [16].

In industrial setup, it is important to convince the management to use AI algorithms and equally important for the management to have an understanding of the results and vulnerabilities of a model. As pointed out in the literature. [8, 29,34], it is explainability to manage has an overarching theme that encompasses justification, control, improvement and evaluation of models.

4   Rubric for Implementation of XAI

4.1   Low Effort

As production logistics concerns with short throughput times and high planning reliability together with fulfilling customer demands all of which has cost attached to it [32]. Therefore, it is important to do a cost benefit analysis [25] of the model to be explained before implementing XAI methods to it. Accordingly, the cost to explain the model should not exceed, and in most cases should be far below than the profit incurred from a particular model. Ideally the fewer resources are used in explaining the model the better it is [29].

The cost to explain a model could also be a one-time cost if the explanation is *model agnostic*. Model agnostic explanation refers to the explanation that can be used to explain any model and not just a specific model.

4.2   High Fairness

Binns [9] on their work on fairness in XAI discuss how *fair* should be defined: equal probability of all explainees benefiting from the explanation or minimizing risk for the least advantaged stakeholder [7,18]. Among many definitions of formalisation of fairness, Dieterich et al. proposed 'equality of opportunity' which is a well-suited definition in case of many stakeholders. Following this multi intra and interfactories stakeholders, this presents itself as the most suited explanation of fairness as shown in Fig. 1.

Fig. 1. Characteristics proposed for XAI in production logistics.

Production logistics inherently is a multiple stakeholder scenario where different stakeholders are engaged in a supply chain. These stakeholders could be personnel responsible for inbound and outbound logistics together with external suppliers.

4.3   High Comprehensibility

Comprehensibility refers to the aid that explanation provides in human understanding of an AI/ML model [29]. This has also been discussed as *plausibility* in the literature [15], but the research team for this work believes that plausibility which refers to as a measure regarding the acceptance of the explanation. Comprehensibility, thus, encompasses the plausibility aspect of the model.

Interpretability is discussed in the XAI literature as an extent to which the explanation is understood by humans [17]. The research team upon discussion decided that in production logistics interpretability could be seen as a part of comprehensibility and does not need to be differentiated (Table 1).

Table 1. Relevant literature corresponding to the XAI characteristics

XAI characteristic	References
Low Effort	Nyhuis et al. [32], Layard et al. [25], Meske et al. [29]
High Fairness	Binns [9], Barocas et al. [7], Haian et al. [18], Dietrich et al. [12]
High Comprehensibility	Meske et al. [29], Furnkranz et al. [15], Guidotti et al. [17]
High Fidelity	Arbatli et al. [6], Andrews et al. [3], Maskowska-Kaczmar et al. [28], Zilke et al. [44], Ribero et al. [37]
High Generalizability	Meske et al. [29], Ras et al. [35], Ribeiro et al. [37]
Legal	Montjoye et al. [11]

4.4   High Fidelity

Fidelity in the context of XAI refers to the degree to which the method applied agrees to the input-output mapping of the particular AI technique. The property is considered the most important of all characteristics for explaining an AI model [3,6,28,37,44]. Ribeiro et al. [37] call this property local fidelity as it is not possible for an explanation to be true for the complete model other than when it is indeed explanation of the complete model itself which brings in the word *locally*. This means how a model behaves in the vicinity of the prediction made. Thus, there exists a trade-off between explanability or interpretability and fidelity. This has been discussed in the literature. However, in context of production logistics local fidelity would be sufficient as global fidelity of complex models is difficult to achieve.

Depending upon the management to which the explanation is to be presented from the factory level to shop floor level, the trade-off between explanability and fidelity is made.

4.5   High Generalizability

According to Meske et al. and Ras et al. [29,35] refers to the range of methods which the XAI technique can be used to explain or interpret. Higher the generalizability more the usefulness of the XAI would be. Literature also discusses *explanatory power* [35,37] as an important characteristic for XAI which refers to how generic an explanation is. For example, an explanation that is able to extend to general models has more explanatory power than one that is specific to a model. In other words, model agnostic explanations have more explanatory power than model specific explanations. The research team views this property as a subset of comprehensibity and generalizability.

4.6   Legal

Privacy is an important aspect mentioned the existing literature in the personalized explanation space which includes the risk of meta-data of personnel involved in the process or draw conclusions about behaviour of personnel [11]. However, the research team believes that in the context of production systems and specifically logistics, it is crucial to secure the data and metadata of upstream and downstream suppliers which may include performance data, cost-related figures, etc. Data sharing and explanability in context of the model developed is therefore has legal concerns which encompasses the abovementioned criteria.

Therefore, we used the term *legal* instead of only privacy concerns for the production domain.

5   Conclusion

Recently, XAI has been used in the result critical fields of medicine and healthcare. However, current challenges in production logistics make the use of XAI increasingly relevant. Accordingly, this study explored the use of XAI for production logistics and identified a rubric for its implementation including six characteristics of XAI in production logistics. Additionally, the study identified the reasons for applying XAI in production logistics. Finally, the authors present a rubric for implementing explainable AI in the domain. In future work, it would be interesting to see how a real-world production logistics problem is solved using the rubric presented. Validation of the presented rubric is also an important future work.

References

1. Adadi, A., Berrada, M.: Peeking inside the black-box: a survey on explainable artificial intelligence (XAI). IEEE Access (2018)
2. Ahmad, M.A., Eckert, C., Teredesai, A.: Interpretable machine learning in healthcare. In: Proceedings of the 2018 ACM International Conference on Bioinformatics, Computational Biology, and Health Informatics (2018)
3. Andrews, R., Diederich, J., Tickle, A.B.: Survey and critique of techniques for extracting rules from trained artificial neural networks. Knowl. Based Syst. (1995)
4. Anjomshoae, S., Najjar, A., Calvaresi, D., Främling, K.: Explainable agents and robots: results from a systematic literature review. In: 18th International Conference on Autonomous Agents and Multiagent Systems (AAMAS 2019), Montreal, Canada, 13–17 May 2019. International Foundation for Autonomous Agents and Multiagent Systems (2019)
5. Antoniadi, A.M., et al.: Current challenges and future opportunities for XAI in machine learning-based clinical decision support systems: a systematic review. Appl. Sci. **11**(11) (2021)
6. Arbatli, A.D., Akin, H.L.: Rule extraction from trained neural networks using genetic algorithms. Nonlinear Anal. Theory Methods Appl. (1997)
7. Barocas, S., Selbst, A.D.: Big data's disparate impact. Calif. Law Rev. **104**, 671 (2016)
8. Berente, N., Gu, B., Recker, J., Santhanam, R.: Managing Ai. MIS Q. (2019). Call for Papers
9. Binns, R.: Fairness in machine learning: lessons from political philosophy. In: Conference on Fairness, Accountability and Transparency. PMLR (2018)

10. Caruana, R., Lou, Y., Gehrke, J., Koch, P., Sturm, M., Elhadad, N.: Intelligible models for healthcare: Predicting pneumonia risk and hospital 30-day readmission. In: Proceedings of the 21th ACM SIGKDD International Conference on Knowledge Discovery and Data Mining (2015)
11. De Montjoye, Y.A., Radaelli, L., Singh, V.K., Pentland, A.S.: Unique in the shopping mall: on the reidentifiability of credit card metadata. Science (2015)
12. Dieterich, W., Mendoza, C., Brennan, T.: Demonstrating accuracy equity and predictive parity performance of the compas risk scales in broward county (2016)
13. Dua, S., Acharya, U.R., Dua, P.: Machine Learning in Healthcare Informatics. Springer, Heidelberg (2014). https://doi.org/10.1007/978-3-642-40017-9
14. Esteva, A., et al.: A guide to deep learning in healthcare. Nat. Med. (2019)
15. Fürnkranz, J., Kliegr, T., Paulheim, H.: On cognitive preferences and the plausibility of rule-based models. Mach. Learn. **109**(4) (2020)
16. Gilpin, L.H., Bau, D., Yuan, B.Z., Bajwa, A., Specter, M., Kagal, L.: Explaining explanations: an overview of interpretability of machine learning. In: 2018 IEEE 5th International Conference on Data Science and Advanced Analytics (DSAA). IEEE (2018)
17. Guidotti, R., Monreale, A., Ruggieri, S., Turini, F., Giannotti, F., Pedreschi, D.: A survey of methods for explaining black box models. ACM Comput. Surv. (CSUR) (2018)
18. Hajian, S., Domingo-Ferrer, J.: A methodology for direct and indirect discrimination prevention in data mining. IEEE Trans. Knowl. Data Eng. (2012)
19. Howard, A., Zhang, C., Horvitz, E.: Addressing bias in machine learning algorithms: a pilot study on emotion recognition for intelligent systems. In: 2017 IEEE Workshop on Advanced Robotics and its Social Impacts (ARSO). IEEE (2017)
20. Jordan, M.I., Mitchell, T.M.: Machine learning: trends, perspectives, and prospects. Science (2015)
21. Khandani, A.E., Kim, A.J., Lo, A.W.: Consumer credit-risk models via machine-learning algorithms. J. Bank. Financ. (2010)
22. Klumpp, M., Hesenius, M., Meyer, O., Ruiner, C., Gruhn, V.: Production logistics and human-computer interaction-state-of-the-art, challenges and requirements for the future. Int. J. Adv. Manuf. Technol. **105**(9) (2019)
23. Knoll, D., Prüglmeier, M., Reinhart, G.: Predicting future inbound logistics processes using machine learning. Procedia CIRP (2016)
24. Kusner, M.J., Loftus, J., Russell, C., Silva, R.: Counterfactual fairness. Adv. Neural Inf. Process. Syst. (2017)
25. Layard, P.R.G., et al.: Cost-Benefit Analysis. Cambridge University Press, Cambridge (1994)
26. Le, H.H., Viviani, J.L.: Predicting bank failure: an improvement by implementing a machine-learning approach to classical financial ratios. Res. Int. Bus. Financ. (2018)
27. Linardatos, P., Papastefanopoulos, V., Kotsiantis, S.: Explainable ai: a review of machine learning interpretability methods. Entropy **23**, 18 (2020)
28. Markowska-Kaczmar, U., Wnuk-Lipiński, P.: Rule extraction from neural network by genetic algorithm with pareto optimization. In: Rutkowski, L., Siekmann, J.H., Tadeusiewicz, R., Zadeh, L.A. (eds.) ICAISC 2004. LNCS (LNAI), vol. 3070, pp. 450–455. Springer, Heidelberg (2004). https://doi.org/10.1007/978-3-540-24844-6_66
29. Meske, C., Bunde, E., Schneider, J., Gersch, M.: Explainable artificial intelligence: objectives, stakeholders, and future research opportunities. Inf. Syst. Manag. (2022)

30. Nagy, G., Illés, B., Bányai, Á.: Impact of industry 4.0 on production logistics. In: IOP Conference Series: Materials Science and Engineering, vol. 448. IOP Publishing (2018)
31. Nazar, M., Alam, M.M., Yafi, E., Mazliham, M.: A systematic review of human-computer interaction and explainable artificial intelligence in healthcare with artificial intelligence techniques. IEEE Access (2021)
32. Nyhuis, P., Wiendahl, H.P.: Fundamentals of Production Logistics: Theory, Tools and Applications. Springer Science & Business Media, Heidelberg (2008). https://doi.org/10.1007/978-3-540-34211-3
33. Panigutti, C., Perotti, A., Pedreschi, D.: Doctor XAI: an ontology-based approach to black-box sequential data classification explanations. In: Proceedings of the 2020 Conference on Fairness, Accountability, and Transparency (2020)
34. Rai, A., Constantinides, P., Sarker, S.: Next generation digital platforms: toward human-ai hybrids. Mis Q. (2019)
35. Ras, G., van Gerven, M., Haselager, P.: Explanation methods in deep learning: users, values, concerns and challenges. In: Escalante, H.J., et al. (eds.) Explainable and Interpretable Models in Computer Vision and Machine Learning. TSSCML, pp. 19–36. Springer, Cham (2018). https://doi.org/10.1007/978-3-319-98131-4_2
36. Ravì, D., et al.: Deep learning for health informatics. IEEE J. Biomed. Health Inform. (2016)
37. Ribeiro, M.T., Singh, S., Guestrin, C.: Why should i trust you? Explaining the predictions of any classifier. In: Proceedings of the 22nd ACM SIGKDD International Conference on Knowledge Discovery and Data Mining (2016)
38. Singh, A., Wiktorsson, M., Hauge, J.B.: Trends in machine learning to solve problems in logistics. Procedia CIRP (2021)
39. Stepin, I., Alonso, J.M., Catala, A., Pereira-Fariña, M.: A survey of contrastive and counterfactual explanation generation methods for explainable artificial intelligence. IEEE Access 9 (2021)
40. Strandhagen, J.W., Alfnes, E., Strandhagen, J.O., Vallandingham, L.R.: The fit of industry 4.0 applications in manufacturing logistics: a multiple case study. Adv. Manuf. 5(4) (2017)
41. Wang, N., Pynadath, D.V., Hill, S.G.: Trust calibration within a human-robot team: comparing automatically generated explanations. In: 2016 11th ACM/IEEE International Conference on Human-Robot Interaction (HRI). IEEE (2016)
42. Woschank, M., Rauch, E., Zsifkovits, H.: A review of further directions for artificial intelligence, machine learning, and deep learning in smart logistics. Sustainability (2020)
43. Wu, S.D., Roundy, R.O., Storer, R.H., Martin-Vega, L.A.: Manufacturing logistics research: taxonomy and directions. Technical report, Cornell University Operations Research and Industrial Engineering (1999)
44. Zilke, J.R., Loza Mencía, E., Janssen, F.: DeepRED–rule extraction from deep neural networks. In: Calders, T., Ceci, M., Malerba, D. (eds.) DS 2016. LNCS (LNAI), vol. 9956, pp. 457–473. Springer, Cham (2016). https://doi.org/10.1007/978-3-319-46307-0_29

A Procedural Method to Build Decision Support Systems for Effective Interventions in Manufacturing – A Predictive Maintenance Example from the Spring Industry

Ferdinand Deitermann[1]([✉]) [ID], Lukas Budde[1] [ID], Thomas Friedli[1], and Roman Hänggi[2]

[1] University of St. Gallen, 9008 St. Gallen, Switzerland
ferdinand.deitermann@unisg.ch
[2] University of Applied Sciences OST, St. Gallen, Switzerland

Abstract. Predictive maintenance as one of the most prominent data-driven approaches enables companies to not only maximize the reliability of production processes but also to improve their efficiency. This is especially valuable in today's volatile environment. Nevertheless, companies still struggle to implement digital technologies to track and improve their manufacturing processes, which includes data driven decision support systems. Based on practitioner interviews we identified the lack of guidance as a root cause. Additionally, literature reveals a shortcoming of methods especially suited for the needs of the manufacturing industry. This study contributes to this field by answering the question of how a procedural method can look like to guide practitioners to build decision support systems for effective interventions in manufacturing. Applying a design science research approach, the manuscript presents a seven-step procedural method to build decision support systems in manufacturing. The approach was designed and field tested at the example of a predictive maintenance model for a spring production process. The findings indicate that the incorporation of all stakeholders and the uncovering and use of implicit process knowledge in humans is of utmost importance for success.

Keywords: Decision support systems · Predictive maintenance · Data-driven applications · Data mining · Industry 4.0

1 Introduction

The importance of managing manufacturing volatility has become ever more present due to recent events such as the COVID-19 pandemic and the Ukraine war. Despite them being external events, the ability to deal with internal disruptions and disturbances has become more important as well [1, 2]. According to Heil [3] and Peukert et al. [4] externally caused disruptions account for less than 30% of all disruptions. Hence, internal disruptions are important. These are, for example machine failures, quality defects, or personnel failures [4]. To cope with such internal events, two approaches are suitable:

© IFIP International Federation for Information Processing 2022
Published by Springer Nature Switzerland AG 2022
D. Y. Kim et al. (Eds.): APMS 2022, IFIP AICT 663, pp. 198–209, 2022.
https://doi.org/10.1007/978-3-031-16407-1_24

reactive or preventive [4]. The first approach describes measures reacting to an already occurred event, while the latter describes measures that will prevent disruptions from occurring [4]. Of particular importance are cyber-physical solutions, which are expected to "significantly contribute to the better transparency and to the more robust functioning of supply chains" [1]. This is due to their ability to quickly and reliably unveil potential events, while at the same time reducing potential negative consequences [1].

"One of the most prominent data-driven approaches for monitoring industrial systems aiming to maximize reliability and efficiency" is Predictive Maintenance (PdM) [5]. PdM "consists of assets or systems monitoring to predict trends, behavior patterns, and correlations by statistical or machine learning models aimed at developing prognostic methods for fault detection and diagnosis" [5]. Introducing PdM can reduce maintenance costs by up to 30% and at the same time reduce breakdowns by up to 75% [6, 7]. Bunzel [8] even states that 50% of the preventive maintenance costs are a waste. PdM can increase efficiency significantly, as maintenance accounts for a total of 15–60% of the total costs of manufacturing operations [9, 10]. Establishing a ratio: Mobley [10] states that "the U.S. industry spends more than $200 billion each year on maintenance". As a result, PdM 1) can reduce machine breakdowns, which in turn reduces the possibilities of internal disturbances and 2) has the potential to reduce manufacturing costs [10, 11]. Therefore, PdM is one potential solution to solve the trade-off between cost efficiency and increase in robustness. As a result, the study focuses on this particular measure.

Despite a variety of use cases of data-driven improvements, companies are far from implementing such approaches [5]. Interviews with practitioners from three different companies reveal that one reason is the lack of a "roadmap" or "user manual" that guides an implementation. These statements show that current approaches lack a manufacturing focus and are too complex to apply.

Hence, we want to answer the research question of *"how can a procedural method look like to guide practitioners to build decision support systems for effective interventions in manufacturing?"* We do so by following the design science research (DSR) approach from Hevner [12]. The practical contributions include both the procedural method and insights about the role of humans. Additionally, scientific contributions include the necessary steps to implement data-driven improvements in a manufacturing environment, and the importance of implicit human knowledge.

The remainder of this article is structured as follows: After the introduction, related literature on data-driven improvement approaches and PdM is discussed. Subsequently, the research methodology and the artifact development are introduced. Afterwards, the field testing is described. Lastly, we briefly discuss the theoretical and practical implications of this paper, as well as its limitations and possible future research.

2   Research Background

All major countries with a strong manufacturing industry have identified the integration of digital technology into manufacturing processes as important for future competitiveness. In Germany the concept is called Industry 4.0 [13], China initiated China 2025 [14], and in the USA, the National Institute of Standards and Technology has coined the term smart manufacturing [15]. Although the concepts differ, all promote the use of modern

IT technologies and data in manufacturing [16], with one of the key technologies being big data analysis [17]. Despite the announcement a decade ago (e.g., 2011 in Germany) [13], companies still struggle to implement the technologies [5].

Big data analytics refers to a set of data with high volume and complex structure that cannot be handled by traditional methods of data processing [17]. It aims to transform data into meaningful and usable information [18]. Four levels of analytic capabilities are apparent: descriptive, diagnostic, predictive, and prescriptive [19–22]. Descriptive answers the question of "what happened". At this first level of data analytics, no root-causes analysis is conducted [22]. Diagnostic addresses the question of "why did it happen" and identifies root-causes [22]. Predictive addresses the question of "what will happen" and seeks to predict potential future outcomes based on drivers of observed phenomena [22]. Prescriptive addresses the question of "what should be done" combining results of the previous stages [22]. We aim to develop a procedural method for stage three (prescriptive), since PdM can be of great value for companies (see Sect. 1) and companies so far struggle to make use of data, resulting in stage 4 being out of scope for a significant number of companies.

A literature review reveals many approaches for data mining and exploitation (i.e., [23–33]). One of the most famous is the Cross Industry Standard Process for Data Mining (CRISP-DM) [34]. It is industry-independent consisting of six iterative phases: business understanding, data understanding, data preparation, modeling, evaluation, and deployment [25, 34]. It emphasizes the following aspects as essential to succeed with big data projects: understanding the business problems, a well-planned project map, adoption of innovative visualization techniques, top management involvement, and a data-driven decision making culture [22]. Another approach is the Data Value Chain, a framework to manage data holistically from capture to decision making [31]. The chain provides a framework to examine how to bring disparate data together in an organized fashion and create valuable information that can inform decision making at the enterprise level [31]. The flexible analytics framework (FlexAnalytics) proposes several potential data-analytics placement strategies. It is applicable for data pre-processing, runtime data analysis and visualization, as well as for large scale data transfer [33]. Another well-known method is "Sample, Explore, Modify, Model and Assess" (SEMMA), which focuses to integrate data mining tools [35]. However, the lack of integration into organizational management results in a decreased importance [35].

To assess the suitability of existing methods, we derived literature-based criteria (i.e., [36]) and from practitioners (see Fig. 1). On the one hand, the assessment reveals that all analyzed approaches strive for general validity. Consequently, they fail to address the specific needs of the manufacturing industry. An example for this shortcoming is the CRISP-DM approach: Several attempts to increase the approach were undertaken [35]. One of the most acknowledged (i.e., Analytics Solutions Unified Method for Data Mining/Predictive Analytics (ASUM-DM)), developed by IBM, however, is not open source available [35, 37]. To still categorize ASUM-DM we used the works from Mockenhaupt [30] and Angée et al. [29]. On the other hand, existing solutions are complex, expensive, and too comprehensive for a simple bottom-up approach and not adapted for and tested in manufacturing companies. We found, for example, that process understanding is not considered as starting point of data-based decision making and process optimization.

However, the involvement of human operators is considered key (i.e., research stream Human-In-The-Loop [38]) [39]. As a result, a procedural method that is suited for the manufacturing industry describing interactions between humans and non-human agents is lacking [39].

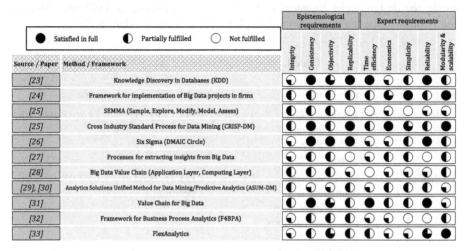

Fig. 1. Comparison of data mining approaches

3 Research Approach

We opted for a DSR approach to design a procedural method that provides guidance to build decision support systems for effective interventions in operations. DSR originates from information systems (IS) research [40] and is well established in the field [41–43]. It supports the development of a "well-tested, well-understood and well-documented innovative generic design that has been field tested to establish pragmatic validity" [44]. The approach is well suited for operations management research as well [44]. For this particular study it is suited, as we intend to develop a generic method (see [45] for different types of artifacts), which is applicable to data-driven improvements.

Various processes and guidelines to conduct DSR exist [41, 43]. While the framework from Hevner et al. [46] is the most cited by IS researchers [47], the three cycle view from Hevner [12] provides a more detailed and improved version [48], which is why we rely on this version. It is divided into three cycles: relevance cycle, rigor cycle, and design cycle [12].

The DSR process starts with the relevance cycle by providing the "problem space" [46]. In this study, the application context is motivated by problem owners (POs) from three companies (i.e., two industrial companies and one smart factory solutions provider). The authors conducted interviews of about one hour each with a different number of participants (see Table 1). Based on the POs' statements, and supported by related literature, the research team derived requirements for an artifact: 1) proper guidance to implement PdM, 2) include context aware information [49] also considering the human role, and 3) include a quality and maturity assessment of collected data.

The rigor cycle provides "past knowledge to the research project to ensure its innovation" [12]. The knowledge base for the conceptual development of this study is provided in Sect. 2. Its findings led to a first procedural method, which was evaluated by POs during the design cycle. Eventually, the results of the conducted DSR are added as contribution to the scientific community [12], which closes the rigor cycle.

Table 1. Overview of empirical data

Purpose	Data item	Duration	Source	Date
Problem statement and understanding	Interviews with three companies with problem owners	1 h each	CEO, COO, IT, Head of Operations	01.2018–03.2018
Evaluation	Workshop with operations management from case study company to discuss, and concretize use-case and project plan/procedural method	8 h	CEO, IT, Head of Operations	01.2018–03.2018
Evaluation	Interview with case study company	2 h	Head of Operations, Operators	
Field testing	Shadowing (process immersion: global view)	8 h	Head of Operations, Operators	03.2018–04.2018
Field testing	Shadowing (process immersion: material flow)	8 h	Head of Operations, Operators	
Field testing	Shadowing (process immersion: machine control)	8 h	Head of Operations, Operators	
Field testing	Data list (process and machine data)	–	Head of Operations, Manufacturing IT	
Field testing	Machine and process data, documentation of operator´s actions	–	Machine and process data	

(*continued*)

Table 1. (*continued*)

Purpose	Data item	Duration	Source	Date
Field testing	Analytic results	–	Machine and process data	04.2018–05.2018
Field testing	7 workshops (various iterations to optimize model, extend data volume, variables and increase robustness of model)	4 h each	Head of Operations, Manufacturing IT, Operators	06.2018–12.2018
Evaluation and finalization	Final interview with problem owners from case study company	1 h	Head of Operations	01.2019
Evaluation	Final meeting with problem owners from all three companies	2 h	Head of Operations,	06.2019

The design cycle represents the core of DSR, aiming to develop the artifact and rigorously evaluate it, "until a satisfactory design is achieved" [12]. The first procedural method was evaluated and refined with POs during an eight-hour workshop. Afterwards, it was transferred to the field testing (i.e., relevance cycle). It was applied to a specific use-case of PdM by conducting an interview, a series of workshops, and utilizing company data (see Sect. 5). To ensure the completeness of the artifact, the outcome of the application of the procedural method and the method itself were validated with the POs (final interview and meeting). We stimulated a guided discussion a) to validate the procedural method and b) about success factors in each step. Based on the predefined requirements, the artifact was approved (i.e., giving proper guidance, including sufficient context aware information, and assessing the quality and maturity of data). Additionally, the POs highlighted the importance of implicit knowledge of humans in all steps of the method (e.g., step 7: the capability to visually assess the cutting burr quality). Moreover, the solution provider representatives stated that the artifact is suited for other use cases, and that they will incorporate it in their service offerings.

4   Development of the Artifact

The development of the artifact followed two phases: First, we searched the literature for existing methods and models to implement data-driven solutions. Based on this knowledge and the goal to develop a procedural method that is applicable and understandable for practitioners, we derived the first artifact. The design cycle was further enriched by the initial interviews with POs. Second, we evaluated and refined the first artifact during an eight-hour workshop with POs and based on an interview with one PO and manufacturing experts (i.e., operators). The outcome was the definition of the procedural method, which was at the same time the project plan. It comprises seven major steps and incorporates iterative elements (see Fig. 2).

Step 1: Establishing a sound process understanding
The interviews revealed the establishment of a thorough understanding of the underlying process as an essential precondition of all optimization efforts in the manufacturing industry. It ensures the analysis of the original problem without premature conclusions and that the right data is gathered. Consequently, it is important that not only manufacturing experts (e.g., process engineers) develop a thorough process understanding, but all stakeholders. This includes, for example machine operators, data-scientists, IT-experts, and project managers.

Step 2: Identification and classification of available data
The second step of the procedural method intends to identify and classify the data, which is available in the current configuration of the production equipment. The following information have been proven to be relevant: object that is described by data (e.g., torque of axis a); group to which the object belongs (e.g., process quality, material); type of data (e.g., boolean, string, array); availability (e.g., yes, yes under certain circumstances, no); frequency of measurement (e.g., every 1 ms, 5 ms, 1 s); type of measurement device (e.g., sensor, camera system, manual input). The resulting output of step two is a list of available data that can be used for further analysis.

Step 3: Understanding quality-critical factors
During step three, two aspects are relevant: 1) Identifying factors that have the potential to influence the quality of the produced part, and 2) determining if and which data is available within the current configuration of the production equipment to describe manifestations of the identified potential factors. The following example describes this: The incorrect fastening of screws (i.e., overtightened or not tight enough) can result in a substandard product quality. To describe the manifestation of the fastened screw, the torque used to fasten the screws would be an appropriate metric, which can be tracked by sensors. The output of step three is a list with quality-critical factors and its data sources to describe the manifestation.

Step 4: Formulation of hypotheses
The fourth step combines the collected knowledge from the previous steps to formulate admissible hypotheses. A hypothesis needs to clearly state two aspects: 1) the influence of a certain element of a machine on the output quality of a product and 2) the metric to measure deviations from the ideal manifestation.

Step 5: Data collection, verification, and complementation
Step five is composed of collecting the data with which the hypotheses in step four were formulated. Subsequently, it is necessary to validate if the collected data describes the causal relationship from the hypothesis. Additionally, the right frequency to collect the

data has to be determined (e.g., every 1 ms). Finally, the causal relationship has to be analyzed for moderating effects (e.g., temperature and vibrations).

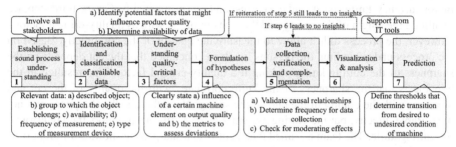

Fig. 2. Procedural method

Step 6: Visualization & analysis
In order to assess the data and identify trends and anomalies, time series graphs can be applied. IT tools can support the handling of greater data amounts during this step. If no insights are generated, an iteration of step five is necessary. Such an iteration can lead to the collection of different data or frequencies. If an iteration of step five does not result in insights, a reanalysis of the hypotheses (i.e., step 4) has to be undertaken.

Step 7: Prediction
The last step of the procedural method is the definition of thresholds that allow to predict the transition from a desired to an undesired condition of a machine. As a result, the previous steps 1–6 enable the project team to predict the optimal point in time to maintain the machine or change a tool. It is recommended that many different systems settings are tested to validate the prediction model.

5 Field Testing

To field test the procedural method we conducted a case study in the spring industry (i.e., several workshops, relevant machine and process data, and documentations) (see Fig. 3). In consultation with the company, we chose the process of welding and cutting the wire to produce springs. The objective was to identify and develop a data-based use case for more effective quality related operator machine interventions.

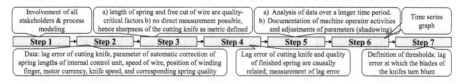

Fig. 3. Application of artifact

First, we established a process understanding for the spring production process and visualized it (step 1). Afterwards, we identified and classified available data to describe the process (step 2). Based on the extensive implicit knowledge of the operators the following data were chosen: lag error of cutting knife, parameter of automatic correction of spring lengths of internal control unit, speed of wire, position of winding finger, motor currency, knife speed, and the corresponding spring quality. For the third step, we identified the length of the spring and the free cut of the wire as quality-critical factors. However, the process didn´t allow to measure the quality of the cut directly. Based on the process understanding, the persons involved concluded that the cut depends on the sharpness of the cutting knife, making it a quality-critical factor. This resulted in the hypothesis that the sharpness of the knife correlates with the quality of the cut and therefore with the quality of the burr of the spring. Nevertheless, the sharpness was not measurable directly, but the cutting system´s drive controller monitors the lag error of the cutting knife. The team assumed that a cut with a sharp knife shows a different time series of the lag error than a cut with a blunt knife (step 4). To test the hypotheses of the causal relationship between lag error of the cutting knife and the quality of the burr, the lag error was measured over a defined time period. We tested the hypotheses with different materials and systems stats to strengthen the traceability and generalizability of the prediction model (step 5). Plotting the lag error of the knife over time revealed that the graphs of the sharp and blunt knife differ (step 6). During step 7 thresholds of the lag error at which the blades of the knifes should be renewed were defined for certain instances. The instances were highly dependent on the input material and thresholds were difficult to derive due to a self-adjusting control system of the machine, preventing clearly distinguishable graphs. The implicit knowledge and visual inspection capability of the operators (i.e., for the burr) was a vital mean.

6   Conclusion

This study yielded a seven-step procedural method to guide practitioners to build decision support systems for effective interventions in operations. We conducted interviews to evaluate the artifact and field tested it in a spring production process.

During our study, the first step *establishing a sound process understanding* turned out to be of utmost importance. That is due to the involvement of different human stakeholders, which subsequently allows to capture the implicit knowledge of humans. First, the management board needs to back such projects, as it displays the relevance of such projects. This in turn leads to employee commitment. Second, the establishment of a process understanding with all stakeholders results in less fearful employees as they are part of the project team. Constant updates over the duration of the project ensure the commitment. Third, the implicit knowledge of humans is a vital part of the process understanding and needs to be extracted in all steps. Hence, the right execution of the first step, i.e., the correct involvement of all stakeholders is key for all subsequent steps.

This study contributes to science as it is empirically grounded in the manufacturing environment. Hence, addressing the specific needs of the manufacturing industry. Additionally, our work touches on the research of human-centric smart manufacturing, highlighting the requirement of built-in human-in-the-loop control and the knowledge about when and how to involve human operators. The procedural method contributes to practice, providing structured guidance to implement decision support systems.

A limitation of this study is the evaluation and field testing in one company and with one specific process only. However, a smaller sample allows for more in-depth research. In future studies this limitation may be addressed by applying the procedural method to different manufacturing processes in different companies.

References

1. Monostori, J.: Supply chains robustness: challenges and opportunities. Procedia CIRP **67**, 110–115 (2018)
2. Bernard, G., Luban, K., Hänggi, R.: Resilienz in der Theorie. In: Luban, K., Hänggi, R. (eds.) Erfolgreiche Unternehmensführung durch Resilienzmanagement. Springer, Heidelberg (2022)
3. Heil, M.: Entstörung betrieblicher Abläufe (1995)
4. Peukert, S., Lohmann, J., Haefner, B., Lanza, G.: Towards increasing robustness in global production networks by means of an integrated disruption management. Procedia CIRP **93**, 706–711 (2020)
5. Arena, S., Florian, E., Zennaro, I., Orrù, P.F., Sgarbossa, F.: A novel decision support system for managing predictive maintenance strategies based on machine learning approaches. Saf. Sci. **146**, 105529 (2022)
6. Gao, R., et al.: Cloud-enabled prognosis for manufacturing. CIRP Ann. **64**(2), 749–772 (2015)
7. Matyas, K., Nemeth, T., Kovacs, K., Glawar, R.: A procedural approach for realizing prescriptive maintenance planning in manufacturing industries. CIRP Ann. **66**(1), 461–464 (2017)
8. Bunzel, M.: As much as half of every dollar you spend on preventive maintenance is wasted. IBM, 4 May 2016
9. Zonta, T., da Costa, C.A., da Rosa Righi, R., de Lima, M.J., da Trindade, E.S., Li, G.P.: Predictive maintenance in the Industry 4.0: a systematic literature review. Comput. Ind. Eng. **150**, 106889 (2020)
10. Mobley, R.K.: An Introduction to Predictive Maintenance. Elsevier, Amsterdam (2002)
11. Coleman, C., Damodaran, S., Deuel, E.: Predictive maintenance and the smart factory: predictive maintenance connects machines to reliability professionals through the power of the smart factory, Deloitte Consulting LLP (2017)
12. Hevner, A.R.: A three cycle view of design science research. Scand. J. Inf. Syst. **19**(2), 4 (2007)
13. Steinhoff, C.: Aktueller Begriff Industrie 4.0, Wissenschaftliche Dienste (2016)
14. Babel, W.: Industrie 4.0, China 2025, IoT. Springer Fachmedien Wiesbaden, Wiesbaden (2021)
15. Thoben, K.-D., Wiesner, S., Wuest, T.: "Industrie 4.0" and smart manufacturing – a review of research issues and application examples. Int. J. Autom. Technol. **11**(1), 4–16 (2017)
16. Tao, F., Qi, Q., Liu, A., Kusiak, A.: Data-driven smart manufacturing. J. Manuf. Syst. **48**, 157–169 (2018)
17. Kang, H.S., et al.: Smart manufacturing: past research, present findings, and future directions. Int. J. Precis. Eng. Manuf.-Green Technol. **3**(1), 111–128 (2016). https://doi.org/10.1007/s40684-016-0015-5
18. Kletti, J.: MES - Manufacturing Execution System. Springer, Heidelberg (2015)
19. O'Donovan, P., Leahy, K., Bruton, K., O'Sullivan, D.T.J.: An industrial big data pipeline for data-driven analytics maintenance applications in large-scale smart manufacturing facilities. J. Big Data **2**(1), 1–26 (2015). https://doi.org/10.1186/s40537-015-0034-z

20. Shuradze, G., Wagner, H.-T.: Towards a conceptualization of data analytics capabilities. In: 2016 49th Hawaii International Conference on System Sciences (HICSS), 2016 49th Hawaii International Conference on System Sciences (HICSS), Koloa, HI, USA, 05 January 2016–08 January 2016. IEEE (2016)
21. Shao, G., Shin, S.-J., Jain, S.: Data analytics using simulation for smart manufacturing. In: Proceedings of the Winter Simulation Conference 2014, 2014 Winter Simulation Conference - (WSC 2014), Savanah, GA, USA, 07 December 2014–10 December 2014. IEEE (2014)
22. Banerjee, A., Bandyopadhyay, T., Acharya, P.: Data analytics: hyped up aspirations or true potential? Vikalpa J. Decis. Mak. **38**(4), 1–12 (2013)
23. Fayyad, U., Piatetsky-Shapiro, G., Smyth, P.: From data mining to knowledge discovery in databases. AI Mag. **3**(17), 37 (1996)
24. Dutta, D., Bose, I.: Managing a big data project: the case of Ramco cements limited. Int. J. Prod. Econ. **165**, 293–306 (2015)
25. Shaerer, C.: The CRISP-DM model: the new blueprint for data mining. J. Data Warehous. **5**(4), 13–22 (2000)
26. Köhler, M., Frank, D., Schmitt, R.: Six Sigma. In: Pfeifer, T., Schmitt, R. (eds.) Masing Handbuch Qualitätsmanagement. Hanser, München (2014)
27. Gandomi, A., Haider, M.: Beyond the hype: big data concepts, methods, and analytics. Int. J. Inf. Manage. **35**(2), 137–144 (2015)
28. Hu, H., Wen, Y., Chua, T.-S., Li, X.: Toward scalable systems for big data analytics: a technology tutorial. IEEE Access **2**, 652–687 (2014)
29. Angée, S., Lozano-Argel, S.I., Montoya-Munera, E.N., Ospina-Arango, J.-D., Tabares-Betancur, M.S.: Towards an improved ASUM-DM process methodology for cross-disciplinary multi-organization big data & analytics projects. In: Uden, L., Hadzima, B., Ting, I.-H. (eds.) Knowledge Management in Organizations, vol. 877. Springer, Cham (2018). https://doi.org/10.1007/978-3-319-95204-8_51
30. Mockenhaupt, A.: Datengetriebene Prozessanalyse. In: Mockenhaupt, A. (ed.) Digitalisierung und Künstliche Intelligenz in der Produktion. Springer Fachmedien Wiesbaden, Wiesbaden (2021)
31. Miller, H.G., Mork, P.: From data to decisions: a value chain for big data. IT Prof. **15**(1), 57–59 (2013)
32. Vera-Baquero, A., Colomo-Palacios, R., Molloy, O.: Business process analytics using a big data approach. IT Prof. **15**(6), 29–35 (2013)
33. Zou, H., Yu, Y., Tang, W., Chen, H.-W.M.: FlexAnalytics: a flexible data analytics framework for big data applications with I/O performance improvement. Big Data Res. **1**, 4–13 (2014)
34. Schröer, C., Kruse, F., Gómez, J.M.: A systematic literature review on applying CRISP-DM process model. Procedia Comput. Sci. **181**, 526–534 (2021)
35. Schäfer, F., Zeiselmair, C., Becker, J., Otten, H.: Synthesizing CRISP-DM and quality management: a data mining approach for production processes. In: 2018 IEEE International Conference on Technology Management, Operations and Decisions (ICTMOD), 2018 IEEE International Conference on Technology Management, Operations and Decisions (ICTMOD), Marrakech, Morocco, 21 November 2018–23 November 2018. IEEE (2018)
36. Greiffenberg, S.: Methoden als Theorien der Wirtschaftsinformatik. In: Uhr, W., Esswein, W., Schoop, E. (eds.) Wirtschaftsinformatik 2003/Band II: Medien - Märkte - Mobilität, s. l. Physica-Verlag HD, Heidelberg (2003)
37. Brenner, W., van Giffen, B., Koehler, J., Fahse, T., Sagodi, A.: Stand in Wissenschaft und Praxis. In: Brenner, W., van Giffen, B., Koehler, J., Fahse, T., Sagodi, A. (eds.) Bausteine eines Managements Künstlicher Intelligenz. Springer Fachmedien Wiesbaden, Wiesbaden (2021)
38. Nunes, D.S., Zhang, P., Sa Silva, J.: A survey on human-in-the-loop applications towards an internet of all. IEEE Commun. Surv. Tutor. **17**(2), 944–965 (2015)

39. Cimini, C., Pirola, F., Pinto, R., Cavalieri, S.: A human-in-the-loop manufacturing control architecture for the next generation of production systems. J. Manuf. Syst. **54**, 258–271 (2020)
40. Winter, R., Aier, S.: Design science research in business innovation. In: Hoffmann, C.P., Lennerts, S., Schmitz, C., Stölzle, W., Uebernickel, F. (eds.) Business Innovation: Das St. Galler Modell. BIUSG, pp. 475–498. Springer, Wiesbaden (2016). https://doi.org/10.1007/978-3-658-07167-7_25
41. Dresch, A., Lacerda, D.P., Antunes Jr, J.A.V.: Design Science Research. Springer, Cham (2015)
42. Gregor, S., Hevner, A.R.: Positioning and presenting design science research for maximum impact. MIS Q. **37**(2), 337–355 (2013)
43. Winter, R.: Design science research in Europe. Eur. J. Inf. Syst. **17**(5), 470–475 (2008)
44. van Aken, J., Chandrasekaram, A., Halman, J.: Conducting and publishing design science research. J. Oper. Manage. **47**, 1–8 (2018)
45. March, S.T., Smith, G.F.: Design and natural science research on information technology. Decis. Support Syst. **15**(4), 251–266 (1995)
46. Hevner, A.R., March, S.T., Park, J., Ram, S.: Design science in information systems research. MIS Q. **28**(1), 75 (2004)
47. Hjalmarsson, A., Rudmark, D., Lind, M.: When designers are not in control – experiences from using action research to improve researcher-developer collaboration in design science research. In: Winter, R., Zhao, J.L., Aier, S. (eds.) DESRIST 2010. LNCS, vol. 6105, pp. 1–15. Springer, Heidelberg (2010). https://doi.org/10.1007/978-3-642-13335-0_1
48. Cahenzli, M., Deitermann, F., Aier, S., Haki, K., Budde, L.: Intra-organizational nudging: designing a label for governing local decision-making. In: itAIS2021: XVIII Conference of the Italian Chapter of AIS - Digital Resilience and Sustainability: People, Organizations, and Society, Trento, Italy (2021)
49. Schmidt, B., Wang, L.: Cloud-enhanced predictive maintenance. Int. J. Adv. Manuf. Technol. **99**(1–4), 5–13 (2016). https://doi.org/10.1007/s00170-016-8983-8

Towards an Inclusion of a PMS-Based Mechanism for Cyber-Physical Production Systems

Abdelaziz Ouazzani-Chahidi[1,3]([⊠]), Jose-Fernando Jimenez[2], Lamia Berrah[1], and Abdellatif Loukili[3]

[1] LISTIC Laboratory, Université Savoie Mont Blanc., Annecy, France
{abdelaziz.ouazzani-chahidi,lamia.berrah}@univ-smb.fr
[2] SYMME Laboratory, Université Savoie Mont Blanc., Annecy, France
jf.jimenez@univ-smb.fr
[3] Industrial Technologies and Services Laboratory, Sidi Mohamed Ben Abdallah University, Fez, Morocco
abdellatif.loukili@usmba.ac.ma

Abstract. Cyber-physical systems, or Cyber-physical production systems in the manufacturing domain, are considered a fundamental technological enabler on the industry 4.0 revolution. In fact, these are interconnected physical and virtual components that provide real time monitoring on the manufacturing execution, for an intelligent management and advanced decision-making to ensure efficiency and reactivity improvement. Traditionally, on manufacturing operation, performance management systems have managed production by piloting the operations towards the expected objectives. However, this approach is limited on cyber physical systems due to the following difficulties: a) synchronous and asynchronous behavior on a real time context causing an unsuitable periodic calculation of performance indicators; and b) human limitations for real-time decision-making due to the complexity of problem and need of prompt analysis and action during execution. The main objective of this paper is to characterize five possible localizations of a potential performance management mechanism on the architectural arrangement of cyber-physical production systems, ranging from traditional centralized to distributed approaches. The purpose of this study is to assess the possible localizations of this mechanism thought the main performance steps including the objectives and results definition, the execution monitoring, the current state analysis, the performance reporting and the launching of the corrective actions.

Keywords: Cyber-physical systems · Industrial performance · Performance management systems · Industry 4.0

1 Introduction

Nowadays, industrial companies are rapidly adopting the digital transformation by integrating new technological enablers, such as internet of things, cyber-physical system,

D. Y. Kim et al. (Eds.): APMS 2022, IFIP AICT 663, pp. 210–218, 2022.
https://doi.org/10.1007/978-3-031-16407-1_25

artificial intelligence, among others [1]. The implementation of these technologies seek to follow better and smarter process for improving product quality through automation. Production systems involve a set of technological devices and human management/labors, which include machines, products, services, informational systems, communication systems, human operators, supervisors, among many others [2]. A Cyber-physical system (CPS), or cyber-physical production systems (CPPS) on the manufacturing domain, are the most promising technology that will enhance manufacturing operations from the productive, efficiency, reactivity and adaptability perspectives [3]. In addition, the cyber-physical system is fast becoming a key technology in Smart manufacturing systems, providing a collaborating entities which are in intensive connection with the surrounding physical world and its on-going processes [4]. In other terms, CPS can be considered as a real-time and embedded system that requires specific applications, including highly precise timing, flexible sensor and actuator interfaces, and robust safety characteristics.

Recent industrial technological advances have made it possible to exploit the advantages of CPPS on the production floor [5]. For example, some of the benefits are related to the information and communication technologies [6]. In particular, CPPS promote product customization through an intelligent composition of manufacturing systems, based on real-time data collection, taking into consideration objectives such as variation in product characteristics, reliability, cost, lead time, etc. [7]. Another benefit is related to the efficiency and sustainability of performance [8, 9]. For example, it would boost the sustainable development on factories as an effective management and use of resources to reduce the negative impact of industry on the environment. Overall, CPPS would improve the operations planning and execution. For instance, CPPS is able to speed up the production setup process, able to reducing the complexity in production and improve the employee's safety [10]. These not exhaustive benefits would definitely improve the efficiency ad adaptability on the highly completive dynamic market.

Smart manufacturing systems are considered as new intelligent systems that provide many capabilities to the production system, processes, and machines. These systems combine different technologies and techniques: statistics, data mining, modelling and artificial intelligence methods [11] for responsiveness and rapid decision-making.

Considering the constant expansion and development of new technologies and the profusion of data, the complexity of managing industrial performance is increasing in the industry. Perhaps, it is not possible to integrate a performance management system (PMS) into a CPPS, due to the lack of reactiveness of traditional PMS and the volatile demand of CPPS. For this reason, the main objective of this paper is to characterize five possible localizations of a potential performance management mechanism on the architectural arrangement of cyber-physical production systems, ranging from traditional centralized to distributed approaches. The purpose of this study is to assess the possible localizations of this mechanism thought the main performance steps including the objectives and results definition, the execution monitoring, the current state analysis, the performance reporting and the launching of the corrective actions.

2 Industrial Performance Management: State of the Art

Performance management is shown to be a critical condition for the efficiency and effectiveness of any business, facilitating control and correction, by comparing current performance results with desired performance levels [12]. The PMS can be defined as the set of procedures and indicators that make it possible to precisely and continuously measure the performance of a company [13]. According to [14] PMS is the set of structured measures used to quantify the efficiency and effectiveness of actions. [15] emphasized the integration of the performance indicator in a PMS, Performance indicators are defined as a set of quantifiable and strategic measures in a performance measurement system that reflect the factors reviews of a company's success. The main context for the evolution of the performance measurement system dates back to the 1980s, when the need for a better tool for performance measurement systems was identified [16] Since that time, several publications have emphasized the need for more balanced, integrated, strategic and dynamic performance measurement systems [14, 20]. This has resulted in the development of frameworks, methodologies, models and tools to trigger the development of new performance measurement systems. Among the methods developed to define and implement indicators, and mainly used in industrial performance management [20], we find the Balanced Score Card which is a strategic planning tool developed by [21], the performance Prism [14] considered by its developers as the second generation of the Balanced Score Card and the management framework. There are other types of systems, such as the Ecograi model, that is a method of designing and implementing advanced manufacturing systems [22], also the "integrated performance management system" proposed by [23], and the system Pyramid of Performance system developed by Judson to link an organization's strategy to its operations, among many others . Thus, it can conclude that a PMS consists of a set of procedures and indicators, which accurately and permanently measure the performance of activities, processes and the whole of organization [17].

Various studies have also assessed the industrial performance in industry 4.0 (I4.0) context, considering that the CPS is the most significant technology exploited in the I4.0 [15]. Furthermore, [26] have explored the effects of I4.0 technology components on organizational performance, and mentioned that the impact of the advanced technologies promises to be significant on the industrial performance. The literature show that technology components allow enterprise to be more productive, certainly they increase the complexity of the production process, but they also allow increase the operational production flexibility, production agility and responsiveness, production quality, customer satisfaction, production robustness, production efficiency, production reliability, and production profitability [27, 28]. In the same way, [29], mentioned the relationship between integrating 10 pillars of I4.0 enabling technologies, and the performance of a smart factory, revealed that I4.0 technologies provides some opportunities, like the process flexibility, increasing production capacity, improving product quality and reducing the error of machine and humans.

Few are the articles that have addressed industrial performance especially in the CPPS, [30] proposed to monitor the performance of a conveyor belt via a CPS demonstrator, that allows to simulate on a small scale the generation and processing of data, as well as visualize the performance parameters. Moreover, [31] highlights the benefits of implementing real-time indicators in CPPS, which speed up decision-making and the detection of anomalies, at the end of his work, the author mentioned the importance of real-time data in predictive maintenance and also in the analysis of the energy consumption of the machine.

3   PMS-Based Mechanism: Analysis for Inclusion

The CPPS is a set of physical and virtual components arranged within an organized architecture that pilots on real-time the execution of a manufacturing system [33] In practice, this components assembly feature an autonomous interaction that permits to react to unexpected event or configurate to improve the manufacturing performance. Therefore, a performance management for a CPPS is fundamental to fulfil the organization objectives. Figure 1 presents the reference framework of a CPPS to analyze the inclusion of the PMS-based mechanism.

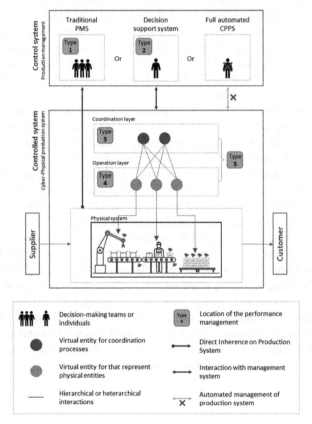

Fig. 1. Reference framework of a CPPS and potential types of inclusion

For establishing the analysis reference framework for this study, it is defined a general architecture of a CPPS. Therefore, the CPPS is conceptually defined from the external view and the internal view of the system. From the external view, the CPPS is constructed to fulfil an assigned organizational objective and amongst an organizational environment. Then, while the organizational objective is to manage optimally and reactively the production execution by conducting of the human, products, equipment and other production components in real time, the organizational environment is that the system is encompassed under an ERP system of the manufacturing domain that responds to a cascading instruction from corporate and middle management, and transversely as part of a supply chain that fulfils the logistics of the reference organization. From the internal view, the CPPS is defined by the components, the structural arrangement and the components behavior or functionalities. The components, which are generally hosted under coordination, operations and physical layers, are physical objects (i.e., products, machines, conveyors, tools, etc.), human individuals (i.e., supervisors, operators, maintenance engineer, etc.), virtual components (i.e., digital twins o virtual object that represent physical objects), virtual applications (i.e., schedulers, analytics applications, other virtual objects that do not represent physical objects) and interaction devices (i.e., Human-machine interfaces, screen, leviers, etc.), set together to support the distributed coordination of the manufacturing execution. The structure is an arrangement which could be hierarchically, hierarchically, or semi-hierarchically positioned. The behavior or functionalities is the behavior that each component feature, and definitively the collective interaction of components emerge into a collective behavior of the system.

Certainly, the CPPS is a complex system composed of atomic physical and virtual elements, form a structure arrangement, comprise an individual behavior, and derive an emergent collective comportment, functioning towards pre-settled objectives. Then, the complexity of including a PMS-based mechanism resides on the localization of the mechanism and the functionality characteristics. In this paper, we put aside this complexity as we analyze the inclusion from the operational actors either computational, managerial or hybrid perspective. For this paper, even it is certain that each individual could influence the collective behavior of the CPPS, the actors are the identified components, set or components or layers that can influence the management of the system as well the performance of it. Then, it is identified 5 types of inclusion derived from the structure and behavior from the CPPS. Although, the types of a PMS-based mechanism are 1) Manual performance management, 2) Computer system-aided performance management, 3) coordination system performance management, 4) distributed system performance management, and 5) coordination-distributed performance management. Figure 1 shows the localization of each type of mechanism. The conducted analysis is guided through the advantages and disadvantages, as well as the contribution or limitation on each phase of the performance management process.

4 Discussion and Conclusions

The management of performance within a production system is changing drastically due to the deployment of cyber-physical production systems on manufacturing shop-floors. Some common characteristics can be identified that set the guidelines for designing a PMS-based mechanism. Still, there is also some constraint to consider reaching efficiency within the management of performance.

First, it is clear that PMS-based mechanism on CPPS must fit to new system architectures. CPPS are currently featuring adaptive architectures that configure dynamically according to environment conditions. These changes are responding the optimality and reactivity needs (Table 1).

Table 1. Type of PMS-based mechanism to include into a cyber-physical production system

	Types of inclusion				
	Traditional production management		PMS-like mechanism on CPPS		
	Manual Performance Management	Computer-System aided Performance Management	Coordinated System Performance Management	Distributed system Performance Management	Coordination distributed Performance management
Advantages	Complete control of manufacturing process and actions from the performance team.	Decision support systems for supervisor(s) or operator(s). Features actions alternatives and recommendations options.	Automated centralized performance management. Complete control of performance that features optimal results.	Automated distributed management. Collective management with adaptability features	Automated management. Features global and local performance management of system and virtual entities
Disadvantages	Process loosely supported from information systems. Functioning under ad doc reporting and delay reactivity.	Full responsibility to supervisor or operator on production actions. Human limitation on the decision making process.	Lack of human judgement on automated actions. Difficulties for dealing with unexpected scenarios.	Lack of human judgement on automated actions Difficulties for achieving optimal results faced to main objectives	Need of clear policy and system functioning for avoiding system breakdown and synchronization issues
Objectives and expected results acknowledgment	Objectives settled strictly cascaded with corporate purposes. Lack of objectives adaptability when business requires	Objectives are included on supporting systems for immediate performance comparison. Forced quantification of objectives.	Complete systems acknowledge of objectives, which are quantified and frequently disaggregated. Fully global performance objectives	Fully local objectives looking for reactiveness behaviour Creation of virtual entities with shared and autonomous goals	Two types of objectives : Global objectives and local objectives. Local goals are disaggregated to impact global objectives
Behaviour and indicators monitoring	Performance measured in key performance indicators. Do not feature manufacturing behaviour and business patterns.	Indicators are monitored further on a semi-continuous time line. Preliminary what-if scenarios for behaviour acknowledgement.	Global indicator of performance, sometimes disaggregated. Global behaviour monitoring regardless specific occurrences.	Particular awareness to specific behaviours Creation of additional indicators for behaviour monitoring	Behaviour is the resulted interaction of coordinated and collaborated action of the system. Profusion of data
Current state analysis towards objectives	Manual performance monitoring and comparison to objectives. Limited analysis of the current scenario.	Computational analysis and recommendations for control. Continuous comparison of performance objectives.	Global indicators analysis Estimated indicators due to static characteristics at the end of production execution.	State monitored for virtual entities Comparison on a global emergence behaviour and a local virtual entities behaviour	Global and local analysis in a descriptive, predictive and prescriptive analysis
Results and reports communication	Results presented in wall-mounted dashboard. Reports are briefed on team meetings and executive reports.	Computational treatment of data and results. Periodical reports for decision support system display.	Periodic reporting of indicators and recommended actions. User interfaces and interaction with system	Temporal reports for virtual entities actions and collaboration. Reports and results are presented due emergence comportment.	Continuous featuring behaviour through user interfaces. Reports include recommended scenarios
Launching improvement or actions	Actions mainly based under disrupted scenarios. Actions instructed through team meetings.	Actions are fully human instructed, or due a recommendation option from system. Potential improvement actions.	Automated action launching based on global reports and estimated indicators.	Individual action of virtual entities according to its own autonomy. Collective action due to cooperation of virtual entities.	Action are launched continuously in a global and a local level.

Still, a dynamic management system force to adopt a mechanism that adapt accordingly and, perhaps, changes as well with on centralized and distributed architectures. Therefore, it will be possible to monitor global processes and local decentralized processes, such for example global schedule task and local maintenance of machines. Second, CPPS features an autonomous intelligence that will interact with the human decision makers. These characteristics features represent a challenge to the mental process of decision makers due to the demand of the CPPS to interact with a human operator. Then, it is needed that the PMS-based mechanism involves a human interaction requirement for involving in synergy with the autonomous intelligent production systems. This is a completely new characteristic for the management of performance as this is not traditionally included in PMS systems. The human interaction requirements become a new consideration that will involve supervisors, configurators, operators within the piloting of a manufacturing execution. Then, a coupled human-system function must be developed for getting an optimal efficiency of production management. Third, the centralized inclusion of PMS-based mechanism is similar to the traditional management of performance, except that is executed by a fully automated system or a semi-automated system (i.e., type 2 or type 3). However, there is new requirement to develop and deploy distributed approaches for managing the performance. The distributed approaches (i.e., type 4) contribute to the reactivity and adaptability of the system for productivity, as well to performance. However, the principle of distributed approaches focuses on certain part or entities within the architecture regardless the rest of entities. This characteristic complicates the global performance management as not necessarily the distributed management of performance will contribute to the overall performance.

Nevertheless, it is needed to develop collaboration, communications, and negotiation protocols to distributed approaches. Then, it might be embedded a PMS-based module on each virtual entity to manage collectively the performance. It is clear that it will not be simply, but it might be a good start for featuring reactive features for performance with distributed approaches. Fourth, we think that is soon to consider approaches that follow a coupled centralized and distributed approaches for managing the performance (i.e., type 5). From the literature review, this approach is still in development, and it is not clear the features and functioning. However, it will be a proper contribution to propose a PMS-based mechanism for this type of architectures. Finally, either the type of approach for managing the performance, it is recommended to tackled the PMS-based mechanism by identifying where would be allocated the general steps of a Performance management system. Then, allocating this functionalities, the PMS-based mechanism will convoke this function to execute the management of performance within productions systems. Our next work will be devoted to the practical comparison, in a real industrial environment, between the different types proposed, to ultimately choose the most optimal to drive performance in CPPS.

References

1. Gawankar, S.A., Gunasekaran, A., Kamble, S.: A study on investments in the big data-driven supply chain, performance measures and organisational performance in Indian retail 4.0 context. Int. J. Prod. Res. **58**(5), 1574–1593 (2020)
2. Žižek, S.Š., Nedelko, Z., Mulej, M., Čič, Ž.V.: Key performance indicators and Industry 4.0 – a socially responsible perspective. Naše Gospod. Econ. **66**(3), 22–35 (2020)
3. Singh, H.: Big data, industry 4.0 and cyber-physical systems integration: a smart industry context. Mater Today Proc. **46**, 157–162 (2021)
4. Monostori, L., et al.: Cyber-physical systems in manufacturing. CIRP Ann. **65**(2), 621–641 (2016). https://doi.org/10.1016/j.cirp.2016.06.005
5. Arsene, C.G., Constantin, G.: Industry 4.0: key questions in manufacturing. MATEC Web Conf. (2019)
6. Kamble, S.S., Gunasekaran, A.: Big data-driven supply chain performance measurement system: a review and framework for implementation. Int. J. Prod. Res. **58**(1), 65–86 (2020)
7. Cardin, O.: Contribution à la conception, l'évaluation et l'implémentation de systèmes de production cyber-physiques (2017)
8. Bakkari, M., Khatory, A.: Industry 4.0: strategy for more sustainable industrial development in SMEs, p. 9 (2017)
9. Nagy, J., Oláh, J., Erdei, E., Máté, D., Popp, J.: The role and impact of Industry 4.0 and the internet of things on the business strategy of the value chain—the case of Hungary. Sustainability **10**(10), 3491 (2018)

10. Gallo, T., Santolamazza, A.: Industry 4.0 and human factor: how is technology changing the role of the maintenance operator? Procedia Comput. Sci. **180**, 388–393 (2021)
11. Lee, J., Lapira, E., Yang, S., Kao, A.: Predictive manufacturing system - trends of next-generation production systems. IFAC Proc. **46**(7), 150–156 (2013)
12. Taticchi, P., Tonelli, F., Cagnazzo, L.: Performance measurement and management: a literature review and a research agenda. Meas. Bus. Excell. **14**(1), 4–18 (2010)
13. Vernadat, F., Shah, L., Etienne, A., Siadat, A.: VR-PMS: a new approach for performance measurement and management of industrial systems. Int. J. Prod. Res. **51**(23–24), 7420–7438 (2013)
14. Neely, A., Adams, C., Crowe, P.: The performance prism in practice. Meas. Bus. Excell., 6–13 (2001)
15. Kang, N., Zhao, C., Li, J., Horst, J.A.: A hierarchical structure of key performance indicators for operation management and continuous improvement in production systems. Int. J. Prod. Res **21**, 6333–6350 (2016)
16. Ante, G., Facchini, F., Mossa, G., Digiesi, S.: Developing a key performance indicators tree for lean and smart production systems. IFAC-Pap. **51**(11), 13–18 (2018)
17. Sorooshian, S.: Study on unbalanceness of the balanced scorecard. Appl. Math. Sci. **8**, 4163–4169 (2014). https://doi.org/10.12988/ams.2014.45337
18. Sorooshian, S., Aziz, N.F., Ahmad, A., Jubidin, S.N., Mustapha, N.M.: Review on performance measurement systems. Mediterr. J. Soc. Sci. (2015)
19. Sangwa, N.R., Sangwan, K.S.: Development of an integrated performance measurement framework for lean organizations. J. Manuf. Technol. Manag. **29**(1), 41–84 (2018)
20. Sarraf, F., Nejad, S.H.: Improving performance evaluation based on balanced scorecard with grey relational analysis and data envelopment analysis approaches: case study in water and wastewater companies. Eval. Program. Plann. **79**, 101762 (2020)
21. Kaplan, R.S., Norton, D.P.: The balanced scorecard - measures that drive performance. Balanc. Scorec. **11** (1992)
22. Doumeingts, G., Clave, F., Ducq, Y.: ECOGRAI — a method to design and to implement performance measurement systems for industrial organizations — concepts and application to the maintenance function. In: Rolstadås, A. (ed.) Benchmarking — Theory and Practice. IAICT, pp. 350–368. Springer, Boston, MA (1995). https://doi.org/10.1007/978-0-387-34847-6_39
23. Bititci, U.S., Carrie, A.S., McDevitt, L.: Integrated performance measurement systems: a development guide. Int. J. Oper. Prod. Manag. **17**(5), 522–534 (1997)
24. Kamble, S.S., Gunasekaran, A., Raut, R.: A performance measurement system for industry 4.0 enabled smart manufacturing system in SMMEs-a review and empirical investigation. Int. J. Prod. Econ., 107853 (2020)
25. Gamache, S., Abdul-Nour, G., Baril, C.: Development of a digital performance assessment model for Quebec manufacturing SMEs. Procedia Manuf. **38**, 1085–1094 (2019)
26. Calış Duman, M., Akdemir, B.: A study to determine the effects of industry 4.0 technology components on organizational performance. Technol. Forecast. Soc. Change **167**, 120615 (2021)
27. Bueno, A., Godinho Filho, M., Frank, A.G.: Smart production planning and control in the Industry 4.0 context: a systematic literature review. Comput. Ind. Eng. **149**, 106774 (2020)
28. Hizam-Hanafiah, M., Soomro, M.A., Abdullah, N.L.: Industry 4.0 readiness models: a systematic literature review of model dimensions. Information **11**(7), 364 (2020)
29. Büchi, G., Cugno, M., Castagnoli, R.: Smart factory performance and Industry 4.0. Technol. Forecast. Soc. Change **150**, 119790 (2020)
30. Mörth, O., Emmanouilidis, C., Hafner, N., Schadler, M.: Cyber-physical systems for performance monitoring in production intralogistics. Comput. Ind. Eng. **142**, 106333 (2020)
31. Morella, P., Lambán, M.P., Royo, J.A., Sánchez, J.C.: The importance of implementing cyber physical systems to acquire real-time data and indicators. J **4**(2), 147–153 (2021)

32. Ribeiro, L.: Cyber-physical production systems' design challenges. In: 2017 IEEE 26th International Symposium on Industrial Electronics (ISIE), Edinburgh, United Kingdom, June 2017, pp. 1189–1194 (2017)
33. Jiménez, J.-F.: Dynamic and hybrid architecture for the optimal reconfiguration of control systems: application to manufacturing control (2017)

Multiple Operational Status Classification Based on One-Versus-One SVM in FDM 3D Printer

Yebon Lee and Sujeong Baek$^{(\boxtimes)}$

Hanbat National University, Daejeon 34158, Republic of Korea
sbaek@hanbat.ac.kr

Abstract. FDM 3D printers are commonly used in various fields because they can efficiently manufacture complex shaped products. However, producing even a small product is usually time consuming because the printer operation comprises several stages: heating, aligning, printing, and re-aligning. Working sensors and actuators also differ according to operational states; therefore, it is necessary to distinguish multiple operational states correctly using the sensor information. In this regard, we propose a sensor-signal based multiple status classification for distinguishing FDM 3D printer operations into four categories. To analyze the operational status, we install a total 51 sensors and record temperature, triaxial angular velocity, triaxial acceleration, triaxial geomagnetism, and current signals. For multi-classification, one-versus-one support vector machine algorithm is used, which shows good performance in class-imbalance. As a result, the proposed method shows a higher classification performance in every operational state. Using the findings of this study, the current operational information can be automatically identified, and our research outcome is expected to be used as a basis for effective monitoring of 3D printer operation, such as generating fault detection model of each operational status.

Keywords: FDM 3D printer · Operational status classification · Fault detection · SVM

1 Introduction

In recent years, the use of 3D printers in various industries, such as semiconductor manufacturing, space, automotive, and medical care, has increased because they can manufacture complex shaped products, which are impossible to manufacture using traditional subtractive manufacturing without assembly or bonding tasks [1–4]. Printers can be classified into several categories, depending on the applied material and printing method. Fused deposition modeling (FDM) is widely used for additive manufacturing, which is relatively inexpensive and has a high printing speed [5, 6]. FDM printers make products by melting thermoplastic filaments and stacking them layer-by-layer [7].

Whereas FDM 3D printers can be used for product fabrication relatively easily even by a beginner, producing even a small product is usually time consuming. The printers also usually require a long preparation time before main printing, including heating and

© IFIP International Federation for Information Processing 2022
Published by Springer Nature Switzerland AG 2022
D. Y. Kim et al. (Eds.): APMS 2022, IFIP AICT 663, pp. 219–226, 2022.
https://doi.org/10.1007/978-3-031-16407-1_26

aligning; therefore, typical FDM printers possess several operational stages: heating, aligning, printing, and re-aligning. According to operational states, in addition to the different roles, moving actuators and activated sensors are also different. For example, a bearing nut or a stepper motor in an extruder is mainly operated in the printing stage [8, 9]. This kind of differences would negatively affect the effectiveness and efficiency of an entire machine monitoring and management. However, various studies have focused on the main printing stage only [10–13], since it is quite simple to conduct. That is, it will be helpful to distinguish multiple operational states correctly using the sensor information.

Thus, we propose operational status classification for an FDM printer using the one-versus-one (OVO) SVM algorithm, which shows good classification performance with class-imbalance. The developed classification model is applied to check what tasks the printer is performing when printing an object under normal operating conditions. To this end, sensors are installed at five points inside the 3D printer to collect time series data, and the entire normal operation process was classified into four states. To improve the accuracy of multiple state classification, the magnitude of the magnetic field and amount of current are measured concurrently, in addition to acceleration, angular velocity, and temperature. Accordingly, this paper is structured as follows. Section 2 describes the 3D printer and installed sensors used to collect data, Sect. 3 presents the classification algorithm and corresponding results, and Sect. 4 summarizes conclusions and future work.

2   Experimental Setting and Data Collection

2.1   The Used FDM 3D Printer and the Printed Object

Section 2 introduces the FDM printer and sensors, which are attached to the printer and used for data collection. The FDM 3D printer was Cubicon single, shown in Fig. 1-(a), and the dedicated sliding program, Cubicreator 4, was used to make the object. The printed object was set to a cube shape, as shown in Fig. 1-(b). The output material was polylactic acid (PLA), and the related printing parameters were optimized according to previous research, the objective of which was to obtain the optimal output conditions for a low-end FDM type 3D printer [14]: 30% internal density, 0.1 mm layer height, and two external wall lines.

(a) FDM 3D printer   (b) The printed object

Fig. 1. 3D printer and object printed in the experiment: (a) FDM 3D printer (Cubicon single), (b) a cube shaped object

2.2 Sensor Data for Analyzing Printer Operation Status

In this study, an attitude and heading reference system sensor was used to measure the posture angle of the moving object and collect additional motion information. Sensors are manufactured by ROBOR, and each sensor measures 10 data types: temperature, three-axis angular velocity (roll, pitch, and yaw), three-axis acceleration (x, y, and z axis), and three-axis magnetometers (x, y, and z axis). Further details regarding the sensor information is listed in Table 1.

Table 1. The detailed specification of output sensor

Measurement type in a sensor	Unit	Total number of sensor signals
Temperature	°C	5
Acceleration (x-axis)	g	5
Acceleration (y-axis)	g	5
Acceleration (z-axis)	g	5
Geomagnetic (x-axis)	μT	5
Geomagnetic (y-axis)	μT	5
Geomagnetic (z-axis)	μT	5
Euler angle (roll)	deg	5
Euler angle (pitch)	deg	5
Euler angle (yaw)	deg	5
Current	A	1

To effectively analyze the operation status in the FDM printer, the attachment position of each sensor must be optimized. For example, there is a criterion for determining the optimal position of vibration sensors for condition monitoring, which includes sensitivity to generated vibrations and safe installation [15]. Based on the previous studies, we attached the sensors to the upper part of the nozzle head, side of the bed, and inner three surfaces of the chamber, as illustrated in Fig. 2. We also installed a current sensor to obtain the value of the current from an input power supply.

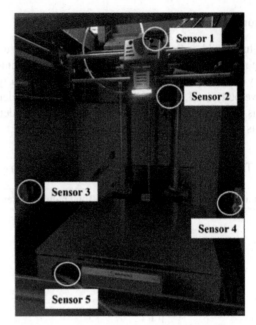

Fig. 2. Sensor positions in the 3D printer

3 SVM-Based Status Classification of FDM Printer

3.1 Data Collection and Preprocessing

There are various fault types, depending on the operational status of an FDM printer, such as blockage by unappropriated remaining filament and layer deformation during printing due to untightened screws. In addition, identical root causes can be regarded as different faults depending on the working state. Therefore, it is necessary to identify the operational status in consideration of these different characteristics, which are unique to an operating status, in an FDM printer. Therefore, we classified the 3D printer operation into four states based on the movement characteristics. First, 'State 1' is defined as a heating step, in which the temperature of the bed and nozzle are increased according to the user setting. 'State 2' is called an alignment step for adjusting the gap between the bed and the nozzle, and 'State 3' is regarded as the printing step, in which the filament is extruded to produce an output. 'State 4' is the last step, called the re-aligning step, in which each actuator is reset to its initial position.

While the printer was working, multiple sensor data was collected from States 1–4. The data collected every 0.5 s (at a sampling rate of 2 Hz) by the 51 types of sensors were automatically stored in the MySQL-based MariaDB table to efficiently manage the large amount of data. During the generation of one cube-shaped object with 20 repetitions, an average of 3,818 length data was generated (variance: 4,749.5); a total of 20 objects were made, thereby 20 datasets were collected. The amount of data for each state is proportional to the time required for each state, as shown in Table 2. In particular, the variance of the length of State 1 (Heating) is significantly larger than that of other states

Table 2. The average amount of data per operating status

Operating status	The length of each status (points)	
	Mean	Variance
State 1. Heating	501.2	4037.4
State 2. Aligning	393.6	525.5
State 3. Printing	2873.0	290.8
State 4. Re-Aligning	52.1	1.8

because the initial temperature at the start of the printing operation is not always fixed. For example, a length of State 1 is usually shorter when 3D printing operations are continuously conducted. On the other hands, at the first operation of the day, the printer may consume a relatively longer time for achieving the pre-determined temperature of a heating bed and an extruder from the room temperature. In addition, all data sets were standardized with an average of 0 and a variance of 1.

3.2 Status Classification

The SVM algorithm is one of the supervised learning methods that construct an optimal hyperplane, which maximizes the margin between two classes. It has the advantage of being able to perform classification efficiently because it is generally less time-consuming than neural networks [16]. However, in this study, four status labels are required to be distinguished instead of two; Therefore, SVM method for multi-classification was used. The multiple classification method is largely divided into OVR (one-versus-rest) and OVO. OVR performs k (the number of state classes) binary classification for distinguishing one class from the rest. That is, a binary classification determines whether a specific measurement is included in a target class or not (for example, the measurement is labelled as class 1 or not). Contrarily, the OVO strategy consists of $k \cdot (k - 1)/2$ classifiers that perform each binary classification [17]. As shown in Fig. 3, a specific measurement can have $k \cdot (k - 1)/2$ decision results according to each hyperplane. For example, the '1' measurement (in Fig. 3) is finally labelled as 'yellow class', because 2 out of 3 decision results were 'yellow' by hyperplane 1 and 3 (where k = 3). However, a measurement is not completely classified by the OVO SVM classifiers if it has different decisions from every hyperplane, which is observed as a gray area in Fig. 3. When the classes are unbalanced, OVR shows a relatively low performance due to simple classification methodology, while the computation speed is fast. Conversely, OVO with more classifiers shows a higher performance, but is computationally slow [18]. Considering the 3D printer operational status with class imbalance, an OVO SVM algorithm is adopted for the proposed multi-class classification.

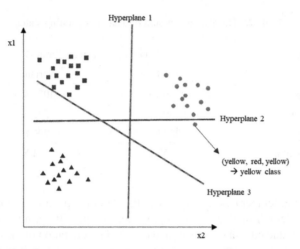

Fig. 3. An example of the OVO SVM classification method

In this study, the training and test datasets were split into a ratio of 9:1. The hyper-parameters were optimized based on a grid-search strategy for improving each state classification accuracy as shown in Table 3. We controlled Gamma and C, which indicate an amount of acceptable degree of a hyperplane curvature and classification error individually, with 3 levels. The finally derived hyper-parameter setting (C and Gamma) was chosen to 5 and 0.005, respectively. In this parameter setting, the training and testing accuracies of the constructed model were 99.6% and 99.3%, respectively. In particular, the classification accuracies for State 1, 2, 3, and 4 were 99.8%, 98.7%, 99.3%, and 99.1%, respectively. To consider the different number of measurements in each state, the F1-score was calculated to be 98.9%. In summary, the model accuracies of the training and testing phases were high enough, and the F1-score showed good performance despite the class imbalance among the four statuses [19].

Table 3. The F1-score according to hyper-parameters of the SVM classification model (Bold indicates the best accuracy in the experiment)

	C = 0.1	C = 1	C = 5
Gamma = 0.1	87.7	91.8	91.9
Gamma = 0.01	95.9	98.3	98.8
Gamma = 0.005	96.2	98.4	**98.9**

4 Conclusion

In this study, the entire FDM printer operation was classified according to four different stages, that is, heating, aligning, printing, and re-aligning, to distinguish each operational status by analyzing sensor data. Acceleration, angular velocity, temperature, magnetic field, and current data were collected for status classification. In addition, sensors were attached to five optimal locations, thereby collecting 51 sensor data. As a result, an F1-score performance of 98.9% was obtained when classifying the four normal operating states of the FDM printer using the OVO-SVM algorithm. Despite there being a class imbalance owing to the different working times among the four states, the proposed classification algorithm showed statistically high accuracy in every operational state.

However, it is difficult to generalize the classification results because we used a simple shaped object (the cube), which resulted in a simple movement of the nozzle. In the future, to overcome these limitations, we intend to classify the work states to be independent of the shape of the printed objects by using different shaped objects in which the nozzle head movement and printing time are different from those of the existing model. In addition, it would be helpful to perform machine maintenance and monitoring which is specialized for each operational state during 3D printer operation.

Acknowledgement. This work was supported by project for Industry-Academic Cooperation Based Platform R&D funded Korea Ministry of SMEs and Startups in 2020. (Project No. S3025721) and supported by project for Industry-Academic Cooperation Based Platform R&D funded Korea Ministry of SMEs and Startups in 2020 (Project No. S3025825).

This paper was also supported by Korea Institute for Advancement of Technology (KIAT) grant funded by the Korea Government (MOTIE). (P0012744, HRD program for industrial innovation).

References

1. Na, D.J.: Current status and future prospects of 3D printing technology. KOSEN report (2019)
2. Oh, W.K.: Customized model manufacturing for patients with pelvic fracture using FDM 3D printer. J. Korea Contents Assoc. **14**(11), 370–377 (2014)
3. Singh, S., Ramakrishna, S., Singh, R.: Material issues in additive manufacturing: a review. J. Manuf. Proc. **25**, 185–200 (2017)
4. Tlegenov, Y., Hong, G.S., Lu, W.F.: Nozzle condition monitoring in 3D printing. Rob. Comp. Integr. Manuf. **54**, 45–55 (2018)
5. Surange, V.G., Gharat, P.V.: 3D printing process using fused deposition modelling (FDM). Int. Res. J. Eng. Technol. **3**(3), 1403–1406 (2016)
6. Mehrpouya, M., Dehghanghadikolaei A., Fotovvati, B., Vosooghnia, A., Emamian, S., Gisario, A.: The potential of additive manufacturing in the smart factory industrial 4.0: a review. Appl. Sci. **9**(18), 3865 (2019)
7. Durgun, I., Ertan, R.: Experimental investigation of FDM process for improvement of mechanical properties and production cost. Rapid Prototyp. J. **20**(3), 228–235 (2014)
8. Günaydın, K., Türkmen, H.S.: Common FDM 3D printing defects. In: International Congress on 3D Printing (Additive Manufacturing) Technologies and Digital Industry, Turkey, pp. 1–8 (2018)
9. Liao, J., Shen, Z., Xiong, G., Liu, C., Luo, C., Lu, J.: Preliminary study on fault diagnosis and intelligent learning of fused deposition modeling (FDM) 3D printer. In: 14th IEEE Conference on Industrial Electronics and Applications (ICIEA), pp. 2098–2102. IEEE, China (2019)
10. Kim, J.S., Lee, C.S., Kim, S.M., Lee, S.W.: Development of data-driven in-situ monitoring and diagnosis system of fused deposition modeling (FDM) process based on support vector machine algorithm. Int. J. Prec. Eng. Manuf. Green Technol. **5**(4), 479–486 (2018)

11. Kadam, V., Kumar, S., Bongale, A., Wazarkar, S., Kamat, P., Patil, S.: Enhancing surface fault detection using machine learning for 3D printed products. Appl. Syst. Innov. **4**(2), 34 (2021)
12. Sampedro, G.A., Agron, D.J., Kim, R.G., Kim, D.S., Lee, J.M.: Fused deposition modeling 3D printing fault diagnosis using temporal convolutional network. In: 1st International Conference in Information and Computing Research (iCORE), pp. 62–65. IEEE, Philippines (2021)
13. He, K., Yang, Z., Bai, Y., Long, J., Li, C.: Intelligent fault diagnosis of delta 3D printers using attitude sensors based on support vector machines. Sensors **18**(4), 1298 (2018)
14. Lee, S.J., Baek, S.J.: Kano model based important quality of products printed by entry-level 3D printers. In: Proceedings of 2021 Spring Korean Society of Mechanical Engineers, pp. 31–32. The Korean Soc. Mech. Eng. Rep. Korea (2021)
15. BISOPE Homepage. https://m.blog.naver.com/vs72/222006593687. Accessed 24 Mar 2022
16. Kim, G.H., Kim, Y.W., Lee, S.J., Jeon, G.J.: A hierarchical clustering method based on SVM for real-time gas mixture classification. J. Korean Inst. Intell. Syst. **20**(5), 716–721 (2010)
17. Guo, J., Chen, Y., Zhu, M., Wang, S., Liu, X.: An efficient support vector machine algorithm for solving multi-class pattern recognition problems. In: Proceedings of the 2nd International Conference on Computer Modeling and Simulation, vol. 2, pp. 461–465. IEEE (2010)
18. Su, J., Zhang, Y.: Triple-O for SHL recognition challenge: an ensemble framework for multi-class imbalance and training-testing distribution inconsistency by OvO binarization with confidence weight of one-class Classification. In: Adjunct Proceedings of the 2021 ACM International Joint Conference on Pervasive and Ubiquitous Computing and Proceedings of the 2021 ACM International Symposium on Wearable Computers, pp. 401–407. Association for Computing Machinery, USA (2021)
19. Lin, Y.D., Liu, Z.Q., Hwang, R.H., Nguyen, V.L., Lin, P.C., Lai, Y.C.: Machine learning with variational autoencoder for imbalanced datasets in intrusion detection. IEEE Access. **10**, 15247–15260 (2022)

The Impact of Design Complexity on Additive Manufacturing Performance

Kyudong Kim[1] , Kijung Park[1(✉)] , and Hyun Woo Jeon[2]

[1] Department of Industrial and Management Engineering, Incheon National University, Incheon, Republic of Korea
{sooe07,kjpark}@inu.ac.kr
[2] Department of Industrial and Management Systems Engineering, Kyung Hee University, Yongin-si, Republic of Korea
hwjeon@khu.ac.kr

Abstract. Complexity in a manufacturing system can lead to unnecessary costs due to an increase in manufacturing uncertainty that negatively affects the reliability and controllability of the system. Despite the importance of understanding complexity in manufacturing, the conceptualization of complexity for an additive manufacturing (AM) system and its impact on operational performance have not been clearly articulated in the literature. As a response, this study characterizes a complexity measure relevant to AM and identifies the impact of the complexity on operational performance in an AM system. For this, design complexity for AM is defined by considering both the volume ratio and area ratio of a part design. Then, a virtual AM plant for aircraft parts is built by a discrete event simulation to derive the average order lead time of each part design. A linear regression analysis is performed to understand the impact of the calculated design complexity on the AM performance. As a result, this study shows that design complexity negatively affects the average order lead time of the AM system. The findings from this study indicate that the design aspects of complexity for an AM based system should be properly managed to improve its operational performance.

Keywords: Additive manufacturing · Design complexity · Discrete event simulation · Regression analysis

1 Introduction

Many concepts and metrics of complexity for a manufacturing system have been widely discussed in previous studies [1–3]. Complexity is related to an increase in uncertainty that negatively affects the reliability and controllability of a manufacturing process [1, 3]. Despite a consensus of the negative impact of complexity on operational performance [2], the complexity of additive manufacturing (AM) has not been fully discussed in the literature. Moreover, existing studies relevant to AM have not sufficiently investigated how AM complexity affects the operational performance of an AM system that handles multiple AM machines for various part designs.

© IFIP International Federation for Information Processing 2022
Published by Springer Nature Switzerland AG 2022
D. Y. Kim et al. (Eds.): APMS 2022, IFIP AICT 663, pp. 227–234, 2022.
https://doi.org/10.1007/978-3-031-16407-1_27

Focusing on the above issues, this paper aims not only to propose a complexity measure for AM but also to investigate the impact of AM complexity on the operational performance of an AM system. First, this study proposes a design complexity measure to quantify the complexity underlying in a part design for AM. Next, a virtual AM plant for aircraft parts, which handles multiple fused filament fabrication (FFF) machines for carbon fiber reinforced polyether-ether-ketone (CFR-PEEK), is modeled for discrete event simulation to estimate the average order lead time of each part design. Then, a regression analysis is performed to identify whether the proposed design complexity measure has a statistically significant impact on the operational performance obtained from the simulation model.

2   Literature Review

Design complexity for AM has been addressed based on the computer-aided design (CAD) of a part because a CAD model contains geometric information for digital manufacturing [4, 5]. Conner et al. [6] evaluated design complexity by considering three geometric parameters: (1) the volume ratio of a part to its bounding box, (2) the surface area ratio of a sphere with equivalent volume to a part, (3) the number of holes in a part. Pradel et al. [7] proposed a design complexity measure through the ratio between the surface area of a part and the volume of a design space between functional surfaces. Valentan et al. [8] used three design parameters for a part (i.e., the number of triangle in the standard tessellation language (STL), the surface area of a part, and the volume of a part) to represent design complexity. Johnson et al. [9] addressed five design complexity metrics: (1) the number of surface of a part, (2) the number of triangle in STL of a part, (3) the volume ratio of a part to the volume of a bounding box, (4) the area ratio to the surface area of a cube, and (5) the area ratio to the surface area of a sphere. Fera et al. [10] proposed a design complexity metric, which is defined as a ratio between part volume and envelope convex volume. Joshi and Anand [11] calculated a complexity score for measuring design complexity based on AM parameters (i.e., sharp corners, thin regions and thin gaps, support structure volume, and part volume and height) and subtractive manufacturing parameters (i.e., internal corners, number of free form surfaces, tool inaccessibility, and machining volume of stock).

With the efforts to define and quantify design complexity for AM, there also have been attempts to examine the impact of design complexity on AM performance in the literature. Johnson et al. [9] addressed that design complexity metrics have no significant effects on processing time for CAD modeling. Baumers et al. [12] showed that design complexity has a weak impact on energy consumption for an AM machine. Pradel et al. [7] revealed that an increase in the surface area of a part negatively affects printing time and material cost for an AM machine. Chen et al. [13] stated that a higher level of design complexity significantly negative impacts on the build quality of AM.

Although a relationship between design complexity and AM performance for a single AM machine has been explained in the literature, the impact of design complexity on an entire AM system has not been sufficiently discussed so far. As a response, this study proposes a design complexity measure for AM. Then, a discrete event simulation model is built to identify the impact of design complexity on operational performance in an AM system that handles multiple AM machines and multiple part orders.

3 Methodology

3.1 Development of Design Complexity for AM

A design complexity measure for AM is proposed in this section. This study employed the volume ratio and the area ratio defined in [14] to quantify design complexity for AM because they comprehensively characterize the geometric features of a part design. The volume ratio (V_R) is expressed as:

$$V_R = V_P/V_B(0 < V_R \leq 1), \tag{1}$$

where V_P is the volume of a part design, and V_B is the volume of a bounding box for the part design. A bounding box is defined as a box given by the maximum length, width, and height of the part design [14]. The volume ratio becomes 1 (i.e., the lowest complexity level) if the volume of the part is the same as the volume of its bounding box. Similarly, the area ratio (A_R) is defined as:

$$A_R = A_S/A_P(0 < A_R \leq 1), \tag{2}$$

where A_P is the surface area of a part design, and A_S is the surface area of a sphere that has the same volume as its part design.

A design complexity measured for AM is proposed by combining the above two elements in Eq. (1) and Eq. (2). The design complexity (DC) measure for AM is expressed as:

$$DC = 1/(V_R A_R) \tag{3}$$

If an AM machine fabricates a simple part design such as a cube or a sphere, the value of the proposed measure becomes close to 1, which indicates a low complexity level. On the other hand, the proposed measure has a large value if a part design includes various design features (e.g., holes and complex shapes).

3.2 Impact of Design Complexity on AM Performance

In order to estimate the operational performance of an AM system, a virtual AM plant, which handles 15 part designs for aircraft part type (i.e., bracket, door hinge, engine cover, fork fitting, and seat buckle) (see Fig. 1), is modeled for discrete event simulation. The part designs are collected from Thingiverse [15], which is an open source platform for CAD models. The CAD model of each part design is resized by the Simplify3D [16] slicing software to have the same part volume (= 10 cm^3) to identify the impact of design complexity on operational performance at the same condition.

A virtual AM plant is created based on a simulation model in Kim et al. [17] with the following assumptions and conditions. AM machines are assumed to be Apium P220 [18], which is an industrial FFF based 3D printer and compatible with CFR-PEEK. The AM plant consists of 20 parallel FFF machines for CFR-PEEK, and only uses CFR-PEEK as a material to produce aircraft parts. The plant employs a make-to-order strategy, which allows orders to immediately start manufacturing when they arrive at the AM system. If all AM machines are processing to fabricate parts, an incoming order waits in a centralized queue until any FFF machine is available within the AM system. Each order type consists of multiple parts of the same part design, and the inter-arrival time of each order is assumed to follow a normal distribution: N ($\mu = 4.0$ h, $\sigma = 0.5$ h). In addition, one of 15 aircraft part designs is randomly assigned to an order type with an equal chance. The part quantity of each order follows a uniform distribution: $u_{[15units, 25units]}$. The printing time of each aircraft part is assumed to follow a normal distribution: N ($\mu = t$ in Fig. 1, $\sigma = 100$ s). The estimated printing time (t) of each aircraft part design is obtained by Simplify3D [16]; the default process parameter settings of Apium P220 for CFR-PEEK are used to derive the estimated printing time information provided by Simplify3D [16] (see Fig. 1).

Aircraft part design	Bracket A	Bracket B	Bracket C	Door hinge A	Door hinge B
t (sec)	10140	9480	11040	8940	9540
V_R	0.08	0.23	0.16	0.52	0.38
A_R	0.29	0.44	0.33	0.35	0.28
Aircraft part design	Door hinge C	Engine cover A	Engine cover B	Engine cover C	Fork fitting A
t (sec)	10440	15180	16380	13140	10140
V_R	0.18	0.23	0.06	0.13	0.25
A_R	0.37	0.10	0.27	0.24	0.28
Aircraft part design	Fork fitting B	Fork fitting C	Seat buckle A	Seat buckle B	Seat buckle C
t (sec)	12540	11460	14700	10740	11040
V_R	0.10	0.24	0.16	0.33	0.44
A_R	0.31	0.33	0.28	0.34	0.29

Fig. 1. Aircraft part designs and their information

When the fabrication of an aircraft part for an order is completed, the part temporarily waits in the AM plant if the part quantity for the order is multiple; the order leaves the AM system only when the assigned part quantity is satisfied. The AM plant is assumed to be operated for one year (= 52 weeks). In addition, the simulation model runs 100 replications to obtain steady-state statistics. The simulation model is built using Simio 11 [19].

The average order lead time of each aircraft part design obtained by the simulation model is considered to evaluate the operational performance of the AM system. The average order lead time (LT_i) of each aircraft part design (i) is expressed by:

$$LT_i = \frac{\sum_{j=1}^{N_i} DT_i^j - AT_i^j}{N_i}, \tag{4}$$

where AT_i^j denotes the arrival time of order j for aircraft part design i, DT_i^j is the departure time of order j for aircraft part design i for customer delivery, and N_i indicates the total number of completed orders for aircraft part design i.

In order to calculate the design complexity of each aircraft part design, the design information for the volume, area, and bounding box of each part design is obtained from Makexyz [20], which is an online 3D printing service platform. Then, the volume ratio (V_R) and area ratio (A_R) of each part design are derived by Eqs. (1–2) (see Fig. 1). Based on the obtained the volume ratio (V_R) and area ratio (A_R) of each part design, the design complexity of each part design is calculated by Eq. (3). To identify the statistically significance of the proposed design complexity on the average order lead time for the AM system, the single linear regression analysis is performed using Minitab 20.3 [21].

4 Results

Table 1 summarizes the results of the design complexity (DC_i) and the average order lead time (LT_i) derived for each aircraft part design (i).

Table 1. Design complexity and average order lead time for each aircraft part design

Part design (i)	Bracket A	Bracket B	Bracket C	Door hinge A	Door hinge B
DC_i	43.33	9.99	19.15	5.47	9.48
LT_i (hours)	4.46	4.17	4.79	3.98	4.21
Part design (i)	Door hinge C	Engine cover A	Engine cover B	Engine cover C	Fork fitting A
DC_i	14.94	44.61	61.87	31.90	14.06
LT_i (hours)	4.58	6.40	6.89	5.59	4.45
Part design (i)	Fork fitting B	Fork fitting C	Seat buckle A	Seat buckle B	Seat buckle C
DC_i	33.29	12.59	22.58	8.87	7.67
LT_i (hours)	5.39	4.96	6.20	4.71	4.81

Table 2 and Fig. 2 show that the design complexity measure is a statistically significant predictor of the average order lead time ($p < 0.05$). The positive coefficient of the design complexity in Table 2 indicates the negative impact of design complexity on the average order lead time; the average order lead time of the AM system increases as the design complexity associated with the AM system increases. Although the complexity measure itself cannot explain all variations in the average lead time (R-sq = 58.76%), the moderate prediction power indicates that the proposed design complexity measure can serve as a good input variable along with other operational input variables to predict the average order lead time of an AM system.

Table 2. Regression results ($a = 0.05**$)

Major statistics	Result
Regression equation	$LT = 4.13 + 0.04 \cdot DC$
R-sq	58.76%
Test for β_0	$t = 15.94, p = 0.00**$
Test for β_1	$t = 4.30, p = 0.00**$

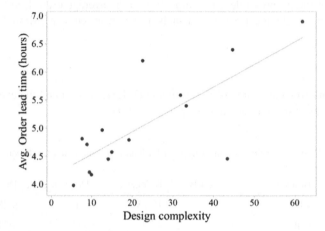

Fig. 2. Linear regression plot for average order lead time on design complexity

5   Conclusions

This study defined design complexity for AM to investigate its impact on operational performance from an entire AM system aspect. First, a design complexity measure for AM was proposed based on the volume ratio and the area ratio of a part design. Then, the discrete event simulation of an AM system that handles AM orders for 15 aircraft part designs was built to obtain the average order lead time of each part design. Then, a single linear regression analysis was performed to identify the statistically significant impact of the proposed design complexity on the average order lead time. The results of this study showed that design complexity associated with an AM system negatively affects the average order lead time of the AM system and is a critical source of causing inefficient AM operations.

The findings from this study support that complexity is may not be free for AM [7]. Although AM has design freedom to fabricate parts [22], complexity inherent in a part design should be properly managed to improve operational performance for an AM system. For the future work of this study, the original simulation model should be extended to reflect a large AM plant scale and other performance measures. Then, operational strategies for AM to mitigate the impact of complexity on an AM system will be investigated to provide guidelines for best AM operations.

Acknowledgement. This work was supported by the National Research Foundation of Korea(NRF) grant funded by the Korea government(MSIT) (No. NRF-2022R1C1C1012140) for Kijung Park.

References

1. Wu, Y., Frizelle, G., Efstathiou, J.: A study on the cost of operational complexity in customer–supplier systems. Int. J. Prod. Econ. **106**(1), 217–229 (2007). https://doi.org/10.1016/j.ijpe.2006.06.004

2. Park, K., Okudan Kremer, G.E.: Assessment of static complexity in design and manufacturing of a product family and its impact on manufacturing performance. Int. J. Prod. Econ. **169**, 215–232 (2015). https://doi.org/10.1016/j.ijpe.2015.07.036

3. Frizelle, G.: Getting the measure of complexity. Manuf. Eng. **75**(6), 268–270 (1996)

4. Li, W., Mac, G., Tsoutsos, N.G., Gupta, N., Karri, R.: Computer aided design (CAD) model search and retrieval using frequency domain file conversion. Addit. Manuf. **36**, 101554 (2020). https://doi.org/10.1016/j.addma.2020.101554

5. Stern, A., Rosenthal, Y., Dresler, N., Ashkenazi, D.: Additive manufacturing: an education strategy for engineering students. Addit. Manuf. **27**, 503–514 (2019). https://doi.org/10.1016/j.addma.2019.04.001

6. Conner, B.P., et al.: Making sense of 3-D printing: creating a map of additive manufacturing products and services. Addit. Manuf. **1**, 64–76 (2014). https://doi.org/10.1016/j.addma.2014.08.005

7. Pradel, P., Bibb, R., Zhu, Z., Moultrie, J.: Complexity is not for free the impact of component complexity on additive manufacturing build time. In: Rapid Design, Prototyping & Manufacturing (RDPM 2017), Newcastle, pp. 1–7 (2017)

8. Valentan, B., Brajlih, T., Drstvenšek, I., Balič, J.: Development of a part complexity evaluation model for application in additive fabrication technologies. Strojniški vestnik J. Mech. Eng. **57**(10), 709–718 (2011). https://doi.org/10.5545/sv-jme.2010.057

9. Johnson, M.D., Valverde, L.M., Thomison, W.D.: An investigation and evaluation of computer-aided design model complexity metrics. Comput.-Aid. Des. Appl. **15**(1), 61–75 (2017). https://doi.org/10.1080/16864360.2017.1353729

10. Fera, M., Macchiaroli, R., Fruggiero, F., Lambiase, A.: A new perspective for production process analysis using additive manufacturing—complexity vs production volume. Int. J. Adv. Manuf. Technol. **95**(1–4), 673–685 (2017). https://doi.org/10.1007/s00170-017-1221-1

11. Joshi, A., Anand, S.: Geometric complexity based process selection for hybrid manufacturing. In: 45th SME North American Manufacturing Research Conference, Los Angeles, pp. 578–589 (2017). https://doi.org/10.1016/j.promfg.2017.07.056

12. Baumers, M., Tuck, C., Wildman, R., Ashcroft, I., Hague, R.: Shape complexity and process energy consumption in electron beam melting: a case of something for nothing in additive manufacturing? J. Ind. Ecol. **21**(S1), S157–S167 (2017). https://doi.org/10.1111/jiec.12397

13. Chen, R., Imani, F., Reutzel, E., Yang, H.: From design complexity to build quality in additive manufacturing—a sensor-based perspective. IEEE Sens. Lett. **3**(1), 1–4 (2019). https://doi.org/10.1109/lsens.2018.2880747

14. Joshi, D., Ravi, B.: Quantifying the shape complexity of cast parts. Comput.-Aid. Des. Appl. **7**(5), 685–700 (2010). https://doi.org/10.3722/cadaps.2010.685-700

15. Thingiverse. https://www.thingiverse.com

16. Simplify3D® version 4.1. https://www.simplify3d.com/software/release-notes/version-4-1-0/

17. Kim, K., Noh, H., Park, K., Jeon, H.W., Lim, S.: Characterization of power demand and energy consumption for fused filament fabrication using CFR-PEEK. Rapid Prototyp. J. **28**(7), 1394–1406 (2022). https://doi.org/10.1108/rpj-07-2021-0188
18. Apium P220 datasheet. https://apiumtec.com/en/case-studies-datasheets
19. SIMIO 11. https://www.simio.com/software/simulation-software.php.
20. Makexyz. https://www.makexyz.com
21. Minitab 20.3. https://www.minitab.com/en-us/products/minitab/
22. Yang, S., Zhao, Y.F.: Additive manufacturing-enabled design theory and methodology: a critical review. Int. J. Adv. Manuf. Technol. **80**(1–4), 327–342 (2015). https://doi.org/10.1007/s00170-015-6994-5

Relaxing RGV Scheduling Problem
for Approximate Assessment
of Transportation Rate

Shota Suginouchi[1]([✉]) [ID], Kazuki Honda[1], Tomoya Hattori[2], Takahiro Sakai[2],
and Hajime Mizuyama[1] [ID]

[1] Aoyama Gakuin University, 5-10-1 Fuchinobe, Sagamihara 252-5258, Japan
`suginouchi@ise.aoyama.ac.jp`
[2] Murata Machinery, Ltd., 2 Hashizume Nakajima, Inuyama 484-0076, Japan

Abstract. How to quickly assess the transportation rate of an RGV system in the early design phase is an important issue. Thus, we propose an approach for evaluating the transportation rate of an RGV system based on mathematical optimization. We first present a formulation of the RGV transportation scheduling problem. The objective function is minimizing the makespan, whose reciprocal corresponds to the transportation rate. Then, we translate the original scheduling problem into four relaxation problems to shorten the calculation time. We further conduct computational experiments for characterizing the proposed approach.

Keywords: RGV systems · Heuristics · Mixed Integer Programming

1 Introduction

RGVs (Rail Guided Vehicles) are widely used in factories and distribution centers combined with an automated storage and retrieval system (AS/RS) to transport palletized materials between the AS/RS and other facilities efficiently. A typical RGV system is composed of a rail, several stations connecting the rail with the AS/RS or other facilities, several RGVs running along the rail, etc. The number of transportation jobs accomplished per unit time, i.e., the transportation rate, depends on various factors such as the physical layout of the system, the number of RGVs, and the distribution of the origin-destination pairs. The customer is primarily concerned with whether the transportation rate reaches the requirement under various constraints. Hence, in the business inquiry phase negotiating over various design options, the provider needs to evaluate the transportation rate of candidate designs of the system quickly.

Evaluating the transportation rate is not straightforward. For example, increasing the number of RGVs improves the rate but the effect gradually

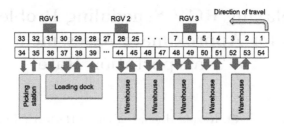

Fig. 1. Example of RGV system

decreases, and finally, becomes negative. This is because multiple RGVs share a single rail. While an RGV is loading/unloading a job from/to a station, it must stop in front of it. Accordingly, if the next RGV traveling behind it approaches the station, the next one must also stop and wait for the first one to complete the loading operation. That is, traffic jams may occur. The higher the number of installed RGVs, the more frequent such jamming and thus the lower the effect of increasing RGVs. Though this qualitative effect trend is understood, we usually need to rely on extensive numerical simulation to quantify the effect, and it takes a long time.

Thus, in this paper, we propose an approximate approach for assessing the transportation rate of an RGV system but in a relatively short time based on mathematical optimization. RGV systems can be classified into two types: orbital type and shuttling type. Some authors formulated the scheduling problem of shuttling type RGV systems [1, 2] and others estimated the transportation rate of orbital type systems based on simulation [3]. Ordinary single-loop AGV systems do not use a rail but are similar to the orbital type in the mathematical sense, and their guide-path design problems are dealt with by mathematical optimization [4–6]. However, to our best knowledge, no paper has tackled a scheduling problem for the orbital type by mathematical optimization approach. We formulate a mixed integer linear programming problem that determines a transportation schedule for an orbital type RGV system. The objective function is minimizing the makespan, whose reciprocal corresponds to the transportation rate. The solution consists of a sequence of jobs and a matching between RGVs and jobs. The larger the problem size, the longer the calculation time to obtain the exact solution, which increases exponentially. Hence, we also provide four relaxation problems by removing some constraints and decision variables from the original problem in stages, and evaluate the performance of the assessment approach using those relaxed problems through numerical experiments.

2   Discretized Model of RGV System

Figure 1 shows a discretized model of an example RGV system. In this model, the rail is divided into multiple cells, whose length is determined so that only one RGV can occupy a cell. Each RGV moves from one cell to another in the specified direction along the rail, that is, cells 1, 2, etc. The time for the RGV to pass through a cell depends on the cell because the RGV needs to slow down for example at corners. The velocity of the RGV also depends on whether it holds a job or not. Each RGV can hold at most one job and can load/unload a job only while it stops at a cell connected with a loading/unloading station which is indicated by an upwards/downwards arrow in the figure. Further, it takes a specified time for the RGV to complete the loading/unloading operation. Even when an RGV is running at a slower speed, or stops, in front of another RGV, the latter cannot overtake the former.

The problem is to assess the transportation rate of this RGV system, on the assumption that the distribution of the origin-destination pairs of the jobs is known. We address this problem by solving the RGV scheduling problem for a set of jobs created according to the distribution. More specifically, we evaluate the transportation rate by the reciprocal of the obtained makespan.

3   RGV Scheduling Problem and Its Relaxation

3.1   Original Scheduling Problem

We first provide a formulation of the original RGV scheduling problem below.

Instance $\mathcal{I} = (\mathcal{C}, \mathcal{V}, \mathcal{J}, (IC_v)_{v \in \mathcal{V}}, (F_j, G_j)_{j \in \mathcal{J}}, (T_{0,c}, T_{1,c}, W_{0,c}, W_{1,c})_{c \in \mathcal{C}}, \mathcal{L})$

$\mathcal{C} \subset \mathbb{N}$: Set of rail cells

$\mathcal{L} \subset \mathbb{N}$: Set of laps

$\mathcal{V} \subset \mathbb{N}$: Set of RGVs

$IC_v \in \mathcal{C}$: Initial position of RGV v

$T_{0,c} \in \mathbb{R}_0^+$: Time for an RGV to pass through cell c when it does not hold a job

$T_{1,c} \in \mathbb{R}_0^+$: Time for an RGV to pass through cell c when it holds a job

$W_{0,c} \in \mathbb{R}_0^+$: Time for an RGV to load a job at cell c

$W_{1,c} \in \mathbb{R}_0^+$: Time for an RGV to unload a job at cell c

$\mathcal{J} \subset \mathbb{N}$: Set of jobs

$F_j \in \mathcal{C}$: Origin cell of job j

$G_j \in \mathcal{C}$: Destination cell of job j

Solution $x_{v,l,c} \in \mathbb{R}_0^+$: Arrival time of RGV v at cell c in its lth lap

$s_j \in \mathbb{R}$: Start time of job j

$c_j \in \mathbb{R}$: Completion time of job j

CT : Makespan

$sc_{v,l,j} \in \{0,1\}$: Indicator variable whether RGV v starts job j in its lth lap

$cc_{v,l,j} \in \{0,1\}$: Indicator variable whether RGV v finishes job j in its lth lap

$h_{v,l,c} \in \{0,1\}$: Indicator variable whether RGV v holds a job when it arrives at cell c in its lth lap

Objective Function and Constraints

$$\min CT \tag{1}$$

$$\text{s.t.} c_j \leq CT \qquad\qquad\qquad \forall j \tag{2}$$

$$v' = \begin{cases} |\mathcal{V}| & (\text{if } v = 1) \\ v - 1 & (\text{otherwise}) \end{cases} \tag{3}$$

$$l' = \begin{cases} l - 1 & (\text{if } v = 1 \wedge c \neq |\mathcal{C}| \wedge 2 \leq l) \\ l + 1 & (\text{if } v \neq 1 \wedge c = |\mathcal{C}|) \\ l & (\text{otherwise}) \end{cases} \tag{4}$$

$$c' = \begin{cases} 1 & (\text{if } c = |\mathcal{C}|) \\ c + 1 & (\text{otherwise}) \end{cases} \tag{5}$$

$$x_{v',l',c'} \leq x_{v,l,c} \qquad \forall (v,l,c) \in \{(v,l,c) | 2 \leq l \vee (l = 1 \wedge IC_v \leq c)\} \tag{6}$$

$$l'' = \begin{cases} l + 1 & (\text{if } c = |\mathcal{C}|) \\ l & (\text{otherwise}) \end{cases} \tag{7}$$

$$ah_{l,c} = \begin{cases} 1 & (\text{if } l = |\mathcal{L}| \wedge c = |\mathcal{C}|) \\ 0 & (\text{otherwise}) \end{cases} \tag{8}$$

$$x_{v,l,c} + T_{0,c} \times (1 - h_{v,l,c}) + T_{1,c} \times h_{v,l,c} + \sum_{\forall j \in \{j | F_j = c\}} W_{0,c} \times sc_{v,l,j}$$

$$+ \sum_{\forall j' \in \{j' | G_{j'} = c\}} W_{1,c} \times cc_{v,l,j'} \leq x_{v,l'',c'} + M \times ah_{l,c} \qquad \forall (v,l,c) \tag{9}$$

$$c'' = \begin{cases} |\mathcal{C}| & (\text{if } c = 1) \\ c - 1 & (\text{otherwise}) \end{cases} \tag{10}$$

$$l''' = \begin{cases} l - 1 & (\text{if } c = 1) \\ l & (\text{otherwise}) \end{cases} \tag{11}$$

$$ph_{v,l,c} = \begin{cases} 0 & (\text{if } c \leq IC_v - 1 \wedge l = 1) \\ 1 & (\text{otherwise}) \end{cases} \qquad \forall (v,l,c) \tag{12}$$

$$h_{v,l,c} - ph_{v,l,c} \times h_{v,l''',c''} - \sum_{\forall j \in \{j | F_j = c\}} sc_{v,l,j}$$

$$+ \sum_{\forall j' \in \{j' | G_{j'} = c\}} cc_{v,l,j'} = 0 \qquad \forall (v,l,c) \tag{13}$$

$$h_{v,1,IC_v} = 0 \qquad\qquad\qquad\qquad \forall v \tag{14}$$

$$x_{v,l,F_j} \leq s_j + M \times (1 - sc_{v,l,j}) \qquad\qquad \forall (v,l,j) \tag{15}$$

$$s_j \leq x_{v,l,F_j} + M \times (1 - sc_{v,l,j}) \qquad\qquad \forall (v,l,j) \tag{16}$$

$$x_{v,l,G_j} + W_{1,G_j} \times cc_{v,l,j} \leq c_j + M \times (1 - cc_{v,l,j}) \qquad \forall (v,l,j) \tag{17}$$

$$c_j - W_{1,G_j} \times cc_{v,l,j} \leq x_{v,l,G_j} + M \times (1 - cc_{v,l,j}) \qquad \forall(v,l,j) \ (18)$$

$$\sum_{v=1}^{|\mathcal{V}|} \sum_{l=1}^{|\mathcal{L}|} sc_{v,l,j} = 1 \qquad \forall j \ (19)$$

$$\sum_{v=1}^{|\mathcal{V}|} \sum_{l=1}^{|\mathcal{L}|} cc_{v,l,j} = 1 \qquad \forall j \ (20)$$

$$\sum_{l=1}^{|\mathcal{L}|} (sc_{v,l,j} - cc_{v,l,j}) = 0 \qquad \forall(v,j) \ (21)$$

$$0 \leq s_j \leq c_j \qquad \forall j \ (22)$$

$$x_{v,1,IC_v} = 0 \qquad \forall v \ (23)$$

Equation (1) expresses the objective function, which minimizes the makespan. The constraints are Eqs. (2)–(23). Equation (2) defines that the makespan CT is the latest completion time c_j of all jobs j. Equations (3)–(6) express that RGV v cannot overtake RGV v' running in front of it. Equations (7)–(9) express that when an RGV holds/does not hold a job, the time for it to pass through cell c is $T_{1,c}/T_{0,c}$. These equations also consider the time to load/unload a job. Equations (10)–(13) express that RGVs cannot hold two or more jobs at the same time. Equation (14) guarantees that RGVs do not hold any job at the initial condition. Equations (15) and (16) define the relationship between the starting time s_j of job j and the arrival time x_{v,l,F_j} of RGV v which carries out the job j at cell F_j in lth lap. Similarly, Eqs. (17) and (18) define the relationship between the completion time c_j of job j and the arrival time x_{v,l,G_j} of RGV v at cell (l, G_j). Equation (19) and (20) guarantee that a job is transported once. Equation (21) guarantees that any job cannot be interrupted once started until finished. Equation (22) expresses that RGVs can unload a job only after loading the job. Equation (23) designates the initial position of every RGV v.

3.2 RP1: Relaxation of No Overtaking Constraints

We next relax the RGV scheduling problem in stages to shorten the calculation time. Relaxation Problem 1 (RP1) relaxes Eqs. (3)–(6) from the original problem. Accordingly, RGV v is permitted to overtake RGV v' running in front of it. The number of RP1's constraints is lesser than that of the original problem but the number of RP1's decision variables is the same as that of the original.

3.3 RP2: Relaxation of No Preemption Constraints

RP2 further allows RGVs to preempt the job at any cell on the way to its destination. The number of RP2's decision variables is lesser than that of RP1. RP2 needs some notations in addition to those used in the original problem. The formulation of the RP2 is as follows:

Instance $A_{j,c} \in \{0,1\}$: Indicator variable whether cell c is the origin F_j of job j

$B_{j,c} \in \{0,1\}$: Indicator variable whether cell c is the destination G_j of job j
$D_{j,c} \in \{0,1\}$: Indicator variable whether the RGV holding job j passes cell c
Solution $x_{v,j} \in \{0,1\}$: A decision variable whether RGV v carries out job j
$y_{v,c} \subset \mathbb{N}$: Number of times that RGV v passes cell c without holding a job
$z_{v,c} \subset \mathbb{N}$: Number of times that RGV v passes cell c with holding a job
$AA_{v,c} \subset \mathbb{N}$: Number of times that RGV v loads a job at cell c
$BB_{v,c} \subset \mathbb{N}$: Number of times that RGV v unloads a job at cell c
$ct_v \subset \mathbb{N}$: Time when RGV v finishes all jobs allocated to it
Objective Function and Constraints

$$\min CT \tag{24}$$

$$\text{s.t.} ct_v \le CT \qquad \forall v \tag{25}$$

$$\sum_v x_{v,j} = 1 \qquad \forall j \tag{26}$$

$$AA_{v,c} = \sum_j A_{j,c} \times x_{v,j} \qquad \forall(v,c) \tag{27}$$

$$BB_{v,c} = \sum_j B_{j,c} \times x_{v,j} \qquad \forall(v,c) \tag{28}$$

$$z_{v,c} = \sum_j D_{j,c} \times x_{v,j} \qquad \forall(v,c) \tag{29}$$

$$z_{v,c} - z_{v,c'} \le y_{v,c'} \qquad \forall(v,c) \in \{(v,c)|c' \le c-1\} \tag{30}$$

$$z_{v,c} - z_{v,c'} - 1 \le y_{v,c'} \qquad \forall(v,c) \in \{(v,c)|c \le c'\} \tag{31}$$

$$ct_v = \sum_c (T_{0,c} \times y_{v,c} + T_{1,c} \times z_{v,c} + W_{0,c} \times AA_{v,c} + W_{1,c} \times BB_{v,c}) \quad \forall v \tag{32}$$

3.4 RP3: Average Occupied Time per RGV

RP3 does not require solving an optimization problem, and instead needs a straightforward calculation. RP3 calculates the average traveling time per RGV. The makespan CT means the average traveling time per RGV and is expressed by Eqs. (33)–(36) with using the number of times that an RGV passes cell c with holding a job z_c and the number of times that an RGV passes cell c without loading a job y_c.

$$CT = \{\sum_c (T_{1,c} \times z_c + \sum_j W_{0,c} \times A_{j,c} + \sum_j W_{1,c} \times B_{j,c})\}/|\mathcal{V}| \tag{33}$$

$$z_c = \sum_j D_{j,c} \qquad \forall c \tag{34}$$

$$z_c - z_{c'} \le y_{c'} \qquad \forall c \in \{c|1 \le c' \le c-1\} \tag{35}$$

$$z_c - z_{c'} - 1 \le y_{c'} \qquad \forall c \in \{c|c \le c' \le |\mathcal{C}|\} \tag{36}$$

3.5   RP4: Maximum Occupied Time of Cells

RP4 also needs only a straightforward calculation. The makespan CT is the maximum occupied time of cells and is expressed by Eq. (37).

$$CT = \max_{c}(\sum_{j} T_{1,c} \times D_{j,c} + \sum_{j} W_{0,c} \times A_{j,c} + \sum_{j} W_{1,c} \times B_{j,c}) \qquad (37)$$

Table 1. Experimental conditions

	Exp. 1	Exp.2
The number of RGVs	5,6	5,10,15
The number of jobs	7,8,...,12	20,30,...,100
The number of trials	20	10
Loading/Unloading time $W_{0,c}$, $W_{1,c}$ [sec]	5.5–6.7	5.5–6.7
Travel time when not holding a job $T_{0,c}$ [sec]	0.3–1.5	0.3–1.5
Travel time when holding a job $T_{1,c}$ [sec]	0.4–1.5	0.3–1.5

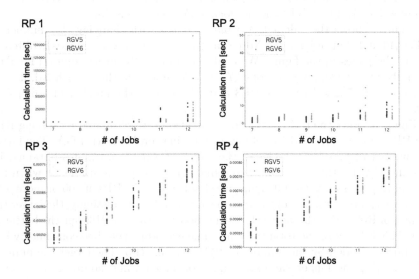

Fig. 2. Calculation time of RP1, 2, 3 and 4

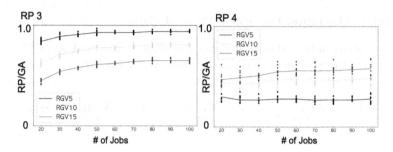

Fig. 3. The ratio of the objective function value obtained by RPs to that by GA

4   Numerical Experiments

We next investigate the features of the proposed approach through computational experiments taking up the example system shown in Fig. 1. Table 1 shows the experimental conditions. The system configuration and experimental conditions do not correspond to a real system but assume a fictive one. In the experiments, we employ Genetic Algorithm for solving the original problem of a large size, and CPLEX [7] for others, on 8 Core Apple M1 CPU 16GB memory computer. The distribution of the origin-destination pairs are as follows: Warehouse → Picking station is 20%, Picking station → Warehouse is 20%, Warehouse → Loading dock is 40%, and Loading dock → Warehouse is 20%.

Figure 2 shows the calculation time obtained with changing the number of RGVs $|\mathcal{V}|$ and that of jobs $|\mathcal{J}|$. Note that the scale of the vertical axis is different among the panes in the figure. We could not obtain the exact solution for RP1 and RP2 when the number of jobs $|\mathcal{J}|$ is 13 or more. On the other hand, it took only less than 5[msec] to solve RP3 and RP4 even if the number of jobs $|\mathcal{J}|$ is 100.

Figure 3 shows the ratio of the transportation rate estimated by solving RP3 and RP4 to that obtained by solving the original problem with GA. The larger the number of jobs $|\mathcal{J}|$, the lesser the gap between the estimates obtained by RPs and GA. Further, a certain gap remains but the gap is stabilized when the number of jobs is close to 100. Thus, we should solve the RPs of 100 or more jobs to obtain a stable estimate of the transportation rate. Interestingly, the larger the number of RGVs $|\mathcal{V}|$, the worse the estimation accuracy in RP3 but the better in RP4. This is because the total traveling time excluding the time consumed while jamming is divided by the number of RGVs $|\mathcal{V}|$ in RP3. The larger the number of RGVs $|\mathcal{V}|$, the longer the extra time consumed while jamming in general. Whereas, the estimate provided by RP4 does not depend on $|\mathcal{V}|$ since it focuses on the cells instead of RGVs. Thus, RP3 and RP4 complement each other and both should be adopted for assessing the transportation rate.

5   Conclusions

In this paper, we presented a formulation of the scheduling problem for an orbital type RGV system and its relaxation problems. To obtain a stable estimate of the transportation rate, a scheduling problem of 100 or more jobs should be solved. The calculation time for solving RP1 and RP2 increases exponentially. RP3 and RP4 of up to 100 jobs can be solved within a reasonable time.

Future research directions include to apply a machine learning technique to establish a transportation rate prediction model using the solution data obtained by solving the relaxation problems as the training data.

References

1. Hu, W., Mao, J., Wei, K.: Energy-efficient rail guided vehicle routing for two-sided loading/unloading automated freight handling system. Eur. J. Oper. Res. **258**(3), 943–957 (2017)
2. Hu, P., Chen, H., Wang, X., Shi, M.: Model and algorithm for co-scheduling of stackers and single RGV during retrieval process in AS/RS. In: IOP Conference Series: Materials Science and Engineering, vol. 688 (2019)
3. Lee, S., Souza, R., Ong, E.: Simulation modelling of a narrow aisle automated storage and retrieval system (AS/RS) serviced by rail-guided vehicles. Comput. Ind. **30**, 3241–253 (1996)
4. Sinriech, D., Tanchoco, J.M.A.: Solution methods for the mathematical models of single-loop AGV systems. Int. J. Prod. Res. **31**, 705–725 (1993)
5. Chen, M.T., McGinnis, L., Zhou, C.: Design and operation of single-loop dual-rail inter-bay material handling system. Int. J. Prod. Res. **37**(10), 2217–2237 (1999)
6. Asef-Vaziri, A., Laporte, G., Sriskandarajah, C.: The block layout shortest loop design problem. IIE Trans. **32**, 727–734 (2000)
7. IBM Web page: https://www.ibm.com/analytics/data-science/prescriptive-analytics/cplex-optimizer. Accessed 9 Apr 2022

Direct Part Marking (DPM) Supported by Additively Manufactured Tags to Improve the Traceability of Castings

Snehal Desavale, Farhad Ameri$^{(\boxtimes)}$, Luis Trueba, and Ogoma Igveh

Department of Engineering Technology, Texas State University, San Marcos, USA
{s_d378,ameri,l.trueba,ogi1}@txstate.edu

Abstract. Manufacturers are increasingly required to trace and track their products throughout different stages of product lifecycle. Various identification techniques such as barcodes, RFID tags, magnetic strips, and optical character recognition (OCR) can be used to support traceability. This research is focused on using Direct Part Marking (DPM) for permanent identification of castings using 2D codes. 3D printed codes were used as pattern inserts in a series of experiments. The objective was to identify the most suitable 3D printing technology for creating permanent marks on castings manufactured using the nobake sand casting process. It was concluded that Polyjet technique creates more dimensionally accurate 3D printed tags and the generated markings are more readable compared to other tested methods.

Keywords: Direct part marking · Foundry traceability · Part identification

1 Introduction

Traceability of manufactured products refers to the capability to track and trace raw materials, parts, and finished goods throughout the production and distribution processes [1]. Tracing is the ability to extract the history of a particular product by retrieving the records held upstream in the supply chain while tracking is the ability to follow the downstream path of a product along the supply chain. Traceability provides manufacturers with real-time visibility into the operations involved in manufacturing of the products [2]. Manufacturers often strive to use modern tools and technologies to automate the traceability process to the extent possible. Automated identification and data capture (AIDC) technologies are widely used in industry to automatically identify objects, collect contextual data about the identified objects, and record the data in computer systems for future use and trace and track activities.

Some of the commonly used identification techniques include barcodes, two-dimensional (2D) codes, RFID tags, magnetic strips, and optical character recognition (OCR). Finished and semi-finished products with identifiers, such as barcodes and RFID tags, can be readily monitored at various stages of production and distribution with the aid

© IFIP International Federation for Information Processing 2022
Published by Springer Nature Switzerland AG 2022
D. Y. Kim et al. (Eds.): APMS 2022, IFIP AICT 663, pp. 244–251, 2022.
https://doi.org/10.1007/978-3-031-16407-1_29

of scanners. If identification systems are designed and implemented properly, AIDC systems can provide part-level visibility and maximize data value to quickly spot production problems or trends and take proactive actions [1].

Barcodes and 2D codes are typically printed on paper labels and attached to products or their packaging. In some cases, the codes are permanently marked on parts or products. Direct part marking (DPM) is a method of marking objects permanently with product information, which may include serial and part numbers, batch number, production date, and other useful information. DPM is particularly useful in harsh environments where labels would not last. Even the most durable label can fade, fall off, or disintegrate when exposed to extreme temperatures, chemicals, liquids, and other harsh environmental conditions. Direct part marking, due to its permanent nature, has proven to be an effective identification method in these situations.

This research focuses on foundry traceability. Due to the high temperatures of the molten metals and the rough surface quality, using RFID tags or barcode stickers is not practical for identification of castings. Therefore, DPM becomes the preferred method for part-level identification in foundry. One of the requirements of traceability in foundry operations is the ability to record the raw material batch, metal composition, and the complete history of pattern making and metal pouring process [3]. The information related to production history can be encoded using various coding standards and marked on castings during their production. The selected method for the DPM process in this work is to print the codes using various additive manufacturing (AM) techniques as tags that can be inserted onto patterns during the mold making operation and before metal pouring. DotCode was selected as the 2D code for permanent marking of castings. Marking of castings is challenging since sand casting often generates rough surfaces, which negatively influences the readability of the codes. Also, the size of the marking needs to be relatively small for aesthetic reasons.

The main research questions that motivate this work are: (1) what is the best 3D printing technology to produce quality tags for sand casting? and (2) what are the optimum casting parameters that result in the most readable codes with a minimum of post-processing steps?

The remainder of this paper is organized as follows. The next section provides a brief overview the related works. The DotCode standard is discussed next. The overall research method is discussed in Sect. 4. In Sect. 5, the results of the 3D printing experiments are presented, and Sect. 6 focuses on casting experiments. The paper ends with conclusions.

2 Related Work

There are different methods available for DPM including etching, dot peening, and laser marking. The focus of this paper is on creating permanent marks on castings manufactured using the *nobake sand casting process*. Although techniques such as laser marking or dot peening can still be applied to castings as a post-productions step, part marking directly during the casting process would be beneficial since its extends the scope of tracking activities to include the molding, casting, shakeout, and cleaning steps. Researchers have used multiple methods for marking of castings including sand embossing using paraffin-actuated reconfigurable pin-type tooling [4] or using CNC machined inserts [5]. An alternative process that has been used for creation of mold inserts is 3D printing which is advantageous for several reasons such as eliminating the need for using special purpose tools, and enabling rapid creation of 3D printed inserts based on the digital models of the codes. Uyan *et al.* [6] have successfully used 3D printed code inserts to be used during the mold making process. They used wax printing technique on ProJet MJP 3600W machine. Although this technique generates tags with high surface quality and accuracy, it requires some extra preprocessing that can be time consuming. In this work, three more affordable3D printing techniques are used and compared for printing of 2D code inserts.

3 DotCode

There are various standards for 2D codes including QR Code, Data Matrix, Maxi Code, Aztec, and DotCode. Figure 1 shows some of the commonly used 2D codes. In this research, DotCode was selected for direct part marking. DotCode is a 2D matrix symbology consisting of dots arranged in a rectangular array. One advantage of DotCode is that there is no maximum capacity to the amount of data that can be stored in a single code. However, the limit is often imposed by the printers that are restricted to a size limit of 124 dots in either direction. To ensure that the scanner can read the code without picking up any additional pattern around the code, a DotCode must be surrounded by a "quiet zone", which is three dots wide, on all four sides of the printed code. Smaller and tighter dot geometry results in smaller tags, but also a tag that is more difficult to consistently fabricate and cast into the part.

Fig. 1. Different types of 2D codes generated using the laser engraving method (left) and an example DotCode (right).

4 Research Method

In this work, three-dimensional (3D) printed tags were used as pattern inserts for direct marking of castings. Three different 3D printing technologies, namely, fused deposition modeling (FDM), stereolithography (SLA), and PolyJet were evaluated. The tags were printed in extruded (bumps) and protruded (dimples) patterns. Tags were also printed in different dimensions to test if changes in dimensions have any impact on the readability of the codes. The tag measurements were 50 × 30, 40 × 30, 30 × 20 mm. The quality of the printed tags was compared qualitatively and quantitatively to identify the most suitable 3D printing technology with minimal deviation from the original geometry. For quantitative comparison, a digital 3D measurement system was used to measure the diameter of the dots and their distances with adjacent dots. Tags with lower variation in diameter and distance were deemed better in quality. Finally, each of the tags were used on the cope and drag surfaces (separately) of a plate pattern to mark aluminum castings with DotCodes. The readability of the codes was tested using a code scanner mobile app.

5 Tag Printing Experiments

FDM Method: Three different FDM printers, namely, Craftbot, Makerbot Replicator z18, and Voxelizer were used. The Craftbot 3D printer gave better output for bigger tags, but the results were not as desirable for smaller tags. The Makerbot Replicator z18 did not generate desired tag quality for either bump or dimple patterns. The Voxelizer 3D printer managed to get better results than other FDM 3D printers for the bump pattern. Some of the printed tags using Voxelizer are shown in Fig. 2.

Fig. 2. Tags with bump (left) and dimple (right) patterns printed using Voxelizer.

SLA Method: Most of the dimple patterns were not printed as desired using the SLA print method. The issue encountered was with resin getting stuck in the dimples. It was difficult to remove resin from dimples even after machine washing and manual cleaning. Tags were printed multiple times to get accurate results. In the end, only one tag was produced with satisfactory results. SLA printing was a time-consuming method as it took 2 h and 20 min, including washing and curing, to generate one set of tags in all dimensions. Figure 3 shows some of the tags printed using SLA technique.

PolyJet Method: As shown in Fig. 4, all of the tags printed using the PolyJet method were of very good print quality; the material appeared strong and solid. The bumps and dimples both printed well.

Fig. 3. Tags with bump (left) and dimple (right) patterns printed using SLA method.

	Technology	Std Dev	Mean
Bump	FDM	0.097	1.1
40*30	Polyjet	0.061	1.04
mm	SLA	0.07	1.02
Dimple	FDM	0.11	1
40*30	Polyjet	0.043	1.01
mm	SLA	0.122	1.125

Fig. 4. Tags printed using PolyJet method (left) and the measurements obtained from VR-5200 digital measurement system (right).

A digital 3D measurement system (Keyence VR-5200) was used to measure the dimensions of the printed tags. The diameter of the dots (bumps and dimples) and their spacing were the dimensions of interest that were measured for various tag sizes. The mean and the standard deviation for those dimensions were used to measure of the accuracy of the prints. More accurate prints have mean values closer to the nominal values and with smaller standard deviation. Figure 4 (right) shows the measurements obtained for one set of tags. Based on the measurements obtained using VR-5200, the PolyJet tags demonstrated higher quality and accuracy. The next best technology was SLA.

6   Casting Experiments

The objective of this experiment was to mark castings using the 3D printed tags and evaluate the readability of the 2D codes created on the surface of the castings. Steps involved in the casting process included pattern making, sand preparation, molding, melting, pouring, cooling, shake-out, degating, finishing, and inspection. The sand types that are often used for sand casting include green sand and resin bonded sand. As compared to green sand molds, resin bonded sand molds and cores have better mechanical properties and generally produce more dimensionally accurate castings. In this project, AFS GFN 80 round silica sand with a phenolic urethane nobake binder was used. The castings were made of aluminum alloy A356.

Fig. 5. Mold pattern with tags inserted (left); the drag (lower half of the mold) after drawing the pattern (right).

Figure 5 (left) shows the 3D printed tags attached to the match plate pattern. One of the challenges during pattern preparation was to ensure that all tags were sitting flat on the pattern. PolyJet and FDM tags were sturdier and therefore, stayed relatively flat on the surface. SLA tags were curled after curing, and they did not lie flat on the pattern surface.

Another challenging step was drawing the pattern from the mold without damaging the bump and dimple features on the sand. While drawing the patterns, some of the tags adhered to the sand. The tags remaining in the mold needed to be carefully removed so that the sand around the tag did not become damaged. Figure 5 (right) shows the drag (lower half of the mold) after drawing the pattern.

After producing the castings, it was observed that all dots associated with the SLA tags were damaged. Hemispherical dots and the dots with fillets survived the metal casting process. This observation confirmed the initial assumption that dimple and bumps with a hemispherical shape or fillets yield better results and cylindrical shapes with sharp edges must be avoided. During the casting process, tags placed in the drag were accurately reproduced, but cope-placed tags were not.

After solidification and shake-out, several post-processing steps were needed to obtain readable markings. A mild detergent-water solution and metal brush were used to clean the residue without damaging the markings. Figure 6 (left) shows the markings after the first cleaning step. The *Scandit* mobile app was used to read the codes after cleaning. However, due to low contrast between the bumps and dimples and the flat surface of the code, the app was not able to provide a reading. To improve the contrast, three methods were used: Cleaning with a Scotch-Bright disk, light grinding with abrasive paper, and painting followed by light grinding.

Scotch-Bright Disk: 3M's Scotch-Bright is a line of abrasive products applied to clean the metal surfaces. Disks of Scotch-Bright mounted on a die grinder were used to abrasively clean the metal surfaces to improve contrast.

Abrasive Paper: A 320 grit silicon carbide abrasive paper was used to remove surface oxidation and dirt while also leveling out the surface. Aluminum is a relatively soft metal, so it did not take too much effort to level off the surface. After following these cleaning methods, some of the part markings were readable under oblique lighting conditions, but not all were readable.

Application of Flat Black Paint: This step involved spraying flat black paint and further polishing the surface. Figure 6 (right) shows the markings after the secondary preparation step. This step significantly improved the readability with the Scandit app. Markings produced with PolyJet tags with bump patterns were immediately recognized without using any special light setting while markings with dimple patterns required use of light at a 30–40° angle to be scanned. The Scandit app has a small scanning area, and it therefore works better for smaller tags (30 mm × 20 mm). As a result, markings made with 30 mm × 20 mm PolyJet tags were easily read by the app. For larger tags, it was necessary to move the reader further away from the casting, which consequently increased the time needed by the app to capture an accurate image and generate a correct reading.

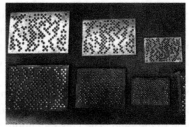

Fig. 6. Tags after initial cleaning (left) and after painting and polishing (right).

Markings made with FDM-printed tags did not work well even after post-processing steps since most of the dots were connected to each other while 3D printing.

7 Conclusions and Future Directions

The experimental study was undertaken to evaluate which 3D printing technology produces better quality DotCode tags for use as pattern inserts in direct part marking of metal castings. DPM is a reliable method of permanent identification of parts exposed to harsh environments. Direct marking of sand castings is challenging since the 2D codes are often not immediately readable and some extra steps are needed to improve the readability. One of the objectives of this work was to simplify the process by reducing the post-processing steps.

Several experiments were conducted using different 3D printing methods and sand casting setups. Both bump and dimple code patterns were used in the experiments. In nearly all experiments, extra steps were needed after casting to improve the contrast and readability of tags. Post casting processes included surface cleaning using abrasive media and painting the tags with flat black paint. Use of paint significantly improved the readability as the matt finish of the paint was more easily read than the reflective surface of the cleaned metal. Also, oblique lighting improved readability.

The Scandit mobile application was used to read the tags. Markings made with PolyJet tags were read most easily with those made with SLA tags being the next easiest to read. Polyjet and SLA tags remained flat after printing and post processing. SLA produced accurate prints except that some tags had resin remaining and adhering in the holes of the tags. SLA produced the bump pattern best as it gave accurate output regardless of size of the tags. The SLA tags were curled and created difficulty in the casting process. It was concluded that FDM technology is not suitable for DotCode printing since the codes generated using FDM tags were the most difficult to read. FDM printing might work for larger tags, though. Overall, it was concluded that PolyJet technology is the best method in terms of sturdiness of the 3D printed tag, the quality of print, as well as suitability for the sand casting process. It was also observed that bump patterns produced with PolyJet tags were easiest to read because they did not require special lighting whereas the dimple patterns did.

Several avenues remain for further research in this area. For example, different types of 3D printing technologies such as digital light processing (DLP), selective laser sintering (SLS), and drop on demand (DOD) could be investigated to produce 3D tags. While DotCode was used in this experiment, DataMatrix codes may prove more robust because the marking is still readable when approximately 17% of the code is damaged. Use of pattern parting compounds such as liquid parting may also improve tag performance as pattern drawing was a major source of marking damage experienced in this study. Different metals such as stainless steel, copper-based alloy, iron, nickel-based alloys can be tested to measure the performance and durability of tags over several alloy systems. In addition, compatibility of the tags with green sand should be investigated. Marking parts with cylindrical surfaces is another challenge that needs to be addressed. Finally, industrial scanners will be used in future research instead of mobile phone apps to better replicate industrial use.

References

1. Bechini, A., Cimino, M., Marcelloni, F., Tomasi, A.: Patterns and technologies for enabling supply chain traceability through collaborative E-business. Inf. Softw. Technol. **50**(4), 342–359 (2008)
2. Winkel, T., Stein, D.: Casting inspection and traceability for total quality assurance. Foundry and Management Technology (2016)
3. Wadhwa, R.: Methodology for internal traceability support in foundry manufacturing. In: Prabhu, V., Taisch, M., Kiritsis, D. (eds.) APMS 2013. IAICT, vol. 414, pp. 183–190. Springer, Heidelberg (2013). https://doi.org/10.1007/978-3-642-41266-0_23
4. Vedel-Smith, N.K., Lenau, T.A.: Casting traceability with direct part marking using reconfigurable pin-type tooling based on paraffin–graphite actuators. J. Manuf. Syst. **31**(2), 113–120 (2012)
5. Saveraid, G.C.: Cast data matrix symbols performance characterization. Ph.D. thesis, Iowa State University (2010)
6. Uyan, T., Jalava, K., Orkas, J., Otto, K.: Additively Manufactured Tags for Cast Part Traceability Using Two-Dimensional Digital Code Direct-Part-Marking. American Society of Mechanical Engineers Digital Collection (2020)

Development of a STEP-NC – Enabled Interoperable and Open Architecture CNC Controller

Julien Bechtold$^{(\boxtimes)}$, Christophe Danjou, and Walid Jomaa

Polytechnique Montréal, Montréal, QC H3T 1J4, Canada
bechtold.julien@gmail.com

Abstract. Most of modern computer numerical control (CNC) machine tools (CNCMTs) use standard G-code (ISO 6983) – based controllers. However, during the generation of G-codes by Computer-Aided Manufacturing (CAM) software, several machining information could be lost, which hinder the development of smart interoperable CNCMTs required for modern manufacturing environment. The STEP-NC (STEP compliant Numerical Control), which is a machine-tool control language governed by the ISO 14649 standard, was developed to overcome the G-code programming limitations. Over the last two decades, several research studies attempted to develop a new generation of CNCMTs controllers taking advantage of STEP-NC capabilities. Nevertheless, these controllers are customized for specific applications, complex to replicate, costly, and not yet accepted in the manufacturing industry. In this paper, an easy to replicate, noninvasive, and low-cost interpreted open architecture STEP-NC controller is developed. This controller uses a Single Board Computer which can be directly connected to a commercial lathe. The controller software is developed based on C++ and can interpret a ISO14649 STEP-NC file, generate a toolpath, simulate the toolpath, and communicate with the CNCMT. The developed STEP-NC controller was successfully tested by simulating the toolpath during the machining of a test part available in the ISO standard.

Keywords: STEP-NC · Open architecture controller · CNC machine tools · Machining

1 Introduction

Since the invention of numerically controlled machine-tools in the 1950s, their uses have steadily increased in the manufacturing industry until the beginning of the 1980s, were the first CNCMTs appeared. As of that date, the capabilities and performance of CNCMTs have evolved significantly. From its creation in the 1960s and normalization as ISO 6983 [1], the so-called G-code language is mainly used for programming CNCMTs. However, G-code is a low-level programming language containing basic information related to the toolpath and commands the machine must execute during the machining. Besides, G-codes allow only one-way communication between the controller and the CNCMT, that

© IFIP International Federation for Information Processing 2022
Published by Springer Nature Switzerland AG 2022
D. Y. Kim et al. (Eds.): APMS 2022, IFIP AICT 663, pp. 252–259, 2022.
https://doi.org/10.1007/978-3-031-16407-1_30

is it does not allow any systematic feedback from the CNCMT to the Computer Aided Manufacturing (CAM) and/or the Computer Aided Design (CAD) levels. This limitation pushed CNCMTs manufacturers to add specific functions and commands requiring the use of post-processors to generate G-code programs compatible with their CNCMTs. It is worth noting that, current commercial controllers are totally closed and cannot be modified by the customer, they act like a black box.

STEP-NC, as a new standardized machine-tool control language, was developed to resolve many of the G-code and current controllers' limitations. It was standardized as the ISO 14649 [2] which is an extension of STEP (Standard for the Exchange of Product model data), standardized as ISO 10303 [3]. With STEP-NC it is possible to use a single standardized language throughout the numerical manufacturing chain, from the CAD to the CNC controller. In addition, STEP-NC can ensure a bidirectional communication transfer without any loss of information. Figure 1 shows the current manufacturing chain and the concept of STEP-NC-enabled interoperable manufacturing chain.

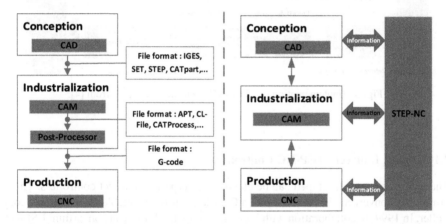

Fig. 1. Current manufacturing chain (left), manufacturing chain with STEP-NC (right)

With the STEP-NC standard, only one file is used along the numerical manufacturing chain. It is a high-level language which, in addition to how to make information (such as the tool path) as for the G-code, can store additional relevant information about what-to-make (features, operations, machining strategies, tool geometry, …) [4]. Today, there is no commercial CNC controller working based on STEP-NC program. In the new era of industry 4.0, the scientific community seeks to develop STEP-NC – based open architecture controllers (OAC) to meet the economical and performance needs of modern manufacturing systems. To this end, the main contribution of the present article is the development of a new STEP-NC controller, allowing intelligent monitoring of CNCMT and easier integration of STEP-NC in a production environment.

In the next section, a state of the art of STEP-NC-based controllers will be introduced. Then, in Sect. 3, the developed software and hardware of the STEP-NC controller will be described and discussed. Finally, Sect. 4 will be dedicated to the validation of the proposed solution.

2   State of the Art

The first STEP-NC controller prototypes have been developed earlier in 2003 and their evolution has continued until today. Three types of concepts were documented in the open literature and are summarized in Fig. 2 [4].

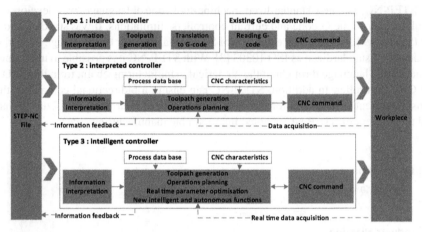

Fig. 2. Implementation of STEP-NC controllers, adapted from [4]

2.1   Type 1: Indirect STEP-NC Controllers

The first prototypes developed can be classified as type 1 or indirect controllers. These prototypes convert STEP-NC data into a G-code, so it is executable on a standard controller. In 1999, in collaboration with Siemens group, the European consortium ESPRIT [5] were among the first organizations able to run a single STEP-NC file on multiple types of CNCMTs using the Sinumerik 840D controller from Siemens Inc. Even so, this approach still suffers some limitations such as the use of G-code and the resulting loss of information after generating the toolpath. Furthermore, there is still a need for the post processor and for proprietary closed controllers. It is worth noting that this approach was useful to prove the feasibility of STEP-NC controllers at the beginning, but it cannot so far be a viable solution.

2.2   Types 2 and 3: Interpreted and Intelligent STEP-NC Controllers

Type 2 or interpreted controllers are capable of interpreting and executing STEP-NC files without using any G-code. The most relevant prototype of type 2 STEP-NC controller present in the literature are summarized in Table 1.

Presently, researchers are working on developing controllers with intelligent function, such as CLM feature [6] or automatic real time parameter correction [7]. However, a fully smart controller (Type 3) does not yet exist. It is the final goal of the STEP-NC

Table 1. Most relevant type 2 STEP-NC prototype controllers

Reference	Language	Hardware	Limitation
[4, 8]	C++	2 PC	Complex and costly architecture
[9]	C++	PC	Complex and costly architecture, no toolpath simulation or visualization
[10]	C	Microcontroller	More difficult to code, less user-friendly
[11]	C++	PC	Complex architecture with external control cards and acquisition cards
[12]	LabVIEW	PC	Custom control cards, proprietary software
[13]	C++	SBC	Lack of toolpath visualization, not tested on a commercial CNCMT

community, it should be able to optimize machining parameters in real time, to be a web-based and collaborative between machines and manufacture.

Conclusively, STEP-NC controllers are currently: (1) Complex and hard to replicate: most prototypes use a PC with additional (and mostly custom) controller and acquisition cards to communicate with the CNCMT. (2) High cost: a PC and custom controller cards are costly (estimated at more than 5000 $). (3) Cumbersome: most prototypes use a hardware that is external to the body of the CNCMT. Dharmawardhana, et al. [13] proposed a relevant solution based on a Single Board Computer (SBC) and proves that it is possible to make economical and compact STEP-NC controllers. The lack of toolpath visualization and simulation are however missing, and the facts that they use an Arduino Mega in addition to a RPi induce additional challenges during the integration of the controller.

To this end, the present research work aims to the development of an open architecture interpreted STEP-NC controller for a CNCMT with an emphasis on the miniaturization, integration, reproducibility, and cost effectiveness.

3   Development

As we have seen in the last chapter, there is a need to develop an open architecture interpreted STEP-NC controller. The emphasis will be put on developing a cheap and compact controller that is easy to replicate. The developed STEP-NC controller is devoted to control turning operations on a CNC mini-lathe.

3.1   Design of the Architecture

The software of the controller is developed based on the open-source C++ programming language which is compatible with a wide range of hardware. The C++ is an object-oriented and low-level programming language making the translation of STEP-NC information more accurate and intuitive since STEP-NC is an object-oriented language too. Moreover, compared to other programming languages, the C++ enable higher computation speed and more performant programming capabilities. Once the software language is chosen, it is necessary to focus on the hardware architecture.

The SBC is used as a hardware support for the developed controller. One of the well-known is the RPi. SBC which consists of a single electronic board including all PC components. The RPi SBC is not expensive, compact, and especially it has input/output ports called General Purpose Input/Output (GPIO) which allows communication directly with a CNCMT and other sensors without any additional control board. The RPi 4B model is selected for the hardware support. It has a quad-core ARM processor clocked at 1.5 GHz, 8 GB of RAM, and a 40-pin GPIO. This SBC meets the requirements of the controller and the objective of the project, that it is available for about 100 CA\$ and supports several languages, including C++ and Python. Thanks to its GPIO, it can communicate with external sensors and/or actuators. Furthermore, it offers many connectivity possibilities thanks to its Ethernet, camera, USB and HDMI Port and Wi-Fi connection.

To be able to communicate with the driver, the controller must send 5 V pulses. But the GPIO of the RPi works only with 3 V. So, a shifter card is used to upgrade the RPi from 3 V to 5 V. To protect the RPi and to facilitate the connection, a Breakout Board (BOB) is used, allowing the interface between the RPi and the driver. A BOB for 5 axis MOCN with optical couplers is available for less than 20 CA\$. The prototype controller is illustrated in Fig. 3.

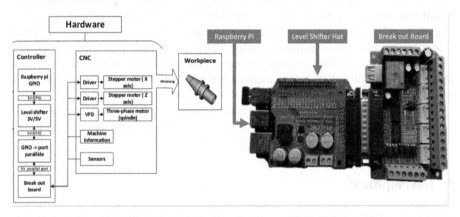

Fig. 3. Designed hardware of the developed STEP-NC controller.

Since the BOB as well as the GPIO can both send and receive signals, sensors or other actuators can therefore be connected to the controller in future development.

The signals sent by the RPi to the drivers must be sent in real time. Thus, the operating system (OS) must deal with real time signals. Contrary to a Windows system, which requires a paid and closed module to be transformed into a real time operating system (RTX of Venture COM is often used), the RPi OS has an open and free real time patch that can be installed.

3.2 Development of the Controller

The structure of the controller is as follows: First the STEP-NC file interpreter read all information that is stored in the STEP-NC file and instantiates the corresponding C++ objects. Then, the toolpath is generated as well as all the actions necessary to produce the workpiece by using the interpreted data and the characteristics of the machine-tool. The toolpath is then sent to the low-level controller. This is the part of the software that must work in real time since it oversees sending the information to the CNCMT. It is composed of two modules: The Numerical Control Kernel (NCK) and the Programmable Logic Control (PLC). The NCK interprets the information of the tool path and generates the signals that allow the movement of the axes of the CNCMT. To generate those signals, the NCK interpolate the toolpath and calculate the speed of the tool, considering the maximum acceleration allowable by the CNCMT. The general structure of the NCK and the algorithms used are given in Theory and Design of CNC [14]. The Programmable Logic Control (PLC) manages all the auxiliary actuators such as the spindle speed, the tool magazine, or the activation of the coolant system. All these instructions are sent to the motor drivers of the CNCMT and will allow the desired part geometry to be produced.

The functionalities of the software are as follows: The "Interpretation" function allows the reading and translation of the information included in the STEP-NC file. It, then, generates the toolpath and all the information necessary for moving the axes and managing the machine-tool's functions. The "Automatic" function allows the execution of the STEP-NC file and the machining of the part by sending the corresponding operational signals to the CNCMT actuators. The "Manual" function allows the manual movement of the CNCMT axes via the keyboard connected to the RPi. The "Visualization" function displays the visualization of the part, the toolpath, and the interpolated points. The "Animation" function generates a simulation video of the movement of the axes in real time. The "Edit" function allows modifying some defined parameters, for example the dimensions of the stock part or the start position of the tool. The "Information" function allows displaying additional information included in the STEP-NC file, such as the name of the workingsteps or the workpiece parameters.

4 Case Study

The integration of the new controller with the EMCO PC TURN 55 CNC mini-lathe is in progress. Hence, in this paper, we merely present a simulation of the machining of a test part available in the ISO standard [14].

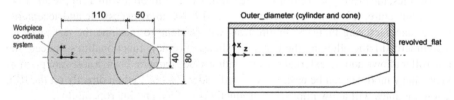

Fig. 4. Turning test piece from Annex D ISO14649 part 12 [15]

The test part that will be used is illustrated in Fig. 4. It is composed of three features: OUTER_DIAMETER for the cone, OUTER_DIAMETER for the cylinder and a REVOLVED_FLAT for the end face. To machine these features, several operations are defined. First the end face is machined with a rough facing, then the two OUTER_DIAMETER features are machined using a rough contouring operation. Finally, a finishing path is performed.

Once the STEP-NC file is imported, the information is read and is interpreted, and the toolpath is generated in approximately 500 ms. Figure 5 shows the generated toolpath.

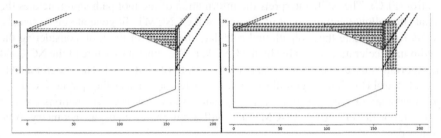

Fig. 5. Toolpath visualization of the test part. Stock dimension: left (length 165 mm, diameter 88 mm), right (length 175 mm, diameter 96 mm)

It is noteworthy to mention that, with the developed controller, it is possible to modify the size of the stock before the machining, using the edit function. The toolpath can be automatically recalculated without needing to manually machine the stock or modifying the CAD. The right image on Fig. 5 shows the toolpath for a cylinder stock different from the recommended stock (Fig. 5 - left image). In the future it is possible to add automatic probing to measure the size of the stock to adapt the toolpath.

5 Conclusion

A new STEP-NC OAC controller is developed, allowing to interpret STEP-NC files, to generate the toolpath and to communicate with a CNC machine-tool. The open-source C++ code and the proposed hardware make this controller more accessible and simpler to integrate compared to previous controllers which use home – made electronic cards and proprietary software. Moreover, with its cost less than 200$, it is among the less expensive developed STEP-NC controllers as it cost less than a tenth of the price of other controllers.

Besides, the prototype confirms the feasibility of a controller with a simple and low-cost architecture. It is a step towards making STEP-NC more accessible and acceptable in the manufacturing industry. Future tests will be done to machine the test piece on a commercial lathe allowing the test and validation of new functionalities. Indeed, the controller allows adding external sensors and/or video camera. From a software point of view, many modules can be easily developed under C++ or Python directly on the RPi. These modules will allow improving productivity, safety, and interoperability.

References

1. ISO 6983-1:1982 Commande numérique des machines — Format de programme et définition des mots adresses —, ISO (1982)
2. ISO 14649-1: Overview and fundamental principles, ISO (2003)
3. ISO 10303 Systèmes d'automatisation industrielle et intégration — Représentation et échange de données de produits, ISO (1994)
4. Suh, S.H., Lee, B.E., Chung, D.H., Cheon, S.U.: Architecture and implementation of a shop-floor programming system for STEP-compliant CNC. Comput. Aided Des. **35**(12), 1069–1083 (2003). https://doi.org/10.1016/s0010-4485(02)00179-3
5. Mueller, P., Hyu, Y.T.: ESPRIT Project EP 29708 STEP-Compliant Data Interface for Numerical Controls (STEP-NC), STEP-NC consortium (2001)
6. Brecher, C., Verl, A., Lechler, A., Servos, M.: Open control systems: state of the art. Prod. Eng. Res. Devel. **4**(2–3), 247–254 (2010). https://doi.org/10.1007/s11740-010-0218-5
7. Zhao, Y.F., Habeeb, S., Xu, X.: Research into integrated design and manufacturing based on STEP. Int. J. Adv. Manuf. Technol. **44**(5–6), 606–624 (2008). https://doi.org/10.1007/s00170-008-1841-6
8. Choi, I., Suh, S.H., Kim, K., Song, M., Jang, M., Lee, B.E.: Development process and data management of TurnSTEP: a STEP-compliant CNC system for turning (in English). Int. J. Comput. Integr. Manuf. **19**(6), 546–558 (2006). https://doi.org/10.1080/09511920600622072
9. Lee, W., Bang, Y.B., Ryou, M.S., Kwon, W.H., Jee, H.S.: Development of a PC-based milling machine operated by STEP-NC in XML format. Int. J. Comput. Integr. Manuf. **19**(6), 593–602 (2006). https://doi.org/10.1080/09511920600623674
10. Calabrese, F., Celentano, G.: Design and realization of a STEP-NC compliant CNC embedded controller. In: 2007 IEEE Conference on Emerging Technologies and Factory Automation (EFTA 2007), 25–28 September 2007, pp. 1010–1017 (2007). https://doi.org/10.1109/EFTA.2007.4416894
11. Po, H., Hongya, F., Zhenyu, H., Dedong, H.: A closed-loop and self-learning STEP-NC machining system. In: 2014 IEEE/ASME International Conference on Advanced Intelligent Mechatronics, 8–11 July 2014, pp. 1598–1603 (2014). https://doi.org/10.1109/AIM.2014.6878312
12. Latif, K., Yusof, Y., Nassehi, A., Alias Imran Latif, Q.B.: Development of a feature-based open soft-CNC system. Int. J. Adv. Manuf. Technol. **89**(1–4), 1013–1024 (2016). https://doi.org/10.1007/s00170-016-9124-0
13. Dharmawardhana, M., Ratnaweera, A., Oancea, G.: STEP-NC compliant intelligent CNC milling machine with an open architecture controller. Appl. Sci. **11**(13) (2021). https://doi.org/10.3390/app11136223
14. Suh, S.-H., Kang, S., Chung, D.-H., Stroud, I.: Theory and Design of CNC Systems (2008)
15. ISO 14649-12: Process date for turning, ISO (2003)

Risk Analysis in Manufacturing Processes: An Integrated Approach Using the FMEA Method

Luís Basto[1]([✉]), Isabel Lopes[1] [iD], and Cláudia Pires[2]

[1] ALGORITMI Research Centre, University of Minho, Guimarães, Portugal
luis.basto@dps.uminho.pt

[2] CATIM – Centro de Apoio Tecnológico à Indústria Metalomecânica, Porto, Portugal

Abstract. Risk management is a requirement of today's management system standards. FMEA is one of the most commonly used tools to perform risk assessment. However, neither FMEA nor other risk assessment tools were originally developed to assess risk jointly by several management areas to analyze failure events that can originate failure modes of different types. This paper aims to present an integrated approach for risk analysis, in manufacturing processes, using the FMEA method. The proposed approach considers the involvement of the quality, environment, health and safety, and maintenance management areas. A linkage between Machinery FMEA (operation failures) and Process FMEA is proposed, which allows to better prioritize maintenance actions. This integrated approach is intended to be implemented in a network aimed at collaboration among areas, an important aspect in the context of Industry 4.0.

Keywords: Collaborative tool · Machinery FMEA · Process FMEA · Risk management

1 Introduction

According to ISO 31000:2018, which provides the guidelines for risk management, *risk* is defined as the "effect of uncertainty on objectives", while *risk management* is defined as the "coordinated activities to direct and control an organization with regard to risk" [1].

The importance of risk management has grown in manufacturing industries with the last revision of ISO 9001, the international quality management standard, in 2015. ISO 9001:2015 highlights risk-based thinking as an essential approach for an effective quality management system [2]. Besides this, ISO 14001, for environmental management [3], ISO 45001, for safety and health management [4], and IATF 16949, for quality management in the automotive industry [5], also require companies to carry out risk analysis.

FMEA, HAZOP, HACCP, APR, and FTA are qualitative and/or quantitative methods to support risk management [6–8]. According to Badreddine *et al.*, these techniques were

© IFIP International Federation for Information Processing 2022
Published by Springer Nature Switzerland AG 2022
D. Y. Kim et al. (Eds.): APMS 2022, IFIP AICT 663, pp. 260–266, 2022.
https://doi.org/10.1007/978-3-031-16407-1_31

not designed to cope with multiple management areas at once, although the same source of hazard can affect targets in many areas, such as the environment, health and safety, and quality [8]. FMEA is a methodology that identifies failure modes and associated causes and effects. Each failure mode criticality is assessed by quantifying its occurrence, severity, and detection (using usually values between 1 and 10). FMEA can be used to address product reliability [9], environmental aspects, such as toxic emissions and land contamination [10], as well as health and safety incidents, such as falls and electric shocks [11]. Process FMEA is a type of FMEA concerned with product quality in manufacturing processes [9].

In an industrial context, the risk management approach is departmentalized, which means that each company sector performs risk analysis and management in its unique perspective (e.g., quality, safety, environment).

Risk management integration in the context of standardized management systems – mainly of quality, environment, and safety – is addressed in the literature [7, 8, 12, 13]. However, these works do not propose a specific integrative approach for risk analysis for this issue or, when they do, it only addresses the effects integration level. Romdhane et al. proposed an extension of the FMEA method to take into account different management areas, integrating at the effect level, by determining severity levels for the following targets: people, equipment, environment, production, and management [12]. Zeng et al. used FMEA in the construction sector to jointly analyze risks associated with occupational health and safety, environment, and/or quality [13]. The authors consider, as failure modes, failures related to product quality, hazardous events to the environment, and accidents and dangerous events on occupational health and safety. Each failure mode can affect more than one area (for example, high noise can affect workers' safety, as well as the environment). The authors state that an integrated risk analysis could reduce effort and resource inputs.

FMEA can also be used to enhance maintenance planning, an important aspect that is addressed by Filz et al. [14] and Lolli et al. [15]. In production processes, equipment failures frequently cause problems of different natures, such as defects. However, maintenance records are not linked to quality records and no connection between equipment failures and defects is established.

This paper presents an integrated approach for risk analysis, in manufacturing processes, using the FMEA method. This approach addresses the areas of quality, environment, health and safety, and maintenance. A linkage between Machinery FMEA (which is concerned with machinery operation failures) and Process FMEA is proposed. This allows for maintenance actions to be prioritized considering the effects of equipment failures in the process. This integrated approach is intended to be achieved through the collaboration of different departments, which is in line with the concept of Industry 4.0, and is being developed with the support of a Portuguese metalworking company, to test and validate the proposed solutions.

This work mainly focuses on the risk identification and evaluation functions presented in a previous work [16], which defines the specifications and functions of the dynamic and collaborative risk assessment tool under development. For this tool, the FMEA method was chosen since, nowadays, many organizations have been using it in the development of their processes [17]. It is, however, important to highlight that, despite published manuals and ongoing training describing the method, few organizations can take full advantage of FMEA [17]. This method is developed differently from team to team with a significant degree of subjectivity, creating inconsistencies, such as in the failure modes definition [17, 18]. Therefore, in this paper, a clear structure is presented for different individuals to elaborate FMEA more objectively.

This paper is organized as follows: Sect. 2 presents the proposed approach for integrated risk assessment of manufacturing processes, both conceptually and through practical examples; Sect. 3 includes the conclusions and future work.

2 Integrated Risk Analysis Using the FMEA Method

2.1 The Concept

Impacts related to different departments can have a common cause. For instance, a specific equipment failure can cause a gas leakage, affecting personnel and the environment, and also affecting product quality. Departmental risk analysis does not take into consideration that a specific event can originate failure modes of different types, which gives rise to an incomplete view and evaluation of risks, besides increasing the time of execution. To avoid these issues, an integrated risk analysis is needed.

The conceptual model for the integrated risk analysis of manufacturing processes is presented in Fig. 1. This approach is centered on the Process FMEA, where failure modes – the way the failure is observed in the process, whether by quality, safety, or environmental perspective – are registered. These failure modes can be due to the same event or cause. In this Process FMEA, the causes of failure modes can be grouped into Ishikawa's Ms – Machine, Man, Method, Measure, Milieu (Environment), and Material – as it is presented in AIAG & VDA FMEA Handbook [11] under the name of Work Elements. Concerning the Machine group, a Machinery FMEA can be developed to assess the machine reliability and to support maintenance planning. Therefore, the root cause of a failure mode registered in the Process FMEA is defined. In the Machinery FMEA, failure modes are concerned with functional failures during equipment operation and are registered at the component level (although they could also be registered at the module or machine level). A manufacturing process can involve more than one machine, each with its Machinery FMEA, which will be associated with the analyzed process and linked to the Process FMEA.

In the Process FMEA, failure modes are divided into three categories – Quality, Safety, and Environment – and the respective failure modes are expressed as follows:

- *Quality:* concerning product defects, such as a certain dimension above or below the specified limits, burrs, and marks;
- *Safety:* concerning hazardous events or exposures that can cause injury or ill health to workers, such as falls, gas leakages, and fires;
- *Environment:* concerning hazardous events that can damage the environment.

These failure modes in the process lead to undesired effects, such as injury and ill health to workers, environmental damage, and internal or external failure costs (i.e., non-quality costs associated with scrap, rework, returned parts, etc.). These undesired effects impact stakeholders – whether they are internal or external clients, administration, society (mainly due to environmental issues), or company collaborators – and can, therefore, be grouped by the stakeholders they impact on.

According to Ford's FMEA Handbook, a failure mode can be an effect of a previous operation or a cause of a subsequent operation [19]. This statement allows linking Process FMEAs of interrelated processes (i.e., when one process output is another one's input), fomenting the implementation of a process-based approach, as prescribed in ISO 9001:2015 [2].

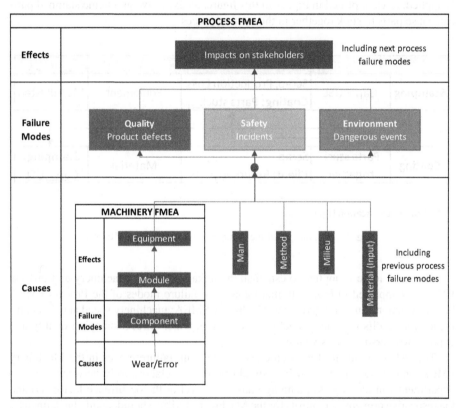

Fig. 1. The conceptual model for the integrated risk analysis of manufacturing processes.

2.2 Practical Examples

To illustrate the proposed approach with practical examples, two interrelated processes from the metalworking industry were considered, as shown in Fig. 2. In this figure, the stamping process transforms the metal sheet into stamped parts, which are then transformed into finished parts by the coating process.

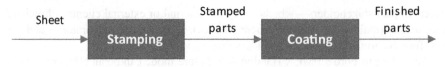

Fig. 2. Interrelated processes.

A defective output of the stamping process can affect the subsequent process (in this case, the coating process). In this way, a linkage between the respective Process FMEAs is applied, as exemplified in Fig. 3. In this figure, an excessive gap in the stamped parts can cause parts to stick together in the coating process.

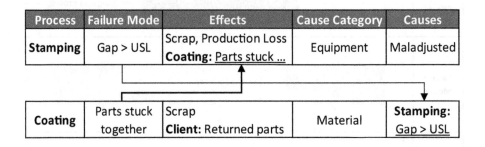

USL: Upper Specification Limit

Fig. 3. An example of the linkage between process FMEAs.

The same logic is applied to establish the linkage between Machinery and Process FMEA, exemplified in Fig. 4. In this figure, two failure modes of the Process FMEA have a common cause, related to the Machinery FMEA: machinery speed above recommendation results in serious machinery vibration, which affects stamping quality and exposes workers to excessive noise.

The risk assessment of a specific event, involving failure modes in the Machinery FMEA and in the Process FMEA, should be done collaboratively between areas or departments. In the process planning phase, the level of the occurrence factor (O) and the respective preventive controls for the Machinery FMEA should mainly be defined by the maintenance department and used on the Process FMEA, since the occurrence factor is related to the failure cause. The level of the detection factor (D) should be defined by the maintenance department and other departments involved in the process, taking into account the respective detection controls. In the example presented in Fig. 4, the failure event could be detected at the machine level – by identifying the excessive SPM (Strokes Per Minute) or the damaged component – or in the process – by the failure modes occurrence, i.e., identification of the defective parts or the excessive noise. The level of the severity factor (S), related to the end effects, is intended to be defined in the Process FMEA, considering all the effects on different areas, and used on the Machinery FMEA (nevertheless, a corrective cost and time of the machinery failure could also be used to better assess the severity level).

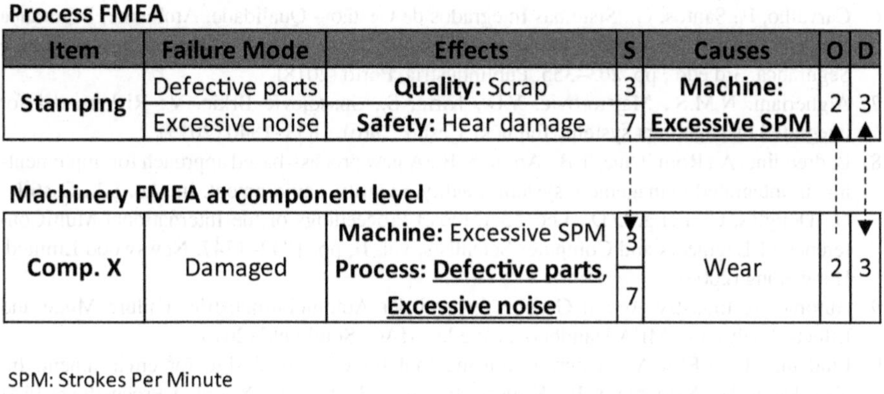

Process FMEA

Item	Failure Mode	Effects	S	Causes	O	D
Stamping	Defective parts	**Quality:** Scrap	3	**Machine:**	2	3
	Excessive noise	**Safety:** Hear damage	7	**Excessive SPM**		

Machinery FMEA at component level

Comp. X	Damaged	**Machine:** Excessive SPM	3	Wear	2	3
		Process: Defective parts, Excessive noise	7			

SPM: Strokes Per Minute

Fig. 4. An example of the proposed linkage between machinery and process FMEA.

3   Conclusions and Future Work

This paper presents an integrated approach for risk analysis, in manufacturing processes, using the FMEA method. It was shown how risk identification and evaluation can be integrated, considering the areas of quality, environment, health and safety, and maintenance. To illustrate the proposed approach, practical examples from the metalworking industry are presented.

For future work, this approach is intended to be operationalized through a computer application. The collaborative network has to be defined to facilitate communication among the different departments. It should also be noted that the proposed approach can be extended to non-manufacturing processes.

Acknowledgment. The authors would like to express appreciation for the companies involved. This work has been supported by Norte 010247 FEDER 046930 – CORIM I&DT.

References

1. International Organization for Standardization: Risk management — Guidelines (ISO Standard No. 31000:2018), 2nd edn. ISO, Geneva (2018)
2. International Organization for Standardization: Quality management systems — Requirements (ISO Standard No. 9001:2015), 5th edn. ISO, Geneva (2015)
3. International Organization for Standardization: Environmental management systems — Requirements with guidance for use (ISO Standard No. 14001:2015), 3rd edn. ISO, Geneva (2015)
4. International Organization for Standardization: Occupational health and safety management systems — Requirements with guidance for use (ISO Standard No. 45001:2018), 1st edn. ISO, Geneva (2018)
5. International Automotive Task Force: Automotive Quality Management System Standard (IATF Standard No. 16949:2016), 1st edn. AIAG, Southfield (2016)

6. Carvalho, F., Santos, G.: Sistemas Integrados de Gestão – Qualidade, Ambiente, Segurança e outros Sistemas de Gestão. In: Sistemas Integrados de Gestão – Qualidade, Ambiente e Segurança, 3rd edn., pp. 263–355. Publindústria, Porto (2018)
7. Algheriani, N.M.S., Majstorovic, V.D., Kirin, S., Spasojevic Brkic, V.: Risk model for integrated management system. Tehnički vjesnik **26**(6), 1833–1840 (2019)
8. Badreddine, A., Romdhane, T.B., Amor, N.B.: A new process-based approach for implementing an integrated management system: quality, security, environment. In: Ao, S.I., Castillo, O., Douglas, C., Feng, D.D., Lee, J.-A. (eds.) Proceedings of the International MultiConference of Engineers and Computer Scientists, vol. II, pp. 1742–1747. Newswood Limited, Hong Kong (2009)
9. Automotive Industry Action Group, Verband der Automobilindustrie: Failure Mode and Effects Analysis - FMEA Handbook, 1st edn. AIAG, Southfield (2019)
10. Lindahl, M.: E-FMEA - a new promising tool for efficient design for environment. In: Yoshikawa, H., Yamamoto, R., Kimura, F., Suga, T., Umeda, Y. (eds.) Proceedings First International Symposium on Environmentally Conscious Design and Inverse Manufacturing, pp. 734–739. IEEE Press, New York (1999)
11. Jahangoshai Rezaee, M., Yousefi, S., Eshkevari, M., Valipour, M., Saberi, M.: Risk analysis of health, safety and environment in chemical industry integrating linguistic FMEA, fuzzy inference system and fuzzy DEA. Stoch. Env. Res. Risk Assess. **34**(1), 201–218 (2020)
12. Romdhane, T.B., Ammar, F.B., Badreddine, A.: Une approche par la logique floue pour l'optimisation multicritère de la prise de décision appliquée à l'AMDEC. J. Decis. Syst. **16**(4), 505–544 (2007)
13. Zeng, S.X., Tam, C.M., Tam, V.W.Y.: Integrating safety, environmental and quality risks for project management using a FMEA Method. Eng. Econ. **21**(1), 44–52 (2010)
14. Filz, M., Langner, J.E.B., Herrmann, C., Thiede, S.: Data-driven failure mode and effect analysis (FMEA) to enhance maintenance planning. Comput. Ind. **129** (2021). Article 103451
15. Lolli, F., Gamberini, R., Rimini, B., Pulga, F.: A revised FMEA with application to a blow moulding process. Int. J. Qual. Reliab. Manage. **33**(7), 900–919 (2016)
16. Lopes, I., Meira, D., Pires, C.: Development of a risk assessment tool for manufacturing processes. In: Silhavy, R. (ed.) CSOC 2021. LNNS, vol. 228, pp. 161–170. Springer, Cham (2021). https://doi.org/10.1007/978-3-030-77448-6_14
17. Aguiar, D.C., Salomon, V.A.P., Mello, C.H.P.: An ISO 9001 based approach for the implementation of process FMEA in the Brazilian automotive industry. Int. J. Qual. Reliab. Manage. **32**(6), 589–602 (2015)
18. Estorilio, C., Posso, R.K.: The reduction of irregularities in the use of "process FMEA." Int. J. Qual. Reliab. Manage. **27**(6), 721–733 (2010)
19. Ford Motor Company: Failure Mode and Effects Analysis - FMEA Handbook (with Robustness Linkages). Version 4.2. Ford Motor Company, Dearborn (2011)

Intelligent Warping Detection for Fused Filament Fabrication of a Metal-Polymer Composite Filament

Jungyoon Moon[1] , Kijung Park[1(✉)] , and Sangin Park[2]

[1] Department of Industrial and Management Engineering, Incheon National University, Incheon, Republic of Korea
{mjy,kjpark}@inu.ac.kr
[2] Department of Mechatronics Engineering, Incheon National University, Incheon, Republic of Korea
sangin.park@inu.ac.kr

Abstract. Fused Filament Fabrication (FFF) for a metal-polymer composite filament is receiving attention as an effective means to manufacture complex metal parts. However, warping deformation is one of the main problems that reduce part quality in the FFF of a metal-polymer composite filament. In this regard, an appropriate quality monitoring system for the warping deformation of FFF is essential to effectively manage the quality of metal-polymer composite 3D printing outputs. This study presents an intelligent warping detection process for FFF using a metal-polymer composite filament through vision monitoring and automatic object detection. First, five FFF samples are manufactured using the Ultrafuse-316L metal-polymer composite filament. Each fabrication process is recorded by a camera to construct an image dataset for warping deformation. Then, the YOLO v5 algorithm is applied to a training set (80%) of the image dataset to learn labeled FFF output and warping deformation areas. The constructed object detection model for warping deformation is tested using a validation set (20%) of the original image dataset. This study provides a basis to develop an intelligent quality management system for the FFF of a metal-polymer composite filament.

Keywords: Object detection · Fused Filament Fabrication · Metal-polymer composite · Warping · Image mining

1 Introduction

Additive manufacturing (AM) has received increasing attention as a potential tool for cost-effectiveness and sustainable manufacturing [1]. The Fused Filament Fabrication (FFF) method is an AM technique to extrude a polymer filament at a high temperature and to deposit the molten material layer by layer [2]. FFF is one of the popular AM methods due to its compatibility with various materials [2]. In particular, the recent advance of FFF to use metal-polymer composite filaments provides a new opportunity to fabricate complex metal parts with affordable manufacturing cost [3]. Nowadays various metal applications such as metal tooling parts and prototypes are easily manufactured by FFF for metal-polymer composite materials [4].

Warping deformation is a common error type for FFF that occurs due to material shrinkage during an FFF process and results in bending distortion of a fabricated output [5]. Since the warping deformation of metal-polymer composite outputs significantly reduces part quality after post-processing (i.e., sintering process) for the outputs, detecting warping deformation during an early stage of FFF is essential to avoid unnecessary material consumption and printing time taken for final outputs with warping defects. Previous studies relevant to reducing warping deformation during FFF mainly focused on the impact of FFF process parameters that cause warping deformation [6–8]. On the other hand, recent studies relevant to the warping deformation of FFF have attempted to develop an intelligent process through data or image mining to detect warping deformation of FFF outputs. For example, Li et al. [9] proposed a back-propagation neural network (BPNN) model to diagnose warping deformation based on the vibration data of an FFF machine. Saluja et al. [10] developed a closed-loop system to identify warping deformation in an FFF process through a convolutional neural network (CNN) model.

Recently, the YOLO (You Look Only Once) object detection algorithm has received a great deal of attention in defect detection and quality monitoring due to its successful detection performance for various application areas [11–13]. Defect detection based on an object detection model can be applied to AM to provide useful information of defects during an AM process such as defect location and size of a being fabricated object. Paying attention to the aforementioned issues, this study employs the YOLO v5 object detection algorithm [14] to identify warping deformation during FFF using a metal-polymer composite filament.

2 Methods

2.1 Experimental Settings

Pinter223 [15], an open-source FFF machine, was remodeled to fabricate a metal-polymer composite filament. Ultrafuse-316L [4], which is a popular commercial metal-polymer composite filament for FFF, was used for experiments. For data collection, the GoPro Hero9 [16] camera was positioned at the front side of the FFF machine to record the fabrication process of each experimental sample (see Fig. 1). The part design illustrated in Fig. 2 was adopted to fabricate five samples through FFF.

2.2 Data Collection and Labeling

The recoded videos of the whole FFF process for each sample were transformed to an image dataset for a warping detection model. The image dataset was extracted by capturing one image frame per second from the fabrication process video of each sample. As a result, a total of 7,029 warping images were collected for a supervised learning-based warping detection model. Furthermore, the region of interest (ROI) method [17] was employed to resize 2407 * 1520 (pixels) original images to 640 * 640 (pixels) images for model training.

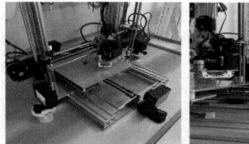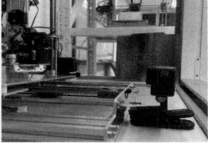

Fig. 1. Machine settings to record fabricated outputs during FFF

Fig. 2. Design of a sample and its fabricated output with a brim

Next, data labeling was conducted to train a warping detection model based on YOLO v5 [14]. YOLO v5 requires a label per image in a YOLO format, which consists of the center coordinates of bounding boxes (x, y), width (w), and height (h). To identify the whole fabrication and warping areas, the number of classes for bounding boxes was set to two (i.e., "part" and "warp") for the YOLO v5 model. Figure 3(b) illustrates these two target detection areas (i.e., the green bounding box for "part" class and the red bounding boxes for the "warp" class). In order to input image data with predefined labels into YOLO v5, this study conducted label annotation for the YOLO format.

2.3 Training and Validation of Warping Detection Model

The constructed image dataset was randomly separated into a training set (80% of the dataset) and a validation set (20% of the dataset). The training and validation sets consisted of 5,623 and 1,406 images, respectively. A training model for warping detection was built based on the YOLO v5s model, which shows the fastest data learning process of all available YOLO v5 model variants. Moreover, the transfer learning method [18] was adopted to reduce training time and to improve detection performance. The pre-trained weight obtained by transfer learning was trained by the COCO dataset [19], which is a popular benchmark dataset in the computer vision field. The hyper-parameter of YOLO v5s was set to the default settings in the YOLO v5 library [11], including 640 image sizes in pixels, 64 batch sizes, and 100 epochs.

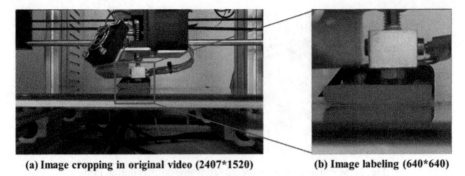

(a) Image cropping in original video (2407*1520)   (b) Image labeling (640*640)

Fig. 3. ROI resizing and labeling process

The following precision, recall, and mean average precision (mAP) [20] measures were employed to evaluate the performance of the derived warping detection model. These measures were calculated based on intersection over union (IoU) [21], which is a criterion of judging true or false, in Eq. (1).

$$\text{IoU} = \frac{|Ground\ truth \cap Prediction|}{|Ground\ truth \cup Prediction|}, \tag{1}$$

where the ground-truth (*Ground truth*) is an area of the labeled bounding boxes of trained images, and the prediction (*Prediction*) is an area of the predicted bounding boxes of trained images. Through this IoU values, the true positive (TP), false positive (FP), and false negative (FN) were determined for *Precision* and *Recall* [22] in Eqs. (2–3).

$$Precision = \frac{TP}{TP + FP} \tag{2}$$

In Eq. (2), the precision measure is defined as a ratio between correctly recognized true positives and all predicted positives. A high precision value indicates that the object detection model can precisely predict object locations and areas.

$$Recall = \frac{TP}{TP + FN} \tag{3}$$

In Eq. (3), the recall measure is defined as a ratio between correctly recognized positive prediction and all ground-truth of positives and negatives through the model. A high recall value means that the object detection model is close to the ground-truth of object locations and areas.

$$mAP = \frac{1}{c}\sum_{i=1}^{c} AP_i, \tag{4}$$

where AP is calculated as a gap between *Precision* and *Recall*, and c is the number of label types. The mAP is categorized into two types: $mAP_{0.5}$ (IoU criterion at 0.5) and $mAP_{0.5:0.95}$ (averaged over IoU criterion in a range from 0.5 to 0.95).

3 Results

Figure 4 shows the originally labeled areas and the detected warping areas obtained by the warping detection model using the validation dataset. The performance of the warping detection model is shown in Table 1. The total recall, precision, $mAP_{0.5}$ and $mAP_{0.5:0.95}$ of the warping detection model in all the classes were achieved at 0.99, 0.989, 0.992, and 0.785, respectively.

The generated warping detection model can detect warping deformation along with a printing part close to labels and bounding boxes in the validation dataset. However, the gap between $mAP_{0.5}$ and $mAP_{0.5:0.95}$ for "Warp" indicates this gap may be occurred because the bounding boxes of the "Warp" label are too small to detect precisely. Nevertheless, this issue seems not to largely affect to the visualized results of the warping detection model as shown in Fig. 4.

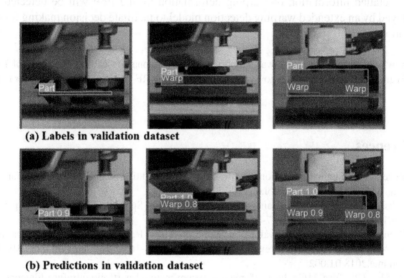

(a) Labels in validation dataset

(b) Predictions in validation dataset

Fig. 4. Comparison of ground-truth (a) and prediction (b) in validation dataset

Table 1. Performance of warping detection model

Classes	Recall	Precision	$mAP_{0.5}$	$mAP_{0.5:0.95}$
Warp	0.98	0.981	0.990	0.627
Part	0.99	0.998	0.995	0.942
Total	0.99	0.989	0.992	0.785

4 Conclusions and Discussion

This study applied an objective detection algorithm to intelligently identify warping deformation during a FFF process using a metal-polymer composite filament. First, five FFF samples using Ultrafuse-316L were printed to record their FFF process. An image dataset was constructed from the recorded fabrication process of each sample. To train a warping detection model, the image dataset was labeled by the YOLO format. Next, the warping detection model based on YOLO v5 was trained to identify a warping area along with a sample part. The derived warping detection model showed the overall good performance in the model evaluation measures.

This study would serve as a basis for an intelligent quality management system for AM. For future work, an extended model of warping detection for FFF will be studied to achieve a dynamic quality management system through automatic vision monitoring. More detailed information of warping deformation during FFF will be detected and displayed by an extended warping detection model to facilitate decision making for AM operations.

Acknowledgement. This work was supported by the National Research Foundation of Korea (NRF) grant funded by the Korea government (MSIT) (No. NRF-2022R1C1C1012140) for Kijung Park.

References

1. Beyer, C.: Strategic implications of current trends in additive manufacturing. J. Manuf. Sci. Eng. **136**(6) (2014). https://doi.org/10.1115/1.4028599
2. Gibson, I., et al.: Additive Manufacturing Technologies. Springer, Cham (2021). https://doi.org/10.1007/978-3-030-56127-7
3. Brenken, B., Barocio, E., Favaloro, A., Kunc, V., Pipes, R.B.: Fused filament fabrication of fiber-reinforced polymers: a review. Addit. Manuf. **21**, 1–16 (2018). https://doi.org/10.1016/j.addma.2018.01.002
4. BASF - Ultrafuse 316L. https://forward-am.com/material-portfolio/ultrafuse-filaments-for-fused-filaments-fabrication-fff/metal-filaments/ultrafuse-316l/. Accessed 15 July 2022
5. Armillotta, A., Bellotti, M., Cavallaro, M.: Warpage of FDM parts: experimental tests and analytic model. Robot. Comput.-Integr. Manuf. **50**, 140–152 (2018). https://doi.org/10.1016/j.rcim.2017.09.007
6. Wang, T.-M., Xi, J.-T., Jin, Y.: A model research for prototype warp deformation in the FDM process. Int. J. Adv. Manuf. Technol. **33**(11), 1087–1096 (2007). https://doi.org/10.1007/s00170-006-0556-9
7. Nazan, M., Ramli, F., Alkahari, M., Sudin, M., Abdullah, M.: Optimization of warping deformation in open source 3D printer using response surface method. In: Proceedings of Mechanical Engineering Research Day 2016, pp. 71–72 (2016)
8. Alsoufi, M.S., Elsayed, A.: Warping deformation of desktop 3D printed parts manufactured by open source fused deposition modeling (FDM) system. Int. J. Mech. Mechatron. Eng. **17**(11) (2017)
9. Li, Y., Zhao, W., Li, Q., Wang, T., Wang, G.: In-situ monitoring and diagnosing for fused filament fabrication process based on vibration sensors. Sensors **19**(11), 2589 (2019). https://doi.org/10.3390/s19112589

10. Saluja, A., Xie, J., Fayazbakhsh, K.: A closed-loop in-process warping detection system for fused filament fabrication using convolutional neural networks. J. Manuf. Process. **58**, 407–415 (2020). https://doi.org/10.1016/j.jmapro.2020.08.036

11. Li, J., Su, Z., Geng, J., Yin, Y.: Real-time detection of steel strip surface defects based on improved yolo detection network. IFAC-PapersOnLine **51**(21), 76–81 (2018). https://doi.org/10.1016/j.ifacol.2018.09.412

12. Zhang, C., Chang, C.C., Jamshidi, M.: Concrete bridge surface damage detection using a single-stage detector. Comput.-Aid. Civil Infrastruc. Eng. **35**(4), 389–409 (2020). https://doi.org/10.1111/mice.12500

13. Li, Y., Huang, H., Chen, Q., Fan, Q., Quan, H.: Research on a product quality monitoring method based on multi scale PP-YOLO. IEEE Access **9**, 80373–80387 (2021). https://doi.org/10.1109/ACCESS.2021.3085338

14. Jocher, G., et al.: ultralytics/yolov5: v3. 1-bug fixes and performance improvements. Zenodo (2020). https://doi.org/10.5281/zenodo.3983579

15. Pinter223.   http://www.samdimall.com/goods/goods_view.php?goodsNo=1000000636. Accessed 24 June 2022

16. GoPro   Hero9.   https://gopro.com/shop/cameras/hero9-black/CHDHX-901-master.html. Accessed 20 July 2022

17. Bradley, A.P., Stentiford, F.W.: JPEG 2000 and region of interest coding. In: Digital Image Computing Techniques and Applications, pp. 1–6 (2002)

18. Torrey, L., Shavlik, J.: Transfer Learning in Handbook of Research on Machine Learning Applications. IGI Global, Hershey (2009)

19. Lin, T.-Y., et al.: Microsoft COCO: common objects in context. In: Fleet, D., Pajdla, T., Schiele, B., Tuytelaars, T. (eds.) ECCV 2014. LNCS, vol. 8693, pp. 740–755. Springer, Cham (2014). https://doi.org/10.1007/978-3-319-10602-1_48

20. Liu, L., Özsu, M.T.: Encyclopedia of Database Systems, vol. 6. Springer, New York (2009)

21. Rezatofighi, H., Tsoi, N., Gwak, J., Sadeghian, A., Reid, I., Savarese, S.: Generalized intersection over union: a metric and a loss for bounding box regression. In: Proceedings of the IEEE/CVF Conference on Computer Vision and Pattern Recognition, pp. 658–666 (2019)

22. Bama, S.S., Ahmed, M., Saravanan, A.: A survey on performance evaluation measures for information retrieval system. Int. Res. J. Eng. Technol. **2**(2), 1015–1020 (2015)

A Two-Phased Approach to Energy Consumption Prediction for Fused Filament Fabrication of CFR-PEEK

Heena Noh[1] , Kijung Park[1(✉)] , and Gül E. Kremer[2]

[1] Department of Industrial and Management Engineering, Incheon National University, Incheon 22012, Republic of Korea
{nhn,kjpark}@inu.ac.kr
[2] School of Engineering, University of Dayton, Dayton OH 45469, USA
gkremer2@udayton.edu

Abstract. With increasing attention on fused filament fabrication (FFF) applications for high-performance polymers, understanding the energy characteristics of FFF is critical to pursue a sustainable additive manufacturing system. In this regard, this study proposes a two-phased energy prediction approach to FFF. A full factorial design of experiments for FFF is planned to collect data for build time, filament volume, and energy consumption by varying major process parameters (i.e., layer thickness, infill density, and printing speed). Carbon fiber reinforced polyether-ether-ketone (CFR-PEEK), which is an emerging high-performance polymer for advanced engineering applications, is used for a material of the experiments. In the first phase, two machine learning methods (i.e., decision tree and random forest) are employed to estimate the material addition rate (MAR) of FFF, which indicates the amount of deposited material volume per unit time. Then, a statistical regression model of energy consumption on the estimated MAR is built to predict the energy consumption of FFF for CFR-PEEK. The results show that the decision tree model has better prediction performance to predict the MAR of FFF than the random forest model. In addition, the energy consumption model through the predicted MAR shows that an increase in the MAR reduces energy consumption. The two-phased prediction approach based on the MAR provides better performance than the direct energy prediction from process parameters through a machine learning technique. The findings of this study provide a basis to characterize energy dynamics in FFF for CFR-PEEK.

Keywords: Fused filament fabrication · CFR-PEEK · Material addition rate · Energy consumption · Machine learning

© IFIP International Federation for Information Processing 2022
Published by Springer Nature Switzerland AG 2022
D. Y. Kim et al. (Eds.): APMS 2022, IFIP AICT 663, pp. 274–281, 2022.
https://doi.org/10.1007/978-3-031-16407-1_33

1 Introduction

Additive manufacturing (AM) implements layer-by-layer fabrication using various materials to produce components from computer aided design (CAD) models [1]. Fused filament fabrication (FFF) is a representative AM technique, which is widely used in practice due to its cost-effectiveness, ease of use, and compatibility with various thermoplastic materials [1]. In particular, FFF for carbon fiber reinforced polyether-ether-ketone (CFR-PEEK) has received attention in various domains such as aerospace, automobile engineering, and medical devices due to its superior strength and mechanical stability [2]. The FFF of CFR-PEEK requires higher energy consumption than common polymers due to the high temperature and resultant long fabrication time of CFR-PEEK required for material extrusion [3]. Therefore, estimating the energy consumption of FFF using CFR-PEEK is critical to manage the energy intense AM process for CFR-PEEK in practice. However, most studies relevant to FFF not only relied on common polymers such as acrylonitrile-butadiene-styrene (ABS) and polylactide (PLA) but also mainly focused on the effects of process parameters on energy consumption [4–8].

This study proposes a two-phased approach to effectively predict the energy consumption of FFF for CFR-PEEK. A machine learning algorithm is employed first to estimate a material addition rate (MAR), the amount of deposited material volume per time, from major process parameters of FFF. Then, resultant energy consumption is predicted based on the estimated MAR through a regression model. For this, a full factorial experimental design for all combinations of major process parameters (i.e., layer thickness, infill density, and printing speed) is performed to collect the build time, filament volume, and energy consumption of FFF for CFR-PEEK. Then, two popular machine learning techniques (i.e., decision tree and random forest) are used to build models to predict the MAR of FFF, and the best MAR prediction model is selected. Through the predicted MAR, the energy consumption is fitted by a linear regression model.

2 Literature Review

Existing studies for the energy consumption of FFF have employed analysis of variance (ANOVA) to identify the effects of process parameters on energy performance. For example, Al-Ghamdi [5] performed ANOVA and multi-response optimization to identify the best parameter combination of FFF for ABS in energy consumption, product mass, and build time. Elkaseer et al. [6] examined the effects of process parameters (i.e., infill density, layer thickness, printing speed, extruder temperature, and surface inclination angle) on the energy consumption, dimensional accuracy, surface roughness, and productivity of FFF for PLA. Galetto et al. [7] employed ANOVA for the impact of FFF parameters (i.e., layer thickness, infill density, printing speed, extruder temperature, number of shells, and retraction speed) on the build time, energy consumption, surface roughness, and dimensional accuracy of FFF for PLA. Although the above studies suggest optimal parameter settings for energy consumption based on their ANOVA results, the resultant process parameters are difficult to be generalized due to different machine specifications and specific process parameter settings in each study. On the other hand, recent studies have employed the MAR of FFF to generalize energy characteristics in FFF. Liu et al.

[9] examined the relationship between the MAR and the energy consumption of different AM processes. Lunetto et al. [1] suggested regression models based on the MAR to characterize the specific energy consumption of FFF using ABS and polycarbonate ABS. They found that the specific energy consumption decreases as the MAR increases.

Despite the effectiveness of using the MAR measure to develop a general energy consumption model for FFF, a high-performance polymer such as CFR-PEEK that requires a much higher energy demand than other polymers has not been sufficiently investigated in the literature. Indeed, the prediction of energy consumption in the FFF of an advanced polymer is essential in practice not only to achieve environmental sustainability but also to save the total energy cost.

From this point of view, this study proposes a two-phased approach to estimate the energy consumption of FFF for CFR-PEEK. In the first phase, two machine learning algorithms (i.e., decision tree and random forest) are respectively employed to estimate the MAR from major FFF parameters (i.e., layer thickness, infill density, and printing speed). A machine learning model that shows better prediction performance for the MAR is selected to estimate the energy consumption of FFF for CFR-PEEK. Then, a linear regression model is built for energy prediction based on the estimated MAR. Finally, this study compares the energy prediction performance between the proposed approach and a machine learning approach to direct energy prediction from FFF process parameters.

3   Methodology

3.1   Experimental Settings

This study used a seat buckle design (volume $= 3$ cm^3) (see Fig. 1), which was collected from the Thingiverse online CAD sharing platform [10], for experiments. The stereolithography (STL) file of the CAD was imported to the Simplify 3D slicing software [11] to generate a G-code file that reflects parameter settings for FFF. Experimental samples were fabricated by Apium P220 [12], which is an industrial FFF-machine for high-performance polymers. The fabrication of each experiment was performed using Apium PEEK CFR, which has the density of 1.38 g/cm^3 and the tensile strength of 190 MPa [13]. The extruding nozzle and printing bed of the machine was set up to maintain 510 °C and 120 °C, respectively, during the FFF process. In addition, a brim was generated for each fabrication to ensure part quality (see Fig. 1b).

3.2   Design of Experiments (DOE)

The DOE of this study aims to collect energy consumption data from the FFF of CFR-PEEK given varied parameter settings. For this, three major FFF parameters (i.e., layer thickness, infill density, and printing speed) were selected as input variables for experiments. These factors have been examined as parameters significantly affecting the energy consumption of FFF in the existing literature [4–8]. Each input parameter has three levels as shown in Table 1.

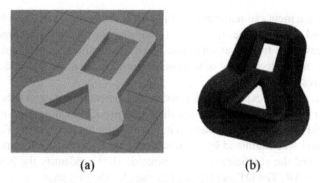

(a)   (b)

Fig. 1. Sample design and its fabricated output.

Table 1. Process parameters for DOE.

Process parameter	Unit	Level 1	Level 2	Level 3
Layer thickness	mm	0.1	0.15	0.2
Infill density	%	20	60	100
Printing speed	mm/min	1000	1100	1200

A full factorial design was planned to fabricate samples for all possible parameter combinations; a total of 27 experiments (3 levels × 3 levels × 3 levels) were randomly ordered to fabricate samples with different parameter settings. For each fabrication, the build time, filament volume, and energy consumption of each sample were collected for analysis. The energy consumption (Wh: Watt-hour) of each experiment was measured by Wattman HPM-100A Power Analyzer [14] during the FFF process. For calculating MAR values, build time (s: seconds) and consumed filament volume (cm³) were recorded for each fabrication using the machine data system. The MAR value of each experiment is computed through Eq. (1).

$$MAR = filament\ volume\left(cm^3\right)/\ build\ time\ (s) \tag{1}$$

3.3   Two-Phased Energy Consumption Prediction

A two-phased prediction approach to energy consumption was proposed to effectively estimate the energy consumption of FFF for CFR-PEEK. In the first prediction phase, a machine learning method was used to estimate the MAR of FFF for CFR-PEEK that is resulted from process parameter settings. Herein, two representative machine learning techniques, decision tree (DT) [15] and random forest (RF) [16] were examined to select the best model for prediction. The process parameters and the MAR were considered as predictor variables at the root node of a DT and a target variable at the leaf node of a DT, respectively. The minimum number of samples needed to split each internal node was set to two, and that of samples required to be at the leaf node was restricted to one. In the RF method, a meta estimator fits multiple decision trees on various sub-samples of the dataset, and then combines the results to improve the predictive accuracy [16]. The number of trees in the forest was set to ten. The minimum number of samples needed to split each internal node and that of samples required to be at the leaf node were set to two and one, respectively.

Two-thirds of all the experiment data were used as a training dataset to build a model, and the remaining dataset was used to test the model in each machine learning technique. The DT and RF models used the same datasets for training and testing. Each machine learning method was examined by the mean squared error (MSE), the mean absolute error (MAE), and the coefficient of determination (R^2) to identify the best prediction model for the MAR. The DT and RF models used for the first phase were implemented using the scikit-learn library in Python [18].

In the second phase, the energy consumption of FFF was fitted by a regression model using the estimated MAR as a predictor. The regression model was adopted from a general model of energy consumption in the previous studies [3, 19]. The regression model of energy consumption on the MAR is expressed by Eq. (2):

$$EC = \beta_{0(EC)} + \beta_{1(EC)} \cdot MAR_{inv},\tag{2}$$

where EC (unit: Wh) is the energy consumption of FFF, MAR_{inv} (unit: s/cm^3) is the inverse value of a material addition rate $(= 1/MAR)$, $\beta_{0(EC)}$ represents an intercept, and $\beta_{1(EC)}$ represents a coefficient of the energy consumption model. The statistical significance of the regression model was tested by $\beta_{1(EC)}$ at the *p-value* of 0.05. The regression model was derived using Minitab 21 [17].

Finally, the effectiveness of the proposed two-phased prediction approach was verified by comparing the proposed approach and energy prediction directly derived from the process parameters through a machine learning technique selected in the first phase.

4   Results

Table 2 shows the performance measures of the MAR estimation models. The DT method has better prediction performance than the RF method in all the measures. Thus, the DT model was selected to estimate the MAR of FFF for CFR-PEEK in this study.

Table 2. Estimation of MAR.

Measure	Decision Tree	Random Forest
MSE	4.9276	9.3187
MAE	2.0780	2.8849
R^2	0.9912	0.9834

The MAR of each parameter combination predicted by the decision tree model was transformed into *1/MAR* to build a linear regression model in Eq. (2). Figure 2(a) and Table 3 show the linear regression results. The *p*-value shows that MAR is a statistically significant predictor of energy consumption (see Table 3). In addition, the derived regression model has a high prediction power ($R^2 = 0.958$). As shown in Fig. 2(b), the decrease in the energy consumption of FFF for CFR-PEEK is accelerated as the MAR increases.

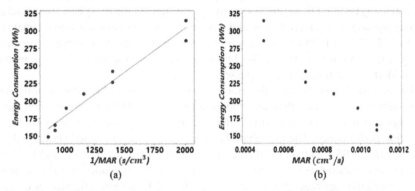

Fig. 2. Fitted regression plot (a) and energy consumption plot (b) on MAR.

Table 3. Fitted energy consumption model on MAR.

Equation	$EC = 52.13 + 0.126 \cdot MAR$
F-value	159.79
p-value	0.00 ($p < 0.05$)
R^2	0.958

Table 4 shows the performance measures of the decision tree model of energy consumption, which directly uses the process parameter values for the model. The DT model shows a lower prediction performance ($R^2 = 0.898$) than that of the final energy prediction model from the two-phased approach ($R^2 = 0.958$).

Table 4. Estimation of energy consumption on process parameters through decision tree.

Measure	Decision Tree
MSE	281.8005
MAE	15.0489
R^2	0.898

5 Conclusions

This study proposed a two-phased prediction approach to estimate the energy consumption of FFF for CFR-PEEK, which can have a better prediction power than the direct prediction of energy consumption based on process parameters. For this, the DOE considering three process parameters (i.e., layer thickness, infill density, and printing speed) was planned to collect data for build time, filament volume, and energy consumption from experimental samples. This study employed the MAR of FFF to represent the process efficiency resulted from process parameter settings. In the first phase, two machine learning methods (i.e., decision tree and random forest) were examined to estimate the MAR of FFF for CFR-PEEK. Then, a linear regression model was derived to estimate energy consumption from the MAR obtained from the best machine learning method for the MAR estimation in the first phase.

The results showed that the decision tree model for the MAR estimation has better prediction performance than the random forest model. The linear regression model of energy consumption on the estimated MAR in the second phase also showed good prediction performance. The two-phased prediction approach provided better final performance ($R^2 = 95.8\%$) than the direct energy prediction using the DT model directly using process parameters ($R^2 = 89.8\%$). Thus, it can be concluded that the proposed energy prediction approach for the FFF of CFR-PEEK is more effective in estimating energy consumption for the FFF of CFR-PEEK. The findings from this study also demonstrate that the MAR provides a basis to characterize energy dynamics in FFF; the MAR of FFF can effectively explain the energy performance of FFF depending on parameter settings.

Nonetheless, this study should be further extended to reflect the following tasks. First of all, the replicates of each experiment should be employed to derive more statistically significant results that consider possible experimental noises. Second, the proposed energy consumption approach should be improved by a meta-optimization process for parameter tuning of each machine learning method to ensure the best prediction condition of the model. Moreover, different part designs and other high performance materials should be jointly considered to develop a more reliable and general energy prediction approach for various FFF applications in practice.

Acknowledgement. This work was supported by the National Research Foundation of Korea (NRF) grant funded by the Korea government (MSIT) (No. NRF-2022R1C1C1012140) for Kijung Park.

References

1. Lunetto, V., Priarone, P.C., Galati, M., Minetola, P.: On the correlation between process parameters and specific energy consumption in fused deposition modelling. J. Manuf. Process. **56**, 1039–1049 (2020). https://doi.org/10.1016/j.jmapro.2020.06.002
2. Park, K., Kim, G., No, H., Jeon, H.W., Okudan Kremer, G.E.: Identification of optimal process parameter settings based on manufacturing performance for fused filament fabrication of CFR-PEEK. Appl. Sci. **10**(13), 4630 (2020). https://doi.org/10.3390/app10134630

3. Kim, K., Noh, H., Park, K., Jeon, H.W., Lim, S.: Characterization of power demand and energy consumption for fused filament fabrication using CFR-PEEK. Rapid Prototyp. J. **28**(7), 1394–1406 (2022). https://doi.org/10.1108/rpj-07-2021-0188

4. Mognol, P., Lepicart, D., Perry, N.: Rapid prototyping: energy and environment in the spotlight. Rapid Prototyp. J. **12**(1), 26–34 (2006). https://doi.org/10.1108/135525406106 37246

5. Al-Ghamdi, K.A.: Sustainable FDM additive manufacturing of ABS components with emphasis on energy minimized and time efficient lightweight construction. Int. J. Lightweight Mater. Manuf. **2**(4), 338–345 (2019). https://doi.org/10.1016/j.ijlmm.2019.05.004

6. Elkaseer, A., Schneider, S., Scholz, S.G.: Experiment-based process modeling and optimization for high-quality and resource-efficient FFF 3D printing. Appl. Sci. **10**(8) (2020). https://doi.org/10.3390/app10082899. Article 2899

7. Galetto, M., Verna, E., Genta, G.: Effect of process parameters on parts quality and process efficiency of fused deposition modeling. Comput. Ind. Eng. **156**, 107238 (2021). https://doi.org/10.1016/j.cie.2021.107238

8. Peng, T., Yan, F.: Dual-objective analysis for desktop FDM printers: energy consumption and surface roughness. Procedia CIRP **69**, 106–111 (2018). https://doi.org/10.1016/j.procir.2017.11.084

9. Liu, Z., et al.: Investigation of energy requirements and environmental performance for additive manufacturing processes. Sustainability **10**(10), 3606 (2018). https://doi.org/10.3390/su1 0103606

10. Thingiverse. https://www.thingiverse.com

11. Simplify 3D. www.simplify3d.com/software/release-notes/version-4-1-2

12. Apium. https://apiumtec.com/download/apium-p220-datasheet

13. Apium. https://apiumtec.com/download/apium-cfr-peek-datasheet

14. Adpower. https://bit.ly/3LOZm3S

15. Wei, Y., et al.: A review of data-driven approaches for prediction and classification of building energy consumption. Renew. Sustain. Energy Rev. **82**, 1027–1047 (2018). https://doi.org/10.1016/j.rser.2017.09.108

16. Zhang, W., Wu, C., Li, Y., Wang, L., Samui, P.: Assessment of pile drivability using random forest regression and multivariate adaptive regression splines. Georisk Assessment Manage. Risk Eng. Syst. Geohaz. **15**(1), 27–40 (2021). https://doi.org/10.1080/17499518.2019.167 4340

17. Minitab. https://www.minitab.com/en-us/products/minitab

18. Scikit-learn. https://scikit-learn.org/stable/supervised_learning.html#supervised-learning

19. Gutowski, T.G., Branham, M.S., Dahmus, J.B., Jones, A.J., Thiriez, A., Sekulic, D.P.: Thermodynamic analysis of resources used in manufacturing processes. Environ. Sci. Technol. **43**(5), 1584–1590 (2009). https://doi.org/10.1021/es8016655

Simulation and Model-Driven Production Management

Sequential Optimization of a Temporary Storage Location for Cooperative Twin Overhead Shuttles in a Rail-Based Automated Container Terminal

Bonggwon Kang[1], Bosung Kim[2], and Soondo Hong[2(✉)]

[1] Major in Industrial Data Science and Engineering, Department of Industrial Engineering,
Pusan National University, Busan 46241, South Korea
[2] Department of Industrial Engineering, Pusan National University, Busan 46241, South Korea
soondo.hong@pusan.ac.kr

Abstract. Twin overhead shuttle cranes (OSs) transport containers in a rail-based automated container terminal (RACT). Terminal operators separate a job into a main job and an auxiliary job based on a temporary storage location. Since the temporary storage location determines the frequency of the job separations and the workload of each OS, they use simulation-based decision-making to investigate the impact of the interference between the twin OSs. It is time-intensive to optimize an objective function with manually designed experiments, so this study proposes a sequential optimization approach, Bayesian optimization (BO), to determine the optimal temporary storage location within a limited simulation run. The BO adaptively draws the surrogate model of simulation outcomes and actively suggests the most promising solution comparing the current optimal solution. An experiment demonstrates that the BO predicts the outcomes of a RACT simulation and ensures a near-optimal solution within a limited simulation run.

Keywords: Twin overhead shuttles · Bayesian optimization · Rail-based automated container terminal · Simulation

1 Introduction

To improve the efficiency and reliability of container handling, Lee, et al. [1] developed a rail-based automated container terminal (RACT). In the RACT, an overhead shuttle (OS) performs a similar function as a yard crane (YC) in a typical container terminal [2]. Flatcars transfer containers between a quay crane and an OS along guided ground rails. The storage yard consists of multiple overhead rails with twin OSs for each rail. Figure 1 illustrates the conceptual layout.

D. Y. Kim et al. (Eds.): APMS 2022, IFIP AICT 663, pp. 285–292, 2022.
https://doi.org/10.1007/978-3-031-16407-1_34

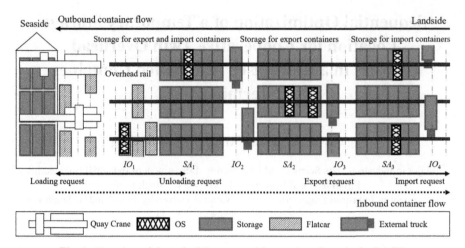

Fig. 1. Top view of the twin OS system with container flows in the RACT.

Since the twin OSs in a rail cannot pass each other, terminal operators separate each job into a main job and an auxiliary job based on a temporary storage location. The job separation procedure aims to smooth the synchronization between the twin OSs. The temporary storage location determines the frequency of job separations and the workload of each OS.

The workloads of the OSs are black-box functions due to complex and unknown constraints. Therefore, terminal operators commonly use discrete-event simulations to mimic yard operations, e.g., container handling equipment scheduling, vehicle congestion, interference between yard cranes, and the like, and obtain the optimal decision within a certain planning period [3–6]. However, the expensive objective function to evaluate hinders obtaining an optimal solution within a limited time [7, 8].

In this study, we suggest a sequential optimization approach, Bayesian optimization (BO), to determine the optimal temporary storage location within a limited simulation run. The BO adaptively draws the surrogate model of simulation outcomes, and then actively suggests the most promising optimal solution comparing the current best solution based on an acquisition function controlling the trade-off between exploration and exploitation of searches.

The main contributions of this study are as follows: (1) We investigate the temporary storage location determination problem in a RACT, unlike most studies which mainly treat crane scheduling with a fixed temporary storage location; and (2) We propose a sequential optimization approach, BO, to determine the temporary storage location. A simulation experiment evaluates the proposed model compared to optimal solutions.

This study is structured as follows: Sect. 2 introduces the detailed job separation procedure and the two optimization approaches to minimize the maximum workload of twin OSs in a RACT. Section 3 describes the experiment and the results of the proposed approaches compared to an optimal solution. Section 4 concludes and suggests future research.

2 Problem Methodology

2.1 Container Flows with a Job Separation Procedure

In the RACT, there are four input/output (I/O) points and three stacking areas (see Fig. 1). A transfer request can be to or from an inbound or outbound container. The inbound (import and unloading) containers move from a vessel to an ET (external truck). The outbound (export and loading) containers move from an ET to a vessel. OSs transport them to and from flatcars at seaside and to and from ETs at landside. Requests for export and unloading containers are storage requests and requests for import and loading are retrieval requests. To complete a transfer request, the OSs repeat four basic operations: empty travel, pick-up, loaded travel, and drop-off.

A job separation procedure is for collaborative operations between the twin OSs whereby one OS transfers a container from its original location to a temporary storage location and the other OS transfers it from the temporary storage location to the container's destination. The job separation procedure balances the workloads of OSs and alleviates interference between twin OSs.

Gharehgozli, et al. [9] showed that using two temporary storages decreases rehandlings, the extra jobs to remove the stacked containers on a target container. We fix the sizes of the temporary storages according to Little's law, $L = \lambda \times W$, where L denotes the estimated size, W denotes the mean dwelling time of stacked containers in the temporary storages, and λ denotes the mean arrival rate.

2.2 Temporary Storage Location Determination Model

To optimize a temporary storage location, we formulate a temporary storage location determination model (TSLDM) based on MIP. The TSLDM clarifies our optimization problem with linear constraints. We use the following definitions.

Indices and Sets

N = Set of nodes representing all terminal sections, $N = \{SA_1, SA_2, SA_3, IO_1, IO_2, IO_3, IO_4, B_u, B_l\}$.
SA = Set of nodes representing stacking areas, $SA = \{SA_1, SA_2, SA_3\}$, $SA \subset N$.
IO = Set of nodes representing I/O points, $IO = \{IO_1, IO_2, IO_3, IO_4\}$, $IO \subset N$.
i, j = Index of nodes representing all terminal sections.
T, t = Set of job types and its index, $T = \{U, L, I, O\}$, $t \in T$.
K, k = Set of OSs and its index, $K = \{OS_{sea}, OS_{land}\}$, $k \in K$.
PU, u = Set of unloading storage candidates and its index, $u \in PU$.
PL, l = Set of loading storage candidates and its index, $l \in PL$.
V, v = Set of vessels and its index, $v \in V$.

Parameters

F_{vi}^t = Number of requests of job type t from node i of vessel v.
UR_v = Ratio of unloading operations using a temporary storage of vessel v.

LR_v = Ratio of loading operations using a temporary storage of vessel v.
t_{ijk} = Processing time of OS k from node i to j.
ut_{ijku} = Processing time of OS k from node i to j using unloading storage u.
lt_{ijkl} = Processing time of OS k from node i to j using loading storage l.

Decision Variables

MF = Maximum workload of OSs

$x_u = \begin{cases} 1 \text{ If unloading storage } u \text{ is used,} \\ 0 \text{ Otherwise.} \end{cases}$

$y_l = \begin{cases} 1 \text{ If loading storage } l \text{ is used,} \\ 0 \text{ Otherwise.} \end{cases}$

F_{vijk} = Number of container flows of OS k from node i to j except auxiliary flows of vessel v.

FU_{vijku} = Number of auxiliary flows of OS k from node i to j using unloading storage u of vessel v.

FL_{vijkl} = Number of auxiliary flows of OS k from node i to j using loading storage l of vessel v.

Objective function

$$(\text{TSLDM}) \quad minimize \ MF \tag{1}$$

Subject to

$$MF \geq \sum_{i \in N} \sum_{j \in N} F_{vijk} \cdot t_{ijk} + \sum_{i \in N} \sum_{j \in N} \sum_{u \in PU} FU_{vijku} \cdot ut_{ijku} \ \forall k \in K, + \sum_{i \in N} \sum_{j \in N} \sum_{l \in PL} FL_{vijkl} \cdot lt_{ijkl}, \tag{2}$$

$$F_{vijk} \geq f_{vi}^U \cdot (1 - UR_v), \quad \forall v \in V, \forall i \in \{IO_1\}, \qquad \forall j \in \{SA_1\}, \forall k \in \{OS_{sea}\}, \tag{3}$$

$$F_{vijk} \geq f_{vi}^L \cdot (1 - LR_v), \quad \forall v \in V, \forall i \in \{SA_1\}, \qquad \forall j \in \{IO_1\}, \forall k \in \{OS_{sea}\}, \tag{4}$$

$$\sum_{j \in SA} \sum_{k \in K} F_{vijk} \geq f_{vi}^I, \ \forall v \in V, \forall i \in IO, \tag{5}$$

$$\sum_{j \in IO} \sum_{k \in K} F_{vijk} \geq f_{vi}^O, \ \forall v \in V, \forall i \in SA, \tag{6}$$

$$FU_{vijku} \geq \sum_{w \in N} f_{vw}^U \cdot UR_v \cdot x_u, \quad \forall v \in V, \forall i \in \{IO_1\}, \forall j \in \{B_u\}, \qquad \forall k \in \{OS_{sea}\}, \forall u \in PU, \tag{7}$$

$$FU_{vijku} \geq \sum_{w \in N} f_{vw}^U \cdot UR_v \cdot x_u, \quad \forall v \in V, \forall i \in \{B_u\}, \forall j \in \{SA_3\}, \qquad \forall k \in \{OS_{land}\}, \forall u \in PU, \tag{8}$$

$$FL_{vijkl} \geq \sum_{w \in N} f_{vw}^L \cdot LR_v \cdot y_l, \quad \forall v \in V, \forall i \in \{SA_2\}, \forall j \in \{B_l\}, \qquad \forall k \in \{OS_{land}\}, \forall l \in PL, \tag{9}$$

$$FL_{vijkl} \geq \sum_{w \in N} f_{vw}^L \cdot LR_v \cdot y_l, \quad \forall v \in V, \forall i \in \{B_l\}, \forall j \in \{IO_1\}, \qquad \forall k \in \{OS_{sea}\}, \forall l \in PL, \tag{10}$$

$$\sum_{u \in PU} x_u = 1, \tag{11}$$

$$\sum_{l \in PL} y_l = 1, \tag{12}$$

$$x_u + y_u \leq 1, \qquad \forall u \in PU. \tag{13}$$

The TSLDM aims to minimize the maximum workloads of OSs (constraints (1) and (2)). Constraints (3) and (4) calculate the unloading and loading flows without a job separation procedure. Constraints (5) and (6) calculate the import and export flows. Constraints (7), (8), (9), and (10) calculate the unloading and loading flows with job separations considering the temporary storage. Constraints (11) and (12) determine the temporary storage locations. Constraint (13) ensures that the temporary storage locations should not be overlapped.

2.3 Sequential Optimization of a Temporary Storage Location

The BO consists of a surrogate function and an acquisition function. We use the Gaussian process (GP) as a surrogate function, which is suitable to take into a noise variance [10]. The GP is identified as a multivariate Gaussian distribution drawn by its kernel function and statistically approximates a posterior distribution of the maximum workloads of the twin OSs according to the decision variables i.e., the locations of temporary storages for loading and unloading requests. Based on the posterior distributions, an acquisition function carefully determines where to sample with a limited number of trials. We use maximum expected improvement (MEI) as an acquisition function to maximize the quality of solutions considering noise measurements. Because the BO treats an objective function with a continuous domain, we apply a *naïve rounding* approach which rounds the recommended temporary storage locations to the nearest discrete locations at the end [11].

We let $f(x)$ denote an underlying simulation's response over the input variable x:

$$f(x) \sim GP\big(m(x), k(x, x')\big), \tag{14}$$

where $f(x)$ is specified by mean function $m(x)$ and covariance function $k(x, x')$. We utilize the most commonly used covariance function, the radial basis function, as kernel function k. We derive the posterior distribution for unknown x_{n+1} based on Bayesian statistics [10] as:

$$P(f(x_{n+1})|D_{1:N}) = N\big(u_n(x_{n+1}), \sigma_n^2(x_{n+1})\big) \tag{18}$$

EI (Expected Improvement) provides x_{n+1}^* with the maximum excted improvement by controlling the trade-off between exploration and exploitation of searches according to the posterior distribution:

$$x_{n+1}^* = argmax_{x \in \chi} \, EI_n(x). \tag{19}$$

EI quantifies the expected improvement over the input variables toward the optimal decision [12], γ denotes the trade-off between exploitation and exploration, y^+ denotes the current best observations, Φ denotes the probability density function, Φ denotes the cumulative density function, and Z denotes the standard normal distribution. Then,

$$EI_n(x) = \begin{cases} \big(u_n(x) - y^+ - \gamma\big)\Phi(Z) + \sigma_n(x)\phi(Z) & \text{if } \sigma(X) > 0 \\ 0 & \text{if } \sigma(X) = 0' \end{cases} \tag{20}$$

where

$$Z_n = \begin{cases} \frac{u_n(x) - y^+ - \gamma}{\sigma_n(x)} & \text{if } \sigma(X) > 0 \\ 0 & \text{if } \sigma(X) = 0 \end{cases}. \tag{21}$$

3 Experiment and Results

We build a single-bay simulation model and specify a maritime demand using four factors: the average of loading and unloading containers (N_{sea}), the portion of import containers (RI), the portion of unloading containers (RU), and the portion of landside containers (RL). We assume a demand pattern where RI, RU, and RL are 50%, 50%, and 40%, respectively. For example, we can obtain the number of containers from the landside by multiplying RL to N_{sea}. N_{sea} are 30, 50, and 70 with different vessel specifications. We randomly generate the different sets of 20 vessels where a vessel requires a uniformly distributed number of transfer requests within the intervals $[0.8 \times N_{sea}, 1.2 \times N_{sea}]$. We observe the cumulative maximum workload of twin OSs over different instances and evaluate the proposed approaches compared with known optimal solutions.

Table 1 summarizes the means and standard deviations of the maximum workloads. The BO with the larger simulation budgets ensured the reduced maximum workload with its small standard deviation. The BO with different simulation budgets ($b = 25$, 50, and 100) obtained the average optimality gaps as 5.79, 2.99, and 1.03% respectively. The BO with $b = 100$ consistently converged to the near-optimal solution in the range between 0.08 and 1.89%. Notably, the TSLDM obtained the average optimality of 20.79% with a high variation in solution qualities because could not consider the impacts of time-variant interferences among the twin OSs and vehicles.

Table 1. Maximum workload and optimality gaps obtained by the TSLDM and the BO.

| Instance | Maximum workload (hours) | | | | | Optimality | | | |
	Optimal	TSLDM	BO (b = 25)	BO (b = 50)	BO (b = 100)	TSLDM	BO (b = 25)	BO (b = 50)	BO (b = 100)
1	1157.02	1559.77	1281.35	1169.72	1171.85	34.81%	10.75%	1.10%	1.28%
2	1179.02	1421.16	1343.83	1197.65	1180.01	20.54%	13.98%	1.58%	0.08%
3	1219.65	1322.67	1288.19	1251.96	1234.16	8.45%	5.62%	2.65%	1.19%
4	1193.88	1313.48	1207.42	1251.52	1216.41	10.02%	1.13%	4.83%	1.89%
5	1134.90	1209.12	1210.43	1145.98	1142.43	6.54%	6.66%	0.98%	0.66%
6	1219.12	1651.14	1235.72	1246.25	1223.37	35.44%	1.36%	2.23%	0.35%
7	1197.79	1622.68	1210.07	1228.12	1217.99	35.47%	1.03%	2.53%	1.69%
8	1190.89	1337.65	1226.05	1323.11	1210.78	12.32%	2.95%	11.10%	1.67%
9	1211.77	1644.86	1241.81	1226.73	1221.03	35.74%	2.48%	1.23%	0.76%
10	1119.70	1215.87	1253.52	1138.17	1127.46	8.59%	11.95%	1.65%	0.69%
Mean	1182.37	1429.84	1249.84	1217.92	1194.55	20.79%	5.79%	2.99%	1.03%
Std.v	32.99	166.54	41.32	53.48	35.12	12.42%	4.62%	2.91%	0.58%

4 Conclusions

It is time-consuming to run simulations based on manually designed experiments to optimize an underlying objective function. Time is also a factor when significant variations in maritime demands or unexpected breakdowns of equipment occur.

For prompt and effective simulation-based decision-making in yard operations, we propose a sequential optimization model, BO, for determining the location of temporary storages to minimize the maximum workload of twin OSs. The results of our experiment demonstrate that the BO consistently obtains near-optimal solutions, whereas the TSLDM with linear constraints cannot provide the optimal solutions with their high variations.

An integrated analysis of the collaborative operations of twin OSs considering scheduling and routing methods for vehicles merits further research. We suggest that a sophisticated discretization approach could overcome the limitation of the *naïve rounding* approach used in this study which can cause the BO to repeatedly search previously observed points and become stuck. We also suggest expanding the proposed BO to improve collaborative operations between twin YCs in traditional vertical terminals in the future.

Acknowledgments. This work was supported by the 2022 BK21 FOUR Program of Pusan National University and a National Research Foundation of Korea (NRF) grant funded by the Korean government (MSIT) (No. NRF-2020R1A2C2004320).

References s

1. Lee, E.K., Jeong, D.H., Choi, S.H.: A Study on the new concept container terminal for processing containers of mega sized container ships. J. Shipp. Logist. **30**(3), 671–696 (2014)
2. Fibrianto, H.Y., Kang, B., Hong, S.: A job sequencing problem of an overhead shuttle crane in a rail-based automated container terminal. IEEE Access **8**, 156362–156377 (2020)
3. Chang, D., Jiang, Z., Yan, W., He, J.: Integrating berth allocation and quay crane assignments. Transp. Res. Part E Logist. Transp. Rev. **46**(6), 975–990 (2010)
4. Sacone, S., Siri, S.: An integrated simulation-optimization framework for the operational planning of seaport container terminals. Math. Comput. Model. Dyn. Syst. **15**(3), 275–293 (2009)
5. He, J., Zhang, W., Huang, Y., Yan, W.: A simulation optimization method for internal trucks sharing assignment among multiple container terminals. Adv. Eng. Inform. **27**(4), 598–614 (2013)
6. Legato, P., Mazza, R.M., Gullì, D.: Integrating tactical and operational berth allocation decisions via simulation–optimization. Comput. Ind. Eng. **78**, 84–94 (2014)
7. Zhou, C., Ma, N., Cao, X., Lee, L.H., Chew, E.P.: Classification and literature review on the integration of simulation and optimization in maritime logistics studies. IISE Trans. **53**(10), 1157–1176 (2021)
8. Amaran, S., Sahinidis, N.V., Sharda, B.,Bury, S.J.: Simulation optimization: a review of algorithms and applications. Ann. Oper. Res. **240**(1), 351–80 (2016)
9. Gharehgozli, A.H., Vernooij, F.G., Zaerpour, N.: A simulation study of the performance of twin automated stacking cranes at a seaport container terminal. Eur. J. Oper. Res. **261**(1), 108–128 (2017)

10. Rasmussen, C.E.: Gaussian processes in machine learning. In: Bousquet, O., von Luxburg, U., Rätsch, G. (eds.) Advanced Lectures on Machine Learning. ML 2003. LNCS, vol. 3176, pp. 63–71. Springer, Berlin, Heidelberg (2004). https://doi.org/10.1007/978-3-540-28650-9_4
11. Luong, P., Gupta, S., Nguyen, D., Rana, S., Venkatesh, S.: Bayesian optimization with discrete variables. In: Liu, J., Bailey, J. (eds.) AI 2019: Advances in Artificial Intelligence. AI 2019. LNCS, vol. 11919, pp. 473–84. Springer, Cham (2019). https://doi.org/10.1007/978-3-030-35288-2_38
12. Jones, D.R., Schonlau, M., Welch, W.J.: Efficient global optimization of expensive black-box functions. J. Glob. Optim. **13**(4), 455–492 (1998)

Determining Due Dates for Rush Orders

A Simple and Effective Order Acceptance Procedure

Christopher Mundt$^{(\boxtimes)}$ ⓘ, Eilis Bernadette Beck, and Hermann Lödding

Hamburg University of Technology, Hamburg, Germany
{christopher.mundt,eilis.beck,loedding}@tuhh.de

Abstract. Determining realistic delivery dates is difficult for make-to-order man-ufacturers, especially when customers demand both long and short delivery times (rush orders). In this article, we show a procedure for determining delivery dates for rush orders by extending an approach developed for standard orders. Our procedure only uses early available order information and visualizes it in a throughput diagram. A simulative evaluation proves its effectiveness by achieving both short delivery times and a high delivery compliance.

Keywords: Order acceptance · Throughput diagram · Rush orders

1 Introduction

Logistical objectives, such as the delivery time, are important decision criteria for customers of make-to-order manufacturers in particular, which is confirmed by recent studies among German manufacturing companies [1, 2].

Many make-to-order manufacturers offer different delivery time classes, such as standard orders or rush orders [2]. This enables them to meet different delivery time requirements. Often, customers are even accepting higher prices for shorter delivery times [3, 4].

Even without rush orders, determining realistic delivery times is difficult, since the incoming order load is uncertain. To begin with, it is unclear whether an offer is accepted by the customer or not. Furthermore, in the early stage of order acceptance management, detailed production schedules with the corresponding routings and work stations are not yet available for planning. Moreover, there is uncertainty about the work content of an order.

Rush orders make planning even more difficult as they are received at short notice. In many cases capacity may already be utilized when rush orders occur. Also, prioritizing rush orders over standard orders increases the throughput times of standard orders [3]. If rush orders are not taken into account in production planning, they will lead to backlogs and schedule deviations, especially of standard orders.

This article introduces a scheduling procedure with throughput diagrams that reserves production capacities for rush orders, so that companies can schedule rush orders at short notice without overloading production. In the following, a brief overview of the

© IFIP International Federation for Information Processing 2022
Published by Springer Nature Switzerland AG 2022
D. Y. Kim et al. (Eds.): APMS 2022, IFIP AICT 663, pp. 293–301, 2022.
https://doi.org/10.1007/978-3-031-16407-1_35

fundamentals and the state of research is given (Sect. 2), the scheduling procedure for rush orders is explained (Sect. 3) and the evaluation results are presented (Sect. 4), before a conclusion is drawn (Sect. 5).

2   Fundamentals and Current State of Research

Rush orders are prioritized over standard orders in the workstation queues [5]. Often sequencing by due dates is used to implement this prioritization [6]. Based on the operating curve theory [7] and the funnel model [5], Trzyna employs balance equations to model the effect of rush orders on the throughput times of standard orders [4]. Logistic operating curves illustrate this relation. At low work in progress (WIP) levels, rush orders do not have significantly shorter throughput times than standard orders, since all orders can be processed without long waiting times. Conversely, rush orders have much shorter throughput times than standard orders at high WIP levels, due to their prioritization. However, rush orders thereby also delay standard orders and thus extend their throughput time [3, 4].

Because of the turbulence that rush orders can cause, companies should consciously decide whether and to what extent rush orders offer an advantage [4, 8].

In order acceptance management, rush orders pose an especially great challenge, because of their short term occurrence and their influence on standard orders. Due to the arrival of rush orders on short notice, the available capacities may already be fully utilized. Production may be overloaded, if rush orders will be accepted anyway. Delays, especially for standard orders, would be the consequence, if capacities cannot be adjusted in the short preparation time available. Different approaches from the fields of mathematical optimization, machine learning and procedures based on production models exist to address these challenges.

Procedures based on mathematical optimizations reschedule orders in many cases. They require a comparatively large amount of input data at the work system level, which is usually not available at the early stage of scheduling. The mathematical descriptions are similarly complex, which makes implementation difficult (cf. [9–11]).

Procedures based on machine learning often optimize scheduling at the work system level. Moreover, these methods require comparatively large amounts of detailed input data, such as work plans and capacity requirements at the work system level, which are usually not available at the early scheduling stage. The use of machine learning requires technical expertise, which is not available in many companies (cf. [12, 13]).

The procedure described in this paper is based on models of logistic objectives, such as the funnel model. This approach is also pursued by Kingsman et al., Land and Trzyna (cf. [4, 14, 15]). Especially, in such procedures some authors avoid overloading production by reserving capacity for rush orders (cf. [4, 16]). However, this approach contains the risk of capacity utilization losses, if fewer rush orders are received than expected. Some of these existing scheduling procedures do not consider rush orders separately.

Trzyna, however, takes a different approach to schedule rush orders in his dissertation [4]. His procedure is based on reserving capacities for rush orders. It uses a cumulative input graph in a throughput diagram after a previous throughput scheduling. The procedure checks whether sufficient capacity is available on the planned start date of a rush order. During the capacity check, Trzyna allows the planned capacity to be exceeded within limits. Since the focus of the dissertation is on rush orders rather than on order acceptance, Trzyna simplifies the order acceptance process. He assumes an existing pool of orders, thereby neglecting the uncertainty about incoming orders, the customer response time and the customers' delivery time requests. Additionally, scheduling takes place at work station level, which requires the existence of detailed production schedules.

A procedure previously presented by the authors, inspired by the method of Trzyna, shows how companies can schedule standard orders using a throughput diagram [17]. The procedure requires comparatively few input parameters and enables effective scheduling on the level of the entire production. Figure 1 shows the respective throughput diagram of the procedure.

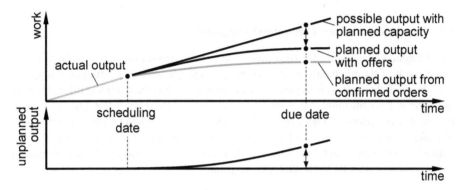

Fig. 1. Throughput diagram for the basic scheduling procedure [17]

The procedure compares the planned output and the possible output with the planned capacity. The planned output includes both confirmed orders and offers awaiting a decision by the customer. The capacity requirements of the latter are discounted by the expected acceptance rate. The difference between the possible output with planned capacity and the planned output with offers results in the unplanned output, which is used for capacity allocation for incoming requests. In addition to capacity allocation, the procedure also determines the delivery time of an offer on the basis of the customer's requested delivery time and the average throughput time of production.

This approach is associated with the risk of capacity utilisation losses due to capacity reservation under uncertainties. If more offers than assumed are rejected by the customer, the reserved capacities can often not be used due to the short time in advance. However, the procedure can show a high schedule compliance and the capacity utilisation losses can be significantly reduced by releasing orders according to ConWIP [17] or by a short-term capacity reduction. However, rush orders have not been taken into account in this procedure so far.

3   Scheduling Rush Orders in a Throughput Diagram

The following sections describe a scheduling procedure for rush orders. Therefore, the construction of the necessary throughput diagram is described (3.1) and the scheduling procedure itself is presented (3.2).

The basic idea is to allocate part of the capacity for rush orders and thus avoid competition with standard orders, as for example suggested by Trzyna (cf. [3]). This approach presents the opportunity to offer short delivery times without sacrificing the schedule of standard orders. Main objectives of the procedure are (1) to secure the logistic objectives of delivery reliability and utilization, (2) a simple implementation with as little input data as possible and (3) a transparent representation of the scheduling situation.

3.1   Construction of the Throughput Diagram

The scheduling procedure for rush orders, like the original procedure, is based on the comparison of the planned output with the planned capacity in a throughput diagram. The object of observation is the entire production, as well as the complete offer and order throughput. Possible units to measure the output are standard hours (total work content), the number of orders or other capacity equivalents. The planned output contains orders in different statuses, such as released orders, orders waiting for release, orders in the indirect departments, and open offers with a work content adjusted by the acceptance rate. Figure 2 shows such a throughput diagram.

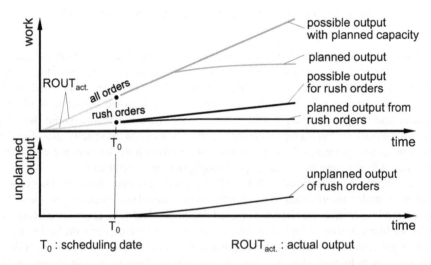

Fig. 2. Throughput diagram for scheduling involving rush orders

The possible output with planned capacity starts with the actual output on the scheduling date and results from the integration of the planned capacity over time. The curve rises linearly at a constant planned capacity and its slope corresponds to the capacity. In order to avoid the turbulences caused by rush orders, the possible output with maximum planned capacity is split into two parts, the possible output for standard orders and the possible output for rush orders. Therefore, the maximum planned output from capacities is multiplied with the rush order share resulting in a capacity reserved for incoming rush orders (1). The possible output from planned capacities for standard orders is reduced accordingly by the rush order share (2).

$$OUT_{pos,rush}(t) = OUT_{act,rush}(T_0) + \sigma_{rush} \cdot (t - T_0) \cdot CAPA_{plan} \qquad (1)$$

$$OUT_{pos,std}(t) = OUT_{pos}(t) - OUT_{pos,rush}(t) \qquad (2)$$

with

$OUT_{pos,rush}$: possible output with planned capacity for rush orders.
$OUT_{pos,std}$: possible output with planned capacity for standard orders.
OUT_{pos} : possible output with planned capacity.
$OUT_{act,rush}$: actual output of rush orders.
σ_{rush} : rush order share.
t : time.
T_0 : scheduling date.
$CAPA_{plan}$: planned capacity.

The unplanned output is the difference between the possible output and the already planned output. It is essential for the procedure to decide on the schedule of further orders.

3.2 Scheduling Rush Orders

Scheduling is carried out separately for rush orders and standard orders. Beforehand planned throughput times for standard and rush orders are determined according to the equations presented by Trzyna [4]. Standard orders are scheduled in the basic scheduling procedure described in Sect. 2 with the planned capacity for standard orders as a reference [17].

The scheduling procedure for rush orders determines the delivery time of the offer, its preliminary planned due date, and after customer feedback the final planned due date of the order.

Step 1 - Determining a Realistic Delivery Time. Firstly, the procedure determines the possible delivery time of a rush order based on three conditions.

Condition 1. The procedure detects the first date at which the cumulative unplanned capacity for rush orders achieves or exceeds the expected work content of the offer. Scheduling the offer on any earlier date would lead to backlogs and therefore lateness.

Condition 2. The procedure checks, if the throughput time of the offer is not shorter than the necessary throughput time for rush orders as determined by the procedure of Trzyna [4] to avoid unrealistic short throughput times.

Condition 3. The procedure takes the delivery time, requested by the customer, into account. This ensures that the order is not scheduled earlier than desired by the customer.

The possible delivery time is then calculated by adding a delivery time buffer to the throughput time. The delivery time buffer is intended to provide additional protection against uncertainties in production and associated delays. The company can promise this possible delivery time to the customer in the offer.

Step 2 – Adding the Offer to the Planned Output. The offer can now be added to the planned output to update the throughput diagram. The procedure determines the work content that has to be scheduled and calculates the estimated due date of the offer. The work content is discounted with the acceptance rate, thus taking the possible rejection of offers by the customers into account. The procedure calculates the estimated due date for an offer starting from the scheduling date. An estimate of the customer response time is added to the scheduling date since the delivery time does not begin until the customer has placed an order. Moreover, the previously determined delivery time, minus the delivery time buffer, is added, as the delivery time buffer is not taken into account in internal order scheduling. Note that both the acceptance rate and the customer response time may vary between standard and rush orders.

Step 3 – Adjusting the Planned Output after the Customer Response. After the customer response, offers are removed from the schedule in the case of acceptance as well as in the case of rejection. For confirmed orders, the procedure determines the planned due date of the order. In contrast to offers, orders are considered with their entire expected work content in the planned output. The planned due date for confirmed orders is based on the actual confirmation date. Again, the previously determined possible delivery time minus the delivery time buffer is added to the actual confirmation date.

4   Evaluation by Simulation

The following sections describe the evaluation of the presented scheduling procedure for rush orders. Firstly, the simulation model is described and assumptions are being made. Secondly, the results of the simulation experiments are presented.

4.1 Simulation Model

Simulation experiments were carried out to evaluate the procedure in a basic state and to show the potentials of the procedure in combination with production control. The simulation experiments were carried out with a simulation model in the Plant Simulation software. In addition to production, the simulation model also includes areas upstream of production, such as the offer preparation process.

The simulated factory consists of seven work stations, each of which can process one order. These work stations are arranged in a job shop layout. Each work station performs a unique operation and has its own queue. Sequencing and order release can be varied to explore different configurations of the PPC. All workstations prioritize the orders according to the planned order due date to fast-track rush orders. This is a simplification.

Especially if the position of workstations in the routings varies, companies should use an earliest operation due date policy instead. The order release is either Constant Work in Process (ConWIP) or due date based. Capacities are purposely not controlled in the experiments in order to be able to assess the unmodified effect of the scheduling procedure on the logistical objectives.

Orders are divided into rush orders and standard orders. On average, the simulated share of rush orders is 20%. In the short term, the share of rush orders can differ, as each incoming request is randomly assigned. This causes varying inter arrival times between rush orders. Rush and standard orders differ in particular in the average customer response time and the maximum delivery time accepted by the customer. The average customer response time for standard orders is five shop calendar days and for rush orders three shop calendar days. Rush order customers accept a maximum delivery time of six days. Below this value, customers accept an order with an acceptance rate of 50%. Customers of standard orders have no restriction on the maximum delivery time and accept any order with an average acceptance rate of 50%. A delivery time buffer of one day is used for both order types.

Both rush and standard orders are further divided into ten variants. In the long run, the proportion of variants is equally distributed, but for each new order the variant is randomly selected. The average work content across all variants is seven hours. The work content varies between the variants with a coefficient of variance of one.

The simulation experiments were simulated with a balanced ratio of expected load to capacity. In each experimental run, 10,000 customer requests were simulated. The offer request rate fluctuated in the short term, due to varying inter arrival times.

4.2 Simulation Results

The aim of the simulation experiments is to evaluate the procedure in terms of delivery compliance, throughput times and utilization. For this purpose, the process was simulated (1) in a basic state and (2) in combination with a ConWIP control. Table 1 shows the results of the simulation experiments.

In the basic state, an order release according to the planned start date and a sequencing according to the planned due date were selected. A high delivery compliance of nearly 99% could be observed for the different order types. The throughput times are short and do not fluctuate excessively. As for the standard procedure, utilisation losses were observed. Especially rush orders are vulnerable to this. These losses result from the fact that capacities are released at short notice due to a higher than assumed share of rejected offers for rush orders. These capacities cannot subsequently be reassigned.

Afterwards, the procedure was combined with order release according to ConWIP with an unlimited advance release window. The sequencing after the planned due date was maintained in order to still prioritize rush orders in production. Compared to the basic state, the following changes occur:

(1) The overall utilization is increasing from 87.7% to 95%. In particular, capacity utilization for rush orders increases from 68.5% to 88.3%.
(2) Delivery reliability increases to 100% due to the combination with ConWIP control. Orders are completed slightly earlier on average due to the advance release window.

(3) Average throughput times increase slightly. This is due to the advanced release window, but it has no negative impact on the delivery times.

(4) The effect of the ConWIP control on the variance of throughput times is very small.

The implementation of the ConWIP control is consequently even more important in the presence of rush orders.

Table 1. Results of the simulation experiments

Simulation experiment	Order type	Logistical objectives			
		Delivery compliance	Throughput time		Utilization
			Mean	SD	
Basic state	All Orders	98.7%	2.3 SCD	1.4 SCD	87.7%
	Rush Orders	98.6%	0.3 SCD	0.6 SCD	68.5%
	Standard Orders	98.7%	2.6 SCD	1.3 SCD	92.5%
With ConWIP	All Orders	100%	2.6 SCD	1.4 SCD	95.0%
	Rush Orders	100%	0.7 SCD	0.7 SCD	88.3%
	Standard Orders	100%	3.0 SCD	1.1 SCD	96.7%

SD: Standard Deviation SCD: Shop Calendar Day

5 Summary and Outlook

The presented paper shows how companies can schedule rush orders using a throughput diagram. This procedure enables companies to schedule rush orders, taking backlogs, previous orders and the expected load of open offers into account. Compared to other procedures, rush orders are taken into consideration from the beginning, so that rescheduling is not necessary. In addition, the procedure works with very little information that is already available at an early stage.

In an evaluation we were able to show the general effectiveness of the procedure, especially if it is combined with a ConWIP control. Without a ConWIP control, a very high delivery reliability and short throughput times can be achieved. However, there were losses in capacity utilisation due to a higher than expected proportion of rejected offers for rush orders at short notice.

Yet the advance release window included in the ConWIP control can avoid more than half of these losses and further improve delivery reliability.

Nevertheless, further simulation experiments are necessary to investigate the process in greater detail. For example, it is not yet clear how robust the procedure reacts to deviations in the planning values. For example, the influence of a systematically higher proportion of rush orders, than taken into account, is unclear. The robustness has to be investigated in further simulation studies.

Acknowledgement. The Authors would like to thank Deutsche Forschungsgesellschaft (DFG) for funding the project "Model-based order acceptance and scheduling" (Project No. 405645389).

References

1. Nyhuis, P. (ed.): Aktuellen Herausforderungen der Produktionsplanung und–steuerung mittels Industrie 4.0 begegnen: Studienergebnisse, PZH Verlag, Garbsen (2016)
2. Schilp, J. (ed.): PPS-Report 2021: Studienergebnisse, Fraunhofer Publica, Augsburg (2021). https://doi.org/10.15480/882.4120
3. Trzyna, D., Lödding, H.: Fundamentals of order acceptance and scheduling of rush orders. In: 22nd International Conference on Production Research, ICPR (2013)
4. Trzyna, D.: Modellierung und Steuerung von Eilaufträgen in der Produktion. Hamburg (2015)
5. Bechte, W.: Theory and practice of load-oriented manufacturing control. Int. J. Prod. Res. **26**, 375–395 (1988)
6. Conway, R., Maxwell, W.L., Miller, L.W.: Theory of Scheduling. Addison-Wesley, Reading, Mass. (1967)
7. Nyhuis, P., Wiendahl, H.-P.: Fundamentals of Production Logistics. Springer, Berlin (2009). https://doi.org/10.1007/978-3-540-34211-3
8. Lödding, H., Engehausen, F.: Eilaufträge strategisch einsetzen. Zeitschrift für wirtschaftlichen Fabrikbetrieb **114**, 449–454 (2019). https://doi.org/10.3139/104.112122
9. Zhang, L., Wong, T.N.: An object-coding genetic algorithm for integrated process planning and scheduling. Eur. J. Oper. Res. **244**(2), 434–444 (2015). https://doi.org/10.1016/j.ejor.2015.01.032
10. He, X., Dong, S., Zhao, N.: Research on rush order insertion rescheduling problem under hybrid flow shop based on NSGA-III. Int. J. Prod. Res. **58**(4), 1161–1177 (2020). https://doi.org/10.1080/00207543.2019.1613581
11. Psarommatis, F., Zheng, X., Kiritsis, D.: A two-layer criteria evaluation approach for rescheduling efficiently semi-automated assembly lines with high number of rush orders. Procedia CIRP **97**, 172–177 (2021). https://doi.org/10.1016/j.procir.2020.05.221
12. Li, N., Qiao, F., Ma, Y., Liu, J.: Research on scheduling method for urgent orders based on genetic algorithm. In: 2020 Chinese Automation Congress (CAC), pp. 3933–3938. IEEE (2020). https://doi.org/10.1109/CAC51589.2020.9326759
13. Mezgebe, T.T., Demesure, G., Bril El Haouzi, H., Pannequin, R., Thomas, A.: CoMM: a consensus algorithm for multi-agent-based manufacturing system to deal with perturbation. Int. J. Adv. Manuf. Technol. **105**(9), 3911–3926 (2019). https://doi.org/10.1007/s00170-019-03820-0
14. Kingsman, B.G., Tatsiopoulos, I.P., Hendry, L.C.: A structural methodology for managing manufacturing lead times in make-to-order companies. Eur. J. Oper. Res. **40**(2), 196–209 (1989). https://doi.org/10.1016/0377-2217(89)90330-5
15. Land, M.J.: Cobacabana (control of balance by card-based navigation): a card-based system for job shop control. Int. J. Prod. Econ. **117**(1), 97–103 (2009)
16. Hendry, L., Land, M., Stevenson, M., Gaalman, G.: Investigating implementation issues for workload control (WLC): a comparative case study analysis. Int. J. Prod. Econ. **112**, 452–469 (2008). https://doi.org/10.1016/j.ijpe.2007.05.012
17. Mundt, C., Lödding, H.: Order acceptance and scheduling with a throughput diagram. In: Lalic, B., Majstorovic, V., Marjanovic, U., von Cieminski, G., Romero, D. (eds.) APMS 2020. IAICT, vol. 591, pp. 351–359. Springer, Cham (2020). https://doi.org/10.1007/978-3-030-57993-7_40

Combining Agile Hardware Development with Additive Manufacturing: Implications for a Manufacturing Firm's Business Model

Daniel Omidvarkarjan[1]([✉]), Robin Streuli[2], Omid Maghazei[3], Torbjørn Netland[3], and Mirko Meboldt[4]

[1] Inspire AG, Zurich, Switzerland
omidvarkarjan@inspire.ethz.ch
[2] Turbo Systems Switzerland Ltd., Baden, Switzerland
[3] Department of Management, Technology, and Economics, ETH Zurich D-MTEC, Zurich, Switzerland
[4] Product Development Group Zurich (pdlz), ETH Zürich D-MAVT, Zurich, Switzerland

Abstract. Manufacturing firms are increasingly adopting Agile approaches for the development of physical products. In combination with advanced production technologies such as Additive Manufacturing (AM), Agile offers unprecedented opportunities to cope with increasing uncertainties, risks and complexities involved in hardware development operations. Following the case study method, this paper sets out to investigate the implications of combining Agile hardware development (AHD) and AM for the business model of a high-end manufacturer of photography equipment. A comparison of the business model canvas for plan-driven versus Agile development at the case company revealed that the two approaches featured significant differences, which required adaptations in every building block of the canvas. This study's implications are threefold. First, this study empirically examines the potential of AHD approaches and highlights that the adoption of AHD engages with virtually all organizational functions of a manufacturing firm. Thus, AHD calls for holistic approaches during implementation. Second, this study shows that regular product take-backs are required to account for product iterations becoming frequently outdated. This result implies a closed-loop manufacturing system for operations and supply chain management. Third, this paper discusses strategies for both product design and product take-back processes, which could further enhance companies' AHD operations.

Keywords: Agile hardware development · Additive manufacturing · Business model canvas · Closed-loop manufacturing system

1 Introduction

In recent years, product development has increasingly become more volatile, uncertain, complex, and ambiguous [1]. Popularly abbreviated as VUCA [2], this trend represents a major challenge for many firms in the hardware industry because they are required

© IFIP International Federation for Information Processing 2022
Published by Springer Nature Switzerland AG 2022
D. Y. Kim et al. (Eds.): APMS 2022, IFIP AICT 663, pp. 302–309, 2022.
https://doi.org/10.1007/978-3-031-16407-1_36

to deliver new products with more customer value faster than ever to remain competitive [3]. To cope with such challenges, iterative development approaches have been identified as promising strategies, among which Agile has received remarkable attention from both academics and practitioners [4]. Agile refers to a group of new product development (NPD) methodologies that employ short, iterative development cycles with Scrum being the most widespread framework. The primary goal is to rapidly create customer value while ensuring high responsiveness to change throughout the NPD process [5]. Compared to traditional, plan-driven product development approaches (such as the Stage-Gate and waterfall process), Agile is well suited for highly uncertain and complex contexts, in terms of both technical implementation and customer requirements [5].

Despite being virtually the industry standard in the software industry, Agile hardware development (AHD) is an emerging phenomenon in both research and practice [6]. A recent survey by Atzberger [7] revealed that firms in the manufacturing industry still struggle to fully adopt AHD in their NPD and broader operations. The authors have concluded that, among other barriers, dealing with AHD's hardware-specific restrictions represents the main barrier to AHD adoption. Evidence shows that existing Agile methods from software must be adapted to address the characteristics of hardware product development [8].

One notable context that stands out and has been repeatedly discussed in both research and practice is the integration of Additive Manufacturing (AM) technology in AHD [9, 10]. Originally developed as a technique for rapid prototyping, AM has evolved into a mature manufacturing technology [11]. With its unique technological properties, AM is highly compatible with the iterative development rhythm of AHD. In essence, AM's manufacturing costs are theoretically independent from lot size [12], which makes the flexible production of constantly evolving product designs during AHD economically feasible. Various case studies have shown that an iterative development approach is often suggested for AM products [13] because AM can significantly alter how manufacturing firms create value [14]. For the company Tailored Fits, adopting AM for ski boot production transformed the firm's value creation from hardware manufacturing toward a software-driven, service-centric business model (BM) [15]. This pattern can also be observed in other industries [16].

2 Case Study

Although some studies [9, 10] have provided early empirical insights into the combination of AM and AHD, extant works on the adoption of AHD in manufacturing firms remain few and far between. For example, it is unclear how firms' value chains outside of research and development (R&D) are affected by the implementation of AHD. This paper's main objective is to explore the implications of AHD for a manufacturing firm's BM. This empirical investigation is based on the following case study.

2.1 Case Description

The case company is a small manufacturer of high-end photography equipment from Switzerland, serving a small niche of professionals and wealthy enthusiasts in the field of medium format photography. Its products can be characterized as high-mix, low-volume luxury goods. They are mostly produced with conventional manufacturing technologies (i.e., aluminum milling) together with external partners. The minimum batch sizes required for milling represent a major challenge for the case company because exploratory product ideas can hardly be pursued without a substantial investment. To overcome this barrier, the firm combined AM and AHD for the development of a novel product for an emerging market (in this case, large format videography). As depicted in Fig. 1, the NPD project took place between June 2017 and December 2018 and included three development sprints of four to five weeks each. Within every iteration, the resulting product increment was internally tested by lead customers to acquire user feedback. An initial product release took place after the second iteration. Based on the market feedback, the product was substantially redesigned after 12 months. Selective laser sintering, a polymer-based AM process, was used to produce all development prototypes and final product units. These parts were manufactured by an external partner.

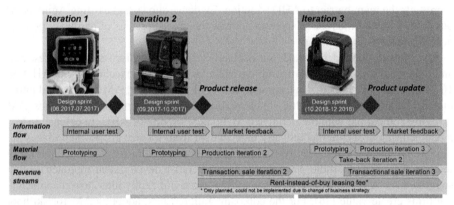

Fig. 1. Overview of the AHD project analyzed within the case study with an idealized illustration of information, material flows, and revenue streams (product photos © ALPA of Switzerland)

2.2   Research Methodology

This study is aimed to compare the BM of products developed with a traditional, plan-driven process to one using the AHD approach at the case company. The business model canvas (BMC) is used as a framework for this comparison. Originally presented by Osterwalder and Pigneur [17], BMC is widely established in practice for the design and visualization of BM. It comprises nine building blocks, which collectively cover the four main areas of BM design (the who, the what, the how, and the why). This standardized structure facilitates comparison among different BM variations and enables the generation of transferable BM patterns [18]. Both of this study's BMCs were created based on 12 interviews and two workshops. These were conducted with firms' managers, including CEO and head of products, as well as firms' suppliers, from March to June 2021. The workshops were structured using the methodology provided by the BMC's creators [18]. Based on the information of the interviews and workshops, the authors created the BMC for both the plan-driven and AHD approach.

3 Results

Table 1 displays the comparison of the two BMCs for the case company, with the traditional, plan-driven process depicted on the left and the AHD approach shown on the right. The results show that the introduction of AHD led to a significant change in almost all the aspects of the firm's BM.

Table 1. Comparison between the BMC for the plan-driven approach and the BMC for AHD.

	Plan-driven development approach	Agile development approach
Customer segments	• Established market (medium format photography) • Variety of customer groups (professionals, enthusiasts, noble amateurs)	• Emerging market (large format videography) • Focus on lead users, early adopters (innovative professionals)
Value proposition	• Longevity, precision, durability • Investment (high reselling value)	• Co-innovation and co-design, customization • Early access to most innovative products
Customer relationship	• Loose relationship after product sale, partly anonymous (not all customers are known)	• Personal and collaborative, even after product sale (direct & constant exchange of feedback, needs for improvement) • Service-centric
Channels	• Various dealers around the world • Direct sales through web shop	• Primarily direct sales • Collaboration with selected video equipment rental houses
Key resources	• Brand recognition • Dealership network	• Internal AM design competence and tools • Network & relationships with lead users, early adopters
Key activities	• Coordination of external R&D and manufacturing resources • Marketing & sales • Quality check, distribution	• Lead user interaction (feedback acquisition) • Internal product development with AM • Quality check, distribution
Key partnerships	• Dealers • Manufacturing and R&D partners	• Lead users • AM supplier
Revenue streams	• Transactional sales (fixed list prices) • Monetization only after end of product development	• Rent-instead-of-buy* (access to most recent product iteration for a leasing fee) • Early monetization already during product development
Cost structure	• High fixed costs, low variable costs, due to large initial lot sizes for conventional manufacturing, and big upfront R&D expenses	• Low fixed costs, high variable costs, due to on-demand manufacturing with AM, and constant R&D expenses for subsequent product iterations

* Only planned, could not be implemented due to change of business strategy

Comparing the *customer segments* of the two BMCs shows that the AHD approach is shifting the focus towards delivering solutions to a narrow group of highly innovative lead users and early adopters. Furthermore, the AHD project's overall product field (i.e., large format videography) is more dynamic and uncertain than the established market covered by the plan-driven approach (i.e., medium format photography).

The shift in focus is also reflected in terms of *value proposition*—set against the conventional BM with its emphasis on longevity, precision, and durability, the AHD approach is much more tailored to providing lead customers with early access to the most innovative products, including those that have yet to be fully matured. For this particular product field (i.e., high-end videography), having access to the most recent technology and innovations represents a unique selling proposition to differentiate early adopters from their competitors. As such, the case company's lead customers are ready to accept a product that does not constitute a fully robust solution and are even willing to pay a premium to access the product earlier than other potential users. Moreover, the AHD approach offers customers the opportunity to co-innovate and co-design a product for their individual needs because they can drive development by providing user feedback. For instance, the case company included an active cooling solution in the third iteration specifically based on several customers' feedback.

This shift in value proposition also manifests itself in *customer relationships*; by keeping close contact with its customers via direct and frequent exchange of user feedback, the firm established a more personal and collaborative relationship compared to the conventional, plan-driven approach. To enable such a closed feedback loop, the firm was required to move its channels from dealerships toward direct sales. Instead of relying on a large network of individual dealers, the firm recognized the need for direct communication channels with its customers and few selected partners (in this case, video equipment rental houses). Such selected partners would not only support the sales process but also could forward the user feedback they received from the customers to the case company's R&D department.

In terms of *key resources, activities, and partnerships*, the AHD approach, with its user-centric and iterative nature, revolved around acquiring customer feedback and implementation through in-house engineering in subsequent product iterations rather than order fulfillment in the plan-driven approach. Therefore, ensuring access to those lead users and building up the required internal R&D capabilities (i.e., competence in AM design) was of great importance for the case company.

Regarding *revenue streams*, the firm recognized the need to move from classical, transactional sales to a rent-instead-of-buy business model. Because an updated physical product increment is frequently released in short intervals, customers are less willing to purchase each given iteration than they otherwise would be out of fear that it will soon be outdated. To overcome this challenge, the firm initially planned to introduce a leasing fee for which customers would gain access to the most recent iteration (i.e., rent-instead-of-buy). This idea was not implemented in the case company due to a change of business strategy concerning the product's priority. Nevertheless, the early product release provided the firm with the early opportunity to monetize the product during the development process.

In terms of *cost structure*, the plan-driven approach of fully developing a product up front and pre-producing large batches with conventional manufacturing technologies incurs high fixed costs and low variable costs for the case company. Instead, the combination of AHD and AM resulted in low fixed costs and high variable costs. Although low fixed cost was enabled by AM, and thus reduced initial, up-front investment in the stock through on-demand production of small lot sizes, the frequent development iterations increased variable R&D expenses.

4 Discussion

The comparison between the plan-driven approach and the AHD approach in our case study shows that the adoption of AHD in combination with AM has major consequences for a manufacturing firm's BM. In every dimension of the BMC, the introduction of both factors led to a substantial change in BM design for the case company. To the best of our knowledge, this is the first paper to report detailed empirical evidence regarding the combination of AHD and AM in an industrial context. The findings imply that AHD cannot be implemented within only R&D. In contrast, the adoption must be coordinated among all of a firm's organizational functions.

In addition to the required adaptations in BM design, the case study revealed other implications of AHD adoption for operations and supply chain management. When a new product iteration is released to the market, the previously distributed version becomes outdated. For many products and industries, it would be advised to take back outdated iterations through reverse logistics. For instance, this may prevent customers from acting as resellers on secondary gray markets. The case company recognized that its material flows needed to be adapted toward a closed-loop manufacturing system to account for this frequent take-back of physical products. Establishing such a closed loop system is receiving more attention in manufacturing companies, beyond AHD [19]. Many firms consider closed loop manufacturing as part of their strategies related to sustainable and environmental initiatives. Nevertheless, some studies have shown that applying this concept to physical products is still associated with several challenges, such as costly manual disassembly processes, high changeover times, and inefficient use of resources [19]. This study helped the case company identify two potential strategies to enable the efficient take-back of outdated physical product versions within the scope of an AHD project. First, introducing a *high degree of product modularity* allows for updating and exchanging of single components or features without taking back the entire product system. This strategy is highly compatible with AM because its geometrical freedom can be used to freely introduce modularity through flexible hardware interfaces. The case company isolated, for instance, major parts of the electronics in a modular carrier, allowing them to flexibly reconfigure and update the components if needed. Second, product take-back can primarily be steered using *interaction with the customer through BM design* [20]. In particular, the case study suggests that applying a rent-instead-of-buy BM could reinforce product take-back processes. Through such a BM, customers would be obliged to exchange outdated predecessors for updated product versions by shipping them back to the firm.

5 Conclusion and Future Research

This paper investigates the implications of combining AHD and AM in the context of a high-end photography equipment manufacturer. The comparison of the BMC for the plan-driven versus AHD approach revealed that the adoption of AHD causes fundamental changes in the firm's BM, requiring an adaptation in every building block of the BMC. Furthermore, this paper foregrounds the need for closed-loop manufacturing systems to account for regular take-backs due to constantly evolving product iterations. This study shows that AHD could be further enhanced when carried out in tandem with all organizational functions through holistic approaches. Finally, this research discusses strategies for product design and product take-back processes, which could enhance AHD operations.

This paper's main limitation is related to its single case study design. Further research is needed to validate and expand the results in contexts other than the one studied in this paper (i.e., high-end photography with small-scale operations while using AM as the main production technology). By doing so, the interplay of the AHD approach with a firm's product strategy could be better understood, especially when short demand cycles are present. Moreover, a quantitative assessment of AHD's potential versus that of plan-driven approaches provides a promising research direction for future scholars.

References

1. Ciric, D., Lalic, B., Gracanin, D., Palcic, I., Zivlak, N.: Agile project management in new product development and innovation processes: challenges and benefits beyond software domain. In: 2018 IEEE International Symposium on Innovation and Entrepreneurship (TEMS-ISIE), Beijing, 30/03/2018–01/04/2018, pp. 1–9. IEEE (2018). https://doi.org/10.1109/TEMS-ISIE. 2018.8478461
2. Bennett, N., Lemoine, G.J.: What a difference a word makes: understanding threats to performance in a VUCA world. Bus. Horiz. **57**, 311–317 (2014). https://doi.org/10.1016/j.bus hor.2014.01.001
3. Sommer, A.F., Hedegaard, C., Dukovska-Popovska, I., Steger-Jensen, K.: Improved product development performance through Agile/stage-gate hybrids: the next-generation stage-gate process? Res. Technol. Manag. **58**, 34–45 (2015). https://doi.org/10.5437/08956308X580 1236
4. Ovesen, N.: The challenges of becoming Agile: Implementing and conducting Scrum in integrated product development. PhD Dissertation, Department of Architecture and Design, Aalborg University (2012)
5. Boehm, B.W., Turner, R.: Balancing Agility and Discipline. A Guide for the Perplexed. Addison-Wesley, Boston (2004)
6. Bohmer, A.I., Hugger, P., Lindemann, U.: Scrum within hardware development insights of the application of scrum for the development of a passive exoskeleton. In: 2017 International Conference on Engineering, Technology and Innovation (ICE/ITMC), Funchal, 27/06/2017–29/06/2017, pp. 790–798. IEEE (2017). https://doi.org/10.1109/ICE.2017.8279965
7. Atzberger, A., Nicklas, S.J., Schrof, J., Weiss, S., Paetzold, K.: Agile Entwicklung physischer Produkte. Universitätsbibliothek der Universität der Bundeswehr München, Neubiberg (2020)
8. Schmidt, T.S., Atzberger, A., Gerling, C., Schrof, J., Weiss, S., Paetzold, K.: Agile Development of Physical Products. An Empirical Study about Potentials, Transition and Applicability. Universitätsbibliothek der Universität der Bundeswehr München, Neubiberg (2019)
9. Montero, J., Atzberger, A., Bleckmann, M., Holtmannspotter, J., Paetzold, K.: Enhancing the additive manufacturing process for spare parts by applying Agile hardware development principles. In: 2019 IEEE 10th International Conference, pp. 109–116. IEEE (2019). https://doi.org/10.1109/ICMIMT.2019.8712045

10. Reichwein, J., Vogel, S., Schork, S., Kirchner, E.: On the applicability of Agile development methods to design for additive manufacturing. Procedia CIRP **91**, 653–658 (2020). https://doi.org/10.1016/j.procir.2020.03.112
11. Wohlers Associates: Wohlers report 2020. 3D printing and additive manufacturing: Global state of the industry. Wohlers Associates, Fort Collins (2020)
12. Ruffo, M., Tuck, C., Hague, R.: Cost estimation for rapid manufacturing–laser sintering production for low to medium volumes. In: Proceedings of the Institution of Mechanical Engineers, Part B: Journal of Engineering Manufacture (2006). https://doi.org/10.1243/09544054JEM517
13. Klahn, C., Meboldt, M., Fontana, F., Leutenecker-Twelsiek, B., Omidvarkarjan, D., Jansen, J.: Entwicklung und Konstruktion für die Additive Fertigung. Grundlagen und Methoden für den Einsatz in industriellen Endprodukten, 2nd edn. Vogel Communications Group & Co. KG, Würzburg (2021)
14. Fontana, F., Klahn, C., Meboldt, M.: Value-driven clustering of industrial additive manufacturing applications. JMTM **30**, 366–390 (2019). https://doi.org/10.1108/JMTM-06-2018-0167
15. Biedermann, M., Meboldt, M.: Swiss AM Guide 2018: Exploring new applications in additive manufacturing. AM Network, Zurich (2018)
16. Basso, M., et al.: An additive manufacturing breakthrough: a how-to guide for scaling and overcoming key challenges, World Economy Forum, Cologny (2022)
17. Osterwalder, A., Pigneur, Y.: Business Model Generation. Wiley-VCH, Weinheim (2010)
18. Gassmann, O., Frankenberger, K., Choudury, M.: The Business Model Navigator. The Strategies Behind the Most Successful Companies. Pearson, Harlow, England (2020)
19. Bockholt, M.T., et al.: Changeable closed-loop manufacturing systems: a case study of challenges in product take-back. In: Lalic, B., Majstorovic, V., Marjanovic, U., von Cieminski, G., Romero, D. (eds.) APMS 2020. IAICT, vol. 592, pp. 758–766. Springer, Cham (2020). https://doi.org/10.1007/978-3-030-57997-5_87
20. Uhrenholt, J.N., Kristensen, J.H., Rincón, M.C., Jensen, S.F., Waehrens, B.V.: Circular economy: factors affecting the financial performance of product take-back systems. J. Clean. Prod. 335, art. 130319, (2022). https://doi.org/10.1016/j.jclepro.2021.130319

Effects of Multiple Depots on Total Travel Distance in Parallel-Aisle Manual Order Picking Systems

Thao Huong Tran-Vo[1], Thuy Mo Nguyen[2], and Soondo Hong[2(✉)]

[1] Major in Industrial Data Science and Engineering, Department of Industrial Engineering,
Pusan National University, Busan 46241, Korea
[2] Department of Industrial Engineering, Pusan National University, Busan 46241, Korea
soondo.hong@pusan.ac.kr

Abstract. This study introduces an order batching problem in a parallel-aisle warehouse system with multiple depots. In such a system, orders are organized into batches for picking and these batches are distributed across multiple depots, where pickers receive batch-specific picking information and unload all picked items after each trip. We formulate the problem using a mixed-integer linear programming model with the objective of minimizing the total travel distance while ensuring the workload balance among depots. Then, on small-scale instances, we also conduct several experiments to validate the model and to investigate how using multiple depots affects warehouse performance in terms of total travel distance. The results show that multi-depot order picking systems outperform single-depot systems in saving the total travel distance, and the performance can be enhanced by properly defining depot locations.

Keywords: Order picking system · Order batching · Multiple depots · MILP ·
Total travel distance

1 Introduction

The order-picking problem has been considered as one of the most important factors in improving warehouse productivity since this area can consume as much as 60% of a warehouse's total operating cost [1]. Pickers receive picking information from a depot, travel along pre-determined routes to retrieve items, then bring them back to the same depot before downstream workers inspect and package the orders. Pickers, in practical, often combine orders into batches to reduce the number of travel trips as well as to shorten the total travel distance, which is known as an NP-hard problem [2]. The target order picking system (OPS) in this study is a one-block parallel-aisle warehouse. We consider the one-way S-shape routing method which is the most popular in practice and may be helpful to avoid aisle congestion [3, 4].

Integrated picking operations have recently drawn high attention [5], in that warehouse layout design is also considered as a component [6]. Most previous studies were

D. Y. Kim et al. (Eds.): APMS 2022, IFIP AICT 663, pp. 310–318, 2022.
https://doi.org/10.1007/978-3-031-16407-1_37

conducted under the assumption that there is only one depot location, which may lead to congestion and become a bottleneck of the whole warehouse process of picking and its downstream operations. Recently the multi-depot model has been widely used in real manual warehouses to cope with this problem. Operating multiple depots may reduce the waiting time for loading containers and unloading picked items at depots, shorten the completion time, and thus have a high ability to enhance customer service. When using the multi-depot model, the workload balancing among depots must also be considered to achieve high performance in terms of time reduction.

For these aforementioned motivations, in this study, we *first* develop a new order batching problem with multiple depots (MDOB) under the objective of minimizing total travel distance. We present a formulation of MDOB using a mixed-integer linear programming model to find exact solutions for small-scale problems. *Second*, we run several experiments to assess the impact of using multiple depots in order picking systems in terms of total travel distance.

The remaining of this paper is structured as follows: Sect. 2 defines the multi-depot order batching problem and its assumptions. Section 3 proposes the mathematical model of the problem. An example of problem's solution, the small-instance experimental design, and computational results to analyze the impact of multiple depots on travel distance are described and discussed in Sect. 4. Finally, Sect. 5 concludes and makes recommendations for future research.

2   Problem Definition

2.1   Problem Statement

In this study, we consider an OPS with parallel aisles and two cross aisles at the front and the back of parallel aisles. Each parallel aisle has two aisle sides with the same number of item storage locations per side. Several depots are assumed to be in front of parallel aisles. Figure 1 displays a model with six one-way parallel aisles with ten storage locations per aisle side, and there are two depots in the middle of the front cross aisle. The depot workload balance is also necessary to be considered to ensure that all operated depots have a similar amount of work. As customers' shopping habits have changed from ordering large amounts with less variety of items to ordering smaller amounts with more variety of items [3], we focus on the OPS whose order size is 1~3 items.

A batch contains a set of orders picked in a single route. In this study, we assume that pickers apply the sort-while-pick strategy [3, 7] in the picking process, i.e., the capacity of each batch is measured by the number of orders that can be assigned into a batch. Pickers receive batch information from one depot, travel following the assigned route to collect all items of orders in that batch, then return to the same depot for conducting inspection and packaging. Pickers do not need to travel every aisle but if they enter an aisle, they must pass through all of it, following the one-way S-shape routing method. This study is conducted under the assumptions that travel time only depends on travel distance, as pickers' walking speed and picking time are unchanged; and blocking within aisles is also ignored.

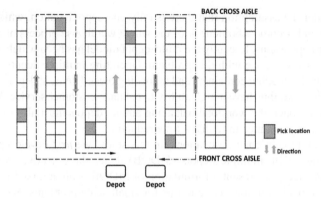

Fig. 1. Multi-depot order picking problem in a six-aisle OPS

2.2 Route Length Calculation

We denote L_a and W_a as the length and width of an aisle, n_{va} as the number of aisles visited by a picker; s and e be the starting aisle and ending aisle passed through by the picker with the route. The length L of the whole route including assigned depot d is:

$$L = L_a n_{va} + W_a(e - s) + W_a(|d - e| + |d - s|) \tag{1}$$

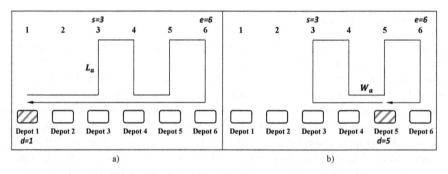

Fig. 2. Routing method in six-parallel-aisle OPS

Considering the routing method for a six parallel-aisle system as shown in Fig. 2 with $L_a = 15$ and $W_a = 3$. The total number of combinations of 12 within-aisle routes and 6 depots is 12*6 = 72. We consider the same route which enters aisle 3 ($s = 3$), travels through aisle 4, 5, and exits at the end of aisle 6 ($e = 6$). If it is combined with depot $d = 1$ (Fig. 2a), the length of the whole route will be $L = 15 * 4 + 3 * (6 - 3) + 3 * (|1 - 6| + |1 - 3|) = 90$, while combined with depot $d = 5$ (Fig. 2b) the length is $L = 15 * 4 + 3 * (6 - 3) + 3 * (|5 - 6| + |5 - 3|) = 78$ units of distance. As a result of this finding, selecting the appropriate depot for each picking trip has the potential to considerably shorten trip length.

3 Mathematical Formulation

We formulate MDOB problem as a mixed-integer linear programming model (MILP), where decision variables answer following questions: which orders are combined into a batch; and which route (including depot) is used to retrieve all the items of orders assigned into a batch. The initial number of batches is set equal to the number of orders to allow the worst case that every single order holds a separate batch. The set of routes and their travel distance when combined with each depot follows the definition given by Eq. (1).

The objective of this study is to minimize the total travel distance to retrieve all orders but still ensure the depot-workload balance. To do that, we set only "total travel distance minimizing" as the prime optimal objective, whereas "workload balancing" is considered as a constraint by setting a lower bound to the amount of workload at each depot. As the depot workload in this study is measured by the number of batches assigned to a depot, its lower bound (w) is the required minimum number of batches on each depot to make workload balance and is defined by the average integer number of batches per depot under the assumption that all batches reach the full capacity.

$$ w = \left\lfloor \frac{\text{total number of orders}}{\text{cart capacity} \times \text{number of depots}} \right\rfloor \tag{2} $$

Indices and parameters:

A = the set of aisles a.

D = the set of operated depots d.

R = the set of routes r.

O = the set of orders o.

B = the set of batches b.

L_{rd} = the length of route r with depot d.

C = the capacity of a cart.

$$ P_{oa} = \begin{cases} 1, \text{if order } o \text{ has at least one pick on aisle } a \\ 0, \text{ otherwise} \end{cases} $$

$$ V_{ra} = \begin{cases} 1, \text{if route } r \text{ visits aisle } a \\ 0, \text{ otherwise} \end{cases} $$

w = the minimum number of batches on each depot.

Decision variables:

$$ X_{ob} = \begin{cases} 1, \text{if order } o \text{ is assigned into batch } b \\ 0, \text{ otherwise} \end{cases} $$

$$ Y_{brd} = \begin{cases} 1, \text{ if batch b takes route r and depot d} \\ 0, \text{ otherwise} \end{cases} $$

$$ (MDOB)min \sum_{b \in B} \sum_{d \in D} \sum_{r \in R} L_{rd} Y_{brd} \tag{3} $$

Subject to:

$$ \sum_{b \in B} X_{ob} = 1, \quad \forall o \in O \tag{4} $$

$$X_{ob} \leq X_{bb}, \quad \forall o \in O, b \in B \tag{5}$$

$$\sum_{o \in O} X_{ob} \leq C, \quad \forall b \in B \tag{6}$$

$$\sum_{d \in D} \sum_{r \in R} Y_{brd} = X_{bb}, \quad \forall b \in B \tag{7}$$

$$X_{ob} P_{oa} \leq \sum_{d \in D} \sum_{r \in R} V_{ra} Y_{brd}, \quad \forall a \in A, b \in B, o \in O \tag{8}$$

$$\sum_{b \in B} \sum_{r \in R} Y_{brd} \geq w, \quad \forall d \in D \tag{9}$$

$$X_{ob}, Y_{brd} \in \{0, 1\}, \quad \forall o \in O, b \in B, r \in R, d \in D \tag{10}$$

The objective function (3) aims to minimize the total travel distance for picking all orders. Constraints (4) ensure that each order is assigned into one batch. Constraints (5) ensure that an order is assigned into a batch only when that batch is active (a batch is indexed by a specific order inside it). Constraints (6) limit the number of orders of each batch. Constraints (7) and (8) choose the route and depot for each batch so that all orders assigned to that batch can be picked. Constraints (9) ensure that the workloads among depots are balanced.

4   Experimental Results and Discussions

In this section, we present a small-scale solution example to help explain the considered problem and validate the proposed model. Then we conduct experiments on various small instances to investigate the effects of multi-depot application on the total travel distance. All experiments are set under some common parameters. We consider two configurations of an OPS with random storage policy, which are 6- and 8-parallel-aisle systems. The length and width of an aisle are 15 and 3 distance units. There are 30 picking locations on each aisle side. The number of one-way S-shape routes with the number of aisles equating to 6 and 8 are 12 and 33 routes, respectively [7]. The number of items per order is uniformly distributed (U[1, 3]). We implement our experiments using the Python API for IBM ILOG CPLEX Optimization Studio 20.1 on a Windows 10 Pro 64-bit server system with Intel(R) Core (TM) i5–10400 CPU @ 2.90 GHz and 16 GB memory.

4.1 A Small-Scale Solution

Table 1 shows the result of a small-size problem on the 6-aisle case in which depot 3 and depot 4 are operated (as illustrated in Fig. 1). The number of picking orders is 20 and the capacity is set at 3 orders per batch. An order picking information is represented by its relationship with aisle (e.g. [1, 1, 0, 0, 0, 0] depicts the order with picking locations belong to aisle 1 and aisle 2).

Table 1. An example of a small-size solution

Batch	Route	Depot	Orders	Distance
1	[1,1,1,0,0,1]	4	([0,1,1,0,0,1],[1,0,0,0,0,0],[0,0,1,0,0,1])	90
2	[0,0,1,1,0,0]	4	([0,0,0,1,0,0],[0,0,1,0,0,0],[0,0,0,1,0,0])	36
3	[0,0,1,1,0,0]	4	([0,0,1,0,0,0],[0,0,1,0,0,0],[0,0,1,0,0,0])	36
4	[0,0,0,0,1,1]	4	([0,0,0,0,0,1],[0,0,0,0,1,0])	42
5	[1,1,0,0,0,0]	3	([1,1,0,0,0,0],[0,1,0,0,0,0],[0,1,0,0,0,0])	42
6	[1,1,1,1,0,0]	3	([0,1,0,1,0,0],[1,0,0,0,0,0],[0,1,1,0,0,0])	78
7	[1,0,0,1,1,1]	3	([0,0,0,1,1,0],[0,0,0,1,1,0],[1,0,0,0,1,1])	90
			Total Travel Distance	**414**

As shown in the result, the optimal solution tries to fulfill a batch's capacity (6 full-capacity batches and only one two-order batch) and assign a best-fit route for all batches. The workloads between two depots are also balanced with 3 batches assigned to Depot 3 and 4 batches assigned to Depot 4. The optimal total travel distance of this problem is 414 units of distance.

4.2 Effects of Multiple Depots on Total Travel Distance

Single-depot and Dual-depot Systems. First, we aim to compare the performances between single-depot and dual-depot (two operated depots) situations by conducting experiments on several different configurations of MDOB with the capacity of each pick tour is equal to 3 orders. Each experiment consists of 20 randomly generated instances and the experiment result is represented by the average value of these instances. The average travel distance per order is used as the measurement for easily comparison. Figure 3 shows the results of four system configurations, in that D1, D2, ..., D8 denote the location of a depot by the index of the corresponding aisle. In each configuration, the diagonal cells (thick-border cells) are the results of the cases using only a single depot (e.g., D1-D1 is the situation of using only Depot 1), while the others are the results of operating two corresponding depots simultaneously. The index color demonstrates the performance comparison, in which the brighter color index indicates a better performance (i.e., the average travel distances are shorter) and vice versa.

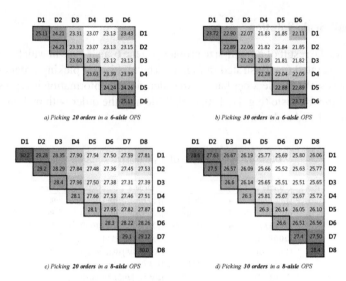

a) Picking **20 orders** in a **6-aisle** OPS   b) Picking **30 orders** in a **6-aisle** OPS

c) Picking **20 orders** in a **8-aisle** OPS   d) Picking **30 orders** in a **8-aisle** OPS

Fig. 3. Single-depot and dual-depot experimental results

For single-depot cases, the results show that travel distance is shortened when the depot location is closer the center of the front cross aisle, which is consistent with the conclusions of previous studies on single depot location [7]. The dual-depot application generally obtains better results than single-depot cases in all four configurations in terms of shortening travel distance. The best result of dual-depot cases can save 2.1~3.3% of the average travel distance on each order compared to the best result of single-depot cases. It leads to the opportunity of improving the problem performance by choosing the best proper locations of operated depots. However, these results also depict that combining the first and the last depot or combining two central depots is not a good choice for reducing travel distance.

Multi-depot Systems. We further investigate the effect of increasing the number of depots on the total travel distance by conducting experiments of picking 30 orders on the 6-aisle and 8-aisle systems with various cases of the number of depots. For each case, we investigate all the possible combinations of depots and the representing result for each combination is the average value of 20 randomly generated instances. The statistical results of these experiments are presented in Fig. 4 observably prove that using multiple depots significantly reduces the travel distance per order as well as the total travel distance compared to using only one depot. But for considered systems in this study in which depots are equipped in front of every aisle (i.e., the number of depots is equal to the number of aisles), the results show that if the number of depots is larger than a half of the number of aisles then operating more depots will not gain more advantages in saving the total travel distance. Besides, most of the outline points from multi-depot cases come from the combinations which include depots at farthest aisles. This emphasizes again that combining edge depots will not yield good performance.

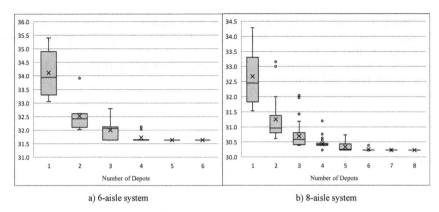

a) 6-aisle system   b) 8-aisle system

Fig. 4. Effect of the number of depots on the total travel distance

5   Conclusions

This study introduces a new order picking problem with multiple depots (MDOB) in that batching, routing, and depot-workload balancing processes are integrated. Orders are grouped into batches then each batch is assigned on a suitable combination of one route and one depot so that the total travel distance to retrieve all orders is minimized while the numbers of batches processed by selected depots are balanced. The concept of depots' workload balancing is expected to give good performance when combined with minimizing travel distances. The problem was formulated by a MILP model. Our experiments on small instances depict that operating a proper number of parallel depots does not only take advantage of reducing the completion time and bottleneck prevention but also gives positive effects on significantly shortening the total travel distance. These results are expected to lay the foundation for many interesting research topics on multi-depot warehouses in the future, particularly large-scale problems and the problem of defining the number of operated depots to achieve the best performance.

Acknowledgment. This work was supported by the National Research Foundation of Korea (NRF) grant funded by the Korean Government (MSIT) (No. NRF-2020R1A2C2004320).

References

1. Drury, J., Turnbull, B.: Towards more efficient order picking. Institute of Logistics (1988)
2. Gademann, N., Velde, S.: Order batching to minimize total travel time in a parallel-aisle warehouse. IIE Trans. **37**(1), 63–75 (2005)
3. De Koster, R., Le-Duc, T., Roodbergen, K.J.: Design and control of warehouse order picking: a literature review. Eur. J. Oper. Res. **182**(2), 481–501 (2007)
4. Hong, S., Kim, Y.: A route-selecting order batching model with the S-shape routes in a parallel-aisle order picking system. Eur. J. Oper. Res. **257**(1), 185–196 (2017)
5. Van Gils, T., Ramaekers, K., Caris, A., de Koster, R.B.M.: Designing efficient order picking systems by combining planning problems: state-of-the-art classification and review. Eur. J. Oper. Res. **267**(1), 1–15 (2018)

6. Cergibozan, Ç., Tasan, A.S.: Order batching operations: an overview of classification, solution techniques, and future research. J. Intell. Manuf. **30**(1), 335–349 (2016). https://doi.org/10.1007/s10845-016-1248-4
7. Hong, S., Johnson, A.L., Peters, B.A.: Large-scale order batching in parallel-aisle picking systems. IIE Trans. **44**(2), 88–106 (2012)

Service Systems Design, Engineering and Management

Towards Adaptable Customer Segments and Reference Geometries

Greta Tjaden[1]([⊠])[iD], Anne Meyer[2][iD], and Alexandru Rinciog[2][iD]

[1] TRUMPF SE + Co. KG, Ditzingen, Germany
greta.tjaden@trumpf.com
[2] TU Dortmund University, Dortmund, Germany
{anne2.meyer,alexandru.rinciog}@tu-dortmund.de

Abstract. For all activities along the product lifecycle, a company should know its (possible) customers. The sheet metal tool manufacturer TRUMPF uses static customer segments and representative sheets with part geometries. Dynamic and use case-specific customer segments and geometries are missing. To overcome these shortcomings, we develop a novel framework for adaptable customer segments and reference geometries: We detail the limitations of the current approach and review literature delineating the research gap. We identify use cases covering the product lifecycle and define requirements for a software system to generate adaptable customer segments and reference geometries.

Keywords: Product life cycle management · Customer segmentation · Reference geometries · Sheet metal processing

1 Introduction

Companies must understand their customers to design products and services according to their needs and preferences. This also applies to TRUMPF SE + Co. KG (TRUMPF), a German manufacturer of machine tools for sheet metal processing. TRUMPF's product portfolio covers the most important production steps in sheet metal processing, including laser cutting, bending, punching, and automation components. Sheet metal products are utilized in engineering, automotive, electrical industry, and many more.

TRUMPF uses customer segments and benchmark sheets to provide detailed knowledge about customers and the products they manufacture. Several departments at TRUMPF use individual, static customer segments that vary in terms of the number of segments, underlying data, and considered parameters. These co-existing customer segments indicate the need for use case-specific customer segments. To compare the performance of 2D laser machines, several benchmark sheets have been developed at TRUMPF. Representative geometries have been placed on these sheets depending on the geometries' complexity and the sheet thickness. The placement of geometries on sheets is called *nesting*.

© IFIP International Federation for Information Processing 2022
Published by Springer Nature Switzerland AG 2022
D. Y. Kim et al. (Eds.): APMS 2022, IFIP AICT 663, pp. 321–328, 2022.
https://doi.org/10.1007/978-3-031-16407-1_38

As the customers and their production requirements change over time, these static approaches are not sufficient. Both in practice and research, there is a demand for dynamic, data-driven techniques for the identification of customer segments and knowledge about their production. To overcome the limitations of the current approaches, we propose a software system for the data-based generation of adaptable customer segments and reference geometries that cover the relevant production steps of sheet metal processing. The major difference between reference geometries and the previously mentioned benchmark sheets is the flexibility. While the benchmark sheets consist of standard-sized sheets with certain sheet thicknesses, the reference geometries will not be limited by these factors. The aim is to represent the majority of the customers' jobs, consisting of customer geometries.

Our contribution is fourfold: (1) We analyze the limitation of the current static approaches of describing who the customers are and what they do. (2) We discuss relevant work and define the research gap, following the typical phases of product life cycle management (PLM). (3) We identify use cases for three different areas in our cross-functional workshop at TRUMPF. The results of this workshop let us expect improvements along the product life cycle. (4) We derive system requirements for generating adaptable customer segments and reference geometries on an up-to-date database, using TRUMPF use cases as an example.

The paper's structure closely follows these contributions: Sect. 2 describes the problem, Sect. 3 surveys the related work, while Sect. 4 describes the TRUMPF use cases and their requirements. In Sect. 5, we provide our conclusions together with a brief outlook.

2   Problem Description

To align activities to customer needs, we need to answer two questions, namely "which customers do we address?", and "what do the addressed customers do?".

The addressed customers vary depending on the use case. We identified three issues with TRUMPF's current static, department-specific customer segments.

Firstly, department-specific customer segments are generated in a time-consuming process. As such, segments are not tailored to particular use cases and are static over time. The absence of up-to-date information can hinder the work of the teams. Furthermore, several departments do much of the same work independently, which constitutes a waste of resources.

Secondly, the existing customer segments do not distinguish between customers with repetitive, long-term orders and those with small lot sizes and almost no repetition. The differing nature of the customers' orders results in different customer requirements.

To prepare the production, geometries are nested on sheets. Nesting can be optimized, for instance, to minimize material waste. Customers with repetitive, long-term orders usually benefit from nesting optimization. In contrast, for customers with little to no repetition, the cost and effort of the nesting optimization usually exceed their benefits.

We hope to solve these issues with a data-driven method for dynamically generating customer segments considering use case-specific requirements.

We can derive relevant requirements for a customer's production from their production organization, their geometries, and how often these geometries repeat. Up to now, TRUMPF has been using benchmark sheets to represent customer geometries. For their development, geometries and nested sheets from customers were analyzed in 2009 to determine the typical concentration of cutting meters depending on the sheet thickness. This work resulted in eight benchmark sheets, providing exemplary geometries with three different degrees of part complexities, nested on standard-sized sheets with sheet thicknesses between 1 and 4 mm, between 4 and 10 mm, and greater than 10 mm.

Since the benchmark sheets are static, the production times of experiments carried out ten years ago can be compared with experiments carried out today. However, the static nature of the benchmark sheets and the focus on the comparability of 2D laser cutting machines lead to the following problems:

1. **Missing Dynamics:** The technical development since their creation has not been captured. An update of the benchmark sheets on current data is time-consuming and costly and would still not cover other technologies.
2. **Limited Scope:** The benchmark sheets only cover one production step (cutting). To allow for a holistic view of customer production, single geometries that cover the most relevant production steps are needed.
3. **Inflexibility:** Related external influences like lot sizes and repetition factors should be incorporated. For instance, questions regarding the optimal combination of machines and automation components for a customer's order spectrum cannot be answered. Instead, numerous sheet sizes and geometries must be considered.

All in all, the benchmark sheets help compare the performance of laser cutting machines. However, they are ill-suited for the assessment of a portfolio, to help customers find the best machine park and hall layout for their orders, or to support development tasks by providing additional information. Adaptable reference geometries could solve the issues and challenges listed above.

3 Related Work

In this section, we review related literature. First, we look at data-driven methods for dynamic customer segmentation in product lifecycle management. Then, we scrutinize the B2B sector's use of customer segmentation. Lastly, we check how the sheet metal industry uses reference geometries.

3.1 Data-Driven Methods for PLM

PLM covers the whole journey of a product, starting with its creation and closing with its degradation. The cycle is usually divided into Beginning of Life (BOL),

Middle of Life (MOL), and End of Life (EOL), e.g. [4,12]. We found literature for BOL for the three sections *market analysis, product development,* and *product manufacturing.* For MOL, the literature covers *sales & distribution,* and *repair.* Our search revealed no data-driven PLM work related to EOL.

BOL: The applications of data-driven methods during *market analysis* include customer identification and customer requirement specification [10,11]. Based on the results of these methods, product features and characteristics, e.g. [11,12], as well as product quality requirements, e.g. [10], can be derived. The authors of [10] introduce data-driven approaches as tools for establishing a customer-centered *product development* practice. Many argue that *product manufacturing* can benefit from data-driven methods, e.g. [4,10,12]. Real-time-schedulers enable the optimization of the production plan but need representative production plans for the training and test phases, e.g. [10]. Information about the customer orders may fill the data gap for such a real-time scheduler. Further applications include simulation and testing [4] and optimization of the supply chain network [12].

MOL: In [11], the authors use customer segmentation as a data-driven method application for *sales & distribution.* Stormi et al. introduce customer segmentation for sales prediction in [9]. The literature dealing with the *repair* section focuses on data-driven applications within the field of predictive maintenance, e.g. [12], and anomaly detection [12]. Grouping customers by common geometry attributes—which implies similar wear of machines—and linking these groups to a maintenance history could help to improve maintenance.

The literature shows that data-driven and adaptable customer segments are important at multiple stages in PLM. Independently from individual phases, the need for an information management system along the whole PLM is stressed, e.g. in [8].

3.2   Customer Segmentation

Clustering customers into similar groups is called customer segmentation and enables customer-specific actions like marketing activities or development projects. However, the literature's focus lies with the B2C market fields and not primarily on B2B, to which sheet metal processing belongs. To the best of our knowledge, sheet metal processing is not yet covered in the literature.

The authors of [9] try to map B2C approaches to B2B, focusing on the market basket analysis, classification, and the Recency, Frequency, Monetary (RFM) model. The RFM value of a customer is calculated based on the determined values for recency (date of the last purchase), frequency (amount of purchases), and monetary (e.g. average purchase monetary value). The RFM model has also been applied with K-means clustering [2] and K-Medoids [5]. The authors of [3] use the Length, Recency, Frequency, Monetary (LRFM) model, which additionally considers the length of the relationship with the customer, to derive marketing strategies from customer segments in the B2B context. They note that the quality of the segments can be increased by considering multiple customer characteristics. Rivera et al. criticize the RFM model, saying it can be confusing

[6]. To make the traditional RFM model more suitable for the B2B context, they use a time-series clustering technique and topological data analysis to forecast the customer segments' demand.

The authors of [9] name customer characteristics suitable for the B2B context, such as purchase behavior, product preferences, frequency, and customer firmographics. The customer purchase behavior and customer value are mentioned in [3]. Simkin et al. similarly identify typical traits of the agrichemical industry, namely product group, location, and business sector, but note that these are not sufficient for creating meaningful customer segments. Additional attributes describing the customers, their needs, their buying behavior, and their decision-making reasoning are required [7].

The literature discussed above proves that customer segmentation is feasible for the B2B context, and provides potential characteristics for distinguishing customers. However, these features alone are not sufficient to alleviate the problem presented in Sect. 2.

3.3   Reference Geometries

We found [1] it to be the only application of reference geometries in literature. Here, the authors use benchmark sheets similar to those at TRUMPF to optimize the layout of a sheet metal processing plant using simulation. Since the considered plant has a lot of repeating sheets, the selection of five of their sheets of varying thicknesses was deemed sufficient for the simulation study. The work does not elaborate on the exact sheet selection mechanism. The authors' approach suffers from the missing dynamics (1), limited scope (2), and inflexibility (3) caveats listed in Sect. 2. Consequently, the highly volatile production of many different, customer-specific geometries with decreasing lot sizes cannot be covered. Instead, the method's applicability is limited to a production setup characterized by reoccurring geometries and sheets using static nesting configurations.

4   Towards Adaptable Customer Segments and Reference Geometries

We want to tackle the problems described in Sect. 2 with a software system that generates adaptable customer segments and reference geometries. The core difference between our proposal and existing approaches is the adaptability to changing use case requirements and databases. We introduce reference geometries as geometries that represent typical orders for customers or customer groups and can be flexibly nested on all types of sheets.

4.1   Use Cases at TRUMPF

The different use cases for customer segments and reference geometries identified at TRUMPF share the need to answer questions based on data, raising the demand for a dynamic approach. We conducted a cross-functional workshop and identified three areas as most relevant for adaptable customer segments and reference geometries: Research & Development, Product & Portfolio Management, and Sales & Consulting.

Research & Development works on the development of new products and the improvement of features of existing ones. In PLM, it covers applications from both BOL and MOL. Extensive knowledge about geometries and edge cases is required, where edge cases represent unusual and above-average complex geometries. This expertise would allow distributing development capacity better.

Moreover, fine-grained availability and understanding of data would accelerate the development of machine learning methods for both services and products. Examples include the training of a real-time scheduler and an algorithm-assisted sorting of produced geometries.

Product & Portfolio Management concentrates on BOL but stands responsible for the entire PLM. This area aims for an economically successful portfolio of products and services. It also decides on further developments, additions, and deletions from the portfolio. Customer segments that are adaptable to the specific use cases like "customers that have a specific machine", "customers that do not use any automation components", or "differentiation of all customers" pave the way for customer segment-centric developments and decisions. Currently, product management is missing a reliable, data-based distinction between regularly used machine functions and those used only on a minority of geometries. This information is required for efficiently using the capacities for further product and service developments. Either the entirety or a focus group of customers could be segmented, and reference geometries with the desired characteristics could be selected, providing more fine-grained information.

Sales & Consulting focus on the distribution of products and services as well as the optimization of existing systems and hence, relate to MOL. In customer projects, they try to balance—beyond others—the contradicting key performance indicators (KPIs) cost per part, throughput, lead time, and delivery reliability. To calculate and weigh these KPIs, fine-grained data about the customers and their production is necessary. Adaptable customer segments in combination with reference geometries may accelerate comparing customers with certain characteristics, supporting these Sales & Consulting activities.

Within the last years, the industry's focus shifted from isolated machines to a holistic view of the production. Since the entirety of the production process affects the listed KPIs, customers need consultation on solutions as a whole, covering machines, automation components, services, and software. Such a perspective requires detailed knowledge about the customer. Reference geometries would allow for a fine-grained production process consideration, leading to better recommendations for overall customer productivity improvement. Adaptable customer segments would enable the assessment of the customer development within their segment and between segments.

4.2 Requirements

In this section, we define the requirements for a software system for the generation of adaptable customer segments and reference geometries on up-to-date data. We derived these requirements from the identified use cases and the reviewed literature. The most important requirement we derive is the adaptability of the customer segments and reference geometries. We further specify this as: **(1) Use case specificity:** The users must be able to select the relevant characteristics and weigh them for their specific use case. **(2) Freeze points:** To observe the development of products and customers over time, freeze points must be introduced to make certain customer segments and reference geometries static at fixed points in time. **(3) Dynamic updatability:** To have up-to-date decision databases, automatic updates of customer segments and reference geometries must be possible, whenever new data are available.

A second important aspect is the accessibility of customer and geometry data. These data are immensely sensitive, and without a convincing concept, customers will hesitate to share them. The software system should fulfill the following requirements: **(4) Confidentiality:** Legal restrictions and non-disclosure agreements must be considered. **(5) Stable decision base:** Upon request of a customer, the deletion of data must be possible (see Confidentiality), while the decision base or a description of the data must stay available to ensure transparency of past decisions in the future. **(6) Format compatibility:** The system must cover a wide range of data formats and types, especially for describing geometries. **(7) Data transfer:** Of course, a safe and continuous data transfer must be established.

To ensure a high user acceptance of the software system, the following requirements should be met: **(8) Understandability:** The adaptable customer segments and reference geometries must be applicable and understandable irrespective of the technical background of the users. **(9) Verifiable Validity:** System users are to be enabled to assess the trustworthiness of the generated customer segments and reference geometries.

5 Conclusion and Outlook

This paper lays down the challenges of describing customers and their activities in the B2B sector in general, and sheet metal processing in particular. We argue that a software system to generate adaptable customer segments and reference geometries can help meet these challenges. Both customer segmentation and reference geometries can be used independently or linked together.

We identified use cases along the product life cycle: Adaptable customer segments and reference geometries help Research & Development to accelerate the development of products and services tailored to the customers and better handle edge cases; Product & Portfolio Management can distribute and use its capacities more efficiently; Sales & Consulting can better cope with the perspective shift to a holistic view of the production processes.

Building upon a literature review and the use cases obtained through the cross-functional workshop at TRUMPF, we derived requirements for such a software system. We specified adaptability as use case specificity, freeze points, and dynamic updatability. To gain access to the data, we must ensure confidentiality, data deletion, format compatibility, and data transfer. The generation approach must be understandable and have a verifiable validity.

Future work needs to focus more on the exact features describing customers and geometries. In our next steps, we will analyze the data necessary to describe the customers and the reference geometries in detail. Using the results of this analysis, we will endeavor to bridge the gap between data already being collected and data required for the adaptable generation of customer segments and reference geometries. Lastly, we will implement minimum viable products to enhance the understanding of the most relevant use cases and their facets.

References

1. Deokar, A.Y., Bavdhankar, A.M., Degaonkar, R.R., Sardar, V.B., Rajhans, N.: Simulation and optimization of layout of sheet metal manufacturing plant (2016)
2. Hosseini, M., Shabani, M.: New approach to customer segmentation based on changes in customer value. J. Mark. Anal. 3(3), 110–121 (2015)
3. Kandeil, D.A., Saad, A.A., Youssef, S.M.: A two-phase clustering analysis for B2B customer segmentation. In: 2014 International Conference on Intelligent Networking and Collaborative Systems, pp. 221–228. IEEE (2014)
4. Li, J., Tao, F., Cheng, Y., Zhao, L.: Big data in product lifecycle management. Int. J. Adv. Manuf. Technol. 81(1), 667–684 (2015)
5. Maulina, N.R., Surjandari, I., Rus, A.M.M.: Data mining approach for customer segmentation in B2B settings using centroid-based clustering. In: 2019 16th International Conference on Service Systems and Service Management (ICSSSM), pp. 1–6 (2019)
6. Rivera-Castro, R., Pilyugina, P., Pletnev, A., Maksimov, I., Wyz, W., Burnaev, E.: Topological data analysis of time series data for B2B customer relationship management. CoRR abs/1906.03956 (2019)
7. Simkin, L.: Achieving market segmentation from B2B sectorisation. J. Bus. Ind. Mark. (2008)
8. Srinivasan, V.: Open standards for product lifecycle management, January 2021
9. Stormi, K., Laine, T., Elomaa, T.: Feasibility of B2C customer relationship analytics in the B2B industrial context (2018)
10. Tao, F., Qi, Q., Liu, A., Kusiak, A.: Data-driven smart manufacturing. J. Manuf. Syst. 48, 157–169 (2018)
11. Wang, L., Liu, Z., Liu, A., Tao, F.: Artificial intelligence in product lifecycle management. Int. J. Adv. Manuf. Technol., 1–26 (2021)
12. Zhang, Y., Ren, S., Liu, Y., Sakao, T., Huisingh, D.: A framework for big data driven product lifecycle management. J. Clean. Prod. 159, 229–240 (2017)

Digitalization of Services for Volunteers in Non-profit Organization

Mike Freitag[1]([✉]) [ID] and Oliver Hämmerle[2]

[1] Fraunhofer Institute for Industrial Engineering IAO, Nobelstr. 12, 70569 Stuttgart, Germany
mike.freitag@iao.fraunhofer.de
[2] Institut für Arbeitswirtschaft und Technologiemanagement IAT, University of Stuttgart, Stuttgart, Germany
oliver.haemmerle@iao.fraunhofer.de

Abstract. Non-profit organizations are also impacted by the digital transformation, and should pursue it systematically. To this end, this paper presents and describes a process model for transformation. This process model focuses specifically on the use of digital tools with strong involvement of volunteers. The process model is based on the service engineering and design thinking approaches, and supports the collaborative, interactive cooperation of volunteers. The process model was validated in the use case of volunteers at a German engineering society. This use case highlights the fact that volunteers would like to see a video conferencing tool used above all else. In addition, there is a call for greater involvement of young volunteers, for example via their own apps or forums.

Keywords: Virtual service engineering · Digital transformation · Smart services · Social entrepreneurship · Virtual volunteering · Public innovation

1 Introduction

The digital transformation has far-reaching effects on the work and organizational processes of the future. This affects not only traditional production and service companies, but also non-profit organizations (NPOs)—for instance, associations, foundations and unions.

Several studies now exist [1–5] on the status and development of digitalization in non-profit organizations in Germany. These studies set out in general terms the empirically determined status of the use of digital technologies and the identified need for change in terms of digital transformation. For example, the IW Consult study [6], in which more than 250 representatives from non-profit organizations were surveyed, confirms the major importance of digitalization for non-profit organizations. 80 percent consider it to be very important or somewhat important. At the same time, however, only slightly more than a quarter of the organizations surveyed felt well-prepared to reap the benefits of digital transformation.

© IFIP International Federation for Information Processing 2022
Published by Springer Nature Switzerland AG 2022
D. Y. Kim et al. (Eds.): APMS 2022, IFIP AICT 663, pp. 329–334, 2022.
https://doi.org/10.1007/978-3-031-16407-1_39

Also the concepts of»social entrepreneurship« and»social business models« has also been widely studied, as a literature search revealed [2, 5, 7]. Especially the Digital-Report of»Haus des Stiftens« [2] in 2020 had to be mentioned here.

This paper offers a procedural approach and addresses the use of digital tools by volunteers at non-profit organizations [8]. It begins with a brief description of the conceptual process model of»Volunteering Service Engineering« and then it presents the results of a survey conducted by the»VDI Württembergischer Ingenieurverein« (Society of Engineers in Stuttgart, Germany) on»Virtual Volunteering« which is assigned to the first steps of this conceptual process model. The paper is concluded with a brief summary in Sect. 3.

2   Volunteering Service Engineering

The focus here is on the generation of new digital offers and interface management between core staff and volunteers. The aim is to ensure the participatory involvement of volunteers in the digital transformation of NPOs. The process model in Fig. 1 shows the key steps in introducing smart services for volunteers in non-profit organizations. The process model is a combination of the service engineering approach [9–14] and design thinking [15]. It focuses on the structured involvement of volunteers in the service development process. The knowledge and experience gained in service engineering can be transferred in simplified form, and adapted if required.

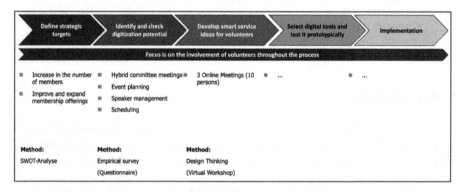

Fig. 1. Process model

The first step is to define the strategic objective of the non-profit organization, for example, an increase in the target group of volunteers, engaging younger members, or increasing digital support for volunteer work [1, 3, 5]. In the second step, the potential for digitalization—for instance by means of surveys or workshops—is identified and reviewed within the NPO. Next, the ideas for Smart Services for Volunteers are brought together and reviewed as to their suitability for the non-profit organization [2–4, 16]. In the fourth step, the selected ideas are implemented and tested as prototypes using digital tools. This is done through subscriptions to online cloud services or the use of open-source tools, for example. The final step is to scale the selected tool, and ensure that all volunteers are qualified to use it. Throughout the process, the focus is on involving volunteers [2, 16–19].

Selected results of quantitative data collected from volunteers at an engineering society in Stuttgart, Germany are described below. The survey of 850 volunteers was used to identify and analyze the NPO's potential for digitalization. This quantitative analysis is to be assigned to process step 2 and 3. The central question is therefore which smart services are suitable for NPO.

2.1 Virtual Volunteering – on the Way to a Digital Future at the VDI Württembergischer Ingenieurverein e.V.

The process model described above was also implemented at the VDI. During **step 1**, strategic goals were defined as part of a workshop. Two key issues emerged here: increasing appeal among young students or professionals and fostering online collaboration and networking during the Covid-19 pandemic. Based on these findings, **step 2 and step 3** of the process model involved the quantitative data collection and analysis of a total of 30 questions, answered by a total of 845 members of an engineering society in the Stuttgart region [20]. 7% of the respondents were students, 4% were employed for max. 4 years, 66% were employed for more than 4 years and 20% were no longer employed.

Configuration of a smartphone app was identified as an important way for VDI members to network and subscribe to information. This would give VDI members the opportunity to read contributions from other members and to publish their own contributions. Figure 2 shows how highly the respondents rated the benefits of such an app.

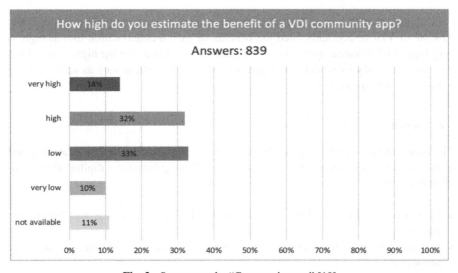

Fig. 2. Survey results "Community app" [19]

As well as providing information on events that can be selected at any time, the app should also allow users to network with one another. In addition, push messages should be customizable. 46% of all VDI respondents rated the benefits of a VDI community app as high to very high. This proportion is particularly pronounced among students and young professionals at 64%, 44% of whom rated the benefit as very high.

Digital offers can also pave the way for joint workshops and simplify the management of collaborative projects. For example, volunteers with varying expertise could develop and implement such projects together by way of a digital Wiki platform. Figure 3 shows how highly the respondents rated the benefits of such a collaboration tool.

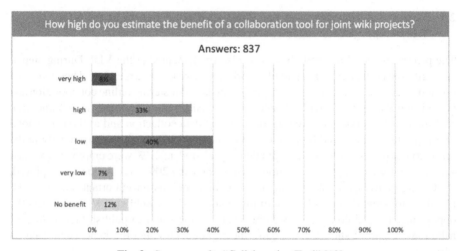

Fig. 3. Survey results "Collaboration Tool" [19]

Collaborative work via a VDI platform is viewed as an interesting option in principle. 41% of all VDI respondents rated the benefits of such a collaboration tool as high to very high. Collaborative work via a VDI platform is rated as having high to very high benefits, especially by students and young professionals, and is seen as an interesting option with anticipated benefits.

2.2 Findings

The needs and requirements of volunteer members can be identified by analyzing and assessing the data collected. For example, the following beneficial digital offers were identified [20]:

- Design of hybrid committee meetings that combine face-to-face and live online meetings
- Self-services for volunteers in event planning and event promotion via email and newsletter
- Possibility of joint digital workshops

The volunteer VDI members surveyed see hybrid committee meetings that combine face-to-face and live online meetings as beneficial. However, the quality of participation in discussions, and reciprocal perception in online participation, should be similar to that of a purely face-to-face committee meeting. There is also a desire for self-services for volunteers in event planning and event application. Furthermore, the volunteers considered the option of conducting digital workshops to be helpful.

3 Summary

To successfully shape the digital transformation of non-profit organizations, it is important to use a strategy and process model for transformation in order to inform, mobilize and involve members in a purposeful manner. In particular, a targeted approach, i.e. one that is people-related and low-threshold, needs to be intensified. The process model presented focuses specifically on the use of digital tools with strong involvement of volunteers. The process model is based on the service engineering and design thinking approaches, and supports the collaborative, interactive cooperation of volunteers. The process model was validated in the use case of volunteers from an engineering society in the Stuttgart region. In summary, it can be said that the status quo of digitalization in the»virtual volunteering« area was recorded in detail. Thanks to the survey conducted at VDI Württembergischer Ingenieurverein, important needs for action were identified. Thus, volunteers at VDI Württembergischer Ingenieurverein primarily favor the use of a video conferencing tool. This allows volunteers to participate both online and face-to-face. In addition, there is a call for greater involvement of young volunteers, for example via their own apps or forums.

References

1. Dufft, N., Kreutter, P.: Digitalisierung in non-profit-organisationen: strategie, Kultur und Kompetenzen im digitalen Wandel. In: Berndt, R., Kreutter, P., Stolte, S. (eds.) Zukunftsorientiertes Stiftungsmanagement, pp. 105–115. Springer, Wiesbaden (2018). https://doi.org/10.1007/978-3-658-19267-9_9
2. Haus des Stiftens (2020): Digital-Report 2020, Non-Profits & IT, abgerufen am, 30 March 2022. unter. https://www.hausdesstiftens.org/wp-content/uploads/Digital-Report-2020.pdf
3. Reiser, B.: Organisatoren des Gemeinwohls. Über die Beteiligung Ehrenamtlicher am Organisationsgeschehen. In: BdW Blätter der Wohlfahrtspflege, vol. 164, no. 2, pp. 67–69 (2017)
4. Simsa, R., Meyer, M., Badelt, C. (eds.): Handbuch der Nonprofit-Organisation: Strukturen und Management, Schäffer-Poeschel (2013)
5. Eimhjellen, I., Steen-Johnsen, K., Folkestad, B., Ødegård, G.: Changing patterns of volunteering and participation. In: Enjolras, B., Strømsnes, K. (eds.) Scandinavian Civil Society and Social Transformations. Nonprofit and Civil Society Studies, pp. 25–65. Springer, Cham (2018). https://doi.org/10.1007/978-3-319-77264-6_2
6. IW Consult (2018): Digitalisierung in NGOs. Eine Vermessung des Digitalisierungsstands von NGOs in Deutschland. Abgerufen am: 30.02.2022 unte. https://www.iwconsult.de/filead min/user_upload/projekte/2018/Digital_Atlas/Digitalisierung_in_NGOs.pdf
7. Jabłoński, A., Jabłoński, M.: Social Business Models in the Digital Economy. Palgrave Macmillan, Cham (2020). https://doi.org/10.1007/978-3-030-29732-9

8. Freitag, M.: Studie Digitale Transformation von Non-Profit-Organisationen–Status quo und Handlungsbedarfe. Fraunhofer IAO, Stuttgart (2021)
9. Meyer, K. (2020): Vom Service Engineering zum Social Service Engineering–Anforderungen an die Schnittstelle zwischen Dienstleistungsentwicklung und Arbeitswissenschaft. Zeitschrift für Arbeitswissenschaft **74**(1), 52–58
10. Yamakami, T.: Servicenics approach: a social service engineering framework. In: Eighth International Conference on Digital Information Management (ICDIM 2013), pp. 358–362. IEEE (2013)
11. Freitag, M., Schiller, C.: Approach to test a product-service system during service engineering. Procedia CIRP **64**, 336–339 (2017)
12. Freitag, M., Westner, P., Schiller, C., Nunez, M.J., Gigante, F., Berbegal, S.: Agile product-service design with VR-technology: a use case in the furniture industry. Procedia CIRP **73**, 114–119 (2018)
13. Freitag, M., Hämmerle, O.: Agile guideline for development of smart services in manufacturing enterprises with support of artificial intelligence. In: Lalic, B., Majstorovic, V., Marjanovic, U., von Cieminski, G., Romero, D. (eds.) Advances in Production Management Systems. The Path to Digital Transformation and Innovation of Production Management Systems. APMS 2020. IFIP Advances in Information and Communication Technology, vol. 591, pp. 645–652. Springer, Cham (2020). https://doi.org/10.1007/978-3-030-57993-7_73
14. Freitag, M., Schiller, C., Hämmerle, O.: Guideline to develop smart service business models for small and medium sized enterprises. In: Dolgui, A., Bernard, A., Lemoine, D., von Cieminski, G., Romero, D. (eds.) APMS 2021. IAICT, vol. 634, pp. 369–375. Springer, Cham (2021). https://doi.org/10.1007/978-3-030-85914-5_39
15. Plattner, H., Meinel, C.; Weinberg, U.: Design-thinking. Landsberg am Lech: Mi-Fachverlag (2009)
16. Falkner, J., Kett, H., Castor, J.: Ein Leitfaden–Smarte Produkte und Dienstleistungen. Wie Sie als Entscheider Schritt für Schritt ins Thema einsteigen. Mittelstand 4.0 Kompetenzzentrum, Fraunhofer Verlag, Stuttgart (2020)
17. Qu, M., Yu, S., Chen, D., Chu, J., Tian, B.: State-of-the-art of design, evaluation, and operation methodologies in product service systems. Comput. Ind. (2016)
18. Ojasalo, J., Ojasalo, K.: Using service logic business model canvas in lean service development. In: Gummesson, E., Mele, C., Polese, F. (eds.) Service Dominant Logic, Network and Systems Theory and Service Science: Integrating three Perspectives for a New Service Agenda. Naples: Conference Proceedings 5th Naples Forum on Service (2016)
19. Pezzotta, G., Pirola, F., Pinto, R., Akasaka, F., Shimomura, Y.: A service engineering framework to design and assess an integrated product-service. Mechatronics 169–179 (2015)
20. Gutmann, O., Schäfer, P.-M.: Auf dem Weg in eine digitale Zukunft–Erfahrungen des VDI Württembergischer Ingenieurverein e.V. In: Studie Digitale Transformation von Non-Profit-Organisationen–Status quo und Handlungsbedarfe, Stuttgart, Fraunhofer IAO, pp. 17–26 (2021)

Reference Model for Product-Service Systems with an Use Case from the Plating Industry

Christian Schiller[1]([⊠]), Mike Freitag[1] [ID], Alexander Leiden[3] [ID],
Christoph Herrmann[3] [ID], Alexander Gorovoj[2], Patric Hering[4], and Sascha Hering[4]

[1] Fraunhofer Institute for Industrial Engineering IAO, Nobelstr. 12, 70569 Stuttgart, Germany
christian.schiller@iao.fraunhofer.de
[2] Institut für Arbeitswirtschaft und Technologiemanagement IAT, Universität Stuttgart,
Nobelstraße 12, 70569 Stuttgart, Germany
[3] Chair of Sustainable Manufacturing and Life Cycle Engineering, Institut of Machine Tools
and Production Technology (IWF), Technische Universität Braunschweig, Langer Kamp 19b,
38106 Braunschweig, Germany
[4] Airtec Mueku GmbH, Im Ganzacker 1, 56479 Elsoff-Mittelhofen, Germany

Abstract. In recent years, digitalization has affected more and more industries to an increasing extent. As a result, new approaches to develop innovative service offers are becoming increasingly relevant. In the article at hand, a reference framework for the development of product-service systems is presented and validated by way of an application example. The reference framework has five levels, which cover both the cyber-physical production system and smart service. Each of the five levels is made up of six development steps, going from the early development phase of target group definition through to the integration of the finished solution. The reference framework thus combines elements of Smart Service Lifecycle Management and the CRISP DM data mining model.

Keywords: Product-service systems · Smart service · Service business model · Cyber-physical production system · Service lifecycle management · Service engineering · SME

1 Introduction

For years, advances in digitalization have provided more and more opportunities for the further development of physical products into cyber-physical systems that can communicate with other products and with the internet, and enable the provision of new services [1]. The smart Product Service Systems (sPSS) created in this way offer a whole new range of potential in terms of value creation, such as the provision of data-based and intelligent services, which are also known as smart services [2]. Characteristic for such systems is their customer-oriented solution approach aimed at generating genuine added value for individual users [3]. They are also characterized by a high degree of complexity, dynamism and their multi-dimensional nature [4].

D. Y. Kim et al. (Eds.): APMS 2022, IFIP AICT 663, pp. 335–342, 2022.
https://doi.org/10.1007/978-3-031-16407-1_40

One of the key benefits of smart services is that they enable a significant improvement in customer engagement. This allows for much better anticipation of customer requirements and more targeted and efficient use of the company's own resources [5]. Smart services also give providers the opportunity to expand their service portfolio and create new business models [6].

However, the development of smart services still poses significant challenges for companies. For instance, in a recent business survey, 55% of companies indicated a need for support in developing new smart services [7]. 53% needed support in developing appropriate business models. Well-defined development processes to help develop smart systems are also desired by many companies, but are not commonplace as yet [8]. As a potential solution approach, this publication presents a six-stage reference framework for the development and configuration of new smart services. After a theoretical derivation and presentation of the approach, it is validated by means of an application example and put into practice. The approach presented was developed as part of a research project on electroplating and therefore focuses on this topic.

2   Procedure Model for the Product-Service System

To support the development and configuration of product-service systems, a six-level reference framework was developed, which in turn was broken down into five individual layers (Fig. 1). The inner four layers describe the cyber-physical production system (CPPS) of the electroplating plant (introduced in [9] and [10]) and the outer layer describes the surrounding service by way of service engineering [11–13]. The layers also indicate the degree or the state of the digital transformation of a product-service system. The dots here show the layers affected in the current development step. The reference framework combines elements of Smart Service Life Cycle Management and the CRISP DM model [14], thus bringing together the two spheres of service and CPPS in one reference framework. A detailed presentation of this reference framework can be found in Leiden et al. [15]. Only a brief description is provided in this paper.

The physical system, i.e. the corresponding elements of the electroplating plant, constitutes the core of the system. From this, data are collected in the second layer by means of sensors. These data are analyzed in the next layer of the cyber system, in either a data-based or model-based manner. The decision-support layer represents the transition to service: at this point, interaction between people and IT systems begins. These systems must be made appealing to users through appropriate forms of visualization, so as to achieve a high level of acceptance. The final layer is the service, which builds on the previous layers and incorporates the requirements from operations into the service.

As well as providing methodological support for the development of smart services, the reference framework can measure the current extent of their digital transformation. Upon assessment, the more layers a user can cover with their systems, the more advanced the current status of their digital transformation.

In the following, the individual steps of the reference framework are explained in detail from both a service and CPPS perspective, and the special features are presented.

Definition of the target group (1) During the first step, the customer target group is defined. Who will the new smart service and the corresponding business model address?

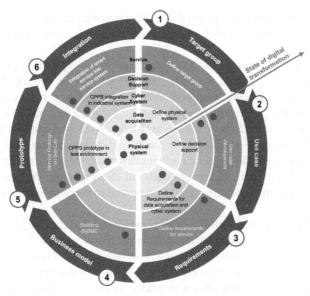

Fig. 1. Reference framework for the development of product-service systems (based on [15]).

According to Osterwalder and Pigneur [16], it is necessary to differentiate between target groups if their needs require and justify an individual offer. Can they be reached through different distribution channels, do they require different relationship types, do they have significantly different levels of profitability, or are they willing to pay for different aspects of an offer? In electroplating, depending on the service concept, a distinction can be made, for example, between in-house and contract electroplating or between small, medium and large companies. Further target group definitions can be made in terms of the respective company's liquidity or in the differentiation between "makers" and "outsourcers" (make-or-buy decision). The physical system in question is derived from the target group, as it is highly dependent on it. For example, larger companies with series production require completely different equipment than small, highly flexible contract electroplating shops. While in the case of the former, the focus is on integration into the production system that is as efficient as possible and fits into the cycle time, contract electroplating requires adaptable systems that can easily adapt to meet current needs with the least possible effort.

Development of the use case (2) The second step requires the establishment of a specific use case for the previously defined target group. It should outline how the service has been provided to date (if already in place), how often it has been provided, and what the targets are. In addition, one or more unique selling points of the existing business model idea need to be clarified. This step also involves defining the specific value proposition. The benefits to the customer of the new or enhanced smart service are clarified, along with the specific customer problems that can be solved. The use case and the value proposition also result in the requirements for decision support and thus the interface with the CPPS. At this early stage, the requirements from the service can be translated very easily into the CPPS environment. In particular, if mixed reality approaches are to be used for decision support in view of a smart augmented reality service, the specific features of these technologies [17] must be given appropriate consideration during this step.

Definition of requirements (3) Based on the previous steps, the requirements from the service and CPPS point of view are finalized in order to develop the prototype. The methods to be used in the cyber system are determined and, if necessary, different variants for the prototypes are proposed. The decision to use a data-based or model-based approach significantly affects the requirements for data collection systems. Thus, the data collection system must be designed accordingly and its integration within existing IT systems must be ensured. This is particularly important with regard to the final integration step, as the IT systems can differ enormously. In electroplating, the plant technology and related IT are highly operator-specific compared to other industries (e.g. machine tools).

Business modeling (4) A well-developed business model is an important part of complete service engineering, and the starting point for the subsequent integration process [18]. Thanks to its easy-to-follow structure, Osterwalder & Pigneur's business model canvas [16] is of particular interest, especially for start-ups and smaller companies. An added advantage is that a defined business model canvas can be further developed into a service business model canvas at any time, if required, and if sufficient data are available.

Development of a prototype (5) The aim is to develop the smart service. A smart service like this is designed and developed step by step using service engineering [2]. During the process, the product, process and resource model of a smart service are first designed and prototyped. The prototype is then tested in a test environment at a Technical Readiness Level (TRL) [19] of four to five [20]. To this end, the CPPS is fully set up as a prototype in an appropriate test environment, e.g. on a research partner's site. Either the same test environment can be used for the service, or a separate one, allowing the services to be evaluated in a particularly simple way. However, when using different test environments, it must be ensured that the environments are appropriately compatible and that the interfaces between the CPPS and service sphere can be tested intensively. If no test environment is available, productive systems at customer sites may also be used. However, it should be noted that the systems to be tested are still in development and if they are used by the customer directly, they risk jeopardizing acceptance among potential customers given that the systems are not yet functional.

Integration of the Smart Service (6) The final step in the procedure is the integration of the developed Smart Services within the operational systems. The service is integrated within the process landscape of the parties involved, and appropriate resources are provided. The basis is the business model developed to this end during the previous step. The CPPS is transferred from the prototype system to operational IT systems and installed at the customer's site. Any additional hardware that may be required will be introduced along with the corresponding software. The decisive factor compared to the prototype system is the achievement of a high TRL of between 8 and 9. This usually involves more testing of the hardware and software systems to be used, but ensures that the system is ready for use.

3   Use Case from the Electroplating Industry

In this chapter, part of the approach presented above is validated by means of a use case together with the German company Airtec Mueku GmbH. The company in the use case described is a supplier of exhaust air purification technologies, which are used, among other things, in electroplating. The aim is to add digital components to the classic service portfolio, thus enhancing value creation.

The first step in the reference framework is to define the target group. In the use case presented, there is a major interface with the second step, i.e. the development and scope of the use case. This is specifically due to the fact that there was no deviation in the target group from the existing product portfolio. Rather, the focus was on extending the business model, which ultimately characterizes the use case. Additional service offers for existing customers are intended to increase sales and enhance customer satisfaction. In addition, building customer loyalty is a key feature of the new digitally-supported offer. Extending the business model to include further target groups is not the main focus. Instead, increased and more targeted use of data, as well as the use of augmented reality and other remote solutions are intended to achieve, among other things, better planning capability and resource efficiency, optimized spare parts management and optimized error analysis. This affords the customer increased machine availability and a higher level of safety. In addition, positive effects can be expected in terms of CO_2 emissions. Furthermore, the provider's performance becomes more transparent for the customer, bringing clear benefits for both parties.

During the third step of the reference framework, the requirements for the product-service system to be developed are defined. In the context of this publication, the focus is on eliciting the requirements for the business model. In principle, several approaches may be considered in order to back up the use case outlined above with a business model. For instance, performance-based payment, usage-based payment, subscription models, guaranteed availability or external condition monitoring could be considered. The corresponding business model approaches were reviewed and analyzed as part of a customer survey. The analysis revealed a clear preference among customers for external condition monitoring combined with predictive maintenance.

Once requirements have been elicited, business modeling is used to substantiate the use case. The four-step procedure to develop a business model for small and medium-sized enterprises (SMEs) from [21] was used as a guide. Unfortunately, the substantiated business model cannot be presented here.

At the time of writing, the use case has reached the fifth step of the reference framework, i.e. development of the prototype for the new product-service system and the associated smart service. To this end, three scenarios were developed and visualized with the aid of process models. The process models were created using the Service Blueprinting method, as the customer perspective is particularly emphasized here. The design of the processes was based closely on the results of the customer survey (see step three of the use case). In addition, several workshops were held with the managing director, the service director, representatives from marketing, and experts from service engineering to finalize the processes.

The respective scenarios address the different levels of willingness to pay among various customer groups. Thus, a distinction is made between cost-focused, standard-focused and quality-focused customers. Both the costs and the scope of service provision differ in each case. The first scenario addresses more cost-conscious customers and offers only a basic package of services and digital technologies. The second scenario is focused on standard customers and has extensive use of technologies for service delivery. In particular, the use of AR technology plays a role here. The third scenario is the most cost-intensive. In return, there is an even more intensive use of digital technologies and service delivery here. This also makes it possible to significantly extend the warranty of the machines compared with the first two scenarios (Fig. 2).

	Scenario 1	Scenario 2	Scenario 3
Low-priced for the customer	+++	++	+
Scope of service delivery	+	++	+++
Customer support	++	+++	+++
Warranty	++	++	+++
Digital technologies available	+	++	+++

Fig. 2. Differentiation of the different scenarios.

The process models also form the basis for the development of the resource model. With its help, it is possible to calculate as accurately as possible the human, intangible and material resources required to successfully deliver the new solution.

The integration of the Smart Service as step six of the reference framework will occur at a later stage in the project.

4   Summary

In the context of this publication, a six-step reference framework for the development of new smart services was first presented. This comprises five layers, where the inner four layers represent the cyber-physical production system of an electroplating plant, and the outer layer represents the surrounding service. As such, this combines elements of Smart Service Lifecycle Management and the CRISP DM model. Not only does the reference framework provide methodological support to develop smart services, it also allows companies to measure the extent of their digital transformation. As the number of layers covered in the model increases, so does the system's degree of digitalization. When developing the reference framework, specific attention was also paid to practical applicability for SMEs.

In the second part of the publication, the reference framework is put into practice. The company from the use case produces peripheral systems for the electroplating industry, and would like to build better, more regular relationships with existing customers, perform remote diagnostics, intensify data usage, and optimize sales by means of a digitalized service offer. With the help of the reference framework, it was possible to develop a promising solution concept that can be tailored to several customer types, each with different requirements in terms of quality and cost. This new solution has not yet been put into practice but the integration is planned in the near future. Consequently, a final assessment of the reference framework presented for the case at hand is still pending but is expected soon.

Acknowledgements. This work has been partly funded by the German Federal Minis-try of Education and Research (BMBF) through the Project "SmARtPlaS (No. 02K18D112). The authors wish to acknowledge the Commission, the Ministry and all the project partners for their contribution.

References

1. Abramovici, M. (Hrsg.): Engineering smarter Produkte und Services, Plattform Industrie 4.0 Studie, acatech–Deutsche Akademie der Technikwissenschaften, München (2018)
2. Freitag, M., Hämmerle, O.: Die Entwicklung von Smart Services im Maschinen-und Anlagenbau: Ein Leitfaden. Fraunhofer IAO, Stuttgart (2021)
3. Maleki, E., Belkadi, F., Bernard, A.: A meta-model for product-service system based on systems engineering approach. Procedia CIRP **73**, 39–44 (2018). https://doi.org/10.1016/j. procir.2018.04.016
4. Kuhlenkötter, B., et al.: New perspectives for generating smart PSS solutions–life cycle, methodologies and transformation. Procedia CIRP **64**, 217–222 (2017). https://doi.org/10. 1016/j.procir.2017.03.036
5. acatech (Hrsg.), Smart Service Welt. Umsetzungsempfehlungen für das Zukunftsprojekt Inter-netbasierte Dienste für die Wirtschaft. Abschlussbericht. Acatech–Deutsche Akademie der Technikwissenschaften, München (2015)
6. Bullinger, H.J., Ganz, W., Neuhüttler, J.: Smart services–Chancen und Herausforderungen digitalisierter Dienstleistungssysteme für Unternehmen. In: Bruhn, M., Hadwich, K. (eds.) Dienstleistungen 4.0. Springer Gabler, Wiesbaden (2017). https://doi.org/10.1007/978-3-658-17550-4_4
7. Meiren, T., Friedrich, M., Schiller, C.: Smart Services–Mit digital unterstützten Dienstleis-tungen in die Zukunft. Studie. Fraunhofer IAO, Stuttgart (2021)
8. Friedrich, M., Schiller, C.: Smarte Produkt-Service-Systeme–Eine Bestandsaufnahme unter deutschen Unternehmen. Studie. Fraunhofer IAO, Stuttgart (2022)
9. Leiden, A., Herrmann, C., Thiede, S.: Cyber-physical production system approach for energy and resource efficient planning and operation of plating process chains. J. Clean. Prod. 125160 (2020)
10. Leiden, A., Kölle, S., Thiede, S., Schmid, K., Metzner, M., Herrmann, C.: Model-based analysis, control and dosing of electroplating electrolytes. Int. J. Adv. Manuf. Technol. **111**(5–6), 1751–1766 (2020). https://doi.org/10.1007/s00170-020-06190-0
11. Qu, M., Yu, S., Chen, D., Chu, J., Tian, B.: State-of-the-art of design, evaluation, and operation methodologies in product service systems. Comput. Ind. **30**(77), 1–4 (2016)
12. Pezzotta, G., Pirola, F., Pinto, R., Akasaka, F., Shimomura, Y.: A service engineering frame-work to design and assess an integrated product-service. Mechatronics **31**(31), 169–179 (2015)
13. Ojasalo, J., Ojasalo, K.: Using service logic business model canvas in lean service devel-opment. In: Gummesson, E., Mele, C., Polese, F. (eds.) Service Dominant Logic, Network and Systems Theory and Service Science: Integrating three Perspectives for a New Service Agenda. Naples: Conference Proceedings 5th Naples Forum on Service (2016)

14. Shearer, C.: The CRISP-DM model: the new blueprint for data mining. J. Data Warehousing **5**, 13–22 (2000)
15. Leiden, A., Freitag, M., Schwanzer, P., Karl, A., Schiller, C., et al.: Entwicklung von Smart Services–Ein Bezugsrahmen und Anwendung in der Galvanotechnik. In: Sörgel, T. (ed.), Jahrbuch Oberflächentechnik 2020. Leuze, Bad Saulgau (2020)
16. Osterwalder, A., Pigneur, Y.: Business Model Generation–A Handbook for Visionaries, Game Changers and Challengers, Wiley, New Jersey (2010)
17. Milgram, P., Kishino, F.: A taxonomy of mixed reality visual displays. IEICE Trans. Inf. Syst. **12**, 1321–1329 (1994)
18. Burger, T.: Testen in der Dienstleistungsentwicklung, Stuttgarter Beiträge zum Testen in der Dienstleistungsentwicklung: Band I. Fraunhofer Verlag. Stuttgart (2014)
19. ISO, 2013. ISO 16290. Space engineering–Definition of the Technology Readiness Levels (TRLs) and their criteria of assessment. Beuth, Berlin
20. Freitag, M., Schiller, C.: Approach to test a product-service system during service engineering. Procedia CIRP **64**, 336–339 (2017). https://doi.org/10.1016/j.procir.2017.03.059
21. Freitag, M., Schiller, C., Hämmerle, O.: Guideline to develop smart service business models for small and medium sized enterprises. In: Dolgui, A., Bernard, A., Lemoine, D., von Cieminski, G., Romero, D. (eds.) APMS 2021. IAICT, vol. 634, pp. 369–375. Springer, Cham (2021). https://doi.org/10.1007/978-3-030-85914-5_39

How Does Manufacturing Strategy Contribute to Servitization Orientation? The Moderating Effect of Firm Size

Davide Gamba[1,2]([✉]) [iD], Tommaso Minola[1] [iD], Matteo Kalchschmidt[1] [iD],
and Federico Adrodegari[3] [iD]

[1] Department of Management, Information and Production Engineering, University of
Bergamo, Via Pasubio 7b, 24044 Bergamo, Dalmine, Italy
{davide.gamba,tommaso.minola,matteo.kalchschmidt}@unibg.it
[2] MEI Srl, Via Ing. Caproni 50, 24036 Bergamo, Ponte San Pietro, Italy
[3] Department of Mechanical and Industrial Engineering, University of Brescia, Via Branze 38,
25123 Brescia, Italy
federico.adrodegari@unibs.it

Abstract. This study theoretically articulates and empirically validates a model
of relationships between a firm's manufacturing strategy – proxied through competitive priorities – and servitization orientation. In addition, it analyzed the moderating effect of firm size on this relationship. The model was developed and tested
through hierarchical regression analysis on the Sixth International Manufacturing
Strategy Survey (IMSS-VI) data. The results indicate that different manufacturing
strategies positively affect servitization orientation. In addition, firm size positively
moderates the effect of exploitative manufacturing strategy. This research is one of
the first quantitative studies that examine how different manufacturing strategies
influence servitization orientation according to firm size.

Keywords: Manufacturing Strategy (MS) · Servitization orientation ·
Small-medium sized enterprises (SMEs) · Competitive priorities · International
manufacturing strategy survey (IMSS)

1 Introduction

The fourth industrial revolution that dominates manufacturers' innovation opportunities
includes the concept of servitization [1], leading many product-centric firms to shift their
business model from products to product-service systems [2]. Servitization assumes that
companies that initially offer just products begin adding more and more services to their
total offering [3].

Transitioning to a servitized business model requires an organizational-level orientation to services. The latter is depicted by the organization's investments in new
service development, employees' upskilling for service delivery, and the development
of products for enhancing service operations [4].

© IFIP International Federation for Information Processing 2022
Published by Springer Nature Switzerland AG 2022
D. Y. Kim et al. (Eds.): APMS 2022, IFIP AICT 663, pp. 343–351, 2022.
https://doi.org/10.1007/978-3-031-16407-1_41

Companies must effectively define a clear manufacturing strategy to plan their long-range objectives [5]. Manufacturing strategy (MS) is a pattern of decisions to develop certain manufacturing properties as a competitive weapon to move from where it is to where it wants to be [6]. This definition implicitly emphasizes the competitive priorities concept, which refers to factors on which MS is based and how firms want to compete. Some competitive priorities reflect exploitative MS, which implies better products than competitors, while others reveal explorative MS that implies newer and more innovative products [7]. Firms that bring together exploitation and exploration are called ambidextrous [8].

Managers must allocate available resources to develop a subset of prioritized competitive priorities to win orders in the market [9]. In this sense, small and medium enterprises (SMEs) lack internal resources compared to large companies [10]. Thus, prioritizing competitive capabilities is crucial for SMEs to ensure servitization orientation. In addition, literature shows that servitization success is associated with appropriate slack resource allocations that guarantee to increase the chance of growing and obtaining positive service performance [11].

However, to the best of our knowledge, studies have been absent about the relationship between firms' competitive priorities (i.e., manufacturing strategy) and servitization orientation and the different outcomes for SMEs and large manufacturers. Thus, we focus on the relationship mentioned, emphasizing the moderating role of firm size. Based on quantitative data from the International Manufacturing Strategy Survey (IMSS), we developed the two hypotheses of this study (see Fig. 1):

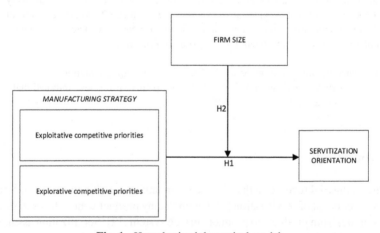

Fig. 1. Hypothesized theoretical model.

H1. The firm's exploitative/explorative MS's importance positively impacts the firm's servitization orientation.

H2. Firm size moderates the relationship between the firm's exploitative/explorative MS and the firm's service orientation. Specifically, as firm size increases (i.e., internal resources increase), the positive relationship between the firm's exploitative/explorative MS and the firm's service orientation is augmented.

The next section is devoted to the research model specification. Then empirical results are presented and discussed in Sect. 3. Last, final remarks and limitations are listed in the conclusion part.

2 Research Model Specifications

2.1 Sampling and Data Collection

The survey approach was chosen to test the proposed theoretical model as a suitable research method. Data from the sixth round of the International Manufacturing Strategy Survey (IMSS-VI) [12] were used to test the research hypotheses. IMSS is a periodic data gathering of a large and representative sample of worldwide manufacturing business units (ISIC 25–30). This initiative was launched in 1992 by the London Business School and Chalmers University. Data collection is carried out every 4 to 5 years through the cooperation of an international network of operations management scholars. IMSS-VI collected data between 2013 and 2014 in 22 countries, including 961 valid responses from 7,167 initial contacts. Previous studies have used the IMSS-VI data to analyze several servitization aspects [5, 8, 13–16].

We inspected all data items for any missing values. All variables considered include less than 5% of missing values. Thus, the missing values of a variable could be replaced with the respective mean of valid values if these were missing completely at random (MCAR) [17]. We performed Little's MCAR test [18] to verify this hypothesis. It is a χ^2 test of the null hypothesis that the data are MCAR. The χ^2 statistic was insignificant (p = 0.32), so the data could be considered MCAR.

2.2 Measures Development and Validation

Table 1 describes the model's three constructs based on IMSS-VI: exploitative competitive priorities, explorative competitive priorities, and servitization orientation.

Table 1. Constructs measurement.

Construct	Item from IMSS-VI
Exploitative MS Cronbach's $\alpha_{proposed} = 0.678$	A3.b) Better product design quality *(FL = 0.85)*
	A3.c) Better conformance to customer specifications *(FL = 0.60)*

(continued)

Table 1. (*continued*)

Construct	Item from IMSS-VI
Explorative MS *Cronbach's* α *proposed* = 0.768	A3.j) Offer new products more frequently *(FL = 0.79)*
	A3.k) Offer products that are more innovative *(FL = 0.79)*
Servitization orientation *Cronbach's* α *proposed* = 0.816 *Cronbach's* α *refined* = 0.850	S3.a2) Expanding the service offering to your customers (e.g., by investing in new service development) *(FL = 0.89)*
	S3.b2) Developing the skills needed to improve the service offering *(FL = 0.83)*
	S3.c2) Designing products so that the after-sales service is easier to manage/offer (e.g., design for maintenance) *(dropped after confirmatory factor analysis)*

Quality was the competitive priority used to measure exploitative manufacturing strategy, while innovation was employed as a proxy to measure explorative manufacturing strategy [7–9]. Both were operationalized as reflective constructs and captured the importance of the competitive priority to win orders in the last three years using a 1 (none) to 5 (high) Likert scale. On the other hand, servitization orientation was operationalized as a reflective construct to describe the current implementation of service action programs using a Likert scale from 1 to 5 [5].

All constructs of the proposed model were subject to confirmatory factor analysis (CFA), providing overall acceptable model fit (χ^2/df = 40.391, CFI = 0.986, TLI = 0.974, RMSEA = 0.053 [0.036, 0.071]), except for χ^2/df which shows that the model does not fit the data. Hence, we refined the model by dropping item S3.b2 from the servitization orientation construct reaching an acceptable model (χ^2/df = 8.861, CFI = 0.998, TLI = 0.996, RMSEA = 0.022 [0.000, 0.051]). All items' factor loading (FL) exceed the satisfactory level of 0.60. Cronbach's alphas indicating that all constructs were reliable being near to or greater than 0.70.

Starting from Exploitative MS and Explorative MS constructs, we created a categorical variable to describe each business unit's MS position according to the value of the two latent variables generated from CFA. Each respondent was clustered in one of the four groups in Table 2.

Table 2. MS categorical variable description.

MS cluster	Description
Steady *N = 319*	Exploitative MS$_i$ < Exploitative MS$_{mean}$ & Explorative MS$_i$ < Explorative MS$_{mean}$
Exploitative *N = 119*	Exploitative MS$_i$ ≥ Exploitative MS$_{mean}$ & Explorative MS$_i$ < Explorative MS$_{mean}$

(*continued*)

Table 2. (*continued*)

MS cluster	Description
Explorative $N = 166$	Exploitative MS_i < Exploitative MS_{mean} & Explorative MS_i ≥ Explorative MS_{mean}
Ambidextrous $N = 357$	Exploitative MS_i ≥ Exploitative MS_{mean} & Explorative MS_i ≥ Explorative MS_{mean}

A specific IMSS-VI item measures the business unit size, collecting last year's number of employees. According to the definition proposed by the European Commission [19], we create a dummy variable to discriminate between small-medium size (less than 250 employees) and large size (250 or more employees).

Last, following reviewed studies, we introduced three controlling variables as they could influence MS and servitization orientation. First, the business unit's industry was defined using five dummy variables (ISIC26, ISIC27, ISIC28, ISIC29, and ISIC30) [15]. Second, the business unit's country endowment was measured using the natural logarithm of the GDP per capita in 2012 obtained from the World Bank's databank [20]. Last, the region is operationalized as a dummy variable: developed countries (i.e., Europe and North America) versus developing countries (i.e., Asia and South America) [5].

3 Results

We employed hierarchical regression to analyze the data. It refers to the process of adding or removing predictor variables from the regression model in steps, which is an important method for revealing the moderating effect [21]. The model was developed in Stata 17.

The maximum variance inflation factor (VIF) among the observed variables was 1.80, indicating that multicollinearity was not problematic among the sample data. Table 3 shows the hierarchical regression results.

Table 3. Regression results of servitization orientation.

Models	Dependent variables	
	Servitization orientation	
	Model 1	Model 2
Independent variables		
MS strategy - Exploitative	0.065**	0.008
MS strategy - Explorative	0.263***	0.274***

(*continued*)

Table 3. (*continued*)

Models	Dependent variables	
	Servitization orientation	
	Model 1	Model 2
MS strategy - Ambidextrous	0.333***	0.379***
MS strategy - Steady * Firm Size - Large	–	0.021
MS strategy - Exploitative * Firm Size - Large	–	0.090**
MS strategy - Explorative * Firm Size - Large	–	−0.045
MS strategy - Ambidextrous * Firm Size - Large	–	−0.045
Control variables		
Industry ISIC 26	0.0.024	0.021
Industry ISIC 27	0.062*	0.056*
Industry ISIC 28	0.100***	0.096***
Industry ISIC 29	0.026	0.021
Industry ISIC 30	−0.027	0.025
Country – Per capita GDP	−0.137***	−0.135***
Region – Developing countries	0.157***	0.156***
Regression indexes		
R^2	0.215	0.219
Adj R^2	0.201	0.208
F for the regression	26.01***	19.05***

* $p < 0.10$, ** $p < 0.05$, *** $p < 0.01$. Regression coefficients are standardized betas.

Model 1 tested H1 analyzing the direct impact of MS strategy on servitization orientation. Results show that all MS strategy categories positively impact servitization orientation. In particular, business units that pursue ambidextrous MS are the more oriented toward servitization.

Model 2 tested H2 analyzing the moderating effect of firm size on the relationship between the firm's MS and service orientation. Results show that only the effect of exploitative MS is significantly moderated by firm size. The R^2 increased from model 1 to model 2 is poor, making clear that the proportion of variance explained by the introduction of firm size as moderator is very little. In order to reveal the nature of the moderating effect of firm size on the relationship between the firm's MS and service orientation, we plotted the predictive margins of the moderating effect of firm size in the exploitative MS case (see Fig. 2).

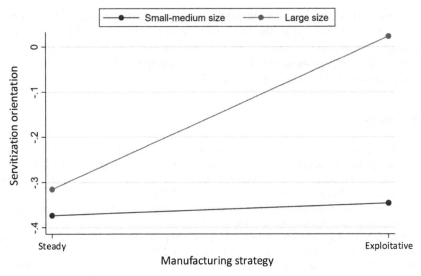

Fig. 2. Predictive margins of exploitative manufacturing strategy on servitization orientation contingent on firm size.

4   Conclusions

Servitization is challenging as firms need to reconfigure their business models, introduce new resources, and realign existing ones. This study investigated the role of MS – proxied through a firm's competitive priorities – as a predictor of a servitization orientation.

Results show that exploration MS has a greater impact on servitization than exploitation MS. While exploitation leverages current resources to optimize products, exploration rely on new knowledge and partners to innovate manufactured goods. Firms more prone to explorative MS (e.g., launching a new product more frequently than their competitors) are more oriented to servitize their business model. Last, the analysis identifies that ambidextrous MS – the combination of exploitative and explorative MS – is the best predictor of firms' servitization orientation.

Firm size explains the impact just of exploitative MS on servitization orientation. This result confirms that large firms have enough resources to invest in new service development and improve service-oriented skills than SMEs.

This paper is not exhaustive, and it presents a set of limitations. Due to the limited number of industries involved, the abovementioned findings cannot be fully generalized. In addition, IMSS-VI collected cross-sectional that did not catch the different firms' behaviors over time. Last, the IMSS-VI dataset does not collect the recent fourth industrial revolution trends.

Based on the findings and limitations described, this study opens a set of potential further research. Firstly, given that manufacturing is rapidly growing, especially with digital technologies (e.g., cloud manufacturing), results should be confirmed by replicating analysis on more recent datasets that could include respondents from different industrial sectors (e.g., the construction industry). Secondly, the use of longitudinal datasets is strongly suggested. Thirdly, future research opportunities arise by expanding the current proposed model. For example, the firm's servitization outcomes could be included by analyzing MS's impact on financial and non-financial service performance. Finally, the present work's findings should be deepened considering that SMEs are typically more servitization-oriented than large companies [22].

References

1. Thoben, K.D., Wiesner, S., Wuest, T.: Industrie 4.0 and smart manufacturing-a review of research issues and application examples. Int. J. Autom. Technol. **11**(1), 4–16 (2017)
2. Adrodegari, F., Saccani, N.: A maturity model for the servitization of product-centric companies. J. Manuf. Technol. Manag. **31**(4), 775–797 (2020)
3. Viljakainen, A., Toivonen, M.: The futures of magazine publishing: servitization and co-creation of customer value. Futures **64**, 19–28 (2014)
4. Shah, S.A.A., Jajja, M.S.S., Chatha, K.A., Farooq, S.: Servitization and supply chain integration: an empirical analysis. Int. J. Prod. Econ. **229**, 107765 (2020)
5. Dohale, V., Gunasekaran, A., Akarte, M.M., Verma, P.: Twenty-five years' contribution of benchmarking: an international journal to manufacturing strategy: a scientometric review. Benchmarking Int. J. **27**(10), 2887–2908 (2020)
6. Miltenburg, J.: Setting manufacturing strategy for a factory-within-a-factory. Int. J. Prod. Econ. **113**(1), 307–323 (2008)
7. Chaudhuri, A., Boer, H.: The impact of product-process complexity and new product development order winners on new product development performance: the mediating role of collaborative competence. J. Eng. Technol. Manag. **42**, 65–80 (2016)
8. Chang, Y.Y., Hughes, M.: Drivers of innovation ambidexterity in small-to medium-sized firms. Eur. Manag. J. **30**(1), 1–17 (2012)
9. Netland, T.H., Frick, J.: Trends in manufacturing strategies: a longitudinal investigation of the international manufacturing strategy survey. In: Brennan, L., Vecchi, A. (eds.) International Manufacturing Strategy in a Time of Great Flux, pp. 1–16. Measuring Operations Performance. Springer, Cham (2017). https://doi.org/10.1007/978-3-319-25351-0_1
10. Kowalkowski, C., Witell, L., Gustafsson, A.: Any way goes: identifying value constellations for service infusion in SMEs. Ind. Mark. Manag. **42**(1), 18–30 (2013)
11. Böhm, E., Eggert, A., Thiesbrummel, C.: Service transition: a viable option for manufacturing companies with deteriorating financial performance? Ind. Mark. Manag. **60**, 101–111 (2017)
12. IMSS. www.manufacturingstrategy.net. Accessed 13 Apr 2022
13. Szász, L., Demeter, K., Boer, H., Cheng, Y.: Servitization of manufacturing: the effect of economic context. J. Manuf. Technol. Manag. **28**(8), 1011–1034 (2017)
14. Szász, L., Seer, L.: Towards an operations strategy model of servitization: the role of sustainability pressure. Oper. Manag. Res. **11**, 51–66 (2018)
15. Sousa, R., da Silveira, G.J.: The relationship between servitization and product customization strategies. Int. J. Oper. Prod. Manag. **39**(3), 454–474 (2018)
16. Sousa, R., da Silveira, G.J.: Advanced services and differentiation advantage: an empirical investigation. Int. J. Oper. Prod. Manag. **40**(9), 1561–1587 (2020)
17. Hair, J.F., Hult, G.T., Ringle, C.M., Sarstedt, M.: A Primer on Partial Least Squares Structural Equation Modeling (PLS-SEM), 2nd edn. Sage publications, Thousand Oaks (2021)
18. Little, R.J.A.: A test of missing completely at random for multivariate data with missing values. J. Am. Stat. Assoc. **83**(404), 1198–1202 (1988)
19. European Commission. https://ec.europa.eu/growth/smes/sme-definition_en. Accessed 13 Apr 2022

20. World Bank. https://databank.worldbank.org. Accessed 13 Apr 2022
21. Tian, Y., Jia, Y., Sun, H., Li, D., Yang, Y., Malik, S.A.: The moderating effect of service capability on the relationship between service delivery and business performance of manufacturing companies. Afr. J. Bus. Manag. **6**(6), 2169–2180 (2012)
22. De Souza, M., Trento, L.R., Dauer, M.: Servitization as a startup driver: a case study in a technology park. In: Leiras, A., González-Calderón, C., De Brito Junior, I., Villa, S., Yoshizaki, H. (eds.) Operations Management for Social Good. POMS 2018, pp. 957–966. Springer Proceedings in Business and Economics. Springer, Cham (2020). https://doi.org/10.1007/978-3-030-23816-2_94

Effects of Importer Country's GDP in Brazilian Agriculture Exports: Chicken Meat, Coffee, Maize, Soybean and Soybean Cake

Daniel Laurentino de Jesus Xavier(ID) and João Gilberto Mendes dos Reis(✉)(ID)

RESUP - Research Group in Supply Chain Management - Postgraduate Program in Production Engineering, Universidade Paulista, São Paulo, Brazil
daniel.xavier3@aluno.unip.br, joao.reis@docente.unip.br

Abstract. It is strategic for countries that produce agricultural goods to identify the factors that can impact the global trade market. Brazil is one of the main agricultural commodities exporters and can benefit from different approaches to trade data analysis. This paper aims to study the correlation between Importer Country's GDP and the Brazilian main agricultural commodities (Soybeans, Sugar Raw Centrifugal, Chicken meat, Soybeans cake, Green Coffee, Cattle boneless meat (beef & veal), and Maize. To do so, we collected exports data from 2011 till 2020 from FAO and their respective Importer Country's GDP from World Bank and analyzed then using Multiple Linear Regression. We found evidence of a positive correlation with Importer Country's GDP from exports of Green Coffee, Soybean and Chicken meat and a negative correlation with Soybean cake and Maize. It was not found correlation on exports of cattle boneless meat (beef & veal) and sugar raw centrifugal.

Keywords: Linear regression · Importer Country's GDP · Agricultural commodities

1 Introduction

The agribusiness trade is very important to the global economy and represents the main export sector for Brazil. According to data from Brazil's Ministry of Agriculture, Livestock and Supply (MAPA), agribusiness was responsible for almost half of Brazil's exports in 2020, with a 48% share, representing a trade balance surplus of US$ 87.76 billion [1].

The top five Brazilian agribusiness sectors exported year were the Soybean Complex (US$ 35.24 billion and 35% of exports), Meat (US$ 17.16 billion and 17% of exports), Forest Products (US$ 11, 41 billion and 11.3% of exports), Sugar and Alcohol Complex (US$ 9.99 billion and 9.9% of exports) and Cereals, Flours and Preparations (US$ 6.89 billion and 6.8% of exports) [1].

© IFIP International Federation for Information Processing 2022
Published by Springer Nature Switzerland AG 2022
D. Y. Kim et al. (Eds.): APMS 2022, IFIP AICT 663, pp. 352–357, 2022.
https://doi.org/10.1007/978-3-031-16407-1_42

Due to its strategic importance, it is crucial to comprehend which economic factors can impact international agribusiness. De Winne e Peersman [2] examined the macroeconomic consequences of disruptions in global food commodity markets and found evidence of impact on US GDP. Santos et al. [3] studied the correlation between the common stocks of Brazilian agribusiness companies with several factors, including Brazil's GDP. The authors found a negative relationship, even during economic crisis.

Although these studies explore relations between agribusiness and GDP, it is more common to find studies on the GDP of the exporter country, but not so usual to find studies that use Importer Country's GDP, which reinforces the importance of this study.

In this study, we adopted the multiple linear regression technique to understand the relation between Importer Country's GDP and the trade relations over seven important global commodities: Soybean, Soybean Cake, Green Coffee, Cattle Boneless Meat (Beef & Veal), Chicken Meat, Sugar Raw Centrifugal and Maize. We seek to comprehend if the Importer Country's GDP can influence the agribusiness trade. These commodities are chosen because of their importance on Brazil's exports, representing 74% of all agriculture exports from 2011 and 2020.

The data analysis is conducted using Stata and Excel and the measures were coefficient and standardized Error.

This paper is divided as follows: The introduction addresses the article proposal and some background; methodology presents the procedures of the research; results section presents the findings of the research; discussion shows the implications and analysis; and finally the conclusion section points out the final remarks of the study.

2   Methodology

To conduct this study, we use the Food and Agriculture Organization of the United Nations (FAO) database to extract data on Brazil's exports of the last decade, from 2011 until 2020, using the amount of trade in US dollars [4]. The FAO database gathers information provided by the countries. The data was exported to a CSV (Comma-separated values) file and later on organized using Microsoft Excel software.

Afterward, we make some amendments to the data settings. Autonomous regions such as Taiwan, Hong Kong, and Macau were sum with mainland China. Moreover, we decided to establish a minimum value of 1,000 US dollars trade per year. We also selected products that represented at least 5% of all agricultural products exported during the period.

The products are Soybeans, Sugar Raw Centrifugal, Chicken meat, Soybeans cake, Green Coffee, Cattle Boneless Meat (Beef & Veal), and Maize. These adjustments had the purpose to avoid outlier data and fluctuations that can distort the analysis. Despite these minor modifications our sample represents at least 74% of trade for all categories.

For the GDP information, we use the World Bank database [5] to obtain data from the countries that purchased the selected products. The data were added to the matrix, relating each country to its respective GDP for that year. The generated matrix has as columns: the year, the importer country, each selected product, and the GDP of the importer country in US dollars.

To perform the data analysis, the matrix was loaded into the Stata 16.0 software from StataCorp LLC [6]. The matrix has 1279 lines. Each line is related to a country and a year, from 2011 to 2020, and the columns represent the imports value by-product and the GDP of that year. We applied the multiple linear regression technique, and obtained 63 observations by the model.

According to Fávero [7], "the linear regression technique (simple and multiple) offers, as a priority, the possibility of studying the relationship between one or more explanatory variables, which are presented in linear form, and a quantitative dependent variable". Applying this technique, we seek to verify if there is a relationship between the GDP of the importer country and the trade value of one or more Brazilian agricultural products.

We use neperian logarithm (LN) on each of the raised variables to generate new logarithmic (e base) variables creating a linear effect. Therefore, Importer Country's GDP is set as LNGDPimp, Soybean Cake is set as LNCake, Green Coffee is set as LNCoffee, Maize is set as LNMaize, Cattle Boneless Meat (Beef & Veal) is set as LNBeef, Chicken Meat is set as LNChiken, Soybean is set as LNSoya and Sugar Raw Centrifugal is set as LNSugar.

$$
\begin{aligned}
LnGDPj = \gamma 0 + \beta_1 \; LNCake + \beta_2 \; LNCoffee + \beta_3 \; LNMaize + \beta_4 \\
LNBeef + \beta_5 \; LNChicken + \beta_6 \; LNSoya + \beta_7 \; LNSugar + \varepsilon i
\end{aligned}
\tag{1}
$$

where, LnGDPj = sample size, N = population, Z = abscissa of the normal standard, p = estimated homogeneity, e = sample error.

At first, we use the sum command in order to obtain statistical information on all variables, dependent and explanatory. This command shows the observation quantities, mean, standard deviation, and minimum and maximum values for each variable. The results are shown in the next section.

Then we use the stepwise command, pr (0.10), and the reg command to perform the regression, using the logarithmic variable of the Importer Country's GDP as the quantitative dependent variable. The logarithmic values of each agricultural product's exports to its respective country are the explanatory variables we used. The results are presented in Sect. 3 and validated according to Gujarati in reference [9]. Table 1 summarizes the statistical data.

3   Results

Both Sugar Raw Centrifugal (LnSugar) and Cattle boneless (LnBeef) are not statistically significant and the final equation obtained is represented in Eq. 2.

Table 1. Sumarized statistical data

Variable	Obs	Mean	Std. Dev.	Min	Max
LNCake	372	1.052.811	1.866.948	6.921.658	1.464.935
LNCofee	598	9.916.319	1.690.997	6.934.397	1.440.094
LNmaize	435	1.028.425	176.685	6.911.747	1.393.238
LNBeef	474	9.700.381	19.324	6.907.755	1.539.253
LNchicken	814	952.426	1.778.179	6.917.706	142.384
LnSoya	308	112.185	202.707	6.910.751	1.712.877
LnSugar	535	1.038.033	1.928.087	6.915.723	1.442.697
LNGDPimp	1,279	2.500.226	2.167.128	1.955.627	3.069.596

$$LnGDPj = \gamma 0 + \beta_1 \; LNCake + \beta_2 \; LNCoffee + \beta_3 \; LNMaize + \beta_4 \\ LNChicken + \beta_6 \; LNSoya + \varepsilon i \tag{2}$$

The number of observations adopted by the model was 63 - which means values without zero for all the categories.

The coefficient of determination R^2 was 0.8067. According to Moreira et al. [8], R^2 is an indicator of the adopted model fitness to explain the correlations. It can vary from 0 to 1. The closer to one indicates that the model is suitable to explain all the data variability. The result can be interpreted as 80% of Importer Country's GDP can be explained by the variables used (trade products. However, According to Gujarati in reference [9], one of the disadvantages of R^2 is the fact that the value naturally grows as we increase the number of dependent variables. As a complement, according to the author, we should also consider the adjusted R^2, which is commonly used to evaluate two or more regression models with the same dependent variable. The adjusted R^2 we found is 0.7898, or 79% of Importer Country's GDP can be explained by the trade products.

Table 2 shows the results of the multiple linear regression technique applied to trade data using logarithmic variables.

Table 2. Multiple linear regression results

LNGDPimp	Coef.	Std. Err.	t	P>—t—	[95% Conf.	Interval]
LNCake	−.165979	.0442037	−3.75	0.000	−.2544954	−.0774626
LNCofee	.5518952	.0852398	6.47	0.000	.3812054	.722585
LNmaize	−.1252941	.0593424	−2.11	0.039	−.2441251	−.006463
LnSoya	.3034753	.0489467	6.20	0.000	.2054613	.4014894
LNchicken	.2923714	.0513913	5.69	0.000	.189462	.3952808
_cons	1.809.418	1.231.322	14.69	0.000	156.285	2.055.986

Data shows that Coffee represents the main correlation with Importer Country's GDP, with a positive coefficient of correlation of 0.552, followed by Soybean (0.303) and Chicken meat (0.292). We also found evidence of a negative correlation with Importer Country's GDP on Soybean cake and Maize, with a coefficient of correlation of -0.165 and -0.125 respectively.

We found evidence that a 1% increase on Importer Country's GDP represents a 0.55% increase on Coffee exports, 0.30% on Soybean exports and 0.29% on Chicken meat exports. On the other hand, a 1% increase on Importer Country's GDP represents a 0.17% decrease on Soybean cake exports and 0.13% on Maize exports to this country.

The information shows that is possible to use multiple regression technique, to better understand the global trade demand for some agribusiness products. It is intuitive to assume that the more a country increases its GDP, the more it buys all products, but we only found evidence of that correlation on Coffee, Soybean and Chicken Meat.

More counterintuitive is the fact that a negative correlation happens with Soybean Cake and Maize. In other words, the more a country increases its GDP, the less it buys those products. One possible explanation for that is that both Soybean Cake and Maize are used as animal food, so as a country increases its GDP, it can represent a shift in consumer behavior of animal protein, preferring to import those products over local production.

It is quite remarkable that Brazilian farmers can use Importer Country's GDP, as a relevant metric in trade analysis, opening up a field of opportunities for regression studies on the subject.

4   Conclusions

Brazil is one of the major agriculture producers and the agribusiness is its main export sector, but international trade is a complex system involving several variables, therefore it is important to apply multiple techniques and different approaches to find insights that might value information for strategic decisions.

In this context, this work analyzed data from Brazilian exports of Soybean, Soybean Cake, Green Coffee, Cattle Boneless Meat (Beef & Veal), Chicken Meat, Sugar Raw Centrifugal and Maize from FAO [4]. We also gathered data on Importer Country's GDP from World Bank [5]. The data refers to 2011 until 2020. The relation between the Brazilian commodities and Importer Country's GDP was analyzed it using multiple linear regression technique.

We found evidence of a positive correlation with Importers GDP from exports of Green Coffee, Soybean, and Chicken Meat. It was not found correlation from exports of Cattle Boneless Meat (Beef & Veal) and Sugar Raw Centrifugal. We also found evidence of a negative correlation with Soybean Cake and Maize.

We suggest for further studies, a more detailed approach to beef and sugar commodities, in order to identify which other variables may impact their exports. Another important study would be to understand why Soybean Cake and Maize presents a negative correlation to Importer Country GDP. We also suggest the use of exported volume as a variable, in order to check if the monetary variation could affect the results. The results allow us to raise questions for further studies. The Brazilian agriculture production can properly adapt to world demands? Did possible international restrictions on agricultural products impact the results? These questions can be addressed in future research.

Acknowledgments. This study was financed in part by the Coordenação de Aperfeiçoamento de Pessoal de Nível Superior - Brasil (CAPES). Finance Code 001.

References

1. Exportações do agro ultrapassam US$ 100 bilhões pela segunda vez na história. https://www.gov.br/agricultura/pt-br/assuntos/noticias/exportacoes-do-agro-ultrapassam-a-barreira-dos-us-100-bilhoes-pela-segunda-vez
2. Winne, J.D., Peersman, G.: Macroeconomic effects of disruptions in global food commodity markets: evidence for the United States. Brook. Pap. Econ. Act. **2016**(2), 183–263 (2016)
3. Santos, J.O.d., Santos, F.A., Volpato, L.A., Volpato, B.L.: Análise do desempenho do retorno das ações ordinárias de empresas do setor do agronegócio em cenários econômicos adversos. Revista de Ciências da Administração **23**(61), 37–51 (2021). https://periodicos.ufsc.br/index.php/adm/article/view/79157. Number: 61
4. FAOSTAT. https://www.fao.org/faostat/en/#data/TM
5. DataBank | The World Bank. https://databank.worldbank.org/home.aspx
6. StataCorp LLC: Stata Statistical Software (2019)
7. Fávero, L.P., Belfiore, P.: Manual de Análise de Dados - Estatística e Modelagem Multivariada com Excel®, SPSS® e Stata®, 1 edn. Elsevier (2017)
8. Moreira, M.S., Rodrigues, M.P., Ferreira, C.F., Nienov, O.H.: Regressão linear simples e múltipla. In: Capp, E., Nienov, O.H. (eds.) Bioestatística quantitativa aplicada, pp. 197–216. UFRGS (2020)
9. Gujarati, D.N., Porter, D.C.: Basic Econometrics, 5th edn. McGraw-Hill Irwin, Boston (2009)

Industrial Digital Transformation

Building Trust in Business Ecosystems: The Interplay of Technology and Community in Governing Data Sharing

Ulriikka Järvihaavisto[(⊠)] and Mikael Öhman

Department of Industrial Engineering and Management, School of Science, Aalto University, P.O. Box 15500, 00076 Espoo, Aalto, Finland
{ulriikka.jarvihaavisto,mikael.ohman}@aalto.fi

Abstract. Data sharing remains one of the biggest challenges for emerging industrial ecosystems. Lack of trust, and perceived risks are holding companies back, as no one wants to go first and get it wrong. At the core of this challenge is a lack of understanding how data sharing could, and should be governed in business ecosystems. Despite growing scholarly interest in data sharing and data markets, research on the governance mechanisms of data sharing is scarce. In this paper, we analyze the governance of data sharing in two emerging business ecosystems. Based on our findings, we elaborate on the complementary role of community- and technology-based governance mechanisms. We discuss our findings in light of emerging industry 4.0 business ecosystems.

Keywords: Data sharing · Governance · Business ecosystems

1 Introduction

In recent years, ecosystems and digital platforms have received increasing attention from both management scholars and business practitioners. Adner [1] defines ecosystems as "the alignment structure of the multilateral set of partners that need to interact in order for a focal value proposition to materialize". Digital platforms on the other hand are often seen as a core technology on top of which different ecosystems operate. Despite the increasing interest on the phenomena, we see surprisingly little research on ecosystems and platforms conducted in the industrial context.

The industrial context differs from purely digital contexts, as it typically entails existing system architectures that connect hardware and machines, legacy software, strong existing organizational identities [2] and different business models. Empirical evidence on data sharing in emerging industrial business ecosystems is scarce [3]. And can as such be considered as one of the biggest challenges in industrial business ecosystem emergence. An underlying reason for this challenge is a lack of understanding on how data sharing should be governed in business ecosystems [4].

D. Y. Kim et al. (Eds.): APMS 2022, IFIP AICT 663, pp. 361–369, 2022.
https://doi.org/10.1007/978-3-031-16407-1_43

Even though data sharing, and data markets have drawn attention from business scholars, governance mechanisms of data sharing have barely been discussed. Further, when discussed, data sharing is often discussed solely from a technology governance perspective, neglecting the impact of community governance mechanisms. In this study we seek to understand how technology- and community governance mechanisms complement each other in the governance of data sharing.

We approach this question through conducting a polar case study with two emerging business ecosystems, where one case starts with an existing community and develops the platform technology, and the other starts with the technology, and seeks to develop the community. We base our analysis on a recent systematic literature review on the governance of data sharing in business ecosystems [5], which identified three interrelated governance mechanisms: usability, transparency and exchangeability. Based on our findings, we discuss learnings for industrial business ecosystems that seek to redeem the promises of industry 4.0.

2   Data Sharing Governance in Business Ecosystems

Before reviewing prior work on the three governance mechanisms of data sharing [5], we consider two concepts that are directly linked to all of them: data ownership and sovereignty. Data ownership is often considered as a governance issue of its own [6]. Ownership can be defined as the legally enforceable right to determine the terms and conditions of data use [7–13]. When the data source is an individual, or the data shared is personal data, ownership itself is not questioned [8]. However, distinguishing between personal and non-personal data can be problematic [14, 15].

Data sovereignty is derived from the concept of data ownership [7, 10, 12, 13], and denotes that the data owner should be able to maintain control over the shared data [11]. If an intermediary, such as a disseminator or data broker is involved in data sharing, maintaining the owner's data sovereignty becomes the responsibility of the intermediary [7]. Sovereignty is also determined by system architecture [13] and interaction topology [11].

2.1   Usability

Usability is about what is shared, to whom it's shared, and for how long it is shared. Usability has been discussed in the literature especially in the perspective of data source: how do you share enough data for it to be useful, but little enough to avoid unwanted purposes [16]. Ensuring privacy is a key part of usability [10, 17, 18]. This is discussed especially in the healthcare sector, where personal data is concerned [16, 19]. Data granularity is a key issue that supports privacy and affects the willingness to share data [17]. However, strict limitations on usability might stifle innovation [16]. Indeed, from the perspective of the data user, usability has attracted surprisingly little academic attention. In the platform ecosystem literature, data use case is seen as a governance factor, meaning that data users need to have a clear idea what data is important to them and why [6]. In community governance perspective, continuously maintaining definitions of data use cases and related stakeholders are seen key aspects of data governance [6]. Further, intermediaries between data source and user can in some cases improve usability [14].

In addition to intermediaries, we can identify two technological approaches facilitating usability: confidentiality approaches and federated analysis. They ensure that the shared data contains only the necessary information, which is important especially when the purpose of data use is to derive aggregate insights from large datasets. In confidentiality approaches, data is generalized by reducing the level of detail in a dataset [10, 18], or by fragmentation of the database, all the while preserving aggregate usability [20]. Federated analysis is used for the purpose of training AI models [8]. It entails aggregating model parameters from locally stored data sets, meaning that the data is technically not shared, only the insight. Even though, it is yet rarely used in practice, it is seen to provide great opportunities in the future use.

2.2 Transparency

Transparency is about whether and to what extent there is a visibility into what data are used for, by whom data are used, and for how long [17]. In the perspective of the data source, it should be clear how the shared data is used [8, 12, 21], especially when sharing personal data [22]. In addition, the data user should have information of data provenance [6, 7, 23]. Thus, trust in the source of the data [11], in the history of the data [7, 8] and in the quality of data [24] is important both in the perspective of data source and user. Including metadata in data sharing facilitates transparency in transactions [6].

Furthermore, distributed ledger technologies (often in combination with federated architectures) also facilitate transparency through auditability in data sharing. Distributed ledger technologies can also be used for ensuring sovereignty and provenance [9, 23, 25]. The link between transparency and trust is also reflected in the technological discussion, where blockchain is referred to as a "trust technology" [9].

2.3 Exchangeability

Exchangeability defines the incentives to share data. Especially when the data user can be expected to profit from the data, data source is expected to require some kind of compensation from sharing the data [12]. Compensation for sharing personal data typically comes in the form of access to services [14], discounts [12], or some form of tokens [8]. However, also monetary compensation is often expected [22]. With more altruistic purposes for the use of data, data sharing can be governed by consent [9, 16], which may be extended to third parties [21]. However, questions concerning consent and compensation typically become harder to answer when re-using or aggregating data [16].

Blockchain-enabled smart contracts can be used to reduce transaction costs of data sharing by streamlining processes and removing the need for intermediaries [8, 23, 25], and ensuring transaction validity [26]. The caveat is that the data sharing agreement needs to be computationally representable [23] for it to be machine-readable and -executable [11].

3   Methodology and Empirical Case Studies

Industry 4.0 business ecosystems are still in their infancy, and currently organized mostly in a centralized manner. In order to understand how manufacturing industries can evolve towards more extensive data sharing and (de-centralized) ecosystemic cooperation, we study two non-manufacturing contexts where this is happening. We use a longitudinal, explorative polar case study as our research method [27]. For evaluating the generalizability of our findings, understanding and explicating the context embedded nature of knowledge is of key importance [28].

The studied empirical cases, the Streamr Community and Barcelona Green Shops, are part of the Atarca EU Horizon 2020 project that studies accounting technologies for anti-rival coordination and allocation. Through our involvement in the project, we have been able to study the evolution of the two de-centralized ecosystems that utilize distributed ledger technologies. From the perspective of ecosystem evolution, the cases have one fundamental difference (making them polar opposites in our study): Whereas Streamr Community builds the technology with the collaborative community emerging around it, Barcelona Green Shops starts with an existing community, building the collaborative technology for it.

Longitudinal (and still ongoing) data collection extends over the entire EU-project. Collected data includes 3 workshops, meeting notes from 5 project meetings. For this report we conducted two 1-h interviews with key case informants, focusing explicitly on governance aspects related to data sharing. Further, we included secondary data such as project reports, community websites and white papers in the analysis. Based on the framework by Järvihaavisto & Öhman [5], we performed both within case- and cross case analysis.

Case: Streamr community
Streamr (https://streamr.network/) is developing core technology for decentralized real-time data sharing. Leveraging the core technology, the formation of decentralized platforms and services is a collective effort by the Streamr community. So far, community contributions have mainly been technical, ranging from providing a part of the technical infrastructure to taking part in software development. However, to some extent these contributions have also included various technology governance activities (decision making, decision support).

The challenge faced by the Streamr Community is to extend the realm of contributions beyond the traditional programming-related tasks. This is of special importance as dedicated non-programming contributions are increasingly important to the long-term viability of Web3 projects (DLT-based, including cryptocurrencies) in general. Streamr is pioneering new ways of sharing and giving acknowledgements using shareable, non-transferable non-fungible tokens.

Case: Barcelona Green Shops
Barcelona Green Shops focus on creating a business platform that enhances networking and information sharing among "Green shops of Barcelona" community members. The community, formed around sustainable (and local) products, is managed by Rezero (https://rezero.cat/en/) and consists of shopkeepers, their clients, and suppliers. NGO Novact (https://novact.org/) facilitates the building of the platform in the ATARCA

project. Due to community's focus on sustainability and local producers, the ecosystem is geographically concentrated in the Barcelona region.

The challenge faced by Barcelona Green Shops is to incentivize the existing community stakeholders to participate in the platform that promotes coordination, information sharing, and community building among the shops. To achieve this, Barcelona Green Shops uses Barcelona's social currency REC. Moreover, the social currency facilitates the consumers' green and sustainable consumption, manifesting the Green Shops' sustainability impact, while building feedback channels (product demand and quality) among all members of the Barcelona Green Shop community.

4 Findings

We use the abbreviations BGS for Barcelona Green Shops and SC for Streamr Community. We highlight the key distinction between the cases, i.e. the different starting points of the cases; with BGS starting from the community and building the technology, and with SC starting with the technology, and building the community.

As both of the ecosystems are in their early stages of their emergence, the governance is centralized. Rezero/Novact and Streamr company decides the rules who get to participate and how the data can be shared in the platforms. However, in both cases, the governance is expected to be de-centralized in the future, as the members take ownership in the web3 platforms. According to our interviewees, de-centralizing the current central governance is a key future challenge.

Usability

Starting from the purpose of the shared data, we find that the primary purpose of BGS is to enable sharing of data on suppliers amongst shops. SC on the other hand does not hold any preconceived ideas about the purpose of the shared data. Going one step further, SC even distances itself from any responsibility for what data is shared on the platform. Elaborating on the purpose in the BGS case, we note that the purpose of data sharing is derived from the overarching purpose of the community. In order to promote sustainable and local production, which reaches consumers through community-centred small shops, the BGS network has to be able to compete in economic terms against major retail players. This is achieved through sharing information of suppliers, and enabling coordination in procurement. Conversely, while SC does not promote any specific purpose for data sharing, the technological focus is clearly on real-time data. Based on this we present our first finding:

In a community-based ecosystem, the type of shared data is derived from community purpose, whereas in a technology-based ecosystem, the type of shared data is derived from the focus of technology.

Transparency

In BGS the parties sharing data include shops, suppliers and customers. Despite sharing the overarching purpose (as mentioned above), the different parties mostly do not have an a priori relationship with each other, so trust is an issue. The shared identity promoted by Rezero, however, acts as a common anchor for initial trust, and as a mediator, on which more in-depth relationships can be built. In SC data is produced by sharers and used by subscribers. The anonymity, or pseudonymity offered by the network means that trust cannot be based on social relations. In practice, the technology in SC offers the tools for data provenance and privacy, which is then implemented in apps that facilitate data sharing. Based on this we present our second finding:

> *In a community-based ecosystem, with a trusted mediator, data sovereignty can be based on relational trust, whereas in a technology-based ecosystem, data sovereignty must be explicit and hard-wired.*

Exchangeability

In BGS, the shop keepers have joint incentive to share data: in collaboration they can join their market forces in order to compete with large global merchandise stores and promote sustainable and local production within their area. Data sharing in the platform is not monetized, but incentivized by offering "merit" tokens to regular contributors as a sign of appreciation. In SC, the company offers their DLT technology for users with different motivations to share and consume data, and transactions can be monetized in the platform. In SC, the incentives for sharing data are not known, however, SC encourages members to use and develop their platform by rewarding active contributors through appreciation by offering tokens and immaterial demonstrations of appreciation. Based on this we conclude that:

> *If there is a common, social goal among the community members in the ecosystem, data sharing doesn't necessarily need to be monetized. On the other hand, monetization of data sharing can be used for financing the platform maintenance and development.*

5 Discussion

There are no major technological barriers for data sharing in industrial context. Different DLT technology platforms, such as Streamr, enable ecosystems to share large data sets, even real-time data that suits industrial needs. However, in order for the data to flow in the ecosystem, there needs to be incentives for members to share. With a community-based purpose for data sharing, as in the Barcelona Green Shops case, the motivation for data sharing is tangible even though the data transaction itself is not monetized. Similar shared purpose can be seen in healthcare [16, 19], where patient data is readily shared (based on consent) for the purpose of medical research. However, the challenge in this type of community-based governance is how to maintain and finance common infrastructure and development of data sharing tools/platforms.

In technology-based ecosystems, transactions can only be incentivized through monetization, which does not further community building, and by extension industrial ecosystem emergence. Tokenization can be used, but the (relational or social) value of tokens is reliant on community building efforts. However, due to business-criticality, competitive advantage, and context specificity (potentially combined with risk aversiveness), reaching an agreement on the exchange value of industrial data is challenging. Thus, fostering community-based data sharing in industrial ecosystems is of key importance. The challenge is that communities take time and effort to build and sustain. Our argument in this paper is that when starting with technology-based governance perspective, community building will be the challenge for achieving sustainable business ecosystem. However, when starting with community-based governance perspective, financing and maintaining common infrastructure will be the key challenge for sustainable data sharing ecosystems, see Fig. 1.

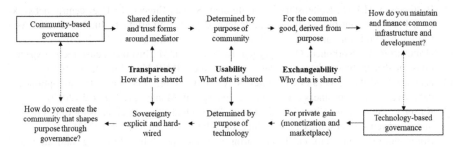

Fig. 1. Data sharing through community- and technology-based governance

In industry 4.0 context, sustainability, quality, and standardization could be community purposes (along with their respective non-profit industry organizations) that incentivize industrial organizations to share their data within the business ecosystem, without the need for monetization of sharing. Also, increasing market power to counter dominant players could also be a unifying purpose for smaller industrial players (as in the BGS case). Through our case-study, we advance theoretical understanding of data sharing governance in business ecosystems. However, the generalizability of the results are limited [27], warranting further research in different contexts where data is shared in business ecosystems.

References

1. Adner, R.: Ecosystem as structure: an actionable construct for strategy. J. Manag. **43**, 39–58 (2017)
2. Järvihaavisto, U., Smeds, R.: Becoming an ecosystem actor: coping with identity ambiguity in industrial organizations. In: Egos (2019)
3. Koutroumpis, P., Leiponen, A., Thomas, L.D.W.: Markets for data. Ind. Corp. Chang. **29**, 645–660 (2020)
4. Gawer, A.: Digital platforms and ecosystems: remarks on the dominant organizational forms of the digital age. Innovation 1–15 (2021)
5. Järvihaavisto, U., Öhman, M.: Data sharing in business ecosystems: a systematic literature review. In: 22nd International Working Seminar on Production Economics (2022)
6. Lee, S.U., Zhu, L., Jeffery, R.: Data governance for platform ecosystems: critical factors and the state of practice. In: Twenty First Pacific Asia Conference on Information Systems Langkawi 2017 (2017)

7. Janev, V., Vidal, M.E., Endris, K., Pujic, D.: Managing knowledge in energy data spaces. In: Web Conference 2021–Companion World Wide Web Conference WWW 2021, pp. 7–15 (2021)
8. Jabarulla, M.Y., Lee, H.-N.: Healthcare system for combating the COVID-19 pandemic: opportunities and applications. Healthcare **9**, 1–22 (2021)
9. Lemieux, V.L., Rowell, C., Seidel, M.D.L., Woo, C.C.: Caught in the middle? Strategic information governance disruptions in the era of blockchain and distributed trust. Rec. Manag. J. **30**, 301–324 (2020)
10. Wong, K.S., Kim, M.H.: Privacy protection for data-driven smart manufacturing systems. Int. J. Web Serv. Res. **14**, 17–32 (2017)
11. Bastiaansen, H.J.M., Kollenstart, M., Dalmolen, S., van Engers, T.: User-centric network-model for data control with interoperable legal data sharing artefacts. In: 24th Pacific Asia Conference on Information Systems PACIS 2020 Proceedings, pp. 1–14 (2020)
12. Grundstrom, C., Korhonen, O., Väyrynen, K., Isomursu, M.: Insurance customers' expectations for sharing health data: Qualitative survey study. JMIR Med. Inform. **8** (2020)
13. Zrenner, J., Möller, F.O., Jung, C., Eitel, A., Otto, B.: Usage control architecture options for data sovereignty in business ecosystems. J. Enterp. Inf. Manag. **32**, 477–495 (2019)
14. Kaiser, C., Stocker, A., Viscusi, G., Fellmann, M., Richter, A.: Conceptualising value creation in data-driven services: the case of vehicle data. Int. J. Inf. Manag. **59**, 102335 (2021)
15. Borgogno, O., Colangelo, G.: Data sharing and interoperability: fostering innovation and competition through APIs. Comput. Law Secur. Rev. **35**, 105314 (2019)
16. Saksena, N., Matthan, R., Bhan, A., Balsari, S.: Rebooting consent in the digital age: a governance framework for health data exchange. BMJ Glob. Heal. **6**, 1–8 (2021)
17. Ahmadian, A.S., Jürjens, J., Strüber, D.: Extending model-based privacy analysis for the industrial data space by exploiting privacy level agreements. In: Proceedings of the ACM Symposium on Applied Computing, pp. 1142–1149 (2018)
18. He, B.Y., Chow, J.Y.J.: Optimal privacy control for transport network data sharing. Transp. Res. Part C Emerg. Technol. **113**, 370–387 (2020)
19. Blasimme, A., Fadda, M., Schneider, M., Vayena, E.: Data sharing for precision medicine: policy lessons and future directions. Health Aff. **37**, 702–709 (2018)
20. Livraga, G., Viviani, M.: Data confidentiality and information credibility in online ecosystems. In: 11th International Conference on Digital Ecosystems MEDES 2019, pp. 191–198 (2019)
21. Choi, W., Chun, J.W., Lee, S.J., Chang, S.H., Kim, D.J., Choi, I.Y.: Development of a mydata platform based on the personal health record data sharing system in Korea. Appl. Sci. **11** (2021)
22. Rantanen, M.M., Koskinen, J.: Humans of the European data economy ecosystem–what do they demand from a fair data economy? In: Kreps, D., Komukai, T., Gopal, T.V., Ishii, K. (eds.) Human-Centric Computing in a Data-Driven Society. HCC 2020. IFIP Advances in Information and Communication Technology, vol. 590, pp. 327–339. Springer, Cham (2020). https://doi.org/10.1007/978-3-030-62803-1_26
23. Khatoon, A.: A blockchain-based smart contract system for healthcare management. Electron **9**, 1–23 (2020)
24. Järvihaavisto, U., Öhman, M., Smeds, R.: Towards a serious game on data sharing in business ecosystems. In: Dolgui, A., Bernard, A., Lemoine, D., von Cieminski, G., Romero, D. (eds.) APMS 2021. IAICT, vol. 633, pp. 500–509. Springer, Cham (2021). https://doi.org/10.1007/978-3-030-85910-7_53
25. Cai, T., Wu, Y., Lin, H., Cai, Y.: Blockchain-empowered big data sharing for internet of things. Int. J. Web Serv. Res. **18**, 58–69 (2021)
26. Oh, H., Park, S., Choi, J.K., Noh, S.: Deposit decision model for data brokers in distributed personal data markets using blockchain. IEEE Access **9**, 114715–114726 (2021)

27. Yin, R.K.: Case Study Research: Design and Methods. Sage Publications Ltd., Thousand Oaks, CA (2009)
28. Öhman, M.: Design science in operations management: extracting knowledge from maturing designs (2019). http://urn.fi/URN:ISBN:978-952-60-8487-9

Exploring Challenges in the Integration of Additive Manufacturing

Christopher Gustafsson(✉) ⓘ, Anna Sannö ⓘ, Jessica Bruch ⓘ,
and Koteshwar Chirumalla ⓘ

Mälardalen University, Hamngatan 15, 631 05 Eskilstuna, Sweden
{christopher.gustafsson,anna.sanno,jessica.bruch,
koteshwar.chirumalla}@mdu.se

Abstract. The purpose of this paper is to identify the challenges in the integration of additive manufacturing (AM) that management faces in large manufacturing companies. Based on a case study consisting of a focus group, interview, informal meetings, direct and participant observations, company documents, reports, presentations, and field notes, seven dimensions containing 20 challenges were identified. The challenges were mentioned by 10 participants from four functional organizations. Thereafter, the 20 challenges were sorted into the three stages of integration. The results suggest a newly emerging theme that builds upon an existing framework. Organizational change was a unanimous concern by all functional organizations when contemplating integrating AM into the whole organization. Most of the challenges appear in the pre-integration stage and the post-integration stage compared to the integration stage which only highlighted two challenges. Future research should investigate solutions that contain proper actions and capabilities to overcome the identified challenges to enhance facilitating the integration of AM step-by-step.

Keywords: Additive manufacturing · Industrial 3D Printing · Integration · Challenges · Management

1 Introduction

Additive manufacturing (AM) is a key technology in the future of manufacturing [1]. AM is defined as the "...*process of joining materials to make parts from 3D model data, usually layer upon layer, as opposed to subtractive manufacturing and formative manufacturing technologies.*" [2]. With its ability to add materials layer-by-layer it is now possible to produce and manufacture complex products that were never possible through conventional manufacturing (CM). Complex products can utilize and benefit AM with, for example, reduced cost, reduced lead time, reduced weight, reduced carbon footprint, as well as improved performance [3].

To unlock the full potential of AM in the manufacturing industry AM needs to be integrated into the whole organization consisting of functional organizations such as

© IFIP International Federation for Information Processing 2022
Published by Springer Nature Switzerland AG 2022
D. Y. Kim et al. (Eds.): APMS 2022, IFIP AICT 663, pp. 370–379, 2022.
https://doi.org/10.1007/978-3-031-16407-1_44

operations, purchasing, sales, technology, etc. Integration is referred to as interaction processes involving information exchange and co-production to combine different parts into one whole meaning [4]. Information exchange and co-production are crucial to ensure the integration of AM into the whole organization and not solely in the individual functional organizations [5].

There are two main problems in the context of integrating AM. Firstly, the complexity of AM can influence and change how products are developed, for example, new materials, process selection, technology selection, redesign, manufacturing strategy, quality management, build or manufacture, post-processing, and application, compared to CM [6, 7]. Secondly, the issues with the integration are still challenging for many manufacturing companies. Especially those who are much less familiar with AM, those who are being introduced to it for the first time, and those wanting to scale up [8]. There is usually a bottleneck when integrating AM into the whole organization, the level of knowledge in the industry professionals in the different functional organizations, amount of ongoing and finished AM-related development projects, and if someone is working full-time with AM in the company [9].

The management perspective of AM is receiving increased attention from scientific journals but still lacks clear definitions. Previous research has highlighted that "...*AM seems to have different impacts for large companies, which need further investigation."* [10, p. 1432]. There is a need to investigate the integration of AM into large companies in the manufacturing industry through case study research since industry professionals in management positions still experience challenges [10, 11].

To this background, the purpose of this paper is to identify the challenges in the integration of AM that management faces in large manufacturing companies. This would then provide an understanding of what large manufacturing companies should consider in terms of challenges when integrating AM.

2   Frame of Reference

Integration could be seen as the next step from introduction, application, adoption, and implementation toward industrialization [6]. Previous research has focused on the challenges of integrating various technologies, for example, AM and metal casting [12], and on integrating AM in a learning factory [13]. An AM implementation framework consists of general factors that are important to consider when categorizing challenges related to the integration of AM [11]. The general factors can be summarized into:

- *External forces* (e.g., competitive pressures, environmental legislation, customer requirements),
- *AM strategy* (e.g., the alignment between business, manufacturing, and research and development strategy),
- *AM supply chain* (e.g., AM system vendors, material suppliers, customers, location of manufacture),
- *System of operations* (e.g., design for AM, AM process planning, quality control, AM cost accounting systems, integration),
- *Organizational change* (e.g., business size, organizational structure, workforce experience, workforce skill, organizational culture), and

- *AM technology* (e.g., AM standards, technology maturity, technology benefits and tradeoffs, rapid prototyping legacy).

Furthermore, challenges faced by Danish and German manufacturers in adopting AM have been identified [14]. Identified barriers to implementing AM in the Indian automotive sector have been analyzed [9]. Factors that are important to consider when implementing AM from a management perspective have been identified [10]. Additional barriers have been identified in the integration of AM technologies into manufacturing systems [5]. In several studies [5, 9–11], it is not recognized that the challenges can be different depending on the point in time. This differentiation has been considered in the adoption of AM in the context of AM service providers [14] and the implementation of AM for mass customization in the dental industry [15] but not for the integration of AM in the commercial vehicle sector. A definition of implementation along with a life-cycle model in terms of a three-stage sequence (in this research *stages of integration*) has been constructed [16].

1. Pre-installation, in this research *pre-integration*, represents the resources that are relevant to the success or failure of integrating AM which are evaluated.
2. Installation and commissioning, in this research *integration*, ensure the successful and consistent realization of a working order after having AM integrated.
3. Post-commissioning, in this research *post-integration*, include continuous improvements of technical and business-related activities with having AM integrated.

3   Research Methodology

This research was conducted following the case study guidelines [17] as it allows for in-depth exploration of the challenges in the integration of AM. This research was conducted in collaboration with one large-sized heavy equipment manufacturing company with more than 10 000 employees in the commercial vehicle sector that has factories located in Sweden and globally. They develop and produce heavy equipment machines and tools that are used globally by their customers. The company was chosen based on opportunistic sampling [18] since the company 1) develops and manufactures complex products, 2) utilizes AM in different development projects of varying complexity, and 3) has previous experience in AM.

Qualitative data was collected in the case study as it provides descriptions of the studied phenomenon [19]. Data were collected from one focus group [20] held online with nine participants (Participants A–I) and one separate interview held online with one respondent (Participant J) which covers four functional organizations (Table 1). The participants and the respondent were asked two questions in consecutive order related to 1) the challenges of integrating AM into the company and 2) why AM has not progressed more or not matured enough in the company.

Additional data were collected during one year from informal meetings with six of the participants (Participants B–F & J), direct and participant observations (both internal at the company and external, for example, tours in some of the company's factories, online seminars, and workshops), company documents, reports, presentations, and field notes to add potentially new findings and complement currently collected data. Reviewing the literature served as a base for building up the frame of reference.

The gathering of the focus group and the interview were recorded (video and audio) and transcribed manually. Through the Gioia method, thematic analysis was used to analyze the collected data [21]. All transcribed data were labeled and listed in spreadsheets for each participant. Thereafter, the labeled data were color-coded, grouped into themes, and categorized into aggregated dimensions. Lastly, the challenges highlighted by the functional organizations were presented and sorted into the three stages of integration based on the life-cycle model [16]. An additional gathering with the focus group was completed to report back on the initial results of the research.

Table 1. Summary of the participants from the focus group and the interview

Designation	Job role	Functional organization	Work experience (years)
Participant A	Head of parts & uptime	Sales	1
Participant B	Project leader aftermarket purchasing	Purchasing	5
Participant C	Manufacturing technology development & governance manager	Operations	3
Participant D	Global head of research engineers	Technology	4
Participant E	Research strategy manager	Technology	3
Participant F	Head of advanced manufacturing engineering & research	Operations	2
Participant G	Global commodity director uptime	Purchasing	9
Participant H	Head of virtual product development	Technology	17
Participant I	Head of purchasing controls	Purchasing	11
Participant J	Strategy & future solutions manager	Technology	4

4 Results

It was observed that the company had many ongoing and finished development projects related to AM. Most of the finished development projects were small-scale, focused on polymer materials, and focused on small-sized parts and components with low complexity, small batch sizes, and relatively low cost. Additionally, there were a few ongoing large-scale development projects concerning metallic materials and focused on small- and medium-sized parts and components with varying complexity, small batch sizes, and varied costs. Further, the company had no one working full-time with AM. The company's business strategy was not oriented toward AM. The consistency in the realization of AM-related development projects was missing.

The results of the thematic analysis highlighted several challenges from a management perspective consisting of 20 themes that have been categorized into seven aggregated dimensions (Table 2). Next, the challenges were sorted into the three stages of integration to enhance the understanding of when in time such challenges appear and from which functional organization such challenge was addressed (Table 3). Most of the challenges appear in the pre-integration stage and the post-integration stage and only two challenges are in the integration stage.

Table 2. Thematic analysis of empirical findings

Examples of 1st order concepts	2nd order themes*	Aggregated dimensions
"*For example, if we reduce the weight of a [product] by 10 kg on a 20 ton machine we would potentially generate a very low reward.*" (Participant D)	Identifying and generating value with AM	Added value
	Impact of AM on the value chain	
"*How do we control the intellectual property [with AM parts]?*" (Participant B)	Intellectual property	External factors
	Benchmarking and competition with AM	
"*One challenge is about how we can make it easier to scale up. How do we go from a pilot to a broader application and scale this for different parts of the organizations and so on?*" (Participant F)	Industrialization of AM	AM strategy
	Identifying and defining business cases	
	Limited resources for AM	
"*I can say from a technology [perspective], the benefits [of AM in the commercial vehicle sector] are not clearly understood.*" (Participant D)	Benefits, abilities, and suitability of AM	AM technology

(*continued*)

Table 2. (*continued*)

Examples of 1st order concepts	2nd order themes*	Aggregated dimensions
	Maturity of AM	
"…*are we prepared to invest in certain AM technologies and how far in our supply chain? Do we keep that on our suppliers, or do we take it to the service vans to print it?*" (Participant G)	Location of manufacture	AM supply chain
	AM suppliers	
	Financial vulnerability	
"*That was a big challenge that we didn't even have the software and skills in our engineering teams.*" (Participant I)	Material, quality, and process perspectives	System of operations
	Testing, experimentation, and evaluation	
	Design for AM	
	Operational planning and organization	
"*I hear from Operations [functional organization] sometimes why are we not printing stuff or different parts. We want Technology [functional organization] to tell us what to print and things like that. It seems that we are kind of waiting for each other in different functional organizations to take the first step to … 'ok let's go for this now and try it.' Perhaps that makes us sometimes get stuck.*" (Participant C)	Competence, know-how, and skills in AM	Organizational change
	Prioritization, engagement, and taking initiatives with AM	
	Decision-making	
	Resilience, communication, and coordination	

5   Discussion

The results showed several identified challenges in the integration of AM that different functional organizations face in a large manufacturing company and when those challenges occur in the three stages of integration. The results suggested that a new theme emerged in added value which builds upon previous research [11]. The added value perspective seemed to be an important area for the company in its daily work and overall business strategy. However, it is not clear how added value is defined and used in the context of integrating AM [5, 9–14]. It is suggested that added value could consider the sustainability and product-service-related perspectives [10, 15].

Organizational change was a unanimous concern by all functional organizations. It is suggested that the company should address the concern by answering the following question: *"What has to change in my business in order for it to be successful?"* [10, p. 1427]. Especially if the company wants to have continued consistency in the realization of development projects related to AM even though AM is not yet integrated into their organization. On the other hand, there was a varied consensus regarding challenges related to AM strategy and AM technology. According to previous research [10, 11, 14, 15], one issue could be the limited knowledge of AM strategy- and AM technology-related challenges.

Table 3. Challenges are sorted into the functional organizations and stages of integration: pre-integration stage (I), integration stage (II), and post-integration stage (III)

Aggregated dimensions	Themed challenges	Functional organizations			
		Operations	Purchasing	Sales	Technology
Added value	Identifying and generating value with AM		I		I
	Impact of AM on the value chain				I
External forces	Intellectual property		III		
	Benchmarking and competition with AM				III
AM strategy	Industrialization of AM		I		I
	Identifying and defining business cases	I	I		I
	Limited resources for AM				I
AM technology	Benefits, abilities, and suitability of AM		I		I
	Maturity of AM		I	I	
AM supply chain	Location of manufacture		I		
	AM suppliers		II		
	Financial vulnerability				III

(*continued*)

Table 3. (*continued*)

Aggregated dimensions	Themed challenges	Functional organizations			
		Operations	Purchasing	Sales	Technology
System of operations	Material, quality, and process perspectives		III		III
	Testing, experimentation, and evaluation		III		III
	Design for AM		III		III
	Operational planning and organization		II		II
Organizational change	Competence, know-how, and skills in AM	I	I		I
	Prioritization, engagement, and taking initiatives with AM	III	III		III
	Decision-making		I	I	
	Resilience, communication, and coordination		III		III

It is not surprising that few challenges are present in the integration stage since previous research [14, 15] also highlighted a few challenges with similar distribution over all three stages during the adoption and implementation. However, there might be challenges affecting all three stages simultaneously [15]. Some examples of actions to overcome the challenges are suggested for one challenge in each of the stages of integration. When identifying and defining business cases it is suggested to seek help from AM service providers or AM research institutes [14]. Next, to overcome operational planning and organization challenges it is important to make sure that industry professionals have access to necessary resources (e.g., available workforce, software, money). To prioritize, get engagement, and increase the number of initiatives with AM it is suggested that industry professionals get the opportunity to prioritize such initiatives in their daily work.

6 Conclusions

This paper has identified challenges in the integration of AM that management faces in large manufacturing companies. This research has provided an understanding of what large manufacturing companies should consider in terms of challenges when integrating AM. A new dimension has been added to previous research [11]. Organizational change is seemingly unavoidable and was unanimously highlighted by several functional organizations of the company. The identified challenges were similarly distributed over all three stages of integration.

Identified challenges may be similar across the commercial vehicle sector in the manufacturing industry and generalization of results in other sectors and industries may be limited. The results might be useful for managers and other decision-makers when planning to integrate AM, planning suitable mitigation strategies, and making more informed decisions related to the integration of AM.

Future research should include insights from engineers, operators, and technicians. Additionally, similar research should be replicated at other large manufacturing companies to further enhance generalizability. This research mainly used qualitative data; hence, future research should include quantitative data or a mix of both. Furthermore, future research should investigate 1) if there are additional challenges affecting all stages of integration simultaneously [15], 2) the relationships between the identified challenges and their influence on the integration of AM [9], and 3) solutions that highlight actions (e.g., mitigation mechanisms) [14] and capabilities, to overcome the identified challenges to enhance facilitating the integration of AM step-by-step.

Acknowledgment. This research project has been funded by the Knowledge Foundation within the framework of the ARRAY++ Research School and the participating companies, and Mälardalen University, Sweden. The people that contributed with their knowledge are gratefully thanked for making these experiences available.

References

1. Oztemel, E., Gursev, S.: Literature review of industry 4.0 and related technologies. J. Intell. Manuf. **31**(1), 127–182 (2018). https://doi.org/10.1007/s10845-018-1433-8
2. ISO/ASTM 52900:2015 Additive manufacturing—General principles—Terminology: Fabrication additive—Principes généraux—Terminologie. Switzerland: ISO/ASTM International 2015
3. Gibson, I., Rosen, D., Stucker, B., Khorasani, M.: Additive Manufacturing Technologies, 3rd edn. Springer Nature, Switzerland AG (2021). https://doi.org/10.1007/978-3-030-56127-7
4. Gustavsson, M., Säfsten, K.: The learning potential of boundary crossing in the context of product introduction. Vocat. Learn. **10**(2), 235–252 (2017). https://doi.org/10.1007/s12186-016-9171-6
5. Yi, L., Gläßner, C., Aurich, J.C.: How to integrate additive manufacturing technologies into manufacturing systems successfully: a perspective from the commercial vehicle industry. J. Manuf. Syst. **53**, 195–211 (2019). https://doi.org/10.1016/j.jmsy.2019.09.007
6. Reiher, T., Lindemann, C., Jahnke, U., Deppe, G., Koch, R.: Holistic approach for industrializing AM technology: from part selection to test and verification. Prog. Addit. Manuf. **2**(1–2), 43–55 (2017). https://doi.org/10.1007/s40964-017-0018-y
7. Gao, W., et al.: The status, challenges, and future of additive manufacturing in engineering. Comput. Aided Des. **69**, 65–89 (2015). https://doi.org/10.1016/j.cad.2015.04.001
8. Schniederjans, D.G.: Adoption of 3D-printing technologies in manufacturing: a survey analysis. Int. J. Prod. Econ. **183**, 287–298 (2017). https://doi.org/10.1016/j.ijpe.2016.11.008
9. Dwivedi, G., Srivastava, S.K., Srivastava, R.K.: Analysis of barriers to implement additive manufacturing technology in the Indian automotive sector. Int. J. Phys. Distrib. Logist. Manag. **47**(10), 972–991 (2017). https://doi.org/10.1108/IJPDLM-07-2017-0222

10. Niaki, M.K., Nonino, F.: Additive manufacturing management: a review and future research agenda. Int. J. Prod. Res. **55**(5), 1419–1439 (2017). https://doi.org/10.1080/00207543.2016.1229064
11. Mellor, S., Hao, L., Zhang, D.: Additive manufacturing: a framework for implementation. Int. J. Prod. Econ. **149**, 194–201 (2014). https://doi.org/10.1016/j.ijpe.2013.07.008
12. Lynch, P., Hasbrouck, C.R., Wilck, J., Kay, M., Manogharan, G.: Challenges and opportunities to integrate the oldest and newest manufacturing processes: metal casting and additive manufacturing. Rapid Prototyp. J. **26**(6), 1145–1154 (2020). https://doi.org/10.1108/RPJ-10-2019-0277
13. Centea, D., Singh, I., Yakout, M., Boer, J., Elbestawi, M.: Opportunities and challenges in integrating additive manufacturing in the SEPT learning factory. In: 10th Conference on Learning Factories, CLF2020, pp. 108–113. Graz, Austria (2020). Procedia Manufacturing. https://doi.org/10.1016/j.promfg.2020.04.080
14. Chaudhuri, A., Rogers, H., Soberg, P., Pawar, K.S.: The role of service providers in 3D printing adoption. Ind. Manag. Data Syst. **119**(6), 1189–1205 (2019). https://doi.org/10.1108/IMDS-08-2018-0339
15. Deradjat, D., Minshall, T.: Implementation of rapid manufacturing for mass customization. J. Manuf. Technol. Manag. **28**(1), 95–121 (2017). https://doi.org/10.1108/JMTM-01-2016-0007
16. Voss, C.: Implementation: a key issue in manufacturing technology: the need for a field of study. Res. Policy **17**(2), 55–63 (1988). https://doi.org/10.1016/0048-7333(88)90021-2
17. Yin, R.K.: Case Study Research: Design and Methods. 6 th edn. SAGE, Thousand Oaks, CA (2018)
18. Patton, M.Q.: Qualitative Research & Evaluation Methods, 3rd edn. SAGE, London (2002)
19. Creswell, J.W.: RESEARCH DESIGN: Qualitative, Quantitative, and Mixed Methods Approaches, 4th edn. SAGE, Thousand Oaks, CA (2014)
20. Coghlan, D., Brydon-Miller, M.: Focus Groups. In: The SAGE Encyclopedia of Action Research, pp. 1−7. SAGE, London (2014). https://doi.org/10.4135/9781446294406
21. Gioia, D.A., Corley, K.G., Hamilton, A.L.: Seeking qualitative rigor in inductive research: notes on the gioia methodology. Organ. Res. Methods **16**(1), 15−31 (2012). https://doi.org/10.1177/1094428112452151

Agile and Digital Transformation in Manufacturing: A Bibliometric Review, Current Research Trends and Future Avenue

Milena Savkovic[✉] [iD], Danijela Ciric Lalic [iD], Bojan Lalic [iD], Maja Miloradov [iD], Jelena Curcic [iD], and Nenad Simeunovic [iD]

Faculty of Technical Sciences, University of Novi Sad, 21000 Novi Sad, Serbia
milena.savkovic@uns.ac.rs

Abstract. Digital transformation has become commonplace in the manufacturing industry, forcing companies to abide by the "laws" established by Industry 4.0. The term adaptability could relate to agility, which brings us to the link between agile manufacturing and digital transformation. This posed a question: do these two concepts affect each other's success and implementation? Likewise, does their relationship affect other factors in the manufacturing industry? This article aims to study the connection between agility and digital transformation in manufacturing. Based on the relationship between these two concepts, the authors tented to map current research and establish new research avenues through bibliometric analysis of all articles indexed in Scopus's bibliographic database. We identified the most relevant and productive authors, countries, and institutions researching the relation between agile and digital transformation in manufacturing. Trend analysis and thematic evaluation were performed to indicate respect for the research terms and their effect on other topics.

Keywords: Agility · Manufacturing · Digital transformation · Industry 4.0 · Bibliometric analysis

1 Introduction

The fourth industrial revolution can be seen in the digital transformation in all industries and the consumer market [1]. Today's manufacturing firms are forced into agility and digital business transformation to maintain market success and operate sustainably [1, 2].

A dynamic and uncertain business environment provokes manufacturing companies to be agile and thrives in digital transformation simultaneously. Agile manufacturing, the 21st-century manufacturing paradigm [3], could be explained as a methodology that fosters high-quality products and provides high value to the customer at its core. Some authors claim that agile manufacturing support socially and environmentally responsible business and responds to uncertainty and change [3–8]. The all-encompassing way agile

© IFIP International Federation for Information Processing 2022
Published by Springer Nature Switzerland AG 2022
D. Y. Kim et al. (Eds.): APMS 2022, IFIP AICT 663, pp. 380–388, 2022.
https://doi.org/10.1007/978-3-031-16407-1_45

manufacturing could be defined in a strategic context is a "business-wide mindset that emphasizes routinely flexible structures and infrastructures" [9].

Some of the topics of the APMS 2022 conference are "Industrial Digital Transformation", "Sustainable Production Management", "Smart Manufacturing & Industry 4.0", "AI & Data-driven Production Management", etc. All topics can be linked to Industry 4.0. And the struggle of companies to adapt to new paradigms. The key topics this conference has been covering in the last few years (e.g. Industry 4.0, Lean manufacturing, Flexibility, Sustainability, Smart manufacturing, etc. [10]) indicate that the APMS is one of the research drivers in digital and agile manufacturing.

This article aims to study the scientific production around digital transformation and agility in manufacturing through bibliographic data analysis of all articles indexed in Scopus, containing the terms "agile/agile methods/agile methodology/agile manufacturing", "manufacturing" and "digital transformation/digitalization/digitization" in all article title, abstract and keywords. Scopus is the largest, multidisciplinary database consisting of peer-reviewed scientific content. Based on the relationship between these two concepts, the authors tented to map current research and establish new research avenues through bibliometric analysis of all articles indexed in Scopus's bibliographic database. The bibliometric study was conducted using the "bibliometrics" R Package. VOSviewer software was used for graphical analysis and representation of the bibliographic data. We contribute to manufacturing literature by evaluating the publication of digital transformation and agile in this field to comprehend research trends through bibliometric analysis.

This article is organized into four chapters. The introductory part defined the problem, need and aim of the paper. The methodology then explains how the research was conducted and why we use the bibliometric R tool. The third section presents the key research findings and a brief discussion. Finally, the paper is summarized in conclusion, and directions for future research are also suggested.

For this research, we consider the following questions to be answered to help identify the dynamics of manufacturing literature and provide future research avenues in the era of digital and agile industrial enterprise challenges. The authors proposed research questions as follows:

1. *What is the evolutionary path of scientific documents on agile and digital manufacturing to date?*
2. *What are the most productive countries, authors and affiliations in this field?*
3. *Exploring the link between agile and digital in the manufacturing industry, what are the main trends and key themes?*

2   Research Methodology

This article proceeds with standard "bibliometric workflow", suggested by Zupic and Čater [11, 12]. The first step is (1) a *Scheme of study* where we defined research questions and identified tools and techniques for accessing bibliometric analysis. This step is described in the introductory section. Then we performed the second step – (2) *Data collection*, which included source selection, filter and export data. In order to determine the research trend in this area of publications, the dataset was obtained from the Scopus database, which is widely used in bibliometric studies [13]. The data were downloaded from the Scopus core collection for the period 2006–2022 using the following search query: *(TITLE-ABS-KEY(agile) OR TITLE-ABS-KEY("agile manufacturing") OR TITLE-ABS-KEY("agile methods") OR TITLE-ABS-KEY("agile methodology") AND TITLE-ABS-KEY(manufacturing) AND TITLE-ABS-KEY("digital transformation") OR TITLE-ABS-KEY(digitalization) OR TITLE-ABS-KEY(digitization)) AND (LIMIT-TO(DOCTYPE,"cp") OR LIMIT-TO (DOCTYPE,"ar")) AND (LIMIT-TO(LANGUAGE,"English"))*. A filter was used to find documents containing any search terms in the title, abstract, and keyword. The search was restricted to English-language articles. Document types observed were only conference proceedings and articles. (3) *Bibliometric analysis* was the third step, including software selection and analysis. The bibliometric analysis was conducted using the "bibliometrix" R Package tool. This analysis enables scientists to get an overview in one place, identify gaps in knowledge, extract new research ideas and set out their intended contribution to the field [14]. Firstly, annual scientific production, the most productive countries, authors and relevant affiliations were analyzed. After that, we performed trend analysis and thematic evaluation. (4) *Visualization* was the fourth step, which refers to selecting tools and techniques for appropriate visualization [15]. VOSviewer software was used for the graphical analysis of the bibliographic data [16]. Finally, the fifth step – (5) *Interpretation*, refers to the explanation of findings.

3 Results and Discussion of Findings

3.1 The Main Information About the Database

The final sample consisted of 154 documents published in 107 sources (44 articles and 110 conference papers) during the timespan 2006:2022. These documents were (co)authored by 447 people, out of which there were only ten single-authored documents and 467 multi-authored documents, with the average number of authors per document at 3.1. Records are concentrated around main research areas: engineering, computer science, business, management and accounting and decision sciences. Scopus assigns indexed articles to one or more research areas.

Figure 1 shows the annual production, and Fig. 2 shows the average citation per year for a relation between the terms agile, agile methodology/methods, agile manufacturing and at the other hand digital transformation, digitalization and digitization, observed in the manufacturing sector. Figure 1 clearly emphasizes increased literature production over time, especially in 2018, with 26 documents per year. Only 20 papers were published in the first 11 years in the observed time frame, increasing the number of published works already in 2017. The year 2018 can be considered the first relevant year for the scientific community because more papers were published than in the previous 11. However, after 2018, the number of published documents was constant and, then again, in 2021 – an increasing trend in the publication. Figure 2 indicates a significant increase in the annual citation rate of publications linking agile and digital transformation topics in the manufacturing domain from 2016 to 2021. The first significant growth in average citations is observed in 2016 and the second in 2021. The decline in average citations can be seen in 2019 and a substantial increase in 2020. These results may be related to the beginning COVID 19 pandemic and thus the growing need for digital and flexible ways of doing business.

The trend line is shown in red on both charts, pointing to a specific pattern that can be seen from the behavioral observation of the set of data. From 2016 to 2021, there is a steady increase in the average citation of documents per year. From 2006 to 2015, citations did not exceed 0.5%, considered a weak scientific contribution in this area. Also, most of the papers were published from 2017 until the end of the observed period.

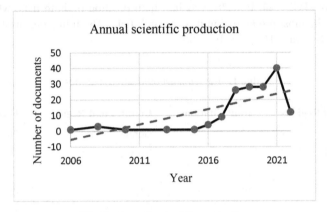

Fig. 1. Annual scientific production

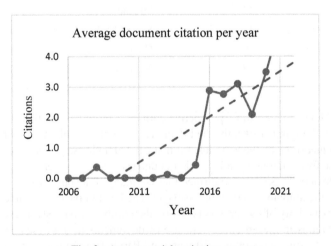

Fig. 2. Average articles citation per year

3.2   Most Productive Countries, Authors and Affiliations

This section provides information regarding core countries, authors and relevant affiliations of manufacturing literature in the field of digital and agile. Table 1 shows the top ten most productive countries, observing the total citations (TC) and frequency (F) over a time span. Country productivity was measured by two indicators - total citation of each country and distribution of publication frequencies according to country. The most productive countries, by total citation, were Sweden, followed by New Zealand, Norway, Portugal, Turkey, etc. Germany was in the first place, perceived by country frequency in the scientific world, followed by Norway, the United States, the United Kingdom, France, etc. According to both observed indicators, countries that appear in the top ten were Sweden, Germany, Norway, and China. It can be seen from the table that Germany (TC = 44, F = 78) was in a high position on both lists, which makes this country the most productive in this research field. The following most productive country was Norway (TC = 38, F = 22).

Table 1. Top ten most productive countries

Country and Regions	Total Citations	Country and Regions	Frequency
Sweden	95	Germany	78
New Zealand	59	Norway	22
Germany	44	USA	21
Norway	38	UK	14
Portugal	35	France	12
Turkey	23	Italy	12
China	12	Finland	11
Morocco	11	Switzerland	11
Malaysia	9	China	9
Romania	7	Sweden	7

Table 2 shows the ten most productive authors. The indicators that influenced the ranking were the number of published documents due to the observed period and the local impact measured by the h - index. From the list of authors, we can conclude that six authors come from Germany, and the other countries mentioned were Sweden, Norway, USA and Mexico. These facts confirmed that Germany contributed to the development of science in the domain observed in this paper. The local impact by h - index shows the scientific productivity of the authors based on the number of published research papers and their citations in the observed database of documents in this research. An author who stands out from others on this list was Vinit Parida from Luleå University of Technology, Sweden. His research interests were innovation, manufacturing, digitalization, entrepreneurship, high tech, sustainable industry, etc.

The top ten most relevant affiliations were shown in Table 3, according to the number of documents published during the timespan. The most pertinent affiliation was Reutlingen University with seven published documents from 2006 - to 2022 in the field of agile and digital manufacturing, one of Germany's leading universities offering international

Table 2. Top ten most productive authors

Authors	Authors Country	Local Impact by h - index	Number of Documents
V. Parida	Sweden	4	4
D. J. Powell	Norway	2	4
A. Zimmermann	Germany	3	4
J. Bogner	Germany	3	3
S. Bondar	Germany	2	3
J. C. Hsu	USA	2	3
D. Jugel	Germany	3	3
M. Möhring	Germany	3	3
A. Pfouga	Germany	2	3
D. Romero	Mexico	2	3

academic programs with close ties to industry and commerce. Besides Reutlingen University, this list included three more affiliates recognized as important in the scientific community. Affiliates from Norway, Sweden and the United States are in the most relevant affiliation, which confirms they are one of the leading countries researching this topic.

Table 3. Top ten most relevant affiliation

Affiliations	Country	Number of Documents
Reutlingen University	Germany	7
Norwegian University of Science and Technology	Norway	5
Aalen University	Germany	3
California State University	USA	3
Luleå University of Technology	Sweden	3
RWTH Aachen University	Germany	3
University of Rostock	Germany	3
Aalborg Universitet	Denmark	2
Delft University of Technology	Netherlands	2
University of St. Gallen	Switzerland	2

It is interesting to mention Denmark, the Netherlands and Switzerland as part of this list, then only Switzerland being on the list of the most productive countries in Table 1 in terms of frequency. None of the authors from these countries were on the list of the most productive authors (Table 2).

All universities shown in Table 3 have a strong connection with the industry, and their relevance in the research field of agile and digital manufacturing industry signified the importance of this topic and the challenges facing manufacturing companies.

3.3 Trend Analysis and Thematic Evaluation

This section presents trend analysis and thematic evaluation of the research topic. Trend analysis, shown in Fig. 3, explains the evolution of keyword plus from 2008 to 2022. The observed parameter was keyword plus, which can tell us about the content and scientific concepts presented in the documents in the database. The most frequent terms in the last three years were virtual manufacturing, information system, systems engineering (2018.), agile manufacturing system, digital transformation, automotive industry, software design (2019), internet of things, embedded systems, industry 4.0, digital technologies (2020), agile, manufacturing companies, digitization, lean manufacturing, industrial research (2021).

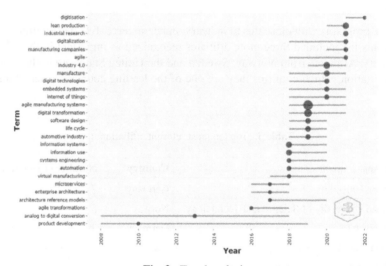

Fig. 3. Trend analysis

Figure 4 presents the historical development of agile and digital manufacturing literature. Thematic evolution depicts the history of themes and how these themes evolved, using the authors keywords. The first segment is from 2006–2020 and the second is from 2021–2022. Themes have evolved with time. Today, the concepts of agility and manufacturing are mentioned in the context of digitalization, which can be seen from the figure.

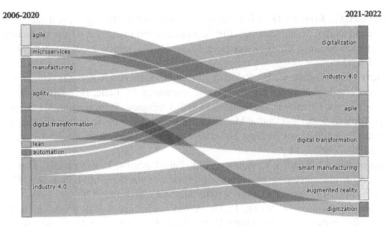

Fig. 4. Thematic evaluation

4 Conclusions and Further Research

To remain in a dynamic market and stay concurrent, companies are adopting agile and adaptive management methods and changing existing business models, i.e., operating more agile and digitally. This paper presents the scientific production of manufacturing literature about agile and digital transformation using bibliometric analysis. The research covers annual scientific production and citation per year to point out the topic's relevance, the most productive countries, authors and affiliations researching agile and digital manufacturing areas, and trend analysis and evolution of themes to show the current topics and future direction. The results of this research provide the directions for future research in sustainable and competitive manufacturing. This research is limited to analyzing only the Scopus database. Further works can be developed by analyzing databases such as Web of Science, Science Direct, among others.

References

1. Ghobakhloo, M.: Industry 4.0, digitization, and opportunities for sustainability. J. Cleaner Prod. 252 (2020). https://doi.org/10.1016/j.jclepro.2019.119869
2. Delic, M., Lalic, B., Gracanin, D., Lolic, T., Ciric, D.: Exploring the link between project management approach and project success dimensions: a structural model approach. Adv. Prod. Eng. Manag. **16**, 99–111 (2021)
3. Yusuf, Y.Y., Sarhadi, M., Gunasekaran, A.: Agile manufacturing: the drivers, concepts and attributes (1999)
4. Goldman, S.L., Nagel, R.N.: Management, technology and agility: the emergence of a new era in manufacturing (1993)
5. Kidd, P.T.: Agile Manufacturing: a strategy for the 21st century
6. Rakic, S., Pavlovic, M., Marjanovic, U.: A precondition of sustainability: industry 4.0 readiness. Sustainability **13**(12), 6641 (2021). https://doi.org/10.3390/su13126641
7. Ciric, D., Lolic, T., Gracanin, D., Stefanovic, D., Lalic, B.: The application of ICT solutions in manufacturing companies in Serbia. In: Lalic, B., Majstorovic, V., Marjanovic, U., von

Cieminski, G., Romero, D. (eds.) Advances in Production Management Systems. Towards Smart and Digital Manufacturing. IFIP Advances in Information and Communication Technology, vol. 592, pp. 122–129. Springer, Cham (2020). https://doi.org/10.1007/978-3-030-57997-5_15

8. Pavlović, M., Marjanović, U., Rakić, S., Tasić, N., Lalić, B.: The big potential of big data in manufacturing: evidence from emerging economies. In: Lalic, B., Majstorovic, V., Marjanovic, U., von Cieminski, G., Romero, D. (eds.) Advances in Production Management Systems. Towards Smart and Digital Manufacturing. IFIP Advances in Information and Communication Technology, vol. 592, pp. 100–107. Springer, Cham (2020). https://doi.org/10.1007/978-3-030-57997-5_12

9. Gunasekaran, A., Yusuf, Y.Y., Adeleye, E.O., Papadopoulos, T., Kovvuri, D., Dan'Asabe G. Geyi,: Agile manufacturing: an evolutionary review of practices. Int. J. Prod. Res. **57**(15–16), 5154–5174 (2019). https://doi.org/10.1080/00207543.2018.1530478

10. Keepers, M., Romero, D., Wuest, T.: The APMS conference & IFIP WG5.7 in the 21st century: a bibliometric study. In: Ameri, F., Stecke, K.E., von Cieminski, G., Kiritsis, D. (eds.) Advances in Production Management Systems. Towards Smart Production Management Systems. IFIP Advances in Information and Communication Technology, vol. 567, pp. 1–13. Springer, Cham (2019). https://doi.org/10.1007/978-3-030-29996-5_1

11. Zupic, I., Čater, T.: Bibliometric methods in management and organization. Organ. Res. Methods **18**(3), 429–472 (2015). https://doi.org/10.1177/1094428114562629

12. Ciric, D., Lalic, B., Marjanovic, U., Savkovic, M., Rakic, S.: A bibliometric analysis approach to review mass customization scientific production. In: Dolgui, A., Bernard, A., Lemoine, D., von Cieminski, G., Romero, D. (eds.) Advances in Production Management Systems. Artificial Intelligence for Sustainable and Resilient Production Systems. IFIP Advances in Information and Communication Technology, vol. 634, pp. 328–338. Springer, Cham (2021). https://doi.org/10.1007/978-3-030-85914-5_35

13. Rojas-Lamorena, Á.J., del Barrio-García, S., Alcántara-Pilar, J.M.: A review of three decades of academic research on brand equity: a bibliometric approach using co-word analysis and bibliographic coupling. J. Bus. Res. **139**, 1067–1083 (2022). https://doi.org/10.1016/j.jbusres.2021.10.025

14. Donthu, N., Kumar, S., Mukherjee, D., Pandey, N., Lim, W.M.: How to conduct a bibliometric analysis: an overview and guidelines. J. Bus. Res. **133**, 285–296 (2021). https://doi.org/10.1016/j.jbusres.2021.04.070

15. Nasir, A., Shaukat, K., Hameed, I.A., Luo, S., Alam, T.M., Iqbal, F.: A bibliometric analysis of corona pandemic in social sciences: a review of influential aspects and conceptual structure. IEEE Access **8**, 133377–133402 (2020). https://doi.org/10.1109/ACCESS.2020.3008733

16. Aria, M., Cuccurullo, C.: Bibliometrix: an R-tool for comprehensive science mapping analysis. J. Inf. **11**(4), 959–975 (2017). https://doi.org/10.1016/j.joi.2017.08.007

Sustainable Production Management

Achieving Global Sustainability Through Sustainable Product Life Cycle

Foivos Psarommatis[1](✉) ⓘ and Gökan May[2] ⓘ

[1] SIRIUS, Department of Informatics, University of Oslo, Gaustadalléen 23 B N-0373, Oslo, Norway
foivosp@ifi.uio.no
[2] Department of Mechanical Engineering, University of North Florida, Jacksonville, Florida, USA

Abstract. Sustainable product life cycle management aims at minimizing the negative impacts on the environment, society, and economy by managing different stages of a product's existence. Proper management of the product life cycle thus leads to a reduction in several types of waste such as materials, energy, and time. While there is significant progress on the key enabling technologies and resources for sustainability within the last decade, the traditional models used for product life cycle sustainability are outdated thus hindering a successful shift toward a circular economy and hence these outdated models should be updated properly to cover the needs of the modern manufacturing landscape. In this paper, we challenge the traditional way of managing a product's life cycle and propose a new sustainable product life cycle approach with the emphasis on multiple life cycles of products as well as their components and materials through iterative repurposing and reuse, and by integrating the disposal concept from the early phases of conception and design for achieving global sustainability. We highlight that by adopting the proposed approach, it is possible to achieve a longer period of actual use of products and save a significant amount of resources.

Keywords: Sustainability · Re-use · Re-purpose · Product life cycle · Global · Sustainable product life cycle

1 Introduction and Literature Review

From an engineering perspective, product life cycle (PLCs), which are associated primarily with the creation of new products, cover the phases of a product's entire life from inception through design and manufacturing, service and distribution, and the manufactured product's end of life [1, 2] This traditional and limited view was originally developed for manufacturers. It aims to achieve maximum profits and value at each phase of a product's life cycle and hence focuses on economic indicators rather than environmental and societal impacts [3].

Sustainable development is a principle that seeks to satisfy the needs of the present while conserving and enhancing resources for future generations [4]. To accomplish

© IFIP International Federation for Information Processing 2022
Published by Springer Nature Switzerland AG 2022
D. Y. Kim et al. (Eds.): APMS 2022, IFIP AICT 663, pp. 391–398, 2022.
https://doi.org/10.1007/978-3-031-16407-1_46

this goal, it is important to gradually change approaches to development and use proper methods and key enabling technologies to create more sustainable products [5, 6]. Sustainable product life cycle (SPLC) management is a method for managing the different phases of a product's existence to minimise negative impacts on the three pillars of sustainability: environment, society, and economy [7]. In this context, SPLC enhances the reuse, remanufacturing, and recycling of all materials involved in the creation of products [8] Moreover, repurposing directs products or materials for use in different functions than they were originally designed and produced for [9]. Determining alternative uses for outdated assets leads to cost savings in terms of both disposal and materials. While sustainability-oriented key enabling technologies and resources have made significant progress within the last decade [10], the traditional models used for PLC sustainability are outdated and thus hinder a successful shift toward a circular economy. Accordingly, these outdated models should be updated to address the needs of the modern manufacturing landscape [11].

The concept of PLCs has formed a fundamental component of marketing theory for more than seven decades. Following its initial proposition in 1950 [12] and significant growth in the 1960s thanks to the influence of a prominent article by Levitt, [13] it has remained a central element in different disciplines from marketing to new product development despite its flawed nature criticised by leading academics for decades 11, 12. The PLC we refer to and challenge in this study, however, is associated with the creation of a product that begins with the extraction of raw materials and ends with the materials from this product being reused, recovered, recycled, or disposed of [16] Properly managing the PLC thus reduces several types of waste, such as materials (e.g., mineral resources), energy, and time [17].

According to Hood, [18] to decrease overall waste society should be more open to repurposing previously owned products. Geissdoerfer et al. (2017) [11] define the Circular Economy as "a regenerative system in which resource input and waste, emission, and energy leakage are minimised by slowing, closing, and narrowing material and energy loops". Circularity can only be achieved by integrating an SPLC approach from the initial product design to the repurposing of waste and by fostering the reuse and recycling of materials to minimise negative impacts on the environment as much as possible [17, 18]. Single-use products and materials, such as plastic packaging in the food industry, are one of the major contributors to global waste and should be eliminated to improve sustainability [16, 21]. Hence, it is of paramount importance to improve the design of new products by revising the outdated models of the PLC theory with the addition of a sustainability dimension [22].

Although widely accepted, the PLC theory has many flaws. A major critique is that the traditional PLC theory considers products to have only one life cycle before recycling and therefore does not give enough consideration to product reuse and repurposing. However, not all products must advance to end of life and disposal; instead, they can return to the growth phase via repurposing and reusage, hence achieving multiple iterative life cycles. Finally, the traditional PLC models used today are outdated and unable to fully cope with the current social, environmental, and economical challenges of the modern world [23] In this paper, therefore, we address this gap and propose a new SPLC approach that emphasises multiple life cycles of products and their components and materials through iterative repurposing and reuse and that integrates the disposal concept from the early phases of conception and design to achieve true global sustainability.

Guided by these aforementioned obstacles, this paper challenges traditional PLC management and seeks to achieve global sustainability by adding new inner cycles for repurposing and reusability that consider multiple product lives simultaneously and by removing the notion of disposure from the main cycle and incorporating it into the design phase.

2 Sustainable Product Life Cycle

The PLC perception affects the sustainability of a product's design as well as its production, distribution, use, and recycling. The traditional PLC was developed without considering the needs of contemporary and future societies and markets and is therefore obsolete and unable to describe modern concepts arising from modern needs. Furthermore, a fault of the traditional PLC is the disposal and waste of products within their life cycle; Sect. 2.1 provides further information on this aspect. The PLC is an outlook and is foundational to the sustainable creation of products. If this fundament is incorrect or outdated, then the product will not be sustainable.

2.1 Proposed Sustainable Product Life Cycle Framework

The proposed SPLC was developed in consideration of the latest concepts that contribute to sustainability—such as zero defect manufacturing [22, 23], product reusability, and repurposing—and how to better exploit products and knowledge [26]. The radical change our proposed SPLC brings is that it considers multiple lives for a product rather than only one. Traditionally, the PLC has consisted of a single life cycle, starting with the conceptualisation of the product until its disposal or recycling. Usually when a product reaches the disposal stage, the recycling phase still has significant remaining useful life (RUL); therefore, the product is terminated not based on the product's operability but on the personal responsibility of the user. Often the product can operate normally, and even when a product cannot operate as designed, its included components can be used elsewhere. Therefore, two key concepts our upgraded SPLC model introduces are reusability and repurposing.

Figure 1 illustrates the proposed SPLC model, which is intended to function as a roadmap for sustainable designing, manufacturing, living, and thinking. The figure is colour coded to demonstrate the different PLC stages. The main cycle (blue) is the traditional PLC model, which has existed for many years and significantly affected the adoption of circularity. We modified the traditional PLC slightly by removing the notion of disposure from the main cycle and incorporating the concept of zero waste and sustainability into the design and develop phase. This enrichment to the design phase is mandatory since it is crucial for circularity and because if the product is not designed in a specific way, then reusage and repurposing will not be possible, as occurs at present. From our SPLC, it is evident that the disposal step (marked in red) has been removed from the cycle. Disposing a product is an undesirable step that disrupts the cycle and must be avoided as it is not sustainable to create waste of any form. The second

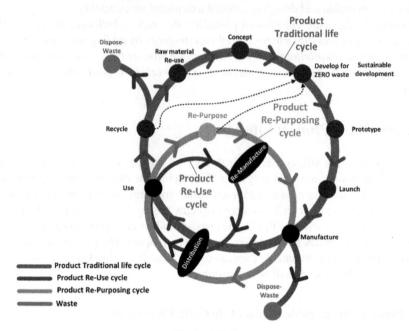

Fig. 1. SPLC

innovation of our SPLC model occurs at the use phase of the product. Traditionally, products are used and then recycled or disposed of. To increase the sustainability and exploit 100% of a product's RUL, we added the repurpose and reuse cycles (signified by purple and green, respectively). Products are currently treated as if they have a single life and are then recycled or disposed of; however, a product or part of a product can have multiple lives until it reaches the global end of life. Once the first life of a product has concluded, our model proposes two pathways. If the product can be used for its original purpose, then remanufacturing is performed if necessary and the product is reused. If the product cannot operate as originally intended or its use is no longer required, then the product or components of the product are repurposed. Reusing or repurposing 100% of the consumed resources for manufactured products will significantly increase the global sustainability of modern life. The reuse and repurpose loop continues until the global end of life of each product or component is reached. Because recycling focuses only on materials, other types of resources, such as manufacturing time, cannot be recycled; therefore, these extra cycles will help exploit better not only the natural resources but also the human effort and manufacturing time. Additionally, a knowledge cycle arising from the use, repurpose, reuse, recycle, and product design phases provides valuable information and feedback for the development of new sustainable products compatible with SPLCs. The proposed SPLC aims to improve all three pillars of sustainability, economy, environment, and society. Utilizing all the remaining useful life of a product not only the material waste is reduced but also the resources spent (money, human time etc.) are utilized more efficiently and they are not wasted.

2.2 Product Remaining Useful Life

Utilising the entire RUL of a product is crucial for improving global sustainability [27]. Figure 2 illustrates the difference between a single PLC and multiple PLCs. It also demonstrates the existing single-PLC situation that our proposed model addresses. The waste that using a single PLC creates is tremendous and includes not only material-based wastes but also human effort, manufacturing time, and other types of time wastes that cannot be recycled, thus leading to a dramatic reduction of sustainability. From Fig. 2, it is evident that adopting the proposed approach would achieve a longer period of product use and save a significant quantity of resources.

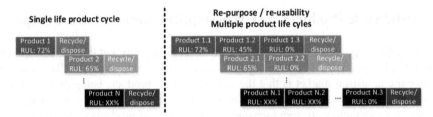

Fig. 2. Single versus multiple PLCs

2.3 Sustainability Levels

Sustainability is a term that is difficult to measure [28], but it is possible to estimate how the sustainability level is affected by different actions. Figure 3 depicts the basic concepts of both traditional PLCs and the proposed SPLCs. The sustainability level is a measure that considers the performance of all three pillars of sustainability (economy, environment, and society) at the same time. It is evident from the figure that the concepts and mentality of traditional PLCs correspond to extremely low levels of sustainability. The bottom of the chart contains any form of waste, which is unwanted and should be avoided as much as possible. The next row contains products that are used only once and then recycled. Recycling prevents the scale from swinging immediately towards the negative side but is not a sustainable solution. The goal is to not create waste, and therefore new methods and outlooks are required.

The proposed SPLC introduces the concepts of repurpose and reuse, which offer significantly higher sustainability levels. Repurpose corresponds to a lower level of sustainability than reuse because more effort is required to change the purpose of the initial product or components. To reuse a product, in many cases almost no significant effort is needed. In general, sustainability will only be achieved by changing mindsets and inventing ways to avoid creating waste, whether material or any other type.

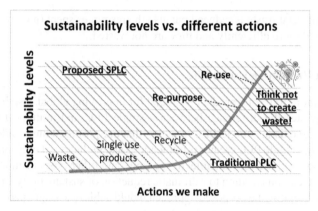

Fig. 3. Sustainability levels versus actions

3   Sustainable Product Life Cycle Implications and Future Steps

Adopting the proposed SPLC will increase global sustainability, but this increase comes with many implications. The main implication that will occur and potentially disrupt or change the industrial market is that the number of new products being produced will be significantly reduced because manufactured products will be reused or repurposed. Manufacturers should shift from focusing on producing new products to developing and establishing systems and procedures for remanufacturing and reusing products. To this end, new methods and manufacturing systems should focus on remanufacturing products, maintaining high-level quality, and utilising zero defect manufacturing [22, 23]. At the same time consumers should be familiarized with re-using and re-purposing concepts to embrace re-using products and in general buying products with re-used or repurposed components. Data-driven technologies and Industry 4.0 technologies in general are key for the successful implementation of our proposed model as these technologies help achieve the required knowledge for building the SPLC model.

Furthermore, the product design is critical for implementing the proposed SPLC model. Manufacturers must design collaboratively with other manufacturers or at minimum have a plan for incorporating existing products into their new products. Collaborating could provide opportunities to repurpose the products of other manufacturers when they have reached their first end of life (not the global life cycle). Therefore, new collaborative design methodologies are needed and would capture the reuse and repurpose concepts. To achieve the collaboration design and simultaneously maintain the intellectual property rights of each manufacturer, new communication and collaboration platforms are needed to facilitate this procedure. Enhanced methods, protocols, and standardisation procedures should be created to successfully implement the repurposing and reuse of products.

Numerous products that are intentionally designed to be single use, such as packaging in the food and other industries, currently exist. These types of products disrupt the sustainability cycle and require radical changes in terms of the product design.

4 Conclusion

In this paper, we focused on the shortcomings of the traditional PLC concept and proposed a new approach for an SPLC as an enabling factor toward achieving true global sustainability. The novelty of the new SPLC model is manifold. First, it considers multiple lives for a product rather than only one. Second, it removes disposal from the main cycle and incorporates it into the design phase. Finally, it adds new repurpose and reuse cycles. This new SPLC model will help advance further developments in fields that cope with the social, environmental, and economical challenges of the modern world. Manufacturing companies' top management must embrace the concepts of reuse and repurpose, think globally, and not create waste.

Acknowledgments. The presented work was partially supported by the projects Eur3ka and QU4LITY, EU H2020 projects under grant agreements No 101016175 and No 825030 accordingly. The paper reflects the authors' views, and the Commission is not responsible for any use that may be made of the information it contains.

References

1. Kos, K.: Modularity: A Key Concept in Product Life-cycle Engineering. Handbook of Life-cycle Engineering (1998). pp. 511–530
2. Klöpffer, W.: Life cycle assessment. Environ. Sci. Pollut. Res. **4**, 223–228 (1997). https://doi.org/10.1007/BF02986351
3. Tipnis, V.A.: Product life cycle economic models — towards a comprehensive framework for evaluation of environmental impact and competitive advantage. CIRP Ann. **40**, 463–466 (1991). https://doi.org/10.1016/S0007-8506(07)62030-7
4. Brundtland, G.H.: Our common future—call for action. Environ. Conserv. **14**, 291–294 (1987). https://doi.org/10.1017/S0376892900016805
5. Curran, M.A.: Life Cycle Assessment Handbook: A Guide for Environmentally Sustainable Products (2012). https://doi.org/10.1002/9781118528372
6. Heijungs, R., Huppes, G., Guinée, J.B.: Life cycle assessment and sustainability analysis of products, materials and technologies. Toward a scientific framework for sustainability life cycle analysis. Polym. Degrad. Stab. **95**(3), 422–428 (2010). https://doi.org/10.1016/j.polymdegradstab.2009.11.010
7. Niemann, J., Tichkiewitch, S., Westkamper, E., et al.: Design of sustainable product life cycles. Design Sustain. Prod. Life Cycles 1–209 (2009). https://doi.org/10.1007/978-3-540-79083-9
8. Kiritsis, D.: Closed-loop PLM for intelligent products in the era of the Internet of things. Comput. Aided Des. **43**, 479–501 (2011). https://doi.org/10.1016/J.CAD.2010.03.002
9. Liu, W., Beltagui, A., Ye, S.: Accelerated innovation through repurposing: exaptation of design and manufacturing in response to COVID-19. R&D Manag. **51**, 410–426 (2021). https://doi.org/10.1111/RADM.12460
10. Dušková, M.: Key enabling technologies and measuring of the company performance in relation to sustainable development: evaluation model design. Int. J. Innov. Sustain. Dev. **15**, 1–34 (2021)
11. Geissdoerfer, M., Savaget, P., Bocken, N.M.P., Hultink, E.J.: The circular economy – a new sustainability paradigm? J. Clean. Prod. **143**, 757–768 (2017). https://doi.org/10.1016/J.JCLEPRO.2016.12.048

12. Dean: Pricing policies for new products (HBR Classic). Harv. Bus. Rev. **28**, 45–50 (1976)
13. Levitt, T.: Exploit the product life cycle (1995)
14. Mercer, D.: A two-decade test of product life cycle theory. Br. J. Manag. **4**, 269–274 (1993). https://doi.org/10.1111/J.1467-8551.1993.TB00063.X
15. Mitchell, S.L., Clark, M.: Reconceptualising product life-cycle theory as stakeholder engagement with non-profit organisations. J. Market. Manag. **35**, 13–39 (2019). https://doi.org/10.1080/0267257X.2018.1562487
16. Law, K.L., Narayan, R.: Reducing environmental plastic pollution by designing polymer materials for managed end-of-life. Nat. Rev. Mater. **7**(2), 104–116 (2021). https://doi.org/10.1038/s41578-021-00382-0
17. Machac, J., Steiner, F., Tupa, J.: Product life cycle risk management. Risk Manag. Treatise Eng. Practit. (2017). https://doi.org/10.5772/INTECHOPEN.68797
18. Hood, B.: Make recycled goods covetable. Nature **531**(7595), 438–440 (2016). https://doi.org/10.1038/531438a
19. Rosenboom, J.-G., Langer, R., Traverso, G.: Bioplastics for a circular economy. Nat. Rev. Mater. **7**(2), 117–137 (2022). https://doi.org/10.1038/s41578-021-00407-8
20. Kiser, B.: Circular economy: Getting the circulation going. Nature **531**(7595), 443–446 (2016). https://doi.org/10.1038/531443a
21. Cabernard, L., Pfister, S., Oberschelp, C., Hellweg, S.: Growing environmental footprint of plastics driven by coal combustion. Nature Sustain. **2021**, 1 (2021). https://doi.org/10.1038/s41893-021-00807-2
22. Sovacool, B.K., Newell, P., Carley, S., Fanzo, J.: Equity, technological innovation and sustainable behaviour in a low-carbon future. Nat. Hum. Behav. **2022**, 1–12 (2022). https://doi.org/10.1038/s41562-021-01257-8
23. Dong, Y., Zhao, Y., Wang, H., et al.: Integration of life cycle assessment and life cycle costing for the eco-design of rubber products. Sci. Rep. **12**, 1–19 (2022). https://doi.org/10.1038/s41598-021-04633-6
24. Psarommatis, F., May, G., Dreyfus, P.-A., Kiritsis, D.: Zero defect manufacturing: state-of-the-art review, shortcomings and future directions in research. Int. J. Prod. Res. **7543**, 1–17 (2020). https://doi.org/10.1080/00207543.2019.1605228
25. Psarommatis, F., Sousa, J., Mendonça, P., et al.: Zero-defect manufacturing the approach for higher manufacturing sustainability in the era of industry 4.0: a position paper. Int. J. Prod. Res. (2021). https://doi.org/10.1080/00207543.2021.1987551
26. Psarommatis, F., Bravos, G.: A holistic approach for achieving sustainable manufacturing using zero defect manufacturing: a conceptual framework. Procedia CIRP **107**, 107–112 (2022). https://doi.org/10.1016/J.PROCIR.2022.04.018
27. El Jamal, D., Ananou, B., Graton, G., et al.: Similarity-based brownian motion approach for remaining useful life prediction, pp. 1–7 (2021). https://doi.org/10.1109/ICCAD52417.2021.9638776
28. Shuaib, M., Seevers, D., Zhang, X., et al.: Product sustainability index (ProdSI). J. Ind. Ecol. **18**, 491–507 (2014). https://doi.org/10.1111/JIEC.12179

Circularity Practices in Manufacturing—A Study of the 20 Largest Manufacturing Companies in Sweden

Filip Skärin$^{(\boxtimes)}$ ⬡, Carin Rösiö⬡, and Ann-Louise Andersen⬡

Jönköping University, Gjuterigatan 5, 553 18 Jönköping, Sweden
filip.skarin@ju.se

Abstract. In line with the accelerating global warming crisis, the concept of circular economy (CE), wherein the utilization and lifetimes of resources and materials are maximised, has gained a significant increase in attention. For manufacturing companies, adapting to a CE is particularly important due to high CO_2-e emissions. In order to increase the knowledge regarding how manufacturing companies have adapted to a CE, sustainability reports wherein the companies themselves report upon their circularity practices can be examined. This study has aimed at investigating the publicly available sustainability reports of the 20 largest manufacturing companies in Sweden, with the purpose of identifying which, and on what level of implementation, circularity practices are mentioned. The 10R framework was used as a foundation for categorizing and analysing the identified circularity practices. The findings in this study include a total of 38 unique circularity practices, whereas 13 are categorized as visioned or planned, and 36 are categorized as ongoing or already realised circularity practices. The circularity practices were primarily related to reducing, reusing, and recycling. Suggestions of further research include elaborately describing the circularity practices as well as further exploring the implementation of repairing, refurbishing and remanufacturing amongst manufacturing companies.

Keywords: Circularity · Circularity practices · Circular economy · Manufacturing · Sustainability

1 Introduction

During the past 150 years, the linear economy characterised by a "take-make-use-dispose" product and material view has dominated [1, 2]. In line with the accelerating global warming crisis, the approach of circular economy (CE) has gained a significant increase in attention, wherein the utilization and lifetimes of resources and materials are maximised [3]–[5]. Nowadays, CE is generally accepted as a significant support to sustainable development [1, 6, 7]. For manufacturing companies, the strive towards a CE is highly relevant as they play a major part in the global warming crisis. For instance, in 2019, manufacturing companies were responsible for 32% of Sweden's entire CO_2-e

D. Y. Kim et al. (Eds.): APMS 2022, IFIP AICT 663, pp. 399–407, 2022.
https://doi.org/10.1007/978-3-031-16407-1_47

emissions [8]. In order to realize CE, circularity practices such as reuse, refurbish, repair and remanufacture can be adapted and implemented [9]. However, the descriptions of circularity practices are largely focused on products in previous research. Similarly, hitherto conducted research has also been directed towards describing the circularity practices from a supply chain perspective (e.g. [10]) and developing circular business models [11]. A particular emphasis on the circularity practices in manufacturing is yet to be realised. Therefore, further clarifications regarding the contents of circularity practices directly related to manufacturing operations is needed.

CE has also become an interesting topic for companies, as indicated by the increased focus on CE in publicly stated sustainability reports (e.g. [10, 12]). Hence, investigating sustainability reports enables an up-to date description by the companies' themselves regarding their circularity practices. In Sweden, the sustainability report is a public document required to be annually presented by companies if fulfilling two of the following requirements: (i) having a total asset of more than 175 million SEK ($\approx$17.2 million USD), (ii) net sales of more than 350 million SEK ($\approx$ 34.4 million USD) or (iii) average 250 employees or more [13]. Previous research has not emphasized on describing circularity practices mentioned in sustainability reports amongst manufacturing companies. Hence, the purpose of this study is to identify which, and on what level of implementation, circularity practices in manufacturing are mentioned in sustainability reports. The remainder of the paper is structured as follows: chapter 2 describes the theoretical framework, including circularity focus in sustainability reports and circularity practices. Section 3 presents the methodology for fulfilling the purpose. Section 4 presents the identified circularity practices, and in Sect. 5 these are discussed. Lastly, in Sect. 6, conclusions and suggestions of further research are presented.

2   Related Research

2.1   Circularity Focus in Sustainability Reports

Investigating sustainability reports has previously been carried out in order to identify and describe circularity practices. For instance, Sihvonen & Partanen [14] explored how Asian, European and North American information and communications technology companies have addressed CE in their sustainability report. The focus regard eco-design practices regarding quantitative environmental targets. CE was addressed in terms of the product life cycle phases pre-use, use and post-phase, including recover, reduce, reuse and recycle [14]. Rhein and Sträter [15], on the other hand, studied the sustainability reports of 10 global companies which products are most frequently found in oceans and on coasts, focusing on a the self-commitment of those companies and reconstructuring the CE concept and the circularity practices reduce, reuse and recycle. Moreover, Calzolari et al. [10] focused on the adaptation of CE practices, in particular reduce, reuse, recycle and recover were distinguished as CE practices, within 50 European Multi-National Enterprises within the sectors agri-food, services, energy and manufacturing.

The latter included companies such as Volkswagen AG, Daimler, Siemens and Unilever. They found an increase from 3 mentions in 2013 to 25, i.e. half of the companies in 2018. Production/manufacturing was found to be primarily related to reuse of parts and components, usage of renewable energy and increase of production systems efficiency [10].

2.2 Circularity Practices and R-Frameworks

The R-framework originates from the introduction of 1R in the 1980s. This stemmed from the lean manufacturing, and focused primarily on the reduction of wastes [16]. During the 1990s, an evolved R-framework covering the circularity practices reduce, reuse and recycle was adopted by many companies in order to establish greener manufacturing. However, as this R-framework, frequently termed as 3R, does not ensure the possibility to adapt a four-stage product life-cycle, including pre-manufacturing, manufacturing, use and post-use, it is nowadays frequently reckoned as not alone capable of ensuring sustainable manufacturing [17, 18]. Instead, incorporating 6 circularity practices, i.e. the 6R framework is commonly referred to. This framework includes the addition of recover, redesign and remanufacturing from the previous 3R framework. By implementing the circularity practices included in the 6R framework, a closed-loop which entails cradle-to-cradle perspective of products and resources can be implemented within the supply chain in order to set the foundation for sustainable manufacturing [18]. However, in recent years the R-framework has been developed even further. This has led to a numerous Rs being added to the aforementioned 6Rs. For instance, Potting et al. [19], presents an additional 4Rs, resulting in a total of 10Rs. The general rule of thumb in Potting et al.'s [19] reasoning implies that a higher degree of circularity aids in maximising the utilization of resources, hence limiting the environmental impacts of manufacturing companies. Nevertheless, there is a discrepancy amongst the hitherto conducted research regarding the terminology used in these descriptions of the R-framework. Potting et al. [19] uses similar, but not identical terms, as the previously discussed 6Rs, whilst also adding refuse, rethink, repurpose and recover to the R-framework (Table 1).

Table 1 The 10R framework, adapted from Potting et al. [19]

Circularity practice category	Description
R0—Refuse	Make the product unessential through function removal or by including function and ability in other products
R1—Rethink	Rethinking the usage of products, e.g. through minimizing natural resource and material usage
R2—Reduce	Efficiently manufacturing of the products, e.g. through minimizing natural resource and material usage

(continued)

Table 1 (*continued*)

Circularity practice category	Description
R3—Reuse	The product is reused by another consumer while still remaining original abilities
R4—Repair	Repair the product to enable original abilities to properly function
R5—Refurbish	Refurbishing the product to original condition
R6—Remanufacture	Dismantle the product to enable original abilities to properly function
R7—Repurpose	Use discarded product or its parts in new product (with other abilities and functions)
R8—Recycle	Process the product to obtain material which can be used in manufacturing of new products
R9—Recover	Recover energy through material incineration

3 Methodology

In this research, a document study was carried out in order to investigate sustainability reports (see Fig. 1). The sample, and also the unit of analysis, included the 20 largest manufacturing companies in Sweden according to their net turnover in 2020. Sustainability reports from the sample were gathered from the companies' websites, and their most recent reports from 2020 were read in its entirety. During the reading, parts related to circularity were extracted. The sustainability reports were read in English if available, however, in the cases were solely a Swedish version of the report was available, the excerpted parts were translated into English after reading the reports in order to synchronize the data analysis. The parts related to circularity practices, e.g. in terms of quotes and paragraphs, were thereafter sorted and categorized using the software NVivo. This was based on the previously mentioned 10R framework, which was chosen due to its extensiveness in comparison to other R-frameworks (e.g. 3R and 6R). However, as the 10R framework described by Potting et al. [19] focuses on products, not circularity practices in manufacturing, solely the structure of the framework was used. Instead, the purpose of this study has been to provide new insights into the specific contents of each circularity practice category, as well as the level of implementation of these circularity practices. A circularity practice in manufacturing was defined as a circularity practice occurring within the manufacturing facility. Only the circularity practices related to the production of products was included, as well as e.g. reparations of the product, however, circularity practices related to product design, implementing circular business models and so on was not included. Once the initial categorization was completed, a second refinement of the circularity practices was carried out to further cluster and clarify the practices. Lastly, each circularity practice was categorized either as a visioned/planned practice or as an ongoing/realised practice. This categorization was inspired by Calzolari et al. [10], and chosen since it was deemed to provide sufficient separation between the identified circularity practices in terms of level of implementation.

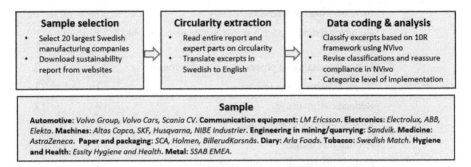

Fig. 1 The methodological process and sample, adapted from Calzolari et al. [10]

4 Circularity Practices in Manufacturing

By studying the sustainability reports of the 20 largest manufacturing companies in Sweden, a total of 38 unique circularity practices in manufacturing were identified (see Table 2). The majority of the identified circularity practices in this study have been categorised as ongoing/released practices. In total, 13 of the identified circularity practices were categorized as visioned/planned practices, whilst 36 ongoing/realised circularity practices. In terms of visioned/planned circularity practices, *"Reduce resource usage"*, *"Reduce generated waste"* and *"Reduce GhG (greenhouse gas) emissions"* were the most frequently mentioned practices, and also the only practices mentioned by more than one single company. The circularity practices *"Reduce GhG emissions"*, *"Reuse materials"*, *"Reduce generated waste"* and *"Reduce energy usage"* were mentioned by the most companies in terms of a realised/ongoing practice. Furthermore, repairing, refurbishing and remanufacturing were only identified in terms of a single circularity practice each, in comparison to the other circularity practice categories wherein more specified descriptions of circularity practices were possible to attain from the results.

Table 2 Identified circularity practices in manufacturing

Category Circularity practices		Total	V/P	O/R
R0—Refuse	No practice identified			
R1—Rethink	Apply sustainable chemical management	1		1
	Implement circular production processes	1		1
	Increase available data from production	1		1

(continued)

Table 2 (*continued*)

Category	Circularity practices	Total	V/P	O/R
	Increase usage of renewable energy	7	1	6
	Rethink existing production to make more sustainable & circular	1	1	
	Use new sustainable processes and technologies	3	1	2
R2—Reduce	Reduce chemical usage	1		1
	Reduce energy usage	8		8
	Reduce environmental impact	2	1	1
	Reduce fuel usage	1	1	
	Reduce greenhouse gas (GhG) emissions	11	2	9
	Reduce resource usage	9	3	6
	Reduce generated waste	11	3	8
	Reduce water usage	3		3
R3—Reuse	Reuse components	6	1	5
	Reuse heat and steam	2	1	1
	Reuse materials	10	1	9
	Reuse packaging material	2		2
	Reuse products	1		1
	Reuse water	2		2
R4—Repair	Repair own products (as service)	3		3
R5—Refurbish	Refurbish own products and parts	7		7
R6—Reman	Remanufacture products, parts and components	3		3
R7—Repurpose	Repurpose packaging materials	1		1
	Repurpose product	1		1
	Repurpose residual products	4		4
R8—Recycle	Recycle energy	1		1
	Recycle hazardous waste	2		2
	Recycle heat from wastewater and machines	1		1
	Recycle metals	3		3
	Recycle packaging materials	2	1	1
	Recycle thermoplastics	1		1
	Recycle in general	3		3
	Recycle waste	5	1	4
	Recycle water	2		2

(*continued*)

Table 2 (*continued*)

Category Circularity practices		Total	V/P	O/R
R9—Recover	Recover for incineration (energy recovery)	7		7
	Recover for landfill	2		2
	Recover—undefined (only disposal mentioned)	1		1

5 Discussion

The circularity practices mentioned in the sustainability reports have been found to be recurrently vaguely described by the companies, which might signal a lack of focus on circularity practices in manufacturing. This as the sustainability report otherwise would provide an opportunity for manufacturing companies to clearly describe their adaptation to a CE and related circularity practices. Hence, the neglection of focus on circularity practices in sustainability reports might be an explanation for the amount of unique circularity practices identified in this study and the low frequency of many circularity practices. Similarly are the results of this study indicating a lack of a structured way of working with circularity in manufacturing. For instance, the usage of a R framework in order to coordinate circularity practices was only mentioned by three companies. However, only one of these companies refer to a specific R framework (5R, including reduce, reuse, repair, remanufacture and recycle), whilst the other two briefly mention the following of a few circularity practice categories. This is further strengthening the probability regarding the lack of focus on circularity practices in manufacturing amongst the studied companies.

The majority of the identified circularity practices in this study have been categorised as ongoing/released practices, a finding which is correlating with the conclusions from e.g. Tiscini [12], implying that circularity indeed has increased in frequency in sustainability reports and is currently being adapted by many companies. Studying sustainability reports has proven to be a sufficient method for identifying and categorizing circularity practices according to level of implementation. Although, as the description of the circularity practices often are described at a low degree in the sustainability reports, difficulties in interpreting the report were present, causing the need to further describe the identified circularity practices. This study provides valuable insights in indicating the circularity trends amongst Swedish manufacturing companies. However, further case studies are needed to precisely identify how far companies have come in their adaptation to CE through circularity practices, as well as describing in detail the challenges with implementing circularity practices.

Furthermore, the identified irregularities in terms of frequency amongst the circularity practices might stem from the 3R framework, i.e. reduce, reuse, recycle, still being the most dominantly focus areas amongst manufacturing companies. Nevertheless, using the 10R framework as a foundation provided the possibility for creating a detailed description of the identified circularity practices. Though, as previously mentioned, the definitions in the 10R framework, as presented by Potting et al. [19], was not used. Instead, this study was carried out with the intention of exploring the circularity practices without any predetermined description of the contents of the circularity practices. Due to this, differences in the formulation of the circularity practices are clearly visible, hence, the results should not be considered comparable in terms of amount of unique circularity practices in each circularity practice category, rather as solely transparently describing the circularity practices reported by manufacturing companies. The circularity practices are also frequently entangled with each other, primarily related to reduce, which can be considered both as a consequence of other circularity practices and as individual practices. This might be considered as an influencing factor partly causing the comparatively high frequency in circularity practices related to e.g. reduce. Likewise can the literal interpretation of circularity practices be recognized as an issue. For instance, reduce energy has been interpreted as either a direct intention or realised act to reduce energy usage, and also, as described by one of the companies: *"Energy efficiency is aimed at reducing the amount of energy required to produce products and provide services."* [20, p. 106], and is thus also including energy efficiency.

6 Conclusions

In this study, the sustainability reports of the 20 largest manufacturing companies in Sweden have been investigated in order to identify and categorize the circularity practices related to manufacturing. The analysis was based on the 10R framework, an extension of the 6R framework and was chosen since it enables a more detailed description of the circularity practices. A total of 38 unique circularity practices were identified in this study, whereas 13 of these were categorized as visioned or planned practices, and 36 as ongoing or already realised practices.

As identified in this study, multiple circularity practices which are not directly related to the products are mentioned by the companies. For instance, several companies have addressed the work towards managing residual materials from production and reusing heat from production. This implies that solely fulfilling circularity practices from directly related to products are not sufficient in order to achieve circularity. Primarily since circularity often involves a resource perspective, hence the aim should regard extending the lifetimes of all resources used by companies.

Further research could focus on elaborately describing the circularity practices, as these are seldom described in detail in sustainability reports. Further exploration if less frequency circularity practices are neglected by companies, or solely not included in the sustainability report, could also be carried out.

References

1. Franco, M.A.: Circular economy at the micro level: a dynamic view of incumbents' struggles and challenges in the textile industry. J. Clean. Prod. **168**, 833–845 (2017)
2. Pitt, J., Heinemeyer, C.: Introducing ideas of a circular economy. In: Stables, K., Keirl, S. (eds.) Environment, Ethics and Cultures. International Technology Education Studies, vol. 5, pp. 245–260. SensePublishers, Rotterdam (2015). https://doi.org/10.1007/978-94-6209-938-8_16
3. Webster, K.: What might we say about a circular economy? Some temptations to avoid if possible. World Futur. J. Gen. Evol. **69**(7–8), 542–554 (2013)

4. Bocken, N.M.P., de Pauw, I., Bakker, C., van der Grinten, B.: Product design and business model strategies for a circular economy. J. Ind. Prod. Eng. **33**(5), 308–320 (2016)
5. Bressanelli, G., Saccani, N., Perona, M., Baccanelli, I.: Towards circular economy in the household appliance industry: An overview of cases. Resources **9**(11), 1–23 (2020)
6. Ghisellini, P., Cialani, C., Ulgiati, S.: A review on circular economy: The expected transition to a balanced interplay of environmental and economic systems. J. Clean. Prod. **114**, 11–32 (2016)
7. Lieder, M., Rashid, A.: Towards circular economy implementation: A comprehensive review in context of manufacturing industry. J. Clean. Prod. **115**, 36–51 (2016)
8. Statistiska Centralbyrån, 2021. https://scb.se/hitta-statistik/sverige-i-siffror/miljo/utslapp-av-vaxthusgaser. (accessed Sep. 23, 2021)
9. Schroeder, P., Anggraeni, K., Weber, U.: The Relevance of Circular Economy Practices to the Sustainable Development Goals. J. Ind. Ecol. **23**(1), 77–95 (2019)
10. Calzolari, T., Genovese, A., Brint, A.: The adoption of circular economy practices in supply chains—an assessment of European multi-national enterprises. J. Clean. Prod., 312(127616), (2021)
11. Gusmerotti, N.M., Testa, F., Corsini, F., Pretner, G., Iraldo, F.: Drivers and approaches to the circular economy in manufacturing firms. J. Clean. Prod. **230**, 314–327 (2019)
12. Tiscini, R., Martiniello, L., Lombardi, R.: Circular economy and environmental disclosure in sustainability reports: empirical evidence in cosmetic companies. Bus. Strateg. Environ., 1–16 (2021)
13. Swedish Parliament, "Årsredovisningslag (1995:1554)." https://www.riksdagen.se/sv/dok ument-lagar/dokument/svenskforfattningssamling/arsredovisningslag-19951554_sfs-1995-1554#K6P10 (January 27, 2022)
14. Sihvonen, S., Partanen, J.: Eco-design practices with a focus on quantitative environmental targets: An exploratory content analysis within ICT sector. J. Clean. Prod. **143**, 769–783 (2017)
15. Rhein, S., Sträter, K. F.:Corporate self-commitments to mitigate the global plastic crisis: Recycling rather than reduction and reuse. J. Clean. Prod. 296, 126571 (2021)
16. Wu, H.Q., Shi, Y., Xia, Q., Zhu, W.D.: Effectiveness of the policy of circular economy in China: A DEA-based analysis for the period of 11th five-year-plan. Resour. Conserv. Recycl. **83**, 163–175 (2014)
17. Badurdeen, F., Iyengar, D., Goldsby, T.J., Metta, H., Gupta, S., Jawahir, I.S.: Extending total life-cycle thinking to sustainable supply chain design. Int. J. Prod. Lifecycle Manag. **4**(1–3), 49–67 (2009)
18. Jawahir, I.S., Bradley, R.: Technological Elements of Circular Economy and the Principles of 6R-Based Closed-loop Material Flow in Sustainable Manufacturing. Procedia CIRP **40**, 103–108 (2016)
19. J. Potting, M. Hekkert, E. Worrell, and A. Hanemaaijer, "Circular economy: Measuring innovation in the product chain" PBL Netherlands Environmental Assessment Agency (2017)
20. SSAB, "Annual report 2020" 2020. https://www.ssab.com/company/investors/reports-and-presentations#first=10&sort=%40customorder descending (accessed Jan. 21, 2022)

A Multiple Case Study on Collaboration for a Circular Economy: A Focus on the Italian Textile Supply Chain

Beatrice Colombo[1,2]([✉]) [ID], Albachiara Boffelli[1] [ID], Paolo Gaiardelli[1] [ID], Matteo Kalchschmidt[1] [ID], Alice Madonna[1] [ID], and Tommaso Sangalli[1]

[1] Department of Management, Information and Production Engineering, University of Bergamo, Via Pasubio 7/B, 24044 Dalmine, BG, Italy
{beatrice.colombo,albachiara.boffelli,paolo.gaiardelli,
matteo.kalchschmidt,alice.madonna}@unibg.it,
t.sangalli@studenti.unibg.it
[2] ENEA – Italian National Agency for New Technologies, Energy and Sustainable Economic Development, Division for Sustainable Materials, Brindisi Research Centre, SS7 Appia Km 706,00, 72100 Brindisi, BR, Italy

Abstract. The establishment of valuable collaborations among supply chain partners is essential for the success of a circular economy. However, there are still many doubts about the most helpful collaboration practices that could support sustainable development. The analysis deals with deepening links between the circular economy and supply chain collaborations that could favor its development. Specifically, the study focuses on recognizing the most diffused collaboration practices among the actors that successfully implemented circular systems. A multiple case study from the Italian textile industry is the methodology chosen to carry out the research. The analysis of five selected companies confirms the creation of valuable collaborations is essential to successfully implement circular practices, highlighting that a holistic approach is needed to establish this new economic paradigm effectively.

Keywords: Circular economy · Supply chain collaboration · Multiple case study

1 Introduction

The textile industry poses one of the biggest environmental challenges, as its overproduction and overconsumption are incredibly impactful in terms of water consumption, use of chemicals, greenhouse gas emissions, land use, and waste production [1, 2]. This system is not sustainable anymore and needs substantial restructuring. Organizations need to address these issues considering environmental and social concerns, whose importance should be equivalent to the economic performance of the business [3]. One feasible solution to improve the situation and reduce the damaging impact of the current system on the environment without shadowing economic viability is the Circular Economy

© IFIP International Federation for Information Processing 2022
Published by Springer Nature Switzerland AG 2022
D. Y. Kim et al. (Eds.): APMS 2022, IFIP AICT 663, pp. 408–415, 2022.
https://doi.org/10.1007/978-3-031-16407-1_48

(CE). Circular business models would reduce the need for primary resources as input and waste production as output [4]; consequently, there would be a relief in the environmental impact of resource extraction, production, and disposal [2]. Nonetheless, the industry's structure does not facilitate such business models as these extensively rely on the cooperation between the different actors. Being these actors particularly numerous and geographically dispersed, there is a noteworthy barrier to the development of CE. Several authors have identified the main collaboration practices that should be developed in the supply chain (SC) to achieve satisfying performance levels; thus, it has been sought to understand the value and effectiveness thereof in the CE context.

This work aims to expand the knowledge around SC collaboration's role in developing successful CE practices, focusing on the textile industry, one of the world's most polluting sectors [2]. This objective has been pursued by attempting to answer the following research question:

"What are the collaboration practices along the SC that foster the successful implementation of CE in the textile industry?"

The present work contributes to the extant literature by proposing insights from five Italian textile companies. This empirical approach differs from what is available in the scientific literature. Indeed, to the best of authors' knowledge, there is scant work and mainly of a conceptual nature about SC collaboration to foster the CE.

The case studies confirm that solid collaborative practices are needed to establish an effective CE business model. Finally, these practices are prioritized, differentiating between primary and subordinate ones.

The work is structured as follows: Sect. 2 reviews the literature on the related concepts, Sect. 3 explains the methodology according to which the case studies have been performed, Sects. 4 and 5 respectively outline the results and critically discuss them against the notions already available in the literature, and finally, Sect. 6 concludes the work by examining its contributions and limitations.

2   Related Literature

2.1   Circular Economy

The most comprehensive definition for CE is the one provided by the Ellen MacArthur Foundation, which refers to it as *"an industrial system that is restorative or regenerative by intention and design. It replaces the 'end-of-life' concept with restoration, shifts towards the use of renewable energy, eliminates the use of toxic chemicals, which impairs reuse, and aims for the elimination of waste through the superior design of materials, products, systems and, within this, business models"* [1]. This description highlights the main features of CE, namely the importance of a regenerative design, the elimination of the concept of waste, and the use of more sustainable resources, generating as few harmful effects as possible for the environment. These objectives align with those proposed by [5] within the 9R framework that summarizes the ten principles of CE: Refuse (R0), Rethink (R1), Reduce (R2), Reuse (R3), Repair (R4), Refurbish (R5), Remanufacture (R6), Repurpose (R7), Recycle (R8), Recover (R9).

2.2 Collaboration Practices Along the Supply Chain

Different actors along the SC carry out various phases, and thus different stages could have objectives that conflict with each other. For this reason, each member could have only a local consideration of its activities and lose its interdependencies to partners' operations, resulting in a lower amount of total benefit for the whole SC [6]. To overcome these problems, [6] identified seven practices that can help improve the collaboration among SC members and, consequently, create sustainable advantages for the value chain, facilitating the development of a collaborative culture inside the business [7]. These seven practices are defined as follows:

1. Information sharing: ideas, plans, procedures, and strategies that a company shares with supply chain members with openness and honesty.
2. Goal congruence: compatibility between partners' objectives and overall supply chain objectives.
3. Decision synchronization: the extent to which partners make decisions by mutual agreement to benefit the entire supply chain.
4. Incentive alignment: shared risks, costs, and gains among supply chain actors by enhancing motivations to act consistently towards common goals.
5. Resource sharing: mutual exchanges and uses of partners' capabilities and assets (e.g., time, capital, know-how, experience, technologies, assets).
6. Collaborative communication: interactions among supply chain members in terms of information flow direction, frequency, mode, and influence potential.
7. Joint knowledge creation: the extent to which supply chain members jointly work to improve the awareness of consumers' needs and recognize the competitive environment characteristics and commit themselves to find solutions to adapt to the identified market conditions.

3 Methodology

Qualitative case study is suitable and necessary when theory does not exist, or it is unlikely to apply, when theory exists, but the context considered is different from a more traditional one, or when cause and effect are not well defined [8]. There are various types of qualitative studies. The one applied with the highest frequency regarding CE implementation in the textile context is the single case study [9]. Nevertheless, this approach could present some limitations regarding the conclusions' generalizability [10]. Therefore, multiple case studies approach has been identified as the most suitable methodology to ensure a reasonable level of external validity and reduce the risk of relying on biased information [10]. To obtain an exhaustive overview of CE implementation and the enabling role of SC partnerships for its success in the Italian textile industry, five cases (Table 1) were selected through a purposive sampling technique [8]. The research focused on four start-ups that have been recently founded and on an incumbent actor engaged in the textile sector over the last 150 years. This diversity in size among the analyzed companies should increase the generalizability of the research findings. Primary sources of information about the cases are interviews that lasted, on average, 60 min. Each interview was recorded and then transcribed for accuracy. All the respondents are co-founders or managers. This aspect was essential to gain insightful and comprehensive notions about the development process of circular SC. All the interviews were semi-structured, and were based on a defined case study protocol sent to the respondents in advance to allow a consistent comparison between the different answers and improve the reliability of the analysis [8]. Questions were open-ended to permit interviewees to freely discuss their experiences and explore some of the considered issues. Data gained from the interviews were triangulated with multiple secondary sources to contextualize and validate the findings [11]. Lastly, data analysis was structured in two distinct phases: the within-case and the cross-case analysis. The results of the cross-case analysis are presented in the next section.

Table 1. Overview of the five cases selected for the investigation.

Company	Year of foundation	Type of company	Role of respondent
A	2017	Start-up	Co-founder
B	2018	Start-up	Co-founder
C	2020	Start-up	Co-founder
D	2020	Start-up	Co-founder
E	1876	Incumbent	Manager

4   Main Results

All the companies have confirmed the basic notion found in the literature that it is almost impossible to implement circular projects in a completely autonomous way. Indeed, none of the analyzed companies has developed CE solutions without the establishment of functional collaborations with their suppliers. A sentence from Company A's founder conveys this concept: *"What I can say with a high degree of certainty is that it is impossible to create circular systems without the proper development of a set of partnerships, establishing dynamics of a symbiotic economy and creating win-win relationships. [...] It is essential moving from SCs that work individually to SCs that work together circularly"*. Furthermore, the findings outlined that it is also essential to expand the collaborations to actors from different fields, such as universities, non-governmental organizations, and customers or organizations that are not primarily engaged in the industrial field, to effectively obtain the variety of resources and competences needed to manage CE systems.

The results of the cross-case analysis are reported in Table 2. Information sharing and resource sharing are the practices that characterize the collaborations of all the five selected companies. Collaborative communication is found in all cases too. However, as this last practice is strongly related to information sharing, it was expected to be encountered in the same number of cases. Therefore, it can be claimed that the collaboration practices identified in the literature are essential for the successful development of CE systems. In particular, information sharing and resource sharing seem to play a primary role, especially when sectors that previously had no contact points start to create synergies for implementing sustainable solutions. The other collaboration practices identified by [6], namely decision synchronization, incentive alignment, collaborative communication, and joint knowledge creation, are still crucial for actors operating in the CE field, even though they were less frequently mentioned during the interviews.

Table 2. Collaboration practices discussed during the interviews.

Practice	Company				
	A	B	C	D	E
Information sharing	✓	✓	✓	✓	✓
Decision synchronization	✓	✓	✓		✓
Incentive alignment	✓		✓		✓
Resource sharing	✓	✓	✓	✓	✓
Collaborative communication	✓	✓	✓	✓	✓
Joint knowledge creation	✓	✓		✓	✓

"✓" = Mentioned.

5   Discussion

Over the last decade, the relationship between CE and SC collaboration has been discussed in academia. However, although it is evident that a functional development of partnerships along the SC is essential for the success of CE [1, 12, 13], there are still many doubts about the most valuable collaboration practices that could support sustainable development.

The case study analysis undoubtedly strengthens the importance of the collaboration between companies to foster CE developments. The respondents cited all the collaboration practices described by [5], which can be considered appropriate in dealing with CE. However, considering the analysis of the cases, goal congruence should be regarded as a prerequisite for this type of partnership rather than a collaboration practice. After this premise, it is essential to specify that information sharing and resource sharing are critical for CE development. The former is defined as the bonding agent that improves the business structure of SC partners and allows SCs to become more agile and reach competitive advantage [14]. The flow of information could be inherent to various aspects of the business, including transactional data, production processes, customer feedback, and research and development issues [6]. As suggested by [15], a high level of trust among partners is essential to share valuable information through the SC effectively. The importance of functional information sharing processes was continuously mentioned during the interviews. Indeed, different cases repeatedly pointed out that frequent visits to partners' production plants or offices are vital for firms to be constantly updated and notified as soon as critical issues emerge, thus preventing the achievement of the desired performance levels. The latter, instead, implies leveraging capabilities and assets through joint investments and commitment by business partners [6]. Joint investments usually refer to both financial and non-financial aspects, including time, money, training, knowledge exchange, experience and technology updates [6]. [16] outlined how time and mutual effort needed to create valuable collaborative partnerships should not be undervalued. Considering the context in which CE systems develop, sharing financial and non-financial resources seems to be a crucial factor for the success of these projects. Indeed, the availability of stable production plants and processes guaranteed by large companies has been fundamental for some of the start-ups in the sample to manufacture their products. On the other hand, the possibility to interact with CE experts and actors available to share their experience and precious tacit knowledge, namely non-financial resources, has been a significant driver for the growth of some of the analyzed companies. Indeed, this aspect allowed them to overcome several issues of both technical and bureaucratic nature. The other collaboration practices cited in the literature were mentioned during the interviews, but they seem not as critical as the two described. However, it would be a misjudgment to consider them unnecessary for the proper establishment of SC collaborations to develop CE practices. For example, joint knowledge creation can be regarded as a beneficial collaboration practice, according to [6], both in terms of knowledge exploration (i.e., the research, acquisition, and application of new knowledge) and knowledge exploitation (i.e., the assimilation and the application of existing knowledge). Naturally, proper coordination of critical decisions affecting business activities and, consequently, partnerships' effectiveness, influences the performance of the parties involved in the collaboration [6]. Furthermore, decision synchronization among business partners is vital as joint planning supports companies on how to best invest their resources to succeed in a determined set of aligned goals [17]. Ultimately, incentive alignment between partners could help act in a coherent way with respect to the defined objectives [17]. Several examples of joint investments, such as specific machineries necessary for processing waste materials, were mentioned during the interviews and they represent a case in point of this collaboration practice. Certainly, some of the cited collaboration practices are linked to each other. In particular, collaborative communication affects the efficacy of the information sharing process. During almost all the interviews, some aspects related to this practice were addressed, but it is more appropriate to consider it as a factor that influences the information sharing process rather than one of the indispensable practices.

All SC collaboration practices are relevant for CE development, albeit with different intensities, and need to be grounded in goal congruence.

6   Conclusions

This paper aims to expand the knowledge about the relationships between CE development and SC collaboration. Specifically, the main objective of the work was to clarify further how SC collaboration affects the establishment of this new economic paradigm. The research question is addressed through a multiple case study approach, that was identified as the most appropriate methodology considering the novelty of the context

[18, 19]. Five companies operating in the Italian textile industry were analyzed. The evaluation of the selected cases clearly outlined the importance of establishing valuable SC collaborations to favor CE development. In particular, it emphasized that information sharing and resource sharing are the two most relevant collaborative practices to advance in the SC. In contrast, decision synchronization, incentive alignment, collaborative communication, and joint knowledge creation play an important but subordinate role.

The results of the analysis provide theoretical as well as practical insights. Concerning the theoretical implications, the study gives empirical evidence of the importance of SC collaboration for the establishment of a CE, highlighting the most crucial collaboration practices. In doing so, the study contributes to the literature on Sustainable Supply Chain Management. Indeed, the obtained results could support practitioners in managing SC collaborations. Moreover, managers and entrepreneurs should encourage collaborations beyond the traditional sector's boundaries to expand the potential synergies among industries that do not have contact points. Indeed, this aspect is fundamental in the CE context, where resources ought to be continuously maintained in the economic cycle. The waste generated by some actors could be considered valuable input for some others. Future developments of this study could address the challenges that these firms face before and after the establishment of the collaboration and the factors affecting the supplier selection process. Lastly, it is essential to highlight that this study has limitations that could be overcome in future works. First, the findings are related to the analysis of five Italian companies operating in the textile industry. The assessment of other firms that have implemented circular solutions and belong to different sectors would increase generalizability. Second, the study of cases located outside Italy and a focus on larger textile industry players would improve the consistency of the findings.

References

1. Ellen MacArthur Foundation: towards a circular economy, economic and business rationale for an accelerated transition (2013)
2. Manshoven, S., et al.: Textiles and the environment in a circular economy (2019)
3. Walker, H., Klassen, R., Sarkis, J., Seuring, S.: Sustainable operations management: recent trends and future directions. Int. J. Oper. Prod. Manag. 34 (2014)
4. Colombo, B., Gaiardelli, P., Dotti, S., Boffelli, A.: Business Models in Circular Economy: A Systematic Literature Review. In: Dolgui, A., Bernard, A., Lemoine, D., von Cieminski, G., Romero, D. (eds.) APMS 2021. IAICT, vol. 632, pp. 386–393. Springer, Cham (2021). https://doi.org/10.1007/978-3-030-85906-0_43
5. Kirchherr, J., Piscicelli, L.: towards an education for the circular economy (ECE): five teaching principles and a case study. Resour. Conserv. Recycl. **150**, 104406 (2019). https://doi.org/10.1016/J.RESCONREC.2019.104406
6. Cao, M., Vonderembse, M.A., Zhang, Q., Ragu-Nathan, T.S.: Supply chain collaboration: Conceptualisation and instrument development. Int. J. Prod. Res. **48**, 6613–6635 (2010). https://doi.org/10.1080/00207540903349039
7. Barratt, M.: Understanding the meaning of collaboration in the supply chain (2004)
8. Yin, R.K.: Case Study Research: Design and Methods. Sage Publications, CA (2009)
9. Jia, F., Yin, S., Chen, L., Chen, X.: The circular economy in the textile and apparel industry: a systematic literature review. J. Clean. Prod. **259**, 120728 (2020). https://doi.org/10.1016/j.jclepro.2020.120728

10. Voss, C., Tsikriktsis, N., Frohlich, M.: Case research in operations management. Int. J. Oper. Prod. Manag. **22**, 195–219 (2002). https://doi.org/10.1108/01443570210414329
11. Yin, R.K.: Validity and generalization in future case study evaluations. Evaluation **19**, 321–332 (2013). https://doi.org/10.1177/1356389013497081
12. Genovese, A., Acquaye, A.A., Figueroa, A., Koh, S.C.L.: Sustainable supply chain management and the transition towards a circular economy: evidence and some applications. Omega **66**, 344–357 (2017). https://doi.org/10.1016/j.omega.2015.05.015
13. Winkler, H.: Closed-loop production systems-a sustainable supply chain approach. CIRP J. Manuf. Sci. Technol. **4**, 243–246 (2011). https://doi.org/10.1016/j.cirpj.2011.05.001
14. Hudnurkar, M., Jakhar, S., Rathod, U.: Factors affecting collaboration in supply chain: a literature review. Procedia - Soc. Behav. Sci. **133**, 189–202 (2014). https://doi.org/10.1016/j.sbspro.2014.04.184
15. Fawcett, S.E., Osterhaus, P., Magnan, G.M., Brau, J.C., McCarter, M.W.: Information sharing and supply chain performance: the role of connectivity and willingness. Supply Chain Manag. **12**, 358–368 (2007). https://doi.org/10.1108/13598540710776935
16. Min, S., et al.: Supply chain collaboration: what's happening? Int. J. Logist. Manag. **16**, 237–256 (2005). https://doi.org/10.1108/09574090510634539
17. Simatupang, T.M., Sridharan, R.: An integrative framework for supply chain collaboration. Int. J. Logist. Manag. **16**, 257–274 (2005). https://doi.org/10.1108/09574090510634548
18. Van Dijk, S., Tenpierik, M., Van Den Dobbelsteen, A.: Continuing the building's cycles: a literature review and analysis of current systems theories in comparison with the theory of Cradle to Cradle. Resour. Conserv. Recycl. **82**, 21–34 (2014). https://doi.org/10.1016/j.resconrec.2013.10.007
19. Murray, A., Skene, K., Haynes, K.: The circular economy: an interdisciplinary exploration of the concept and application in a global context. J. Bus. Ethics **140**(3), 369–380 (2015). https://doi.org/10.1007/s10551-015-2693-2

Controlling Product Variance in a Factory Through the Evaluation of the Factory Life Cycle

Lennart Hingst[(✉)] and Peter Nyhuis

Institute of Production Systems and Logistics, Leibniz University Hannover,
30823 Garbsen, Germany
hingst@ifa.uni-hannover.de

Abstract. The intensification of competition in the global environment means that companies have to respond more actively to the individual wishes of their customers. The introduction of additional product variants in the course of the factory life cycle increases customer perception and enhances product attractiveness on the market. Decisions on the introduction of product variants are made in sales and development. However, the fields of production and logistics often suffering from product diversity only have limited influence. Once a new product variant has been introduced and the associated investments have been made, a cost remanence results when complexity is reduced. After all, an additional product variant may require an increase in capacity if the current production and logistics concept reaches its limits. The resulting follow-up costs have an impact over the entire factory life cycle. Currently, it is not possible to distinguish between value-creating and value-destroying variant-induced complexity. Therefore, this paper presents an approach for determining the necessity of factory planning measures in case a new product variant is introduced to the factory. It supports the development of different factory configurations for the evaluation of the factory life cycle, so that the total costs and environmental impacts resulting from a new product variant in a factory are known prior to its introduction. Ultimately, the different configuration variants serve as a calculation basis for sales for a more transparent decision on the introduction of a new product variant.

Keywords: Factory planning · Variant management · Life cycle evaluation

1 Introduction

"You can have any color you want as long as it is black" [1]. This statement by Henry Ford reflects that in 1912 a seller's market prevailed. Nowadays, oversupply of goods allows buyers to choose from a variety of products [2]. Companies must increasingly differentiate their products from those of their competitors and respond more intensively to the diverse and individual wishes and needs of their customers in order to sell their products. [3] Companies assume that an expanded product portfolio particularly has a

© IFIP International Federation for Information Processing 2022
Published by Springer Nature Switzerland AG 2022
D. Y. Kim et al. (Eds.): APMS 2022, IFIP AICT 663, pp. 416–423, 2022.
https://doi.org/10.1007/978-3-031-16407-1_49

positive impact on customer satisfaction and that an increase in revenue can be realized through increased sales or higher prices [4]. Even if these strategies may be promising, they generate additional effort and costs during implementation [5]. These costs hardly ever occur completely where they were caused: 50–80% of variant-driven costs occur in production and logistics [3]. After all, the complexity of internal production and logistics processes increases with growing product differentiation [6]. Companies often systematically underestimate the additional costs, so that they end up in a cost trap [7]. This is because attempts to reduce complexity or excess capacity cannot reduce the associated costs and environmental impacts to the same extent [8]. The individualization of products is only justifiable if the customer is willing to bear the costs of the increasing complexity. Otherwise, companies are risking the economic but also the environmental sustainability of their factories and thus their competitiveness in the long term. Therefore, potential variant-driven costs and environmental impacts on the factory must be estimated in advance so that they can be discussed controversially with sales and development before the introduction of a new product or variant [2]. In the following, an approach for the systematic determination of the necessity and derivation of factory planning measures in the case of the introduction of a new product variant is developed, in order to be able to work out different factory configurations, whose economic and ecological sustainability can be evaluated using an envisioned prognosis model of the factory life cycle.

2   The Role of Factory Planning in Variant Management

Each individual product within a product family is referred to as a product variant. While the product family of a model targets a specific market segment, the product variants are developed to meet a specific subset of identified customer needs [9]. All product families combined form the cross-model production portfolio. The variance from successor to predecessor model is referred to as product sequence. The product variants are specified in the product structure, which displays the variants among the components and modules of a model. The variant diversity thus results from the variant parts. [10] It is generally increasing due to higher customer expectations in terms of functionality and quality as part of the ongoing trend toward individualization [5]. Other factors can be technology-driven or have a social or technical origin [11]. When introducing a new product variant to an existing factory, three scenarios can be distinguished [12]:

- **Integration:** The new product variant is integrated in the existing production
- **Substitution:** The new product variant replaces the older product in the existing production
- **Adaptation:** The new product variant cannot be integrated and is manufactured in a separate production facility

Based on this, the types of factory planning - development planning, replanning, demolition or revitalization- and the scope of a factory planning project to be initiated can be derived [13]. Factory planning designs personnel, technical-organizational processes as well as their elements and structures and provides the solution space for factory operation [14]. Factory operation runs, manages and controls the processes in the factory in order to ensure target alignment through the interaction of people, technology and organization as well as cooperation within and outside the factory [15]. The factory targets to be achieved in planning and operation are derived from the company targets [14]. So far, profitability of a factory has been regarded as a meta-target so that competitive products can be produced [16]. In light of the climate change and limited resources, factories increasingly have to include environmental sustainability in their target system [17]. The planning and operation of a factory represent two essential phases of the factory life cycle for meeting set factory targets. A large portion of the costs and environmental impacts are determined during factory planning, but they do not occur until operation as a later phase. Since factory operation can last up to several decades, most costs and environmental impacts occur at this point, making it the most relevant life cycle phase from an economic and environmental perspective [18]. Therefore, life cycle-oriented factory planning deliberately includes the operation phase in the decision-making process for the selection of a specific factory configuration. By evaluating how the planned factory configuration copes with uncertainties during factory operation, economic and environmental sustainability is ensured over the considered lifetime of a factory [19].

Due to internal and external change drivers, it is often not possible to avoid a fundamental diversity of variants, so that variant-driven expenses inevitably emerge in factory operation. The different economic aspects have been summarized in Fig. 1 showing that the perceived customer benefit and the associated revenue follows a degressive trend, while the prevailing complexity costs are progressive, so that profit decreases and no value can be created beyond a certain number of variants.

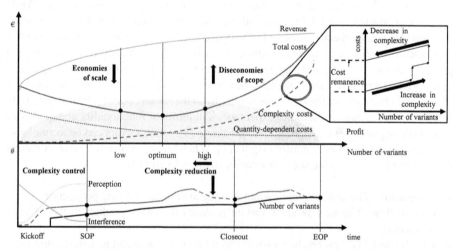

Fig. 1. Economic aspects [4, 7, 8, 20] resulting from an increasing number of product variants whose complexity can be controlled preventively (black) or reduced reactively (blue)

In the literature, variant-driven expenses are also referred to as complexity costs for coping with increased complexity [21]. Expected economies of scale are overestimated when introducing more variants. On the contrary, diseconomies of scope arise, particularly in indirect fields such as logistics, which do not become apparent immediately [4, 22]. The basic task of variant management is to manage the increasing number of product variants caused by diversification and the resulting complexity [23]. In contrast, complexity management does not focus on the product, but analyzes the complexity generated within the overall system [4]. The strategies of variant management are distinguished into complexity reduction, complexity control and complexity avoidance. In complexity reduction, unprofitable variants are removed from the portfolio. Complexity control aims at providing the diversity of variants requested by the customer at low cost [23]. When trying to reduce the variety, or the complexity in general, the investments made and the associated environmental impacts cannot be reduced to the same extent. This asymmetric-dynamic cost behavior is also called cost remanence. Fixed costs which are not reducible or only reducible in the long term are called hysteresis effect or cost trap in this context [4, 8] Furthermore, excess capacities can arise from a previous capacity expansion in addition to cost remanence. The resulting costs for unused capacities are called cost recurrence [4].

The challenge of the cost trap lies in the perception of imminent variant diversity, which increases as product development progresses. At the same time the ability of interference decreases rapidly. Thus, implementation of variants can lead to missed factory targets. However, subsequent attempts to reduce the number of variants is less cost-effective (dashed line). Therefore it is necessary to implement complexity control and to evaluate the impact of variant management measures on the sustainability of the factory at an early stage of product development [20].

3   Challenges of Evaluating the Impact of New Product Variants

An overview of different approaches can be found in the literature review by ELMARAGHY ET AL. on the effective co-development of variants and their manufacturing systems to ensure economic sustainability [24]. The approaches most relevant to this paper are discussed in the following.

In order to make the variants controllable and to create transparency for variant management, SCHUH has developed the variant tree [25]. This can be used to illustrate the diversity across the stages of an assembly process [4]. Based on this, the Variant Mode and Effect Analysis (VMEA) systematically presents variant information and thus supports product planning and design along the value chain [26].

BAYER has developed variant costing using complexity factors to identify the business areas most affected by variant diversity [27]. A process analysis with subsequent variant cost calculation is based on product-related factors in order to identify business units affected by variant diversity the most.

A methodical approach for determining variant-induced costs was developed by BIEDERMANN with the goal of achieving simple implementation in a short time [5]. Complexity costs of reference variants of variant groups are calculated and presented as a variant tree in order to support decision making. BROSCH presents a similar approach with the "Design for Value Chain" methodology (DfVC) using complexity drivers [28].

An approach presented by NEMC (next evolution Management Consulting GmbH) aims to identify variant-driven costs directly in the product development process along the value chain. However, a decision to introduce a product variant has already been made and represents the starting point [6].

Overall, approaches for evaluating the impact of product variants mainly focus on the market cycle and less on the phase before market launch. However, in order to manage complexity in the best possible way, critical aspects must already be taken into account before the planning process is completed. This includes necessary adjustments of the factory configuration to facilitate the production of the product variant. Only if the necessary adjustments and the resulting consequences for factory operation are evaluated during product planning, a cost trap can be avoided and complexity can be successfully controlled. It is therefore necessary to forecast the impact of a new product variant on the economic and environmental sustainability of the factory over the entire product life cycle. Thus, variants are not subsequently reduced but deliberately increased, if factory sustainability is not compromised. Otherwise, a distinction between value-creating and value-destroying variant-induced complexity is not made.

4 Approach for Deriving Factory Planning Measures for the Life Cycle-Oriented Evaluation of New Product Variants

The basic principle of life cycle-oriented factory planning, namely the anticipation of the use phase of a factory with its trends but also possible disruptions for an early consideration during the planning of a factory configuration, addresses precisely the challenges of variant management described above. Emphasis is put on the timely evaluation of costs and environmental impacts in factory operation, which account for a significant share of the complexity expenses. Thus, impacts of new product variants can be predicted or possible future variant scenarios can be thought through and a target value for the number of variants can be set. This provides variant management with complete transparency at the time of decision-making, so that cost remanence is avoided in the best possible way and both the economic and environmental sustainability of a factory can be ensured. The concept of factory life cycle evaluation has already been described in detail [19]. However, the focus has not been on the systematic planning and generation of factory configurations in line with requirements. This is the final missing element of life cycle-oriented factory planning. But the derivation of factory planning measures is very case- and problem-specific, so that the approach visualized in Fig. 2 concentrates on handling new product variants. The impacts of new product variants on the factory are based on the interdependencies of a product with the factory. They cannot be determined in general but rather depend on specific product features and attributes of the elements to be designed in a factory. This is because a factory is also referred to as a socio-technical system, which cannot be designed as a stand-alone planning element [16]. WULF offers a possible classification of product features [12]. For example, physical properties are tangible attributes such as the dimension or weight of a product. Based on the interdependencies of the individual product features with the factory elements, the identified relationships as change dimensions can be described in more detail. For instance, the physical properties of a product show direct dependencies with the technical factory elements. Thus, if there is a physical change in the product, it may have an impact on the storage, transportation or production facilities.

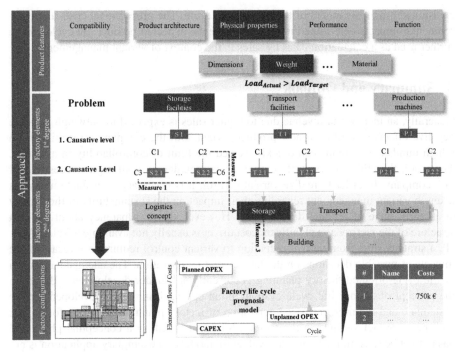

Fig. 2. Approach for Deriving Factory Planning Measures for the Life Cycle-Oriented Evaluation of New Product Variants.

The relevance of the individual change dimensions for factory planning in a specific use case can be determined by analyzing the predominant conditions in a factory. For this purpose, mathematical functions are formulated to analyze the current state of a factory element using inherent attributes and attributes of interdependent factory elements. These functions represent an entry condition for associated cause-effect diagrams in order to investigate, why a particular factory element does not meet the new requirements of a changed product feature (e.g. load-bearing capacity of a storage location for handling a higher weight of a product, while also taking into account load carriers, stock level etc.). This generates an understanding of how certain attributes contribute to the ability of a factory element to cope with the changed requirements and provides the basis for deriving specific factory planning measures in order to upgrade the according factory element. Provided that certain measures are selected to generate a factory configuration variant, further indirect interdependencies between factory elements must be considered, since factory planning decisions in one area of the factory can have a significant impact on another area of the factory (e.g. new shelf bay causes additional spatial demand). For factory elements indirectly impacted by a changed product feature, further mathematical change dimensions can be formulated and cause-effect diagrams established based on the inducing attribute. Once all interdependencies have been considered for a factory configuration and further factory configurations have been developed by deriving alternative factory planning measures, the factory configurations can be evaluated using the envisioned prognosis model of the factory life cycle. The proportional costs and environmental impacts determined in this way over the expected product life cycle can be further used as a calculation basis by sales in the context of variant management.

5 Summary and Outlook

Generally, an increase in revenue due to higher sales is expected to outweigh possible negative effects caused by a new product variant. But the complexity resulting from a high number of variants can quickly exceed the limit of controllability in a factory. Therefore, the ability to control complexity is regarded as a strategic success factor of a company. In order to realize variant control, it is necessary to evaluate measures taken in variant management regarding their impact on the sustainability of the factory at an early stage of product development. However, this transparency about the cost structure of the factory as a significant cost driver is usually not available to sales. After all, a strategy shift from variant reduction to variant control requires a forecast of the impacts of possible decisions on the factory and its operation. The adequate approach of life cycle-oriented factory planning is currently still under development. Based on the concept of factory life cycle evaluation, an approach has been developed for the systematic and requirement-based derivation of factory planning measures for coping with new product variants in the factory. So far, it is still in a conceptual phase and has not yet been combined with the evaluation model. An exemplary application is not possible yet. When implementing the approach, a consistent level of detail as well as a certain generality of the cause-effect diagrams will represent the greatest challenges. Future research will be necessary on the allocation of total costs and the relevance of environmental impacts in product cost accounting.

Acknowledgments. Partially funded by the Deutsche Forschungsgemeinschaft (DFG, German Research Foundation)–412409961. The authors wish to thank Antal Dér and Christoph Herrmann for the valuable discussions.

References

1. Duncan, J.L.: Any colour—so long as it's black: designing the model t ford 1906–1908. Exisle Pub, Wollombi (2008)
2. Maune, G.: Möglichkeiten des Komplexitätsmanagements für Automobilhersteller auf Basis durchgehender IT-gestützter System (2002)
3. Fischer, J.O.: Kostenbewusstes Konstruieren. Springer, Berlin, Heidelberg (2008). https://doi.org/10.1007/978-3-540-78313-8
4. Schuh, G., Riesener, M.: Produktkomplexität managen: Strategien - Methoden - Tools, 3rd edn. Hanser, München (2017)
5. Biedermann, H.: Industrial Engineering and Management. Springer, Wiesbaden (2016)
6. Keuper, F., Schomann, M.: Management von IT und IT-gestütztes Management, 1st edn. Gabler Verlag, Wiesbaden (2008)
7. Albers, S. (ed.): Strategieentwicklung - Produktplanung - Organisation - Kontrolle, 3rd edn. Gabler, Wiesbaden (2007)

8. Hichert, R.: Probleme der Vielfalt. Teil 1: Soll man auf Exoten verzichten? Werkstattstechnik, wt - Zeitschrift fuer Industrielle Fertigung 75, 235–237 (1985)

9. Romero, F., Sanfilippo, E.M., Rosado, P., Borgo, S., Benavent, S.: Feature in product engineering with single and variant design approaches. a comparative review

10. Wiendahl, H.-P., Gerst, D., Keunecke, L. (eds.): Variantenbeherrschung in der Montage. Konzept und Praxis der flexiblen Produktionsendstufe. Springer, Heidelberg (2004). https://doi.org/10.1007/978-3-642-18947-0

11. Schuh, G.: Produktkomplexität managen: Strategien; Methoden; Tools, 1st edn. Carl Hanser Fachbuchverlag, s.l. (2014)

12. Wulf, S., Bewertung des Einflusses von Produkt- und Technologieveränderungen auf die Fabrik. Dissertation, Hannover (2011)

13. Verein Deutscher Ingenieure. Factory planning Planning procedures: VDI 5200 (2011)

14. Wiendahl, H.-P., Reichardt, J., Nyhuis, P.: Handbook Factory Planning and Design, 2015th ed., Springer, Heidelberg (2015). https://doi.org/10.1007/978-3-662-46391-8

15. Schenk, M., Wirth, S., Müller, E.: Factory Planning Manual: Situation-Driven Production Facility Planning, 2010th edn. Springer, Berlin (2014)

16. Nyhuis, P., Heger, C.L.: Adequate factory transformability at low costs. In: International Conference on Competitive Manufacturing (COMA) (2004)

17. Kadner, S., Kobus, J., Stuchtey, M.R., Weber, T.: Circular economy roadmap für deutschland. acatech Studie, R. acatech/SYSTEMIQ, München/London (2021)

18. Gebler, M., Cerdas, J.F., Thiede, S., Herrmann, C.: Life cycle assessment of an automotive factory: Identifying challenges for the decarbonization of automotive production – a case study. J. Clean Prod. 270 (2020)

19. Dér, A., Hingst, L., Nyhuis, P., Herrmann, C.: A review of frameworks, methods and models for the evaluation and engineering of factory life cycles. Advances in Industrial and Manufacturing Engineering (under revision) (2022)

20. Lindemann, U., Reichwald, R., Zäh, M.F.: Individualisierte Produkte - Komplexität beherrschen in Entwicklung und Produktion. Springer-Verlag, Heidelberg (2006). https://doi.org/10.1007/3-540-34274-5

21. Ehrlenspiel, K.: Kostengünstig Entwickeln und Konstruieren: Kostenmanagement Bei der Integrierten Produktentwicklung, 8th edn. Springer, Heidelberg (2020). https://doi.org/10.1007/978-3-642-41959-1

22. Kestel, R.: Variantenvielfalt und Logistiksysteme: Ursachen - Auswirkungen - Lösungen. Deutscher Universitätsverlag, Wiesbaden (1995)

23. Wildemann, H.: Variantenmanagement: Leitfaden zur Komplexitätsreduzierung, -beherrschung und -vermeidung, 26th edn. TCW-Verlag, München (2018)

24. ElMaraghy, H., Schuh, G., ElMaraghy, W., Piller, F., Schönsleben, P., Tseng, M., Bernard, A.: Product variety management. Manufacturing Technology, 629–652 (2013)

25. Schuh, G.: Gestaltung und Bewertung von Produktvarianten ein Beitrag zur Systematischen Planung von Serienprodukten. Dissertation, VDI-Verl., Aachen (1989)

26. Caesar, C.: Kostenorientierte Gestaltungsmethodik für Variantenreiche Serienprodukte: Variant Mode and Effects Analysis (VMEA). Dissertation, VDI-Verl., Aachen (1991)

27. Bayer, T.: Variantenkostenbewertung mit faktorenanalytischen Komplexitätstreibern. Zugl.: Karlsruhe, Univ., Diss., 2010, 1st ed., Hampp, München (2010)

28. Brosch, M.: Eine Methode zur Reduzierung der produktvarianteninduzierten Komplexität. Dissertation, Techn. Univ. Hamburg-Harburg Univ.-Bibl, Hamburg (2014)

Industry 5.0 – Making It Happen in the Agri Industry. The Core Product Service Platform

Bjørnar Henriksen, Carl Christian Røstad$^{(\boxtimes)}$, and Maria Kollberg Thomassen$^{(\boxtimes)}$

SINTEF Technology Management, S.P. Andersens vei 5, N-7465 Trondheim, Norway
{carl.c.rostad,Maria.Thomassen}@sintef.no

Abstract. There is a gap between the "radical" visions for Industry 5.0 and the practical solutions, which are mainly based on enabling technologies, we have seen so far. We still need more practical guidelines and cases to get an understanding of how, or whether Industry 5.0 could be relevant as an approach for manufacturing companies to meet the challenges they are facing. This paper investigates how Industry 5.0 can be the reference for developing capabilities needed for meeting the increasingly challenging market and sustainability requirements. To be able to capture all facets and effects of Industry 5.0, the sustainability, resilience and human centricity principles have to work jointly together aligned with roadmaps. This paper presents a platform for industry 5.0 capability development based upon literature that is tested in two firms in the agricultural industry. "The Core Product Service Platform" describing the products and services to deliver and capabilities needed to become an Industry 5.0 company.

Keywords: Human centricity · Sustainability · Resilience · Innovation capability

1 Introduction

1.1 Background

Manufacturing companies deal with an increasingly complex business environment that requires innovation capabilities. Industry 5.0, at least in theory, addresses this complex business environment, but requires development of certain capabilities.

Industry 5.0 is based on three core principles; resilience, sustainability and human centricity. Even though human centricity to some extent represents a new perspective, these principles are well-known within manufacturing. But as we dig deeper we see that when these three elements create synergies, the result could be companies heading for societal goals and not pure financial profit, hence representing something new. Industry 5.0 focuses on humans (workers, customers etc.) where their motivation for sustainable and responsible manufacturing could even trigger new broader perspectives in manufacturing resulting in new innovation capabilities.

How to succeed in achieving this is challenging as over time, principles, methods and solutions must be developed and become capabilities that enable companies to move

© IFIP International Federation for Information Processing 2022
Published by Springer Nature Switzerland AG 2022
D. Y. Kim et al. (Eds.): APMS 2022, IFIP AICT 663, pp. 424–431, 2022.
https://doi.org/10.1007/978-3-031-16407-1_50

purposefully in the desired direction. The challenge of being able to operationalize Industry 5.0 is something that is high on the research agenda also in the EU [1].

The literature is dominated by the overall theoretical perspectives and studies primarily focusing on enabling technologies. There is limited research addressing how principles may be adopted in a joint manner with focus on the value creation in the intersection between them to enhance competitiveness, based upon enabling technologies. There is a need to develop new solutions, methods and approaches for increased practical uptake of Industry 5.0 principles in industry, especially among SMEs.

1.2 Scope and Research Approach

This paper introduces a new concept, "The Core Product Service Platform", that can help manufacturing companies enhance their innovation capabilities by adopting Industry 5.0. The concept illustrates how Industry 5.0 can be further developed and applied, focusing on the interrelatedness of principles and capabilities.

Cases from the agricultural technology (agritech) sector are used to illustrate the platform concept in a specific context. This paper is based on the research in two R&D projects "WRAPID" and "Feed Carrier", both aiming to improve product development and long-term competitiveness. The importance of Industry 5.0 has increased during the projects' timelines, although the concept had little focus at the start of the projects.

2 Theoretical Perspectives

2.1 Core Principles of Industry 5.0

Academics have brought forth the ideas of putting sustainability into practice, integrate human values with technology [3, 4], and the European Commission has released the important document "Industry 5.0: Towards a Sustainable, Human-centric, and Resilient European Industry" [5]. Industry 5.0 is based on human orientation, sustainability and resilience, with emphasis on considering elements in context, building culture, practical routines and solutions for creating synergies. It emphasizes employees as important drivers for change and the successful profit realization of technology. At the same time, the concept implies stronger focus on social responsibility, shifts focus from shareholder value to stakeholder value and reinforces the role and contribution of industry to society. Moreover, technology is highly integrated with organizations to develop a more competitive, sustainable and green industry, in healthy, robust and sustainable welfare societies.

The human centricity principle means that people are put at the center and take control of technology and innovation processes. Regarding employees, the principle implies not only to provide better processes and working conditions, but also so that employees as citizens are central for that the company becomes a positive contributor to sustainability and social development. This includes e.g. accountability and qualification of employees to take on new roles, and collective social processes and structures, which may refer to the «Norwegian Working Life Model» [2]. An important prerequisite is that the enabling technologies used in production are adapted to the needs and diversity of workers, instead of the worker continuously adapting to technology in constant development. The human-centricity principle may be represented by digitally enhanced work, which is typically based on cognitive support systems such as decision support and context-based guidance, technology-supported learning, and sensor systems.

The sustainability principle implies that companies contribute to a positive societal development beyond the purely (short-term) financial results. The UN's 17 sustainability development goals provide definitions and guidelines for how to drive societal development. Sustainable production means reducing resource use, environmental damage and greenhouse gas emissions in manufacturing. In the long run, this will lead to economic growth, limit climate change and increase the quality of life for people. This means contributing positively to the local environment, but also regionally and globally, looking beyond the company's own production, also taking responsibility for value chains, supplier systems, usage patterns. It is thus stressed that a company's profit may have to give way to what serves society as a whole. Succeeding to do so not only require decision support systems capturing sustainability, but also people with motivation, skills and ability to decide and perform.

The resilience principle addresses a company's ability to adapt to adverse situations with positive results. Geopolitical changes and natural crises such as the Covid-19 pandemic reveal how fragile industries and supply chains may be. Resilience is also important for the individual company's ability to deal with changing market conditions. Adaptability, mass customization, modularity and product platforms are keywords. This principle reflects to a large extent enabling technologies defined in Industry 4.0. However, there is strong focus on technologies that support human-driven processes and more societal goals.

2.2 Innovation Capabilities

To succeed in creating values based on the core principles of Industry 5.0, a company needs to develop its capabilities. Capabilities reflect a company's ability, including for instance knowledge, skills, resources, motivation, and so on. The resource-based view of the firm highlights the importance of the use and configuration of resources available for a company's performance. A company may enhance its capabilities by using its resources for superior performance and Industry 5.0 can help to strengthen capabilities.

The innovation capability reflects a firm's ability to identify new ideas and transform them into new/improved products, services or processes that benefit the firm [17]. This is typically based on elements related to knowledge management, organisational learning, organisational culture, leadership, collaboration, creativity, idea management, and strategy [18]. When developing the innovation capability for a certain purpose or context, specific elements may be emphasized. For example in product-service systems innovation, key elements may include collaboration, innovation methodology, customer interaction, innovative climate, cross-functionality, network partners and competence building [20]. Within these dimensions, capabilities related to technology, organization, processes, routines and so on, provide a more concrete idea of how they become enablers and prerequisites for innovation.

3   A New Industry 5.0 Platform Concept

3.1   The Core Product-Service Platform (CPSP)

A company adopting Industry 5.0 needs a systematic and structured approach, encompassing not only the management team, but the entire organization and key stakeholders such as customers and other partners in the supply chain. A new platform concept is proposed to support the adoption of Industry 5.0 in the context of new products and services. The platform concept is based on the following elements:

- Establishment of a vision and objectives of future products and services based upon Industry 5.0 including sustainability, resilience and human centricity
- Identification of context-specific enabling methods, technologies and tools
- Identification of key capabilities required to fulfil the established vision
- Development of key capabilities to meet defined objectives by utilizing e.g. knowledge, skills, resources, enabling technologies

The proposed Industry 5.0 platform aims to serve as an engine for developing a company's innovation capability. Hence, the human centricity principle where employees are central driving forces in innovation and development is especially critical (Fig. 1).

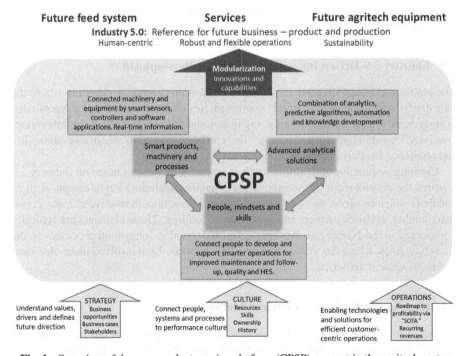

Fig. 1. Overview of the core product-service platform (CPSP) concept in the agritech sector

3.2   The Context – Creating a Vision for the Future Product and Services

To be able to move towards a sustainable, resilient and economically healthy future business, the case companies define clear visions and objectives that are common for the organization and stakeholders. A thorough understanding of the context and of future products and services is necessary to define relevant key capabilities and roadmaps.

The agricultural industry has a major role in contributing to a wide range of sustainability objectives related to for instance food security, animal welfare and soil conservation. EU's Farm to Fork strategy [8] points at sustainable food production, and how digitization of products and services must be able to be used by small and medium-sized farms in a sustainable, productive way that creates smart and flexible agricultural systems. The case companies' feed solutions are crucial in this regard. To succeed, they must take into account an increasingly complex interaction between nature, technology, organization and society's perspective, as well as how the current portfolio can be improved while realizing the next generation of feed product service solutions. Norway's work life is known for close collaboration between employees, unions and managers. The case companies are acutely aware of the importance of involving employees and customers in innovation and improvement activities.

When the companies jointly develop new feed systems in line with overall societal goals, a unique market position is created. However, they also need to have technology and processes that meet market needs that require close interaction with the customers (farmers). This is a major motivation for developing new product service feed systems based on Industry 5.0.

3.3   Industry 5.0-Driven Innovation Capability Development

The platform concept suggests to prioritize innovation capability elements where the Industry 5.0 core principles are jointly combined. Key elements including e.g. knowledge management, organisational learning, organisational culture, leadership, collaboration, creativity, idea management and strategy, that can be developed to enhance sustainability and resilience are thus important.

Creating sustainable agricultural product service feed systems based on Industry 5.0 requires the development of the innovation capability including key elements such as collaboration, innovation methodology, customer interaction, innovative climate, cross-functionality, network partners and competence building. These elements are typically represented in the Norwegian Working Life Model and in innovation processes in the case companies, where the whole organization is motivated and involved in development and improvement activities.

3.4   Enabling Technologies, Tools and Methods

The innovation capability should be developed so that it contributes to the company's desired future direction. The human centricity principle may provide support in the development of new sustainable products, e.g. in the design of new methodologies that employees can use for identifying environmental challenges, collecting and analysing facts, and defining market opportunities. Another example is the involvement of customers in the product-service development of new feed systems. To efficiently involve production and shop-floor employees in the design for sustainable production is another key element, as well as the motivation and ability of the whole organization to drive the development of product-service systems including new technologies.

Industry 5.0 is associated with a wide range of enabling technologies that may support the development of a company's innovation capability. Javaid and Haleem [6] list technologies considered particularly relevant in Industry 5.0, but mainly cover production and personalized products. The European Commission [9] highlights six key categories of technologies:

1. Human-centric solutions and human-machine-interaction
2. Bio-inspired technologies and smart materials
3. Real time based digital twins and simulation
4. Cyber safe data transmission, storage, and analysis technologies
5. Artificial Intelligence (AI)
6. Technologies for energy efficiency and trustworthy autonomy

Digitally enhanced work is also about the use of cognitive support systems, such as decision support and context-based guidance, technology-supported learning, sensor systems. Tools and technologies such as decision support systems, Life Cycle Assessments and predictive analytics, can offer knowledge, increase sustainability and foresee possible contingencies for instance related to the offered products, unexpected events or demand variations etc.

A company's processes, organization, roles and responsibilities of employees, knowledge management and performance management may be included in the development of Industry 5.0 innovation capability. The prioritization of sustainability and resilience in the entire company and among stakeholders may be challenging. This is due the complexity of adding social, cultural and to some extent political aspects in addition to human centricity to the manufacturing context. This means that enabling technologies are not enough. Instead, companies need a variety of tools and solutions to adopt Industry 5.0. Patience is also required as changes of human, social and cultural elements is a maturation process.

The case companies seek to adopt Industry 5.0 in practice supported by the proposed Core Product Service Platform concept. This work involves different ways of using available data, technology, tools and solutions. However, even more importantly is defining specific principles, procedures and processes, based on human centricity, sustainability and resilience, that are adjusted to the companies' contexts. It is also important to take into account that Industry 5.0 is about building a culture where the entire organization sees their activities, and contributes to decisions, in a broader societal perspective. Building such a business culture is challenging and takes time.

4 Conclusion

Industry 5.0 is relevant for many manufacturing companies to meet the challenging competitive situation where resilience and sustainability are critical prerequisites. It is critical to move from theory to practice to see how companies can take advantage of the concept. The proposed platform concept and approach emphasizes the development of a company's innovation capability, i.e. its ability to innovate and develop sustainable products and services. Capability elements related to human centricity is of particular importance to the adoption of Industry 5.0. The Core Product Service Platform is developed in two R&D-projects as a concept for developing companies' innovation capabilities in line with Industry 5.0 thus positioning the companies in a position to meet the challenging competitive situations. The new platform concept is developed to support concretization and adoption of the Industry 5.0 concept. Further research is needed to increase the uptake of Industry 5.0, especially how the concept can be applied for dealing with many of the challenges that manufacturing companies are facing, as well as its implications.

References

1. European Commission (2022): Industry 5.0 Towards a sustainable, human centric and resilient European industry. https://ec.europa.eu/info/research-and-innovation/research-area/industrial-research-and-innovation/industry-50_en. Opplastet 10.02.2022
2. Levin, M., et al.: Demokrati i arbeidslivet. Den norske samarbeidsmodellen som konkurranse-fortrinn. Fagbokforlaget, Bergen (2012)
3. Demir, K.A., Döven, G., Sezen, B.: Industry 5.0 and human-robot co-working. Procedia Comput. Sci. **158**, 688–695 (2019). https://doi.org/10.1016/J.PROCS.2019.09.104
4. Xu, X., Lu, Y., Vogel-Heuser, B., Wang, L.: Industry 4.0 and Industry 5.0-Inception, conception and perception. J. Manuf. Syst. **61**, 530–535 (2021)
5. Breque, M., De Nul, L., Petridis, A.: Industry 5.0: towards a sustainable, human-centric and resilient European industry. Luxembourg, LU: European Commission, Directorate-General for Research and Innovation (2021)
6. Javaid, M., Haleem, A.: Critical Components of Industry 5.0 Towards a Successful Adoption in the Field of Manufacturing. J. Ind Integr. Manag. **5**(3), 327–348 (2020)
7. Martynov V. V., Shavaleeva D. N., Zaytseva, A. A.: Information technology as the basis for transformation into a digital society and industry 5.0. In: 2019 International Conference "Quality Management, Transport and Information Security, Information Technologies" (IT&QM&IS), pp. 539–543 (2019). https://doi.org/10.1109/ITQMIS.2019.8928305
8. https://ec.europa.eu/food/horizontal-topics/farm-fork-strategy_en. Upload 06.04.2022
9. Müller, J.: Enabling Technologies for Industry 5.0: results of a workshop with Europe's technology leaders, publications office. European Commission, Directorate-General for Research and Innovation (2020). https://data.europa.eu/doi/10.2777/082634
10. Breque, M., De Nul, L., Petridis, A.: Industry 5.0: towards a sustainable, human-centric and resilient European industry, publications office. European Commission, Directorate-General for Research and Innovation (2021). https://data.europa.eu/doi/10.2777/308407
11. Renda, A., Schwaag Serger, S., Tataj, D.: Industry 5.0, a transformative vision for Europe: governing systemic transformations towards a sustainable industry. European Commission, Directorate-General for Research and Innovation (2022). https://data.europa.eu/doi/10.2777/17322
12. Akundi, A., Euresti, D., Luna, S., Ankobiah, W., Lopes, A., Edinbarough, I.: State of industry 5.0 -analysis and identification of current research trends. Appl. Syst. Innov. **5**(1), 27 (2022)
13. Lu, Y., et al.: Outlook on human-centric manufacturing towards industry 5.0. J. Manuf. Syst. **62**, 612–627 (2022)
14. Maddikunta, P. K. R., et al.: Industry 5.0: a survey on enabling technologies and potential applications. J. Ind. Inf. Integr., 100257 (2021)

15. Di Nardo, M., Yu, H.: Special issue "industry 5.0: The prelude to the sixth indus-trial revolution". Appl. Syst. Innov. **4**(3), 45 (2021)
16. Sindhwani, R., Afridi, S., Kumar, A., Banaitis, A., Luthra, S., Singh, P. L.: Can industry 5.0 revolutionize the wave of resilience and social value creation? A multi-criteria framework to analyze enablers. Technol. Soc., 101887 (2022)
17. Aas, T.H., Breunig, K.J.: Conceptualizing innovation capabilities: a contingency perspective. J. Entrepreneurship Manag. Innov. **13**(1), 7–24 (2017)
18. Iddris, F.: Innovation capability: a systematic review and research agenda. Interdiscipl. J. Inf. Knowl. Manag. **11**, 235–260 (2016)
19. Wallin, J.: Developing capability for product-service system innovation: an empirical study in the aerospace industry. Chalmers University of Technology (2013)

Circular Economy and Industrial Symbiosis in Sicily

Ludovica Maria Oliveri[1]([✉]), Ferdinando Chiacchio[1], Diego D'Urso[1], Agata Matarazzo[2], Laura Cutaia[3], and Antonella Luciano[3]

[1] Dipartimento di Ingegneria Elettrica, Elettronica ed Informatica, Università degli Studi di Catania, 95125 Catania, Italy
ludovica.oliveri@phd.unict.it
[2] Dipartimento di Economia e Impresa, Università degli Studi di Catania, 95129 Catania, Italy
[3] Italian National Agency for New Technologies, Energy and Sustainable Economic Development – Department for Sustainability, Resource Valorization Lab, ENEA – Casaccia Research Centre, 00123 Rome, Italy

Abstract. Aim of this paper is to present the state of the art of the Industrial Symbiosis in Sicily, a region of southern Italy. The strengths, the limits and the obstacles to its spread of the initiatives carried out by public institutions and private companies are studied. In order to overcome the issues of the previous initiatives, the research proposed in this paper will pivot on a first phase of investigation based on the collection of data and feedback from the main stakeholders (interviews and questionnaires). Such knowledge will be preparatory to understand the main needs of the industries of this territory and will orient to the development of the most valuable and effective tools that can concretely help operators to achieve the goals of the Industrial Symbiosis.

Keywords: Symbiosis · Circular economy · Supply chain · Database · CO2 reduction · Sustainable manufacturing

1 Introduction

The growing demand and the limited supply of resources, especially for some raw materials that are becoming rare, force companies to take into account the risk of dependence on few suppliers and the increase of costs. Moreover, the supply of some raw materials has often very high environmental impacts while the search for new sources can be uneconomical too. In 2014, Working Group on Defining Critical Raw Materials of the European Commission defined 54 critical raw materials for Europe, since 90% are imported from non-EU countries and mainly from China [1]. Events such as the Covid19 pandemic and the recent war in Ukraine have highlighted the impact of this dependence on Asian countries on our economy. Building a Circular Economy and achieving Industrial Symbiosis allow to reduce this subordination, not only, it helps reaching Sustainable Development Goals (SDG) 12 and 13. SDG are a collection of 17 interlinked global goals

© IFIP International Federation for Information Processing 2022
Published by Springer Nature Switzerland AG 2022
D. Y. Kim et al. (Eds.): APMS 2022, IFIP AICT 663, pp. 432–439, 2022.
https://doi.org/10.1007/978-3-031-16407-1_51

designed to achieve a better and more sustainable future for all, they're intended to be achieved by 2030. SDG 12 "responsible consumption and production" is meant to ensure good use of resources, improving energy efficiency, sustainable infrastructure, and providing access to basic services, green and decent jobs and ensuring a better quality of life for all [2]. SDG 13 "climate action" mission's is "take urgent action to combat climate change and its impacts" [3]. As reported in [2], Italy occupies the 25th place in the ranking, regarding SDG 12 the comment is "Significant challenges remain. Score moderately improving, insufficient to attain goal" and SDG13 "Major challenges remain. Score moderately improving, insufficient to attain goal" with a specific attention to CO_2 emission.

According to the definition given in [4], Circular Economy (CE) is a generic term to define an economy designed to regenerate itself. In a CE, "material flows are of two types as described by McDonough and Braungart: biological nutrients, designed to re-enter the biosphere safely and build natural capital, and technical nutrients, which are designed to circulate at high quality without entering the biosphere". The CE is therefore an economic system planned to reuse materials in subsequent production cycles, minimizing waste [5]. Since a company is not always able to reuse its waste internally, which can be transformed into second raw material for another, in this paper we will consider the Industrial Symbiosis (IS) that, according to [6], is the interaction between different industrial plants, grouped in districts or at a distance that still allow to make the operation feasible in order to maximize the reuse of resources (normally considered waste), the sharing of knowledge and skills between companies. IS may be considered as a realization of the CE within the industrial landscape [7].

Digital technologies could be critical enablers of CE by tracking the flow of products, components, and materials and making the resultant data available for improved resource management and decision making across different stages of the industry life cycle [8]. As highlighted in [9] the entire business world is impacted by new technologies that rapidly change and evolve, presenting new challenges and opportunities. This evolution applied in manufacturing is called Industry 4.0 [10]. The relationship between the CE and Industry 4.0 technologies has been explored by [11, 12], they agree that Industry 4.0 adoption has a positive relationship with sustainable production and sustainable production has a positive relationship with CE capabilities. Among these, certainly the one that has a very high potential impact is Artificial Intelligence. In the last decade we saw the development of the Internet of Things (IoT). More commonly used objects have sensors that communicate with each other. The growing use of IoT and artificial intelligence can provide valuable help for the implementation of CE in efficient and green industries of the future. As stated in [13], the come to light of digital and smart technologies provide an opportunity to win the challenge of the CE. The amount of data generated during the production, use and disposal of goods is well suited to the characteristics of Big Data. These can be analyzed by applying big data business analytics and artificial intelligence to highlight trends, optimize logistics and direct the management of production flows with the help of IoT. According to [12] developing big data analytics capability has to become a business priority in order to effectively build competitive sustainable supply chain (SC). Big data facilitates several aspects of circular strategies, such as improving waste-to-resource matching in IS systems via real-time gathering and processing of input-output flows.

In this paper we present the state of the art of IS in Sicily and the initiative created to promote it. We chose the biggest Italian island, because in a small way it represents the average Italian and European supply chain. In the region there are SME (small medium enterprise) dealing with: food transformation, furniture making, electromechanical companies, manufacture of non-metallic and metallic products, manufacture of plastic products, beverages, chemicals, electronics, machinery and equipment, repair and installation, etc. In the period between 2011 and 2015, Sicilian stakeholders and policy makers were involved regional project with Government incentives for the "Development and implementation of a regional platform of industrial symbiosis" [14]. In this paper the results of a survey about the spreading of IS in Sicily is used to identify the current lacks and propose a new approach to help concretely the stakeholders to achieve IS. This paper is structured as follows. Section 2 provide the research context and the literature review regarding CE and IS. Section 3 present the state of the art of IS in Sicily. Section 4 provides the description of the research methodology adopted. In Sect. 5 conclusions and expected results are presented.

2   Research Context

The European Union noted that the enhancement of CE would encourage sustainability and competitiveness of businesses in the long term, helping to:

- preserve resources, including some which are increasingly scarce, or subject to price fluctuation;
- save costs for industries;
- unlock new business opportunities;
- build a new generation of innovative, resource-efficient businesses;
- create local low and high-skilled jobs;
- create opportunities for social integration and cohesion.

The benefits of CE are numerous: reports indicate that CO_2 emissions could be reduced by up to 70% and create new jobs. [15, 16] report success stories of numerous entrepreneurs who are making an impact to develop the CE and who create collaborations that use circular business models from which "circular start-ups" were born. According to [17], moving to CE requires a systemic change in the design of products, business models and SC in order to reduce waste, promote internal reuse of waste, favor the production and design of goods that can be repaired, and enable a flow of goods from consumers back to manufacturing companies (reverse logistics), and more. In [18] is underlined that, despite the growing attention on circular supply chain management, several areas are open for investigation, such as SC integration, collaboration and coordination mechanisms. Industrial symbiosis (IS) can also be considered as an example of CE at the meso level, like the eco-industrial parks. The micro level regards the single company, that, applying CE strategies, can find potential source of growth, increased market share and profitability, despite at the macro level, the CE paradigm involves cities, regions and nations. [19] emphasized how IS generates environmental and economic advantages, such as lower resource consumption, raw materials savings and lower treatment costs. Industrial districts (IDs) are characterized by the localization of many small and medium-sized businesses in a given industry, integrated through a complex network of economic and social interrelationships [20]. In the last decades, the ID as a socio-economic organizational model has been suffering from the effects of globalization [21]. According to [11], we believe that a transition to CE, through IS, has the potential to change the destiny of a declining ID towards new growth. In a recent literature survey of information systems [22], existing tools were categorized into six different types based on their facilitation approach: 1) open online waste markets, 2) facilitated synergy identification systems, 3) industry sector synergy identification, 4) social network platforms and communities, 5) industrial symbiosis repositories, 6) region identification systems for industrial symbiosis. With respect to previous works, this paper presents a methodology that can be used to implement a pilot software platform for improving the IS mechanisms.

3   Industrial Symbiosis in Italy and Sicily

One of the first public initiative, aimed at creating a network of companies, is ENEA's Sun Network. Since 2015, it aims as an Italian reference for operators who want to apply industrial symbiosis. It currently brings together 39 partners from universities, political institutions, research institutions, private companies and technological networks. The activity planned was the "Development and implementation of a regional platform of industrial symbiosis" [14]. In [23] a good summary of the activity done in the project is presented. The Sicilian productive system was then investigated and companies were involved in operative meetings for resources sharing, potential synergies individuation and to acquire data for platform validation (http://www.industrialsymbiosis.it/). Potential synergies verification was performed, from a technical, regulatory, logistic and economic point of view, for a selected group of categories. Operative handbooks on some specific case studies were produced. On the basis of the results, some critical issues emerge: 1) the low grade of diversification of participating companies that was not fully representative of the actual productive system so limiting the information on the potential matches; 2) the disequilibrium between observed supply and demand due to the prevalent interest of participating companies in finding out alternative solutions for the disposal of their residues rather than to find alternative supplies for their processes; 3) the excessive offers of services and expertise; 4) companies concern about a potential increase in controls on their activities. It must be highlighted that there are also private enterprises, such as Sfridoo®, whose mission is to generate industrial symbiosis between companies by offering them projects and market tools to convert waste in a resource. It is clear from several publications [24–26], that there are various activities aimed at achieving the CE and specifically at creating industrial symbiosis in Sicily, but they are limited to innovative and virtuous companies, which have sought other companies to collaborate with. The driving element is the concept of Zero Waste [27], that is to reconvert as much as possible the production scraps into secondary raw materials, looking for who can use them to produce or goods or energy.

A first survey on the spreading of the industrial symbiosis in Sicily, involved 20 private companies. Data collected focus on 1) participation or not to any form of industrial symbiosis and reasons, 2) classification of the residual resource, 3) transfer or acquisition of residual resources, 4) business sectors of companies and 5) value appreciation of residual resources. It has been observed that the 53% of the company that have been interviewed had the opportunity to adapt and obtain excellent results in the field of industrial symbiosis, 15% tried to apply sustainable politics without any success, and for a 32% any approach has been taken. Analyzing the answers, it is deduced that the causes of this failure are different:

- Industries and the main stakeholders are not being aware of the phenomenon of industrial symbiosis;
- Companies reuse all waste and residual production resources internally so they don't need to exploit a corporate interdependence;
- Industries own certain assets that cannot be treated as secondary raw materials due to presumed regulatory problems.

The reasons that push the 53% of the companies to choose an ecological industrial path are essentially focused on the respect for the environment, on the enhancement of local resources and, finally, on the entitlement of competitive advantages (Fig. 1.a). As regards to the residual resource, we have seen that the most shared belongs to the material classification and in only one case to the energy classification. In the IS we distinguish the companies that introduce the residual production resources (output), valued and considered secondary raw material, into the "network", and the companies that are organized to acquire these resources and implement them in their production process (input). From this research, it emerges that the prevalent cases are related to the transfer of residual output to other companies, with only the 22% of companies which choose to acquire the resource (Fig. 1.b).

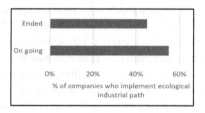

a.

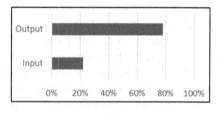

b.

Fig. 1. a. Status of the process of industrial symbiosis; b. Residual resources: moved or acquired (Output/Input).

In the Sicilian system of IS, the main sector of origin of resources is agriculture, followed by the textile sectors for clothing and furnishings and those dedicated to manufacturing and carpentry for construction. The target sectors of the output include activities such as breeding, the manufacture of wooden products and cosmetics, tailoring and the production of non-distilled fermented beverages. It was found that the 67% of the exchange of resources for most companies of the Sicilian territory takes place through an economic enhancement in favor of the producer; this is one of the many economic advantages deriving from IS. The remaining part, representing the 33% of the companies interviewed, chooses the alternative that does not take into account any economic contribution. Choosing an ecological industrial path implies an important behavioral change in entrepreneurs who have to adopt a more careful approach about waste production and an efficient use of resources. While for some companies there are neither barriers nor criticalities, a good percentage of companies still require solutions to specific problems. The difficulties found mostly derive from the lack of harmonization of EU legislation, of consistent incentives and a real circular regulation. In addition, both the limits dictated by distance and the presence of quality problems during the production cycle, still limit the desire of Sicilian companies to create a strong network of IS.

4   Research Proposal

4.1   Methodology

The methodology requires the fulfillment of three different activities: data collection, data analysis and the automation of the process. The first phase will be devoted to the understanding of which district is ready to seize the opportunities generated by CE. The second phase will be dedicated to data analysis and database creation. During the third phase the automation of the platform will be carried out.

Data Collection. A sample of supply chain located in a specific geographical area of Sicily will be selected. The chance to conduct a survey to understand strengths and weaknesses of the previous initiatives which were put in place to promote IS will be one of the main preliminary activities to carry out. Starting from [11] review, the necessary information that will be asked to companies refers to the types and quantities of resources consumed, the types and quantities of waste and by-products produced and the conversion processes, all backed by economic information concerning the exchange. This will allow us to evaluate what resources can be recovered from waste or by-products, what waste or by-products can be used as raw material and last, what technologies and processes are necessary for the conversion. In addition, information regarding availability and requirements of resources in terms of quantity, time and price should be collected. It is important to evaluate the distance among the entities exchanging resources, and the profitability related to the exchanges [7]. Moreover, a detailed study of the production process aimed at reducing waste and enhancing it as a secondary raw material will be proposed to the companies. An important step to achieve is to collect the list of the manufacturing software (ERP, MES, etc.) Which are the most used; in fact, one of the main goals of this research project is to interconnect the software platform object of the next phase -to the companies, offering APIs to query and update the database.

Data Analyses. A database to collect the information about the processes of the industries, the raw materials which they need, their production scraps and waste will be created. This will allow to match the supply of scrap/waste with the demand for secondary raw materials. It also helps to identify which companies can collaborate with each other based also on the geographical position of the companies, with the target to reduce CO_2 emissions.

Criteria of Weakness and Strengths. The analysis of the initiatives in which the companies have been involved will be the starting point of the proposed research. Criteria will be prepared to objectively highlight strengths and weaknesses to use them as a starting point for our work.

Automation of the Platform. In a next step, we aim to implement a set of APIs that will help the companies to update and query the database automatically. All data must be collected and made available for consultation by companies. Access must be simple and intuitive, in Italian, in order not to exclude any user.

5   Conclusions

In this paper, the state of the art of the IS in Sicily has been analyzed. It has been observed that there is a big room of interventions from research institutions, public and private companies to improve the current situation. The diffusion of the internet technologies, such as Internet of Things, Cloud Computing, Artificial Intelligence gives now the opportunity to improve the initiatives that have apparently failed in the past. This study puts the basement for the implementation of a software platform for the IS. The expected results of the next steps of this research project are the following:

- analyze what has been done up to now to promote IS in Sicily;
- build a database that facilitates the exchange of information and favors the dissemination of a culture of CE in the Sicilian supply chain;
- facilitate the transition from linear to CE of SMEs in the area;
- reduce the use of natural resources as raw materials, with the consequent reduction of energy, CO_2 and costs;
- reduce the amount of waste destined for landfills.

References

1. European Comission: enterprise and industry: critical raw materials for the EU, report of the Ad-hoc working group on defining critical raw materials. Eucom. 39 (2010)
2. Sachs, J.D., Lafortune, G., Kroll, C., Fuller, G., Woelm, F.: Sustainable development report (2022)
3. PBB: Work of the statistical commission pertaining to the 2030 agenda for sustainable development (2017)
4. Ellen MacArthur foundation: towards the circular economy (2013)
5. Zilia, F., Bacenetti, J., Sugni, M., Matarazzo, A., Orsi, L.: From waste to product: circular economy applications from Sea Urchin. Sustainability 13 (2021)
6. Chertow, M.R.: Industrial symbiosis: literature and taxonomy. Annu. Rev. Energy Environ. **25**, 313–337 (2000)

7. Low, J.S.C., et al.: A collaboration platform for enabling industrial symbiosis: application of the database engine for waste-to-resource matching. In: Procedia CIRP (2018)
8. Kristoffersen, E., Blomsma, F., Mikalef, P., Li, J.: The smart circular economy: a digital-enabled circular strategies framework for manufacturing companies. J. Bus. Res. **120**, 241–261 (2020)
9. Elia, G., Margherita, A., Passiante, G.: Digital entrepreneurship ecosystem: how digital technologies and collective intelligence are reshaping the entrepreneurial process. Technol. Forecast. Soc. Change 150 (2020)
10. Lasi, H., Fettke, P., Kemper, H.-G., Feld, T., Hoffmann, M.: Industry 4.0. Bus. Inf. Syst. Eng. **6**(4), 239–242 (2014). https://doi.org/10.1007/s12599-014-0334-4
11. Acerbi, F., Sassanelli, C., Terzi, S., Taisch, M.: A systematic literature review on data and information required for circular manufacturing strategies adoption. Sustainability 13 (2021)
12. Lopes de Sousa Jabbour, A.B., Jabbour, C.J.C., Godinho Filho, M., Roubaud, D.: Industry 4.0 and the circular economy: a proposed research agenda and original roadmap for sustainable operations. Ann. Oper. Res. **270**(1–2), 273–286 (2018). https://doi.org/10.1007/s10479-018-2772-8
13. Ramadoss, T.S., Alam, H., Seeram, R.: Artificial intelligence and internet of things enabled circular economy. Int. J. Eng. Sci. **7**, 55–63 (2018)
14. Cutaia, L., et al.: The experience of the first industrial symbiosis platform in Italy. Environ. Eng. Manag. J. **14**, 1521–1533 (2015)
15. Veleva, V., Bodkin, G.: Corporate-entrepreneur collaborations to advance a circular economy. J. Clean. Prod. **188**, 20–37 (2018)
16. Henry, M., Bauwens, T., Hekkert, M., Kirchherr, J.: A typology of circular start-ups: Analysis of 128 circular business models. J. Clean. Prod. 245 (2020)
17. Bressanelli, G., Perona, M., Saccani, N.: Challenges in supply chain redesign for the circular economy: a literature review and a multiple case study. Int. J. Prod. Res. **57**, 7395–7422 (2019)
18. Bressanelli, G., Visintin, F., Saccani, N.: Circular Economy and the evolution of industrial districts: a supply chain perspective. Int. J. Prod. Econ. 243 (2022)
19. Wen, Z., Meng, X.: Quantitative assessment of industrial symbiosis for the promotion of circular economy: a case study of the printed circuit boards industry in China's Suzhou New District. J. Clean. Prod. 90 (2015)
20. Becattini, G.: The Marshallian industrial district as a socio-economic notion (2017)
21. Dei Ottati, G.: Marshallian industrial districts in Italy: the end of a model or adaptation to the global economy? Cambridge J. Econ. **42**, 259–284 (2018)
22. van Capelleveen, G., Amrit, C., Yazan, D.M.: A literature survey of information systems facilitating the identification of industrial symbiosis. In: Otjacques, B., Hitzelberger, P., Naumann, S., Wohlgemuth, V. (eds.) From Science to Society. Progress in IS, pp. 155–169. Springer, Cham (2018). https://doi.org/10.1007/978-3-319-65687-8_14
23. Luciano, A., et al.: Potential improvement of the methodology for industrial symbiosis implementation at regional scale. Waste Biomass Valorization **7**(4), 1007–1015 (2016). https://doi.org/10.1007/s12649-016-9625-y
24. Bruno, G., Vazzano, T., Matarazzo, A., Del Fiume, V.: Pulvirenti: Decarbonizzazione del settore industriale cementiero – produzione di combustibile solido dai rifiuti non pericolosi. In: Proceeding Fourth SUN Conference, pp. 81–83 (2020)
25. Basile, M., Conti, S., Arfò, S., Matarazzo, A.: Cirino: Il riutilizzo del gesso come materia prima seconda in bioedilizia nell'ottica della simbiosi industriale. In: Proceedings Fourth SUN Conference, pp. 84–86 (2020)
26. Fichera, S.S., Arfò, S., Huang, Y.L., Matarazzo, A., Bertino, A.: Circular economy and technological innovation in steel industry. Procedia Environ. Sci. Eng. Manag. **7**, 9–17 (2020)
27. Deselnicu, D.C., Militaru, G., Deselnicu, V., Zăinescu, G., Albu, L.: Towards a circular economy – a zero waste programme for Europe. In: ICAMS Proceedings (2018)

Approach Towards Sustainability Modelling and Sustainability Risk Assessment in Manufacturing Systems

Daniel Schneider[1]($\boxtimes$) ⓘ, Susanne Vernim[1] ⓘ, Thomas Enck[2], and Gunther Reinhart[1]

[1] Institute for Machine Tools and Industrial Management, Technical University of Munich (TUM), Boltzmannstraße 15, 85748 Garching bei München, Germany
daniel.schneider@iwb.tum.de
[2] Commerzbank AG, Kaiserplatz, 60311 Frankfurt am Main, Germany

Abstract. Changing environmental conditions and socio-political expectations progressively pose challenges and risks for manufacturing companies in the European Union. These so-called sustainability risks are becoming increasingly important and pose challenges for both the manufacturing and financial industries. While research on sustainability assessment in production is, in principle, already quite advanced, the concept of sustainability risk has so far been discussed mainly without dedicated reference to production and its systems. Based on a brief presentation of the state of the art, this paper, therefore, presents a research concept for modelling the sustainability of production systems to identify and assess sustainability risks. The approach is divided into three steps and covers the phases of sustainability modelling, data extraction, and employment as a risk management tool. Several research aspects to be considered in the context of this concept development are presented. In conclusion, an outlook on how the proposed approach will be employed in the manufacturing and financial industries is given.

Keywords: Sustainability assessment · Sustainability modelling · Sustainability risk · Manufacturing systems · Resilience

1 Introduction

The greenhouse effect is at the centre of current environmental and political debates, resulting from the excessive consumption of fossil fuels and raw materials. An anthropogenic origin of global warming is now assumed to be certain [1], as is the hypothesis that an intensification of climate change would result in massive economic damage [2]. Sustainability or sustainable development was initially defined as the "development which meets the needs of current generations without compromising the ability of future generations to meet their own needs" [3]. It is usually operationalised through the triple bottom line (TBL), a concept pioneered by Elkington [4] that simultaneously considers economic, environmental, and social issues from a microeconomic perspective. A

© IFIP International Federation for Information Processing 2022
Published by Springer Nature Switzerland AG 2022
D. Y. Kim et al. (Eds.): APMS 2022, IFIP AICT 663, pp. 440–447, 2022.
https://doi.org/10.1007/978-3-031-16407-1_52

particularly relevant group of actors pursuing this sustainable development is manufacturing companies. Consequently, there is growing socio-political pressure – especially in the European Union – for sustainable economic activity (e.g., through the European Commission's Green Deal in 2019). The introduction of financial control mechanisms for more sustainable production, such as a CO_2 tax, as well as the evident scarcity of environmentally relevant resources, additionally indicate an increase in the cost of production. It will be an essential challenge for manufacturing companies to at least partially compensate for this increase in costs through more sustainable operations and counter sustainability-related risks to which they are exposed at an early stage.

2 Theoretical Foundations and Aim of this Publication

Research on sustainability assessment in production is, in principle, already quite advanced but still has specific weak points. These weaknesses were presented by Schneider et al. [5] and are summarised and discussed in Sect. 3. In contrast to the sole assessment of sustainability, sustainability modelling creates an abstract of reality using models, as this reality is usually too complex to be fully represented. However, completeness is not intended; rather, only the essential influencing factors significant for the real process and its context are to be identified and represented [6]. Following [7], a sustainability model of a production (system) should fulfil the following three characteristics: (1) representation of the original (i.e., production system), (2) shortening of the original's attributes to those that seem relevant for the further purpose of use, and (3) pragmatism, since models have a replacement function tailored to specific addressees, time intervals and goals.

The concept of sustainability risk, on the other hand, has so far been discussed mainly at the country/sector level or regarding supply chain or product risks, but not yet with dedicated reference to production and its systems (cf. Section 3.3). Sustainability risks encompass environmental and social responsibility risks in addition to risks concerning the traditional bottom line [7]. The concept of sustainability risks becomes apparent when expressing the TBL mentioned above slightly differently: Normally, the TBL is defined as follows:

$$\text{Maximise:} F + E + S = TBL \tag{1}$$

In this formula, F describes the financial or economical performance, E the environmental performance, and S the social (responsibility) performance. Consequently, to maximise the sustainability of a manufacturing system, all three dimensions need to be considered. Following the general understanding of (financial) risk management, risk costs need to be subtracted from profit. Consequently, the TBL can be expressed monetarily as follows [7]:

$$TBL = F - \text{risk costs of } E - \text{risk costs of } S \tag{2}$$

It becomes apparent that the TBL, if measured in financial terms, is directly dependent on environmental and social risks or in other words: if the environmental and social responsibility risk costs are reduced while everything else is held constant, the TBL will increase [7]. As displayed in Fig. 1, two different types of sustainability risks shall be distinguished in the following depending on their origin: physical risks and transitory risks. Physical risks are bidirectional and can either result from the environment and affect the production (e.g., extreme weather effects) or be caused by the production system and impact the environment (e.g., hazardous emissions and waste). Transitory risks, in contrast, are unidirectional and usually result from the changes in society to become more sustainable and tend to be regulatory and legal in nature (e.g., CO_2 tax). In Fig. 1, the difference between pure sustainability assessment and sustainability risk assessment also becomes apparent: While the former only considers the sustainability performance, the latter looks at the impacts of sustainability-related risks on manufacturing systems due to their sustainability performance.

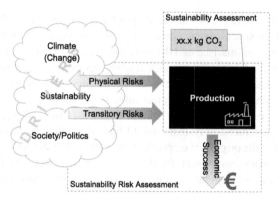

Fig. 1. Distinction between sustainability assessment and sustainability risk assessment

For an efficient sustainability risk assessment of production systems, however, a comprehensive information base is needed to describe the risk-relevant sustainability-related properties of the production system. This requires the sustainability modelling introduced above. Therefore, this paper aims to propose a research approach for modelling multidimensional sustainability to enable the identification and assessment of sustainability risks in production. This shall empower manufacturing companies, on the one hand, to report their sustainability performance to external stakeholders such as banks and customers, and on the other hand, to efficiently manage sustainability and related risks in manufacturing operations.

3   Literature Review and State of the Art

This chapter presents an overview of relevant preliminary work divided into the three sections sustainability assessment and modelling, data availability, and sustainability risks, according to the objectives of the research concept described above. Lastly, a need for action is derived.

3.1 Sustainability Assessment and Modelling of Manufacturing Systems

The state of the art in assessing manufacturing systems' sustainability performance was previously investigated extensively following different approaches [5, 7–11]. It became clear that various use cases for sustainability assessment systems exist, ranging from use as a tool in decision-making processes to operational support for process changes and help in conceptual design phases [5, 9]. Different assessment methodologies were also identified, which can be used to systematise the systems [5, 7, 8, 10]. Similarly, existing sustainability assessment systems have already been systematised according to the company levels considered and the sustainability dimensions covered [5, 11]. However, challenges remain in dealing with sustainability assessment systems. Firstly, there is a persistent lack of a generic sector-appropriate sustainability concept [12]. Secondly, an ongoing disagreement on fundamental aspects of the taxonomy of sustainability indicators becomes apparent [5]. This concerns, in particular, the dimensions and operational levels to be covered during the assessment. For example, few approaches exist for the segment/system, cell, and station level of a company that consider all three dimensions of sustainability according to the TBL. Often, only ecological and economic, or even only ecological, aspects are covered on these levels, while social factors are not or only marginally accounted for [5].

The state of the art of sustainability modelling can be described with less clarity. In particular, this is due to the inconsistent use of the term "model" or "modelling" in connection with the sustainability of production systems. Many publications regarding sustainability assessment also mention the term modelling (e.g., [13–17]). However, the use of the term ranges from being used synonymously with "assessment" to actually representing "modelling" in the sense of the requirements for a (sustainability) model defined above. At the same time, the majority of the actual models presented in these papers are not exhaustively backed by tools and technologies, nor do they support the complete manufacturing life cycle [18].

3.2 Data Availability in Manufacturing Systems for Effective Sustainability Assessment and Modelling

In general, sustainability assessment is very data-intensive [19]. The data basis required for sustainability assessment depends primarily on the assessment object. However, also the choice of the assessment method determines which data are needed for the assessment and in which format they must be available. One of the most widely used types of assessment methods is the so-called material flow-based assessment. The most typical representative of this type is the Life Cycle Assessment (LCA). Despite its high degree of standardisation according to the ISO 14040/14044 standard framework, LCA suffers from a lack of readily available data [20]. For manufacturing use cases, so-called inventory data, i.e., standardised and publicly available data regarding resource consumption and emissions, is typically limited to the production processes of primary materials [21]. This leaves a lack of manufacturing process-related inventory data, which would be essential for accurately assessing and modelling a manufacturing system's sustainability. The following publications, in particular, are among the approaches to solving or improving this problem, not only for LCA but sustainability assessment in general.

Bettoni et al. [22] defined a reference data model for sustainability assessment. Landolfi et al. [23] proposed a Manufacturing as a Service platform architecture to support data sovereignty for sustainability assessments of manufacturing systems. Aizstrauta and Ginters [24] used market data of technologies in their approach to building a sustainability assessment model. Li et al. [19] presented a data-driven approach for improving sustainability assessment in advanced manufacturing. In summary, it becomes apparent through these publications that there is a scientific need for converting and simplifying knowledge-based and data-driven models into analytics models for uniform employment in sustainability assessment [19].

3.3   Identifying and Assessing Sustainability Risks for Manufacturing Systems

The concept of sustainability risk was introduced with a focus on countries or industry sectors [7]. Publications regarding manufacturing companies have only recently appeared. Thereby, the main focus of many of these publications is on sustainability risks affecting procurement and supply chains. For instance, Torres-Ruiz & Ravindran [25] presented a framework for assessing potential sustainability risks of supply chains for different supplier segments. Similarly, Xu et al. [26] developed an assessment framework to evaluate supply chain sustainability by measuring operational risks, social risks, and environmental risks. Another group of publications considers sustainability risks of specific products. For example, Vinodh & Jayakrishna [27] proposed an evaluation model for sequential risk/benefit assessments throughout the product life cycle. Correspondingly, Anand et al. [28] developed a sustainability risk assessment index for the conceptual design phase of a mechanical system. In contrast to those two groups, only a few publications can be found focusing on the risk assessment of manufacturing systems. García-Gómez et al. [29] discussed criteria, methodologies, and requirements for identifying, analysing, and evaluating sustainability risks related to industrial assets. Kazancoglu et al. [30] focused their sustainability risk assessment approach specifically on the process of e-waste recycling for the circular economy. In summary, it can be said that although the topic of sustainability risk is receiving increasing attention in the context of the manufacturing industry, existing approaches are mainly limited to areas adjacent to production. However, an approach that explicitly addresses the sustainability risks of production and its systems is still missing.

3.4   Need for Action

Considering the limitations of the state of research presented above, it is evident that a comprehensive research approach is needed to achieve the goals set out in Sect. 2. On the one hand, this approach must enable the abstract modelling of the sustainability of production systems that is necessary for risk identification and assessment. And on the other hand, it must consider the required data basis and propose a method to determine and capture relevant information efficiently. Thereby, sustainability decision logic and model structures must be modularised to enable and streamline an ongoing sustainability risk assessment in production systems.

4   Concept for Sustainability Modelling and Sustainability Risk Assessment in Manufacturing Systems

The proposed concept comprises the three consecutive steps Modelling, Extracting, and Employing, and is outlined in Fig. 2. For the first step of modelling a manufacturing system's sustainability, a basis must initially be established for abstractly discussing sustainability. To do so, relevant sustainability-related key performance indicators (KPI) are identified and systematised in a use-case-specific taxonomy from the publications presented in [5] and above. The taxonomy is afterwards expanded by the collection and definition of calculation rules for the KPIs. This results in a calculation system to identify and describe the interdependencies between the taxonomy's KPIs.

The second step of determining and extracting relevant data is carried out based on the previously defined calculation system of KPIs. Initially, the required data basis and possibilities for data collection are assessed. Afterwards, the efficient collection of KPI-relevant data is intended. According to the current state of development, the approach is as follows: At the outset, process models and resource libraries are created semi-automatically based on data available in the production system. These are, among others, digital product and plant models containing sustainability-relevant information. Subsequently, a semi-automated matching of the processes and resources with existing Life Cycle Inventory (LCI) databases is conducted. Lastly, the generated process/resource models are linked with the existing LCI data to form an LCA model, thus enabling the automated calculation of KPIs in accordance with ISO 14040/14044.

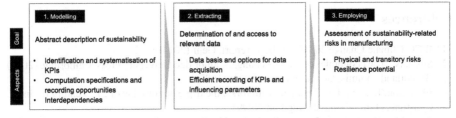

Fig. 2. Concept for sustainability modelling and sustainability risk assessment

The third step of employment uses the achieved KPI model to identify and assess sustainability risks in manufacturing. For this purpose, dimension-specific risk functions are defined and then used to quantify the degree of "damage" to be expected given certain decision functions. Thereby, the severity of damage directly depends on the calculated KPIs' values and, therefore, on the production system itself. The probability of occurrence, however, is mainly dependent on non-manufacturing-related circumstances (e.g., likelihood of stricter climate legislation). Therefore, from a production science perspective, the main focus is on quantifying the potential extent of damage based on the preceding sustainability modelling. The results shall be used, as described above, to report sustainability performance to external stakeholders and to manage sustainability and related risks in manufacturing operations efficiently. The latter serves to increase the sustainability-related resilience of manufacturing companies by identifying improvement possibilities.

5 Conclusion and Outlook

In summary, research on sustainability assessment in production is, in principle, already quite advanced but still has certain weak points. The concept of sustainability risk has so far been discussed mainly at the country/sector level or regarding supply chain or product risks, but not yet with dedicated reference to production and its systems. Therefore, the novelty value of the overall concept lies in the intended use of sustainability assessment to identify and evaluate sustainability risks in production. The proposed concept is currently developed also in cooperation with Commerzbank AG, a major German bank, where it shall be applied in the credit risk management function for corporate customers. The customers are German medium-sized companies in the machinery and plant engineering sector. Emerging sustainability requirements and climate effects impose risks on these manufacturing companies, thus also on the financing bank. These risks, however, can also represent opportunities as high-tech solutions sold by the companies often alleviate the harmful effects of production. They can thus mitigate or reduce the sustainability risks of their respective customers. While risk management in this field used to be focused on well-defined financial risks, it must now increasingly deal with sustainability risks and the sustainability-related resilience of its customers.

Acknowledgement. The authors would like to thank the German Federal Ministry of Education and Research (BMBF) and Jülich Project Management for funding the SynErgie Project (03SFK3E1 2) and Commerzbank AG for the excellent collaboration.

References

1. IPCC Climate Change 2014: Synthesis report, Genf (2014)
2. Stern, N.: The economics of climate change. Cambridge University Press, Cambridge (2007)
3. Brundtland commission our common future (1987)
4. Elkington, J., John, E.: Cannibals with forks: the triple bottom line of 21st century business. Capstone, Oxford, United Kingdom (1999)
5. Schneider, D., Paul, M., Vernim, S., Zaeh, M.F.: Sustainability assessment of manufacturing systems – a review-based systematisation. In: Andersen, A.-L., et al. (eds.) Towards Sustainable Customization: Bridging Smart Products and Manufacturing Systems. Lecture Notes in Mechanical Engineering, pp. 1023–1030. Springer, Cham (2022). https://doi.org/10.1007/978-3-030-90700-6_117
6. Thalheim, B.: Towards a Theory of Conceptual Modelling. Verlag der TU, Graz (2010)
7. Stachowiak, H.: Allgemeine Modelltheorie. Springer, Wien (1973)
8. Anderson, D.R., Anderson, K.E.: Sustainability risk management. Risk Manag. Insur. Rev. **12**, 25–38 (2009)
9. Finnveden, G., Moberg, Å.: Environmental systems analysis tools – an overview. J. Clean. Prod. **13**, 1165–1173 (2005)
10. Ness, B., Urbel-Piirsalu, E., Anderberg, S., et al.: Categorising tools for sustainability assessment. Ecol. Econ. **60**, 498–508 (2007)
11. Moldan, B., Janoušková, S., Hák, T.: How to understand and measure environmental sustainability: indicators and targets. Ecol. Indic. **17**, 4–13 (2012)
12. Singh, R.K., Murty, H.R., Gupta, S.K., et al.: An overview of sustainability assessment methodologies. Ecol. Indic. **15**, 281–299 (2012)

13. Ahmad, S., Wong, K.Y., Rajoo, S.: Sustainability indicators for manufacturing sectors. JMTM **30**, 312–334 (2019)
14. Čuček, L., Klemeš, J.J., Kravanja, Z.: A review of footprint analysis tools for monitoring impacts on sustainability. J. Clean. Prod. **34**, 9–20 (2012)
15. Delai, I., Takahashi, S.: Sustainability measurement system: a reference model proposal. Soc. Responsib. J. **7**, 438–471 (2011)
16. Germani, M., Mandolini, M., Marconi, M., et al.: A method for the estimation of the economic and ecological sustainability of production lines. Procedia CIRP **15**, 147–152 (2014)
17. Krajnc, D., Glavič, P.: A model for integrated assessment of sustainable development. Resour. Conserv. Recycl. **43**, 189–208 (2005). https://doi.org/10.1016/j.resconrec.2004.06.002
18. Nicoletti Junior, A., de Oliveira, M.C., Helleno, A.L.: Sustainability evaluation model for manufacturing systems based on the correlation between triple bottom line dimensions and balanced scorecard perspectives. J. Clean. Prod. **190**, 84–93 (2018)
19. Zhang, H., Haapala, K.R.: Integrating sustainable manufacturing assessment into decision making for a production work cell. J. Clean. Prod. **105**, 52–63 (2015)
20. Ahmed, M.D., Sundaram, D.: Sustainability modelling and reporting: from roadmap to implementation. Decis. Support Syst. **53**, 611–624 (2012)
21. Li, Y., Zhang, H., Roy, U., et al.: A data-driven approach for improving sustainability assessment in advanced manufacturing. In: 2017 IEEE International Conference on Big Data (Big Data), pp. 1736–1745. IEEE (2017)
22. Finnveden, G., Hauschild, M.Z., Ekvall, T., et al.: Recent developments in Life Cycle Assessment. J Environ Manage **91**, 1–21 (2009)
23. Mani, M., Johansson, B., Lyons, K.W., et al.: Simulation and analysis for sustainable product development. Int J Life Cycle Assess **18**, 1129–1136 (2013)
24. Bettoni, A., Alge, M., Rovere, D., et al.: Towards sustainability assessment: reference data model for integrated product, process, supply chain design. In: 2012 18th International ICE Conference on Engineering, Technology and Innovation, pp. 1–10. IEEE (2012)
25. Landolfi, G., Barni, A., Izzo, G., et al.: A MaaS platform architecture supporting data sovereignty in sustainability assessment of manufacturing systems. Procedia Manufacturing **38**, 548–555 (2019)
26. Aizstrauta, D., Ginters, E.: Using market data of technologies to build a dynamic integrated acceptance and sustainability assessment model. Procedia Comput. Sci. **104**, 501–508 (2017)
27. Torres-Ruiz, A., Ravindran, A.R.: Multiple criteria framework for the sustainability risk assessment of a supplier portfolio. J. Clean. Prod. **172**, 4478–4493 (2018)
28. Xu, M., Cui, Y., Hu, M., et al.: Supply chain sustainability risk and assessment. J. Clean. Prod. **225**, 857–867 (2019)
29. Vinodh, S., Jayakrishna, K.: Assessment of product sustainability and the associated risk/benefits for an automotive organisation. Int J Adv Manuf Technol **66**, 733–740 (2013)
30. Anand, A., Khan, R.A., Wani, M.F.: Development of a sustainability risk assessment index of a mechanical system at conceptual design stage. J. Clean. Prod. **139**, 258–266 (2016)
31. García-Gómez, F.J., Rosales-Prieto, V.F., Sánchez-Lite, A., et al.: An approach to sustainability risk assessment in industrial assets. Sustainability **13**, 6538 (2021)
32. Kazancoglu, Y., Ozkan-Ozen, Y.D., Mangla, S.K., Ram, M.: Risk assessment for sustainability in e-waste recycling in circular economy. Clean Technol. Environ. Policy **24**(4), 1145–1157 (2020). https://doi.org/10.1007/s10098-020-01901-3

A Review of Sustainable Composites Supply Chains

Md Rabiul Hasan◉ and Thorsten Wuest(✉) ◉

IMSE West Virginia University, Morgantown, WV 26501, United States
mh00071@mix.wvu.edu, thwuest@mail.wvu.edu

Abstract. The goal of this study is to explore and analyze the progress, methodologies, and maturity level of the composite materials Supply Chain (SC) from a sustainability lens. The SCOPUS database has been used to analyze the existing literature on composite materials SC, and VOS viewer software and MS Excel are used to analyze the data. First, a bibliometric analysis (Co-authorship of countries, Co-authorship analysis of authors, Co-occurrence analysis of keywords, and Bibliographic coupling of documents) has been carried out while following the PRISMA framework to explore and depict the overall growth of this research field. Second, an in-depth review of the selected papers (n = 20) addresses the concrete research questions for future research studies to build a bridge between the research gaps and the efforts to ensure a sustainable SC for composite materials. The outcomes of this research work reveal that the SC of composite materials is right now in its infant phase, which is not a saturated research field yet, and that much more research studies are required to add value to the existing knowledge of this field.

Keywords: Supply chain · Composite materials · Sustainability · Cascade use

1 Introduction

The COVID-19 pandemic has shown a light on the fragility of today's manufacturing SCs. However, the issues behind the limited resiliency of modern SCs across various industries are not new and need to be understood and addressed urgently. The composites manufacturing industry is no exception [1]. Globalized supply combined with increasing restrictions and trade barriers for key materials [2] leads to an urgent focus on better understanding of SC related issues and efforts to reduce dependencies on a limited number of suppliers.At the same time, sustainability is rapidly emerging as a key driver of innovation and competitive advantage. The global goal of net-zero emissions by 2050 [3] as well as increasing awareness of and demand for sustainable products of customers, both end customers, and businesses, is transforming industries. The composites manufacturing industry, while offering products that perform competitively and can contribute to lighter-weight vehicles, faces a particular challenge regarding end-of-life processes. Many composites are based on thermoset polymers posing challenges for recycling, remanufacturing, and other higher cascade use levels. More research is

© IFIP International Federation for Information Processing 2022
Published by Springer Nature Switzerland AG 2022
D. Y. Kim et al. (Eds.): APMS 2022, IFIP AICT 663, pp. 448–455, 2022.
https://doi.org/10.1007/978-3-031-16407-1_53

needed to support the industry in their endeavor to reduce the impact of its products and improve the end-of-life processes.To be effective, both technological innovations, such as new remanufacturing techniques, and SC innovations are necessary to provide a sustainable impact in the composites industry. In this paper, we explore the current state of the art of sustainable SC related research in the composites industry via a literature review. The objective of the paper is to identify research gaps in this field and define concrete research questions that must be addressed moving forward to support the industry's quest of a more resilient and sustainable SC of end-of-life composites materials.

2 Research Methodology

PRISMA framework (Preferred Reporting Items for Systematic Reviews and Meta-Analysis) is used to extract the existing literature on the composite materials SC [4]. To ensure a high quality of the reviewed scholarly works, the SCOPUS database is used for relevant scientific journals and articles. In this research, composites or composite materials are understood as a material that contains two or more constituent materials, in most cases a matrix material and a reinforcement material [5]. Different composite materials terms are also considered for the search terminology. SCOPUS search is conducted to capture the major words that deal with the SC for composite materials in the title, abstract, and keywords section of the articles as follows: (supply chain AND composite material) OR ((supply AND chain AND composite material) AND ((wood OR fiber) OR (particulate OR flake) OR (fiberglass) OR (reinforced AND plastics) OR (polymer AND matrix) OR (ceramic AND matrix) OR (carbon AND matrix) OR (metal AND matrix))) (Fig. 1).

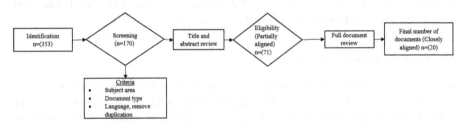

Fig. 1. Prisma framework

The search results have been limited to the "Engineering", "Decision Science", "Mathematics", "Business, Management, and Accounting", and "Economics, Econometrics, and Finance" areas which are aligned with the objectives of this study. The subject area of "Material science" has been excluded due to most of the paper objectives in this field being to investigate the composite materials property rather than the SC. The results are restricted between journal and conference proceedings only. The result is refined based on papers published in the English language also. By applying these search filters and duplication removed, SCOPUS returned 170 documents. By evaluating the title and the abstract section, n = 71 papers give a partial idea about the SC for composite materials. Researchers often include the term "Supply Chain" when describing their works in the abstract section, but those works are not a proper reflection of SC research. For example, Mahdi et al. (2021) pointed out the importance of closed loop SC in their abstract portion, but their paper's goal is to examine different materials properties that can help for reusing, and recycling purposes [6]. So, after a thorough review of the full paper for those initially down-selected, only twenty (n = 20) papers closely meet the inclusion criteria for this study. For the bibliographic part of this study, VOSviewer software is used, and Microsoft Excel is used for the descriptive statistics.

3 Bibliometric Analysis

3.1 Co-authorship of Countries

The collaboration among the authors from different parts of the world can be shown from the co-authorship analysis of the countries. For the co-authorship of the countries, a minimum two number of documents of a country is considered, where only four meet the threshold out of 15 countries. One unanticipated finding is that other than the United Kingdom there is no country from Europe, although the United Kingdom has the highest number of documents (n = 12) with most number of citations (n = 107) as well.

The United Kingdom is followed by Canada (documents = 4, citations = 50, total link strength = 4), Malaysia (documents = 2, citations = 20, total link strength = 1), and United States (documents = 2, citations = 0, total link strength = 0) respectively. But only three of them are connected based on the co-authorship of countries. The cluster of the countries that are connected is shown by a different color in the Fig. 2. Scientific collaboration plays an important role to strengthen the quality of research output. An integrated collaboration research policy that embraces multiple policy levels like local, national, or may be global can improve this linkage [7].

3.2 Co-authorship of Authors

Bote et al. (2013) showed that international collaboration has a great influence on the scientific works of a country [8]. The collaboration network of the authors can be analyzed by the co-authorship analysis of authors. A minimum number of one document and one citation of an author is considered as the threshold. Among the 45 authors, 38 meet the threshold which makes 9 clusters as shown in Fig. 2 (unconnected). Although this study found nine clusters, they are not connected between themselves. From this, it can be inferred that there is little collaboration among the active researchers, and most of the work was conducted isolated from each other.

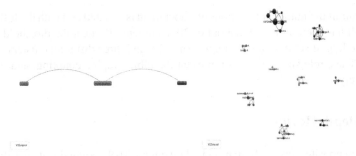

Fig. 2. Co-authorship analysis of countries and authors respectively

3.3 Keywords

Keywords, which give the whole paper impression, so the co-occurrence of the author keywords are considered in this study. Since the final consideration number of papers is quite small (n = 20), the minimum number of occurrences of a keyword is considered as one, which results in 72 keywords. Then the identical keywords are replaced, for example, "composite", "composites", "carbon fiber composite", "glass fibers", "wood plastic composite" etc. which are replaced by the keyword "composite material". This screening process gives 11 keywords, where the minimum number of keyword occurrences is placed at two. From this result, it can be inferred that much more research work is needed to comprehend the SC for composite materials, as the number of keyword occurrences is considered here only two. By network visualization mode, the co-occurrence of author keywords is represented in Fig. 3.

3.4 Bibliographic Coupling of Documents

Bibliographic coupling of documents links between the documents, where each link has a strength which is represented by the positive value. The link strength depends on this value. If the value is higher, their link strength is also better, and vice versa [9].

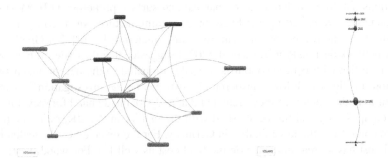

Fig. 3. Co-occurrence of author keywords and bibliographic coupling based on TLS respectively

The minimum number of citations of a document is counted as 5 with the full counting method. It has been observed that out of 20 documents 12 meet the threshold. Figure 3 shows the largest set of connected items (n = 9), and three different clusters have been formed. The circle size and color represent the bibliographic coupling, and the cluster respectively.

4 In-Depth Review

For the composite wastes, Sultan and Mativenga (2019) pointed out that there is no agreement on the waste ownership of the composite materials among the stakeholders. With the exception of the take-back approach has been partially implemented in Germany, Sweden, and the UK. This presents another burning issue for the circular SC of composite materials. This is considered problematic, as there has been a forecasted growth in Carbon Fiber Reinforced Polymer (CFRP) and Glass Fiber Reinforced Polymers (GFRP) due to the manufacture of turbine blades for wind energy [11]. Some argue that the users have the responsibility for the end of life of a product who turned it into waste while in use, while others believe that the government should take over entirely [12]. On this point, Shehab et al. (2020) emphasized the establishment of a market for recycled carbon fibers [13]. Composite waste ending up in landfills is a major problem for the environment and the sustainability ambition of the composites industry. In Europe, landfills, as well as burning composites, are prohibited with strict regulation in selected countries such as Germany, Netherlands, and Finland. There has been increasing awareness of circular pathways of composites. To date, however, this is considered not to be enough. E.g., for GFRP materials recycling, the only commercial facilities in Europe are in Germany. In addition, recycled fibers do not have the same properties compared to virgin materials. For GFRP recycling, mechanical recycling is an attractive method [7]. In the UK, pyrolysis is a technique that is most often used for recycling composites. Recycling CFRP has a beneficial impact on the environment. Shuaib et al. (2015) described that the energy consumed by the pyrolysis method for recycling and remanufacturing the CFRP as less than 10% of the total energy associated with the manufacturing of virgin CFRP materials [11]. However, recycled carbon fiber has its limitations due to degradation in mechanical and surface properties [13]. Most often, it is found that the mixed-integer linear programming method was used to investigate the close loop and reverse SC of composite waste materials [7, 14]. For GFRP reverse supply network design, Rentizelas et al. (2021) suggested that the trade-off between the larger facilities with better economies of scale compared to the decentralized smaller and more facilities with low transportation costs can be the investigation scenario for the future. In their analysis, they predicted that in 2050, the demand for recycling wind blade composites could not be satisfied with the facility in the UK, rather partly will need to come from the large facility in Germany. For the reverse SC, the technology's capital cost has a great influence on the total cost as well [7]. For wood plastic composite, Doustmohammadi and Babazadeh (2020) determined the optimum material flow for the closed-loop SC network to minimize the total cost. It is somewhat surprising that the changes in the transportation cost and production cost parameter do not have a good amount of consequential effect on the total cost of their study [14]. The study by Mondragon et al. (2018) confirmed that the use of composite materials still requires a higher cost than the use of traditional components. They proposed that the reduction of lead time, the number of suppliers, and the complexity of the SC can have a fruitful effect on the use of composite materials in the manufacturing industry [15]. Supplier or vendor selection is another crucial decision for the SCM. Hsu et al. (2012) depicted that the best vendor of recycled material has good scores on the quality of the product and environmental collaboration. Moreover, they showed that the supply risk will affect the delivery service and schedule, cost of the product, and environmental collaboration [16]. The original equipment manufacturer of composite material has multiple suppliers of its own. For minimizing the disruption risks in a SC network, multi-supplier configurations can play an important role. Interestingly, on their hypothesis, Arashpour et al. (2017) found that the multi-supplier configuration increases the total SC cost [17]. For the high-tech industries (where flexible and innovative approaches are common) to maintain the stringent standards among the different echelon of the manufacturers, authentic information and traceability are important. Mondragon et al. (2018) highlighted that with blockchain technology's public and private keys, the information flow will be enhanced among different stages of the composite materials SC [10]. Technology selection for the composite materials SC configuration is very much important. Mondragon et al. (2016) conducted a survey study to find the factors that affect the technology selection. Rapid manufacturing is the one that got the lowest average rating in their survey study among different companies [18]. But in their follow-up publication [19], the enablers who provide engineering services or training have got an above-average rating for this factor. This finding was unexpected and suggests that the factors depend on the type of suppliers also. Besides that, the green SC practice of the composite manufacturers has given them the chance to show their responsibility to the environment. Mahmood et al. (2012) indicated that quality, cost, delivery, and continuous improvement are the desired performance measures for the green SC management among their surveyed companies [20].

5 Limitation and Future Research

The researchers must bear in mind that this study only examined literature curated in the SCOPUS database. Although SCOPUS is considered a comprehensive, and expertly curated abstract and citation database, there are other sources of academic literature that might not have been included in this research due to this limitation. More related research articles may be available by exploring other databases such as Google Scholar, PubMed, Web of Science, ScienceDirect, and so on. By gathering and analyzing the data, a comparison can be done among different databases. Some of the bibliometric analysis that is presented here, is not the only limited options for investigating this topic. Future research can be done by incorporating a large spectrum of search terminology from the combined database results to make the meta-analysis like the dimension reduction of the text data mining, finding the co-relations, and clustering them. This study pointed out some future research works on the following subjects but are not limited to:

- How to improve the resiliency of the multi-echelon composite materials SC?

- How to improve the efficiency of materials and information flow by the use of digital technology like blockchain, big data analytics, etc. for the composite materials SC?
- What will be the optimal composite materials SC network design for high-tech flexible products?
- Sourcing strategies for composite materials.
- What are the demand variabilities of the composite wastes for the closed-loop SC network?
- Coordination mechanism for the forward and reverse SC of composite materials.
- System dynamic analysis of the composite materials SC
- Optimization of the distribution network
- Cascading failure or domino-effect analysis of composite materials SC.
- How to improve the sustainable resource utilization and the green SC of composite materials?
- Information sharing and coordination of composite materials SC
- Enhancing the SC performance including the cost optimization
- Composite SC disruptions, and recovery policy analysis
- Recycling and circular SC path analysis of the composite materials.
- Market demand analysis for the recycled composite materials

6   Conclusion

The use of composite materials is booming around the world, and the complexity of its SC is also increasing. Surprisingly, there is not enough scientific literature on this field. Most of the articles are survey-based and focused on the optimization of the material flows among the different echelon of the suppliers. In recent days, some of the papers which investigated the SC network design for the end life of certain composite materials like wind blades are the first of their kind. So, there is a huge opportunity for the research community to develop and contribute to the composite materials SC or related fields. Collaboration among the wider range of research community, and between researchers with industry is also required to improve this research field in the upcoming days.

Acknowledgements. The authors thank Drs. Hota Gangarao and Rakesh Gupta, both from WVU, for their support and valuable input. Furthermore, ACMA and Dan Coughlin for the valuable discussion and inspiration to investigate the topic.

References

1. Creating a more resilient supply chain (2021). https://compositesmanufacturingmagazine. com/2021/04/creating-a-more-resilient-supply-chain/
2. Blanchard, E.J., Bown, C.P., Johnson, R.C.: Global supply chains and trade policy. National Bureau of Economic Research (2016)
3. Net zero coalition - the United Nations. https://www.un.org/en/climatechange/net-zero-coa lition. Accessed (28 Apr 2022)

4. Zorzela, L., et al.: PRISMA harms group PRISMA harms checklist: improving harms reporting in systematic reviews. BMJ. 352: i157 (2016)
5. Harik, R., Wuest, T.: Introduction to Advanced Manufacturing. SAE International, Warrendale (2020)
6. Mahdi, E., Ochoa, D.R.H., Vaziri, A., Dean, A., Kucukvar, M.: Khalasa date palm leaf fiber as a potential reinforcement for polymeric composite materials. Composite Structures. **265**, 113501 (2021)
7. Rentizelas, A., Trivyza, N., Oswald, S., Siegl, S.: Reverse supply network design for circular economy pathways of wind turbine blades in Europe. Int. J. Prod. Res. 1–20 (2021)
8. Guerrero Bote, V.P., Olmeda-Gómez, C., de Moya-Anegón, F.: Quantifying the benefits of international scientific collaboration. J. Am. Soc. Inf. Sci. Technol. **64**, 392–404 (2013)
9. Eck, N. van, Waltman, L.: VOSviewer Manual-Manual for VOSviewer version 1.6. 15. Universiteit Leiden (2020)
10. Mondragon, A.E.C., Mondragon, C.E.C., Coronado, E.S.: Exploring the applicability of blockchain technology to enhance manufacturing supply chains in the composite materials industry. In: 2018 IEEE International Conference on Applied System Invention (ICASI), pp. 1300–1303. IEEE (2018)
11. Shuaib, N.A., Mativenga, P.T., Kazie, J., Job, S.: Resource efficiency and composite waste in UK supply chain. Procedia CIRP. **29**, 662–667 (2015)
12. Sultan, A.A.M., Mativenga, P.T.: Sustainable location identification decision protocol (SuLIDeP) for determining the location of recycling centres in a circular economy. J. Cleaner Prod. **223**, 508–521 (2019)
13. Shehab, E., Meiirbekov, A., Sarfraz, S.: Challenges in cost modelling of recycling carbon fiber composites. In: Proceedings of the 27th International Conference on Transdisciplinary Engineering (TE2020), Warsaw, Poland. pp. 1–10 (2020)
14. Doustmohammadi, N., Babazadeh, R.: Design of closed loop supply chain of wood plastic composite (WPC) industry. J. Environ. Inf. **35**, 94–102 (2020)
15. Mondragon, A.E.C., Mondragon, C.E.C., Hogg, P.J., Rodríguez-López, N.: A design process for the adoption of composite materials and supply chain reconfiguration supported by a software tool. Comput. Ind. Eng. **121**, 62–72 (2018)
16. Hsu, C.-H., Wang, F.-K., Tzeng, G.-H.: The best vendor selection for conducting the recycled material based on a hybrid MCDM model combining DANP with VIKOR. Resour. Conserv. Recycling. **66**, 95–111 (2012)
17. Arashpour, M., Bai, Y., Aranda-Mena, G., Bab-Hadiashar, A., Hosseini, R., Kalutara, P.: Optimizing decisions in advanced manufacturing of prefabricated products: Theorizing supply chain configurations in off-site construction. Autom. Constr. **84**, 146–153 (2017)
18. Mondragon, A.E.C., Mastrocinque, E., Hogg, P.J.: Factors of technology selection affecting the configuration of supply chains in innovative industries: a survey of UK companies in the composites industry. ARPN J. Eng. Appl. Sci. **11**, 204–209 (2016)
19. Coronado Mondragon, A.E., Mastrocinque, E., Hogg, P.J.: Technology selection in the absence of standardised materials and processes: a survey in the UK composite materials supply chain. Prod. Plann. Control. **28**, 158–176 (2017)
20. Mahmood, W.H.W., Ab Rahman, M.N., Deros, B.M.: Green supply chain management in Malaysian aero composite industry. J. Teknol. **59**, 13–17 (2012)

Digital Supply Networks

An Automated Smart Production with System Reliability Under a Leader-Follower Strategy of Supply Chain Management

Mitali Sarkar[1] , Biswajit Sarkar[2,3]([⊠]) , and Alexandre Dolgui[4]

[1] Information Technology Research Center, Chung-Ang University, 06974 Seoul, South Korea
[2] Department of Industrial Engineering, Yonsei University, 50 Yonsei-ro, Sinchon-dong, Seodaemun-gu, 03722 Seoul, South Korea
[3] Center for Transdisciplinary Research (CFTR), Saveetha Dental College, Saveetha Institute of Medical and Technical Sciences, Saveetha University, 162, Poonamallee High Road, Velappanchavadi, Chennai, Tamil Nadu 600077, India
bsbiswajitsarkar@gmail.com
[4] Automation, Production and Computer Sciences Department, IMT Atlantique, La Chantrerie, France
alexandre.dolgui@imt-atlantique.fr

Abstract. This study deals with the absorption of an automated system in a smart production system, and how the industry tackles several problems. The incorporation of smart machines within smart manufacturing is not only a matter of investments and smart labor but also a matter of tackling them together with the proper trade-off between them. The automated system basically depends on the product's development or product design. In this direction, this research finds that the development of products itself depends on the automated system. A mathematical representation of the automated smart production is provided with a basic aim to reduce the total cost without any specific goal of the industry. A smart supply chain is found here to tackle this automated smart production with a single retailer, even though the players are competitive within them. A Stackelberg game strategy is utilized to solve the model to obtain the optimum total cost and the optimum values of the smart production quantities, and the smart production rate. Due to automated costs, the reduction of setup costs plays an important role. The numerical studies have been conducted to validate this study and obtain that the automated system works properly even though the players compete with each other.

This research was supported by the Yonsei University Research Fund of 2021 (Project Number 2021-22-0305).

Keywords: Smart products · Smart production · Supply chain management · Automated system design · Setup cost reduction · Investments

1 Introduction

The necessity of technological development is increasing for any production system to make it automated and smart. Thus, the industry is also moving towards smart utilization of machines to save the cost, reduction of defective items, and human effort. But always all smart machines may not produce perfect items always. Thus, a research is needed to redesign the smart machines to control defective items. Alavian et al. [1] discussed a smart production system. They developed an automatic system to decide on the manufacturing system. A flexible manufacturing remanufacturing system was developed by Sarkar and Bhuniya [2] for a sustainable supply chain model. They used an investment to improve their manufacturing system.

Sana [3] explained the reliability and production rate. Thus, the production cost increases with the increasing amount of development cost. Jiang et al. [4] studied a remanufacturing system. They represented reliability by the failure rate. The setup cost of a smart manufacturing system is very high.

Sarkar and Moon [5] developed an integrated inventory model (IIM) with setup cost reduction and quality improvement. They considered variable backorder and random demand during lead time. They used a distribution-free approach to solve the model. Al Durgam et al. [6] proposed an IIM with random lead time demand. They used lead time crashing cost to reduce the lead time. Dey et al. [7] used a discrete setup cost reduction policy for their IIM. Table 1 shows the research gap of this study.

Table 1. Comparative study with the existing literature.

Author(s)	Model	Imperfection	Investment	System design
Sana [3]		*	*	
Sarkar and Moon [5]	*Prodction*	*	*	
Dey et al. [7]	*Production*	*		
Sarkar and Chung [9]	*Production*	*	*	
Huang et al. [10]	*Production*	*	*	
This study	*SCM*	*	*	*

The following research questions can be solved by this study:

1. The setup cost of a smart automated production system is very high. How does the manufacturer control the setup cost?

2. How does the automated production system design the improvement of technology mathematically?
3. How does the lead time reduce shortages?

This study is organized as follows: Sect. 2 represents the Mathematical modelling and solution methodology, Sect. 3 consists of numerical experiments, sensitivity analysis, and managerial insights of the model. Conclusions and future works are explained in Sect. 4.

2 Mathematical Model

A smart manufacturing system with artificial intelligence controlled robotic system is used to produce smart electronic products. To maintain the smart production system properly a variable development cost is utilized by the manufacturer. Thus, an investment to improve the autonomated system is used here. Due to the autonomated system the setup cost increases too high which is reduced by applying some investment. The manufacturer sends the finished products using single-setup-multi-delivery (SSMD) policy to the retailer. That means the manufacturer produces all products in a single setup of production system and due to higher holding cost of retailer than manufacturer, send those products in multiple deliveries. Due to huge lead time which is random, the retailer faces shortages of products. To reduce the lead time the retailer uses lead time crashing cost. In this section mathematical model of manufacturer and retailer with their analytical solutions are explained below. The total supply chain cost are optimized analytically.

2.1 Manufacturer's Model

The cost using for the smart manufacturing system are explained in details below. A smart manufacturing system is utilized by the manufacturer. Thus, a flexible production rate (P_f) is used for the system. The unit production cost can be expressed as $\left(A_m + \frac{A_d}{P_f} + \gamma P_f\right)$, where A_m is the material cost, A_d is the development cost, and γ is the tool/die cost. Development cost is dependent on the system design variable (η). The development cost can be expressed as $A_d(\eta) = M + N\eta^g$, where M is the fixed development cost, N is scaling parameter, g is the shape parameter, and η can be defined as $system\ design\ variable = \frac{Number\ of\ failure}{Number\ of\ working\ hours}$. Thus, the manufacturing cost of the system can be written as $\left(A_m + \frac{M+N\eta^g}{P_f} + \gamma P_f\right) D$, where D is the demand of products. The number of defective item (ρ) is directly proportional to the system design variable, i.e., ρ is proportional to η which indicates $\rho = \alpha\eta$. Let E_ϑ denotes the expected number of failure rate of the production system for the lot size ϑ. At the beginning the system was in *in-control* state. i indicates the number of lot. It is known that $\widehat{(\alpha\eta)} = 1 - \alpha\eta \cong$ 1and by Taylor series expansion $\widehat{(\alpha\eta)}^\vartheta = e^{(\ln \widehat{(\alpha\eta)})\vartheta} \cong 1 + (\ln \widehat{(\alpha\eta)})\vartheta + \frac{[(\ln \widehat{(\alpha\eta)})\vartheta]^2}{2}$

(refer to Porteus, [6]). Thus, the expected number of defective can be written as $E_\vartheta = \alpha\eta\vartheta + \widehat{(\alpha\eta)}E_{\vartheta-1} = \alpha\eta\vartheta\frac{(1-\widehat{(\alpha\eta)}^i)}{\alpha\eta} - \alpha\eta\frac{\widehat{(\alpha\eta)}[1+(\vartheta-1)\widehat{(\alpha\eta)}^q - q\widehat{(\alpha\eta)}^{\vartheta-1}]}{(\alpha\eta)^2} = \vartheta - \frac{\widehat{(\alpha\eta)}(1-\widehat{(\alpha\eta)}^\vartheta)}{\alpha\eta} = \frac{\alpha\eta\vartheta^2}{2}$. Therefore, the defective cost for ι shipments during imperfect production can be written as $\frac{wD\iota\vartheta\alpha\eta}{2}$, where w is per unit defective cost. Before start the production, the manufacturing system needs some initial setup. For the smart production system the setup cost is very high. This setup cost can be reduced by using some investment. The discrete investment to reduce the setup cost of the smart production system is $\frac{\delta D}{\iota\vartheta}$ The setup cost and invest-ment of the smart production system is $\frac{S_U e^{-A\delta}D}{\iota\vartheta} + \frac{\delta D}{\iota\vartheta}$, where S_U is the initial setup cost and δ is the investment to reduce setup cost per production run. The manufacturer holds the produced items before sending to retailer. Holding cost per unit item per unit time is H_c. The inventory holding with the manufacturer is needed to be calculated (see for reference Majumder et al. [8]). The manufacturer uses SSMD policy with a fixed transportation cost (G) per shipment. Thus, the total transportation cost for ι shipment is $\frac{GD}{\vartheta}$. Thus, the manufacturer's inven-tory holding and transportation cost is $\frac{H_c\iota\vartheta}{2}\left[\iota\left(1 - \frac{D}{P_f}\right) - 1 + \frac{2D}{P_f}\right] + \frac{GD}{\vartheta}$.

The manufacturer has to optimize the total cost with respect to the decision variables; the number of shipments (ι), the lot size (ϑ), the flexible production rate (P_f), system design variable (η), and investment to reduce setup cost (δ). The total cost of the manufacturer can be written as

$$\Lambda_m(\iota, \vartheta, P_f, \eta, \delta) = \left(A_m + \frac{M + N\eta^g}{P_f} + \gamma P_f\right)D + \frac{wD\iota\vartheta\alpha\eta}{2} + \frac{S_U e^{-A\delta}D}{\iota\vartheta} + \frac{\delta D}{\iota\vartheta}$$
$$+ \frac{H_c\iota\vartheta}{2}\left[\iota\left(1 - \frac{D}{P_f}\right) - 1 + \frac{2D}{P_f}\right] + \frac{GD}{\vartheta}. \tag{1}$$

2.2 Retailer's Model

The retailer uses O_R amount of cost per order to place the order for product delivery to the manufacturer. The demand during lead time of the smart product is random. λ is the lead time and κ is the safety factor. If B_h be the holding cost per unit per unit time, then the holding and ordering cost per cycle of the retailer can be written as $B_h[(\vartheta/2) + \kappa\sigma\sqrt{\lambda} + (1 - \beta)E(\chi - \mu)^+] + \frac{O_R D}{\vartheta} = B_h[(\vartheta/2) + \kappa\sigma\sqrt{\lambda} + (1-\beta)\sigma\sqrt{\lambda}\psi(\kappa)] + \frac{O_R D}{\vartheta}$. Due to the long lead time the retailer faces some shortages which are backordered. Here ν is the per unit backorder cost, and β is the backordered items. To reduce the lead time the retailer uses a crashing cost, which can be written as $\frac{DC(\lambda)}{\vartheta}$. If the expected shortages are $E(\chi - \mu)^+$, then the shortage and lead time crashing cost can be written as $\frac{(\nu+\nu_0(1-\beta))D}{\vartheta}E(\chi-\mu)^+ + \frac{DC(\lambda)}{\vartheta} = \frac{(\nu+\nu_0(1-\beta))D}{\vartheta}\sigma\sqrt{\lambda}\psi(\kappa) + \frac{DC(\lambda)}{\vartheta}$, where $\psi(\kappa) = \phi(\kappa) - \kappa(1 - \Phi(\kappa))$, $\phi(\kappa)$ and $\Phi(\kappa)$ are standard normal distribution and the probability density function of the normal distribution function. The retailer has to optimize the total cost with respect to the decision variable; lot size (ϑ), lead time (λ), and safety factor (κ). The total cost of the retailer (Λ_r) is

$$\Lambda_r(\vartheta, \lambda, \kappa) = \left[\frac{O_R D}{\vartheta} + \frac{DC(\lambda)}{\vartheta} + B_h[(\vartheta/2) + \kappa\sigma\sqrt{\lambda} + (1-\beta)\sigma\sqrt{\lambda}\psi(\kappa)] \right.$$
$$\left. + \frac{(\nu + \nu_0(1-\beta))D}{\vartheta} \sigma\sqrt{\lambda}\psi(\kappa) \right]. \tag{2}$$

2.3 Solution Methodology

Due to the unequal power of supply chain players, Stackelberg game policy is used to solve the model. Even though the leader-follower strategy is there, but both the manufacturer and relater are fair enough for their dealings. The model is solved in two cases: I) Retailer follower and manufacturer leader and II) Manufacturer follower and retailer leader.

2.3.1 Case I Retailer as Follower and Manufacturer as Leader

The optimum values of the decision variables can be obtained as $\Phi^*(k) = 1 - \frac{B_h\vartheta}{B_h(1-\beta)\vartheta + (\nu+\nu_0(1-\beta))D}$, $\vartheta^* = \sqrt{\frac{2[O_R D + DC(\lambda) + (\nu+\nu_0(1-\beta))D\sigma\sqrt{\lambda}\psi(k)]}{B_h}}$, and $\frac{\partial^2 \Lambda_r}{\partial \lambda^2} = -\frac{\sigma}{4\sigma^{3/2}}[\frac{(\nu+\nu_0(1-\beta))\psi(k)}{\vartheta} + B_h k + (1-\beta)\psi(k)] < 0$ and thus Λ_r is concave with respect to λ.

Using the optimum values of retailer, the optimum values of manufacturer's decision variables except the common decision variable, can be obtained as $P_f^* = \sqrt{\frac{2(M+N\eta^g) - H_c\iota\vartheta^*(\iota-2)}{2\gamma}}$, $\eta^* = -\left(\frac{w\iota\vartheta^*\alpha P_f}{2gN}\right)^{\frac{1}{g-1}}$, and $\delta^* = \frac{1}{A}ln(AS_U)$.

2.3.2 Case II Manufacturer as Follower and Retailer as Leader

For this case manufacturer is follower and retailer is leader. The optimum values of the decision variables are $\vartheta^* = \sqrt{\frac{2D(S_U e^{-A\delta} + \delta + G\iota)}{wD\iota^*\alpha\eta + H_c\iota^*[\iota(1-\frac{D}{P_f})-1+\frac{2D}{P_f}]}}$, $P_f^* = \sqrt{\frac{2(M+N\eta^g) - H_c\iota\vartheta^*(\iota-2)}{2\gamma}}$, $\eta^* = -\left(\frac{w\iota\vartheta^*\alpha P_f}{2gN}\right)^{\frac{1}{g-1}}$, and $\delta^* = \frac{1}{A}ln(AS_U)$.

Using decision variables of manufacturer, the optimum values of retailer except the common decision variable can be written as $\Phi^*(k) = 1 - \frac{B_h\vartheta}{B_h(1-\beta)\vartheta + (\nu+\nu_0(1-\beta))D}$, and $\frac{\partial^2 \Lambda_r}{\partial \lambda^2} = -\frac{\sigma}{4\sigma^{3/2}}[\frac{(\nu+\nu_0(1-\beta))\psi(k)}{\vartheta} + B_h k + (1-\beta)\psi(k)] < 0$. Λ_r is concave with respect to λ.

3 Numerical Experiment

Two numerical experiments are take place with same data. The flexibility of a smart production system can reduce the possibility to move to *out-of-control* state which can reduce the production of defective items The contribution of flexible production rate is taken from Sarkar and Chung [9]. To make a production system smart and flexible the setup cost of the manufacturer becomes very high which can be reduced by using some investments. The idea of discrete setup cost reduction for the manufacturer is taken from Huang et al. [10]. Instead of using flexible rate the smart production system produces some defective items for which shortages arise. The shortage cost is included in this study from Sarkar and Moon [5]. For numerical analysis the modified data from Sarkar and Moon [5], Sarkar and Chung [9], and Huang et al. [10] are considered to test the validity of the proposed model. The experiments are done by MATLAB R2020a. Data is enlisted as $D = 600$ units, $\sigma = 7$ units/week, $S_U = \$800/\text{setup}$, $\alpha = 0.2$, $w = \$75/\text{item}$, $A_m = \$50$, $M = \$70$, $N = 90$, $g = 0.2$, $\gamma = \$0.02/\text{unit}$, $A = 3$, $G = \$.1/\text{shipment}$, $H_c = \$.08/\text{unit/year}$, $O_R = \$200/\text{order}$, $C(\lambda) = 22.4$, $B_h = \$55/\text{unit/year}$, $\nu = \$0.4/\text{unit}$, $\nu_0 = \$9/\text{unit}$, $\beta = 0.87$, $\lambda = 3$ weeks. For Case I, the optimum values of retailer's decision variables are $\vartheta = 706.45$ units, $\Phi(k) = 0.61$, $k = 0.28$, and the total cost of the retailer is $\$390.67/\text{cycle}$. Using the same amount of ϑ, the optimum value of other decision variables of the manufacturer are $P_f = 2.75$ units/cycle, $\eta = 0.000001$, $\delta = 2.59$, and the total cost of manufacturer is $\$30,248.50/\text{cycle}$. The total supply chain cost is $\$30,639.17/\text{cycle}$. For Case II, the optimum values of manufacturer's decision variables are $\vartheta = 10.27$ units, $P_f = 63.35$ units/cycle, $\eta = 0.000001$, $\delta = 2.59$, and the total cost of manufacturer is $\$31,507.86/\text{cycle}$. Using the same amount of ϑ, the optimum value of other decision variables of the retailer are $\Phi(k) = 0.99$, $k = 2.51$, and the total cost of the retailer is $\$11,324.79/\text{cycle}$. The total supply chain cost for Case II is $\$42,832.65/\text{cycle}$.

Comparing both cases, it can be conclude that the Case I, i.e., manufacturer is a leader and retailer is a follower gives the better result than the Case II. The total cost of both the players as well as the supply chain total cost is less for Case I than the Case II. The comparison of the decision variables with the exiting research [11,16, and 17], it is found that the proposed model provides better results of values of decision variables comparing with them.

3.1 Sensitivity Analysis

Sensitivity analysis is done only for Case I, because it has the lowest supply chain cost. The changing of total cost of each player corresponding to key parameters are given Table 2 and 3.

- The most sensitive parameter is material cost of the manufacturer among all the cost parameters. The total cost of manufacturer changes almost 50% at both negative and positive direction for 50% changes of the material cost at direction.
- The next sensitive parameter is the retailer's holding cost. The total cost of retailer decreases almost 30% for decreasing of holding cost 50% and increases about 23% for 50% increasing of the holding cost. Whereas the holding cost of the manufacturer fluctuates in the reverse direction. Though the changes are less compare to the retailer's holding cost.
- Ordering cost of the retailer is another sensitive parameter. Retailer's total cost decreases about 25% for 50% decreasing of ordering cost and increases almost 20% for 50% increasing of the cost.

Table 2. Sensitivity of key parameters for manufacturer.

Parameters	Changes (%)	Changes Λ_m	Parameters	Changes (%)	Changes in Λ_m
S_U	−50	−0.00022	A_m	−50	−49.59
	−25	−0.00009		−25	−24.79
	+25	+0.00007		+25	+24.79
	+50	+0.00013		+50	+49.59
w	−50	+0.089	M	−50	−0.17
	−25	+0.032		−25	−0.14
	+25	−0.022		+25	+1.35
	+50	−0.037		+50	+2.53
γ	−50	−0.09	H_c	−50	+2.63
	−25	−0.04		−25	+1.51
	+25	+0.04		+25	−0.0064
	+50	+0.08		+50	+0.102

Table 3. Sensitivity of key parameters for retailer.

Parameters	Changes (%)	Changes Λ_r	Parameters	Changes (%)	Changes in Λ_r
O_R	−50	−25.36	B_h	−50	−29.74
	−25	−11.69		−25	−13.61
	+25	+10.41		+25	+11.97
	+50	+19.87		+50	+22.78

3.2 Managerial Insights

- It is common among almost all the production industries that the flexible production rate is always better than the constant production rate. But to move in the direction of the flexibility there is a huge hazard for system design change and corresponding increasing value of setup cost. The industry manager has to decide that they can tackle this hazard for improving system design or may maintain a traditional production system without any hazard of system design. But utilizing traditional production system cannot produce more degree of accuracy of products properly along with there are huge cost for human labor, which ultimately affects the increasing value of the per unit production cost. Based on this proposed strategy the industry managers can decide which type of production system they need for their product.
- A common finding of any equal and unequal powers of supply chain players is that the total cost must be reduced in case of equal power with joint total cost rather than the unequal power with joint font supply chain cost. However, this study obtains a major total cost reduction for both cases, whoever is

the leader or follower. Therefore, the study of equal power joint total profit was not conducted. In the industry, if the players are unequal in power, still they can get reduced total cost utilizing the recommended strategy of design improvement of the flexible production system.

4   Conclusions

This is the first pioneer attempt to prove the effectiveness of automated production system under a supply chain management. It was proved that flexibility in production system and system designing made a significant effect on the production system to reduce per unit production cost of any smart product. Due to the improvement of the technological development of manufacturer's system design the setup cost was increased, thus, the setup cost reduction strategy was utilized and found a huge amount of savings to control the production cost of the system. Numerically, the savings for this purpose is about 10%. A comparative study was conducted to show the effectiveness of flexible production rate instead of constant production rate and found 5% of savings due to flexibility in the production system. As the demand of these smart products during lead time was a random variable and followed a normal distribution, lead time crashing cost was used which saved 2% of the total cost. Though the research was conducted for the development of the manufacturing system design and its improvement under a supply chain management, but those SCM players are not equal in power, they thought about their own profit only. Even though SCM players do not follow each other, using Stackleburg game policy it was found that both the players were gainer at their optimum level of decisions. This study can be extended with several constraints, which came to improve the machine design and the optimization procedure will be constrained optimization rather than the unconstrained optimization technique. It will be a potential extension if a comparative study can be done within the SCM players having equal and unequal powers with a multi-stage production system.

References

1. Alavian, P., Eun, Y., Meerkov, S.M., Zhang, L.: Smart production systems: automating Decision making in manufacturing environment. Int. J. Prod. Res. **58**(3), 828–845 (2020)
2. Sarkar, B., Bhuniya, S.: A sustainable flexible manufacturing-remanufacturing model with improved service and green investment under variable demand. Expert Syst. Appl. **202**, 117154 (2022)
3. Sana, S.S.: A production-inventory model in an imperfect production process. Eur. J. Oper. Res. **200**(2), 451–464 (2010)
4. Jiang, Z., Zhou, T., Zhang, H., Wang, Y., Cao, H., Tian, G.: Reliability and cost optimization for remanufacturing process planning. J. Clean. Prod. **135**, 1602–1610 (2016)
5. Sarkar, B., Moon, I.: Improved quality, setup cost reduction, and variable backorder costs in an imperfect production process. Int. J. Prod. Econ. **155**, 204–213 (2014)

6. AlDurgam, M., Adegbola, K., Glock, C.H.: A single-vendor single-manufacturer integrated inventory model with stochastic demand and variable production rate. Int. J. Prod. Econ. **191**, 335–350 (2017)
7. Dey, B.K., Sarkar, B., Sarkar, M., Pareek, S.: An integrated inventory model involving discrete setup cost reduction, variable safety factor, selling price dependent demand, and investment. RAIRO-Oper. Res. **53**, 39–57 (2019)
8. Majumder, A., Guchhait, R., Sarkar, B.: Manufacturing quality improvement and setup cost reduction in an integrated vendor-buyer supply chain model. Eur. J. Ind. Eng. **11**(5), 588–612 (2017)
9. Sarkar, M., Chung, B.D.: Flexible work-in-process production system in supply chain management under quality improvement. Int. J. Prod. Res. **58**(13), 3821–3838 (2020)
10. Huang, C.K., Cheng, T.L., Kao, T.C., Goyal, S.K.: An integrated inventory model involving manufacturing setup cost reduction in compound Poisson process. Int. J. Prod. Res. **49**(4), 1219–1228 (2011)

Bilevel Programming for Reducing Peak Demand of a Microgrid System

Young-Bin Woo[1] and Ilkyeong Moon[1,2]

[1] Department of Industrial Engineering, Seoul National University, Seoul, Korea
`ikmoon@snu.ac.kr`
[2] Institute for Industrial Systems Innovation, Seoul National University, Seoul, Korea

Abstract. This paper investigated an electricity control strategy to minimize the electrical peak demand of a microgrid system composed of households. Each household can install a distributed generation system by applying for the subsidy program that the central grid system operator (GSO) encourages. The distributed generation system includes an electricity storage system and residential electricity generators such as photovoltaics and wind turbines. Each consumer seeks to arrange an appropriate schedule that minimizes the overall cost including electricity bills, investment costs, and penalty costs incurred by consumer dissatisfaction. Simultaneously, the GSO wants to minimize the peak demand among households. To address the problem, this paper developed a mixed-integer bilevel programming (MIBP) model. An exact algorithm based on consumer behavior is developed to attain optimal solutions for optimistic consumers. Numerical experiments are presented to illustrate the practical use of the model in the applications.

Keywords: Microgrid system · Peak demand · Bilevel programming

1 Introduction

Electricity consumption has rapidly increased globally over the last few decades. The ever-growing electricity demand affects the stability of electricity grids. If the demand exceeds the capacity reserved by power generators in the grid, critical failures such as overloads of power transmitters or blackout may happen. Hence, it is important to manage the consumption demand so that it can be controlled against the maximum capacity of the grid. The highest demand that occurs over a specified time period is called *peak demand*. Especially in South Korea, daily peak demand has shown a relatively higher growth rate than the daily average electricity consumption [1]. This trend shows that the peak demand is getting

This research was supported by the National Research Foundation of Korea (NRF) funded by the Ministry of Science, ICT & Future Planning [Grant no. NRF-2019R1A2C2084616].

closer to the maximum capacity and that demand within any given day fluctuates significantly. A simple solution is to add a new generator to the grid (i.e., supply-side management) to avoid the peak demand exceeding the maximum capacity. However, the construction of new baseload generation sources, such as nuclear and coal plants, can be a significant financial burden for the grid system operator (GSO). In addition, the simple expansion of grid generators can cause a low utilization rate for some generators.

Another way to deal with the problem of the supply-demand imbalance is demand-side management. In demand-side management, the GSO can level off a fluctuating demand or reduce the peak demand by rewarding (or penalizing) users depending on conditions. If the program proposed by the GSO makes it reasonable for users to change their electricity usage patterns, the realized demand will help match supply and demand as a response to the program. Another way to manage the demand side is to reduce a residential microgrid system by installing small decentralized generators on the grid. If a consumer has a small decentralized generator from renewable energy sources (RES) such as wind turbines and photovoltaics, the consumer in the microgrid system can generate electricity, save electricity for his or her energy storage system (ESS), and trade the surplus electricity within an energy market. With these functions, consumers should control their electricity usage according to the pre-announced central electricity planning strategy. Both the GSO and individual consumers can benefit from such a microgrid system. The GSO can reduce the peak electricity demand level and contribute to decreased carbon emissions by financially supporting consumers in building their RES-based generators. Consumers can save on their electricity bills by generating electricity themselves at lower costs and by making a profit by selling electricity credits that have been locally generated.

However, constructing a microgrid system with financial assistance from the GSO provokes decentralized decisions that assume electricity usage in households is scheduled after the GSO makes its decisions regarding subsidization.

Therefore, the following consecutive questions arise:

- What is the optimal proportion of GSO subsidies for investments in RES-based generators and ESS to reduce peak demand in microgrid systems?
- How should the GSO decide whether or not to install RES and ESS?
- What is the optimal schedule for the electrical appliances installed?

In the microgrid system, participants constitute a Stackelberg leader-follower game, especially in bilevel programming, where consumers' lower-level programs are embedded in the GSO's upper-level program [2,3]. The bilevel program deals with decision-making in various sectors such as the electricity generation market and the chemical industries, where network members interact with each other in a supply chain, but not in a cooperative manner [4].

The proposed mixed-integer bilevel programming (MIBP) generalizes the classical bilevel programming setup by considering binary decisions about investments in RES and ESS at a lower level. To the best of our knowledge, there is no existing research that integrates individual electricity strategies with GSO subsidization. In this study, we develop a solution algorithm for an MIBP that includes discrete decisions based on optimistic consumers–an algorithm that although it has been treated as generally intractable [5]. The performance of the algorithm is evaluated with randomly generated instances.

The remainder of this paper is organized as follows. Section 2 describe the problem and introduce the MIBP model. Section 3 propose an algorithm based on optimistic consumers. In Sect. 4, numerical experiments are conducted. Finally, conclusions are presented in Sect. 5.

2   Problem Definition and Mathematical Formulation

The proposed MIBP consists of a GSO's linear program and consumers' mixed-integer linear program. In the MIBP, we assume that the GSO is the leader and each consumer is the follower. The detailed assumptions of the MIBP are defined as follows: (1) the total time is divided into identical time slots; (2) consumers can install the RES and ESS simultaneously with subsidies from the central GSO; (3) energy potential of RES is predetermined; and (4) electricity loads of appliances are deterministic; The following are the notations used in the MIBP.

Sets

N	set of consumers
A_1^i	set of basic appliances
A_2^i	set of schedule-based appliances
A_3^i	set of model-based appliances
A^i	set of all appliances $(A^i = A_1^i \bigcup A_2^i \bigcup A_3^i)$
T	set of finite time slots
P_a^i	set of predetermined pattern for using schedule-based appliance a

Parameters

l_a	length of operation time of appliance a	$\forall a \in A^i$
E_a	electricity required for the operation of appliance a per one hour	$\forall a \in A^i$
$\overline{E}_a$	maximum electricity of appliance a used per one hour	$\forall a \in A^i$
$\underline{E}_a$	minimum electricity of appliance a used per one hour	$\forall a \in A^i$
π	amortized cost of investment in the RES and ESS	
$\tilde{e}_{at}$	electricity demand of appliance a at time t	$\forall a \in A^i, \forall t \in T$
α	minimum requirements of consumers' utilization	
c_t	unit supply cost of consumer at time t	$\forall t \in T$
p_t	electricity price from the consumer at time t	$\forall t \in T$
ϵ^{dis}	efficiency when electricity is discharged from the ESS	
ϵ^{cha}	efficiency when electricity is charged to the ESS	
C_t^{out}	outside centigrade degree at time t	$\forall t \in T$

Decision variables

e_{it}	quantity of electricity used at time t	$\forall i \in N, \forall t \in T$
e_{iat}	quantity of electricity of appliance a used at time t	$\forall i \in N, \forall a \in A, \forall t \in T$
e_{it}^{in}	inbound quantity of electricity from a supplier at time t	$\forall t \in T$
e_{it}^{out}	outbound quantity of electricity to a supplier at time t	$\forall t \in T$
e_{it}^{cha}	quantity of electricity charged in ESS at time t	$\forall t \in T$
e_{it}^{dis}	quantity of electricity discharged in ESS at time t	$\forall t \in T$
e_{it}^{gen}	quantity of electricity generated by RES at time t	$\forall i \in N, \forall t \in T$
u_{it}	utilization of user at time t	$\forall i \in N, \forall t \in T$
x_i	1, if a consumer invests in ESS and RES; 0, otherwise.	$\forall i \in N$
y	proportion of subsidies	
λ_{iap}	1, if predefined schedule p is selected for appliance a; 0, otherwise.	$\forall i \in N, \forall a \in A_{2i}$ $\forall p \in P_a^i$
C_{it}^{in}	inside centigrade degree at time t	$\forall i \in N, \forall t \in T$

The leader's and follower's optimization problems are presented separately below.

2.1 Leader's Upper-Level Problem

When the capacity of baseload generation sources is given, the GSO decide the percentage of subsidies for followers, as well as a time-varying electricity pricing schedule. The two objectives of the leader's problem are to minimize the maximum peak demands among households and to minimize the cost of the subsidy. The relevant mathematical formulation is developed as follows:

$$\min \ \{\max_t \sum_{i \in N} e_{it}, \sum_{i \in N} \pi y x_i\} \tag{1}$$

$$\text{s.t.} \ \ 0 \leq y \leq 1 \tag{2}$$

$$\{e_{it}\}, x_i \in \ \underset{\substack{\{e_{it}\} \in \mathbb{R}_+^{|t|}, \\ x_i \in \mathbb{B}}}{\arg\min} \ \{(4) : (5)(5) - (20)(20)\}, \quad \forall i \in N \tag{3}$$

Objective function (1) simultaneously minimizes the peak demand and the subsidy required for individuals. Constraint (2) defines the range of proportion of subsidy over investment cost π. Constraint (3) represents the optimal electricity load profile of individual consumers which will be presented in Sect. 2.2.

2.2 Follower's Lower-Level Problem

In the follower's problem, we assume three types of appliances in households. A type-1 appliance is a machine required for daily use (e.g., refrigerators). A type-2 appliance is used based on schedules. (e.g., televisions) Patterns of using each schedule-based machine are predetermined by the users and are known and have been established in this study. A type-3 appliance is a model-based machine. Model-based machines operate to maintain comfortable living environments (e.g., air conditioners and electric heaters). The formulations for the lower-level problem are referred to [6].

Objective Function. In the residential microgrid system, consumer $i \in N$ wants to minimize the overall cost of electricity bills, investment costs, and deductions from the GSO's subsidy support.

$$\min \quad \sum_{t \in T} c_t e_{it}^{in} - \sum_{t \in T} p_t e_{it}^{out} + \pi(1-y)x_i \tag{4}$$

The objective function (4) minimizes the summation composed of electricity bills, the revenue generated from selling surplus electricity to the power market, and subsidies from the GSO. In the operation of RES and ESS, we assume that the quantity of electricity charged (or discharged) is limited by capacity.

Constraints for RES and ESS. In the operation of RES and ESS, we assume that the quantity of electricity charged (or discharged) is limited by the capacity $\overline{B}$.

$$0 \le \sum_{a=1}^{t} \left(\epsilon^{cha} e_{ia}^{cha} - \epsilon^{dis} e_{ia}^{dis} \right) \le \overline{B} \qquad\qquad \forall t \in T \tag{5}$$

$$e_{it}^{in} - e_{it}^{out} + e_t^{gen} = e_{it} + \epsilon^{cha} e_{it}^{cha} - \epsilon^{dis} e_{it}^{dis} \qquad\qquad \forall t \in T \tag{6}$$

$$0 \le e_{it}^{cha} \le \overline{R}x_i \qquad\qquad \forall t \in T \tag{7}$$

$$0 \le e_{it}^{dis} \le \overline{R}x_i \qquad\qquad \forall t \in T \tag{8}$$

$$e_{it}^{out} \le Mx_i \qquad\qquad \forall t \in T \tag{9}$$

$$e_{it} \ge \sum_{a \in A} e_{iat} \qquad\qquad \forall t \in T \tag{10}$$

Constraint (5) mandates that the energy level in ESS at time t should be non-negative and lower than the maximum capacity of ESS. Constraint (6) is the balance equation of electricity, which can be traded with an electricity provider, transferred to the ESS, and generated by RES in the residential area. Constraints (7)–(9) ensure that it is possible to sell energy and store energy only if the RES and ESS are determined to be installed by a consumer. Constraint (10) aggregates the entire electricity load from the operation of appliances at time t.

Constraint for Type-1 Appliances. A type-1 appliance always requires a certain energy level, which is given. For instance, a refrigerator needs a specific level of energy to maintain a low temperature.

$$e_{iat} \ge \tilde{e}_{iat} \qquad\qquad \forall a \in A_1^i, \forall t \in T \tag{11}$$

Constraint (11) indicates that energy is consumed regularly in an appliance a at a time slot t.

Constraints for Type-2 Appliances. An appliance that belongs to a type-2 category is only operated within a consumer's preferred time $t \in [\underline{T}_a, \overline{T}_a]$. Two constraints are required for a type-2 appliance:

$$e_{iat} \geq \sum_{\forall p} E_{apt}\lambda_{iap}, \qquad\qquad \forall a \in A_2^i, \forall t \in [\underline{T}_a, \overline{T}_a] \qquad (12)$$

$$\sum_{\forall p} \lambda_{iap} = 1, \qquad\qquad \forall a \in A_2^i \qquad (13)$$

Constraints (12) and (13) ensure that only one predefined schedule can be determined, based on its association with an appliance, where E_{apt} is the electricity load of the appliance at time slot t relevant to schedule p.

Constraints for Type-3 Appliances

$$C_{it}^{in} = C_{i,t-1}^{in} + \gamma(C_t^{out} - C_{i,t-1}^{in}) + \delta e_{iat} \qquad \forall a \in A_3^i, \forall t \in T \qquad (14)$$

$$\underline{E}_a \leq e_{iat} \leq \overline{E}_a \qquad\qquad \forall a \in A_3^i, \forall t \in T \qquad (15)$$

$$C_t^{target} - \varepsilon \leq C_{it}^{in} \leq C_t^{target} + \varepsilon \qquad \forall t \in T \qquad (16)$$

Constraints (14) and (15) describe energy demanded in order to adjust for environmental conditions such as temperature and humidity at a given time slot. Constraint (14) represents a physical model that expresses the relationship between environmental conditions and electricity consumption. Constraint (15) stipulates that the electricity load of an application should be within the operating range. Constraint (16) represents that the environmental condition over time should be within the desirable condition range.

Constraints on a Consumer's Dissatisfaction

$$u_{it} \geq \sum_{a \in A^i} \sum_{p \in P} \tilde{u}_{apt}\lambda_{iap} \qquad\qquad \forall t \in T \qquad (17)$$

$$\sum_{t \in T} u_{it} \leq 1 - \alpha \qquad\qquad (18)$$

$$0 \leq e_{it}, e_{iat}, e_{it}^{gen}, e_{it}^{in}, e_{it}^{out}, e_{it}^{cha}, e_{it}^{dis}, C_{it}^{in}, u_{it} \qquad (19)$$

$$x_i, \lambda_{iap} \in \mathbb{B} \qquad\qquad (20)$$

In the microgrid system, a consumer's dissatisfaction level is calculated by the predefined dissatisfaction level of schedule p. Constraint (17) defines the dissatisfaction level at time t. Constraint (18) stipulates that the aggregated dissatisfaction level is lower than or equal to the given level. Constraints (19) and (20) define decision variables.

3   Solution Strategy

It is obvious that a consumer should install the equipment by applying for the subsidy program if the profit from operating ESS and RES is greater than the cost of installing ESS and RES. Using this fact, one can obtain the threshold proportion of a subsidy. If decision variable y is equal to the threshold, the consumer is indifferent about installing ESS and RES. If it is assumed that consumers always choose to install the equipment to reduce peak demand (optimistic), we can easily find the global optimal solution. In our problem, Pareto points correspond to peak demand for a whole grid system and subsidy support. If we predetermine y as the threshold that spurs a household to adopt the program, the dominating Pareto point is determined by calculating all the schedules of consumers and the total subsidies. An algorithm for obtaining the Pareto curve is presented in Algorithm 1.

Algorithm 1: Algorithm for the optimal solution for optimistic consumers

---

1: **Step 1:** Finding optimal solutions of lower-level problems (LLPs)
2: **initialize** a list R with 0.
3: **for** $i = 1 \rightarrow N$
4:     **solve** ith LLP with $y = 0$ and let α_i be the optimal function value.
5:     **find** an optimistic solution
$$\{e_{it}^{None}\} \leftarrow \arg\min\{\max_t\{e_{it}\} : \text{OBJ}^{LLP} \leq \alpha_i, (5) - (20)\}.$$
6:     **solve** ith LLP model with $y = 1$ and let β_i be the optimal function value.
7:     **find** an optimistic solution
$$\{e_{it}^{ESS}\} \leftarrow \arg\min\{\max_t\{e_{it}\} : \text{OBJ}^{LLP} \leq \beta_i, (5) - (20)\}.$$
8:     **set** $\hat{y}_i = 1 - (\alpha - \beta))/\pi.$
9:     **add** $\hat{y}_i$ into R in ascending order
10: **Step 2:** Obtaining Pareto points
11: **for** $i = 1 \rightarrow |N| + 1$ **do**
12:     **initialize** $\{\hat{e}_t\}$ and $\hat{B}$ be a zero vector and a zero value.
13:     **get** y from R in order.
14:     **for** $j = 1 \rightarrow |N|$ **do**
15:         **If** $\hat{y}_j \geq y$ **then** $\hat{e}_t \leftarrow \hat{e}_t + e_{jt}^{ESS}, \forall t \in T$ and $\hat{B} \leftarrow \hat{B} + \pi y$.
16:         **Otherwise** $\hat{e}_t \leftarrow \hat{e}_t + e_{jt}^{None}, \forall t \in T.$
17:     **obtain** a Pareto point with $(\max_t\{\hat{e}_t\}, \hat{B})$.

---

4   Computational Experiments

To demonstrate the proposed solution algorithm for solving the MIBP model, we consider a case study on a hypothetical grid system [6]. There are 27 households that can switch their existing energy consumption system to a microgrid system. We refer to an instance of the single microgrid system as baseline data [6]. By changing three sets of data, such as (i) minimum satisfaction level, (ii) RES-based generation potential, and (iii) energy consumption style with three levels, such as "low," "moderate," and "high," a total of 27 instances corresponding to the households are obtained. For (i), α is set by 0.9, 0.7, and 0.5. For (ii), G_t^{max} is changed to 80%, 100%, and 120%. For (iii), energy loads of type-1 appliances are changed to 90%, 100%, and 110% and the set of type-2 appliances used in one household is set according to its level of (iii). Table 1 shows input data for type-2 appliances. All consumers use "a_1^{Type2}" and "a_2^{Type2}" appliances. Consumers in a "moderate" level of (iii) additionally operate a "a_3^{Type2}" appliance. Consumers in a "high" level of (iii) use all the appliance types.

Table 1. Input data for type-2 appliances.

Type-2 appliances	a_1^{Type2}	a_2^{Type2}	a_3^{Type2}	a_4^{Type2}	a_5^{Type2}
$[\underline{T}_a, \overline{T}_a]$	[8,22]	[11,21]	[11,21]	[11,21]	[18,23]
l_a	3	3	3	2	2
E_a	0.8 kWh	1.1 kWh	1.6 kWh	0.9 kWh	1.4 kWh
β_a	0.025	0.025	0.025	0.04	0.04

We assume that the investment cost for installing ESS and RES is \$20,938. To amortize the investment cost of the equipment, we consider the capital charge factor for the land, assuming the interest rate of 8% and a lifetime of 5 years. Thereby the equivalent daily cost of the investment cost is set to 14.15 (\$/day). The electricity cost and price are assumed to be constant and are set to 3.5 (\$/kWh) and 2.8 (\$/kWh), respectively.

To validate that the capacity of ESS affects the reduction of peak demand, we conducted experiments by changing the capacity of ESS to 1.8 kWh (small), 2.4 kWh (medium), and 3.0 kWh (large). The results can be found in Fig. 1. The results show that the Pareto frontier obtained for a large capacity of consumption dominates other Pareto frontiers. This means that increasing the capacity of ESS is effective in reducing peak demand.

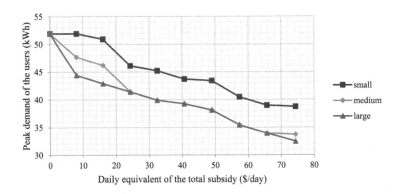

Fig. 1. Pareto frontiers with respect to the ESS capacity

5   Conclusions

We investigated Stackelberg-game-based modeling and optimization for reducing peak demand for a microgrid system. In order to find the optimal solution for optimistic consumers, we developed an exact algorithm. Computational experiments show that the algorithm gets the Pareto frontier of the MIBP model within reasonable time limits. A sensitivity analysis was conducted to validate the effect of ESS capacity on peak demand.

References

1. Ministry of Trade, Industry, and Energy: The 8th Basic Plan for Long-term electiricity Supply and Demand, Korea (2017)
2. Von Stackelberg, H.: Market Structure and Equilibrium. Springer, Heidelberg (2011). https://doi.org/10.1007/978-3-642-12586-7
3. Dempe, S., Kalashnikov, V., Pérez-Valdés, G. A., Kalashnykova, N.: Bilevel Programming Problems. Springer, Berlin (2015). https://doi.org/10.1007/978-3-662-45827-3
4. Sinha, A., Malo, P., Deb, K.: A review on bilevel optimization: from classical to evolutionary approaches and applications. IEEE Trans. Evol. Comput. **22**(2), 276–295 (2018). https://doi.org/10.1109/TEVC.2017.2712906
5. Vicente, L., Savard, G., Judice, J.: Discrete linear bilevel programming problem. J. Optim. Theory Appl. **89**(3), 597–614 (1996). https://doi.org/10.1007/BF02275351
6. Tsui, K.M., Chan, S.C.: Demand response optimization for smart home scheduling under real-time pricing. IEEE Trans. Smart Grid **3**(4), 1812–1821 (2012). https://doi.org/10.1109/TSG.2012.2218835

A Smart-Contract Enabled Blockchain Traceability System Against Wine Supply Chain Counterfeiting

Sotiris P. Gayialis[1]([✉])[iD], Evripidis P. Kechagias[1][iD], Georgios A. Papadopoulos[1][iD], and Elias Kanakis[2]

[1] Sector of Industrial Management and Operational Research, School of Mechanical Engineering, National Technical University of Athens, 15772 Athens, Greece
{sotga,eurikechagias,gpapado}@mail.ntua.gr
[2] Entersoft S.A., 362 Sigrou Avenue, 17674 Athens, Greece
ekn@entersoft.gr

Abstract. The need for effective traceability in the wine industry has dramatically increased in recent years due to the growing consumer awareness of the safety and the quality of products they buy. The loss of visibility as to the origin of a product can cause significant disruptions in the production and distribution of goods but also poses serious fraud risks. More specifically, bad or counterfeit wines may be produced and marketed when they can't be traced at all stages effectively. Fraud, such as adulteration with low-quality raw materials and wines, dilution, replacement of packaging contents and forgery of packages and labels, can be detected at the various stages of the wine supply chain. In order to combat wine supply chain counterfeiting blockchain technology has gained increased popularity as a means of enabling a secure traceability system. This paper presents the development of a smart-contracts-enabled blockchain traceability system that has been specifically designed for the wine supply chain and operates through the Ethereum Network.

Keywords: Blockchain · Ethereum · Smart contact · Traceability system · Counterfeiting · Alcoholic beverages · Wine supply chain

1 Introduction

Counterfeiting in the wine supply chain has always been and continues to remain a significant challenge for the stakeholders and the consumers. In addition to the severe health risks arising from fraudulent activities, emphasis should be laid on the adverse economic consequences for all wine supply chain stakeholders, i.e., cultivators, producers, distributors, wholesalers, retailers, etc. According to the European Commission's science and knowledge service [1], wine fraud costs the regular EU wine sector an estimated 1.3 billion euros per year, around 3% of the total sales value. In 2020, over one million liters of counterfeit alcoholic beverages were seized across Europe, increasing

© IFIP International Federation for Information Processing 2022
Published by Springer Nature Switzerland AG 2022
D. Y. Kim et al. (Eds.): APMS 2022, IFIP AICT 663, pp. 477–484, 2022.
https://doi.org/10.1007/978-3-031-16407-1_56

to over 1.7 million in 2021 – the majority of which was wine – in targeted actions regularly led by the European Anti-Fraud Office (OLAF) as part of joint Europol-Interpol operations known as OPSON [2]. Apart from the economic impact of counterfeiting in spirits and wines, there are other effects such as job losses, which amount to 4800 per year [3]. To identify counterfeit wines, the findings of tests on suspicious wine samples are matched to data on real wine samples kept in the European Union Wine Databank. To achieve precise measurement data, analytical laboratories calibrate their results using a Certified Reference Material (CRM) [4]. However, the controls and checks by the public authorities can achieve limited success as they cannot detect the problem's roots since they cannot trace the wine at various stages of their supply chain.

Determining the percentage of counterfeit wines is considered rather impossible as wines are included in the food and beverage sector, so the data available is not entirely clear. Also, the huge variety in this industry complicates things by highlighting the need for a more detailed industry fragmentation. In addition, exportable wines are often counterfeited within the borders of a country of production before export, making it difficult to detect the counterfeit. However, according to estimates by the World Health Organization, the proportion of counterfeit alcohol on the international market is estimated at around 25% of the total, especially in Southeast Asia and the Eastern Mediterranean, where unregistered alcohol consumption is around 50% or more than total alcohol consumption (45.4% in the Southeast Asia region, 70.5% in the Eastern Mediterranean region) [5].

This paper contributes to the scientific community as well as to the wine industry sector as it presents in detail the development of a smart-contract-enabled blockchain traceability system that has been specifically designed for the wine supply chain. The development of the system is based on a thorough study of the wine industry and the business processes of the wine supply chain, concluding with accurate design specifications. The proposed system operates through the Ethereum Main Net Network, and its various characteristics are presented in this paper. In Sect. 2, it is discussed how a blockchain traceability system can significantly reduce counterfeiting in the wine supply chain. Additionally, the way the system operates is explained, and its interaction with the wine supply stakeholders is shown. Section 3 of the paper presents how the traceability system is being developed by analyzing the required tools and including an indicative smart contract code of the fists phase of development.

2 Applying Blockchain Technology in the Wine Supply Chain

All stakeholders can achieve significant benefits by implementing an effective blockchain traceability system [6]. More specifically, the cultivators and producers can improve the production quality of the wines and reduce or even eliminate the financial damage from the sale of products that do not meet the required specifications. At the same time, the distributors and sellers can achieve secure transportation, the government can ensure that all operations comply with policies and legislations, and the consumer can validate that the wine has not undergone any type of counterfeiting [7].

Many efforts have taken place aiming to combat the wine counterfeiting problem. However, most of them achieved limited success without holistically addressing traceability [8]. The most commonly faced challenges are i) the collection of data, in a secure way, from all parts of the wine supply chain and ii) the creation of non-copyable product labels that serve as the link between the physical products and the digital data [9–11]. This research, aiming to overcome the aforementioned challenges effectively, presents the development of a blockchain-based system that enables the stakeholders to detect all the information related to each individual bottle of wine, including a complete history of dates, locations, and sensor data. Additionally, the consumer can receive a one-of-its-kind digital wine passport that proves the origin and authenticity of the wine. In other words, the system can provide reverse control to each one of the stakeholders of the wine supply chain, from the cultivator to the final consumer, presenting all the authentic information related to the product and ensuring faster and safer transactions. Advanced technologies implemented for effective traceability cover three dimensions: i) secure data sharing using blockchain technology, ii) real-time data collection from the Internet of Things (IoT) sensors and enterprise systems directly transmitted to the blockchain

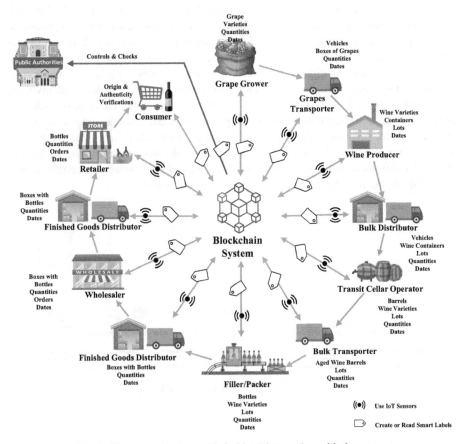

Fig. 1. Wine supply chain stakeholders' interaction with the system

system, and iii) reliable and secure data access through non-copyable labels. Figure 1 presents the interaction of the wine supply chain stakeholders with the blockchain-based system through the aforementioned technologies.

The exchange of all information between the different stakeholders throughout the supply chain will take place using a blockchain network without compromising privacy and security. IoT sensors will be used to collect the necessary data (humidity, temperature, location, etc.) at various stages of the wine supply chain in order to ensure the cultivation, production, and transportation conditions. A crucial part of fraud prevention will be the type of labels, placed on the bottle seals or packages for traceability and authentication. Various smart labels such as NFC tags, RFIDs, and engraved QR Codes will enable access to the bottle's info. The labels will also include advanced marking techniques such as tamper-evident labels, 2D and 3D holograms, digital watermarks, color-shift inks, or invisible printing that will prevent copying or cloning. The increased counterfeiting protection will be achieved by combining smart labels with data veracity control measures (e.g., third-party certification bodies) and short data entry frequency (the time lag between the moment the event occurs and the moment when the related information is written on the blockchain ledger).

Figure 2 presents a sample use case scenario for a wine bottle that moves between the producer, the wholesaler/retailer and the consumer. After each bottle is produced, it receives a unique encrypted bottle identifier (smart label) and is linked to a digital passport that contains all info related to that specific bottle. The digital passport can provide proof of authenticity, provenance, ownership & access to special contents such as info related to the production, sale and transportation that can be added by all involved stakeholders. Each time the bottle moves to another wine supply chain stakeholder, its authenticity is verified, the digital ownership is transferred, and sale and transportation data are added. Involved stakeholders and consumers can, therefore, trace the bottle's supply chain. When the bottle is sold to a consumer, the smart label can be scanned in order to verify its authenticity, provenance, receive a digital ownership certificate and "burn" the bottle in order to show it has now been consumed.

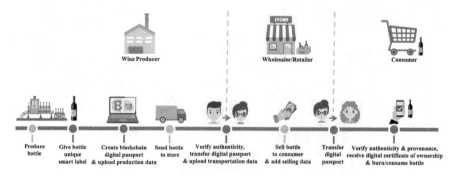

Fig. 2. Sample use case scenario

3   Developing the Blockchain Traceability System

To address the issue of traceability in the wine supply chain, the Ethereum Main Net blockchain network was selected to take advantage of the transparency and decentralized character it offers. The Ethereum network is perhaps the most well-known public blockchain network. Developed in 2015, it is open-source and has been developed specifically for the easy development and implementation of smart contracts [12]. The Smart Contract can be considered a digitized real world contract. It is a code (small program) uploaded to a blockchain network and is executed automatically when certain specific prerequisites are met. When a smart contract is created, it can never be altered. Ethereum has its own cryptocurrency called Ether, which facilitates the transactions of smart contracts since it is integrated into the network. The main advantage of Ethereum is the built-in programming language called Solidity, which has been developed for smart contract applications and is Turing Complete. The cryptocurrency from which it is powered and on which the Ethereum network operates is Ether which is used as "ETH". When each user sends ETH or uses an Ethereum application, they pay a gas fee in "gwei" ($10–9$ ETH) to use the Ethereum network. This end is an incentive for a miner to process and verify what the user is trying to accomplish.

Table 1. Indicative smart contract for the wine producer

Smart Contract's Variables Definition	Smart Contract's Functions	

pragma solidity 0.4.26 ;
 	
contract ProducerData {
  address admin;
  struct Item {
  uint code;
  uint burncode;
  uint8 unittype;
  uint itemsincontainers;
  uint rawmaterialcode;
  string lotnumber;
  uint productiondate;
  uint bestbeforedate;
  uint gln;
  string info1;
  bool status; }
 	
  mapping(uint => Item)
itemArray;
  uint count;
 	
  constructor() public {
admin = msg.sender;
count =0; }
	function insertItem(
	uint code,
	uint burncode,
	uint8 unittype,
	uint itemsincontainers,
	uint rawmaterialcode,
	string lotnumber,
	uint productiondate,
	uint bestbeforedate,
	uint gln,
	string info1,
	bool status) public restricted {
	itemArray[code] = Item(code,
	burncode, unittype, itemsincontain-
	ers,
	  rawmaterialcode, lotnumber,
	productiondate, bestbeforedate,
	gln, info1, status);
	count++ }
	
	function getCount() public re-
	stricted view returns (uint) {
	  return count; }
	
	function getStatus(uint code)
	public view returns (bool,string) {
		function burnItem(uint code, uint
		burncode) public {
		  uint tempcode = itemAr-
		ray[code].burncode;
		  if (tempcode == burncode) {
		  itemArray[code].status = false;
		  } }
		
		  function infoitem(uint code) public
		view returns (
		  uint8, uint, uint, string, uint, uint,
		uint) {
		  return (
		  itemArray[code].unittype,
		  itemAr-
		ray[code].itemsincontainers,
		  itemAr-
		ray[code].rawmaterialcode,
		  itemArray[code].lotnumber,
		  itemArray[code].productiondate,
		  itemArray[code].bestbeforedate,
		  itemArray[code].gln); }
		
		modifier restricted() {
		require(msg.sender == admin);
		  _; }

The code of an indicative smart contract containing wine producers' data and functions is presented in Table 1. The first column of the table includes the tested compiler version and the definition of the variables. The remaining two columns present the smart contract functions and the access modifier. This is just an indicative presentation of the code for demonstration purposes, as many more variables, functions, and stakeholder contracts are necessary for creating the fully functional traceability system.

Additionally, a brief overview of the technological solutions that are part of the blockchain traceability system is presented in Fig. 3. The truffle framework/toolset is used to develop the blockchain traceability system. It is a development toolset based on Ethereum Blockchain, which is used to create DApps (Distributed Applications), i.e., applications structured in the decentralized network through a blockchain server. It allows the development, compiling, testing, and deployment of smart contracts, their penetration into web apps, and the front-end configuration for apps. Ganache, a local personal Ethereum network, is used to test smart contracts before deploying them to the Ethereum Main Net. The users connect to the network through the React Javascript library, used to create the system's user interface, while the Web3.js library collection allows communication with a local or remote Ethereum node using HTTP, IPC or WebSocket. In order for the user to connect to the blockchain server, it is necessary to have a metamask account, a wallet which enables users through a web browser/application, to manage their ETHs and interact with Dapps.

Finally, Etherscan.io, a blockchain explorer is used to give the user access to data from the Ethereum platform. It is a search engine through which the user can monitor the Dapp in real-time by receiving information about the transactions that take place, the smart contracts as well as the costs of any transaction (gas fees).

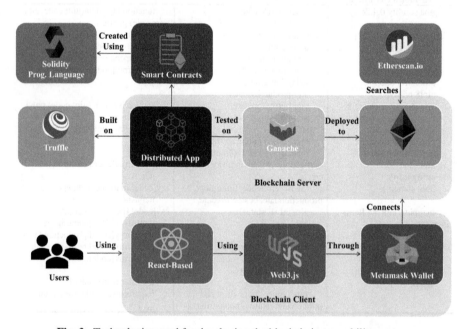

Fig. 3. Technologies used for developing the blockchain traceability system

4 Conclusions

The paper presented ongoing research for the development of a blockchain-based traceability system against counterfeiting in the wine supply chain. After analyzing what technologies are needed and how the system should operate and interact with the supply chain stakeholders, the methodology and the technological tools for developing the system in the Ethereum network were analyzed. The system's first version has been developed as a Dapp based on smart contracts. An indicative smart contract code for the producer's data was also presented in this paper. As it becomes clear from this research, blockchain can become a valuable aid in order to effectively combat the wine supply chain counterfeiting that has severe health and economic consequences. In the next steps of the research, the system will enter its final development phase utilizing all the necessary tools presented in this paper. Afterwards, the system will be tested, in real-life conditions, in wineries and their partners in the supply chain (cultivators, distributors, transporters, wholesalers, retail stores). After testing the system in the wine supply chain, improvements will be made in order to release its final version.

Acknowledgements. The present work is co-funded by the European Union and Greek national funds through the Operational Program "Competitiveness, Entrepreneurship and Innovation" (EPAnEK), under the call "RESEARCH - CREATE - INNOVATE" (project code: T2EDK - 00508 and Acronym: COUNTERBLOCK).

References

1. OECD/EUIPO: Trends in Trade in Counterfeit and Pirated Goods (2019)
2. OLAF: Over 1 million litres of wine and alcoholic beverages seized under OLAF-led operation, Brussels, Belgium (2021)
3. EURACTIV: Fake wines and spirits cost the EU 'at least' 4,800 jobs per year, Brussels, Belgium (2016)
4. Donarski, J., Camin, F., Fauhl-Hassek, C., Posey, R., Sudnik, M.: Sampling guidelines for building and curating food authenticity databases. Trends Food Sci. Technol. **90**, 187–193 (2019). https://doi.org/10.1016/j.tifs.2019.02.019
5. Hammer, J.H., Parent, M.C., Spiker, D.A.: World Health Organization: Global status report on alcohol and health 2018 (2018)
6. Brookbanks, M., Parry, G.: The impact of a blockchain platform on trust in established relationships: a case study of wine supply chains. Supply Chain Manag. Int. J. **27**, 128–146 (2022). https://doi.org/10.1108/SCM-05-2021-0227
7. Li, K., Lee, J.-Y., Gharehgozli, A.: Blockchain in food supply chains: a literature review and synthesis analysis of platforms, benefits and challenges. Int. J. Prod. Res., 1–20 (2021). https://doi.org/10.1080/00207543.2021.1970849
8. Shwetha, A.N., Prabodh, C.P.: A comprehensive review of blockchain based solutions in food supply chain management. In: 2021 5th International Conference on Computing Methodologies and Communication (ICCMC), pp. 519–525. IEEE (2021)
9. Jabbar, S., Lloyd, H., Hammoudeh, M., Adebisi, B., Raza, U.: Blockchain-enabled supply chain: analysis, challenges, and future directions. Multimedia Syst. **27**(4), 787–806 (2020). https://doi.org/10.1007/s00530-020-00687-0

10. Wu, H., et al.: Data management in supply chain using blockchain: challenges and a case study. In: 2019 28th International Conference on Computer Communication and Networks (ICCCN), pp. 1–8. IEEE (2019)
11. Dutta, P., Choi, T.-M., Somani, S., Butala, R.: Blockchain technology in supply chain operations: applications, challenges and research opportunities. Transp. Res. Part E Logist. Transp. Rev. **142**, 102067 (2020). https://doi.org/10.1016/j.tre.2020.102067
12. Sujeetha, R., Deiva Preetha, C.A.S.: A literature survey on smart contract testing and analysis for smart contract based blockchain application development. In: 2021 2nd International Conference on Smart Electronics and Communication (ICOSEC), pp. 378–385. IEEE (2021)

Rescheduling Problem for Heavy Cargo Logistics with Transporters

Kyungduk Moon⬡, Myungho Lee⬡, and Kangbok Lee[✉]⬡

Pohang University of Science and Technology, Pohang, South Korea
kblee@postech.ac.kr

Abstract. We consider a flexible flow shop rescheduling problem with transporters that carry heavy cargoes from a manufacturing site to loading docks. If a transporter is occupied by a heavy cargo, it cannot transport other heavy cargo until the operation at the last stage of the dedicated heavy cargo is completed. This imposes resource constraints for transporters that are practically relevant in heavy cargo logistics. We also consider stage skipping, resource eligibility constraints, sequence-dependent relocation time on transporters, and available time intervals of resources. Assuming that an initial schedule is given, we propose a mixed-integer (linear) programming model for a scheduling problem with multiple objectives including makespan and several rescheduling objectives.

Keywords: Scheduling · Transporter · Resource constraint · MIP

1 Introduction

Heavy cargoes produced in South Korea are transported by specialized cargo ships and transporters from suppliers to domestic customers. For example, steel plates and coils produced by a steel-making company are transported by elevation transporters (E/T cars) to specialized ships called Roll-on/Roll-off (RoRo) ships, and then delivered by those ships to final destinations. In this paper, we demonstrate how practical scheduling problems happening in heavy cargo logistics can be managed by using Mixed-Integer (linear) Programming (MIP) formulation.

Each job representing a delivery batch consists of multiple operations including loading cargoes to a transporter, inspection, and unloading cargoes at a yard. According to operation types, we can assume that there is a list of stages, and each job is processed through a predefined sub-sequence of stages on the given list. The first/last stage is always loading/unloading cargoes, while some stages in the middle (e.g., inspection) may be skipped depending on the job. Processing each operation requires a machine and a transporter as resource. The numbers

© IFIP International Federation for Information Processing 2022
Published by Springer Nature Switzerland AG 2022
D. Y. Kim et al. (Eds.): APMS 2022, IFIP AICT 663, pp. 485–493, 2022.
https://doi.org/10.1007/978-3-031-16407-1_57

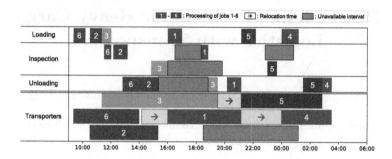

Fig. 1. An illustrative example of heavy cargo transportation schedule

of machines in each stage and transporters could be more than one, and each job has eligibility to machines and transporters. The processing time of each operation depends on its assigned machine and between two consecutive operations is a transportation time. Once a heavy cargo is loaded to a dedicated transporter at the first stage, it cannot be unloaded until the final operation is completed. Between two consecutive jobs assigned to the same transporter is a sequence-dependent relocation time mainly caused by moving from one site to the next. Machines and transporters have specified available time intervals in a scheduling horizon. Given an initial schedule, the objective is to minimize makespan and rescheduling objectives, including machine assignment deviation, transportation assignment deviation, and completion time deviation. Figure 1 shows an illustrative example with three stages (Loading → Inspection → Unloading) and three transporters. Among six jobs (labeled by 1–6 with distinct colors), only Job 4 skipped the second stage.

We deal with the flexible (hybrid) flow shop problem explained in [4], a well-known and practical problem that many authors have studied. Comprehensive survey paper such as [5] exists. Practical requirements such as machine environment, stage skipping, resource eligibility constraints, etc., are listed in those surveys. For another practical requirement beyond surveys, some flexible flow shop problems consider resources for transportation between stages and such resources could be robots [1] or transporters [3]. While most previous papers regard transporters would be released after one transportation between stages, we consider that each transporter is occupied from the first to the last stage since the frequent movement of heavy cargo on transporters is not desired. Moreover, we also consider multiple unavailable periods, which were never considered in this context. Due to the problem's hardness, most previous papers use various metaheuristics as NSGA-III [2]. However, unavailable time intervals within transporters are likely to degrade the performance of existing metaheuristic methodologies because efficiently finding a feasible and reasonably good neighbor solution is hard. Furthermore, slight modification of the incumbent solution significantly may affect the objective value. Thus, we focus more on formulating the problem to efficient MIP formulation that finds a reasonable solution without sticking to local optima.

2   Mathematical Model

Sets	
$\mathcal{G}$	Set of stages ($:= \{1, \ldots, H\}$)
$\mathcal{J}$	Set of jobs to be scheduled
$\mathcal{R}$	Set of transporters ($:= \{1, \ldots, R\}$)
$\mathcal{G}_j$	The sequence of stages of job j ($:= \{\mathcal{G}_j[1], \mathcal{G}_j[2], \ldots, \mathcal{G}_j[H_j]\}$)
	where H_j is the number of stages that job j is processed through,
	$\mathcal{G}_j[1]$ is fixed to be 1, and $\mathcal{G}_j[H_j]$ is fixed to be H ($\forall j \in \mathcal{J}$)
$\mathcal{J}^{\text{init}}$	Set of jobs that belong to an initial schedule ($\mathcal{J}^{\text{init}} \subseteq \mathcal{J}$)
$\hat{\mathcal{J}}_r$	Set of jobs that are eligible to transporter r ($\forall r \in \mathcal{R}$)
$\mathcal{M}_h$	Set of machines of stage h where i-th machine is denoted as (i, h)
	($\mathcal{M}_h$'s are mutually exclusive $\forall h \in \mathcal{G}$)
$\mathcal{E}_{jh}^M$	Set of machines eligible with job j at stage h ($\forall j \in \mathcal{J}, h \in \mathcal{G}_j$)
$\mathcal{E}_j^T$	Set of transporters eligible with job j ($\forall j \in \mathcal{J}$)

Simplifying notation for sets	
$\mathcal{J}_{\neq}^2$	$\{(j, j') : (j, j') \in \mathcal{J} \times \mathcal{J}, j \neq j'\}$
$\mathcal{G}_{\{j,j'\}}$	$\mathcal{G}_j \cap \mathcal{G}_{j'}$ ($\forall (j, j') \in \mathcal{J}_{\neq}^2$)
$\mathcal{E}_{\{j,j'\}h}^M$	$\mathcal{E}_{jh}^M \cap \mathcal{E}_{j'h}^M$ ($\forall (j, j') \in \mathcal{J}_{\neq}^2, h \in \mathcal{G}_{\{j,j'\}}$)
$\mathcal{E}_{\{j,j'\}}^T$	$\mathcal{E}_j^T \cap \mathcal{E}_{j'}^T$ ($\forall (j, j') \in \mathcal{J}_{\neq}^2$)

Parameters	
C_{jh}^{init}	The completion time of job j of stage h in a given initial schedule
	($j \in \mathcal{J}^{\text{init}}, \forall h \in \mathcal{G}_j$)
Q	A sufficiently large number
$\left[a_{ihu}^M, b_{ihu}^M\right]$	The u-th available interval of machine (i, h)
	($\forall u \in \{1, \ldots, \mu_{ih}\}, h \in \mathcal{G}, i \in \mathcal{M}_h$ where μ_{ih} is the number of mutually exclusive available intervals)
$\left[a_{rv}^T, b_{rv}^T\right]$	The v-th available interval of transporter r ($\forall v \in \{1, \ldots, \nu_r\}, r \in \mathcal{R}$
	where ν_r is the number of mutually exclusive available intervals)
$l_{jj'r}$	Relocation time between the end of job j and the beginning of job j'
	if processed by transporter r ($\forall (j, j') \in \mathcal{J}_{\neq}^2, r \in \mathcal{E}_{\{j,j'\}}^T$)
p_{ijh}	Processing time of job j on machine (i, h) ($\forall j \in \mathcal{J}, h \in \mathcal{G}_j, i \in \mathcal{E}_{jh}^M$)
γ_{ijh}^M	1 if assigning job j to machine (i, h) incurs deviation penalty;
	0 otherwise ($\forall j \in \mathcal{J}^{\text{init}}, h \in \mathcal{G}_j, i \in \mathcal{E}_{jh}^M$)
γ_{jr}^T	1 if assigning job j to transporter r incurs deviation penalty;
	0 otherwise ($\forall j \in \mathcal{J}^{\text{init}}, r \in \mathcal{E}_j^T$)
π_1-π_4	Coefficients of penalty for (makespan/machine assignment deviation/ transporter assignment deviation/completion time deviation)
τ_{jh}	Transportation time of job j between stage h and its next
	($\forall j \in \mathcal{J}, h \in \mathcal{G}_j \setminus \{H\}$)
$\hat{q}_{\min}$	a lower bound of the total processing time of transporters
	$\sum_{j \in \mathcal{J}} \sum_{h \in G_j} \min_{i \in E_{jh}^M}\{p_{ijh}\} + \sum_{j \in \mathcal{J}} \sum_{h \in G_j \setminus \{H\}} \tau_{jh}$
$\hat{l}_{\min}$	a lower bound of the total relocation time of transporters; the sum of
	$(|\mathcal{J}| - R)$-smallest elements in $\{\min_{r \in \mathcal{R}, j' \in \hat{\mathcal{J}}_r \setminus \{j\}}\{l_{j'jr}\} : j \in \mathcal{J}\}$

continued

Binary variables

$X_{jj'h}$	1 if job j precedes job j' on the same machine at stage h; 0 otherwise $(\forall(j,j') \in \mathcal{J}^2_{\neq}, h \in \mathcal{G}_{\{j,j'\}})$
Y_{ijh}	1 if job j is assigned to machine (i,h); 0 otherwise $(\forall j \in \mathcal{J}, h \in \mathcal{G}_j, i \in \mathcal{E}^M_{jh})$
y^M_{ijhu}	1 if job j is processed by machine (i,h) within the u-th available interval; 0 otherwise $(\forall j \in \mathcal{J}, h \in \mathcal{G}_j, i \in \mathcal{E}^M_{jh}, u \in \{1, \ldots, \mu_{ih}\})$
y^T_{jrv}	1 if job j is processed by transporter r within the v-th available interval; 0 otherwise $(\forall j \in \mathcal{J}, r \in \mathcal{E}^T_j, v \in \{1, \ldots, \nu_r\})$
β_{jr}	1 if job j is assigned to transporter r; 0 otherwise $(\forall j \in \mathcal{J}, r \in \mathcal{E}^T_j)$
$\theta_{jj'r}$	1 if job j immediately precedes job j' on transporter r; 0 otherwise $(\forall(j,j') \in \mathcal{J}^2_{\neq}, r \in \mathcal{E}^T_{\{j,j'\}})$
θ_{*jr}	1 if job j is the first job of transporter r; 0 otherwise $(\forall r \in \mathcal{R}, j \in \hat{\mathcal{J}}_r)$
θ_{j*r}	1 if job j is the last job of transporter r; 0 otherwise $(\forall r \in \mathcal{R}, j \in \hat{\mathcal{J}}_r)$

Continuous variables (non-negative)

C^M_{ijh}	The completion time of job j at stage h if it is assigned to machine i; 0 otherwise $(\forall j \in \mathcal{J}, h \in \mathcal{G}_j, i \in \mathcal{E}^M_{jh})$
C_{jh}	The completion time of job j at stage h $(\forall j \in \mathcal{J}, h \in \mathcal{G}_j)$
$C_{\max}$	The makespan at the last stage
S^M_{ijh}	The starting time of job j at stage h if it is assigned to machine i; 0 otherwise $(\forall j \in \mathcal{J}, h \in \mathcal{G}_j, i \in \mathcal{E}^M_{jh})$
S_{jh}	The starting time of job j at stage h $(\forall j \in \mathcal{J}, h \in \mathcal{G}_j)$
$\Delta^+_{jh}, \Delta^-_{jh}$	The positive and negative deviation of completion time of job j at stage h $(\forall j \in \mathcal{J}^{\text{init}}, h \in \mathcal{G}_j)$

$$\text{Min } \pi_1 C_{\max} + \pi_2 \sum_{j \in \mathcal{J}^{\text{init}}} \sum_{h \in \mathcal{G}_j} \sum_{i \in \mathcal{E}^M_{jh}} \gamma^M_{ijh} Y_{ijh} + \pi_3 \sum_{j \in \mathcal{J}^{\text{init}}} \sum_{r \in \mathcal{E}^T_j} \gamma^T_{jr} \beta_{jr} + \pi_4 \sum_{j \in \mathcal{J}^{\text{init}}} \sum_{h \in \mathcal{G}_j} (\Delta^+_{jh} + \Delta^-_{jh}) \tag{1}$$

$$\text{s.t. } \sum_{i \in \mathcal{E}^M_{jh}} Y_{ijh} = 1 \qquad \forall j \in \mathcal{J}, h \in \mathcal{G}_j \tag{2}$$

$$X_{jj'h} + X_{j'jh} \geq Y_{ijh} + Y_{ij'h} - 1 \qquad \forall(j,j') \in \mathcal{J}^2_{\neq}, h \in \mathcal{G}_{\{j,j'\}}, i \in \mathcal{E}^M_{\{j,j'\}h} \tag{3}$$

$$X_{jj'h} + X_{j'jh} \leq 1 - Y_{ijh} + Y_{ij'h} \qquad \forall(j,j') \in \mathcal{J}^2_{\neq}, h \in \mathcal{G}_{\{j,j'\}}, i \in \mathcal{E}^M_{\{j,j'\}h} \tag{4}$$

$$\sum_{j' \in \hat{\mathcal{J}}_r \setminus \{j\}} \theta_{jj'r} + \theta_{j*r} = \beta_{jr} \qquad \forall r \in \mathcal{R}, j \in \hat{\mathcal{J}}_r \tag{5}$$

$$\sum_{j' \in \hat{\mathcal{J}}_r \setminus \{j\}} \theta_{j'jr} + \theta_{*jr} = \beta_{jr} \qquad \forall r \in \mathcal{R}, j \in \hat{\mathcal{J}}_r \tag{6}$$

$$\sum_{j \in \hat{\mathcal{J}}_r} \theta_{*jr} \leq 1 \qquad \forall r \in \mathcal{R} \tag{7}$$

$$\sum_{r \in \mathcal{E}^T_j} \beta_{jr} = 1 \qquad \forall j \in \mathcal{J} \tag{8}$$

$$S_{j'h} \geq C_{jh} - Q(1 - X_{jj'h}) \qquad \forall(j,j') \in \mathcal{J}^2_{\neq}, h \in \mathcal{G}_{\{j,j'\}} \tag{9}$$

$$S_{j,\mathcal{G}_j[\rho+1]} \geq C_{j,\mathcal{G}_j[\rho]} + \tau_{j,\mathcal{G}_j[\rho]} \qquad \forall j \in \mathcal{J}, \rho \in \{1, \ldots, (H_j - 1)\} \tag{10}$$

$$S_{j'1} \geq C_{jH} + l_{jj'r} - Q(1 - \theta_{jj'r}) \qquad \forall(j,j') \in \mathcal{J}^2_{\neq}, r \in \mathcal{E}^T_{\{j,j'\}} \tag{11}$$

$$C^M_{ijh} \leq \sum_{u=1}^{\mu_{ih}} b^M_{ihu} y^M_{ijhu} \qquad \forall j \in \mathcal{J}, h \in \mathcal{G}_j, i \in \mathcal{E}^M_{jh} \tag{12}$$

$$S^M_{ijh} \geq \sum_{u=1}^{\mu_{ih}} a^M_{ihu} y^M_{ijhu} \qquad \forall j \in \mathcal{J}, h \in \mathcal{G}_j, i \in \mathcal{E}^M_{jh} \tag{13}$$

$$\sum_{u=1}^{\mu_{ih}} y_{ijhu}^{M} = Y_{ijh} \qquad \forall j \in \mathcal{J}, h \in \mathcal{G}_j, i \in \mathcal{E}_{jh}^{M} \qquad (14)$$

$$C_{ijh}^{M} = S_{ijh}^{M} + p_{ijh} Y_{ijh} \qquad \forall j \in \mathcal{J}, h \in \mathcal{G}_j, i \in \mathcal{E}_{jh}^{M} \qquad (15)$$

$$S_{jh} = \sum_{i \in \mathcal{E}_{jh}^{M}} S_{ijh}^{M} \qquad \forall j \in \mathcal{J}, h \in \mathcal{G}_j \qquad (16)$$

$$C_{jh} = \sum_{i \in \mathcal{E}_{jh}^{M}} C_{ijh}^{M} \qquad \forall j \in \mathcal{J}, h \in \mathcal{G}_j \qquad (17)$$

$$C_{jH} \leq \sum_{r \in \mathcal{E}_j^{T}} \sum_{v=1}^{\nu_r} b_{rv}^{T} y_{jrv}^{T} \qquad \forall j \in \mathcal{J} \qquad (18)$$

$$S_{j1} \geq \sum_{r \in \mathcal{E}_j^{T}} \left(\sum_{v=1}^{\nu_r} a_{rv}^{T} y_{jrv}^{T} + \sum_{j' \in \hat{\mathcal{J}}_r \setminus \{j\}} l_{j'jr} \theta_{j'jr} \right) \quad \forall j \in \mathcal{J} \qquad (19)$$

$$\sum_{v=1}^{\nu_r} y_{jrv}^{T} = \beta_{jr} \qquad \forall r \in \mathcal{R}, j \in \hat{\mathcal{J}}_r \qquad (20)$$

$$C_{jh} - C_{jh}^{\text{init}} = \Delta_{jh}^{+} - \Delta_{jh}^{-} \qquad \forall j \in \mathcal{J}^{\text{init}}, h \in \mathcal{G}_j \qquad (21)$$

$$C_{\max} \geq C_{ijH}^{M} \qquad \forall j \in \mathcal{J}, i \in \mathcal{E}_{jH}^{M} \qquad (22)$$

The objective function (1) is a linear combination of (i) the makespan at the last stage, (ii) machine assignment deviation penalty, (iii) transporter deviation penalty, and (iv) completion time deviation penalty from the given initial schedule. Constraints (2) are for assigning each job to only one eligible machine at each stage that the job is processed on. Constraints (3) and (4) impose a precedence relationship for two jobs assigned to the same machine. Constraints (5)–(7) establish immediate precedence relationships among the jobs assigned to the same transporter. Constraints (8) are for assigning each job to only one eligible transporter. Constraints (9) restrict a job on the same machine to start later than preceding jobs. Constraints (10) tell that a job's starting time at the next stage is greater than the completion time of the previous stage plus the transportation time. Constraints (11) imply that if two jobs are assigned to the same transporter, the succeeding job's starting time is greater than the completion time of preceding job plus the sequence-dependent relocation time. Constraints (12)–(14) restrict a job to be processed within the assigned machine's available interval for each stage. Constraints (15)–(17) define the completion time and starting time of each job at the stages it is processed by. Constraints (18)–(20) imply that the transportation of each job should be processed within the selected transporter's available interval. Constraints (21) define the completion time deviation of previously existing jobs. Constraints (22) define makespan.

3   Results

To evaluate the performance of the proposed MIP, we design an experiment on randomly created instances: small and large. Details for each instance are summarized by Table 1.

Table 1. Experiment parameters

Parameters	Small	Large
The number of stages (H)	3	5
The number of jobs ($|\mathcal{J}|$)	$U(5, 10)$	$U(15, 20)$
The number of transporters ($|\mathcal{R}|$)	3	5
The number of machines in each stage ($[\mathcal{M}_h]$)	[1,2,1]	[2,3,3,2,2]
The number of available intervals (μ_{ih}, ν_r)	$U(1,3), U(1,2)$	$U(1,4), U(1,3)$
The probability that a job skips a stage[†]	20%	30%
The probability that a job is eligible (M,T)[††]	80%, 70%	70%, 65%
Processing time at an eligible machine (p_{ijh})	$\tilde{U}(3,8)$	$\tilde{U}(3,8)$
Transportation time between two stages (τ_{jh})	$\tilde{U}(5,10)$	$\tilde{U}(5,10)$
Relocation time between two jobs ($l_{jj'r}$)[*]	$\tilde{U}(10,20)$	$\tilde{U}(10,20)$
Length of an available interval (M,T)	$\tilde{U}(18,48), \tilde{U}(50,100)$	$\tilde{U}(30,80), \tilde{U}(70,140)$
Length between two available intervals (M,T)	$\tilde{U}(9,24), \tilde{U}(25,50)$	$\tilde{U}(15,40), \tilde{U}(35,70)$

(Abbreviation) M: related to machines, T: related to transporters
(Note) U is a discrete uniform distribution and $\tilde{U} \sim 10 \cdot U$
[†] Jobs do not skip the first and the last stage
[††] Jobs forcefully have eligibility to one random machine at each stage they pass through and one random transporter; eligibility to the others is determined with probability
[*] Relocation time is symmetric (i.e., $l_{jj'r} = l_{j'jr} \ \forall j, j' \in \mathcal{J}^2_{\neq}, r \in \mathcal{E}^T_{\{j,j'\}}$)

Experiments code is implemented by Python MIP package, and we use Gurobi solver ver.9.5.1. We use a desktop computer with Windows 10 OS, AMD Ryzen 9 3900X CPU, and 64GB RAM.

Since our MIP is a rescheduling model, an initial schedule is required. We set $J^{\text{init}} = \emptyset$ and apply the same MIP. We set 3600s seconds as a time limit of an MIP and find initial schedules of instances with objective coefficients $\pi = (1, 0, 0, 0)$ so that only the makespan objective is considered in those initial schedules.

We also provide a lower bound to the makespan. Recall that $\hat{q}_{\min}$ and $\hat{l}_{\min}$ are the lower bounds of the total processing time and of the total relocation time of transporters, respectively. Thus, the makespan of multiprocessing transporters preemptively dealing with the minimum required total working time ($\hat{q}_{\min} + \hat{l}_{\min}$) can be a lower bound to the true makespan. We considered transporter availability while computing the lower bound but disregarded detailed operations of machines and transporter eligibility.

Since all small instances (instance 1–10) could be optimally solved within 6 s, we focus on the results of large instances as presented in Table 2. We examine the objective values at three timestamps (60, 600, and 3600s seconds) and compare the optimality gap to the final lower bound improved from the initial preemptive

Table 2. Computational results of initial scheduling for large instances

	60 s		600 s		3,600 s		LB	
Instance	C_{max}	Gap	C_{max}	Gap	C_{max}	Gap	Init	Final
11	201	11.7%	199	10.6%	195	8.3%	167.5	180.0
12	200	17.9%	200	17.9%	199	17.3%	169.6	169.6
13	344	36.0%	288	13.8%	272	7.5%	226.2	253.0
14†	291	0.0%	291	0.0%	291	0.0%	173.6	291.0
15	289	30.2%	284	27.9%	268	20.7%	219.6	222.0
16	295	23.9%	288	21.0%	281	18.1%	226.8	238.0
17†	236	0.0%	236	0.0%	236	0.0%	197.6	236.0
18	252	29.6%	237	21.9%	237	21.9%	194.4	194.4
19	268	27.3%	252	19.7%	243	15.4%	210.6	210.6
20	358	43.0%	331	32.2%	323	29.0%	250.4	250.4
Avg.	273	22.0%	261	16.5%	254	13.8%	203.6	224.5

†The optimality for instance 14(17) was proven within 182(91) seconds.

lower bound. The average optimality gap at 60 s is 22.0%, which is acceptably good for an initial solution, and it could be further improved to be 13.8% at 3600 s.

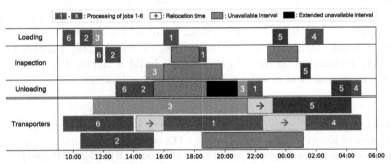

(a) Extended unavailable interval at the last stage (drawn as the black box)

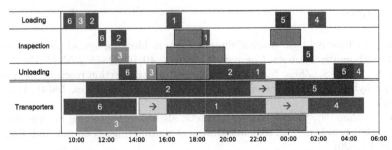

(b) Extended processing time of Job 2 at the last stage

Fig. 2. Rescheduling examples (processing of jobs is labeled by distinct ids and colors)

We demonstrate rescheduling scenarios applied to instance 1 of which the optimal solution from initial scheduling is illustrated in Fig. 1. We consider two scenarios that may happen in practice: (a) extended unavailable intervals of a machine, and (b) extended processing time of an operation. For both scenarios, we set objective coefficients of $\pi = (1, 60, 60, 1)$. All rescheduling problems could be solved within 0.5 s under the same experimental settings to initial scheduling. In Fig. 2(a), due to the extended machine unavailability of 2 h at the last stage, all jobs except Job 1 and 2 are delayed. Nevertheless, every job could be processed without changing resource assignment, which is a desired outcome. In Fig. 2(b), due to the extended processing time of Job 2 by 80 min at the last stage, Job 2 and Job 3 are swapped in machine allocation. All other jobs need not change the resource assignment and could be rescheduled with slight modification of completion times. This is a satisfying result and demonstrates how MIP can effectively handle complicated rescheduling problems.

4   Conclusion

We consider a flexible flow shop rescheduling problem motivated by heavy cargo logistics from manufacturing sites to loading docks. We construct an MIP formulation of the problem, and it finds optimal initial solutions in 6 s for the small problems. Moreover, it finds reasonable initial solutions within 60, 600, and 3600 s with a gap of 22%, 16.5%, and 13.8%, respectively. Moreover, it performs rescheduling in a much shorter amount of time well. We could further develop a model to reduce the current gap for future work. For example, we could propose a heuristic that could work as an initial solution to the MIP. On the other hand, using our problem structure, we could apply parallel machine scheduling techniques to the transporters to build a tighter lower bound. We expect a more practical result by applying these techniques.

Acknowledgements. This paper was supported by the National IT Industry Promotion Agency of Korea (NIPA) funded by the Ministry of Science and Information and Communications Technology of Korea (MSIT). (Grants: S1510-22-1001(001))

References

1. Elmi, A., Topaloglu, S.: A scheduling problem in blocking hybrid flow shop robotic cells with multiple robots. Comput. Oper. Res. **40**(10), 2543–2555 (2013)
2. He, X., Dong, S., Zhao, N.: Research on rush order insertion rescheduling problem under hybrid flow shop based on NSGA-III. Int. J. Prod. Res. **58**(4), 1161–1177 (2020)
3. Lei, C., Zhao, N., Ye, S., Wu, X.: Memetic algorithm for solving flexible flow-shop scheduling problems with dynamic transport waiting times. Comput. Ind. Eng. **139**, 105984 (2020)

4. Pinedo, M.L.: Scheduling: Theory, Algorithms, and Systems, 5th edn. Springer, Cham (2016). https://doi.org/10.1007/978-3-642-46773-8_5
5. Ruiz, R., Vázquez-Rodríguez, J.A.: The hybrid flow shop scheduling problem. Eur. J. Oper. Res. **205**(1), 1–18 (2010)

Monetary Evaluation of Logistical Performance

Tammo Heuer$^{(\boxtimes)}$, Vanessa Teuber, and Peter Nyhuis

Institute of Production Systems and Logistics (IFA), Leibniz University Hannover,
An der Universität 2, 30823 Garbsen, Germany
heuer@ifa.uni-hannover.de

Abstract. Companies can differentiate themselves from competitors through higher logistical performance. It must be valued in monetary terms to realise the advantages of higher logistical performance. According to available information and diverse customer types, different analysis needs to be carried out. In this paper, the unit price potential of a delivery time reduction for customers with stock procurement as an exemplary customer type is modelled for the case of existing customer's process information and analysed based on individual customer-related revenue analysis and thus the logistic operating curves theory. Using storage and procurement models, unit price-delivery time combinations are derived with the same total costs of the customer to deduce the unit price potential of different supplier delivery times. Thus, this model enables supplier to quantify possible unit price increases for lower delivery times for customers with stock procurement.

Keywords: Logistics & distribution networks · Logistical modelling · Logistical performance · Delivery time · Monetary evaluation

1 Introduction

A company has to stand out from its competitors through competitive advantages to succeed in market competition. In addition to high quality and low prices, logistical performance is one way of achieving this [1]. The logistical performance towards the customer consists of the offered delivery time and delivery reliability [2]. In the following, only the delivery time is considered and the delivery reliability is assumed to be constant since the reliability can be regulated by the safety time [3].

Customers are willing to pay higher prices for shorter delivery times [2]. This paper, therefore, deals with the extent to which unit price increases can be achieved by shortening the delivery time. The topic is first placed in the context of the monetary evaluation of logistical performance by describing existing literature approaches in Sect. 2. Then, in Sect. 3, the influence of delivery time on the willingness of customers with stock procurement to pay a certain unit price is logistically modelled based on individual customer-related revenue analysis. The modelling approach and its application via the isocost curve are analysed in Sect. 4. The paper concludes in Sect. 5 with a summary and an outlook on further research activities.

© IFIP International Federation for Information Processing 2022
Published by Springer Nature Switzerland AG 2022
D. Y. Kim et al. (Eds.): APMS 2022, IFIP AICT 663, pp. 494–501, 2022.
https://doi.org/10.1007/978-3-031-16407-1_58

2 Literature Review

When performing unit price analysis for individual customers, a distinction has to be made between customer types. Customers can be divided into two types: consumers and organisational customers [4]. Consumers procure the product for their personal use, so no post-procurement processes need to be considered. The organisational customers procure the products to process them in their own production. For this type of customer, no significant literature analysing the unit price in connection with the delivery time has been published yet.

Organisational customers can be further separated according to their procurement strategy. On the one hand, customers may procure only related to the orders they receive from their customers. In this case, the unit price analysis is complex because, in addition to the influences on the customer's supply chain, the impact on the supply chain of the downstream customer must also be considered. It is necessary because the unit price potential of an enterprise, in this case, also directly includes the unit price potential of the customer. On the other hand, the customer may use stock procurement. This procurement strategy decouples the procurement and the downstream processes. Therefore, a unit price analysis can be carried out detached from further influences of the downstream processes and customers through logistical modelling of the customer's procurement and storing processes.

Schönherr shows four different methods for the monetary evaluation of logistical performance. The choice of the appropriate method depends on the available information. A primary distinction is made between process information and potential information (see Fig. 1) [5].

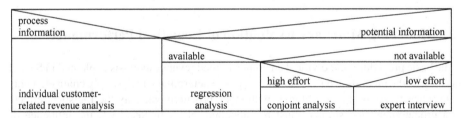

Fig. 1. Classification of methods for the monetary evaluation of logistical performance [5]

Potential information is generally accessible information related to a market or a market segment. If this information is available, it can be analysed using regression analysis regarding the monetary value of the logistical performance. In this process, available data are mapped by a mathematical function and the quality of this mapping is evaluated [6]. Data can be collected through surveys or observations if no potential information is available. Conjoint analyses and expert interviews are used in this case.

The conjoint analysis is an individual analysis in which the market's reaction is concluded based on individual respondents. Product variants with different characteristics, such as unit price-delivery time combinations, are presented to rank them. The resulting total value can be used to conclude the partial value of the individual features. [7] In the expert interview, experts must be able to make well-founded statements about the customers' needs based on experience and knowledge. Expert interviews are always subjective and can only be confirmed with difficulty by models. [8]

If process information is available, the logistical performance can be monetarily evaluated with the help of individual customer-related revenue analysis. As explained in the following paragraph, the customer's supply chain is modelled and thus the customer's cost reduction is quantified in case of a change in the supplier's logistical performance. From the cost reduction, it can be derived by how much the unit price can be increased that the customer has unchanged total costs. The analysis is based on the logistic operating curves theory [9], in which relevant elements of the customer's supply chain are modelled. The impact on the system is investigated through targeted variation of individual parameters. The procedure can be divided into four steps. [5]

In the first step, the primary conditions of the evaluation model are defined. For this purpose, the customer's supply chain is roughly structured and relevant elements are identified. These elements determine the logistic operating curve required for the analysis. In the second step, necessary data for the selected elements, such as the production data for the production operating curve, are selected. Ideally, the customer allows access to all data and missing values can be calculated. If this is not the case, data must be estimated from available industry sector averages or empirical values. The quality of the data directly impacts the validity of the analysis. The logistic operating curves for the current state are then modelled in step three (for further information, see [9]). In the final step, the parameters affected by the change in logistical performance are varied and their corresponding characteristic curves are modelled. By comparing these curve with the current curve, the effect of the change can be identified and the resulting unit price potential determined. [5] With the individual customer-related revenue analysis, precise statements about the unit price potential can be derived if a valid database is available.

3 Modelling Monetary Evaluation of Logistical Performance

The basic procedure of individual customer-related revenue analysis explained in Sect. 2 is used as the modelling basis. The first step is to determine which supply chain elements are relevant. Assuming a customer with stock procurement, only the logistical effects on procurement and storage must be modelled. Next, in Sect. 3.1, the influence of the delivery time on the unit price is modelled as a variable to be influenced by the manufacturing company. Following the possible unit price increases are concluded in Sect. 3.2, which can be used to deduct an isocost curve.

3.1 Modelling of Procurement Cost Components

The cumulative total costs incurred in procurement of one product within a reference period C are made up of purchasing costs CP, material costs CM and stock costs CS.

$$C = CP + CM + CS \tag{1}$$

In the following, it is assumed that fixed order costs CO are generated for each procurement transaction, which represents the administration and transport costs. The purchasing costs CP are then the product of the order costs CO and the number of orders in the reference period. The number of orders itself results from the demand in the reference period DMD and the cost-optimal storage input quantity QIN_{opt}. [10]

$$CP = \frac{DMD}{QIN_{opt}} \cdot CO \tag{2}$$

With help of lot-sizing models, cost-optimal storage input quantity QIN_{opt} can be determined as a function of the order costs CO, the demand in the reference period DMD, the unit costs CU and the stock cost rate i. Order lot sizes can be calculated analogously to optimal production lot sizes, according to Andler and Harris [10–12].

$$QIN_{opt} = \sqrt{\frac{2*CO*DMD}{CU*i}} \tag{3}$$

To calculate the material costs CM, the unit costs CU are multiplied by the demand in the reference period DMD.

$$CM = CU * DMD \tag{4}$$

The stock costs CS, according to Andler and Harris, depend on the mean stock level SL_m, the unit costs CU and the stock cost rate i. The stock cost rate includes the interest for the fixed capital, the maintenance and administration costs of the storage, the risk and venture costs as well as the maintenance costs of the building and technology for storage [11, 12].

$$CS = SL_m*CU*i \tag{5}$$

Stock operating curves help to position strategically between the mean stock level SL_m and the service level $SERL$ that describes the proportion of demand that can be met by the storage level over time. Input variables are the mean order quantity, which here corresponds to the optimal storage input quantity QIN_{opt}, the desired service level $SERL$, the minimum safety-stock level SSL_{min} and the function parameter c_L of the storage operating curve. The function parameter determines the deviation of the function from the ideal state [9, 13]. $c_L = 0,31$ is used as a standard value [14].

$$SL_m = \frac{QIN_{opt}}{2} * SERL^2 + SSL_{min} * \sqrt[c_L]{1 - (1 - SERL)^{c_L}} \tag{6}$$

The safety-stock level SSL_{min} reflects process uncertainties and results from the maximum positive lateness L^+_{max}, the mean demand rate RD_m, the maximum demand rate RD_{max} and the replenishment time [9]. It is assumed that delivery quantity deviations can be compensated as part of the following order. From the customer's point of view, the replenishment time is equivalent to the offered delivery time TD [15].

$$SSL_{min} = \sqrt{\left(L^+_{max} * RD_m\right)^2 + ((RD_{max} - RD_m)*TD)^2} \tag{7}$$

3.2 Deriving Enforceable Unit Price Increases

The cumulative total costs of the customer's procurement of one product within a reference period as a function of delivery time and unit price can thus be calculated by inserting Formula 2–7 into Formula 1:

$$C(TD, CU) = \frac{DMD}{\sqrt{\frac{2*CO*DMD}{CU*i}}}*CO + CU*DMD + \frac{1}{2}*\sqrt{\frac{2*CO*DMD}{CU*i}}*SERL^2*CU*i$$
$$+\sqrt{\left(L_{max}^{+}*RD_m\right)^2 + ((RD_{max} - RD_m)*TD)^2} \cdot \sqrt[cL]{1 - (1 - SERL)^{cL}}*CU*i$$

(8)

From Formula 8, a unit price CU can be determined that the producing company can enforce in the case of delivery time reductions without the customer experiencing increased total costs. Assuming that the customer's total costs remain the same, the unit price CU_2 is calculated as a function of the previous delivery time TD_1, the previous unit price CU_1 and the new delivery time TD_2 examined as follows. The mathematical derivation can be found in the appendix.

$$CU_2(TD_2, TD_1, CU_1) = \left[\frac{-1}{2} \frac{(SERL^2+1)*\sqrt{\frac{CO*DMD*i}{2}}}{\sqrt{\left(L_{max}^{+}*RD_m\right)^2+((RD_{max}-RD_m)*TD_2)^2}* \sqrt[cL]{1-(1-SERL)^{cL}*i}+DMD} \right.$$
$$+\left(\left(\frac{1}{2} \frac{(SERL^2+1)\cdot\sqrt{\frac{CO\cdot DMD\cdot i}{2}}}{\sqrt{\left(L_{max}^{+}*RD_m\right)^2+((RD_{max}-RD_m)*TD_2)^2}* \sqrt[cL]{1-(1-SERL)^{cL}*i}+DMD}\right)^2\right.$$
$$+\frac{(SERL^2+1)*\sqrt{\frac{CO*DMD*i}{2}}*\sqrt{CU_1}}{\sqrt{\left(L_{max}^{+}*RD_m\right)^2+((RD_{max}-RD_m)*TD_2)^2}* \sqrt[cL]{1-(1-SERL)^{cL}*i}+DMD}$$
$$+\left.\left.\frac{\left(\sqrt{\left(L_{max}^{+}*RD_m\right)^2+((RD_{max}-RD_m)*TD_1)^2}* \sqrt[cL]{1-(1-SERL)^{cL}*i}+DMD\right)*CU_1}{\sqrt{\left(L_{max}^{+}*RD_m\right)^2+((RD_{max}-RD_m)*TD_2)^2}* \sqrt[cL]{1-(1-SERL)^{cL}*i}+DMD}\right)^{\frac{1}{2}}\right]^2$$

(9)

4 Analysing the Monetary Evaluation of Logistical Performance

Users are to be supported in selecting attractive unit price-delivery time combinations with the available database and the developed modelling. For this purpose, isocost curves can also be derived from formula 8. For the discrete total cost levels of the customer, they represent the curves of unit price-delivery time combinations between which the customer is indifferent (see Fig. 2). From a unit price-delivery time combination (CU_1, TD_1), an isocost curve ICC_A can be derived. This isocost curve can thus be used to easily determine other unit price-delivery time combinations that the customer would accept under the assumptions made since his total costs would remain unchanged. ICC_B is an equivalent isocost curve with a higher total cost basis. In the example chosen here, with a fictitious dataset, a delivery time reduction from 13 to 7 days results in an increase in the unit price of 0.05€ that can be implemented.

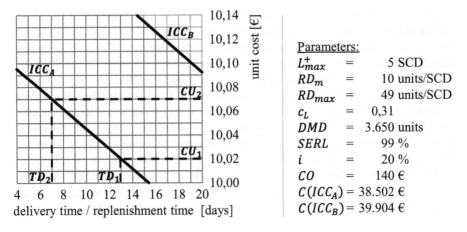

Fig. 2. Determination of unit price-delivery time combinations using isocost curves

A sensitivity analysis of the isocost curve was used to examine the influences of the parameters on the unit price potential. The ratio of unit price and the delivery time does not change, if there is a parallel shift of the isocost curve, as in the case of a change in the order cost CO or the maximum demand rate RD_{max}. An influence on the descent of the isocost curve is the relevant impact in this context, as a change in the relative unit price potential occurs. An increase in the stock cost rate i or the mean demand rate RD_m also marginally increases the descent of the isocost curve, allowing minimal rising unit costs if the reduction in delivery time remains the same. An increase in demand in the reference period DMD leads to a decreasing descent of the isocost curve. The influence of the service level $SERL$ is particularly noticeable. The service level reduction results in an apparent flattening of the isocost curve; at a service level below 35%, a unit price increase can no longer be achieved by reducing the delivery time.

5   Conclusion

According to the available information, different approaches can evaluate logistical performance monetarily. If potential information is available, the individual customer-related revenue analysis can be used through logistical modelling to quantify customers' cost savings with stock procurement concerning a reduction in delivery time. Using iso-cost curves, suppliers can determine which unit price growth would be enforceable at which delivery times for the customer in a cost-neutral manner. The resulting unit price potential depends on the available information, the influence of which was investigated by the sensitivity analysis. In particular, service level $SERL$ has a strong influence on the potential. However, the supplier must consider that they may not be able to negotiate the total unit price growth as assumed in this paper. The cost saving would be split between the supplier and the customer within the negotiation.

Suppose companies can also determine the additional costs for reducing delivery times. In that case, the isocost curves can also be used for revenue-maximising positioning of the delivery time. Therefore, there is a need for research to quantify the costs arising from delivery time reductions. Different order processing strategies can also be considered. For example, when choosing the order processing strategy, it must be considered that a make-to-stock production or a shift of the customer order decoupling point can also enforce a potential growth of the unit prices.

The modelled influence of delivery time on customers' willingness to pay a certain unit price for a reduced delivery time seems relatively low compared to descriptions in the literature (e.g. [2]). However, the high willingness to pay is due to a differing customer classification. In these cases, the high willingness to pay results from situations in which time-critical demands occur in the event of incorrect planning rejects or short-term customer orders. Since these demands are not decoupled, companies in these situations are forced to pay a high price premium to their suppliers to prioritise and fast-track their orders. Further research is therefore needed into the model-based quantification of unit price potential when the customer's production is not decoupled by stock.

Appendix

Using the Power Rule for Exponents, Formula 8 can be simplified as follows:

$$
\begin{aligned}
C = &\left(\sqrt{\left(L^+_{max} + RD_m\right)^2 + ((RD_{max} - RD_m)*TD)^2} * \sqrt[C_L]{1 - (1 - SERL)^{C_L}} * \right. \\
&\left. i + DMD\right)*CU + \left(SERL^2 + 1\right)*\sqrt{\frac{CO*DMD*i}{2}} * \sqrt{CU}
\end{aligned}
\tag{10}
$$

With the following substitutions A and B Formula 10 can be modified to Formula 11:

$$
C(CU, TD) = A*\sqrt{CU} + B(TD)*CU
\tag{11}
$$

$$
A = \left(SERL^2 + 1\right)*\sqrt{\frac{CO*DMD*i}{2}}
\tag{12}
$$

$$
\begin{aligned}
B(TD) = &\sqrt{\left(L^+_{max} + RD_m\right)^2 + ((RD_{max} - RD_m)*TD)^2} * \\
&\sqrt[C_L]{1 - (1 - SERL)^{C_L}} * i + DMD
\end{aligned}
\tag{13}
$$

Equating $C_1(TD_1, CU_1)$ and $C_2(TD_2, CU_2)$ according to Formula 8 using Formula 11 with the substitutions A and B results in:

$$
A*\sqrt{CU_1} + B(TD_1)*CU_1 = A*\sqrt{CU_2} + B(TD_2)*CU_2
\tag{14}
$$

Zeroing Formula 14 in Formula 15 offers the basis for the Quadratic Formula usage that results in Formula 16. The subtraction in Formula 16 can be mathematically excluded. Therefore, Formula 17 quantifies CU_2 as follows:

$$
CU_2 + \frac{A}{B(TD_2)}*\sqrt{CU_2} - \frac{A*\sqrt{CU_1} + B(TD_1)*CU_1}{B(TD_2)} = 0
\tag{15}
$$

$$
\sqrt{CU_2} = \frac{-1}{2}\frac{A}{B(TD_2)} \mp \sqrt{\left(\frac{1}{2}\frac{A}{B(TD_2)}\right)^2 + \frac{A*\sqrt{CU_1} + B(TD_1)*CU_1}{B(TD_2)}}
\tag{16}
$$

$$CU_2(TD_2, TD_1, CU_1) = \left[\frac{-1}{2} \frac{A}{B(TD_2)} + \sqrt{\left(\frac{1}{2} \frac{A}{B(TD_2)} \right)^2 + \frac{A*\sqrt{CU_1} + B(TD_1)*CU_1}{B(TD_2)}} \right]^2 \quad (17)$$

By resubstituting A and B, $CU_2(TD_2, TD_1, CU_1)$ follows according to Formula 9.

References

1. Wiendahl, H.-P., Reichardt, J., Nyhuis, P.: Handbook Factory Planning and Design. Springer, Berlin (2015). https://doi.org/10.1007/978-3-662-46391-8
2. Lödding, H.: Handbook of Manufacturing Control. Springer, Heidelberg (2013). https://doi.org/10.1007/978-3-642-24458-2
3. Schmidt, M., Bertsch, S., Nyhuis, P.: Schedule compliance operating curves and their application in designing the supply chain of a metal producer. Prod. Plan. Control **25**, 123–133 (2014). https://doi.org/10.1080/09537287.2013.782947
4. Homburg, C.: Grundlagen des Marketingmanagements. Springer, Wiesbaden (2020). https://doi.org/10.1007/978-3-658-13654-3
5. Schönherr, M.: Wertorientiertes Logistikmanagement. Springer, Wiesbaden (2016). https://doi.org/10.1007/978-3-658-11671-2
6. Bingham, N.H.: Regression: Linear models in statistics. Springer, Heidelberg (2010). https://doi.org/10.1007/978-1-84882-969-5
7. Breidert, C.: Estimation of Willingness-to-Pay. Springer, Wiesbaden (2007). https://doi.org/10.1007/978-3-8350-9244-0
8. Backhaus, K., Erichson, B., Gensler, S. et al.: Multivariate Analysis: An Application-Oriented Introduction. Springer, Wiesbaden (2021). https://doi.org/10.1007/978-3-658-32589-3
9. Nyhuis, P., Wiendahl, H.-P.: Fundamentals of Production Logistics. Springer, Heidelberg (2009). https://doi.org/10.1007/978-3-540-34211-3
10. Wriggers, F.: Bewertung strategischer Beschaffungsmaßnahmen. Berichte aus dem IFA, 2010, Vol. 02. TEWISS-Verlag, Garbsen (2010)
11. Andler, K.: Rationalisierung der Fabrikation und optimale Losgröße, Reprint 2019. De Gruyter Oldenbourg, Berlin (1929)
12. Harris, F.W.: How many parts to make at once, factory. Mag. Manag. **10**, 152 (1913)
13. Lutz, S.: Kennliniengestütztes Lagermanagement. Fortschritt-Berichte, no. 53. VDI-Verlag, Düsseldorf (2002)
14. Becker, J.: Dynamisches kennliniengestütztes Bestandsmanagement. Berichte aus dem IFA, 2016, vol. 08. TEWISS-Verlag, Hannover (2016)
15. Wagner, G.R.: Lieferzeitpolitik. Springer, Wiesbaden (1975). https://doi.org/10.1007/978-3-663-05205-0

A Survey of Digital Supply Chain Twins' Implementations

Kristine Joy Dy, Jessica Olivares-Aguila$^{(\boxtimes)}$ [ID], and Alejandro Vital-Soto [ID]

Shannon School of Business, Cape Breton University, Sydney, NS B1P 6L2, Canada
{CBU20HXJ,jessica_olivares,alejandro_vital}@cbu.ca

Abstract. This paper examines the implementations of digital twins (DTs) in the context of supply chains (SCs) and disruption risks. The concept of a digital supply chain twin (DSCT) has been a trending topic in recent years, but very little of the literature deals with case studies and actual applications. Therefore, this study concentrates on reviewing the implementations of DSCTs. Moreover, disruption risks associated with the current pandemic have encouraged the adoption of DSCTs to improve SC resilience and agility. For those reasons, this study analyzes the literature according to different industry sectors' implementations (e.g., food, aerospace and automotive, construction, pharmaceutical, and general manufacturing industries). Additionally, literature concentrated on applications for SC risks is studied. This literature review unveils the current developments of DSCTs in the specific industries covered and risks applications. Hence, this work is intended to help SC practitioners and researchers identify challenges and potential research areas for DSCTs.

Keywords: Supply chain · Digital twin · Disruption risks · Literature review

1 Introduction

Supply chains (SCs) are intricate networks that represent the backbone of economies globally. Hence, paralysis in the SC escalates into paralysis of the broader economy. Disruption risks are unforeseen events triggered by incidents such as natural and human-made catastrophes, which lead to disorderly flow within the SC. Uncertainty is difficult to eradicate; hence, awareness and preparedness are imperative to overcoming and quickly recovering from disruption risks (i.e., SC resiliency) [1].

A digital supply chain twin (DSCT) is a virtual replica that represents the network state for any given time to simulate the behaviour of their real counterparts [2, 3]. The combination of a triad – simulation modelling, optimization, and data analytics - comprised the necessary technologies to design a DSCT model. DSCTs allow end-to-end SC visibility to improve resilience and test contingency plans. Implementation of DSCTs will allow for continuous feedback between the cyber and physical systems, which ultimately could help design more efficient SC processes. At the same time, DSCTs will improve the ability to collect real-time data across the SC. Although the

© IFIP International Federation for Information Processing 2022
Published by Springer Nature Switzerland AG 2022
D. Y. Kim et al. (Eds.): APMS 2022, IFIP AICT 663, pp. 502–509, 2022.
https://doi.org/10.1007/978-3-031-16407-1_59

digital twin market size is expected to reach 48.2 billion by 2026 [4], there are a few documented DSCT implementations.

While several literature surveys are available related to DSCTs, they do not concentrate on studying applications for specific industry sectors and SC disruption risks. Therefore, this study fills this gap in the literature.

This article is organized as follows. In Sect. 2, the search methodology is described. Section 3 organizes the available literature according to the different sectors in which DSCTs have been implemented and applications for disruption risks. Section 4 discusses the findings and concludes with future research avenues.

2 Methodology

The search was performed on January 4th, 2022, using the SCOPUS database. Due to space constraints, only journal articles containing the keywords (supply AND chain AND digital AND twin) in the title, abstract, or keywords were selected. The search resulted in 82 articles that were read and classified as frameworks, case studies and real-life implementations. Due to space limitations, only articles related to the scope of the study are included.

3 State-of-the-Art of DSCTs

In this section, the body of literature on DSCTs is classified into two main categories: industry sectors and DSCTs for disruption risks.

3.1 Industrial Sectors

In the literature, there have been several implementations of DSCTs; these applications were grouped according to the sector recurrency.

Food Industry Applications. Over the years, advancements in technology have improved and increased food production, variety, and even global trade. However, food systems are still faced with the growing population, food waste, traceability, and sustainability. The vulnerability of food SCs was also exposed by the COVID-19 pandemic [5]. DTs were considered a promising approach to addressing the many challenges in the food industry [5]. Most of the available research (e.g., [6–9]) in this sector was focused on DTs' applications to the SC transportation function to monitor changes in the quality of fresh produce (biochemical response) using sensors to adapt cooling temperatures throughout the cold chain. Therefore, DTs are a valuable tool to enhance refrigeration and logistics to prevent food wastage, resulting in a greener refrigerated SC [7].

Opportunities for cost reduction during product development using the cyber twin-based model [10] and utilization of artificial intelligence (AI) in the farming industry [11] are other valuable benefits of DTs in the food industry.

To understand the SC dynamics and behaviour, a DT-based analysis of the impact of COVID-19 disruptions on the resilience of a food retail SC was presented in [12]. Similarly, for the food retail SC, Sharma et al. [13] developed a last-mile distribution system for food and essential goods during a pandemic that does not rely upon in-store customer visits or human employees. They used a Robotic Drive Through System and a robotic simulation software tool to create a DT of the robotic work-cell, considering real-world constraints and process requirements.

Aerospace and Automotive Industry Applications. The aerospace industry has one of the most stringent requirements for safety compliance. However, the fast-evolving aircraft SC industry also led to the rapid increase in the spare parts that need to be monitored for airworthiness compliance. In [14], a DT application for inventory management is presented. They implemented a blockchain-based system for the traceability and trackability of aircraft spare parts from original equipment manufacturers throughout the SC. Also, a DT conceptual framework to analyze the creation of a DT for additive manufacturing using blockchain, allowing retracing a component's history faster and in unaltered manner, was proposed in [15].

For the automotive industry, Lugaresi and Matta [16] recommended a method for discovering production system structures and automatically developing digital models starting from the manufacturing systems' event logs. The model was tested in two test cases and one real-life implementation in the automatic assembly line of electric motor vehicles. The study's findings revealed that the model could generate a real-time detailed digital model of the physical counterpart at any time within one minute. In the same way, Sharma et al. [17] proposed to automate and standardize the battery assembly line of electric vehicles using robotic simulation software to create a DT model of the robotic work-cell.

Marmolejo-Saucedo [18] developed a DT that studied the combined vehicle routing and bin-packing problems. These problems were solved by implementing a hybrid optimization-simulation framework. A hypothetical case of an automotive parts manufacturing center in Mexico was developed to verify the proposed DT performance.

Construction Industry Applications. Unlike other sectors, the application of DTs in the construction industry remains ill-defined, without a solid foundation for designing infrastructure [19]. Several studies provided some DSCT applications within this sector. Collectively, these studies outlined the critical role of the Building Information Model (BIM), which was considered the core technology of DTs for construction.

Sacks et al. [19] proposed a data-driven planning and control workflow for designing and constructing infrastructures using DTs. Similarly, Al-Saeed et al. [20] developed a framework to automate the construction manufacturing procedures. A case study was done within a construction product manufacturer located in the UK. That research showed that BIM Digital Objects (BDO) could be a catalyst to automate the processes and workflows, gain financial savings, and reduce material wastage. Lee and Lee [21] also provided a DT framework to simulate and coordinate logistics scenarios and predict accurate delivery in the modular construction industry, which usually operates in just-in-time delivery. That framework created a real-time virtual replica of the modules based on BIM. A geographic system information-based routing application was then used to simulate various logistic scenarios using the virtual replica in real-time.

Greif et al. [22] described the digital silo twin that monitors and tracks the silos' fill level used to store construction bulk materials. The tracking and monitoring capability was possible by installing sensors in the silo. Shifting from a traditional to a smart silo system, it should ideally be cost-effective, safe, and with an integrated system.

Pharmaceutical Industry Applications. In [23], a case study was analyzed on a sterile drug product manufacturing line of the Roche Diagnostics GmbH in Germany to reduce lead-time through improved scheduling while predicting and quantifying the risks during delivery. The result demonstrated the potential of DSCTs in this industry. A DSCT application to forecast several what-if scenarios when facing a disruptive event in the pharmaceutical industry was presented in [24]. A combination of facility location models and dynamic simulation techniques were recommended to aid in the SC's mid- and short-term decision-making. For DT trackability and traceability, the usage of blockchain was suggested in [25]. They analyzed a case study for a pharmaceutical SC.

General Manufacturing Industry Applications. A considerable amount of literature has been published on the applications of DTs in the SC manufacturing industry. DTs are becoming an integral part of a product, asset, and infrastructure operation to achieve a sustainable manufacturing SC [26]. A case study in household appliances manufacturing in China described how enterprises could utilize DTs to promote and shift to a sustainable business model [27]. Applications of DTs are also beneficial to solving information asymmetries problems and accurately optimizing the purchasing and transportation processes of the remanufacturing industry [28]. Advancement in technology also contributes to shortened product life cycles resulting in waste management issues. Tozanliet al. [29] proposed a DT-based simulated product-recovery system for trade-in policymaking to improve reverse logistics and remanufacturing operations in electronics manufacturing.

DTs have been used to optimize the (re)design and process of the drilling operation of printed circuit boards to reduce the manufacturing time [30]. Similarly, Martin et al. [31] demonstrated the significance of DTs in reducing the required time and resources in the design and development of LED luminaires. The project experimented through a case study between a small and medium-sized enterprise (SME) and a large company wherein a method for creating a LED DT using different simulation software and modelling tools was developed. Frankó et al. [32] highlighted the significance of DTs in developing reliable, low-cost, and scalable solutions for asset tracking in less automated environments such as mid-scale manufacturing and warehousing sites.

In make-to-order manufacturing (MTO), a DT-centric architectural framework was proposed for a cyber-physical logistics and production system to provide SC control technical functionalities [33]. Moreover, a simulation and supervised machine learning model for resilient supplier selection in MTO was conceptualized [3]. The study revealed that a DSCT could predict a more reliable on-time delivery of suppliers.

The creation of a blockchain-powered DT was proposed in [34] to cover the entire data flow going from the machine or parcel parameter tracking to the operator monitoring dashboard. The model was tested on two manufacturing SC scenarios - internal (robotized warehouse and transportation) and external logistic (shipment condition monitoring and goods value real-time modification).

Open SC management was proposed in [35]. Using smart designing software and smart manufacturing machines, customers access customized products through DT technology, integrated networks, and smart devices. They implemented the concept of the open SC paradigm in the apparel industry.

3.2 DSCT for Disruption Risks and Resilience

In recent years, there has been an increasing interest in the design and implementation of DTs when managing SC disruption risks. Collaborative intelligent technologies such as cloud manufacturing, IoT, blockchain, data analytics, and DTs can help the manufacturing industry be resilient and viable when facing major disruptions. A Reconfigurable SC or the X-network, which exhibits some crucial design and control characteristics for SC adaptation to ever-changing environments, was proposed in [36].

In [2], a generic structure of a DSCT for managing disruption risks was proposed. At the early stage of SC design and pre-disruption, the model will visualize the potential SC risks, including disruption. In the dynamic mode, the model will use real-time data to simulate the SC disruptions impacts. Disruptions caused by long-term crises such as the pandemic urged businesses and the research community to engage in SC stress testing to examine resilience and viability [37]. Therefore, the current COVID-19 pandemic has highlighted the importance of DSCTs in analyzing the system performance. An off-line DT was developed in [38] to analyze the pandemic's impacts and potential recovery paths on a global SC with upstream facilities in China. Similarly, a DT to predict the impacts of the pandemic was presented in [39]. The DT simulation and optimization can help predict both short- and long-term effects of epidemic outbreaks on the SC [39]. In the same vein, Burgos and Ivanov [12] developed a DT-based analysis of the impact of COVID-19 disruptions on the resilience of a food retail SC with the use of simulation and optimization software.

A DSCT to forecast several what-if scenarios when facing a disruptive event was presented in [24]. DSCTs provide a breakthrough in implementing an interconnected SC structure so that managers can digitally link all the members to get the benefits of increased SC visibility, develop contingency plans, and identify and manage threads in networked SC. Thus, SMEs can benefit from DSCTs by increasing visibility across the SC and predicting risks during disruptions [40].

4   Discussion and Closing Remarks

Although DSCTs have been a trending topic in recent years, most articles concentrate on providing frameworks. Only a small portion of the literature deals with case studies and even a smaller fraction with actual implementations. These studies are paving the way for broader adoption. However, there are still many opportunities and challenges to be addressed. Through the review, several insights have been unveiled:

- DTs have been sparsely implemented for the different SCs functions (e.g., procurement, logistics, distribution, retail)
- Most implementations focus on an asset-centric perspective (e.g., hyper-connected objects and virtual representation). However, an SC-led perspective to enhance sensing and adjusting capabilities of the SC environment is scarcely studied
- The multi-structural composition of SC networks and the implications for the DSCT need to be addressed (e.g., organizational, financial, informational changes)
- Although DTs require on- and off-line interaction between the physical and digital world, a small fraction of studies consider it

- In the food industry, there is a risk of DTs neglecting real-world systems (farms, fields, animals) as it is easier to make decisions on the virtual system
- DSCTs are mainly applied in the manufacturing sectors. However, DT implementations in the service sector are still missing (e.g., healthcare industry)
- While DSCTs offer planning and controlling capabilities at the tactical/operational level, the advantages on the strategic decision-making level to provide business intelligence and enhance the business ecosystem need to be further exploited
- SCs include organizations of different sizes. However, there are many challenges in devising and integrating DSCTs for SMEs
- Closed-loop SC, sustainability, and circular economy objectives can be achieved using DSCTs capabilities
- The current pandemic has boosted the adoption of DTs. Combined with SC risk management, they will allow preparedness and recovery for such events. Therefore, boosting SC resilience and agility
- While there is a variety of commercial software, most of the few DSCT implementations have been devised with anyLogistix software

This literature review will be instrumental for SC practitioners and researchers that would like to know about the DSCTs' advancements in the studied industries and disruption risks. Future research should concentrate on real-case implementations, capitalize on real data to improve the DTs' fidelity and combine technologies such as blockchain to provide more secure data transfer.

References

1. Olivares-Aguila, J., Vital-Soto, A.: Supply chain resilience roadmaps for major disruptions. Logistics **5**(4), 78 (2021). https://doi.org/10.3390/logistics5040078
2. Ivanov, D., Dolgui, A.: A digital supply chain twin for managing the disruption risks and resilience in the era of Industry 4.0. Prod. Plan. Control **32**(9), 775–788 (2021). https://doi.org/10.1080/09537287.2020.1768450
3. Cavalcante, I.M., Frazzon, E.M., Forcellini, F.A., Ivanov, D.: A supervised machine learning approach to data-driven simulation of resilient supplier selection in digital manufacturing. Int. J. Inf. Manag. **49**, 86–97 (2019). https://doi.org/10.1016/j.ijinfomgt.2019.03.004
4. Digital Twin Market - Global Forecast to 2026. https://www.marketsandmarkets.com/
5. Henrichs, E., Noack, T., Piedrahita, A.M.P., Salem, M.A., Stolz, J., Krupitzer, C.: Can a byte improve our bite? an analysis of digital twins in the food industry. Sensors **22**(1), 115 (2022)
6. Shoji, K., Schudel, S., Onwude, D., Shrivastava, C., Defraeye, T.: Mapping the postharvest life of imported fruits from packhouse to retail stores using physics-based digital twins. Res. Cons. Recycl. **176**, 105914 (2022). https://doi.org/10.1016/j.resconrec.2021.105914
7. Defraeye, T., et al.: Digital twins probe into food cooling and biochemical quality changes for reducing losses in refrigerated supply chains. Res. Cons. Recycl. **149**, 778–794 (2019). https://doi.org/10.1016/j.resconrec.2019.06.002
8. Defraeye, T., et al.: Digital twins are coming: will we need them in supply chains of fresh horticultural produce? Trends Food Sci. Technol. **109**, 245–258 (2021)
9. Tagliavini, G., Defraeye, T., Carmeliet, J.: Multiphysics modeling of convective cooling of non-spherical, multi-material fruit to unveil its quality evolution throughout the cold chain. Food Bioprod. Process. **117**, 310–320 (2019). https://doi.org/10.1016/j.fbp.2019.07.013

10. Bamunuarachchi, D., Georgakopoulos, D., Banerjee, A., Jayaraman, P.P.: Digital twins supporting efficient digital industrial transformation. Sensors **21**(20), 6829 (2021)
11. Smith, M.J.: Getting value from artificial intelligence in agriculture. Anim. Prod. Sci. **60**(1), 46–54 (2019). https://doi.org/10.1071/AN18522
12. Burgos, D., Ivanov, D.: Food retail supply chain resilience and the COVID-19 pandemic: a digital twin-based impact analysis and improvement directions. Transp. Res. Part E: Logist. Transp. Rev. **152**, 102412 (2021). https://doi.org/10.1016/j.tre.2021.102412
13. Sharma, A., Zanotti, P., Musunur, L.P.: Drive through robotics: robotic automation for last mile distribution of food and essentials during pandemics. IEEE Access **8**, 127190–127219 (2020). https://doi.org/10.1109/ACCESS.2020.3007064
14. Ho, G.T.S., Tang, Y.M., Tsang, K.Y., Tang, V., Chau, K.Y.: A blockchain-based system to enhance aircraft parts traceability and trackability for inventory management. Expert Syst. Appl. **179**, 115101 (2021). https://doi.org/10.1016/j.eswa.2021.115101
15. Mandolla, C., Petruzzelli, A.M., Percoco, G., Urbinati, A.: Building a digital twin for additive manufacturing through the exploitation of blockchain: a case analysis of the aircraft industry. Comput. Ind. **109**, 134–152 (2019). https://doi.org/10.1016/j.compind.2019.04.011
16. Lugaresi, G., Matta, A.: Automated manufacturing system discovery and digital twin generation. J. Manuf. Syst. **59**, 51–66 (2021)
17. Sharma, A., Zanotti, P., Musunur, L.P.: Enabling the electric future of mobility: robotic automation for electric vehicle battery assembly. IEEE Access **7**, 170961–170991 (2019)
18. Marmolejo-Saucedo, J.A.: Digital twin framework for large-scale optimization problems in supply chains: a case of packing problem. Mob. Netw. Appl. (2021)
19. Sacks, R., Brilakis, I., Pikas, E., Xie, H.S., Girolami, M.: Construction with digital twin information systems. Data-Centric Eng. **1**(6) (2020). https://doi.org/10.1017/dce.2020.16
20. Al-Saeed, Y., Edwards, D.J., Scaysbrook, S.: Automating construction manufacturing procedures using BIM digital objects (BDOs): Case study of knowledge transfer partnership project in UK. Constr. Innov. **20**(3), 345–377 (2020)
21. Lee, D., Lee, S.: Digital twin for supply chain coordination in modular construction. Appl. Sci. (Switzerland) **11**(13), 5909 (2021). https://doi.org/10.3390/app11135909
22. Greif, T., Stein, N., Flath, C.M.: Peeking into the void: digital twins for construction site logistics. Comput. Ind. **121**, 103264 (2020). https://doi.org/10.1016/j.compind.2020.103264
23. Spindler, J., Kec, T., Ley, T.: Lead-time and risk reduction assessment of a sterile drug product manufacturing line using simulation. Comput. Chem. Eng, **152**, 107401 (2021). https://doi.org/10.1016/j.compchemeng.2021.107401
24. Marmolejo-Saucedo, J.A.: Design and development of digital twins: a case study in supply chains. Mobile Netw. Appl. **25**(6), 2141–2160 (2020). https://doi.org/10.1007/s11036-020-01557-9
25. Alles, M., Gray, G.L.: "The first mile problem": deriving an endogenous demand for auditing in blockchain-based business processes. Int. J. Account. Inf. Syst. **38**, 100465 (2020). https://doi.org/10.1016/j.accinf.2020.100465
26. Kamble, S.S., Gunasekaran, A., Parekh, H., Mani, V., Belhadi, A., Sharma, R.: Digital twin for sustainable manufacturing supply chains: current trends, future perspectives, and an implementation framework. Technol. Forecast. Soc. Change **176**, 12144 (2022)
27. Li, X., Cao, J., Liu, Z., Luo, X.: Sustainable business model based on digital twin platform network: the inspiration from Haier's case study in China. Sustainability (Switzerland) **12**(3), 1–26 (2020). https://doi.org/10.3390/su12030936
28. Chen, Z., Huang, L.: Digital twins for information-sharing in remanufacturing supply chain: a review. Energy **220**, 119712 (2021). https://doi.org/10.1016/j.energy.2020.119712
29. Tozanli, O., Kongar, E., Gupta, S.M.: Evaluation of waste electronic product trade-in strategies in predictive twin disassembly systems in the era of blockchain. Sustainability (Switzerland) **12**(13), 5416 (2020). https://doi.org/10.3390/su12135416

30. Balderas, D., Ortiz, A., Méndez, E., Ponce, P., Molina, A.: Empowering digital twin for industry 4.0 using metaheuristic optimization algorithms: case study PCB drilling optimization. Int. J. Adv. Manuf. Technol. **113**(5–6), 1295–1306 (2021). https://doi.org/10.1007/s00170-021-06649-8

31. Martin, G., et al.: Luminaire digital design flow with multi-domain digital twins of LEDs. Energies **12**(12), 2389 (2019)

32. Frankó, A., Vida, G., Varga, P.: Reliable identification schemes for asset and production tracking in industry 4.0. Sensors (Switzerland) **20**(13), 1–24 (2020). https://doi.org/10.3390/s20133709

33. Park, K.T., Son, Y.H., Noh, S.D.: The architectural framework of a cyber physical logistics system for digital-twin-based supply chain control. Int. J. Prod. Res. **59**, 1–22 (2020). https://doi.org/10.1080/00207543.2020.1788738

34. Mazzei, D., et al.: A Blockchain Tokenizer for Industrial IOT trustless applications. Future Gener. Comput. Syst. **105**, 432–445 (2020). https://doi.org/10.1016/j.future.2019.12.020

35. Rahmanzadeh S., Pishvaee, M.S., Govindan K.: Emergence of open supply chain management: the role of open innovation in the future smart industry using digital twin network. Ann. Oper. Res. (2022). https://doi.org/10.1007/s10479-021-04254-2

36. Dolgui, A., Ivanov, D., Sokolov, B.: Reconfigurable supply chain: the X-network. Int. J. Prod. Res. **58**(13), 4138–4163 (2020). https://doi.org/10.1080/00207543.2020.1774679

37. Ivanov, D., Dolgui, A.: Stress testing supply chains and creating viable ecosystems. Oper. Manag. Res. (2021). https://doi.org/10.1007/s12063-021-00194-z

38. Ivanov, D., Das, A.: Coronavirus (COVID-19/SARS-CoV-2) and supply chain resilience: a research note. Int. J. Integr. Supply Manag. **13**(1), 90–102 (2020). https://doi.org/10.1504/IJISM.2020.107780

39. Ivanov, D.: Predicting the impacts of epidemic outbreaks on global supply chains: a simulation-based analysis on the coronavirus outbreak (COVID-19/SARS-CoV-2) case. Transp. Res. Part E: Logist. Transp. Rev. **136**, 101922 (2020). https://doi.org/10.1016/j.tre.2020.101922

40. Nasir, S.B., Ahmed, T., Karmaker, C.L., Ali, S.M., Paul, S.K., Majumdar, A.: Supply chain viability in the context of COVID-19 pandemic in small and medium-sized enterprises: implications for sustainable development goals. J. Enterp. Inf. Manag. **35**, 100–124 (2021)

Multi-period Shelter Location-Allocation Problem with Network and Location Vulnerabilities for the Response Phase of Disaster Management

Sweety Hansuwa[1,2(✉)], Usha Mohan[1], and Viswanath Kumar Ganesan[2]

[1] Department of Management Studies, Indian Institute of Technology, Madras, Chennai, India
sweetyhansuwaiitb@gmail.com
[2] Tata Consultancy Services, IITM Research Park, Chennai, India

Abstract. Natural disasters and man-made calamities are a significant threat in many geographical locations worldwide. The administrative mechanism must plan and ensure the safety as well-being of the humans and other living creatures (or other essential resources) by being prepared during the disaster. This work presents a multi-period shelter location and allocation model that determines when and where to open shelters on the planning horizon. In our work, we define location and network vulnerabilities to measure the impact of a disaster in each geography. We use these vulnerabilities to formulate a Mixed Integer Linear Programming Model (MILP) for the shelter location and allocation problem. We present an extended linear relaxation heuristic and solve the problem using the real-life case data obtained from the major flooding event in and around the Chennai Metropolitan Development Area.

Keywords: Multi-period allocation problem · Shelter location problem · MILP

1 Introduction

The beginning of the year 2022 witnessed around 67 natural disasters. According to the Emergency events database (EM-DAT) statistics, there were 9080 natural disasters from 2001 to 2022. Hence, it is essential for governments worldwide to plan relief operations and effectively manage these disasters in the best possible way. This paper examines two critical dimensions of the relief operations, i.e., shelter (or depot) location selection and allocation of people (or/and other essentials) to safe locations. In our study, we attempt to answer the following questions:

1. Can we design and develop mathematical formulations as multi-period models for real-life disaster relief operations?
2. Can we develop scalable solutions that can quickly solve larger practical instances and provide quality solutions?

© IFIP International Federation for Information Processing 2022
Published by Springer Nature Switzerland AG 2022
D. Y. Kim et al. (Eds.): APMS 2022, IFIP AICT 663, pp. 510–517, 2022.
https://doi.org/10.1007/978-3-031-16407-1_60

The answers to the above questions are demonstrated in this work by formulating the problem as a MILP Model for the multi-period shelter location-allocation problem considering the impact of the disaster as network and location vulnerabilities with the objectives of minimizing unmet demand and the traveling cost. We consider the multiple periods to capture the real-life decision during a rolling horizon approach. That helps in the decision-making process in disaster management. We propose an extended linear relaxation heuristic (ELRH) to solve the problem on real-life case data obtained from the major flooding event in the latter part of 2015 in and around the Chennai Metropolitan Development Area.

2 Literature Review

The shelter location problem has been studied in the literature to provide safer places for evacuees, humanitarian relief operations, medical facilities, inventory management, etc. Shelters (or depots) during the disaster are typically selected among government schools, community halls, public places, etc., that are safe and less vulnerable to the impact of a disaster. Amideo et al. [1] present a review of disaster management using OR and evaluate the shelter location and evacuation routing problems in disaster response. Duhamel et al. [2] discuss the multi-period location-allocation model movement of the affected population assigned to a safer place during the response phase to maximize the assistance to the affected people. Vahdani et al. [7] discuss the multi-period location-routing model for relief distribution while considering the situation of roads after a disaster. Hansuwa et al. [3] formulate the shelter location-allocation problem considering the vulnerabilities of the demand locations and their network connectivities for disaster management's preparedness and response phase. They propose a linear relaxation heuristic (LRH) and compare the heuristic performance with the scenario-based formulation. In this paper, we further extend the work on the shelter location-allocation problem with multiple periods and consider location and network vulnerabilities for the response phase of a disaster. We present an extended LRH to solve the large-scale problems and demonstrate the performance of the heuristic using real-life data.

3 Multi-period Shelter Location-Allocation Problem

This section presents the problem description, assumptions, and the mixed-integer linear programming (MILP) formulation for the multi-period shelter location-allocation (MPSLA) problem for the response phase of disaster management, along with the descriptions of parameters.

Indices

i	the index for affected locations
j	the index for shelter locations
k	the index for capacity levels of shelters
t	the index for time periods

Sets

I	the set of affected locations
J	the set of shelter locations
K	the set of capacity levels of shelter
T	the set of time period level of planning horizon

Parameters

γ_i	the penalty cost on unmet demand at location i
$c_{j,k}$	the capacity of a shelter j at capacity k
$f_{j,k}$	the fixed cost of opening a shelter j at capacity k
$\theta_{i,j}$	the cost of travel/km between location i to shelter j
$d_{i,j}$	the distance between location i to shelter j before disaster
$d'_{i,j}$	the distance between location i to shelter j after disaster
ϑ_i^t	the vulnerability at location i in the time period t, i.e. $\vartheta_i^t \in [0,1]$
b_i^t	the number of affected people at location i in the time period t
$V_{i,j}^t$	the network vulnerability between location i to shelter j in the time period t
B	the total budget
M	a big positive number

Shelter location-allocation (SLA) problems select a safer place for evacuees and assign them to the nearest location. Earlier studies to our understanding solve the SLA problem without considering multiple periods and vulnerabilities of the geographies. In this work, we attempt to address this research gap by considering multiple periods in the planning horizon and using both location and network vulnerabilities. The location or network vulnerabilities may not remain the same as during a disaster. The location vulnerability is defined at four levels for our study based on the Greater Chennai Corporation Report [4]. This work defines network vulnerability based on the definition presented by Gu et al. [5]. Gu et al. [5] discuss the topology-based efficiency indices (TEI) between two points i and j for a network by Eq. 1. We compute the network vulnerability ($V(i,j)$) among locations in terms of the topology-based efficiency indices as discussed in the following Eq. 2.

$$TEI = \frac{1}{|N|\,(|N|-1)} \frac{\sum_{i \neq j \in N}\left(\frac{1}{d_{i,j}} - \frac{1}{d'_{i,j}}\right)}{\sum_{i \neq j \in N}\left(\frac{1}{d_{i,j}}\right)} \tag{1}$$

$$V(i,j) = \frac{1}{2} \frac{\sum_{i \neq j \in N}\left(d'_{i,j} - d_{i,j}\right)}{\sum_{i \neq j \in N}\left(d'_{i,j}\right)} \quad \forall i \in I, \forall j \in J \tag{2}$$

The following is the list of assumptions for our problem definition.

1. A set of susceptible locations and their respective vulnerabilities are available for each period before the start of the response phase of a disaster.
2. A set of shelters with location definitions and their available capacities (in terms of the number of people) with the associated one-time fixed cost of opening the shelters are known.

3. A set of connectivities between various locations and the shelter locations are known and the network vulnerabilities are computed using Eq. 2 for different periods.
4. The shelters are available and can be opened during all time periods. The closure of shelters is not considered in the scope of the model.
5. The number of people to be evacuated from each vulnerable inhabited location is known.
6. The total budget available to open and operate the shelters at various locations is pre-defined.

3.1   Multi-period Shelter Location-Allocation Formulation

This section presents the MPSLA formulation.
    Decision variables

$x_{j,k}^t$ is equal to 1 if shelter j with capacity k in the time period t is open, 0 otherwise
$y_{i,j}^t$ is equal to 1 if location i is assigned to shelter j in the time period t, 0 otherwise
$z_{i,j}^t$ a fraction of demand at location i assigned to shelter j in the time period t
w_i^t the unmet demand at location i in the time period t
$\beta_{i,j}^t$ the cost of travel between location i to shelter j in the time period t

The objective function present in the Eq. 3. The first term minimizes transportation costs that depend on the distance and the network's vulnerability between locations i and j in the planning horizon. The second term minimizes the total penalty cost on unmet demands while considering the vulnerability levels of the demand locations. The penalty cost is increased by $(1+\vartheta_i^t)$ with a level of vulnerability of the demand location. Thus, we define the objective function as:

$$minimize \sum_{t \in T} \sum_{i \in I} \sum_{j \in J} \beta_{i,j}^t + \sum_{t \in T} \sum_{i \in I} \gamma_i \times (1 + \vartheta_i^t) \times w_i^t \qquad (3)$$

subject to the constraints presented in Eqs. 4 to 15.
Constraint 4 ensures only one capacity level is selected when a shelter is opened.

$$\sum_{k \in K} x_{j,k}^t \leq 1 \quad \forall j, \forall t \qquad (4)$$

Constraint 5 ensures that once a shelter opens on the planning horizon, it should remain open for successive periods.

$$\sum_{k \in K} x_{j,k}^t \geq \sum_{k \in K} x_{j,k}^{t-1} \quad \forall j, t = 2, .., |T| \qquad (5)$$

Constraint 6 ensures the total cost of opening a shelter should be less than the entire budget available.

$$\sum_{t \in T} \sum_{j \in J} \sum_{k \in K} f_{j,k} \times x_{j,k}^t \leq B \qquad (6)$$

Constraint 7 ensures each demand location should be allocated to exactly one shelter.

$$\sum_{j \in J} y_{i,j}^t = 1 \quad \forall i, \forall t \tag{7}$$

Constraint 8 ensures that the demand location's assignment to shelter only if it is open.

$$y_{i,j}^t \leq \sum_{k \in K} x_{j,k}^t \quad \forall i, \forall j, \forall t \tag{8}$$

Constraint 9 ensures that the demand of the number of people to evacuate should be satisfied.

$$\sum_{j \in J} z_{i,j}^t + w_i^t = b_i^t + w_i^{t-1} \quad \forall i, \forall t \tag{9}$$

Constraint 10 ensures the initial unmet demand is assumed to be zero.

$$w_i^0 = 0 \quad \forall i \tag{10}$$

Constraint 11 ensures the allocation of demand to the shelter only if it is open.

$$z_{i,j}^t \leq M \times y_{i,j}^t \quad \forall i, \forall j, \forall t \tag{11}$$

Constraint 12 ensures the total evacuated people allocated to the shelter should be less than the shelter's total capacity.

$$\sum_{i \in I} z_{i,j}^t \leq \sum_{k \in K} c_{j,k} \times x_{j,k}^t \quad \forall j, \forall t \tag{12}$$

Constraint 13 computes the worst case scenario while computing the cost of transportation if location i is allocated to shelter j while considering the vulnerability of the network between location i to shelter j. The vulnerability of the network increases the additional cost of transportation by $(1 + V_{i,j}^t)$.

$$\beta_{i,j}^t \geq \theta_{i,j} \times d_{i,j} \times (1 + V_{i,j}^t) - M \times (1 - y_{i,j}^t) \quad \forall i, \forall j, \forall t \tag{13}$$

$$w_i^t \geq 0 \quad \beta_{i,j}^t \geq 0 \quad z_{i,j}^t \geq 0 \quad \forall i, \forall j, \forall t \tag{14}$$

$$x_{j,k}^t \in \{0, 1\} \quad y_{i,j}^t \in \{0, 1\} \quad \forall i, \forall j, \forall k, \forall t \tag{15}$$

4   Extended Linear Relaxation Heuristic (ELRH)

The MPSLA formulation presented in the previous section is a NP-hard problem. Several well-known solution methods are available to solve large-scale MILP formulations. Relaxation methods, particularly linear programming relaxations of MILP, are popular methods for solving large-scale problems. This section presents a heuristic approach using linear programming relaxation for the MPSLA formulation to develop a usable and feasible solution. The binary and specific integer variables in the MPSLA formulation are relaxed to linear variables. The proposed approach solves the MPSLA using a mathematical solver by relaxing the binary and specific integer variables in an iterative process. The variables $\overline{x}_{j,k}^t$, $\overline{y}_{i,j}^t$ are defined as linear variables in relaxed MPSLA formulation and solved as a linear programming problem. Subsequently the $\overline{x}_{j,k}^t$ values are rounded off to the nearest integer, either 1 or 0, when the values of $\overline{x}_{j,k}^t$ It is greater than or less than 0.5, respectively, by considering locations starting with lower fixed cost values for opening the shelter and selecting the locations with the next higher fixed costs. The preset values of shelter location selection variables are used as input to the original two-stage stochastic model by setting $\overline{\overline{x}}_{j,k}^t = 1$, when the $\overline{x}_{j,k}^t > 0.5$ and otherwise, we set $\overline{\overline{x}}_{j,k}^t = 0$. The solver is terminated when the optimality gap between the best MPSLA model bound and the objective function value falls below 10%. The pseudo-code present in Table 1.

Table 1. Extended linear relaxation heuristic

Extended linear relaxation heuristic	
Step 1	Solve the linear relaxation of the MPSLA model (define all binary decision variables as linear variables) and let the output be defined as a solution represented using $(\overline{x}_{j,k}^t, \overline{y}_{i,j}^t)$
Step 2	Define the $\overline{\overline{x}}_{j,k}^t$ values as 0 or 1 ($\overline{x}_{j,k}^t$, is greater than or less than 0.5 respectively) using the output from relaxed MPSLA formulation
	Step 2.1 Sort all the shelter locations in ascending order of budgetary values for all $\overline{x}_{j,k}^t > 0.5$
	Step 2.2 Check the feasibility of constraint (6) by incrementally including each new shelter location from the above-sorted list, and the included shelter locations variables are set as 1
	Step 2.3 The new representation of the set binary variables is defined as $\overline{\overline{x}}_{j,k}^t = 1$ when $\overline{x}_{j,k}^t > 0.5$ otherwise $\overline{\overline{x}}_{j,k}^t = 0$
Step 3	The MPSLA formulation is solved again with the constraints 4–13, and the constraint (16) by using the predefined values of $\overline{\overline{x}}_{j,k}^t$ from Step 2.3
	$x_{j,k}^t \geq \overline{\overline{x}}_{j,k}^t \qquad \forall i, \forall j, \forall k \qquad (16)$
Step 4	Terminate the solver and print the solution when the optimality gap falls below less than 10%

5   Case Study: Chennai Flood 2015

The performance of the ELRH is evaluated using real-life instances obtained during the major flooding event in and around the Chennai Metropolitan Development Area in 2015. CPLEX OPL 12.8 has been used to solve the relaxation of the proposed MILP model in ELRH. The input parameters are population size in the inhabited locations, the vulnerability of locations, vulnerability between inhabited locations and the shelter locations, and the distance between them.

5.1 Data of Chennai Flood 2015

The data used in our experimental study is taken from Greater Chennai Corporation (GCC, 2018) [4]. The number of shelters opened was 176 during the 2015 floods in Chennai, and more than 1.2 lakhs of people were evacuated and accommodated in these shelters for more than 20 days (GCC, 2018 [4]). We have selected 172 shelters (and data were not available for four shelters) with defined capacities given in the source and 184 inhabited locations as demand locations representing inhabited areas for our study. The shelter capacities in terms of the number of people and the fixed cost are defined similarly for our use case as represented in Cap_61 instance of [6]. The data generation for our use cases is defined for a planning horizon of 2 days by considering the flood a natural disaster. The first 48 h (2 days) are crucial during a disaster. The parameter values for the model are taken from the data sets obtained during the Chennai floods of 2015. The demand values are assumed as given for the first day and are reduced by 20% for the second day. We assume that the impact of disaster is more on the initial day and decreases in the following days due to relief operations. We compute the distance based on the network sampling algorithm as discussed by [3].

5.2 Budgets

In our model, we have defined budgets that will capture a monetary value available with the administrative mechanism to effectively plan the deployment of resources during the response phase of a disaster. Hence we define the budgetary spend as a one-time opening cost in our data set. We have generated five scenarios for various budgetary values. We are taking the cost to open the first capacity level of shelter from the Cap_61 instance of [6]. We have assumed that the cost of opening a shelter doubles when the shelter is opened with twice the capacity. We have assumed the three levels of shelter capacities $(c, 2c, 3c)$ where c indicates the capacity and is set a value as 7500. The budgetary levels varied in our experiments from the total cost of opening all the shelters to at least capacity considering 2 days in the planning horizon.

5.3 Computational Results

For our computational study, the number of demand locations(I), the number of shelter locations (J), and the number of periods (T) are 184, 172, and 2 days, respectively. We see that from our experiments in Table 2, the proposed ELRH uses minimal computational effort to get feasible solutions that do not substantially affect the budgetary limits defined for various use cases. The least budget limit is $ 1 million, and the demand satisfied for each level of location's vulnerability is less than 95% for each period. We observe that with the increase in the budget level to $ 3 million, the demand satisfied for across all levels of the location's vulnerability was found to be greater than 99.99%. As the budget levels increased, the demand satisfied was maximum, and the number of shelters used increased to meet the population's relocation needs. The impact of bringing down the budgetary values from $ 3 million to lower values do not significantly increase the computational time of the proposed algorithm except for the first case where the time limit is set to 2 hrs.

Table 2. Experimental results of ELRH

Budget available (in million $)	No of shelters open at varied capacity levels (t = 1)			No of shelters open at varied capacity levels (t = 2)			Demand satisfied (%)		Budget used (in million $)	Objective value	Computa-tional time (s)
	L	M	H	L	M	H	t = 1	t = 2			
1.0	8	21	4	7	20	5	99.99	100	0.9975	261827615.12	7200
1.5	18	22	9	18	18	12	100	100	1.5	6771413.36	663.0
2.0	27	30	12	23	28	13	100	100	1.995	4738844.35	282.45
2.5	36	45	11	25	41	14	100	100	2.4975	3865419.22	120.56
3.0	36	59	12	30	56	14	100	100	3.0	3480247.23	161.33

Lowest: L; Medium: M; High: H

6   Conclusion

This study presents a MILP model for the MPSLA problem, and a linear relaxation heuristic is proposed to solve the problem. The formulation and proposed heuristic have been solved using real-life case data obtained during the major flooding event in and around the Chennai Metropolitan Development Area in 2015. We can extend the current research by considering stochastic aspects of the MPSLA problem and exploring the use of metaheuristics and other solution approaches.

References

1. Amideo, A.E., Scaparra, M.P., Kotiadis, K.: Optimising shelter location and evacuation routing operations: the critical issues. Eur. J. Oper. Res. **279**(2), 279–295 (2019)
2. Duhamel, C., Santos, A.C., Brasil, D., Châtelet, E., Birregah, B.: Connecting a population dynamic model with a multi-period location-allocation problem for post-disaster relief operations. Ann. Oper. Res. **247**(2), 693–713 (2016). https://doi.org/10.1007/s10479-015-2104-1
3. Hansuwa, S., Mohan, U., Ganesan, V.K.: Scenario-based stochastic shelter location-allocation problem with vulnerabilities for disaster relief network design. Eur. J. Ind. Eng. (2022). in press, Accepted Manuscript
4. Greater-Chennai-Corporation. Disaster management plan (2018). https://chennaicorporation.gov.in
5. Gu, Y., Fu, X., Liu, Z., Xu, X., Chen, A.: Performance of transportation network under perturbations: reliability, vulnerability, and resilience. Transp. Res. Part E: Logist. Transp. Rev. **133**, 1–16 (2020)
6. Mostajabdaveh, M., Gutjahr, W.J., Sibel Salman, F.: Inequity-averse shelter location for disaster preparedness. IISE Trans. **51**(8), 809–829 (2019)
7. Vahdani, B., Veysmoradi, D., Shekari, N., Mousavi, S.M.: Multi-objective, multi-period location-routing model to distribute relief after earthquake by considering emergency roadway repair. Neural Comput. Appl. **30**(3), 835–854 (2016). https://doi.org/10.1007/s00521-016-2696-7

Modelling Interdependencies Within Production Planning and Control: An Application-Motivated Approach

Alexander Mütze[1]([mail])[iD], Simon Hillnhagen[2][iD], Matthias Schmidt[2][iD], and Peter Nyhuis[1][iD]

[1] Institute of Production Systems and Logistics, Leibniz University Hannover, Garbsen, Germany
{muetze,office}@ifa.uni-hannover.de

[2] Institute of Product and Process Innovation, Leuphana University Lüneburg, Lüneburg, Germany
{simon.hillnhagen,matthias.schmidt}@leuphana.de

Abstract. In literature on the investigation of cause-effect relationships within production planning and control (PPC), many models and approaches can be found. These range from the didactic description of cause-effect relationships to generally applicable models for describing the effects and impacts of a procedure selection or parameterisation for a PPC task to be fulfilled, right up to explorative simulation studies. Thus, research in the field of production planning and control can be roughly divided into the research areas of conceptual, analytical, empirical and simulation-based investigations.

While each of these approaches makes valuable contributions to prevailing theory, the purpose of this paper is to discuss an application-motivated approach making the complex network of interrelations within PPC easier to penetrate. Because, in particular from the point of view of the practical user, it is of crucial importance to gain a holistic perspective on the relationships and interdependencies within PPC in order to be able to configure it - as well as the entire production system - in the best possible way and in line with the company's objectives. Thus this contribution can be assigned as a conceptual investigation.

Keywords: Production planning and control · Modelling · Production management · Production organisation · PPC

1 Introduction

Several studies show that in industrial practice, there is still a lack of understanding of the concrete impact of PPC tasks and procedures on the logistical

Funded by Deutsche Forschungsgemeinschaft (DFG) - 434659386.

objectives [1,4,19]. At the same time, however, the acceptance of automated PPC solutions, i.e. solutions that in principle relieve the user of the need to understand the complex interdependencies within PPC, is relatively low [1]. Also, market analyses show that the majority of respondents are not satisfied with the process and organisation of their production planning (system) and indicate that the most common problem lies in maintaining a high degree of schedule compliance [4]. The question that arises is thus how the organisation and the process, or overall the configuration of the entire PPC, can be improved to achieve the market goals and ensure the company's profitability.

To tackle this question, there are generalised two points of view on the overarching topic of PPC and production organisation. While one stream tries to increase further the system understanding concerning processes and interactions by building models to describe processes, principals and interrelationships based on knowledge and (physical) relationships (also referred to as white-box modelling), the other stream, more or less assumes that further research in the field of system understanding is more of a dead-end and focus their research activities on topics such as digital twins, AI algorithms, and others (also referred to as black-box modelling) (cf. [5] and [7]).

At this point, this discussion will not be taken up in-depth, but from the authors' point of view, it is crucial to understand which fundamental interactions exist within PPC and how the PPC configuration embeds itself in the overall configuration of production [12]. Thus white-box modelling and in-depth research of fundamental effects are necessary prerequisites for more advanced approaches on the one side, and on the other side, essential for the practical user to gain a clear system understanding.

This contribution is therefore based on the following proposition:

Proposition 1. *Insight must precede application (Max Planck) - A valid understanding of the processes and interactions in PPC is a fundamental prerequisite for both in-depth white-box modelling and the architecture of black-box-based PPC models, algorithms and systems.*

2   Evolution Within the Research Field PPC

Production planning and control has been researched for many decades and has been continuously refined [10,13]. Significant milestones have been the more technical models of Material Requirements Planning (I+II) according to ORLICKY [14] respective WIGHT [20], as well as Hierarchical Production Planning (HPP) and Advanced Planning Systems (APS) [9], but also conceptual or descriptive frameworks such as the Aachen PPC model [18], the manufacturing control model according to LÖDDING [6] and the Hanoverian Supply Chain Model (HaSupMo) [17]. The latter is the basis for this contribution due to the integration of the PPC tasks along the internal supply chain with impact modelling along a company's internal supply chain, i.e. generally speaking, a combination of the modelling approach of the Aachen PPC model with the modelling logic according to LÖDDING.

Through this previous work, a large body of knowledge exists covering, among other things, the question of the tasks to be carried out, the interfaces between PPC and core processes as well as system-theoretical questions about the appropriate degree of integration and the planning hierarchy when carrying out the individual tasks. Among others, a profound overview can be found in [12].

Looking further into the current research landscape, several trends can be identified. Thus scheduling in the context of integration of planning tasks appears as one of them [3]. Furthermore, the trends toward a smarter and more reactive PPC and the exploration of the use of machine learning and artificial intelligence (e.g. reinforcement learning [15]) can be identified, which, presumably, will end in an automated PPC (cf. [8]). The influence of the "simplexity" megatrend can thus be seen, which refers to the straightforward, intuitive operability and thus user-friendliness of simultaneously (e.g., technically) complex systems [2].

3   Research Question and Modelling Principles

Although digitisation significantly impacts PPC, the basis for decision-making is always a valid understanding of interrelationships and interactions. This is particularly important for smaller companies, which cannot rely on highly developed digital solutions for PPC because they lack sufficient data basis regarding quality and/or quantity. Therefore, a broad knowledge base remains essential for mastering and improving the production system.

Thus, this paper follows the **central research question**, how a modelling approach can look like, allowing in practical application to get a comprehensive overview of the interactions within PPC and reducing at the same time the high complexity in order to be easily applicable.

In order to be able to describe the interactions within the PPC in the following and to illustrate the approach, a basic description framework has first to be defined, showing which influencing factors and which output factors exist. Particularly in the range of the PPC, in which a multiplicity of complex interactions exist, it is therefore important to use uniform semantics.

For this purpose, the following definition is applied in this article:

Definition 1. *Logistical objectives are determined by control variables, each resulting from the derivation of so-called actuating variables. Actuating variables, in turn, are determined by the PPC tasks, whereby the PPC procedure selected in each case determines the exact influencing effect on the actuating variable. (based loosely on Lödding [6])*

Thus, it can basically be said that the modelling logic starts with a PPC task and moves from the organisational level to the process level via the selected procedure and the influenced actuating variables, control variables and objectives.

To tackle the research question, the following two main modelling views are introduced, followed by the presentation of the developed application-oriented, integrated approach iteratively combining both views.

4   Modelling Views on the Interdependencies Within PPC

Within PPC, a wide variety of interactions exists, both at individual levels (horizontal) and across levels (vertical), making the overall PPC system a complex network of effects and posing an immense challenge to practitioners. Thus, central aspects in modelling are which targets a company pursues, which tasks affect these targets and, if possible, how exactly individual procedures of a task have an effect. Figure 1 illustrates these levels of consideration through a hierarchisation using the production control task sequencing as an example.

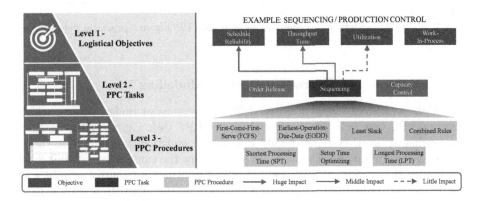

Fig. 1. Levels of consideration towards interactions within PPC (based on [11]).

From a practical point of view, there are generally two central questions or perspectives in the context of PPC modelling and configuration. On the one hand, the question arises how, starting from an unsatisfactory logistical performance, possible levers (PPC procedures and their parametrisation) can be found to counteract this. This viewpoint is referred to in the following as objective-centred (see Fig. 2 left). On the other hand, however, the question can be asked as to what potential the use of a particular PPC procedure has for the logistical achievement of objectives. This viewpoint is referred to as task- and procedure-centred (see Fig. 2 right). Both views are briefly explained in the following.

4.1   The Objective-Centred Modelling View

In the objective-centred modelling view, the focus is clearly on the logistical objectives of the core processes along the company's internal supply chain. This means that the question is posed *via which actuators and which cause-effect relationships a positive or negative effect on the objectives can be achieved*. In industrial practice, the starting point for this is often a poor logistical performance, which is traced back to the variables to be changed, e.g. using a so-called root-cause analysis (cf. [16]), subsequently enabling the target-oriented selection of a PPC procedure.

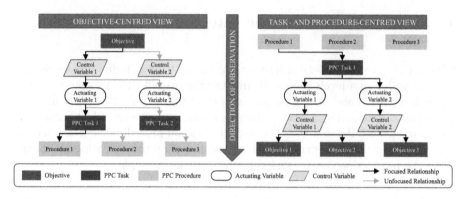

Fig. 2. Views on modelling interdependencies within PPC from a practical perspective.

4.2 The Task- and Procedure-Centred Modelling View

The task- and procedure-centred modelling view aims at understanding which effects a PPC task or a specific procedure of a PPC task, e.g. the setup-optimal sequencing at work systems, finally has on the logistical objectives. As illustrated in Fig. 2 right, it is therefore considered how the cause-effect relationships start from the configured PPC task via the actuating and control variables to the influenced objectives. The central question is, therefore: *How does a PPC task/procedure affect the logistical target achievement?*

5   Integrative Application-Oriented Approach

Considering the two approaches presented, these provide proper results for their respective underlying problem in their "pure form"; however, neither provides a sufficiently comprehensive perspective to support holistic and target-oriented PPC configuration decisions in practice. As indicated in Fig. 2 for the objective-centred view, the direction of investigation and focus exclude possibly important cause-effect relationships from consideration. Thus, the it lacks a loopback from the PPC procedure to be selected to other affected actuating and control variables and objectives. Similarly, for the task- and procedure-centred view, even though the (direct) effect of a PPC procedure on the objectives is examined, no backtracking to possibly similarly acting or indirectly attacked PPC tasks and procedures as well actuating and control variables is conducted.

In order to meet these challenges, different possibilities are conceivable. One option is to develop a comprehensive model that includes all possible interactions between PPC procedures, tasks, actuating and control variables and objectives. A first example of such a model was presented by [12]. Although this offers a comprehensive view, the practitioner has to deal with an extensive network of interactions with the high probability of being unable to handle this complexity.

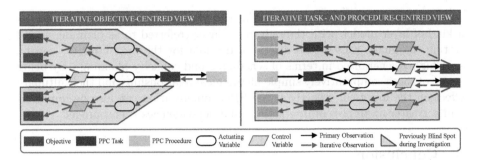

Fig. 3. Integrative application-oriented approach using iterative loopbacks

For this reason, an integrative approach of the two modelling views based on iterative loopbacks is proposed for practical application, as shown in Fig. 3.
As the figure shows, the two modelling views are linked together with a loopback, resulting in two new modes of observation, the iterative object-centred modelling view and the iterative task and procedure-centred view. Through the respective loopback using the prior opposite perspective, a previously existing blind spot of interactions can be included in the observation, whereby the interactions can be considered not only along the ordinal viewing direction but also on the first level of the respective view, resulting in a more comprehensive view. In the iterative objective-centred view, the effect of a possible lever (PPC procedure) on other objectives can be included in the consideration. In the iterative task- and procedure-centred view, there is a loopback to consider possible PPC tasks and procedures that are also affected or have a similar effect on related objectives.

A second essential basis supporting this integrative approach is the knowledge of the hierarchical structure within PPC itself, shown by Fig. 4.

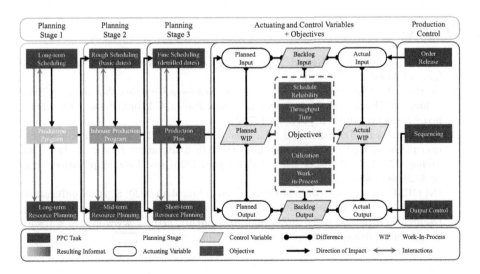

Fig. 4. Planning stages to visualize the hierarchical cause-effect relationships in PPC.

As shown in the figure, the influence of PPC on the objectives can be seen as a kind of layer model, with the outermost layer (referred to as planning stage) setting the guard rails or the degree of freedom for the next layer (as can be seen highly generalised in terms of scheduling and capacity planning). By being aware of these comparatively simple hierarchical relationships and their ultimate effect on the logistical objectives, the PPC configuration can also be improved and a greater awareness of interactions and dependencies is encouraged.

6   Conclusion

The presented, application-oriented integrative approach for modeling interactions within PPC closes the gap of previous, complex models and provides a procedure for the practical user, which allows him to overview the consequences of decisions within the configuration of PPC. By this, it is expected that possible loopbacks, which, e.g. come along with the decision for or against a procedure, are better overlooked and foreseen. Furthermore, the presented approach fits seamlessly into the existing theory for modelling PPC and thus provides a complement to current (frame-) works. By combining the knowledge of the planning stages within PPC, it can also be assumed that better decisions can be made in practice in terms of a holistic and target-oriented PPC configuration.

The presented approach is a conceptual model which has been developed based on various experiences of the authors in industrial practice. A comprehensive evaluation of the approach in practice is currently pending and represents the central limitation of this contribution. However, the approach opens up several possibilities for future research activities: it can be integrated into existing frameworks; also, further research should be done on the simple, practice-oriented PPC configuration, especially to support structural decisions and improve the logistical target achievement of companies.

References

1. Bank, L., et al.: PPS-Report 2021: Studienergebnisse. https://doi.org/10.24406/igcv-n-644067
2. Berthoz, A.: Simplexity: Simplifying Principles for a Complex World. An editions Odile Jacob book, Yale University Press, New Haven, CT, online-ausg edn. (2012). https://doi.org/10.12987/9780300177923
3. Herrmann, J.P., Tackenberg, S., Padoano, E., Gamber, T.: Approaches of production planning and control under industry 4.0: a literature review. J. Ind. Eng. Manag. **15**(1), 4–30 (2022). https://doi.org/10.3926/jiem.3582, http://dx.doi.org/10.3926/jiem.3582
4. INFORM: Trendreport–der maschinen- und anlagenbau 2020: Eine zukunftssichere branche in deutschland? eine umfrage von: Inform institut für operations research und management gmbh juni 2020 (2020). https://www.inform-software.de/produkte/felios/trendreport-maschinenbau

5. Ljung, L.: Black-box models from input-output measurements. In: IMTC 2001. Proceedings of the 18th IEEE Instrumentation and Measurement Technology Conference. Rediscovering Measurement in the Age of Informatics (Cat. No.01CH 37188), pp. 138–146 (2001). https://doi.org/10.1109/IMTC.2001.928802

6. Lödding, H.: Handbook of Manufacturing Control: Fundamentals, Description, Configuration. Springer, Heidelberg (2013). https://doi.org/10.1007/978-3-642-24458-2

7. Loyola-Gonzalez, O.: Black-box vs. white-box: understanding their advantages and weaknesses from a practical point of view. IEEE Access **7**, 154096–154113 (2019). https://doi.org/10.1109/ACCESS.2019.2949286

8. Lucht, T., Drewal, F., Nyhuis, P.: Approaching automation of production planning and control: a theoretical framework. J. Prod. Syst. Logist. **1**(6) (2021). https://doi.org/10.15488/11127

9. Missbauer, H., Uzsoy, R.: Production Planning with Capacitated Resources and Congestion. Springer, New York, NY (2020). https://doi.org/10.1007/978-1-0716-0354-3

10. Mütze, A., Hillnhagen, S., Schäfers, P., Schmidt, M., Nyhuis, P.: Why a systematic investigation of production planning and control procedures is needed for the target-oriented configuration of PPC. In: 2020 IEEE International Conference on Industrial Engineering and Engineering Management (IEEM), pp. 103–107 (2020). https://doi.org/10.1109/IEEM45057.2020.9309885

11. Mütze, A., Lebbing, S., Hillnhagen, S., Schmidt, M., Nyhuis, P.: Modeling interactions and dependencies in production planning and control: an approach for a systematic description. In: von Leipzig, K., Sacks, N., Mc Clelland, M. (eds.) Smart, Sustainable Manufacturing in an Ever-Changing World. Proceedings of the 8th International Conference on Competitive Manufacturing (COMA 2022) (2022)

12. Mütze, A., Lucht, T., Nyhuis, P.: Logistics-oriented production configuration using the example of MRO service providers. IEEE Access **10**, 20328–20344 (2022). https://doi.org/10.1109/ACCESS.2022.3146420

13. Olhager, J.: Evolution of operations planning and control: from production to supply chains. Int. J. Prod. Res. **51**(23–24), 6836–6843 (2013). https://doi.org/10.1080/00207543.2012.761363

14. Orlicky, J.: Material Requirements Planning: The New Way of Life in Production and Inventory Management. McGraw-Hill, New York (1975)

15. Panzer, M., Bender, B., Gronau, N.: Deep reinforcement learning in production planning and control: a systematic literature review. https://doi.org/10.15488/11238

16. Schmidt, M., Maier, J.T., Härtel, L.: Data based root cause analysis for improving logistic key performance indicators of a company's internal supply chain. Procedia CIRP **86**, 276–281 (2019). https://doi.org/10.1016/j.procir.2020.01.023

17. Schmidt, M., Nyhuis, P.: Produktionsplanung und -steuerung im Hannoveraner Lieferkettenmodell. Springer, Berlin, Heidelberg (2021). https://doi.org/10.1007/978-3-662-63897-2

18. Schuh, G., Stich, V.: Produktionsplanung und -steuerung 1: Grundlagen der PPS. SpringerLink Bücher, Springer, Berlin, Heidelberg, 4. aufl. 2012 edn. (2012). https://doi.org/10.1007/978-3-642-25423-9

19. Seitz, M., et al.: PPS-Report 2017/18: Studienergebnisse, Berichte aus dem IFA, vol. 2018. TEWISS, Garbsen (2018)

20. Wight, O.W.: Manufacturing Resource Planning, MRP II: Unlocking America's Productivity Potential. Wiley, New York (1984). rev. ed. edn

Measuring Impacts of Information Sharing on Perishable Product Supply Chain Performance

Natalia Iakymenko[1]([⊠]), Gunrid Kjellmark[2], Daryl Powell[1], and Eivind Reke[1]

[1] SINTEF Manufacturing, S.P. Andersens vei 3, 7031 Trondheim, Norway
natalia.iakymenko@sintef.no
[2] SINTEF Community, S.P. Andersens vei 3, 7031 Trondheim, Norway

Abstract. Information sharing is important for the competitiveness of perishable product supply chains (PPSC). Current research, however, still disagrees if information sharing directly contributes to improved PPSC performance or if it is moderated by other factors. Additionally, few studies measure the impact of information sharing quantitatively. This study addresses these gaps by studying the impacts of information sharing on the performance of ready-mixed concrete supply chains. A single case study was carried out to address the research goal. The data from the case study were analyzed both quantitatively and qualitatively. The results have shown that poor information sharing in PPSC leads to excess waiting times at the ready-mixed concrete factory and at the construction sites. This, in turn, leads to frequent disputes between the two companies regarding the concrete quality.

Keywords: Perishable product supply chain · Information sharing · Ready-mixed concrete

1 Introduction

Information sharing is generally acknowledged as a contributor to organizational and supply chain competitiveness in perishable product industries because supply chain actors need timely and quality information to coordinate intra- and inter-organizational activities [1–3]. There are, however, still some disagreements as to the impact of information sharing on perishable product supply chains (PPSC) performance. Some studies show that although information sharing is essential, it does not necessarily directly lead to improved PPSC performance. Other studies discuss PPSC performance only qualitatively without measuring PPSC performance parameters [2, 3]. Such a perishable product as ready-mixed concrete is not discussed in the PPSC literature—the most studied products are food (vegetables, fruits, meat, etc.) and human blood. Ready-mixed concrete is an extreme example of a perishable product with a shelf life of up to 24 h. Demand for ready-mixed concrete is volatile due to frequent order changes from the contractors. This leads to re-plannings, delivery adjustments, and uncertain waiting times.

© IFIP International Federation for Information Processing 2022
Published by Springer Nature Switzerland AG 2022
D. Y. Kim et al. (Eds.): APMS 2022, IFIP AICT 663, pp. 526–533, 2022.
https://doi.org/10.1007/978-3-031-16407-1_62

Hence, research investigating the impacts of information sharing in the concrete supply chain is needed. The objective of this study is to 1) measure the impacts of information sharing on concrete supply chain performance, 2) understand how information sharing affects the concrete supply chain performance.

This paper is structured as follows. First, we shortly present a theoretical background of information sharing in PPSC. This is followed by the research method and case description. We then present the results. The paper concludes with a discussion, conclusions, and suggestions for future research.

2 Theoretical Background

Perishable products are products whose quality deteriorates over time. They include vegetables, fruits, dairy products, human blood, etc. [4]. Ready-mixed concrete is a perishable product with a very short lifetime. After the concrete is mixed, there are between 1,5 to 24 h or so before it starts to lose its properties. Effective and efficient information sharing between a ready-mixed concrete supplier and a contractor is important to maintain on-time concrete deliveries, high product quality, and avoid waste.

Information sharing in PPSC can be defined as inter-organizational communication or the extent to which critical information is communicated among supply chain partners to improve the ultimate customer satisfaction [2, 6, 7]. Information sharing has been highlighted as an important means of reducing complexity and improving the performance of PPSC [1, 2, 5]. Ferguson and Ketzenberg [1] found that information sharing can reduce uncertainty in demand and supply, significantly improve service levels, decrease inventory levels, lower stockouts, increase product freshness, and greatly reduce product wastage. Shi et al. [8] showed that information sharing in PPSC helps in improving decision-making and minimizing costs across the supply chain.

However, the research is not in total agreement regarding the positive impact of information sharing on PPSC performance. For example, Peng et al. [9, 10] point out that the relationship between information sharing and PPSC performance is influenced by moderating factors that should be further investigated. The latest systematic literature review on PPSC done by Lusiantoro et al. [2] confirms that the relationships between information sharing and PPSC performance are currently unclear.

Given these findings, existing literature calls for more investigation into relationships between information sharing and PPSC performance.

3 Research Method

This study is carried out as a part of the research project aimed at developing solutions for improved on-site concrete casting in terms of time and money spent. This part of the study concentrates on the work of a ready-mixed concrete (RMC) supplier (Company A) and a contractor (Company B). It aims to measure the impacts of information sharing on the concrete deliveries. This requires an in-depth investigation of the fresh concrete deliveries and collection of historical data in the companies, which advocates for the selection of a case methodology [11, 12].

The study was done in two steps. First, quantitative data on concrete deliveries were collected and analysed based on the propositions from Company A. Next, the results of the analysis were discussed with the case companies to get deeper insight into the data analysis results, identify possible contingency factors affecting the results, and validate the results.

Quantitative data include information about each trip of the concrete truck to the construction sites: customer, construction site, concrete quantity, type of concrete, time the order is sent to production, production start and finish, a departure time from the RMC plant, arrival time to the construction site, unloading start and finish times, a departure from the construction site, and arrival to the factory. Company A collected these data with help of GPS, Transport Management System (TMS), tablets, and sensors that can identify when loading and unloading of concrete starts. All data is stored in Excel spreadsheets. To analyze the data, several propositions describing factors that possibly influence concrete deliveries were formulated by the researchers together with Company A. Data analyses were done to test these propositions.

The results of the analysis were then presented to Companies A and B at workshops. Several issues were discussed during the workshops. First, the companies validated the results by pointing out possible mistakes in the data. For example, one of the participants noticed that an unloading time of 1 min is not possible. Consequently, the researchers conducted additional data cleaning to weed out the data errors. Second, the companies provided possible interpretations of the results. Last, the companies discussed how the results of the analysis can be used for improved concrete deliveries in the future.

4 Case Description

The production of RMC starts by blending cement, aggregates such as gravel and sand, and water in a mixer. Ready concrete is then poured into trucks positioned under the mixer. Trucks cycle between the batch plant and construction site until the whole volume of ordered concrete is transported. As the order quantity of concrete is typically larger than the capacity of a single truck, several deliveries need to be scheduled to fulfill an order. The deliveries cannot overlap in time and the time between deliveries should be small.

The work between Companies A and B is challenging. Company B wants to be able to place their orders as close to the delivery time as possible. The timing of the needed delivery often remains uncertain because completion of prerequisite work (reinforcement, concrete forms, etc.) at the site is difficult to forecast reliably. Additionally, the volume of the deliveries is difficult to estimate because the actual site measurements can differ from the measurements based on drawings and plans. On the other hand, Company A tries to time its deliveries so that all projects are served on time. This is further complicated by the RMC properties. RMC is a perishable product and once the water has been added to the mix of dry materials, concrete has several hours until it starts to lose its properties and might jeopardize the strength and stability of the concrete. This leads to frequent disagreements about the timing and quality of the delivered concrete.

5   Results

Below we present the results of the data analysis and the interpretation of the results by the case companies. In total, eleven propositions were tested during the study, but in nine of these propositions, the results were either insignificant or deemed irrelevant for the information sharing. Hence, only two are presented here.

5.1   Time Intervals Between Concrete Deliveries in an Order

The proposition tested was that the time intervals between the last and second last deliveries (t_n in Fig. 1) are different from the time intervals between other deliveries in an order. Company A noticed that time before departure of the last delivery in an order is often longer than the time intervals between previous deliveries in an order.

Figure 1 shows an example of an order which includes six deliveries.

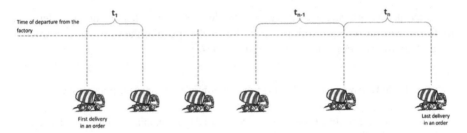

Fig. 1.   Concrete deliveries in a single order and their denotations

In total, 388 orders were analysed. The time between deliveries was calculated as the time between cars leaving Company A's plant. The results of the analysis show that in 268 out of 388 orders, t_n was the longest of all intervals in an order, which corresponds to 69% of orders.

We also analysed how much longer is the waiting time before the last two deliveries (additional waiting time). For the orders where last or second last deliveries are the longest, we calculated the difference between the waiting time before the last delivery (t_n) and the average of the rest of the waiting times in the order ($\mu\,(t_1, t_2 \ldots t_{n-1})$):

$$Additional\ waiting\ time = t_n - \mu(t_1, t_2 \ldots t_{n-1}) \qquad (1)$$

Total additional waiting time for all orders is 166,5 h. This means 166,5 h are spent waiting for the last two deliveries to be shipped to the construction site. It is important to note that administrative time and orders with 3 and less deliveries are not included in our calculations, so waiting time could be higher.

We asked companies to interpret the results. Company A stated that information on the last deliveries are often not known in advance—Company B gives preliminary information that there will be delivery but does not give the precise quantity of the concrete to be delivered, or they might call and ask to change the delivery timing.

Company B stated that they need time to calculate exactly how much concrete they need in the last deliveries—initial calculation might differ from the actual built structure. The timing of the delivery might depend on the setting time of the concrete in previous deliveries.

5.2 Concrete Truck Waiting Times at Different Construction Sites

The proposition tested here was that the concrete trucks waiting times at the construction sites differ depending on the project. Company A noted that they often experience that their trucks spend more time at some construction sites, but they do not know the exact reason why.

The available data on concrete deliveries were divided by project/construction site and average truck waiting times for the different construction sites were calculated:

$$Average\ truck\ waiting\ time\ at\ a\ construction\ site = \frac{\sum Truck\ waiting\ time\ during\ each\ delivery}{Number\ of\ deliveries} \qquad (2)$$

Construction projects with more than 50 deliveries were taken into consideration. Table 1 shows the average waiting times the trucks spend at the different construction sites, standard deviation and number of deliveries.

Table 1. Average truck waiting time for different projects/construction sites

Project #	Average waiting time before unloading at the construction site, min	Standard deviation, min	Number of deliveries
1	2,23	3,89	64
2	5,11	13,65	95
3	3,79	6,24	219
4	2,03	76,73	348
5	4,62	9,53	97
6	2,65	6,98	51
7	4,05	8,57	165
8	3,7	6,54	159
9	4,34	6,95	77
10	6,54	12,45	142
11	2,74	4,24	53
12	4,83	6,58	76
13	3,61	6,59	414
14	4,57	6,88	61

(continued)

Table 1. (*continued*)

Project #	Average waiting time before unloading at the construction site, min	Standard deviation, min	Number of deliveries
15	1,77	3,39	53
16	6,94	16,7	66
17	3,54	7,25	54
18	0,98	2,61	51
19	4,35	6,01	179
20	4,73	8,59	170
21	6,05	8,48	61
22	5,92	9,83	190
23	6,35	13,05	479
24	4,8	8,14	172

The difference in waiting times for different construction sites varies considerably.

Figure 2 shows histogram of waiting time distribution for the analysed construction sites. As we can see, in most occurrences waiting time is between 2,88 and 4,78 min. Even bigger variance is in standard deviations, which can vary from 3 to 77 min. High standard deviations mean that some waiting times at separate construction sites differ considerably from the average at those sites.

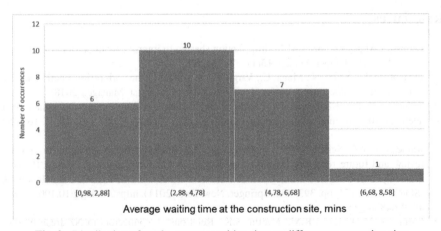

Fig. 2. Distribution of trucks average waiting time at different construction sites

We asked companies to interpret the results. Company B commented that truck waiting time might depend on what is being built (f.eks., several stories apartment building or infrastructure project), as well as the project team, its planning efficiency, and communication between Company A and project teams. Both companies agreed that it would be valuable to conduct in-depth case studies in well-performing projects in order to learn from them. They also agreed that even though performance probably doesn't depend only on information sharing, it is still a big part of it.

6 Discussion and Conclusions

The results have shown negative impacts of poor information sharing on both RMC supplier (Company A) and contractor (Company B). The results have shown that poor information sharing in PPSC leads to excess waiting times at the ready-mixed concrete factory and at the construction sites. Company A is subjected to at least 166 h a year of time waiting to ship the last deliveries in an order. It is also subjected to highly variable waiting times at the construction site, which complicates their production and fleet planning. Due to the uncertainties in delivery precision, both companies are involved in the disputes regarding the product quality and responsibility for the deteriorated product. These findings are in line with previous research showing that information sharing influence PPSC performance. In previous studies, however, PPSC performance was measured in terms of inventory costs, stockouts and product wastage [1, 13]. We add to this research by measuring PPSC in terms of waiting times. For perishable product such as concrete with extremely short shelf life, waiting times are critical.

Finally, our research showed that truck waiting times at the construction sites vary considerably depending on the project/construction site and project team. This is in line with Peng et al. [9, 10] who argue that relationships between information sharing and PPSC performance are affected by moderating factors, and it is difficult to show the direct connection between information sharing and PPSC performance.

References

1. Ferguson, M., Ketzenberg, M.E.: Information sharing to improve retail product freshness of perishables. Prod. Oper. Manag. **15**(1), 57–73 (2006)
2. Lusiantoro, L., Yates, N., Mena, C., Varga, L.: A refined framework of information sharing in perishable product supply chains. Int. J. Phys. Distrib. Logist. Manage. (2018)
3. Wong, C.W., Lai, K., Cheng, T.C.E.: Value of information integration to supply chain management: roles of internal and external contingencies. J. Manag. Inf. Syst. **28**(3), 161–200 (2011)
4. Karaesmen, I.Z., Scheller-Wolf, A., Deniz, B.: Managing perishable and aging inventories: review and future research directions. In: Kempf, K.G., Keskinocak, P., Uzsoy, R. (eds.) Planning Production and Inventories in the Extended Enterprise: A State of the Art Handbook. ISORMS, vol. 151, pp. 393–436. Springer, New York (2011). https://doi.org/10.1007/978-1-4419-6485-4_15
5. Clements, M.D., Lazo, R.M., Martin, S.K.: Relationship connectors in NZ fresh produce supply chains. Br. Food J. (2008)
6. Mohr, J., Spekman, R.: Characteristics of partnership success: partnership attributes, communication behavior, and conflict resolution techniques. Strateg. Manag. J. **15**(2), 135–152 (1994)
7. Zelbst, P.J., Green, K.W., Sower, V.E., Baker, G.: RFID utilization and information sharing: the impact on supply chain performance. J. Bus. Ind. Mark. (2010)

8. Shi, J., Zhang, J., Qu, X.: Optimizing distribution strategy for perishable foods using RFiD and sensor technologies. J. Bus. Ind. Mark. (2010)
9. Peng, G., Trienekens, J.H.: The Relationship between information exchange benefits and performance: the mediating effect of supply chain compliance in the Chinese poultry chain. Int. Food Agribus. Manage. Rev. 15(4), 28 (2012)
10. Peng, G., Trienekens, J., Omta, S.O., Wang, W.: Configuration of inter-organizational information exchange and the differences between buyers and sellers. Br. Food J. (2014)
11. Eisenhardt, K.M.: Building theories from case study research. Acad. Manag. Rev. 14(4), 532–550 (1989)
12. Yin, R.K.: Case Study Research: Design and Methods. Sage Publications, Thousand Oaks (2013)
13. Ketzenberg, M., Bloemhof, J., Gaukler, G.: Managing perishables with time and temperature history. Prod. Oper. Manag. 24(1), 54–70 (2015)

A Decision Support Tool to Assess the Probability of Meeting Customer Deadlines

Hajar Hilali[(✉)] [ID], Yves Dallery, Zied Jemai [ID], and Evren Sahin [ID]

Paris-Saclay University, Centrale Supélec Laboratoire Génie Industriel, Gif-Sur-Yvette, France
hajar.hilali@centralesupelec.fr

Abstract. This research aims to develop a decision support tool to assess the probability of meeting customer deadlines, while considering the different risks associated with the various links in the supply chain (SC). The work was conducted in collaboration with a leading aeronautical industry. The tool developed enables real-time flow management, i.e. from a system initial state, we can define the delivery date of a product and calculate the on-time delivery (OTD) performance indicator over the horizon of our order book. The tool is composed of three essential components: *i)* input data, which includes data related to the characteristics of the system under study (flow diagram, lead time, cost, capacity) and data related to the risks associated with the system links. *ii)* a discrete event simulation (DES) model reproducing the studied system by integrating the risks to identify the delivery date of each product and *iii)* a performance evaluation tool to calculate the distribution of our performance indicator. A multi-scenario analysis was conducted by varying the different parameters of the system and analysing the impact on our OTD. An illustrative example based on real data was presented to show the interest of the developed tool.

Keywords: Supply chain risk management · DES · Performance evaluation

1 Introduction

Every day, the aeronautical SC faces various challenges. On the one hand, there is the need to meet customer commitments, regardless of the situation. On top of this, there is the complexity of the industrial network, with production spread over several continents and permanent interactivity between the components of the SC. Not to mention the length of lead times, which can reach 24 months. This permanent interactivity and the complexity of the SC increase the possibilities of risks and uncertainties. Risk can be described as the occurrence of an unexpected and undesired event that significantly modifies the characteristics of a system. Such an event leads to significant changes in the characteristics of the demand flow or may result from the unavailability of equipment (due to breakdowns), shortages of supply, human or material resources etc. These risks have a direct impact on performance and customer satisfaction.

The objective of this paper is to develop a novel decision support tool to: *i)* firstly assess the probability of meeting customer deadlines, considering the risks throughout

© IFIP International Federation for Information Processing 2022
Published by Springer Nature Switzerland AG 2022
D. Y. Kim et al. (Eds.): APMS 2022, IFIP AICT 663, pp. 534–542, 2022.
https://doi.org/10.1007/978-3-031-16407-1_63

the SC. *ii)* secondly integrate levers to improve performance and agility despite these risks. After a brief state of the art on supply chain risk management (Sect. 2), we will describe the components of our tool in Sect. 3. Finally, we will present a real case study to illustrate the proposed approach (Sects. 4 and Sect. 5).

2 Literature Review

The Supply Chain Risk Management (SCRM) has received much attention in the literature in the last two decades. According to Ho et al. [1], SCRM aims to use quantitative and qualitative risk management methodologies to identify, assess, mitigate and monitor unexpected events or conditions at both macro and micro levels that might negatively impact any part of a SC. The field of SCRM is growing so fast that so far over 38 review articles have been published in this area. These review articles can be split into three main axes: *(i)* the phases of SCRM which are defined by ISO 31000 [2] in five main processes that are: identification, assessment, management, monitoring and communication (Fan and Stevenson [3]; Ho et al. [1]). *(ii)* tools and techniques whether it is related to qualitative models (Hohenstein et al. [4]) or quantitative models (Fahimnia et al. [5]). *(iii)* other review articles either combined the two previous axes such as Ribeiro and Barbosa-Povoa [6] or focused on a narrow scope e.g., price risk (Fischl et al. [7]). Recently, Oliveira et al. [8] conducted a state of the art on the application of simulation and optimisation methods in SCRM phases as well as their contributions regarding the SCRM phases and the performance measurement system (PMS). The authors also identified a major gap in the literature, which is the lack of a systematic process that combines the phases of SCRM, PMS and simulation and optimisation (S&O) methods. The aim is to better represent the dynamic and the complexity of SCs under the impact of risks. It is within this heading of linking between the phases of SCRM, PMS and S&O methods that our paper fits in. In our paper, we have developed a new decision support tool that connects the SCRM to the S&O methods and to the PMS. The developed tool aims to assess the probability of meeting customer deadlines based on the initial state of the system (stocks and work-in-progress), a flow map with possible alternative schemes and a risk map. The tool has been validated in the case of a real aeronautical SC.

3 Description of the Decision Support Tool

The decision support tool we have developed is composed of three essential elements: *i)* input data, which includes data on the characteristics of the system and data on the risks associated with the links in the system. The second component of our tool is *ii)* a DES model reproducing the system under study to identify the end of production date (including transport) of each product. Finally, we have *iii)* a performance evaluation tool to calculate the distribution of our performance indicators and decide whether the performance obtained is acceptable or not. In this section we focus on the description of the three components of the developed decision support tool described in Fig. 1.

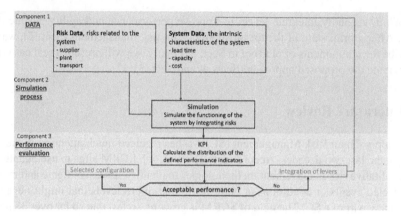

Fig. 1. Architecture of the decision support tool.

3.1 Features of the Studied SC

The SC studied in this paper is composed of: *i)* activities, whether related to a sourcing operation from a supplier, a production operation in an internal plant or a logistics/transportation operation. *ii)* stocks, input and output stocks for each activity.

Each activity $k \in [1..K]$ is characterised by three parameters: *i)* Lead time L_k which represents the time required for an item to move from the activity's upstream stock to the downstream stock. *ii)* Capacity Ca_k which refers to the maximum number of items that can be launched into activity in a single period. *Iii)* Cost Co_k which represents the unit cost associated with the movement of an item through an activity.

Four features characterise the studied SC:

– *Feature a)* A complex industrial scheme: we consider a SC configuration where each manufactured product is: *i)* composed of several components and sub-components *ii)* manufactured in several possible alternative schemes (Fig. 2). Each alternative scheme is characterised by a cost, a total lead time and a carbon footprint. For example, for sub-component 1 (Fig. 2), we have two possible schemes:

   (1) source from two suppliers and complete the manufacture of the sub-component in an internal factory
   (2) buy the sub-component directly from a supplier

– *Feature b)* Means of transportation: the transport operation can be carried out with several types of transport (air, sea, etc.). Each means of transport has a cost, a capacity, a lead time and specific days when it is available
– *Feature c)* The presence of stocks and work-in-progress with different manufacturing/transport times remaining throughout the SC
– *Feature d)* The occurrence of risks in all links of the SC: each activity is characterised by a pair (lead time, probability)
– No risk: nominal lead time and an associated probability (L, P)

– With risks: nominal lead time, additional/early lead time and risk probability (L + S, P) / (L − S, P).

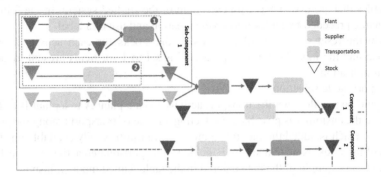

Fig. 2. Overview of the supply chain studied.

3.2 Modelling of Information Flow

We use a DES model implemented in the Simul8 software to represent the flows and stocks of the studied SC. The simulator monitors the arrival of orders and divides the flows into the different possible production modes according to the order book and the allocation entered. The model then reproduces all the SC elements described in the previous section with their associated data and integrates the other management policies of our system (such as batch sizes, mode of transport etc.). Note that the risk-related variability of the operating times of an item in an activity is modelled by probability distributions. The simulator then allows us to obtain the date of entry into final stock for each product (production and transport end date).

To enable a flexible simulation structure, configuration tables for the initialisation of our system, the flow repartition between the possible production modes, the distribution parameters of the activities' operating times and the data related to the transport mode are entered into the database. These tables are transferred at the beginning of the simulation by the simulation environment.

- Order generation and system initialization
  The set of production orders is represented by the vector PO_t at every period $t \in [1..T]$; T is the number of simulation periods. Orders are generated according to a table defining the planning of orders per day over the simulation horizon T.

  In order not to have to modify the simulation model directly in case of data changes, we have opted for a table named activity distribution (D activity) where the parameters of the probability distribution of the operating time of the activity k are indicated.

We have also created a separate table for the initialisation of our system named initial_state which contains for each activity the number of items in upstream stock and the remaining operating times. The use of labels to characterise items is very common in simulation models. They correspond to the qualitative or quantitative variables that are associated with each item of the studied system. In the following, any name preceded by an L refers to the creation and use of a label.

On the reset of our simulation model, the stocks for each activity k are initialised and the label "L item_in progress" is set to 1 for items present in stock at the initialisation.

- Transport mode selection

It should be recalled that the transport activity from a plant A to a plant B or from a plant to the customer is possible by selecting a mode of transport among the possible ones to which is added the fact that a mode of transport is only available on specific days of the week. Note that subset F includes transport-related activities. The Table 1 presents an example of the data entered in the table named mode_transport.

Table 1. Data related to transportation modes.

Transport activity	Total number of modes	Mode	Lead time	Mode status On (1)/Off (0)	Mode_day [days when the mode is available (monday (1) ... sunday (7))]		
k	N	1	L_{k1}	1	3	2	0
		...	...	...	...	...	...
		N	L_{kN}	0	6	0	0

The next program is run before the admission of an item by the activity $k|k \in \mathscr{F}$ (Fig. 3).

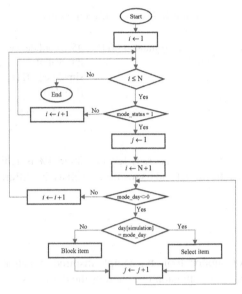

Fig. 3. Identification of the activated transport mode.

3.3 Performance Evaluation

The performance evaluation part was developed using the Excel vba programming language. We use the results of the simulator (production and transport end date for each product) to calculate the probability distribution of the indicator of interest, which is the OTD. It is defined as the number of orders delivered on time divided by the total number of orders. The performance evaluation tool allowed us to validate our prototype by comparing the OTD calculated with our tool with the one calculated in the field and to test and analyse several scenarios by varying the system parameters or by integrating levers.

3.4 DES Model Verification and Validation

Throughout the development of the model, we organised validation meetings every three weeks with the company's supply chain team to validate step by step the structure, the logic implemented, the mathematical and causal relations as well as the behaviour of the model's outputs. We decided with our company partners to work with a dataset of 85 days of historical data. The purpose was to determine whether the model behaves like the system by comparing the empirical distributions of the inputs (processing time and transport time) and outputs (residence time in the system, OTD). We obtained the mean and 95% confidence intervals for the OTD level from the 10 replications of the model. The following table presents the different results obtained (Table 2).

Table 2. Model validation results

Historical OTD level (u_0)	Average simulated OTD level	95% confidence interval of simulated OTD [LB, UB]		ILB-u_0I	IUB-u_0I
93	93.2	89.884	96.515	3.116	3.515

With only 10 replications, an accuracy level of about 4% is achieved. The industrial partners have validated the model and its results as well as the different scenarios studied in the next section.

4   Use Case

We tested our decision support tool on a sample inspired by actual data over a horizon of 85 periods (the temporary division used here is the day).

4.1   The SC Configuration Studied

The SC studied is the one of a leader company in the aeronautic industry. We consider a single product made from nine components, two of these components can be produced using two possible production modes. The product itself can be produced using three possible modes of production. The SC studied has 35 activities in total, distributed as follows: *i)* 14 supplier activities; *ii)* 19 plant activities and *iii)* 2 transport activities. The activities within the plants are either machining or assembly operations. The first step was to model the SC with its current parameters to validate the model compared to the real system it represents and to ensure that the level of OTD calculated from our model is close to that observed in real world (Sect. 3.4).

4.2   Number of Replications

We calculate the number of replications needed by following the steps described in chapter 6 of Kelton et al. [9]. In our case the number of replications needed to reach a precision level of less than 1% is 1500 replications. All the results that will be presented in the following section have been performed based on 1500 replications.

5   Numerical Experiments

Once verified and validated, the developed decision support tool was used to compare the performance of several strategies. We analysed several scenarios by varying: the repartition of flows between the different possible production modes, the production batch size, the transport batch size, the variation of days when a transport mode is available etc. The total computation time is less than 30 min, in the following we will study two scenarios:

- **Reference scenario**: which reproduces the current configuration of the system under study where we have considered the same data and the same repartition of flows between the different possible modes of production as in the field.
- **Scenario A**: in this scenario we have considered a new repartition of the flows between the possible alternative schemes. In this scenario we have activated a lever related to feeding the alternative scheme with the shortest queue.

The following figure shows the probability distribution of the OTD for the reference scenario and for scenario A (Fig. 4).

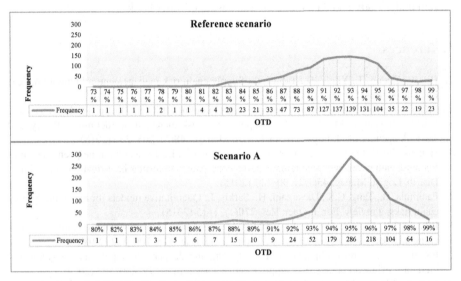

Fig. 4. Probability distribution of the OTD for the reference scenario and scenario A.

As shown in the figure, the mean of the OTD distribution for the reference scenario is 93%. For scenario A, we notice that the curve is pointed and smoother than that of the reference scenario. We also notice that the OTD has gone from an average of 93% in the reference scenario to an average of 95% after the activation of the lever (scenario A) and a standard deviation that has been divided by two compared to the distribution of our reference scenario. The repartition of flows used in the reference scenario between the three possible production modes is (60%, 20%, 20%). This repartition has switched to (50%, 43%, 9%) by selecting to feed the production mode with the shortest queue (scenario A). The challenge is to analyse the cost associated with each scenario and to verify the suppliers' capacity before proceeding to field implementation.

6   Conclusion

In this paper, we propose a new decision support tool, tested in the case of an aeronautical SC, to evaluate the probability of meeting customer deadlines under risk. The tool has three bricks, the first one related to the data, the second one to the DES model and the third one to the performance evaluation tool. The developed decision support tool can easily be transferred to other SCs.

The main limitation of the current study is that economic and carbon footprint aspects are not considered in the evaluation of the different scenarios. Also, there are other performance indicators that need to be explored. Our study also highlights research avenues regarding: *i)* the analysis of new scenarios by varying parameters of the system or by integrating new levers, and *ii)* the development of an optimisation model to determine the optimal repartition of flows between the possible alternative schemes. This optimisation model will be run upstream of the simulator and will use both data related to the system under study and data related to the customer order book.

References

1. Ho, W., Zheng, T., Yildiz, H., Talluri, S.: Supply chain risk management: a literature review. Int. J. Prod. Res. **53**(16), 5031–5069 (2015)
2. ISO 31000: Risk Management: Principles and Guidelines: ISO 31000, pp. 1–24 (2009)
3. Fan, Y., Stevenson, M.: A review of supply chain risk management: definition, theory, and research agenda. Int. J. Phys. Distrib. Logist. Manage. **48**(3), 205–230 (2018)
4. Hohenstein, N.-O., Feisel, E., Hartmann, E., Giunipero, L.: Research on the phenomenon of Supply Chain resilience: a systematic review and paths for further investigation. Int. J. Phys. Distrib. Logist. Manag. **45**(1/2), 90–117 (2015)
5. Fahimnia, B., Tang, C.S., Davarzani, H., Sarkis, J.: Quantitative models for managing Supply chain risks: a review. Eur. J. Oper. Res. **270**(1), 1–15 (2015)
6. Ribeiro, J.P., Barbosa-Povoa, A.: Supply chain resilience: definitions and quantitative modelling approaches: a literature review. Comput. Ind. Eng. **115**, 109–122 (2018)
7. Fischl, M., Scherrer-Rathje, M., Friedli, T.: Digging deeper into supply risk: a systematic literature review on price risks. Supply Chain Manage. Int. J. **19**, 480–503 (2014)
8. Oliveira, J.B., Jin, M., Lima, R.S., Kobza, J.E., Montevechi, J.A.B.: The role of simulation and optimization methods in supply chain risk management: performance and review standpoints. Simul. Model. Pract. Theory **92**, 17–44 (2019)
9. Kelton, W.D., Sadowski, R.P., Zupick, N.B.: Simulation with Arena, 6th edn. McGraw-Hill Education, New York (2015)

Supply Chain Model for Product Repulsion

Subrata Saha[1]([✉]), Izabela Ewa Nielsen[1], and Ilkyeong Moon[2,3]

[1] Department of Materials and Production, Aalborg University, 9220 Aalborg East, Denmark
saha@m-tech.aau.dk, izabela@mp.aau.dk
[2] Department of Industrial Engineering, Seoul National University, Seoul 08826, Republic of Korea
ikmoon@snu.ac.kr
[3] Institute for Industrial Systems Innovation, Seoul National University, Seoul 08826, Republic of Korea

Abstract. This study investigates the effect of product deletion strategy on the profitability of a supply chain while the manufacturer sells both high-and-low quality products. We formulate models to explore optimal supply chain decisions consisting of one manufacturer and one retailer in four scenarios based on the manufacturer's decision to continue both products, only low-quality products, and only high-quality products, or introduce a new product with adjusted quality. The result reflects that a manufacturer can maximize profit by offering only low-quality products or products with adjusted quality based on consumer valuation. If the manufacturer modifies the quality of existing products, total selling quality might be high even if its quality is low when consumers' preferences remain unchanged. Continuation of both products or only high-quality products does not always ensure higher profits.

Keywords: Product elimination · Manufacturing · Quality · Supply chain

1 Introduction

Introducing a new version of a similar type of product or removing an existing one over time is recognized as one of the critical strategic measures by which firms continuously renew themselves to survive in rapidly changing business environments [1,10]. For example, Samsung Galaxy S20, S20 Plus, and Ultra have been discontinued[1] and replaced with some exclusive model such as Samsung Galaxy F series for some specific countries like India[2]. Similar measures are practiced in

---

[1] www.samsung.com/my/smartphones/galaxy-a-series/?product1=sm-a725fzkhxme&product2=sm-a526blvhxme&product3=sm-a326blvhxme.
[2] en.wikipedia.org/wiki/Samsung_Galaxy_F_series.

© IFIP International Federation for Information Processing 2022
Published by Springer Nature Switzerland AG 2022
D. Y. Kim et al. (Eds.): APMS 2022, IFIP AICT 663, pp. 543–549, 2022.
https://doi.org/10.1007/978-3-031-16407-1_64

household appliances or consumer electronics products, where firms have been discontinued as well as introduced new versions to maintain a stable relationship with their consumers [7].

The rapid rate of technological innovation and frequent changes in consumer preferences reduce the lifecycles of products such as personal computers, cellular phones, and new telecommunication services. Product deletion as a critical product management decision equally contributes to strategic organizational development as many others. Various organizations such as Heinz, Procter & Gamble, Kraft, and Unilever shortlist and cull their product portfolios regularly [12]. Product up-gradation, deletion, or replacement with the adjusted quality decision have immense potential to improve overall profitability [9]. A strategic decision to delete products can be used as a "competitive weapon" in critical market situations. For example, a strategic product may be discontinued merely due to its undesirable sales volume or profit, putting meaningful business relations at risk [6,11].

This study presents an analytical model that helps the manufacturers decide when product deletion is favorable. In a two-period supply chain interaction consisting of a single manufacturer and a single retailer supply chain setting, the manufacturers offer both products in the first period. In the second period, the manufacturer decides whether to offer only the high-quality, low-quality or both products. Consequently, we derive the analytical solutions of the optimal wholesale prices, product quality, and product prices for the possible four scenarios. The detailed discussion on the effects of parameters on the profit and product quality can provide a comprehensive overview of marketing and operational aspects they need to consider. We believe that the solutions and corresponding thresholds based on the parameters are beneficial for managers to understand the dynamics and help make product deletion strategies.

The following are the critical contributions of the study: there is extensive empirical and analytical literature on the effect of the strategic introduction of the new product. However, the analytical evaluation of product deletion is sparse. Our analysis clearly demonstrates that the manufacturer's strategic product deletion decision can ensure higher profits for both members. It is sometimes preferable to offer only a product with an adjusted quality instead of continuing with both products.

2   Model Description

We consider a one-to-one supply chain wherein a manufacturer offers both high and low-quality ($i = H, L$) products to a retailer in the first period and sets wholesale prices w_H and w_L, respectively. The product qualities for the low and high-quality products are θ and $t\theta$, $t > 1$, respectively, and the unit cost for producing a low-quality product with quality θ is θ^2, and the that of a high-quality product is $\eta t^2 \theta^2$, $(t > 1)$ where η is the efficiency for the manufacturer in adopting new technology. The quadratic cost function considered in this study is extensively used in the literature [1,3–5]. Followed by the manufacturer decisions, the retailer sets retail prices for low and high-quality products as p_L and P_H, respectively.

We assume that consumers are heterogeneous on product quality (θ) and are uniformly distributed over $[0, b]$, where b represents the degree of market potential among consumers for the product category; therefore, the surplus from purchasing the product with quality θ and retail price p for the consumers whose valuation is U is $U\theta - p$, and consumers make purchase decisions based on both retail price and quality [2]. Each consumer buys at most one unit of either product. Particularly, the consumer's utility is $t\theta U - p_H$ if a unit of the high quality product is bought, $\theta U - p_L$ if a unit of the low quality product is bought, and zero if neither products is bought. We assume the manufacturer offers both product in the first period, the demand function is obtained as follows: $d_L = \frac{p_H - p_L}{t\theta - \theta} - \frac{p_L}{\theta}$ and $d_H = b - \frac{p_H - p_L}{t\theta - \theta}$, $t > 1$. List of notations are presented in Table 1 below:

Table 1. List of notations

Symbol	Description
Subscript	
i	Denotes product type, $i \in \{H, L\}$
j	Denotes scanarios, $j \in \{BHL, OL, OH, AH\}$
Decision variable	
w_i^j	Wholesale price of ith product
p_i^j	Retail price of ith product
t^j	Quality level of the upgraded product relative to that of the existing product ($t^j > 1$)
π_r^j	Profits for the retailer
π_m^j	Profits for the manufacturer
Q_i^j	Total quantity
Parameters	
b	Market potential
η	Quadratic quality cost factor coefficient
θ	Quality of the existing product

In the second period, the manufacturer has four option: (i) offers both products (Scenario BHL), (ii) Only offer a low-quality product (Scenario OL), (iii) Offers only a high-quality product (OH) (iv) Offers an adjusted high-quality product (Scenario AH). Based on the assumption, profit functions for the retailer (π_r) and manufacturer (π_m) are obtained as follows:

$$\pi_r(p_L, p_H) = (p_L - w_L)d_L + (p_H - w_H)d_H$$
$$\pi_m(w_L, w_H, t) = (w_L - \theta^2)d_L + (w_H - \eta t^2 \theta^2)d_H \tag{1}$$

If the manufacturer offers only low-quality products, then the consumers do not have any alternative, and the profit function for the manufacturer and the retailer are obtained as follows:

$$\pi_r = (p_L - w_L)\left(b - \frac{p_L}{\theta}\right) \qquad \pi_m = (w_L - \theta^2)\left(b - \frac{p_L}{\theta}\right) \qquad (2)$$

Finally, if the manufacturer offers only high-quality products, the profit function for the manufacturer and the retailer are obtained as follows:

$$\pi_r = (p_H - w_H)\left(b - \frac{p_H}{t\theta}\right)$$
$$\pi_m = (w_H - \eta t^2\theta^2)\left(b - \frac{p_H}{t\theta}\right) \qquad (3)$$

In the following section, we present optimal decisions for all scenarios.

3   Model Solutions and Discussions

We assume that the manufacturer decides wholesale prices and quality level for a high-quality product and that the downstream retailer decides market prices. In addition, the manufacturer acts as a Stackelberg leader, and the retailer is the follower. We use backward induction to find the optimal decision. Proposition 1 summarizes the optimal decision in Scenario BHL.

Proposition 1. *Optimal decision in Scenario BHL is obtained as follows:*

$$\pi_r^{BHL} = \frac{2b^3 + 15b^2\eta\theta + 18b\eta\theta^2 - 48b\eta^2\theta^2 + 27\eta\theta^3 - 144\eta^2\theta^3 + 128\eta^3\theta^3 + 2(b^2 - 4b\eta\theta - 12\eta\theta^2 + 16\eta^2\theta^2)\sqrt{X}}{432\eta}$$

$$\pi_m^{BHL} = \frac{2b^3 + 15b^2\eta\theta + 18b\eta\theta^2 - 48b\eta^2\theta^2 + 27\eta\theta^3 - 144\eta^2\theta^3 + 128\eta^3\theta^3 + 2(b^2 - 4b\eta\theta - 12\eta\theta^2 + 16\eta^2\theta^2)\sqrt{X}}{216\eta}$$

$$p_L^{BHL} = \frac{\theta(3b+\theta)}{4}, p_H^{BHL} = \frac{5b^2 - \eta\theta^2(3-8\eta) + 19b\eta\theta + (2b\eta+5b)\sqrt{X}}{36\eta}; Q_L^{BHL} = \frac{(b+(3-8\eta)\theta) + 2\sqrt{X}}{12};$$

$$Q_H^{BHL} = \frac{2b - 4\eta\theta - \sqrt{X}}{6}, w_L^{BHL} = \frac{\theta(b+\theta)}{2}, w_H^{BHL} = \frac{2b^2 + 7b\eta\theta - \eta\theta^2(3-8\eta) + 2(b+\eta\theta)\sqrt{X}}{18\eta}, t^{BHL}$$

$$= \frac{b + 4\eta\theta + \sqrt{X}}{6\eta\theta)}.$$

Proof: Because $\frac{\partial^2\pi_r}{\partial p_L^2} = \frac{-2}{\theta(t-1)} < 0$, $\frac{\partial^2\pi_r}{\partial p_H^2} = \frac{-2t}{\theta(t-1)} < 0$ and $\frac{\partial^2\pi_r}{\partial p_L^2} \cdot \frac{\partial^2\pi_r}{\partial p_H^2} - \left(\frac{\partial^2\pi_r}{\partial p_L\partial p_H}\right)^2 = \frac{4}{(t-1)\theta^2} > 0$, the retailer's profit function in Eq. (1) is concave in p_L and p_H. Solving first-order conditions, the retail prices are obtained as follows:

$$p_L = \frac{w_L + b\theta}{2} \qquad p_H = \frac{w_H + bt\theta}{2} \qquad (4)$$

Based on the retailer response, the profit function for the manufacturer is obtained as follows:

$$\pi_m = \frac{(tw_L - w_H)(w_L - \theta^2)}{2\theta - 2t\theta} + \frac{1}{2}\left(b + \frac{w_L - w_H}{(t-1)\theta}\right)(w_H - \eta t^2\theta^2) \qquad (5)$$

Note that the profit function for the manufacturer is a function of three variables, and after solving the first-order equations, possible optimal solutions are obtained as follows:

$$\{w_{1L}, w_{1H}, t_1\} \equiv \left\{ \frac{\theta(b+\theta)}{2}, \frac{b^2 + \eta\theta^2 - b(\eta\theta + \sqrt{b^2 - 4b\eta\theta + 4\eta\theta^2})}{2\eta}, \frac{(b - \sqrt{b^2 - 4b\eta\theta + 4\eta\theta^2})}{2\eta\theta} \right\}$$

$$\{w_{2L}, w_{2H}, t_2\} \equiv \left\{ \frac{\theta(b+\theta)}{2}, \frac{b^2 - b\eta\theta + \eta\theta^2 + b\sqrt{b^2 - 4b\eta\theta + 4\eta\theta^2}}{2\eta}, \frac{b + \sqrt{b^2 - 4b\eta\theta + 4\eta\theta^2}}{2\eta\theta} \right\}$$

$$\{w_{3L}, w_{3H}, t_3\} \equiv \left\{ \frac{\theta(b+\theta)}{2}, \frac{2b^2 + 7b\eta\theta - \eta\theta^2(3 - 8\eta) - 2(b - \eta\theta)\sqrt{X}}{18\eta}, \frac{b + 4\eta\theta - \sqrt{X}}{6\eta\theta} \right\}$$

$$\{w_{4L}, w_{4H}, t_4\} \equiv \left\{ \frac{\theta(b+\theta)}{2}, \frac{2b^2 + 7b\eta\theta - \eta\theta^2(3 - 8\eta) + 2(b + \eta\theta)\sqrt{X}}{18\eta}, \frac{b + 4\eta\theta + \sqrt{X}}{6\eta\theta} \right\}$$

where, $X = b^2 - 4b\eta\theta - 4\eta(3 - 4\eta)\theta^2$. One can verify that the first two solutions are not valid because, in this scenario, the selling quantity of high-quality products becomes zero. To verify concavity, we compute the Hessian matrix, and the value of principle minors for the fourth solution is valid because $|H_1|_{\{w_{4L}, w_{4H}, t_4\}} = \frac{-t}{(t-1)\theta} < 0$; $|H_2|_{\{w_{4L}, w_{4H}, t_4\}} = \frac{1}{(t-1)\theta^2} > 0$; and $|H_3|_{\{w_{4L}, w_{4H}, t_4\}} = \frac{2\eta^2\theta Y}{(b - 2\eta\theta + \sqrt{X})^4}$, where $Y = 25b^4 - 80b^3\eta\theta - 6b^2\eta(24 - (35 - 39\eta)\theta^2 + 8\eta^2\theta(9(3 + \eta)\theta + (9 - \eta(15 + 8\eta))\theta^3 + 88b\eta^3\theta^3(25b^3 + 30\theta b^2)\eta + 8(\eta^2 - \theta(3 - 2\eta)\theta^2)\sqrt{X}$. Therefore, the fourth solution is valid if $Y < 0$. In summarizing, we obtain the above optimal decision

□.

Note that the derivations of the optimal solutions for the other three scenarios are similar; therefore, we omitted the proof. We present the optimal decision for the rest of the scenario in Table 2.

Table 2. Optimal decision in Scenario OL, OH, and AH

Scenario	Scenario OL	Scenario OH	Scenario AH
w_L^j	$\frac{\theta(b+\theta)}{2}$	—	—
w_H^j	—	$\frac{(b+4\eta\theta+\sqrt{X})(7b+4\eta\theta+\sqrt{X})}{72\eta}$	$\frac{2b^2}{9\eta}$
t^j		$\frac{b+4\eta\theta+\sqrt{X}}{6\eta\theta}$	$\frac{b}{3\eta\theta}$
P_L^j	$\frac{\theta(3b+\theta)}{4}$	—	—
p_H^j	—	$\frac{(b+4\eta\theta+\sqrt{X})(19b+4\eta\theta+\sqrt{X})}{144\eta}$	$\frac{5b^2}{18\eta}$
Q_L^j	$\frac{b-\theta}{4}$	—	—
Q_L^j		$\frac{5b-4\eta\theta-\sqrt{X}}{24}$	$\frac{b}{6}$
π_r^j	$\frac{(b-\theta)^2\theta}{16}$	$\frac{(4\eta\theta-5b+\sqrt{X})^2(b+4\eta\theta+\sqrt{X})}{3456\eta}$	$\frac{b^3}{104\eta}$
π_m^j	$\frac{(b-\theta)^2\theta}{8}$	$\frac{(4\eta\theta-5b+\sqrt{X})^2(b+4\eta\theta+\sqrt{X})}{1728\eta}$	$\frac{b^3}{54\eta}$

Product introduction or deletion is a critical strategic activity of any manufacturer to be alive in the market. Some of the essential factors that affect the success of introduction or deletion decisions include product complexity, aspiring regulatory bodies, shrinking product release cycles, market potential, competitor's aggressiveness, complex value chain, etc. [7,8]. The product's value advantage, price, technological sophistication, and innovativeness are common product characteristics that affect the strategic decision. However, analytical research addressing the particular effect of earlier product deletion is relatively sparse. While researchers put lots of emphasis on the issues of how upgraded product conceptualization and development processes affect success, less attention has been given to exploring the strategic effect of a deletion. Note that we proposed a simple solution, and the decision in the first and second periods are independent. Now the graphical representation for the profit functions, sales volume, and quality are presented in Fig. 1.

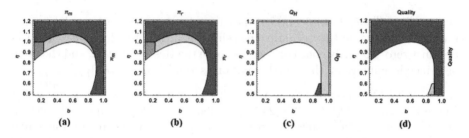

Fig. 1. Maximum (a) manufacturer's profit, (b) retailer's profit, (c) new product quantity sold, (d) product quality in Scenario BHL (red); OL(green); OH (black); and OHA (yellow): $\theta = 0.3$, $b \in (0,1)$, $\eta \in (0.5, 1.2)$ (Color figure online)

It is clear from Fig. 1 that the manufacturer can offer only low-quality products if b is low or high-quality products with adjusted quality. If b is low, consumers are not willing to pay a higher price; therefore, offering a high-quality product or both products might not be profitable, and the results also reflect that fact. Note that the white region represents the area where the manufacturer cannot offer both products or only a new product. In that case, the manufacturer can offer only low-quality products or products with modified quality. Overall, the key insights obtained from the study reflect that the manufacturer can sell a maximum amount of products with adjusted quality, which might also lead to higher profits instead of continuing both products. As noted in the introduction, some manufacturers offer region- or country-specific products by adjusting quality specifications due to low-purchase power, less quality sensitivity, etc. Our results also support the practice.

4   Conclusion and Future Research Direction

In a constantly changing business world, technologies change, customer needs change, competitors change, and environmental regulations change. If the product specification remains the same, the manufacturer will cease to exist with all these changes. In this regard, researchers mostly focus on exploring factors that influence the success of new product introduction; however, product deletion strategy is not explored comprehensively. Therefore, we formulate a stylized two-period supply chain model to study the impact of product deletion strategy.

Only a handful of articles have related product deletion decisions to supply chain management. We proposed a simple model in this study and found that the manufacturer's product decision can benefit the supply chain members and sometimes help them expand the sales volume. Although product deletion is a difficult strategic choice that is affected by multiple factors, therefore, in the future, we will develop a more robust model in a stochastic environment. Moreover, the model outcome needs to be verified with the actual date and feedback to evaluate the feasibility, reliability, and accuracy.

References

1. Amaldoss, W., Shin, W.: Multitier store brands and channel profits. J. Mark. Res. **52**(6), 754–767 (2015)
2. Banker, R.D., Khosla, I., Sinha, K.K.: Quality and competition. Manag. Sci. **44**(9), 1179–1192 (1998)
3. Moorthy, K.S.: Product and price competition in a duopoly. Mark. Sci. **7**(2), 141–168 (1988)
4. Dey, K., Saha, S.: Influence of procurement decisions in two-period green supply chain. J. Clean. Prod. **190**, 388–402 (2018)
5. Dey, K., Roy, S., Saha, S.: The impact of strategic inventory and procurement strategies on green product design in a two-period supply chain. Int. J. Prod. Res. **57**(7), 1915–1948 (2019)
6. Katana, T., Eriksson, A., Hilletofth, P., Eriksson, D.: Decision model for product rollover in manufacturing operations. Prod. Plan. Control **28**(15), 1264–1277 (2017)
7. Kotler, P.: A Framework for Marketing Management. Pearson Education Limited, London (2016)
8. Nielsen, I.E., Saha, S.: Procurement planning in a multi-period supply chain: an epiphany. Oper. Res. Perspect. **5**, 383–398 (2018)
9. Pourhejazy, P., Sarkis, J., Zhu, Q.: A fuzzy-based decision aid method for product deletion of fast moving consumer goods. Expert Syst. Appl. **119**, 272–288 (2019)
10. Shi, X., Shen, B.: Product upgrading or not: R&D tax credit, consumer switch and information updating. Int. J. Prod. Econ. **213**, 13–22 (2019)
11. Varadarajan, R., DeFanti, M.P., Busch, P.S.: Brand portfolio, corporate image, and reputation: managing brand deletions. J. Acad. Mark. Sci. **34**(2), 195–205 (2006)
12. Zhu, Q., Shah, P., Sarkis, J.: Addition by subtraction: integrating product deletion with lean and sustainable supply chain management. Int. J. Prod. Econ. **205**, 201–214 (2018)

Urban Mobility and City Logistics

Smart Cities and Sustainable Development to Relate to the SDG—Review

Helton Almeida dos Santos[1]([⊠]) (iD), Pedro Luiz de Oliveira Costa Neto[1]([⊠]) (iD),
Robson Elias Bueno[1]([⊠]) (iD), Emerson da Silva Santana[2]([⊠]) (iD),
and Moacir de Junior Freitas[2]([⊠]) (iD)

[1] Graduate Studies in Production Engineering, Universidade Paulista, Sao Paulo, Brazil
heltonalmeidasantos@gmail.com, pedroluiz@plocn.com,
robsonebueno@gmail.com
[2] Graduate Studies in Technological Innovation, UNIFESP, São Paulo, Brazil
emersantan@gmail.com, bicimo@uol.com.br

Abstract. Urban planning that leverages improvements in sustainable development and the already proven potential of data and communication technologies are highly adaptable to optimize sustainable cities and improve their performance based on the groundbreaking foundation of smart cities' data-driven technologies [3]. Thus, it is important to review how academic papers reflect the trend of the environmental issue by focusing on a link between smart cities and sustainable development. The main objective of this research is to conduct a bibliometric analysis of articles using an algorithmic research database, as well as a thorough analysis to identify the list of published articles related to the Sustainable Development Goals (SDGs), so that it is possible to identify trends and guide future researches. It is also believed that the relationship between the most mentioned works to the SDGs can be clarified, providing the baseline study for any theme that bring insight to potential solutions using smart city and sustainable development technologies.

Keywords: Smart cities · SDG · Resilience · Sustainable development

1 Introduction

Information and communications technology (ICT) has contributed to the creation of cities with digital infrastructure, referred to as "Wired Cities," "Cyber Cities," "Digital Cities", "Smart Cities," or "Sentient Cities." Although each term is used to describe the city's relationship with ICT in a particular way, these urban cities are increasing impacting on the nature, structure, and performance of urban infrastructure, management, economic activity, and daily life [1].

Although solutions to urban problems are closely related to ICTs, there are aspects where the complementarity of technological initiatives has captured different efforts to achieve urban sustainability. If [2], twenty terms and concepts are analyzed, it is concluded that even though there is an overlap among them in their ideas, concepts, and

© IFIP International Federation for Information Processing 2022
Published by Springer Nature Switzerland AG 2022
D. Y. Kim et al. (Eds.): APMS 2022, IFIP AICT 663, pp. 553–562, 2022.
https://doi.org/10.1007/978-3-031-16407-1_65

visions, as well as distinctive concepts and key differences in terms of planning practices and design strategies, highlights "smart city", and "sustainable city" are evidenced as the most acknowledged in the literature. They also point out that they are often used interchangeably.

Urban planning using sustainable development improvements and the data and communication technologies' proven potential is highly adaptable, leading to a phenomenon known as "data-driven smart sustainable urbanism." This phenomenon is related to the idea of combining and integrating the strengths of sustainable cities and smart cities, using their strategies and solutions to optimize sustainable cities and improve their performance based on cutting-edge data-driven technologies offered by smart cities [3].

Therefore, it is important to verify that the objective of this article is to produce a publication that reflects the trend of the environmental topic and focuses on a link between smart cities and sustainable development. The main objective of this research is accomplished through a bibliometric analysis of a sample of articles from Scopus research database, using the search string "smart city or cities" AND "sustainable development", and through a detailed analysis of the content of some articles. These analyses allow us to determination the relationship between published articles and the Sustainable Development Goals (SDGs) [16].

2 Literature Review

2.1 Smart City

The European Union defines Smart City as a place where traditional networks and services become more efficient using digital and telecommunications technologies for the benefit of its population and businesses [4]. According to the Cities in Motion Index, from the IESE Business School in Spain, the intelligence level of a city is indicated by ten dimensions, according to the flow of interaction, to respond to the social and economic needs of society such as: governance, public administration, urban planning, technology, the environment, international connections, social cohesion, human capital, and the economy [5].

The concepts about smart cities are broad, in which authors consider instrumentalization, interconnection, and intelligence as fundamental. Instrumentation makes it possible to acquire data in practically real-time through physical and virtual sensors. Interconnection is the integration of urban services with data communication platforms. And intelligence is the processing that enables information optimization to improve operational decisions. This set, controlled by Information Technology generates traffic information, statistics on electricity consumption, and urban safety events, optimizing the optimization of city's services. This product of intelligent interaction between the city and citizens contributes to improving operational efficiency and positively influences the quality of life [6].

Another concept of a Smart City is approached through three factors: technological, human, and institutional. This conceptualization is complex it integrates the infrastructure of physical facilities and virtual technologies integrated with intelligence and digital networks providing services for the city's needs (human well-being, government, policy, and regulatory needs) [7].

2.2 Sustainable Development

The Brundtland Commission Report [8] defines sustainable development as the development that meets the needs of the present generation without compromising the ability of future generations to meet their own needs.

Sustainable development has become a kind of keyword in development discourses but is almost always associated with different definitions, meanings, and interpretations [9].

The argument is that sustainable development is the central concept [10] within the global development policy and a way of interacting with the environment without generating risks of damage to resources for the future. It is a concept of development to improve living standards without harming nature and the environment, such as air and water pollution, deforestation, and even conditions that can cause climate change and the extinction of the species [11].

Sustainable development is related to human development goals to achieve social progress, environmental balance, and economic growth [12]. This integration will only be possible be integrating economic, environmental, and social concerns in decision-making processes [13].

Levy and Ellis [14] emphasize that sustainable development should not, as usual, be confused with sustainability, since sustainability is an objective to be pursued. In contrast, sustainable development is the way, or the process, of achieving the objective.

3 Methodology

The work is conceptual and to achieve the objective, which emphasizes quantitative research, the bibliometric method was adopted, which can be considered an essential field of information. This bibliometric is methodical because it organizes itself by developing a means of indicating the questions to be addressed, search strategies to identify the articles searched, and other documents [15]. Accessing specific data of the selected articles such as year, title, authors, keywords, and other data allows statistical procedures for better interpretation and mapping of information behavior [16].

The research was carried out in the Scopus database using the search string smart city OR smart cities AND sustainable development in the keywords, abstract, and the title of the articles. The search was limited by using filters available in the Scopus database such as articles and reviews, open access, already published, in specific areas of environmental sciences, engineering, energy, social sciences, and writing in English. The resulted sample was used to find the relation with the objectives of sustainable development of the United Nations (UN).

The Biblioshiny for Bibliometrix tool helped organize and facilitate data interpretation. The publication period was not defined to permit the identification of the beginning of the authors' use of the search strings and the possible trends in the resulted sample of articles. From the resulted sample of articles, we read the abstracts, for some of them the abstract and conclusions, and for others, the discussion/results to identify and relate to the sustainable development goals (SDGs).

In the first stage of the analysis, we decided to maintain the articles published before defining the 17 sustainability goals by the UN in 2015 they were kept because by the year 2000, was already defined the eight goals to reduce extreme poverty [17].

In the second stage of analysis, articles were removed in which there were no clear definitions of smart city(s) and sustainable development, for example, articles related to games or some articles to define technological indicators (sensors, specific applications, and others).

In the third stage of the analysis, we removed articles discussing the development of indicators for smart cities or sustainable cities, reviews of indicators, reviews or explanations of sustainable objectives, and economic our politicas indicators.

In the fourth stage, for all articles with a tendency toward more than one SDG, only one objective was considered, according to the article's primary focus. For example, if the article deals with a specific sensor that can improve health and well-being (SDG#3), but the objective of the article is to use the sensor in innovation and to be part of infrastructure improvement (SDG#9), then this last SDG was attributed in the number of articles related to the SDG#9.

In the fifth stage, only the ten most cited works of the remaining 231 were presented in Table 2 as a sampling of the result, showing the numbers, title and basic explanation of each SDG, the articles in citation format, and a brief description of the objectives of the articles. Figure 1 present the methodology.

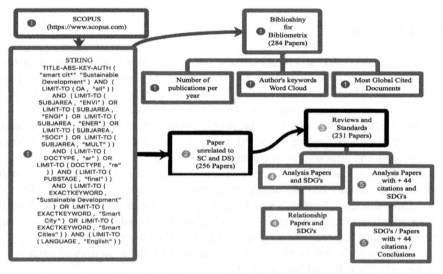

Fig. 1. The methodology used in this article.

4   Results

The application of filter described above indicated 284 journal articles between 2013 and 2022, which emphasis on the year of 2021, with the highest number of publications. The use of the Biblioshiny for Bibliometrix tool allowed organizing the results by classifying the articles.

After the second step of the methodology, we reached 256 articles and applied the third step to classify the articles according to an SDG; 231 articles remained.

Table 1 presenting the summary of articles in which the main subject is closer to meeting an SDG, allowing a view of the focus of the authors and the most researched SDGs.

The results show many researchers with the main focus on UN objectives #9, with 89 articles, #11 with 57 articles, #10 with 27 articles and #7 with 23 articles. The SDGs #1, #2, #5, #12, #14, #16 and #17 have not been explored, showing that new research could explore the use of technology to help create resources to solve problems and achieve these goals.

Table 1. Articles according to the primary objective to meet the SDGs.

SDG		N° Articles
SDG #1	NO POVERTY	0
SDG #2	ZERO HUNGER	0
SDG #3	GOOD HEALTH AND WELL-BEING	13
SDG #4	QUALITY EDUCATION	4
SDG #5	GENDER EQUALITY	0
SDG #6	CLEAN WATER AND SANITATION	2
SDG #7	AFFORDABLE AND CLEAN ENERGY	23
SDG #8	DECENT WORK AND ECONOMIC GROWTH	2
SDG #9	INDUSTRY, INNOVATION AND INFRASTRUCTURE	89
SDG #10	REDUCED INEQUALITIES	27
SDG #11	SUSTAINABLE CITIES AND COMMUNITIES	58
SDG #12	RESPONSIBLE CONSUMPTION AND PRODUCTION	0
SDG #13	CLIMATE ACTION	8
SDG #14	LIFE BELOW WATER	0
SDG #15	LIFE ON LAND	5
SDG #16	PEACE, JUSTICE AND STRONG INSTITUTIONS	0
SDG #17	PARTNERSHIPS FOR THE GOALS	0

The ten most cited articles among the 231 resulting from the third stage are shown in Table 2.

Table 2. Ten most cited articles among the 231 articles

Paper	Times cited
Simon Elias Bibri, John Krogstie. Smart sustainable cities of the future: An extensive interdisciplinary literature review. Sustainable Cities and Society, Volume 31, Pages 183–212, 2017	528
Elvira Ismagilova Laurie Hughes, Yogesh K. Dwivedi, K. Ravi Raman. Smart cities: Advances in research—An information systems perspective. International Journal of Information Management. Volume 47, Pages 88–100, 2019	253
Maria Kaika, Don't call me resilient again!': the New Urban Agenda as immunology … or … what happens when communities refuse to be vaccinated with 'smart cities' and indicators. Environment and Urbanization, Vol 29, 2017	183
Miltiadis D. Lytras, Anna Visvizi. Who Uses Smart City Services and What to Make of It: Toward Interdisciplinary Smart Cities Research. Sustainability, Volume 10, 1998, 2018	175
Mohammad Shorfuzzamana, M. Shamim Hossain, Mohammed F. Alhamid. Towards the sustainable development of smart cities through mass video surveillance: A response to the COVID-19 pandemic. Sustainable Cities and Society, Volume 64, 2021	145
M.A.Sayegh, J. Danielewicz, T.Nannou, M. Miniewicz, P. Jadwiszczak, K. Piekarska, H. Jouhara. Trends of European research and development in district heating technologies. Renewable and Sustainable Energy Reviews, Volume 68, Part 2, Pages 1183–1192, 2017	129
Sandro Nižetića, Petar Solićb, Diego López-de-Ipiña González-de-ArtazacLuigi Patronod. Internet of Things (IoT): Opportunities, issues and challenges towards a smart and sustainable future. Journal of Cleaner Production, Volume 274, 2020	98
Yiheng Chen, Dawei Han, Water quality monitoring in smart city: A pilot project. Automation in Construction. Volume 89, Pages 307–316, 2018	91
Luigi Fusco Girard. Toward a Smart Sustainable Development of Port Cities/Areas: The Role of the "Historic Urban Landscape" Approach. Sustainability, Volume 5, 4329–4348, 2013	89
Ghaffarian Hoseini A., Dahlan N.D., Berardi U., Makaremi N. The essence of future smart houses: From embedding ICT to adapting to sustainability principles. Renewable and Sustainable Energy Reviews, Volume 24, Pages 593–607, 2013	87

Finally, these articles are analyzed in Table 3 are presented, citing the number, title and basic explanation of each SDG, the articles in citation format and a brief justification of the use of the article for the UN goal.

Table 3. SDGs in the articles and a brief justification on the use of the article for the UN goal

SDG's	Articles	Relation to the SDG's
SDG#6 - Clean Water and Sanitation - Ensure availability and sustainable management of water and sanitation for all	Yiheng Chen, Dawei Han, Water quality monitoring in smart city: A pilot project. Automation in Construction. Volume 89, Pages 307–316, 2018	Presents a multi-parameter water monitoring system for the Floating Port of Bristol. The result demonstrates the feasibility of collecting water quality data in real-time online
SDG#9 - Industry, innovation, and infrastructure - Build resilient infrastructure, promote inclusive and sustainable industrialization, and foster innovation	Mohammad Shorfuzzamana, M. Shamim Hossain, Mohammed F. Alhamid. Towards the sustainable development of smart cities through mass video surveillance: A response to the COVID-19 pandemic. Sustainable Cities and Society, Volume 64, 2021	Proposes using mass video surveillance innovation, and technology to combat the COVID-19 pandemic and implement social distancing monitoring. The authors use three deep learning-based real-time object detection models to detect people in videos captured with a monocular camera
	Sandro Nižetića, Petar Solićb, Diego López-de-Ipiña González-de-ArtazacLuigi Patronod. Internet of Things (IoT): Opportunities, issues and challenges towards a smart and sustainable future. Journal of Cleaner Production, Volume 274, 2020	Contributes to a better understanding of innovation and current technological progress in IoT application areas
	Simon Elias Bibri, John Krogstie. Smart sustainable cities of the future: An extensive interdisciplinary literature review. Sustainable Cities and Society, Volume 31, Pages 183–212, 2017	Provides a comprehensive overview of the field of smart and sustainable cities in terms of state-of-the-art research and development, emerging scientific and technological trends, and future planning practices
	Miltiadis D. Lytras, Anna Visvizi. Who Uses Smart City Services and What to Make of It: Toward Interdisciplinary Smart Cities Research. Sustainability, Volume 10, 1998, 2018	Research smart cities and underlines the importance of integrating smart cities and smart villages research with policymaking aimed at sustainability, inclusive growth, and development

(*continued*)

Table 3. (*continued*)

SDG's	Articles	Relation to the SDG's
	GhaffarianHoseini A., Dahlan N.D., Berardi U., Makaremi N. The essence of future smart houses: From embedding ICT to adapting to sustainability principles. Renewable and Sustainable Energy Reviews, Volume 24, Pages 593–607, 2013	Develops a theoretical analysis of smart home case models. The results show that the most significant smart values embodied in smart homes encompass functional automation technologies
SDG#11 - Reduced inequalities - Make cities and human settlements inclusive, safe, resilient, and sustainable	Maria Kaika. Don't call me resilient again!': the New Urban Agenda as immunology … or … what happens when communities refuse to be vaccinated with 'smart cities' and indicators. Environment and Urbanization, Vol 29, 2017	Argues that people and environments being and working together can offer much more efficient, direct, and effective ways to address access to housing, health, education, water, and clean air in urban settlements
	Elvira Ismagilova Laurie Hughes, Yogesh K. Dwivedi, K. Ravi Raman. Smart cities: Advances in research—An information systems perspective. International Journal of Information Management. Volume 47, Pages 88–100, 2019	Analyzes and discusses aspects of smart cities such as smart mobility, smart living, smart environment, smart citizens, smart government, smart architecture, and related technologies and concepts. The discussion also focuses on aligning smart cities with the UN's sustainable development goals
	Luigi Fusco Girard. Toward a Smart Sustainable Development of Port Cities/Areas: The Role of the "Historic Urban Landscape" Approach. Sustainability, Volume 5, 4329–4348, 2013	About a smart sustainable development discusses an integrated smart development model, supported by urban planning, that contributes to urban ecological resilience

(*continued*)

Table 3. (*continued*)

SDG's	Articles	Relation to the SDG's
SDG#13 - Climate Action - Take urgent action to combat climate change, and its impacts	M.A.Sayegh, J. Danielewicz, T.Nannou, M. Miniewicz, P. Jadwiszczak, K. Piekarska, H. Jouhara. Trends of European research and development in district heating technologies. Renewable and Sustainable Energy Reviews, Volume 68, Part 2, Pages 1183–1192, 2017	Articles from a smart, sustainable development discusses an integrated smart development model supported by urban planning that contributes to urban ecological resilience

5 Conclusions

This article presented a theoretical basis for smart city and sustainable development concepts through a literature review based on an algorithm defined within the Scopus research base to identify works specifically targeted to meet sustainable goals (SDGs).

The results show directions and encouragement for further research on SDGs #1, #2, #5, #12, #14, #16, and #17 from technological solutions used in smart cities or sustainable development. Likewise, it encourages studies for intelligent solutions for center-periphery structures in which the population is penalized by local income inequality and income, structural, social, educational, and medical disparities [19]. It is hoped in this work to have presented a contribution to the researchers of our terminology focused on solutions for smart and human cities that privilege the studies of sustainable development objectives.

References

1. De Jong, M., Joss, S., Schraven, D., Zhan, C., Weijnen, M.: Sustainable-smart-resilient-low carbon-eco-knowledge cities; Making sense of a multitude of concepts promoting sustainable urbanization. J. Clean. Prod. **109**, 25–38 (2015)
2. Bibri, S.E.: A novel model for data-driven smart sustainable cities of the future: the institutional transformations required for balancing and advancing the three goals of sustainability. Energy Inform. **4**(1), 1–37 (2021). https://doi.org/10.1186/s42162-021-00138-8
3. Comissão Europeia, Compreender as políticas da União Europeia: Agenda digital Direção-Geral da Comunicação Informação dos cidadãos 1049 Bruxelas BÉLGICA Manuscrito atualizado 2014/11
4. Iese Cities in Motion Index, Cities Economy General Urban Governance (2017)
5. Harrison, C., Eckman, B., Hamilton, R., Hartswick, P., Kalagnanam, J., Paraszczak, J.: Foundations for smarter cities. IBM J. Res. Dev. **54**, 1–16 (2010)
6. Nam, T., Pardo, T.A.: Smart city as urban innovation: focusing on management, policy, and context. In: Proceedings of the 5th International Conference on Theory and Practice of Electronic Governance, pp. 185–194. ACM (2011)
7. Stoddart, H., et al.: A pocket guide to sustainable development governance. Stakeholder Forum (2011)

8. Mensah, J.: Sustainable development: meaning, history, principles, pillars, and implications for human action: literature review. Cogent Soc. Sci. **5**(1), 1653531 (2019)
9. Abubakar, I.R.: Access to sanitation facilities among Nigerian households: determinants and sustainability implications. Sustainability **9**(4), 547 (2017)
10. Browning, M., Rigolon, A.: School green space and its impact on academic performance: a systematic literature review. Int. J. Environ. Res. Public Health **16**(3), 429 (2017)
11. Gossling-Goidsmiths, J.: Sustainable development goals and uncertainty visualization. Thesis submitted to the Faculty of Geo-Information Science and Earth Observation of the University of Twente in partial fulfilment of the requirements for the degree of Master of Science in Cartography (2018)
12. Kolk, A.: The social responsibility of international business: from ethics and the environment to CSR and sustainable development. J. World Bus. **51**(1), 23–34 (2016)
13. Gray, R.: Is accounting for sustainability actually accounting for sustainability … and how would we know? An exploration of narratives of organizations and the planet. Acc. Organ. Soc. **35**(1), 47–62 (2010)
14. Levy, Y., Ellis, T.J.: A systems approach to conduct an effective literature review in support of information systems research. Inform. Sci. Int. J. Emerg. Transdisc. **9**, 181–212 (2006)
15. Ferenhof, H.A., Fernandes, R.F.: Demystifying the literature review as basis for scientific writing: SSF method. Revista ACB (2016)
16. United Nations, Department of Economic and Social Affairs, Sustainable Development. https://sdgs.un.org/goals. Accessed 13 Mar 2022
17. McNaught, C., Lam, P.: Using wordle as a supplementary research tool. HCAS J. TQR **15**, 3 (2010)
18. Hartmanna, D., Bezerra, M., Lodolo, B., Pinheiro, F.L.: International trade, development traps, and the core-periphery structure of income inequality. Economia **21**, 255–278 (2020)

Fads and Misleading Concepts Are Influencing Urban Mobility and City Logistics?

Helcio Raymundo[1] and João Gilberto M. dos Reis[1,2(✉)]

[1] RESUP – Research Group in Supply Chain, Postgraduate Programme in Production Engineering, Universidade Paulista – UNIP, Dr. Bacelar, 1212, São Paulo, SP 04026-002, Brazil
helcioru@uol.com.br, joao.reis@docente.unip.br
[2] Centro de Ciências Sociais Aplicadas, Mackenzie Presbyterian University, São Paulo, Brazil
joao.reis@mackenzie.br

Abstract. The knowledge or information society has brought risks of misinformation for the public and academia. "Greenwashing" in the environmental sciences exists and cannot be ignored. In the fields of "Urban Mobility" and "City Logistics," which share similar processes and the same environment, it is also essential to verify the influence of fads and misleading concepts. Thus, this paper aims to answer this question. To this end, out of a sample of 561 websites, 32 were selected for deep analysis. We conclude that the risk of contamination by fads and misleading concepts is moderate but not negligible, requiring a continuously strong posture in defense of science from the scientific community and society.

Keywords: Fads · Misleading concepts · Urban mobility · City logistic

1 Introduction

Today's society can be characterized as a knowledge or information society anchored in scientific and technological innovation [1], thus enabling us to exert our influences, whatever role we play as stakeholders, such as citizens, planners, decision-makers, or policymakers [2].

Nonetheless, the consumer society (mass society) overlaps with the knowledge or information society [3], powerfully shaped by mass media, continuously propagating the West's hegemonic social, cultural, political, economic, and military values [4], typically relying on arguments from popularity or tradition [5]. Even so, Western values are not free of logical or scientific scrutiny, given that controversies related to "climate change," for example, up until now, remain [6]. In the same way, are still under discussion statements, such as:

- [7]: *'The problems of technological development that produced the environmental crisis have their roots in the typically European way of dealing with nature;'*
- [8]: *'Today's global capitalism developed out of the crisis of European feudalism;'* or

© IFIP International Federation for Information Processing 2022
Published by Springer Nature Switzerland AG 2022
D. Y. Kim et al. (Eds.): APMS 2022, IFIP AICT 663, pp. 563–573, 2022.
https://doi.org/10.1007/978-3-031-16407-1_66

- [9]: '*International law and democracy simply refer to the separation of state and religion.*'

In this sense, it is a matter of concern to note that there may be a variable influence of fads or misleading concepts dictated exclusively by commercial interests. Even more severe is the practice of "brainwashing," such as "greenwashing," a process of conveying a false impression or providing misleading information about how a company's products are more environmentally sound. Practices like these allow some companies to obtain undue advantages and mask fraudulent practices [10].

Thus, to answer the question that gives the title to this paper, it is necessary to know the evolving path of the concept and definitions of "Urban Mobility" and "City Logistics" and verify the influence of fads or misleading concepts. Accordingly, this article aims to answer if fads or misled concepts have influenced "Urban Mobility" and "City Logistics."

To this end, we developed a website screening for "Urban Mobility" (plus "Sustainable Urban Mobility") and "City Logistics" (plus "Urban Freight Transport" and "Urban Logistics"), generating a primary sample of 561 website candidates. From the sample, dismissing those with clear commercial interest, 36 websites were selected for deep analysis, in which we looked for terms or expressions such as "smart cities," "resilience," "greener," or "sustainability" and their speeches without a precise scientific basis of support. Even though these terms and expressions may belong to the academic lexicon, and maybe with ulterior motives, they have been widely used by mass media as something brand new and irresistible in the conquest of hearts and minds of public opinion, as fetish concepts [11], becoming hegemonic and sustaining decisions to buy and sell products and services with these labels [12].

2   Material and Methods

"Urban Mobility" was initially defined as the capability of people to move around in urban environments [13]. However, some authors [14, 15], in a broader and more generously humanistic approach, prefer to understand "Urban Mobility" as a cities' attribute, i. e., depending on (i) the location and distribution of the human activities (in which Urban Planning should play a key role), (ii) the intensity in carrying on these activities (related to social and economics inputs), and (iii) the supply of the passengers' transportation systems.

Beyond that, more recently, the idea of "Sustainable Urban Mobility" arrived as:

- [16]: '*The ability to meet society's need to move freely without sacrificing other essential human or ecological values, today or in the future;*' or, in a functional sense; and
- [17]: '*Organizing urban mobility around the objectives of wider accessibility, reduced automobile dependence, saving energy and reducing carbon emissions, hence increasing the livability of the cities.*'

"City Logistics," in contrast, even evolved from "Urban Freight Transport" to "Urban Logistics" [18], is voiced by a more function-oriented definition, as we can see in [19], as: '*the process for totally optimizing the logistics and transport activities by private companies with the support of advanced information systems in urban areas considering the traffic environment, the traffic congestion, the traffic safety and the energy savings within the framework of a market economy.*'

Despite different definitions, "Urban Mobility" and "City Logistics" are under similar stakeholders, and their relationships can be explained as follows:

- They happen in urban areas, which means that both are subjected to the same inputs and outputs of the urban metabolism process [20];
- The vehicles of their transportation systems share the same scarce spaces in the urban environment, generally called road systems or infrastructure [21], in which public policies would ideally result from high-quality Urban Planning that has been mainly focused on this infrastructure [22]; and
- Climate change affects passenger and freight transportation systems, and their functioning amplifies the harmful effects of climate change [23, 24].

One more element needs to be understood: how are fads and misleading concepts communicated ('transmitted') to "Urban Mobility" and "City Logistics'" stakeholders? Or, in other words: how do the stakeholders 'consume' it? Or: how are fads and misled concepts propagated or spread?

According to mainstream practices supported in the literature, mass media still relies on TV, radio, newspapers, and magazines for exclusive offers, social media for institutional image management and brand strengthening, and sites and emails for direct customer access [25, 26]. Under this condition, we decided to verify the following:

- The existence and influence of fads and misleading concepts in websites supposedly targeted at the general audience and "Urban Mobility" and "City Logistics" stakeholders; and
- The focus of each website and whether they are scientifically oriented, i.e., if the literature supports their statements.

Thus, a simplified research methodology is developed, consisting of website screening on Google Search®. The search results are based on a priority rank system of Google Search®, known as "PageRan®," a way of measuring the "relevance" of websites [27]. The keywords considered are: "Urban Mobility" and "Sustainable Urban Mobility," forming Group 1; and "Urban Freight Transport," "Urban Logistics," and "City Logistics." forming Group 2. The following five sub-items describe the research features and results obtained.

2.1 Urban Mobility

For "Urban Mobility," research was carried out on 02/23/2022, and among 88 websites, 12 were selected for a deep analysis (13.6%), while for "Sustainable Urban Mobility," research was conducted on 03/07/2022, and from 132 websites, 12 were selected (9.1%). The findings are in Table 1 and Table 2.

Table 1. Urban mobility (GROUP 1)- research analysis

#	Name and type of organization	Fads or misleading concepts	Comments
1	**EIT Urban Mobility** Governmental. EU	Not found	(i) Focus on **innovation**; (ii) Scientific approach
2	**WRI** NGO. World	Not found	(i) Focus on **sustainable cities**; (ii) Scientific approach
3	**TUMI** Governmental. Germany	Not found	(i) Focus on **sustainability**; (ii) Some requirements of service and equipment are compulsory; (iii) Some statements may sound prejudiced or colonialist; (iv) Scientific approach
4	**UIA** Governmental. EU	Not found	(i) Focus on **urban changes**; (ii) Scientific-oriented approach
5	**Intertraffic** B2B Portal. World	Partly	(i) Many focuses; (ii) Full of clichés, making it difficult to vouch for scientific accuracy
6	**CIVITAS** Governmental. EU	Partly	(i) Focus on **sustainability & smart mobility**; (ii) There are conflicting concepts; (iii) Scientific approach
7	**UITP** Association. World	Not found	(i) Focus on **public transportation**; (ii) 50% of the associates are operators; 43% manufacturers, 5% government authorities; and 2% others; (iii) Scientific approach
8	**Eltis** NGO. EU	Not found	(i) Focus on **Sustainable Urban Mobility**; (ii) Scientific approach
9	PADAM Mobility Company. Germany	Partly	(i) Focus on **Demand-Responsive Transport**; (ii) A sales-oriented approach could hide scientific accuracy
10	**Urban Insight/Sweco** Company. Sweden	Partly	(i) Many focuses; (ii) A sales-oriented approach could hide scientific accuracy

(continued)

Table 1. (*continued*)

#	Name and type of organization	Fads or misleading concepts	Comments
11	**Interreg Mediterranean** Governmental. EU	Not found	(i) Focus on **"smarter" and "greener;"** (ii) Scientific approach
12	**ITPD** NGO. World	Not found	(i) Focus on **cities for a sustainable and livable future**; (ii) Scientific approach

Table 2. Sustainable urban mobility (GROUP 1) - research analysis

#	Name and type of organization	Fads or misleading concepts	Comments
1	**European Commission** Governmental. EU	Not found	(i) Focus on **Sustainable Urban Mobility Indicators**; (ii) Scientific approach
2	**TUMI** - See Table 1	See Table 1	See Table 1
3	**UBC** NGO. Baltic Cities	Not found	(i) Focus on **sustainable cities**; (ii) Scientific approach
4	**Urban Insight** - See Table1	See Table 1	See Table 1
5	**Flows - Modelling Mobility** Blog. World	Not found	(i) Many focuses; (ii) Scientific approach
6	**Eit** Governmental. EU	Not found	(i) Many focuses; (ii) Scientific approach
7	**CIVITAS** - See Table 1	See Table 1	See Table 1
8	**State of Green** Governmental. Denmark	Not found	(i) Focus on **"green vision;"** (ii) Scientific approach
9	**The Recursive** Online community. Bulgaria	Partly	(i) Focus on **Recursive Innovation**; (ii) A marketing approach could hide scientific accuracy
10	**Smart Cities Dive** B2B Portal. World	Partly	(i) Many focuses; (ii) Full of clichés, hiding scientific accuracy

(*continued*)

Table 2. (*continued*)

#	Name and type of organization	Fads or misleading concepts	Comments
11	TNO – Innovation for Life NGO. World	Not found	(i) Focus on **"smarter"** and **"greener;"** (ii) Scientific approach
12	WWF – World Wildlife Fund NGO. World	Not found	(i) Many focuses; (ii) Scientific approach

2.2   City Logistics

For City Logistics, research was conducted on 02/24/2022, and among 143 websites, four (2.8%) were selected for deep analysis, while for Urban Freight Transport, research was carried out on 03/05/2022, and from 88 websites, four were selected (4.5%). For Urban Logistics, on 03/02/2022, four websites (3.6%) were selected among 110. The findings are in Tables 3, 4, and 5.

Table 3. City logistics (GROUP 2) - research analysis

#	Name and type of organization	Fads or misleading concepts	Comments
1	**CityChangers.org** Online community. World	Not found	(i) Many focuses; (ii) Scientific approach
2	**JLL** Company. England	Partly	(i) Many focuses; (ii) A marketing approach could hide scientific accuracy
3	**DB Schenker** Company. Germany	Not found	(i) Many focuses; (ii) Scientific approach
4	**MIXMOVE** Company. Norway	Not found	(i) Focus on **cloud software for logistics**; (ii) Scientific approach

Table 4. Urban freight transport (GROUP 2) - research analysis

#	Name and type of organization	Fads or misleading concepts	Comments
1	**ICLEI** NGO. World	Not found	(i) Many focuses; (ii); Consultancy with the members; (iii) Scientific approach
2	**POLIS** NGO. Europe	Not found	(i) Focus on **innovative technologies**; (ii) Scientific approach
3	**BESTFACT** NGO. Europe	Not found	(i) Many focuses; (ii) Scientific approach
4	**EEA and Norway Grants** Governmental. Iceland/Lichenstein/Norway	Not found	(i) Many focuses; (ii) Scientific approach

Table 5. Urban logistics (GROUP 2) - research analysis

#	Name and type of organization	Fads or misleading concepts	Comments
1	**MOVILIBLOG** Blog. World	Not found	(i) Focus on **Urban Logistics as a Service**; (ii) Scientific approach
2	Urban Redevelopment Authority Governmental. Singapore	Not found	(i) Focus on **urban logistics**; (ii) Scientific approach
3	**AISIN Mobility** Company. Japan	Not found	(i) Focus on **logistics platforms**; (ii) Scientific approach
4	**UNICEN** Industry-university partnership. Japan/Singapore	Not found	(i) Many focuses; (ii) Scientific approach

3   Results and Discussions

From Tables 1, 2, 3, 4 and 5, among 561 websites generated by the website screening on Google Search® (220 related to "Urban Mobility" and "Sustainable Urban Mobility" and 341 related to "Urban Freight Transport," "Urban Logistics" and "City Logistics"), 36 (6,4%) (24 from Group 1 and 12 from Group 2) were selected for deep analysis. The types of organizations of these 36 websites are shown in Table 6.

Table 6. Types of organization distribution

Type of organizations	"Urban Mobility"	"Sustainable Urban Mobility"	"Urban Freight Transport"	"Urban Logistics"	"City Logistics"
Governmental	**5**	**5**	1	1	0
NGO	3	3	3	0	0
B2B Portal	1	1	0	0	0
Association	1	0	0	0	0
Company	2	1	0	1	**3**
Blog	0	1	0	1	0
Online community	0	1	0	0	1
Industry-university partnership	0	0	0	1	0

In Group 1, governmental organizations prevail, while in Group 2, other types of predominantly private organizations appear. It is an expected result since the nature of the activities involved in Group 1, conducted directly or indirectly by governments, receives funding from climate, environmental, carbon credit, and similar funds. On the other hand, in Group 2, whose activities are private, the participation of companies is relatively greater. It should highlight that European organizations, followed by Japanese and Singapore ones, predominate in the two groups and that "Urban Mobility" was captured by "Sustainable Urban Mobility," which may suggest a sign of the influence of the "sustainability" fad.

The influence of fads and misleading concepts found in the deep analysis and the corresponding comments about focus and approach are shown in Table 7.

Table 7. Possibility of fads and misleading concepts, focus and approach

Expressions	Fads/Misleading concepts		Comments			
	Not found	Partly	Focus		Approach	
			With focus on	Many Focuses	Sales or Marketing	Scientific
Urban Mobility (12)	8	4	10	2	3	9
Sustainable Urban (12) Mobility	8	4	7	5	3	9

(continued)

Table 7. (*continued*)

Expressions	Fads/Misleading concepts		Comments			
	Not found	Partly	Focus		Approach	
			With focus on	Many Focuses	Sales or Marketing	Scientific
GROUP 1 (24)	16	8	17	7	6	19
Urban Freight (04) Transport	4	0	1	3	0	4
Urban Logistics (04)	4	0	3	1	0	4
City Logistics (04)	3	1	1	3	1	3
GROUP 2 (12)	11	1	5	7	1	11
GROUP 1 + 2 (36)	27	9	22	14	7	28

In Group 1, possible fads and misleading concepts are not found in 66.7% of the websites and only partly in 33.3%. In Group 2, 91,7% and 8.3% are the numbers. Regarding "focus," Group 1 shows 70.8% of the websites "with focus," and 29.2% with "many focuses," while in Group 2, we found 41.7% and 58.3%.

Of the 22 websites "with focus" of the two groups, only one is focused on the corresponding keyword ("Urban Logistics"). On the other hand, the remaining 21 websites focus on innovation, sustainable cities, urban changes, sustainability & smart mobility, public transportation, Demand-Responsive-Transport, "smarter" and "greener," cities for sustainable livable future, sustainable urban mobility indicators, "green vision," Recursive Innovation, innovative technologies, Urban Logistics as a Service, logistics platforms, and cloud software for logistics.

Fortunately, the scientific approach predominates in Groups 1 and 2, respectively, with 79.2% and 91.7%.

4 Conclusions

We conclude that issues like "Urban Mobility" and "Sustainable Urban Mobility" involving governments competing for resources from global investment funds can be at moderate risk of being influenced by fads or misled concepts. On the other hand, for "Urban Freight Transport," "Urban Logistics," and "City Logistics," the risk may be lower once fads and misleading concepts differently influence them as a primarily private activity.

Within the limits of our research, we can also conclude that fads and misleading concepts are influencing "Urban Mobility" and "City Logistics" to a moderate degree.

However, and fortunately, among 32 websites investigated, 28 (87.5%) have a scientific-oriented approach.

Thus, more research is needed to verify to what extent the influence described in this paper may be more significant and lessen its harmful effects. For these reasons, the scientific community should be aware and ensure that the needs of governments, public transport operators, logistics operators, decision-makers, policymakers, and the stakeholders involved are always met accordingly to strictly scientific principles.

References

1. Ranga, M., Etzkowitz, H.: Triple helix systems: an analytical framework for innovation policy and practice in the knowledge society. In: Mitra, J., Edmondson, J. (eds.) Entrepreneurship and Knowledge Exchange, pp. 117–158. Routledge, New York (2015)
2. Conrad, E., Cassar, L.F., Christie, M., Fazey, I.: Hearing but not listening? A participatory assessment of public participation in planning. Eviron. Plan. C Gov. Policy 29(5), 761–782 (2011)
3. Minati, G.: Knowledge to manage the knowledge society. Learn. Organ. 19(4), 350–368 (2012). https://doi.org/10.1108/09696471211226707
4. Acharya, A.: After liberal hegemony: the advent of a multiplex world order. Ethics Int. Aff. 31(3), 271–285 (2017)
5. Harding, T.: Common sense fallacy (2014). https://yandoo.wordpress.com/2014/12/28/com mon-sense-fallacy/. Accessed 28 Feb 2022
6. Sarewitz, D.: How science makes environmental controversies worse. Environ. Sci. Policy 7(5), 385–403 (2004)
7. Du Pisani, J.A.: Sustainable development–historical roots of the concept. Environ. Sci. 3(2), 83–96 (2006)
8. Bieler, A., Morton, A.D.: Global Capitalism, Global War, Global Crisis. Cambridge University Press, Cambridge (2018)
9. Marks, S.: The Riddle of All Constitutions: International Law, Democracy, and the Critique of Ideology. Oxford University Press, Oxford (2003)
10. De Freitas Netto, S.V., Sobral, M.F.F., Ribeiro, A.R.B., Da Luz Soares, G.R.: Concepts and forms of greenwashing: a systematic review. Environ. Sci. Eur. 32(1), 1–12 (2020)
11. Bondanella, P.: Umberto Eco and the Open Text: Semiotics, Fiction, Popular Culture. Cambridge University Press, Cambridge (2005)
12. Eco, U.: Faith in fakes. Random House (2014)
13. Mitchell, W.J., Borroni-Bird, C.E., Burns, L.D.: Reinventing the Automobile: Personal Urban Mobility for the 21st Century. MIT press, Cambridge (2010)
14. de Freitas Miranda, H., da Silva, A.N.R.: Benchmarking sustainable urban mobility: the case of Curitiba, Brazil. Transp. Policy 21, 141–151 (2012)
15. Klinger, T., Kenworthy, J.R., Lanzendorf, M.: Dimensions of urban mobility cultures: a comparison of German cities. J. Transp. Geogr. 31, 18–29 (2013)
16. Williams, K.: Spatial planning, urban form and sustainable transport: an introduction. In: Spatial Planning, Urban Form and Sustainable Transport, pp. 15–28. Routledge, Abingdon-on-Thames (2017)
17. Wee, B.: Urban transport and sustainability. In: van Bueren, E., van Bohemen, H., Itard, L., Visscher, H. (eds.) Sustainable Urban Environments, pp. 243–261. Springer, Dordrecht (2012). https://doi.org/10.1007/978-94-007-1294-2_9
18. Rose, W.J., Bell, J.E., Autry, C.W., Cherry, C.R.: Urban logistics: Establishing key concepts and building a conceptual framework for future research. Transp. J. 56(4), 357–394 (2017)

19. Taniguchi, E., Thompson, R.G., Yamada, T., van Duin, R.: City Logistics: Network Modeling and Intelligent Transport Systems. Pergamon, Oxford (2001)
20. Chrysoulakis, N., De Castro, E.A., Moors, E.J. (eds.): Understanding Urban Metabolism: A Tool for Urban Planning. Routledge, Abingdon-on-Thames (2014)
21. Maggi, E., Vallino, E.: Understanding urban mobility and the impact of public policies: the role of the agent-based models. Res. Transp. Econ. **55**, 50–59 (2016)
22. Kennedy, C., Miller, E., Shalaby, A., Maclean, H., Coleman, J.: The four pillars of sustainable urban transportation. Transp. Rev. **25**(4), 393–414 (2005)
23. Song, X.: The potential impacts of climate change on transportation systems. In: CICTP 2020, pp. 4609–4619 (2020)
24. Banister, D.: Cities, mobility and climate change. J. Transp. Geogr. **19**(6), 1538–1546 (2011)
25. Saravanakumar, M., SuganthaLakshmi, T.: Social media marketing. Life Sci. J. **9**(4), 4444–4451 (2012)
26. Venzke, S.: Social media marketing. Datenschutz und Datensicherheit - DuD **35**(6), 387–392 (2011). https://doi.org/10.1007/s11623-011-0096-9
27. Piasecki, J., Waligora, M., Dranseika, V.: Google search as an additional source in systematic reviews. Sci. Eng. Ethics **24**(2), 809–810 (2018)

Fatal Traffic Accidents in São Paulo State, Brazil: Social Characteristics and Social Distance Effects

Sivanilza Teixeira Machado[1,2(✉)] [iD] and João Gilberto Mendes dos Reis[1,3] [iD]

[1] BS in Civil Engineering (in Progress) - Universidade Paulista - UNIP, 1212 Doutor Bacelar Street, São Paulo, SP 04026002, Brazil
sivanilzamachado@ifsp.edu.br, napole.ifsp@gmail.com,
joao.reis@docente.unip.br
[2] NAPOLE - Research Group, Federal Institute of São Paulo – IFSP,
1501 Mogi das Cruzes Avenue, Suzano, SP 08673010, Brazil
[3] RESUP – Supply Chain Research Group, Postgraduate Studies in Production
Engineering/Postgraduate Studies in Business Administration, Universidade Paulista - UNIP,
1212 Doutor. Bacelar Street, São Paulo, SP 04026002, Brazil

Abstract. Every day someone become a victims of road traffic accidents. A traffic accident is a social, economic and health public problem that affects all society. However, the comprehension of its main causes is still a work in process. The influence of traffic volume can be suggested based on the impact of COVID-19 crisis, since that the fatal traffic accident in São Paulo city in 2020 dropped almost 1/3 in relation to 2019. Thus, the objective of this paper is to analyze the number of fatal traffic victims [FTV] in São Paulo State among January 2015 and September 2021. To do so, we used a São Paulo State database over fatal traffic accidents and applied the statistical analysis to provide graphical and cross tabulation results. Our results indicate that São Paulo Metropolitan Region (RMSP) is responsible for 1/3 of the FTV occurred in São Paulo State, and there was a decrease in the number of fatal traffic victims due to public policies applications and social distance caused by COVID-19. Furthermore, it identifies social characteristics that contribute to unsafety traffic such as gender (male), life stage (adult), vehicle (motorcycle), period of the day (night) and days of the week (Saturday and Sunday). We conclude that this research provides information necessary to auxiliary decision-makers to develop urban transportation plans to reduce fatal traffic accidents.

Keywords: Driver behaviour · Risk factors · Road accidents · Urban mobility

1 Introduction

Every year around 1.3 million people die worldwide victims of road traffic accidents which represent 3% of Countries' GDP [1]. Due to this problem, many governments start to implement urban mobility plans to reduce the mortality accident index. In Brazil is not different, the traffic national code established that drivers caught conducting a vehicle

© IFIP International Federation for Information Processing 2022
Published by Springer Nature Switzerland AG 2022
D. Y. Kim et al. (Eds.): APMS 2022, IFIP AICT 663, pp. 574–581, 2022.
https://doi.org/10.1007/978-3-031-16407-1_67

under alcohol influence is judged as a criminal with the clear intention of committing murder. However, we can find other more lenient initiatives inside the country. São Paulo city government, for instance, implemented a reduction of speedy limit in roads and highways, improved traffic signalling, and created bicycle lanes [2].

A traffic accident is a social, economic and health public problem that affects all society. However, the comprehension of its main causes is still a work in process. Some authors suggest that human bad behaviour, lack of road infrastructure, lack of traffic control and monitorization are among the main causes that contribute to fatal traffic accidents [1, 3, 4, 5]. Souza and Oliveira Neto showed a strong correlation between road congestion caused by traffic accidents and the response time in the release of the road (highway) after the traffic accident [4]. In 2010, 43.8 thousand Brazilian died in traffic accidents (22.5 per 100 thousand inhabitants) [2].

The influence of traffic volume can be suggested based on the impact of COVID19 crisis. In 2020, the fatal traffic accident in São Paulo city dropped 29.5% in relation to 2019 [6]. These statistics represent a benefit of the social isolation and restriction law adopted by the local government. However, this association was not tested, and the fact is thousands of people lose their lives every year in traffic accidents.

With these ideas in mind, we highlighted two research questions to be verified in this study: RQ1 – Is the Pandemic Crisis of COVID19 the only one responsible for accidents reduction in São Paulo State, Brazil? RQ2 – Is it possible to find out the main social characteristics that influence the number of fatal traffic accidents in São Paulo State, Brazil?

São Paulo state concentrates more than 40 million people – around 20% of the Brazilian population – where its capital of the same name São Paulo has approximately 12 million inhabitants and add the 39 cities of its metropolitan area have around 50% of the state total population. Therefore, this study is not important only for Brazil but can be a comparison model for many countries around the world that have an equal population or big metropolitan areas.

To answer the research questions the objective of this paper is to analyze the number of fatal traffic victims [FTV] in São Paulo State among January 2015 and September 2021 (last data available) using statistical tools. To do so, we used a São Paulo State database over fatal traffic accidents and Microsoft Excel®, R software and QGIS to organize them and provide the statistical and graphical results.

This paper was structured in four sections: the first part contains the introduction, where the problematic and aims were presented; second, we informed what methodology and analysis data were performed; third, we showed the finds and discussion about FTV; and finally, we present our conclusion of the study.

2 Methodology

As mentioned previously, we analyzed the number of fatal victims' occurrences in transit of the São Paulo State from 2015 up to September 2021. Data was obtained from São Paulo State Government, and it was composed of 31,663 fatal victim occurrences. In the database, we dropped the occurrences without geographic points resulting in a final number of 29,781.

The input data is the year, month, geographic points, gender, age, day of the week, times of the day, city, accident site, model of vehicle, class of victims, death site and kind of the accident, Table 1.

Table 1. Description of the variables

Variables	Category	Description/Terms definition
Year	2015–2021	
Month	Jan–dec	
Geographic points	Latitude; longitude	
Gender	Male; female	
Age	Baby; child; adolescent; young adult, adult, and elderly	Baby $= 0 \sim 2$ years old; Child $= 3 \sim 11$ years old; Adolescent $= 12 \sim 18$ years old; Young Adult $= 19 \sim 24$ years old Adult $= 25 \sim 60$ years old Elderly $=$ above 60 years old
Day of the week	Monday ~ sunday	7 days of the week
Times of the day	Morning ~ midnight	Morning $= 06:00 \sim 11:59$ a.m Afternoon $= 12:00 \sim 05:59$ p.m Evening $= 06:00 \sim 11:59$ p.m Dawn $= 00:00 \sim 5:59$ a.m
City	Adamantina ~ Zacarias	645 cities that composed São Paulo State
Accident site	Municipal roads; highways	
Model of vehicle	Bicycle; bus; car; motorcycle; on foot; other; truck	
Class of victims	Driver; passenger; pedestrian	
Death site	Hospital; accident site; other	Hospital $=$ health establishment; accident site $=$ in municipal roads/highways;
Kind of the accident	Hit; collision; crash; other	Collision $=$ two or more vehicles in the movement were involved Crash $=$ one vehicle in movement and other/object was stopped

Source: Based on the database from São Paulo State Government

2.1 Data Organization and Analysis

Firstly, we organized the data using a spreadsheet in Microsoft Excel. Secondly, we carried out descriptive statistics to analyse the numeric and categorical variables to explore the frequency distribution, proportionality (R 4.0.5 Software), and the density mapping of the FTV occurrence in São Paulo State based on the geographic point (QGIS v 3.24 Software). After, to answer the RQ1, the graphic was applied to determine the decrease value of FTV through simple regression analysis using of R 4.0.5 Software.

In addition, to answer the RQ2, we investigated the association among categorical variables to identify the social characteristics on FTV applying the Chi-squared (χ^2), Eq. 1 [7].

$$\chi^2 = \sum_{i=1}^{I} \sum_{j=1}^{J} \frac{(Oij - Eij)^2}{Eij} \tag{1}$$

where, I = number of variable categories of X; J = number of variable categories of Y; Oij = number of observations (i = categories of variable X; j = categories of variable Y); Eij = expected frequency of observations (i = categories of variable X; j = categories of variable Y). In this analysis, we applied the 95% confidence interval.

3   Results and Discussion

3.1   Fatal Traffic Accident Reduction and Social Distance

Our results indicated that one third of fatal traffic accidents in the State of São Paulo occurred in the São Paulo Metropolitan Region (RMSP), area highlighted in Fig. 1. The RMSP is comprised of 39 municipalities, where live approximately 22 million inhabitants [8]. Traffic accident on the world represent the 1.35 million deaths per year, and the Africa and South-East Asia region presented higher deaths rate than global [1].

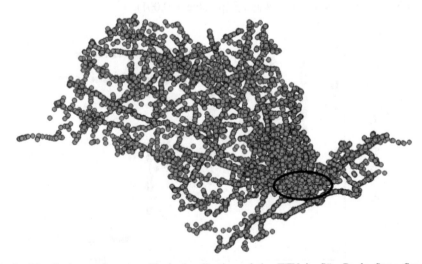

Fig. 1. Distribution and geographical visualization of the FTV in São Paulo State Source: Research results from QGIS Software

Fatal traffic victims' rates in the State of São Paulo have been decreasing since 2015. They dropped more than 10% in 2020 suggesting a relation between traffic volume and fatal accidents, Table 2. The rate of social isolation in São Paulo city, for instance, reached 48%, which represented almost of the 6 million inhabitants out of traffic [9]. Therefore, our study indicates that Pandemic Crisis influenced the drop numbers rather than security measures. This result requires further studies after the end of the emergency of COVID19 to be conclusive.

Table 2. Description statistical of number of deaths in transit by year

Year	n	VAR (%)	Average	SD	Maximum	Minimum
2015	5.054	–	421.17	87.52	508	162
2016	5.032	−0.44	419.33	34.89	481	364
2017	4.612	−8.35	384.33	48.45	490	314
2018	4.256	−7.72	354.67	33.71	404	290
2019	4.462	4.84	371.83	41.62	428	281
2020	3.840	−13.94	320.00	28.95	362	264
2021*	2.525	−34.24	280.56	36.74	342	230

n = number of de FTV per year; VAR % = variation of FTV per year (in percentage); SD = standard deviation; *up to September/2021.

The decrease value of FTV per year during period analysis can be better visualized in Fig. 2, which presents the statistically significant linear model (F-statistics = 62.03; $p < 0.001$), and the parameters α and β (p-value < 0.001).

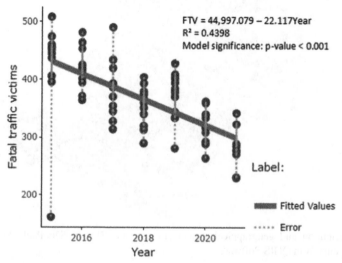

Fig. 2. Decrease value of FTV per year Source: Adapted from R Software

Despite the data being related to São Paulo State, São Paulo city has a great contribution to this scenario, due to the government plan to reduce the speed limit of roads in 2011. According to Sarno's study, in the second semester of 2016, São Paulo city showed a drop of 44,5% in the rate of FTV [5]. This argument is supported by World Health Organization [WHO] which reported that the death risk rises 4.5 times for pedestrians hit when car velocity increases from 50 to 65 km/h [1]. These observations allow us to consider that COVID19 is not the only reason to drop numbers. Perhaps it is responsible for the sharp decay but not for the total reduction.

Public policies to make traffic safer also contributes to the urban mobility plan, encouraging walking and cycling on urban roads, and reducing the number of vehicles. Many people report that they do not use the bicycle as a mode of transport, because they do not feel safe [2].

3.2 Social Characteristics that Influence Fatal Traffic Accidents

Our results also showed that most victims were male (81.5%), and females correspond 18.5% indicating an association between gender and fatal traffic accidents. According to WHO, 73% of road traffic death is related the road user's young male under 25 years old [1] which allows us to characterize the driver profile involved in road accidents. Moreover, we obtained a significant association between gender and period of the day ($\chi^2 = 104.25$; $p < 0,001$), however, surprisingly we did not find the same results between gender and days of the week ($\chi^2 = 9,827.0$; $p = 0.1321$).

Analysing the period of the day with the highest incidence of FTV, it was observed that about 36.5% occur in the evening, followed by 23.5% in the afternoon, 20.5% at dawn and 19.5% in the morning ($\chi^2 = 702.8$; $p < 0,001$). In addition, we observed that most accidents occur on weekends 39.5%, 14.5% on Fridays and the other days of the week around 11.5% each. Both scenarios indicate an association among youths, leisure and traffic imprudence. According to Ferreira et al., the young drivers liked to test the car capacity and velocity, and the speed limit is one the traffic legislative criteria not relevant to them [3]. This behaviour is against what WHO indicated as seven behavioural risk factor on traffic that require legislative criteria such as speed, drink-driving, motorcycle helmets, seat-belts, child restraints, drug-driving and mobile phones [1].

Investigating the existence of an association between the gender of the victims and the life stage (Fig. 3), we noted that approximate 61% of the cases occur by people in the adult stage, following elderly (17%) and young adults (15.5%). Also, the class of victims and life stage ($\chi^2 = 4,285$; $p < 0,05$), we highlighted that almost 39% were related drivers in adult life, 12.5% were pedestrian in adult stage too, and 10.6% were drivers in the young adult stage. WHO reported that the main fatal victim of road traffic injuries is children and young adults aged 5–29 years [1].

Thus, we can infer the reasons are adults make more travels alone and are more exposed to distractions in imprudence both as a pedestrian or a driver. Moreover, young adult drivers usually make mistakes based on their inexperience of conducting a vehicle or under traffic imprudence (speed limit exceed, alcohol influence, etc.) [3, 5].

Regarding the analysis of the types of vehicles involved in FTV, it was noted that the majority are motorcycles and cars, respectively 35.8% and 26.16%. Most victims are represented by drivers, pedestrians and passengers, Table 3. The global results from

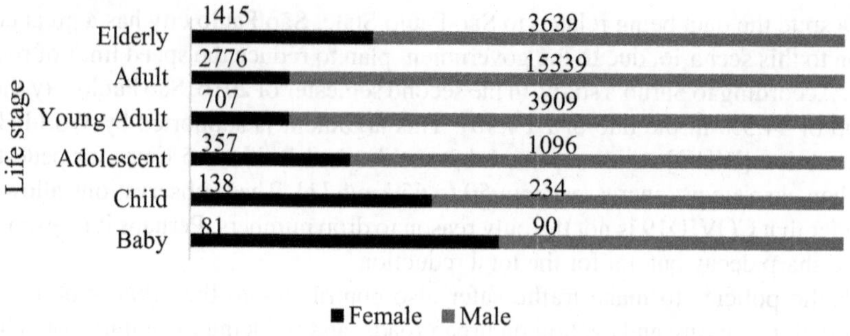

$\chi^2 = 673$; p < 0,001

Fig. 3. Death in transit by life stage and gender, values in percentage.

WHO corroborated our results, highlighting that road traffic death is higher for vulnerable users: pedestrians, cyclists and motorcyclists [1].

Table 3. Percentage of number of FTV by vehicle and class of victim

Vehicle	Driver	Passenger	Pedestrian	na
Car	16.42	8.30	–	1.43
Bicycle	5.88	0.04	–	0.09
Truck	2.84	0.60	–	0.08
Motorcycle	31.62	3.12	–	1.06
Bus	0.19	0.70	–	0.03
Other	0.36	0.08	–	0.05
On foot			23.99	
na	0.35	0.04	–	2.73
Total	**57.66**	**12.88**	**23.99**	**5.47**

$\chi^2 = 45,838$; p < 0,001; na = not available.

We found a significant statistical association between model of vehicles and kind of accidents ($\chi^2 = 39,075$; p < 0,001), collision is 1.6 higher than hit. Analysing each number, vehicles involved in a road accident is led by motorcycle (49.4%), cars (32.8%), bicycle (11%), and others. In relation to foot represent 94.6% road hit. These results reinforce the unsafe condition of São Paulo State roads. We also found a significant association between the class of victims and death site ($\chi^2 = 1,056.5$; p < 0,001), and 52% of victims die in hospitals, 43% on roads and the others in different sites as ambulances during transportation from road to the hospital.

4 Conclusions

This paper analyzed fatal traffic victims in São Paulo State to explore the reason for drop in values in accident numbers and how the accidents are related to social aspects. Our results indicate that there was a decrease in the number of fatal traffic victims due to public policies applications and social distance caused by COVID-19. Furthermore, it identifies social characteristics that contribute to unsafety traffic such as gender (male), life stage (adult), vehicle (motorcycle), period of the day (night) and days of the week (Saturday and Sunday).

The results of this research provide information necessary to auxiliary decision-makers to develop urban transportation plans to reduce fatal traffic accidents. Moreover, the numbers of São Paulo state may be used as a comparison for other states, regions, and cities worldwide.

The limitation of the paper is highlighted by lack of variables like condition of the road/highway infrastructure and the driver behaviour. However, the paper contributed to study of the traffic accident and to determine the factor risk that could be provide a based to decision make in traffic public policies.

References

1. World Health Organization [WHO]. https://www.who.int/publications/i/item/9789241565684
2. Municipal Department of Mobility and Traffic of São Paulo. https://www.prefeitura.sp.gov.br/cidade/secretarias/mobilidade/planmob/index.php?p=189299
3. Ferreira, P.C.P., Santos, M.P.S., Nassi, C.D.: Análise comportamental de motociclistas brasileiros no trânsito urbano. In: XXVIII Congresso de Pesquisa e Ensino em Transporte–Anpet. Curitiba; 2014, pp. 1–11 (2014)
4. Souza, V.N., Oliveira Neto, F.M.: Análise do tempo de duração de acidentes de trânsito em vias arteriais de fortaleza. In: 32 Congresso de Pesquisa e Ensino em Transporte da ANPET. Gramado: ANPET; 2018, pp. 3345–8 (2018)
5. Sarno, C.C.B.: Benefícios imediatos da redução das velocidades máximas permitidas. Nota Técnica 251, Companhia de Engenharia de Tráfego (2016)
6. Companhia de Engenharia de Tráfego. http://www.cetsp.com.br/noticias/2021/05/27/cai-numero-total-de-sinistros-de-transito-na-cidade-de-sao-paulo-em-2020.aspx
7. Fávero, L.P., Belfiore, P.: Manual de análise de dados. 1a. LTC, Rio de Janeiro, 2021, p. 1187 (2021)
8. Instituto Brasileiro de Geografia e Estatística [IBGE]. https://cidades.ibge.gov.br/brasil/sp
9. Governo de São Paulo. https://www.saopaulo.sp.gov.br/coronavirus/isolamento/

Urban Traffic and Pollution in the Metropolitan Region of São Paulo (MRSP): Active Transportation as a Mitigation Measure

Izolina Margarida Souza[1]([✉]) [iD], Alexandre Formigoni[1,3] [iD],
Silvia Pierre Irazusta[1,2] [iD], Ana Paula Paglione Aniceto[1] [iD], Lucas Santos Queiroz[3] [iD],
Eliane Antonio Simões[1] [iD], Rosinei Batista Ribeiro[1] [iD], José Wilson Jesus Silva[4] [iD],
and Fabricio José Piacente[1] [iD]

[1] Centro Paula Souza, Unidade de Pós-graduação, extensão e pesquisa, Mestrado Profissional em Gestão e Tecnologia em Sistemas Produtivos, São Paulo, Brasil
guidariana@hotmail.com, silvia.irazusta@fatec.sp.gov.br,
ana.aniceto2@etec.sp.gov.br, {eliane.simoes,rosinei.robeiro,
fabricio.piacente}@cpspos.sp.gov.br
[2] Fatec Sorocaba - José Crespo Gonzales, Sorocaba, Brasil
[3] Fatec Zona Leste, São Paulo, Brasil
[4] UNIFATEA – Centro Universitário Teresa D'ávila, São Paulo, Brasil

Abstract. Progression of population index and economic development in large urban centers, especially in the Metropolitan Region of São Paulo (MRSP), have caused a high rate of pollutant emissions from industries and mainly from the burning of fossil fuels due to excess of motor vehicles generating, as serious consequences of congestion, degradation of air quality, ecosystem and human health. Measures are being taken in several parts of the world in search of alternatives that can make mobility more sustainable. The purpose of this article is to present, by means of exploratory research and a bibliographic review, an active mobility alternative that can promote reduction of emissions and contribute to improving the quality of air and life of the urban population, from and a new culture and positive public policy actions. To search for articles, database of the "Web of Science" platform was used. Documentary analysis pointed to the use of bicycles as an active mobility resource for contributing not only to reducing emissions and improving air quality, but also to promoting a better quality of life for users by means of practice of physical activity, directly impacting them, in public health.

Keywords: Pollution · Urban mobility · Bicycle

1 Introduction

The arrival of large industries in Brazil in 1930 and their concentration in the Southeast region caused an accelerated growth for cities and provoked a great exodus from the countryside in search of jobs (Matos 2012). Real estate speculation led people to settle

© IFIP International Federation for Information Processing 2022
Published by Springer Nature Switzerland AG 2022
D. Y. Kim et al. (Eds.): APMS 2022, IFIP AICT 663, pp. 582–592, 2022.
https://doi.org/10.1007/978-3-031-16407-1_68

in peripheral regions requiring them to take longer trips to work, compromising urban mobility.

Urban mobility can be understood as the mode of locomotion of people and goods in cities, regardless of the means of transport used, admitting collective, individual, motorized or not transport (Pero and Stefanelli 2015) and is considered a sustainable activity when the movement of people and products occurs rationally, with minimal impacts on the environment (Pedro et al. 2017). By promoting the connection of people relating the city and the opportunities offered such as school, work, entertainment, health, among others, rational urban mobility can favor socioeconomic development, if it uses an inclusive road system that preserves environmental quality (Gomide and Galindo 2013). According to Saldiva (2018), the quality of life of people in large cities is linked to poor transportation management, as a 3-h trip to work or study can harm both physical and mental health, directly impacting public health costs.

According to CETESB (in Portuguese, 2021), the poor air quality in the Metropolitan Region of São Paulo (RMSP) comes from industries, but mainly from vehicles and favors the decline in the quality of life of residents of these regions. In 2019, the RMSP concentrated 48% of the state fleet in just 3.2% of the territory, highlighting that, according to the IBGE (2020), 21.9 million inhabitants reside in the RMSP and that number equivalent to 47% of the state's population. This scenario is responsible for congestion caused by excess vehicles, which lead to poor use of public spaces, noise pollution, impaired mobility, poor quality of life, poor air quality, high number of deaths from accidents and cardiorespiratory diseases (Hess 2018).

The COVID-19 pandemic, which had its milestone registered in Brazil in February 2020, has become yet another great challenge to be managed by all the protagonists of the urban complex, and mobility was one of the most affected aspects, evidenced by factors as weaknesses of the public transport system. These circumstances enabled opportunities for changes both in public policies and in relation to people's behavior (Assagawa and Conti 2020). In view of the pandemic scenario, as in other parts of the world, in the RMSP, there was a great stimulus to the use of active transport, highlighting the use of bicycles, as a recommended and validated vehicle within the premises of the World Health Organization (WHO) for sustainable development, by promoting physical activity, avoiding the emission of polluting gases and favoring social distancing, which are unlikely situations when using public transport (WHO 2020).

The aim of this study, therefore, was to present a critical analysis of the environmental conditions in this region of the State of São Paulo, southeastern Brazil, based on official data and literature. The defense of the active mobility resource for large centers such as RMSP, implies public policy decisions and changes in citizens' habits, in order to contribute to the goals of reducing emissions, improving air quality and the population's life. Urban development, in line with the UN's sustainable development goals.

2 Metodology

As a methodology for this study, an exploratory research was carried out with the objective of understanding phenomena that involve the context of urban mobility and air pollution in the MRSP. A discussion about active transport in the MRSP was carried out, based on a bibliographic review, through the search in the database of the Web of Science Portal (free), considering only peer-reviewed articles published in the period of 2016 to 2021, using the keywords bicycle, mobility and São Paulo. Articles in Portuguese were analyzed, also involving the sub-themes urban mobility and urban area. This research also used documents from databases of official bodies such as IEMA Institute of Energy and Environment (IEMA, in Portuguese), Environmental Company of the State of São Paulo (CETESB, in Portuguese); Traffic Engineering Company (CET, in Portuguese); on websites of international organizations such as the World Health Organization (WHO) and United Nations (UN).

3 Results

The bibliographic survey carried out resulted, according to the adopted exclusion criteria, in 153 publications, of which 66 were publications in Portuguese. When the criterion of topics covered was applied, only 8 articles were obtained, of which, after reading and analyzing the objective of the research, 6 were selected for discussion.

In the study by Diógenes *et al.* (2017), 144 volunteers were interviewed, with the objective of identifying the challenges faced in the diffusion of the bicycle as a means of transport The results pointed out 3 main limitations to the use of the bicycle, the driver's behavior (27%), lack of structure (25%) and urban violence (17%). Proving that there is still much to be done in terms of public policies in favor of bicycle users. In fact, the context of risk experienced by residents of large urban centers highlights the need for more wooded areas in the cycle path regions, which can mitigate the impacts of high temperatures in warmer regions and periods (Meneses and Sales 2018), corroborating the need for better structures to encourage the use of cycle paths. Considering user profile and risk exposure, Harkot *et al.* (2018) make an analysis focused on the mobility of women in relation to the number of users of active mobility, identifying that women make 55% of the trips on foot and only 12% of the trips by bicycle. The explanation would be, again, in the safety structure, since the number of women cyclists is greater when the structures are better.

Multi-criteria decision analysis (MCDA), transport-oriented development (TOD) and hierarchical analytical process (AHP) were the tools used to develop a model for prioritizing urban areas for integrated urban revitalization and sustainable mobility projects. These tools help decision-making by municipal managers to establish investment priorities considering demanded priorities versus resources, since they identify and characterize the troubled scenario of large cities, highlighting traffic and pollutants, as well as the budget constraints faced by agencies. Public (Costa and Lima 2019).

The Bike to Work Day is an event, which began in the United States in 1956, spread to other countries and, in Brazil, began in 2013, whose repercussions have shown that, despite global movements, public policies, warning about the changes necessary for better air and life quality, changing people's behavior is vitally important to overcome these challenges (Kruszielski and Patricio 2016). Events such as the Intermodal Challenge, Solidarity Carriage Week and World Car Free Day, are essential for more people to have the opportunity to experience the benefits that active mobility offers in terms of quality of life and, from there, become fans of this modal. The authors also emphasize the importance of the participation of destinations (employing companies), offering appropriate parking, prizes for cyclist employees, and spa facilities as ways to encourage the use of bicycles.

The use of bicycles in today's society, in addition to being an act of courage, urgency and necessity, is above all an act of resistance (Lucas and Rosin 2019; Felix et al. 2019), considering that in cities there are many spaces destined for parking spaces, large viaducts and other structures that prioritize motorized transport, which contradict the movements in favor of sustainability. In a special way, the work of Lucas and Rosin (2019), demarcate in their research, the actions that took place in São Paulo that segregated the urban space, favored the use of motor vehicles and moved bicycles away from large urban centers and, they also highlight, the importance of the role of cycle activism as a fundamental force for there to be more public policies and actions in favor of the resumption of bicycles as an important means of transport as a master plan and legislation that favors cyclists.

There is a consensus that the current situation of large urban centers is highly harmful to the physical and mental integrity of the people who share these spaces. Alternatives and solutions for improving air, traffic and people's quality of life still do not meet the UN's Sustainable Development Goals (SDGs).

4 Discussion

The growth of the world population along with economic development require more energy generation, results in the high rate of pollutant emissions from the burning of fossil fuels, especially by motor vehicles, in addition to industries, resulting in a high rate of degradation of air quality, which represents a great impact on human health and on resources destined for public health, especially for those who live in large urban centers (Abe and Miraglea 2018).

Air degradation is further aggravated by the common transport model in cities. The "origin and destination" survey deals with an inventory carried out every ten years by the São Paulo Metropolitan Company (Metrô) and, according to the latest data, from 2017, the percentage of trips made by public transport is 54%, while those carried out by individual transport represent 46%, that is, individual transport represents almost 50% of the total trips carried out, a fact that certainly explains the increase in pollution levels.

Although inefficient, the use of private cars is highly valued in our culture (CET, 2019). The emission of gases by the road modal impacts on the environmental panorama, pointing out the need to rethink new ways for the current logistics system. In addition, heavier vehicles still circulate in large numbers in the RMSP, adding to individual vehicles in pollutant emissions in the region (Ferioli and Rodrigues 2018). The result of this scenario is the increase in atmospheric carbon dioxide (CO_2) levels over the years, contributing to the worsening of the greenhouse effect, a phenomenon notably responsible for increasingly severe climate change (Leite 2020). In addition to negative consequences for the balance of ecosystems, these climate changes can aggravate the health problems of the population, directly implying the use of resources for Public Health.

Considering that the poor population is the most vulnerable, this environmental condition will further favor the existing inequalities in the field of health (Nunnenkamp and Corte 2017).

Greenhouse gases (GHG) are gases present in the atmosphere and are mostly composed of carbon dioxide (CO_2) produced by the combustion of fossil sources, as well as nitrogen oxides (NOx) and sulfur oxides (SO_X), among other pollutants (Nunnenkamp and Corte 2017). Motor vehicles are responsible for about 60% of carbon monoxide (CO) emissions (CETESB, 2019). The rises in total CO emissions correspond to the evolution of mortality from respiratory (38%), cardiovascular (17%) and cardiorespiratory (24%) causes in the state of São Paulo between 2000 and 2018 (Saldiva 2012; Leite 2020). One of these studies (Lee *et al.* 2017), with volunteers exposed to a low concentration of CO for a short period of time (45 min), showed that these individuals had a drop in blood pressure and fatigue after inhalation. of the gas. The vulnerable population (elderly, children) and people who are more exposed to GHGs have a higher risk of mortality (Son et al. 2020).

More than 3 million deaths occurred worldwide in 2010 due to gas emissions from anthropogenic sources that are classified as carcinogenic and/or aggravating preexisting diseases (Torres et al. 2020). In the State of São Paulo, the CETESB inventory published in 2020 reports a downward trend in the levels of some pollutants over the last few years, as observed in the concentrations of non-methane hydrocarbons (HCNM) and particulate matter (MP), in 2007, or CO, in 2008 and NOx, in 2009 and SO_2, in 2013. These drops can be attributed, for example, to measures such as the installation of catalysts in cars, which became mandatory to from the 1990s. However, the RMSP still needs urgent actions, both for public policies and for the new habits of people who share urban spaces.

Aggravating these emissions of primary pollutants, there is the possibility of reactions between them, resulting in secondary pollutants. Acid rain, for example, consists of acids formed by the reaction of SO_2 or NO_2 with water present in the atmosphere. Sulfuric (H_2SO_4) and nitric (HNO_3) acids cause problems in metallic structures and monuments in the city, within a radius of up to 10 km from the place of the polluting source. In non-urbanized places, this acid rain can affect flora and fauna, agriculture, in addition to percolating into the soil, contaminating the water table (Callegaro *et al.* 2015).

The global environmental scenario, represented by the worsening of air pollution, has been discussed since the Stockholm Conference in 1972, when debating the need for reductions in the limits of emitted gases. The Paris Agreement, in 2015, the most recent treaty signed and determined that efforts must be made to contain global warming by 2100, with GHG reductions and consequent reduction in global temperature by at least 1.5 °C. At the last conference, COP26, the need for actions aimed at meeting the emission reduction targets towards "zero carbon" was intensified.

The issue of the high level of air pollution is a reality not only in the RMSP, but also in all major urban centers in the world and is an element of concern and discussion in various bodies representing the world, such as the United Nations. (UN) (Estrada Paneque et al. 2016; Arantes 2016; Machado 2019). Also in 2015, the UN Member States published the 2030 Agenda for Sustainable Development and, based on this document, each country determined how it would meet the 17 Sustainable Development Goals (SDGs). Regarding air quality, the number 3 stands out among the SDGs, which deals with health and well-being by reducing the mortality rate from respiratory diseases caused by environmental pollution, and number 11, which deals with Sustainable Cities and Communities, addressing in its chapter 11.6.2 the proposal to reduce the negative environmental impact per capita by the year 2030, reducing the average annual level of inhalable particles in cities, municipal waste management and others (UNITED NATIONS 2021; Fajersztajn et al. 2016; Guerra and Schmidt 2016; Rajagopalan et al. 2018).

The excess of vehicles presents in large urban centers, therefore, is extremely harmful, limits the use of public spaces, prevents the development of local commerce, increases the stress levels of people who waste a lot of time in traffic jams and delays, promotes excessive liberation of GHGs, harming health, quality of life and ecosystems. This perspective highlights the importance of joint actions to mitigate the negative impacts of this context on people's health. Thus, technological advances applied to the production of more sustainable fuels, as well as the development of motor vehicles that use different energy matrices, can contribute to the mitigation of these impacts. (Daemme et al. 2019; CETESB 2020), follows international standards and data - Emission of vehicular pollutants in the state of São Paulo.

Monitoring standards and establishment of limits for polluting agents are well defined by international organizations such as the WHO and the European Union, as well as by CETESB, the environmental control and monitoring body of the State of São Paulo. When making comparisons between CETESB data and the values determined by the WHO and the European Union, it is noted that in the average standard established by CETESB, the levels of pollutants would already be above those established in Table 1, internationally accepted (UNITED NATIONS 2021; Ragagopalan et al. 2018; Guerra and Schmidt 2016).

Based on these data, 5 monitoring patterns were created that can be observed in Table 1, where N1 is considered a good air quality and, N2, which is considered a moderate quality. From there, from N3 to N5, air quality is considered extremely harmful, impacting the health conditions even of people who do not have pre-existing diseases or who are not part of sensitive groups of which they are part, the elderly and children. With respiratory or heart problems (CETESB 2020).

Table 1. Index adopted by CETESB to classify air quality in the state of São Paulo. Source: CETESB (2021)

Quality	Índice	CO (ppm) 8 h	NO$_2$ (μg/m^3) 1 h	SO$_2$(μg/m^3) 24 h	Meaning
N1 – Good Quality	0–40	0–9	0–200	0–20	Does not involve risks to the population
N2 – Moderate quality	41–80	>9–11	>200–240	>20–40	People from sensitive groups (children, the elderly and people with respiratory and heart diseases) may experience symptoms such as dry cough and tiredness. The general population is not affected
N3 – Bad	81–120	>11–13	>240–320	>40–365	The entire population may experience worsening symptoms such as dry cough, tiredness, burning in the eyes, nose and throat and also shortness of breath and wheezing. Even more serious effects on the health of sensitive groups (children, the elderly and people with respiratory and heart diseases)
N4 – Too bad	121–200	>13–15	>320–1130	>365–800	The entire population may experience worsening symptoms, such as dry cough, tiredness, burning in the eyes, nose and throat, as well as shortness of breath and wheezing. More serious the health of groups and diseases (even children with respiratory and heart diseases)
N5 – Extremely harmful	>200	>15	>1130	>800	The entire population can be at serious risk of manifestations of respiratory and cardiovascular diseases

The reports generated, whose data can be monitored on the agency's website. Active mobility, understood as a means of locomotion by human propulsion, carried out on foot or by bicycle, in general, does not have a good infrastructure in most Brazilian cities. Services related to non-motorized transport are not prioritized in the formulation of policies public policies that favor active transport (Pojani and Stead 2018). This fact opposes the UN and WHO premises, with regard to encouraging and valuing active mobility, also because it reduces sedentary lifestyle and provides an opportunity to carry out activities physical activities, improving not only the environment, but the quality of life of citizens. The Vehicle Emissions Prediction Model (VEPM), developed in New Zealand was used to calculate the average emissions of light vehicles per kilometer driven, considering CO, CO_2, NOx gases, volatile organic compounds (VOC) and particulate matter (PM10). The VEPM identified benefits of adopting active transport when applied to a short trip. The change from cars to bicycles in just 5% of trips with a mileage less than or equal to 7km, resulted in a reduction in the use of 22 million liters of fuel and a reduction in CO_2 by 50 thousand metric tons, which represents about 0.4% of the total emission of greenhouse gases emitted by road transport (Lindsay 2011).

Studies show that the number of bicycle users has increased in the RMSP, especially the city of São Paulo. Data from the Origin Destination survey (Pesquisa OD 2017) show that bicycle use increased from 304 to 377 thousand bicycles, corresponding to a 24% increase between 2007 and 2017. Points of São Paulo from the year 2019, it was possible to identify the gradual increase of bicycle users in the West Zone and in the South Zone of the city, representing an increase of almost 30% during the month of April of the year 2020 (Acioli 2020).

The use of bicycles as a means of urban transport is influenced mainly by factors such as the reduction of parking spaces and intense car traffic in large centers. Some French cities, for example, achieved a reduction in traffic jams and the emission of polluting gases and, in the long term, the adoption of this practice was reflected in the better quality of life and health of people (Milheiro 2016). Bicycle use increases blood circulation, aiding reasoning, providing hormonal discharges such as serotonin, promoting improvements in lung capacity over time, in addition to reducing sugar and fat levels, increasing lean mass (Trindade 2016; Ferreira and Costa 2018).

Thus, active transport presents itself as an important part of the solution to the public health challenges of the 21st century, which result from global climate change, air pollution and physical inactivity. By adopting the use of 75 thousand bicycles, it is possible to reduce 6.5 tons of pollutants in the air (Manzoli 2009). In particular, the pandemic increased the number of bicycle users in the south of the city of São Paulo (Aciole 2020).

5   Final Considerations

The accumulative effect of air pollution, in the long term, shortens the life span of the population, increases public spending on health issues and exacerbates long-established inequality, where the periphery needs to move in the chaotic city traffic and is exposed. More time for GHGs. This is also the low-income population that cannot invest in other forms of active locomotion, depending on public transport and transit.

Even with the innovations in the field of product engineering by vehicle manufacturing companies, for example, using new energy matrices, the problems of traffic jams, stress, exclusion and poor quality of life would persist. Active transport is an important part of the solution to the public health challenges of the 21st century. Failure to act on this mobility results in global climate change, air pollution and physical inactivity. The greater the number of motor vehicle users, the greater the number of sedentary and consequently potentially sick people.

No matter how much CETESB controls air quality standards, there is still a lot to be done for people's quality of life. There is an urgent need for changes in society's habits and the implementation of new public policies that favor walking and the use of bicycles as means of locomotion.

Although it is an extremely important issue, practically a question of survival that has driven actions around the world, the gap in the literature that deals with issues of urban mobility and quality of life in cities is evident.

References

Abe, K.C., Miraglia, S.G.E.K.: Avaliação de Impacto a saúde do programa de controle de poluição do ar por veículos automotores no município de São Paulo, Brasil. RBCIAMB. São Paulo (2018)

Acioli, I.S.D., et al.: O papel da bicicleta durante e após a pandemia do novo coronavírus. 34°. Congresso de Pesquisa e ensino de transporte da ANPET 2020. http://www.anpet.org.br/. Accessed 14 Mar 2021

Arantes, A.: COP 21: Conquista para o meio ambiente e alternativa para o desenvolvimento capitalista. Sch. J. Princípios, São Paulo Ed. **140** (2016)

Assagawa, B., Conti, D.M.: A COVID-19 e as perspectivas da mobilidade urbana no Brasil. XXII ENGEMA–Encontro Nacional sobre Gestão Empresarial e Meio Ambiente. São Paulo (2020). ISSN: 2359-1048

Back, D.F., Silva Neto, W.L.B.: Rodízio de veículos em São Paulo: política pública insuficiente na redução de ozônio troposférico (2018). http://www.singep.org.br/7singep/resultado/14.pdf. Accessed 02 Apr 2022

Allegaro, R.M., Andrzejewski, C., Gomes, D.R., Turchetto, F., Mezzomo, J.C., Griebeler, A.: Efeitos da chuva ácida em recursos florestais. Caderno de Pesquisa, série Biologia **27**(3), 13–20 (2015)

CET Companhia de Engenharia de Tráfego. São Paulo. Mobilidade no Sistema Viário Principal Volumes e Velocidades (2019). http://www.cetsp.com.br/sobre-a-cet/relatorios-corporativos.aspx. Accessed 21 May 2022

CETESB São Paulo: Qualidade do ar do estado de São Paulo 2020/CETESB; Coordenação geral Maria Lucia Gonçalves Guardani; Cordenação técnica Clarice Aico Muramoto; Equipe técnica Clarice Aico Muramoto et al. São Paulo: CETESB (2021)

Daemme, L.C., Penteado, R., Vicentini, P.C., & Errera, M.R.: Impacto da redução do teor de enxofre da gasolina s800 para s50 nas emissões da frota brasileira; XXVII Simpósio Internacional de Engenharia Automotiva, pp. 914–929. Blucher, São Paulo (2019)

Diogenes, K.C.A., Araujo, M.A.F., Bizzarria, F.P.A., Tassigny, M.M.: Perspectiva de mobilidade urbana sustentável e a adesão ao modo cicloviário. ENGEMA (2016)

Estrada Paneque, A., Gallo Gonzalez, M., Nunez Arroyo, E.: Poluição ambiental, sua influência sobre os seres humanos, em particular: o sistema reprodutivo feminino. Universidad y Sociedad Cienfuegos **8**(3), 80–86 (2016)

Fajersztajn, L., Veras, M., Saldiva, P.H.N.: Como as cidades podem favorecer ou dificultar a promoção da saúde de seus moradores? Metrópole E Saúde Estud. Av. **30**(86) (2016). Jan-Apr

Felix, R., Riondet, D.C., Lima, J.P.: Modelo de Avaliação de áreas urbanas para receber projetos integrados de revitalização e mobilidade sustentável. EURE 2019 **45**(134), 77–98 (2019)

Ferioli, E.D.V., Rodrigues, G.A.: Os impactos da poluição atmosférica proveniente da precária infraestrutura logística brasileira - um revés do uso demasiado do modal rodoviário. Rev. Interface Tecnol. **15**(1), 272–284 (2018)

Ferreira, S.S.I., Costa, K.C.G.: Avaliação da função pulmonar em ciclistas; Universidade Tiradentes–AL BIO, p. 13 (2018)

Gomide, A.Á., Galindo, E.P.: A mobilidade urbana: uma agenda inconclusa ou o retorno daquilo que não foi. Estud. Av. **27**(79), 27–39 (2013)

Graeme, L., Macmillan, A., Woodward, A.: Moving urban trips from cars to bicycles: impacto n health and emissions. Aust. N. Z. J. Public Health **35**(1) (2011)

Guerra, J., Schmidt, L.: Concretizar o wishfull thinking–DOS ODS À COP21. Ambient. Soc. **19**(04), 18 (2016). páginas, Oct-Dec

Harkot, M.K, Lemos, L.L., Santoro, P.F.: Como as mulheres de São Paulo usam a cidade? Uma análise a partir da mobilidade por bicicleta. Mujeres en arquitetura, vol. 2. https://doi.org/10. 18389/dearq23.2018.05

Hess, S.C.: (ORG); Ensaios sobre a Poluição e Doenças no Brasil, 1 a ed., p. 344, Editora Outras Expressões (2018)

INSTITUTO DE ENERGIA E MEIO AMBIENTE (IEMA): Padrões de Qualidade do Ar: Experiência Comparada Brasil, EUA e União Européia. São Paulo: Instituto de Energia e Meio Ambiente (2012). http://www.energiaeambiente.org.br/2012/09/padroes-de-qualidade-do-ar-experi encia-comparada-do-brasil-eua-e-uniao-europeia/. Accessed 20 Nov 2021

Lee, G.W., et al.: Diminuição da pressão arterial associada à exposição no veículo ao monóxido de carbono em voluntários coreanos. Environ. Health Prev. Med. **22**(34), 8 (2017). páginas. https://doi.org/10.1186/s12199-017-0622-y

Leite, V.P., Debone, D., Miraglia, S.G.K.: Emissões de gases de efeito estufa no estado de São Paulo: Análise do setor de transportes e impactos na saúde. Vittalle–Revista de Ciências da Saúde **32**(3), 143–153 (2020)

Machado, J.R.: Estimativa das Emissões de Gases de Efeito Estufa de Fontes Móveis no Jardim Botânico do Rio de Janeiro; Engenharia Agrícola e Ambiental, da Universidade Federal Fluminense (TCC), Escola de Engenharia, Niterói, p. 57 (2019)

Manzoli, A.: Análise das emissões veiculares em trajetos curtos com localização por GPS; Escola de Engenharia de São Carlos da Universidade de São Paulo (Doctoral Thesis), p. 200 (2009)

Matos, R.: Migração e urbanização no Brasil. Revista Geografias 7–23 (2012). https://doi.org/10. 35699/2237-549X.13326

Meneses, J.R., Sales, L.G.: Caminhos cicláveis: conforto térmico como fator de melhoria do uso das ciclovias de Vilhena, RO. Cadernos de Arquitetura e Urbanismo. Paranoá (2018)

Milheiro, V.: Bicicleta e Qualidade e Vida nas Cidades. Revista UILPS, Instituto Politécnico de Santarém **4**(2), 16 (2016)

Nunnenkamp, C.H., Corte, A.P.D.: Emissão de gases de efeito estufa e proposta de projeto para compensação: um estudo de caso e-commerce. Biofix Sci. **2**(1), 9 (2017)

Objetivos de Desenvolvimento Sustentável–Agenda 2030. https://odsbrasil.gov.br/objetivo/obj etivo?n=11. Accessed 08 Sep 2021

Patricio, L.C.B., Kruszielski, L.: Dia de bicicleta ao trabalho: uma potencial ferramenta para planejamento e promoção da mobilidade sustentável. Revista de gestão ambiental e sustentabilidade (2016)

Pedro, L.M., Silva, M.A.V., Portugal, L.S.: Desenvolvimento e mobilidade sustentáveis; Transporte, Mobilidade e Desenvolvimento Urbano; capítulo 2; 20 páginas; Editora Elsevier Brasil (2017)

Pero, V., Stefanelli, V.: A Questão da Mobilidade Urbana nas Metrópoles Brasileiras. Especial Mobilidade Urbana Rev. Econ. Contemp. **19**(3), 366–402 (2015). Sep-Dec

Pesquisa ORIGEM DESTINO 2017. Disponível em Relatório pesquisa. http://www.metro.sp.gov. br/pesquisa-od-arquivos/ebook_OD_2017-final.pdf. Accessed 01 Sep 2021

Pojani, D., Stead, D.: Policy design for sustainable urban trasport in the global South. Policy Des. Pract. **1**(2), 90–102 (2018). https://doi.org/10.1080/25741292.2018.14542912021

Rosin, L.B., Leite, C.K.S.: A bicicleta como resistência: o paradigma rodoviarista e o papel do ativismo ciclista no município de São Paulo/SP. Cad. Metrop. São Paulo **21**(46), 879–902 (2019). set/dez. https://doi.org/10.1590/2236-9996.2019-4609

Saldiva, P.H.N., Arbex, M.A., Santos, U.P., Martins, L.C.: Jornal Brasil de Pneumologia. A poluição do ar e o sistema respiratório. https://www.scielo.br/j/jbpneu/a/sD3cLkXqQwmDFpg zsyj7gBm/?lang=pt. Accessed 17 Sep 2021

Saldiva, P.: Vida urbana e saúde; editora contexto, p. 128 (2018)

Son, J.Y., Lane, K.J., Miranda, N.L., Michelle, L., Bell, M.L.: Health disparities attributable to air pollutant exposure in North Carolina: influence of residential environmental and social factors, Health Place **62**, 102287 (2020). https://doi.org/10.1016/j.healthplace.2020.102287

Torres, L.M., Pinheiro, C.P.S., Azevedo, S.D., Rodrigues, P.R.S., Sandim, D.P.R.: Poluição atmosférica em cidades brasileiras: uma breve revisão dos impactos na saúde pública e meio ambiente. Naturae **2**(1), 23–33 (2020)

Trindade, R.: Avaliação do modal bicicleta para a redução da emissão de dióxido de carbono (CO2) em Curitiba/PR; Meio Ambiente Urbano e Industrial, Programa de Mestrado Profissional em Meio Ambiente Urbano e Industrial (Master Dissertation), Universidade Federal do Paraná (UFPR), Universität Stuttgart and Serviço Nacional de Aprendizagem Nacional (SENAI), p. 123 (2016)

UNITED NATIONS: The Sustainable Development Goals Report (2016). Disponível em: https://unstats.un.org/sdgs/report/2016/The%20Sustainable%20Development%20Goals% 20Report%202016.pdf. Accessed 2021/05/21

WHO (2016): WHO's Urban Ambient Air Pollution database Update 2016. World Health Organization, Geneza, Switzerland. https://www.who.int/airpollution/data/cities-2016/en/. Accessed 21 May 2021

Comparing Urban Transportation Services in São Paulo, Brazil. A Decision Making Model Using AHP

Gabriel Santos Rodrigues[1]([✉]) [iD], João Gilberto Mendes dos Reis[1] [iD], and Sivanilza Teixeira Machado[2] [iD]

[1] RESUP - Research Group in Supply Chain Management - Postgraduate Program in Production Engineering, Universidade Paulista, São Paulo, Brazil
biel.rodrigues@outlook.com
[2] Instituto Federal de Educação, Ciência e Tecnologia de São Paulo - Câmpus Suzano, Suzano, Brazil

Abstract. Metropolitan Area of São Paulo is the main Brazilian urban region, where approximately 21 million people generate 42 million trips daily being 54% by Public Transportation. This paper aims is to investigate how transport attributes affect the way of commuters use Public Transportation. To do so, a model using the AHP (Analytic Hierarchy Process) a multi-criteria decision was established. We used six criteria: Environment; Safety; Cost; Accessibility; Confort and Speed and five alternatives: Bus, Metropolitan Train, Subway, Ridesharing, and Bike-sharing. The results showed an advantage for Bike-sharing (34.9%), Metropolitan Train (23.5%), Subway (23%), Bus (10.4%), and finally Ridesharing (8%).

Keywords: Passenger transport · AHP · Multi criteria decision making and urban mobility

1 Introduction

Metropolitan Area of São Paulo is the main Brazilian urban region, comprising 39 cities where approximately 21 million people live and accounts for about 18% of the country's GDP [1,2]. According to Companhia do Metropolitano de São Paulo - METRÔ in 2017 42 million trips are generated daily, the main reasons are work 44%, education 35%, and personal matters 7% [1]. Regarding the mode, they are conveyed by motorized means 67% and 33% by non-motorized modes.

Among the motorized modes, in the MASP, car trips, as the main mode, are the ones with the highest volume in 2017 (40.1%) and motorcycles (3.8%) [1]. Individual transport uses a large amount of public space in large and medium-sized cities [3], which creates congestion. In addition, this type of transport is responsible for about 80% of the costs of traffic accidents [3]. Thus, it is

D. Y. Kim et al. (Eds.): APMS 2022, IFIP AICT 663, pp. 593–600, 2022.
https://doi.org/10.1007/978-3-031-16407-1_69

necessary to have urban planning that involves the use of public transport and non-motorized methods of transport such as walking and cycling.

For cities, the choice of collective public transport systems is a complex task with numerous variables [3]. Schmidt [4] states that with a dense transport network it is possible to reach destinations in different ways, reducing travel times. Scott [5] states that to improve the acceptance of public transport, it is necessary to understand what makes passengers choose this mode.

According to Cruz [6] active mobility can be a positive strategy to encourage healthier behaviors, raise awareness about the use of urban spaces and discourage the indiscriminate use of the car, favoring efficient and sustainable transport. For Costa et al. [7] the bicycle can allow greater accessibility to the public transport system.

Bicycles are responsible for 377 thousand daily trips in the MASP and the reasons that lead to their use are: the short distance to be covered (50.9%), physical activity (18%), and the high cost of the transport fee (15.9%). The majority (72%) do not have segregated infrastructure (cycle lanes and/or cycle lanes) during travel [1]. People walk mainly because of the short distances (88.6%), the high cost of transport fares (5%) and physical activity (2%) [1].

The objective of this article is to identify and measure the decision factors that determine the choice of urban transport mode. For this, a decision model is adopted using the Analytic Hierarchy Process. The criteria considered in the model are Environment, Safety, Cost, Accessibility, Comfort and Speed and the available systems are: Bus, Metro, Metropolitan Train, Ridesharing and Bicycle.

2   Analytic Hierarchy Process

Analytic Hierarchy Process (AHP) is a multi-criteria decision method developed by Professor Thomas Saaty based on the hierarchy of the importance degree of a criteria over the others that is applied when a decision needs to be made [8].

In AHP, the decision problem must be divided into hierarchical levels to facilitate understanding and evaluation. In this evaluation, the use of qualitative and quantitative criteria in the structuring of the problem is allowed [8]. For Vieira [9] the AHP is built by three principles: construction of hierarchies, when the hierarchy of complex processes is created; prioritization and logical consistency.

Afterwards, it is necessary to define which criteria is more important than the other based on the opinion of decision-makers [10], making a parity comparison - two by two - of one criteria over the other in the observation of the specialists, in this case, the authors, and this determines the relative importance between them [11]. This process is shown through the following mathematical equation also known as the judgment matrix:

$$A = \begin{bmatrix} 1 & a_{1,2} & a_{1,3} & \cdots & a_{1,n} \\ a_{2,1} & 1 & a_{2,3} & \cdots & a_{2,n} \\ a_{3,1} & a_{3,2} & 1 & \cdots & a_{3,n} \\ \vdots & \vdots & \vdots & \ddots & \vdots \\ a_{n,1} & a_{n,2} & a_{n,3} & \cdots & 1 \end{bmatrix} \tag{1}$$

To define these preferences, the verbal form may be easier to measure than numerical values. For this reason, Saaty also created an intensity scale that correlates the verbal judgments with the number of judgments that must be filled in the judgment matrix. This scale is in the Table 1.

Table 1. Parity comparison scales

Scale	Meaning
1	Equally important
3	Moderate importance
5	Strong importance
7	Very strong importance
9	Extremily important
2–4–6–8	Intermediate values

Peinaldo [12], and Lucena e Mori [13] point out there must be the principle of reciprocity when performing a comparison when using this scale, that is, When criteria A is much more important than B on scale 5, criteria B must be 5 times less important than the criteria an i.e. 1/5. To facilitate the understanding of this scale and methodology. Lucena e Mori [13] adapted Saaty's original table to a more didactic form, as can be seen below.

After that, where the weight of each element is decided in the decision-making model, the software superdecisions was used. The software calculates the alternatives and checks whether the mathematical model is consistent or inconsistent. When the model shows inconsistency and there is a need for some adjustment, it goes back to the previous step and defines a new value in the decision matrix. To be consistent the model must have a CR (Consistency Ratio) that must be < 0.1.

To calculate the Consistency Ratio (CR) this number that determines if a model is consistent or inconsistent, the first step is to calculate the Consistency Index (CI) (Eq. 2).

$$CI = \frac{(\lambda max - n)}{(n - 1)} \tag{2}$$

where the λ max is the biggest eigenvalue of the pairwise comparison. After calculating the CI, it is possible to calculate the CR, this number is obtained by dividing the CI by the RI (Eq. 4). The Random Index (RI) and the RI is obtained in the table developed by Saaty in 1991 (Table 2).

$$CR = \frac{CI}{RI} \tag{3}$$

Table 2. Random index

n	1	2	3	4	5	6	7	8	9	10
RI	0.00	0.00	0.58	0.90	1.12	1.24	1.32	1.41	1.45	1.49

2.1 Methodology

The decision tree, Fig. 1, is composed of the following attributes: Decision problem that is the highest degree of complexity and is at the highest level, the criteria that are the factors that influence the decision defined by the decision-maker and the alternatives that are the actions possible to be taken to solve the decision problem [10].

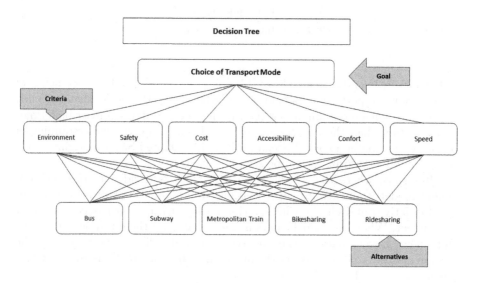

Fig. 1. Decision tree

For this study, the weights were given by the authors themselves according to data available in the literature for the following six criteria:

- **Environment:** Which transport mode has the lowest environmental impact per user.
- **Safety:** Which transport mode has the lowest risk of accidents in its use.
- **Cost:** Which transport mode has the lowest tariff cost for the user.
- **Accessibility:** The ease of the user finding access to use the transport system.
- **Confort:** What is the capacity of users in the transport.
- **Speed:** Based on commercial vehicle speed.

The alternatives are: Bus, Metropolitan Train, Subway, Ridesharing and Bike-sharing.

For the Environment criteria, we defined priorities through data obtained by Carvalho [14] and made the following relationship: Emission of the transport/Ridesharing system, which is the most polluting transport mode.

The mode of transport that emits the most gases is Ridesharing (0.1268), Bus (0.016), Metropolitan Train and Subway (0.0035), and Bike-sharing is the last one because it does not emit gases.

For the Safety criteria, we defined priorities through accident risk data obtained by the TPC Guide [3], which evaluated all modalities as Non-existent to Subway, Low to Train, high to Buses and Ridesharing, and very high to Bike-sharing.

The fare cost Criteria was evaluated by the tariffs in effect for daily plans in June 2021 for Metro, Bus, Metropolitan Train, and Bike-sharing. For ridesharing, an average daily rate was used. The most expensive is the Ridesharing we used the Basic fare to 10km (R$ 63.65 or 100%) [15], the Bus, Subway and Metropolitan train we used the daily rate (R$ 16.80 or 26.30%) [16] and Bike-sharing we used the daily rate (R$ 1.00 or 0.03%) [17].

For the accessibility criteria, we used the coverage criterion, being that for Bus and Ridesharing we use the MASP area coverage which is 7,944 Km^2 [2], for Metropolitan Train the network of lines (273 km - June 2021) [18], for subway the network of lines (101 Km - June 2021) [19] and Bike-sharing the area with bikes available (684 Km^2).

For the comfort criteria, the passenger comfort scale in public transport was agreed, which is 6 pass/m^2 as a base and it was created through a qualitative scale criteria where the number of passengers = 1 to 2 great, 3 to 4 very good, 5 to 6 good/ideal, 7 to 8 bad, 8 or + very bad.

After that, we researched the average number of passengers for the system and classified them by scale. The numbers used were for buses (7.65) [20], Metropolitan train (8.1) [21], Metro (7.1) [22], Ridesharing (1.4) [23], and Bike-sharing (1.0).

For the Speed criteria, we used the following parameters: for bus we used the average of bus services (21,5 km/h), train (50 km/h), and metro (35km/h) speeds, avaliable of the TPC Guide [3], for ridesharing speeds, the official average speed data of the city of São Paulo (18,84 km/h) [24] and bike-sharing we used the average speed of an experienced cyclist (17,5 km/h) [25].

3   Results and Discussion

Our results is presented in Table 3.

In (Table 3), we can observe a preference for Bike-sharing (34.9%). The main motives is that they are cheaper and cleaner, do not generate emissions. However, they are not suitable for long distances and are subject to the weather.

Costa [7] recognize that bicycles are used mainly for commutes of 1.5 km and 4.5 km. For short distances, walking is preferred by commuters due to the time it takes to park the bikes while for far distances the physical effort does not favor the use of bicycles.

Table 3. Results

Name	Normalized by cluster	Limiting
Bike-sharing	0.34927	0.261953
Ridesharing	0.07996	0.059971
Subway	0.23054	0.172908
Metropolitan train	0.23563	0.176721
Bus	0.10460	0.078447

Barriola [26] carried out in Mexico a study and suggested that cities should invest in ridesharing systems to improve the population's quality of life and reduce carbon emissions. To the ITDP (Institute for Transportation and Development Policy) [27] encourage the use of bicycles and also improve the ease of walking around the city. In addition to the environmental benefits, it increases the access of poor people to economic activities.

In second place is Metropolitan Train (23.5%) and third one Subway (23%). In São Paulo the Subway and Metropolitan Train are integrated in a network, what differs is the interval (90 s to the subway and 6 to 10 min to train) and the distance between the stations (1 km to subway and 2.5 km to train, in average). The train is faster than subway and its network is bigger.

Moraes [28] says that Subway and Metropolitan Train are important interventions that reduce congestion by increasing the average speed of travel, which, despite having a high cost of implementation, brings social benefits to the population.

Buses with 10.4% also produce social benefits. A bus network can greatly improve with the implementation of corridors and BRTs and a lower implementation cost than the Subway and Metropolitan Train [28]. Diesel-powered buses, even emitting polluting gases, are responsible for only 13% of greenhouse gas emissions in São Paulo [29].

Finally, Ridesharing (7.99%) can not be considered a solution in displacements because it has a low passenger capacity and is polluting in addition to the average traffic speed in Sao Paulo being 18.84 km/h. Martins et al. [30] claim that Ridesharing affects urban transport, on the one hand, it helps people mobility at night and in low-demand region. However, for Silva and Balassiano [31], ridesharing also competes with the public transport system but has the potential to remove cars from circulation, especially in places with low transport supply and difficulty in parking private cars.

4   Conclusions

The importance of the social benefits of collective public transport is relevant for the city. In addition to bicycles that are sustainable, they can insert more people into economic activities and improve their quality of life. The high-capacity transport systems occupying the following areas indicate their importance Metro and Train, as they are non-polluting and faster, can make public transport more attractive than individual transport. Even buses pollute less than individual transport.

However, the metro-railway transport modes have a relatively lower expansion capacity due to their complexity, so transport by bus, which can preferably be inserted into priority systems such as exclusive lanes, corridors and BRTs, the latter still very incipient at MASP is also important. to enhance and encourage public transport modes.

Ridesharing has its good side of removing private vehicles from circulation and its bad side of impacting and removing passengers from public transport and the researchers still do not have a consensus on the effect of this.

In this way, it is suggested that in works the impacts of carpooling in public transport and how to facilitate the integration of the bicycle in transport are carried out.

Acknowledgments. This study was financed in part by the Coordenação de Aperfeiçoamento de Pessoal de Nível Superior - Brasil (CAPES). Finance Code 001.

References

1. METRÔ: Pesquisa Origem e Destino 2017 50 Anos - A mobilidade da Região Metropolitana de São Paulo em detalhes (2019)
2. EMPLASA: Plano de Desenvolvimento Urbano Integrado - RMSP. Tech. rep., São Paulo (2019). http://multimidia.pdui.sp.gov.br/rmsp/docs_pdui/rmsp_docs_pdui_0018_diagnostico_final.pdf
3. Amicci, A.G.N., et al.: Guia TPC: orientações para seleção de tecnologias e implementação de projetos de transporte público coletivo (2018)
4. Schmidt, M., Schöbel, A.: The complexity of integrating routing decisions in public transportation models (2010)
5. Scott, R.A., George, B.T., Prybutok, V.R.: A public transportation decision-making model within a metropolitan area. Decis. Sci. **46**, 1048–1072 (2016)
6. Cruz, F.J.A.d.O.: A prática da mobilidade ativa na perspectiva do estudante universitário (2019)
7. Costa, T. B.; Siqueira, M.F.L.R.C.L.A.: Integração bicicleta-transporte público no contexto de grandes cidades brasileiras (2019)
8. Quadros, C.E.P.d., Adamatti, D.F., Longaray, A.A.: O Processo de Análise Hierárquica (AHP) e a teoria das Inteligências Múltiplas (MI): uma revisão de literatura com meta-síntese sobre a relação entre o método e a teoria 8 (2021)
9. Vieira, G.H.: Análise e Comparação dos Métodos de Decisão Multicritério AHP Clássico e Multiplicativo. Ph.D. thesis, Instituto Tecnológico de Aeronáutica (ITA), São José dos Campos (2006)
10. Wolff, S.C.: O método AHP: revisão conceitual e proposta de simplificação. Ph.D. thesis, Rio de Janeiro, Brazil (2008)
11. Alves, J., Alves, J.: Definição de localidade para instalação industrial com o apoio do método de análise hierárquica (AHP), pp. 13–26 (2015)
12. Peinado, H.: Método AHP para tomada de decisão multicritério. No. 103 in Coleção Fundamentum, EDUEM, Maringá (2016)

13. Lucena, A.F.E., Mori, L.M.D.: Uso do analytic hierarchy process (AHP) para Hierarquização de Métodos de Mensuração do Grau de Aplicação da Construção Enxuta. Revista Gestão Industrial, 14(4) (2018)
14. Carvalho, C.H.: Emissões Relativas de Poluentes do Transporte Motorizado de Passageiros nos Grandes Centros Urbanos Brasileiros (2011)
15. Uber: Baixe e solicite uma viagem com o app da Uber (2021). https://www.uber.com/br/pt-br/ride/
16. SPTrans: Aviso ao publico 001–21. Tech. Rep. 001/21, São Paulo (2021)
17. Bici, T.: Aluguel de bicicleta em São Paulo: praticidade e segurança (2021). https://bikeitau.com.br/sao-paulo/
18. CPTM: a-companhia—CPTM (2021). https://www.cptm.sp.gov.br/a-companhia/Pages/a-companhia.aspx
19. Metrô: Relatório Integrado 2020. Tech. rep., São Paulo (2021)
20. SPTrans: Relatorio de Administracao 2018. Tech. rep. (2018)
21. Barbosa, B.: Alívio na lotação de Metrô e CPTM deve ficar para 2017 (2016). https://www.mobilize.org.br/noticias/9120/alivio-na-lotacao-de-metro-e-cptm-deve-ficar-para-2017.html
22. G1: Linha 3-Vermelha do Metrô é a mais lotada de passageiros em SP no período da manhã — São Paulo—G1 (2019). https://g1.globo.com/
23. Voitch, G.: São Paulo tem média de 1,4 ocupante por carro - Jornal O Globo (2011). https://oglobo.globo.com/brasil/sao-paulo-tem-media-de-14-ocupante-por-carro-2695421
24. CET: Mobilidade no Sistema Viário Principal Volumes e Velocidades 2019. Tech. rep. (2019)
25. Sevilha, A.: Entenda como são os níveis de pedal — Lobi Cicloturismo e Aventura (2018). https://www.lobi.com.br/entenda-como-sao-os-niveis-de-pedal/, https://www.lobi.com.br/entenda-como-sao-os-niveis-de-pedal/, section: andar de bicicleta
26. Barriola, X.: The impact of gasoline shortages on public bike-sharing systems. Academia Revista Latinoamericana de Administración 34(4), 561–577 (Oct 2021). https://www.emerald.com/insight/content/doi/10.1108/ARLA-01-2021-0017/full/html
27. ITDP: Active Mobility. https://www.itdp.org/key-issues/health-safety/active-mobility/
28. Moraes, A.C.d.: Congestionamento urbano: custos sociais (2013)
29. CETESB: Emissões Veiculares no Estado de São Paulo - 2018. Tech. rep., São Paulo (2018)
30. Martins, D.: Análise sobre o impacto dos aplicativos de ridesourcing nas ações dos planos de mobilidade urbana (2019)
31. Silva, M., Balassiano, R.: Uber - Uma análise do serviço oferecido ao usuário na cidade do Rio de Janeiro (2018)

Urban Mobility in Brazil: An Comparison Overview in Thirteen State Capitals

João Gilberto Mendes dos Reis[1,2], Gabriel Santos Rodrigues[1],
and Sivanilza Teixeira Machado[3(✉)]

[1] RESUP - Research Group in Supply Chain Management, Postgraduate Program in
Production Engineering, Universidade Paulista - UNIP, R. Dr. Bacelar, 1212-4fl,
São Paulo 04026002, Brazil
joao.reis@docente.unip.br
[2] Centro de Ciências Sociais Aplicadas, Mackenzie Presbyterian University,
São Paulo, Brazil
joao.reis@mackenzie.br
[3] NAPOLE - Research Group, Federal Institute of São Paulo - IFSP,
Mogi das Cruzes. 1501, Suzano SP 08673010, Brazil
sivanilzamachado@ifsp.edu.br

Abstract. Urban mobility is related to public transport system planning, geographic city size, economic power, and the ability to manage the resources of each city. In Brazil, cities are obliged by law to create an urban mobility plan, but they really work? How Brazilian state capitals are acting to face the challenges to provide an efficient urban mobility plan? This paper aims to evaluate urban mobility considering infrastructure, quality of services, cost and fares, accessibility, environment and safety in Brazilian cities. To do so, we selected a sample of thirteen state capitals and data were collected from Urban Mobility Information System. The analysis was made using graphs and cross-tabulation. Our results show that the sample cities prioritize road transport systems, the fleet of vehicles requires modernization, and it is missing investment in dedicated bus lanes to have a more agile and efficient transport system.

Keywords: Brazilian state capitals · Public transport · Urban mobility

1 Introduction

Urban mobility has been advanced in the last two decades in Brazilian cities due to government actions to control and improve traffic in cities [1,2]. However, even the guidelines created for the development of an Urban Mobility Plan, cities fail to deal with socioeconomic inequality [1,3,4].

Indeed, the cities' have grown without planning which generates many issues for local governments regarding basic sanitation, education, health, security, and mobility. Urban mobility cope with urban space and displacements carried out by people and loads inside the cities. In Brazil, the Urban Mobility Plan is an obligation established by Law 12,587 in January 2012. This law has five main objectives, and we highlighted three most important: (i) reduction of inequalities and promotion of social inclusion; (ii) promotion of the improvement of urban conditions for the population concerning accessibility and mobility; and (iii) sustainable development with the environmental liability reduction [5]).

Urban mobility can be evaluated by many factors, such as the city's transport and traffic infrastructure, information systems, between physical and payment systems, etc. The lack of infrastructure and quality in public transport services has a straight impact on people's lives and causes immobility [2,3]. The evidence of traffic immobility should be analyzed by congestion rate and the average operational speed at peak times. For instance, São Paulo in 2019 had an average operating speed of 17.93 km/h in the morning and 15.08 km/h in the afternoon [6].

Quality of services, infrastructure, cost and fares, accessibility, and sustainability in urban mobility is related to public transport system planning, geographic city size, the economic power of each city and its ability to manage resources and apply public policies to promote the well-being of the inhabitants. In this study, we established the following research question: How Brazilian state capitals are acting in the face of the urban mobility plan required by Law?

Brazil is a multicultural country with five distinct regions, 27 states and 5,568 cities [4]. Political, economic, and social inequality are presented in all cities. Thus, analyzing the urban mobility policy of each city allows us to reflect on the behaviour of collective spaces, and how the city develops in terms of transport infrastructure, integrated transport system, accessibility, public safety, and contributes to the economic activity of the municipality.

This paper aims to evaluate urban mobility in thirteen Brazilian state capitals considering infrastructure, quality of services, cost and fares, accessibility, environment and safety.

2   Methodology

The data in this research was obtained from the Urban Mobility Information System [UMIS] (2020) database that compares urban mobility plans among main Brazilian state capitals. Table 1 shows the thirteen capitals that we consider in the study.

The variables compared in this study are (1) **Infrastructure:** the public transport services offered by the city, physical integration, number of terminals, stations and embark and disembark points, fleet, exclusive lanes for public transport, and active mobility; (2) **Quality of services:** operational speed of the public transport system in the municipality, the average age of the fleet, information system for users, and user satisfaction; (3) **Costs and fares:** the current and previous fare, gratuity transportation level, and fare for transportation integration; (4) **Accessibility:** actions carried out by the municipality to promote mobility, specific legislation, special transport services; (5) **Environment:** use

Table 1. Population and GDP per capita information

Region Capital/State	Population+	GPD Per capita (USD*)
Palmas/TO	0.31	7,464.46
João Pessoa/PB	0.83	5,506.00
Campo Grande/MS	0.92	7,210.47
Porto Alegre/RS	1.49	11,870.81
Goiânia/GO	1.56	7,457.55
Recife/PE	1.66	7,100.91
Curitiba/PR	1.96	10,621.08
Manaus/AM	2.26	8,307.84
Belo Horizonte/MG	2.53	8,268.23
Fortaleza/CE	2.70	5,396.25
Salvador/BA	2.90	4,746.42
Brasília/DF	3.09	19,389.48
Rio de Janeiro/RJ	6.78	11,289.16

* USD = 4.68 (april 13, 2022); +Value in Million;

of less polluting energy sources in public transportation or taxi, carrying out environmental vehicle inspection by the municipality; and (6) **Safety:** traffic control and inspection, number of traffic agents and inspection equipment, and traffic ticket collected in 2019.

Data were organized in an MS Excel spreadsheet, tabulated, and analyzed using graphs and cross-tabulation. We calculated the mean, standard deviation, maximum and minimum values for quantitative variables.

3   Results and Discussion

3.1   Public Transportation Service and Infrastructure

Transport services are managed by the municipal, state, and federal levels and by a public consortium or a cooperation agreement. Of the 13 Brazilian state capitals, Recife/PE is the only one that does not offer transport services operated by municipal buses.

We observed that cities with a population of fewer than 2 million inhabitants prioritize road transport systems. This result is a reflection of Brazilian transportation policy over the years [3].

Regarding rail transport, Fortaleza/CE offers the same types of services as Rio de Janeiro/RJ with 2.2 times less population (Train, Subway, Light Rail). While Salvador/BA and Brasilia/DF have a population of 2.90 and 3.09 million people, respectively, only offer the Subway system (Fig. 1).

João Pessoa/PB and Porto Alegre/RS cities offer Train service that is managed by the Federal Government. In addition, the Subway service provided in

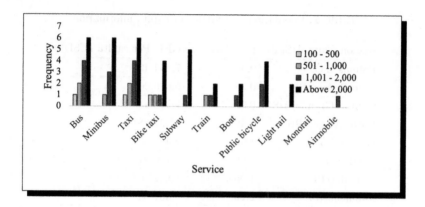

Fig. 1. Distribution of transportation modo service by population of the capital

Recife/PE and Belo Horizonte/MG, Salvador/BA and Palmas/TO do not offer intercity transport services, while the other cities do. However, the system transport management is the responsibility of the State or the Federal government.

The average of age of bus fleet of vehicles is old and should be modernized to meet demand for passenger transport. Mainly, in cities with over 2 million inhabitants, that should acquire articulated and bi-articulated vehicles.

The fleet of vehicles in cities with populations from 100 to 1 million inhabitants are conventional buses, taxis, bike taxis and school buses. The main difference between cities with up to 500 and 1 million inhabitants was the number of vehicles. On the other hand, cities up to 2 million inhabitants added in fleet of vehicles Articulated bus, Bi-articulated bus, Mini bus, and Charter for passenger transport, as well as, cities above 2 million inhabitants also added other modes of transport, such as Subway (composition), Boat and Light Rail (composition).

Regarding the physical integration among different modes of urban transport, nine cities have information over "paracycles or bicycle racks, public bicycle stations in terminals and urban collective public transport stations", five "multimodal integration terminal, such as between the Bus, Metro, Rail or Waterway system" and three "Car parking at terminals and urban collective public transport stations". However, João Pes-soa/PB, Curitiba/PR and Manaus/AM reported not having any type of physical integration.

Considering all cities studied, of the total bus terminals (231), around 80% have an accessible ramp for people with disabilities but only 32.5% are accessible with information for people with visual impairments. Also, around 40% of the terminals have physical integration, and 48% of the embark and disembark points have no shelter for the user, Table 2.

Regarding the transport infrastructure (Table 2), Salvador/BA reported that it has 87 bus terminals in the municipality, João Pessoa/PB, Campo Grande/MS, and Manaus/AM reported that having only one bus terminal for attending the population. Observing the urban mobility infrastructure to promote the public passenger transport, Curtibita is a reference Brazilian city in bus rapid transit

Table 2. Description statistical of number of terminals, stations, and embarkation/disembar-kation point

	Average	SD	Maximum	Minimum
Number of bus terminals	17.77	22.94	87	1
Number of accessible bus terminals with ramps and boarding platforms	15.25	24.71	87	0
Number of accessible bus terminals with information for people with visual impairments	6.25	7.55	21	0
Number of bus terminals with physical integration	7.67	7.62	21	0
Number of metro-railway stations	11.25	12.57	30	0
Number of accessible metro-rail stations with ramps and boarding platforms	11.17	12.60	30	0
Number of accessible metro-rail stations with information for visually impaired people	5.78	10.84	30	0
Number of metro-railway stations with physical integration	7.45	10.43	29	0
Total of modes transport stops*	4,533.83	2,648.84	9,919	766
Total of modes transport stops with shelter for users*	2,343.25	1,494.60	5,424	433

* all modes of transport; SD = standard deviation

[BRT] with 72.2 Km, followed by Brasília (30 Km). Almost 85% of Brazilian capitals have dedicated bus lanes, such as Brasília (135 Km), Fortaleza (106 Km), Rio de Janeiro (56 Km), Belo Horizonte and Recife, both with 40 Km approximately.

3.2 Service Quality, Costs and Tariffs

The average operating speed (km/h) in the city's exclusive bus lanes at peak hours was 24.5 km/h. Brasília showed the maximum speed (40 km/h) and João Pessoa the minimum speed (18.6 km/h). In comparison, the average operational speed (km/h) of the collective public transport system on mixed-traffic roads at peak times were lower (18.7 km/h), and the maximum and minimum speed was 27.9 km/h and 14 km/h, respectively related Palmas and Fortaleza cities. This reflects the inefficiency of public transport and that affects the quality of life of users [2].

The average number of modes of transport stops with information to users about itineraries is 999.5, and the city with the highest number of modes of transport stops was Curitiba (2,829), and the lowest was Manaus (five bus stops). Likewise, the average of modes of transport stops with information to users about timetables was 687, with the city of Campo Grande being the largest (1,500) and Manaus being the smallest (five modes of transport stops).

In addition, the average of modes of transport stops with information to the users about fares was 379.57. Salvador has the highest (1,100 modes of transport stops) and Manaus with the lowest information system with five. The average of modes of transport stops with information to users about modes of interaction with other transportation modes was 1,035.67, and Campo Grande showed a maximum of 1,500 modes of transport stops and Belo Horizonte a minimum of 507.

Palmas, Campo Grande, Curitiba, and Rio de Janeiro responded that they do not apply user satisfaction surveys. However, among cities that carry out, Brasilia is the municipality with the longest time (2013) and Manaus (2014), while Goiana, Fortaleza, and Salvador were recently carried out (2020).

The average adjustment in fare transport was 6.17% from the last to the current one, and the largest adjustment was made by the Manaus city (13.16%) and the smallest by Rio de Janeiro (2.47%), Fig. 2.

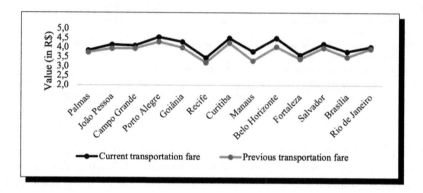

Fig. 2. Average variation in the transport fare from different Brazilian capital

Regarding the payment system integration, João Pessoa, Campo Grande, and Rio de Janeiro only use fare integration over time. Goiana uses the terminals' physical integration and Curitiba applies both integrations (terminals and time). Most Brazilian cities use integration by time and number of integrations between urban transportation modes.

Analyzing gratuities and discounts on public transport, 92% of cities serve students, with the exception of Campo Grande; 77% serve people with disabilities and reduced mobility, and 46% serve people aged 60 to 65.

3.3   Accessibility, Environment and Safety

All cities stated that they had a Master Plan and Zoning or Land Use and Occupation Law, with Goiana being the oldest (2007) and Belo Horizonte being the most recent. But according to the database, Palmas, Goiana, Recife, and Fortaleza cities responded that it is being prepared the Urban Mobility Plan, whereas João Pessoa prepared the Mobility Plan in 2020, and it was not approved yet. Other cities have already implemented the Urban Mobility Plan, the oldest Plan was the Curitiba (2008) and the most recent was the Belo Horizonte and Rio de Janeiro (2019).

Around 89% of the cities reported that they were not covered by the Urban Mobility Plans of Metropolitan Regions, except for Fortaleza and Brasilia. The government adopted some actions to promote accessibility in cities. So, we observed that most cities have public works inaccessible areas, followed by public projects and specific municipal legislation on accessibility. Moreover, it appears that about 50 to 60% of municipalities have the budget resources to promote accessibility, carry out accessibility campaigns and have plans to adapt the existing infrastructure, Fig. 3. Despite actions aimed at accessibility, only 23% of municipalities reported that they have free transport for people with disabilities. Historically, accessibility has been a challenge for public transport in Brazil (3).

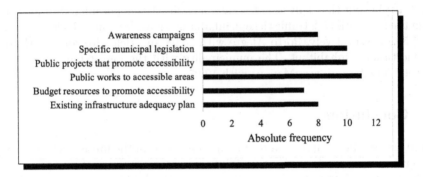

Fig. 3. Government actions to promote accessibility in cities

Concerning the impact of mobility on the urban environment, when asked about the use of vehicular technology or alternative energy sources, Goiana, Curitiba, and Brasilia responded positively, however, Goiana did not highlight any of the actions taken and also informed that it did not perform an environmental vehicle inspection.

Curitiba reported that 2.8% of the fleet uses biodiesel as an energy source, 2.2% of the fleet uses hybrid energy (electricity + diesel). Moreover, 98.08% of the taxi fleet uses ethanol as an energy source and 16.70% uses natural gas as an energy source. In addition, the city also carries out periodic environmental vehicle inspections on buses.

Brasília reported that 0.2% of the fleet uses electricity as a source of energy, 19% of the fleet that uses biodiesel as a source of energy, and carries out environmental vehicle inspections in cars, taxis and buses.

When asked about traffic control measures, the municipalities presented the following result: the average number of traffic agents in the cities was 381.33, with the Brasília city having the highest number of agents and Campo Grande with the lowest number; the average speed inspection equipment was 290.67 and Brasília is the most equipped municipality (1,325) against Palmas with 22 equipment.

All cities use physical speed reduction devices (undulation, plateau, sounder, and baffles). Although, most cities use electronic devices to control speed and establish a speed limit of 30 km/h (Zone 30), except for Manaus. Another measure adopted by most cities is changing the geometry of the road by narrowing or changing the alignment, and almost 50% of them use pavement differentiation to reduce car speed.

These actions are important for traffic safety in cities, however, there is still a high number of traffic tickets. Brazil shows a high victim traffic accident index [1]. Regarding the traffic tickets collected in 2019, Salvador, Brasília, and Rio de Janeiro did not inform the values. We noted that Fortaleza was the municipality that collected the most in traffic tickets (160.96 million), followed by Belo Horizonte (130 million), and Curitiba (129.99 million). The municipality with the lowest collection of traffic tickets was Palmas (11.76 million).

Carrying out the analysis of the rate of traffic tickets per inhabitant, Curitiba is in the lead with 66.2 traffic tickets/inhabitant, Fortaleza, and Recife with 59.54 and 59.13 respectively, Porto Alegre with 54.08 and Belo Horizonte with 51.37 traffic tickets /inhabitant. The municipality with the lowest number of traffic tickets /inhabitants was Manaus with 12.97.

4   Conclusion

Thirteen Brazilian capitals were compared in terms of the infrastructure, quality of services, costs and tariffs, accessibility, environment, and safety. Our analysis indicated that the road transportation is prioritized, but it is a necessity for the modernization of the fleet of vehicles.

There are many capitals with dedicated bus lanes, however, the operational speed is very low, reaffirming the inefficiency of the transport system. Furthermore, the infrastructure and vehicles of the capital attended few aspects of accessible and environmental urban transportation systems, but it is far from being considered an accessible and environmentally friendly city.

References

1. Rubim, B., Leitão, S.: O plano de mobilidade urbana e o futuro das cidades. Estudos Avançados **27**(79), 55–66 (2013)
2. Rolnik, R., Klintowitz, D.: Mobilidade na cidade de São Paulo. Estudos Avançados **25**(71), 89–108 (2011)
3. Ramos, D.V., Chicati, M.L., Machado, A.F., Deimling, K.A.D.S., De Mello, W.B.: A evolução do transporte público de passageiros por ônibus: uma revisão da literatura. Synergismus scyentifica UTFPR **12**(1), 254–261 (2017)
4. IBGE–Instituto Brasileiro de Geografia e Estatística: Panorama: Cidades (2018). https://cidades.ibge.gov.br/brasil/sp
5. BRASIL (2012). http://www.planalto.gov.br/ccivil_03/_ato2011-2014/2012/lei/l12587.htm
6. Companhia de Engenharia de Tráfego: Mobilidade no Sistema Viário Principal: Volumes e Velocidades (2019)

Author Index

Printed in the United States
by Baker & Taylor Publisher Services